Rowboat to Prague

Alan Levy

AN ORION PRESS BOOK

GROSSMAN PUBLISHERS   *New York*   *1972*

ROWBOAT
TO PRAGUE

Acknowledgments ⌐

To thank my Czechoslovak sources by name would only do them more harm than knowing me has already done. More I cannot wish them than that one day they may be free to read this—the fruit of their labors and mine—as well as anything else they choose to read. For similar reasons, certain characters, most notably the boy Václav and his father, have been altered or disguised to protect their identities.

I can, however, acknowledge (in order of their appearance aboard our rowboat) Messrs. Maurice Feldman, Herbert Rosenberg, Theron Raines, and Howard Greenfeld as well as the many couriers and friends-of-friends who brought these pages in and out of Prague during 1968, 1969, and 1970. I also want to give special thanks to a casual acquaintance, Mr. Alden Todd, who bumped into me on West 40th Street, Manhattan, one Saturday in 1967. Todd bade me "bon voyage" and gave me the best farewell advice anyone gave me. Where everyone else was saying "Take care!", Todd said: "Take notes!"

Published sources are generally acknowledged in footnotes or text where their material appears.

To Sadelle & Irwin Wladaver, who left early,

and to Alexander Dubček, who stayed,

and to Jirka Šlitr, "Jo, To Jsem Ještě Žil"

Contents ⌉

PART ONE

Odyssey: Rowboat to Prague

"This apparatus," he said, taking hold of a crank handle and leaning against it, "was invented by our former Commandant. I assisted at the very earliest experiments and had a share in all the work until its completion. But the credit of inventing it belongs to him alone. Have you ever heard of our former Commandant? No? Well, it isn't saying too much if I tell you that the organization of the whole penal colony is his work. We who were his friends knew even before he died that the organization of the colony was so perfect that his successor, even with a thousand new schemes in his head, would find it impossible to alter anything, at least for many years to come."

Franz Kafka, *In the Penal Colony*

Chapter 1]

Thursday 14 April 1966—
Friday 7 July 1967

I TOOK MY FAMILY ROWING ON CENTRAL PARK LAKE
the day I broke the news to them that we would be moving to a magic
yellow city with a hundred gold spires and tiny blue cobblestones that
workmen hammered back into place every morning. It was the summer of 1967 and Erika, two going on three, wanted to know: "Will
we be able to see the Empire State Building at night?"

"Not even by day," I said. But I quickly added that every day they
would be able to visit a real castle or choose among four fulltime puppet theatres—two of which were perhaps the best in the world. Every
hour, in fact, they could see a Town Hall clock whose twelve mechanical apostles, on a turntable, come out to toll the time while a skeleton
clangs a small gong, an elderly courtier nods sagely, and a rooster
crows. I even related the ghastly legend (more true than untrue) of the
fifteenth-century craftsman who made that clock for an Emperor of
Bohemia. The Emperor so admired it that, to prevent his unique mas-
terwork from ever being duplicated, he had the clockmaker's eyes put
out. The clockmaker outlived the Emperor and, when his own day of
reckoning neared, he petitioned the Emperor's son to let him touch his
clock once more before dying. The old man was carried to the clock.
He passed his hands over it just once—and the clock stopped for two
centuries.

"But now it works," I assured both my daughters. Then I told them
that the Czech schools didn't bus you there. You were called for by a
special trolley that had potty seats.

This was an unabashed pitch to Monica—at three going on four, the
opinion-maker—in the hope that Erika would follow. Our rowboat
drifted with oars locked and resting. Erika puckered at the enormity of
a two-year-old's precious routine being upended, but Monica nibbled
at the bait.

"I would like to ride on that trolley," she announced. "But is this the boat we're taking to Prague?"

Before I could answer, my wife Valerie cried: "Watch your head, Daddy! We're in a tunnel and going on the rocks!"

I ducked and lunged for the oars. I didn't know it then, but from that moment on, we were Czechoslovaks, paddling upstream in a flimsy vessel amidst the tides and glaciers of steel that seem always to engulf dreamers in darkness.

Richard Nixon and Miloš Forman have never met, although the ubiquitous Mr. Nixon visited Prague as a private citizen in 1966. But I credit both the President of the United States and the director of *Loves of a Blonde* with inspiring our move to Prague. I visited Mr. Nixon for a ladies' magazine in early 1962, when he was between defeats for President and for Governor of California. At the time, the Nixons were living in Brentwood, California, in a rambling Tudor house with fruit grove, avocado trees, swimming pool, and five television sets. One night, we were sipping excellent martinis made by the host himself at the refreshing Republican ratio of 4-to-1. We were talking about age. I had just survived the trauma of turning 30 (I had been sick in bed for a week with no discernible ailment). Mr. Nixon was facing up to what he termed his own "seventh crisis": he would be fifty in a few months.

"The thirties are really your best years," he assured me. "You have more wisdom than you had in your twenties. You may not be as quick as you were, but you have more stamina than you'll ever have again. In your thirties, you have immense drive; you're tireless. You don't have to worry about the effects of tension—until at least the late thirties. I handled the Alger Hiss case in my early thirties, and I couldn't have handled it better at any other time in my life."

Not being a Nixon man, I took a deep gulp of gin and patted an ancient floppy-eared cocker spaniel who turned out to be a national historical monument. Checkers had padded in to pay homage to his master's voice, which purred on smoothly:

"Another thing about the thirties: You're able to take risks and you ought to be willing to. In the thirties, you should be willing to experiment, to risk everything, to plunge completely into a cause. The thirties are the time to take that trip around the world even if your life savings are involved. It's the time to write that book or compose that symphony.

"In their forties, many people seem to be looking down the tunnel. They've had a scare or two—maybe a physical scare, maybe they've lost a job. They're scarred and they're scared—not all, but many of them. They've fought battles and they have less zeal.

"I'm lucky. I don't suffer from the effects of the forties and I won't have to worry about the fifties because it's just not in my nature to be anything but a battler. But I see the pressure of the forties in young congressmen. If they get to forty-five without a bold move toward the governorship or the Senate, they never go up. The bold move can fail, but the important thing is that it's made. The man who makes it, even if he loses, will be heard from again. But I've observed that people who get past forty-five without making such a move just aren't chance-takers. They're safe-players."

Thus spake "the old Nixon," a voice often scorned, but whose prescription made resounding good sense in charting my future. Mr. Nixon's words were transformed into an ultimatum to be heeded by age thirty-five, by which deadline I had promised myself an unfettered year or two in a new place where I could try my hand as a playwright.

With Monica born in late 1963 and Erika in late 1964, the base for the dream began to sprout prerequisites. My own standards were three-fold: *a beautiful city* (we are neither suburbanites nor islanders) *where my neighbor would NOT be an American writer* (I had long wanted to come to grips with the English language in a semi-private confrontation undissipated by incessant cocktail chatter) and *where the cost of living would be less than that of New York, Paris, or London.* (In 1962, as a childless couple in Manhattan, our break-even income was $6,000 a year; by 1967, as a family of four, it was somewhere between $15,000 and $18,000.) On the whole, our family planning and Mr. Nixon's timetable meshed conveniently. The children would be too young in 1967 to be seriously embroiled in academic life anywhere. In fact, we wanted them out of New York City before any of the highly competitive nursery schools could reject them. Monica and Erika already had a frisky four-year-old boyfriend whose parents' marriage was going on the rocks because their only child "lacked sufficient bezazz," in the words of a progressive headmaster who'd interviewed him at nap time.

In the spring of 1966, I was thirty-four and had not yet found the city of my dreams when I was handed a plane ticket from JFK to PRG. (Pan-Am and Air India already had regular one-stop jet flights between New York and Prague.) My benefactors were the Friends of the Cincinnati Orchestra who, in the interests of publicity, had invited me to be their guest on a packaged charter-flight Culture Tour of Eastern Europe. I wound up my assignments, filed my income tax returns, kissed my family goodbye, and flew to the first destination, Prague, a week ahead of the Cincinnatians. Thus, I would be on hand to welcome them to Prague and could then travel with them to Bratislava, Vienna, Budapest, Moscow, and Leningrad (though the International Air Transport Association's "affinity" rules insisted that I must part from the charter flight in Helsinki and take scheduled transport across the Atlantic).

I landed one night at Ruzyně Airport, whose International Passenger Terminal was a wooden shed. Ruzyně looked like one of those grisly Arctic refueling bases of the pre-jet age, but you knew you weren't at Gander or Goose Bay when the roof lit up with a neon red star alternating with a hammer and sickle. A taxi took me to the Hotel International, a dour Stalin Gothic mausoleum built in the 1950's at the wrong end of the number 18 tram line, almost an hour from the center of town. The International was not a bad place for sleeping, but its only sparkle came from an East German automatic shoeshine machine with instructions in seven languages. The directions in English began: "1. Insert the coin. 2. Lift a little the feet."

There was more promise however, in a message to call Miloš Forman.

He wasn't famous back in early 1966. I vaguely coupled his name with a first feature called *Black Peter* that had been praised in a minor key at 1965's New York Film Festival at Lincoln Center. I had missed it, but I'd been told that I hadn't missed much. The lion's share of festival acclaim had gone to another Czech entry, *The Shop on Main Street,* directed by two older moviemakers, Ján Kadár and Elmar Klos. *Shop* had opened up American art cinemas to a trickle and then a flood of Czech imports.

A mutual friend in New York had sent a letter of introduction to Ján Kadár on my behalf. But Kadár, ironically, was in Santa Monica— where, a few days later, he would accept the Oscar for the best foreign-language film. With Number One away, Czechoslovak Filmexport had simply turned the letter over to Number Two—Forman, whose *Loves of a Blonde* had just started on its Continental rounds. It was proving to be to the youth of Europe what *The Catcher in the Rye* once was to a generation of young Americans.

Forman's telephone was out of order when I tried to call him, but he knocked on my hotel door early the next morning and introduced himself. He was determined to show that Prague's film industry was not inhospitable to Western visitors.

"I am at your disposal for the next two days," he said in fluent English. "What do you want to see?"

"Both your films," I said.

"Nonsense," he said. "Movies you can see in a dark room anywhere, anytime, and in America you'll be able to see both with English titles. But Prague you can only see now!"

I showed him my itinerary, to which he awarded a rating of "standard. So I will show you places not on your itinerary."

My first impression of Miloš, from the way he moved perhaps, was of a smoldering-eyed, dark-maned young lion in a black leather jacket. But that may have been because lions were all about me. A lion was the emblem of the Kingdom of Bohemia and it remains the emblem of Communist Czechoslovakia—with one post-1948 change of headdress: *The lion's crown was replaced by a red star.* Since other vestiges of royal tradition remain (the basic unit of money, for instance, is still the crown), this was an affront to taste rather than a bow to ideology. Even to Miloš, who laughs at most absurdity, the red-starred lion was an unpardonable insult, like the Stalin Gothic hotel where we met.

By the rustle he provoked among the lady clerks in that funereal lobby, I gathered that my thirty-four-year-old host radiated a certain animal magnetism. And so, when he had led me to his illegally parked Hillman Minx and zoomed us away with a hot-rod swerve, I asked: "Are you married, Miloš?"

"Of course," he replied.

"How long?"

"A couple years," he said.

"Any kids yet?"

"Of course," he said, dead serious. "Two. Boys, of course."

"That was quick," I remarked.

"Twins," he elaborated, and I waited in vain for him to add "of course." But, one near-accident later, he added proudly, "Identical twin boys. It used to be like being drunk, seeing double. Until now— one bruises where the other doesn't."

We sped down the Boulevard of the Yugoslav Partisans and around the Circle of the October Revolution. At the Avenue of the Heroes of Peace, Miloš managed to cut off two rickety old trams with a sharp left turn. Then he shook his left fist at the irate motormen clanging their bells at him and pointed in the opposite direction with his right hand: "The entrance to Prague Castle is one block over that way. But it's on your tour. If I took you there now, you wouldn't want to see anything else."

I said: "Take me anywhere you like, but with one hand on the wheel, please."

The little car slalomed along a steep, winding, cobblestoned hill. When we touched down again, Miloš veered off to the left and gestured at eighteen flights of marble stairs leading up another hill to a marble pedestal. Any statue that stood there would have a perfect view of the curving Vltava (or Moldau, in German) and the city of Prague on both sides of the river. But the pedestal was bare.

"Here is where Stalin stood," said Miloš. "It was the largest statue of Stalin in the world and it was unveiled in 1955. I must show you a photo of it some time. *Stalin,* you know, means 'man of steel.' He had his hand inside his coat—in the Napoleonic pose. The Czech joke was: 'Why is he reaching into his pocket?' Answer: Because he admired his statue so much that he wanted to buy it for himself. He reached for his wallet and asked how much the statue cost. When they told him, the Man of Steel turned to stone.

"The next year, Khrushchev made his speech at the Twentieth Congress about the Personality Cult. Everywhere else they took down their Stalin statues—but Novotný kept waiting and hoping until maybe the early 1960's, when he decided Stalin wasn't coming back to life. By then, Stalin was an embarrassment, so President Novotný tried to have him spirited away one night. He must have thought that if we woke up and Stalin wasn't there, we wouldn't notice or maybe wouldn't remember.

"But the statue was too heavy and the workmen couldn't see what to do at night. So when we came into town the next morning, only Stalin's head was missing. It took them many more nights to dismantle him and finally they had to use dynamite to demolish the rest of him. But they continued to do all this only at night, with floodlights now. And hundreds and thousands of people used to come out at night just to watch the workmen work. Nobody said anything, nobody cheered—

it was still too dangerous. We just stood and kept a vigil. They kept on dynamiting him and then they'd use this giant vacuum cleaner to suck up his dust. And each day, people coming to work would see Stalin shriveling away. Talk about de-Stalinization! It was beautiful!

"The biggest secret in Prague is: Where did they take the head of Stalin? Nobody knows. Some say it was sent to Russia. But others say it is kept in one of the Party buildings here, all ready to be put back up if anything ever changes in Moscow."

We sped across the Vltava and swept through a handsome plaza called—in Russian!—Red Army Square. (Prague boasts two Red Army Squares: the Russian-named *náměstí Krasnoarmejců,* and the other, *náměstí Rudé Armády,* named in Czech.) Swinging past the Philosophical Faculty of Charles University, Miloš beckoned to the stately concert hall that goes by three names: Communism calls it the House of Artists; Czechs call it Dvořák Hall; Germans call it the Rudolfinium. On its rooftop Hall of Fame were weatherbeaten busts of great composers.

During the Nazi occupation, Miloš told me, a couple of local workmen had been ordered to take Felix Mendelssohn off the roof. "Which one is he?" they asked. They were told: "The Jewish one with the long nose and the Semitic features." And so they climbed up and removed Richard Wagner.

Miloš gave a deep bass chuckle at his own story. It was still on my mind after he had aimed the Hillman at a parking space near the National Theatre, led me into the riverfront Café Slavia, bought me a cup of the thick, bitter Turkish coffee that the Czechs drink, and talked about film and family for a while. Thus, when Miloš worked the conversation back to "what else would you like to see in Prague?", I was ready for him.

"Whatever you want to show of me of the Czech film industry, of course. But also, if there is one nearby, a World War II concentration camp."

As a second-generation American Jew, I had never been willing to entrust this mission to a German guide. I had often thanked fate for my lucky accident of birth and wondered whether, if we had still been living in Central Europe in the 1930's, my parents would have known when to get out. Or, if such an unimaginable situation ever arose again, would I be able to detect the handwriting on the wall? (In 1939, some New York relatives of mine sent money to import some kinfolk from Poland. But the scheming kin used the passage money in their

home town instead to open a shop. Both it and they were liquidated.)
The best drill I knew for thinking clearly about the unthinkable was
to confront the reality of it or as much as is left of it, so that you may
possibly smell it coming when and if history starts to repeat itself.
Miloš' story of Wagner and Mendelssohn had reminded me of my nag-
ging obligation to—just once—inspect the hell that Hitler had reserved
for me.

Miloš leaped at the idea: "It's good! Whatever I can show you at
Barrandov Studios, you can see in New York, Hollywood, London.
And I am a poor guide to the studio. I never made one minute of
Blonde in Love or *Peter and Paula** inside a studio. I learned to stay
away when I made short films. You are surrounded always by technicians. In the studio, *they* feel at home. *They* feel like the boss. *They*
tell the director what he can and cannot do. So tomorrow, instead of
the studio, I will take you for an outing in the country."

The next morning, we set out for the "privileged ghetto" of
Theresienstadt. Miloš told me about it as he drove. In 1941, the Nazis
evicted the inhabitants of Maria Theresa's old fortress town (*Terezin*
in Czech) and the next year they remodeled it into a showcase ghetto.
With its own Jewish officials and a semblance of community life,
Theresienstadt was used to reassure Red Cross inspectors and other
visitors who harbored the notion that Jews were being mistreated. Jews
with German decorations from World War I were eligible for deportation to Theresienstadt; wealthy Jews could and did buy their way into
"protective custody" there. Such was Theresienstadt's repute that two
escapees from other concentration camps actually made their way
there, where indeed there were an orchestra, family living, and even a
Jewish mayor. The only snag was that, every month, a few of the families were "shipped out" to make way for new arrivals and were never
heard from again. And, by 1944, the myth could no longer be maintained. The Third Reich's extermination "needs" took precedence
over its pretenses.

Sooner or later, the only ways out of Theresienstadt were by the
firing squad or transfer to Auschwitz and other death camps. At Theresienstadt itself, 33,500 perished; for another 84,500, it was an anteroom to extermination.

We were almost there when I asked Miloš a question that was inevitable: "How was it for you during the war?"

* European titles of *Loves of a Blonde* and *Black Peter.*

He put both hands on the wheel and drove with uncharacteristic restraint. "I am half-Jewish," he said after a long minute. "My mother died in Auschwitz. My father died in Buchenwald."

I sat there, stunned and sheepish. Then I apologized for the tactless errand I had suggested. Miloš said: "It is all right, Alan." I urged that we go somewhere else—"a castle or someplace." Miloš stepped on the gas and said emphatically: "It is all right."

Theresienstadt is now a state cemetery and a museum: The Memorial to National Suffering. It has been preserved as it was when liberated, a walled city of the dead. Nobody lives there now, except its caretakers. Crossing a moat, passing beneath stone portals painted with the emblem of the Third Reich, hurrying past a sign proclaiming in German that "WORK IS FREEDOM," you have left life and decency far behind.

In a barracks the size of my bedroom, sixteen triple-tiered wooden bunks were numbered 1 through 48. I found it hard to imagine forty-eight men living so close together. Miloš said: "Then try to imagine four hundred eighty. There were ten men to each bed." In a tiny cell that Miloš shut me into, I spent the longest sixty seconds of my life groping in blackness and colliding with walls. When Miloš freed me, I blinked and said I would have gone crazy in four more minutes. Miloš said: "There were eighteen men in here at a time. Crazier!" In the museum building, formerly the German soldiers' caserne, we saw a pair of slippers made of women's hair and Miloš lost his aplomb for a moment. "Fantas-tic," he muttered. "Fantas-tic."

On a deserted street lined with trees and paved with gravel, Miloš fell into step behind me. Then, passing a row of officers' houses, I felt stones pelting my ankles. Miloš was still keeping in step with me, but at a modified goose-step. Before I could say "Cut it out!", the houses ended and I was confronted by, of all things, a swimming pool.

"The S.S. commandant, Jöckl, built it for his two daughters," Miloš explained. "Those two little girls playing in water were the last living things you ever saw."

Turning a corner we entered a little park, cool and green on first view, but nothing here was what it seemed. "You just passed through the Gate of Death," Miloš informed me. "Between 1943 and 1945, no prisoner who goes in here ever comes out alive." There was a gallows just inside the entranceway. But Miloš led me to a dirt strip near the base of a stone wall pocked with bullet holes. Before me flowed a little stream in which I was surprised to see clear water. Admonishing me to stand where I was, Miloš jumped the stream and, in a dozen strides, mounted a rough-hewn platform shaded by a wood-slatted roof. It had looked like a bandstand until Miloš called to me: "Here stood the firing squad."

Then he cackled—a cackle more startling than gunfire, and said: "Ahaha! You are standing at attention!"

Miloš spoke more than truth. I was rigid, body and soul. This chilling psychodrama, unrehearsed and improvised, was my first glimpse of a good director's instinct for compelling audiences, actors, and everybody around him to experience whatever he feels.

On the road back to Prague, Miloš filled in some details of his life. It was easy for me to imagine myself in his shoes, for he and I were both born in 1932, eight days apart:

"One day my parents aren't there and I start to live with uncles and then with other families. They tell me my parents are in a concentration camp. And what does 'camp' mean to me but Boy Scout camp? And so I think they are lucky and hope they are happy. . . .

"For rest of the war, I am in danger. But it was kept from me. People who look after me were in much more danger.

"For me, war is adventure—new people, new friends, new kids. People take care of me, but not much care. I am free. I am ten, eleven, twelve and coming home at midnight like a gypsy boy. I enjoy the war!

"After three, four years, when they tell me my parents are dead, they are just somebody I used to know. I never realized what it was about."

Not until 1948, when he was a sixteen-year-old at boarding school and he saw a back-number newsreel with freight carloads of naked, emaciated bodies being removed from a death camp: "Everybody in that picture is moving, except those bodies are not moving and maybe one of them is my mother. . . ."

Having been reached so dramatically, it is not surprising that Miloš' language became film. But what never failed to surprise me, once I'd caught up with his movies in New York, was that the abrasiveness of being a teen-ager in a family could be captured so graphically— in both *Loves of a Blonde* and *Black Peter*—by an orphan who had never experienced it. When I asked Miloš about this many months later, he said slowly: "Maybe it's true that with your work you replace what you want to have in your life."

In the New York winter of 1966–67, while Valerie and I were first weighing the feasibility of moving to Prague, a letter of introduction from Miloš to us preceded the arrival of one of his best friends. "Jirka Šlitr* is the most talented person I know, a true Renaissance man," wrote Miloš, who is no paragon of modesty. Then came an invitation to a two-man art show at the Benevy Gallery on First Avenue. One of the two was Jiří Šlitr, who had been granted an exit visa for the event.

At the opening, my wife and I couldn't get near the art or the artists. A couple of afternoons later, we went back with the children and were captivated by a wall of Šlitr's line drawings: intricate, inked mazes which you circled and stalked with puzzlement until, in the instant when you achieved perfect focus, there dawned before your eyes the Prague Castle in much of its grandeur or a dull party in all its sullen sprawl.

I dropped a note to him at the King Edward Hotel in Times Square. When he appeared at our home in the Village for dinner several nights later, he bore a gift: the drawing of the dull party that I had especially praised.

"But it said 'SOLD' by the time we got there," I remarked.

"So I made another one," he said blandly in very precise, singsong English.

Jiří Šlitr's fame in Czechoslovakia was not primarily as a graphic artist, but as co-founder, co-author, and co-star of the Semafor, the liveliest popular musical theatre in Prague. It was there that, back in 1959, he and his partner, Jiří Suchý, had unleashed musical comedies and revues with a jazz beat and a George Abbott pace which signaled a cultural revolution in itself. Until then, Prague staging (of drama as well as musicals) had been very Viennese in tempo: actors standing around on stage holding genteel and rather leisurely discussions, sometimes punctuated by a song. Šlitr composed the music. Suchý, whose straw hat and jaunty singing style had prompted Paris critics to hail him (during an engagement at Jean-Louis Barrault's *Théâtre des Nations* festival) as "the Czech Chevalier," wrote book and lyrics. He also published volumes of poetry and essays. I had never caught their act,

* Jiří = George. Jirka = Georgie. *Šlitr* is pronounced *Schlitter.*

but I knew that in Prague they were known as "The Poet and the Painter" or just plain "S + Š."

For nearly eight years, S + Š had been writing forty to fifty songs per annum. Eighteen of the three hundred and fifty had achieved, on Supraphon Records, six-figure sales—no small achievement in a land of only fourteen million people. S + Š's earnings were published and marveled at all over Eastern Europe. The press called them "crown millionaires." And Šlitr, at least, was intent, almost too intent, on becoming a "dollar celebrity" too. Which was one reason why Miloš had sent him to me.

Jiří Šlitr was a debonair bachelor with graying hair and a black bowler (his onstage trademark) framing a pair of darting, lecherous eyes. He seldom smiled or laughed, but he registered his constant amusement at life with an "umhmm-umhmm-umhmm" let's-get-on-with-it sort of calculating murmur. He reminded me (offstage and later onstage) of a young Jack Benny, though he was already, at forty-two, three years older.

Jirka Šlitr and I became good friends that winter. I asked him what he'd like to see and his interests led us to a New York I'd never really known. We stood on line for two hours in the neon-lit snowdrifts of West 125th Street for the Wednesday night amateurs at the Apollo. We squirmed through a West 78th Street psychodrama as a girl named Phoebe unraveled her penchant for little men. We munched sweet potatoes, bought from a pushcart, on a Sunday stroll through the Lower East Side.

During our walks and talks, we bounced ideas off each other and he was frequently humming little snatches of his own catchy melodies. Now and then, I would ask him about them and he would quote an intriguing Suchý lyric or two. *"Life to me is but a shabby vest/ Gray and boring as you plainly know,"* he would chant softly on the IRT. Or: "A rather topical blues song for a girl: *'My love gave me a sweater made of barbed wire. . . .'*" Šlitr's music reminded me of Irving Berlin at his *Suppertime* best.

By the time Šlitr was packing to go home, several letters and cables had crossed the Atlantic and it was agreed that in Prague I would collaborate with S + Š on an American version of one of their plays, a musical fable of money and greed that hit me like "funny Kafka." Miloš Forman, who had directed it in Prague, endorsed the project and asked for first crack at directing our American version.

"Umhmm-umhmm-umhmm," was Šlitr's response to the good news about Forman. "Wouldn't we be better off with some famous Broadway director like Joshua Logan? I mean, I want it to be a *big* hit."

"So do I," I replied quickly, "so let's stick with Miloš."

The next summer Šlitr went west again, this time for an extended engagement at the Czechoslovak Pavilion of Expo '67 in Montreal. I flew north twice to visit him and there I also met two of his best friends from Prague. One was his frequent wine-drinking companion: the puppeteer and film animator Jiří Trnka (the feature-length *Emperor's Nightingale;* the savage political short, *The Hand*). With his gray handlebar mustache and a friendly-looking mole on his right cheek, Trnka resembled a jovial woodcutter from one of the storybooks he illustrated. Such was the deference paid to him by younger artists that, for three consecutive nights in Montreal, Šlitr, 12 years his junior, accompanied Trnka (who spoke no English) to Michelangelo Antonioni's *Blow-Up* in order to interpret this film which Trnka found so compelling.

Šlitr's other companion was named Sylva. Just turning thirty, Sylva's skill with languages enabled her to perform in English or French (and she was doing both in Montreal) or German or Russian or Polish or Serbo-Croatian as well as Czech. At Expo, she was the onstage hostess in the Czechoslovak Pavilion's *Kinoautomat,* or "Computerized Cinema of Consensus."

Perhaps you saw her there, too, telling you to "push the green button on the arm of your seat if you want [the hero] to let the lady into his flat and the red button if you want him to keep her out. The majority vote will decide which way the film goes next. You have thirty seconds. All right, stop the computer!" And here Sylva would fulfill everyone's occasional fantasy—for, lo and behold, the computer would (after making its instant tabulation) stop.

Then the show would go on—but strictly in accordance with the audience's wishes. For the computer and the movie were programmed to tell a complete and logical story no matter how the audience voted at each of the six crises when Sylva interrupted the continuity.

Sylva had not set out to be a stage performer when she studied history and languages at Charles University in the 1950's. She had contemplated a career in journalism. "But it was difficult to write for newspapers," she told me in Montreal, "if your thinking and feelings were different from the official line. So I took an opportunity that came along to perform with Magic Lantern at the Brussels World's Fair in 1958. Later, I traveled with the Black Theatre of Prague whenever it went abroad on tour.

"I also write children's stories and—being one of the lucky ones who can travel outside our country—I used to write occasional foreign dispatches for the Czech press. But I stopped doing this when I mailed back a story on the Wall from our Berlin engagement. I said the Wall was ugly, which I didn't consider a controversial observation. But, when my article appeared, it said the Wall was not only necessary, but beautiful.

"After I came back to Prague, my friends said to me: 'How could you have written something like that?' I decided I would never give anyone a chance to do such a thing to me again."

Sylva's romance with Jirka Šlitr had been going on for seven years. Even though it was ending in Montreal that summer, we didn't know it then.

In Montreal, we also met Sylva's and Šlitr's and Trnka's boss, Miroslav Galuška, forty-five. A dashing, silver-haired, jut-jawed Boy Scout of a Slav, Galuška bore a startling resemblance to our own General William C. Westmoreland. Galuška was a onetime film writer who became a diplomat, Foreign Ministry press chief (1952–58) and then Ambassador to the Court of St. James (1958–61) before taking up journalism as deputy chief editor of the official Communist party newspaper, *Rudé Právo.** President Novotný always considered *Rudé Právo* his own house organ and Galuška was being groomed for editor-in-chief until his own independent brand of Marxism-Leninism asserted itself. ("Lenin, after all, promised the end of all administrative pressure on the press and the introduction of full freedom.") In 1963, Galuška was shunted to the less influential chief editorship of a new weekly called *Kulturní Tvorba* (*Cultural Creation*). By his sixth issue,

* *Rudé Právo* is *Red Justice*. Wherever feasible, I don't use Czech or Slovak names that are meaningless to the reader. The trade unions' daily, *Práce*, is identified as *Work;* the People's (Catholic) Party paper, *Lidová Demokracie*, is called *People's Democracy* herein. But certain other names remain in Czech. In translation the controversial weekly *Literární Listy* becomes too trivial (*Literary Leaves*) and the orthodox daily *Rudé Právo* too ironic.

Galuška had earned a political (and perhaps even personal) kiss of death: a denunciation by President Novotný. Already, however, Galuška had enough admirers and Novotný enough insecurity that it was deemed punishment enough to shift him out of sight in 1964, by banishing him to Canada as Ambassador/Commissioner General in charge of the Czechoslovak Pavilion for Expo '67.

Relegating dissidents to influential posts abroad is a Czechoslovak habit which often backfires. Galuška had immediately set about fitting his punishment to the crimes he had committed. Rallying his artistic friends, he had organized a sparkling jewelbox of a pavilion that was the hit of the fair.

When Galuška had left Prague, it had been made abundantly clear that his was a one-way ticket to Montreal. Returning to Czechoslovakia would be tantamount to hanging himself. At the time I met him in Montreal, he was even looking rather cursorily for a newspaper job somewhere in Canada. But he had made such a record for himself that he was thinking much more seriously of returning home in triumph when Expo would end in the fall of 1967 and lending his weight to the forces that were already chipping away at the Novotný monolith.

One such force was Jiří Suchý, who—in Šlitr's absence, but with his consent and collaboration—had been moving their Semafor Theatre farther and farther into the realm of political satire. On my next exploratory visit to Prague, I met Jirka Suchý for the first time. On this planet, he was the same statistical age as Forman and myself. But it must have taken several eons elsewhere for that maniacal smile to ripen into pure green-cheese lunacy, for that shy moonface to glow, for those shifty eyes to beam inner madness.

On a rainy Saturday, Suchý took me home to his apartment in Prague 6, a quarter-mile from the Formans, for an afternoon of cold cuts, open-faced sandwiches, Pilsen beer, phonograph records, and talk about friends, acquaintances, children, and our collaboration. The Suchý flat was an eclectic fantasy of antique and modern. I was ushered into a sitting room where low-slung modern furniture of the kind no grown man can relax in had been covered with a white fur that made it not only bearable, but comfortable. Around me were some Old Masters and medieval church art, plus an unadorned mahogany-paneled wall before which a movie screen could descend from above. The motif of the Suchý apartment was the unexpected: In each room, you felt obliged to ask *where* to put yourself. But, once you had found your niche, everything worked.

This livable museum was a happy collaboration between Jirka Suchý and his auburn-haired wife Běla, who sometimes designed theatre costumes and record jackets but who mostly devoted herself to their handsome son, Kubik (short for Jan-Jakub and named after Rousseau, not Astor). Kubik's being two weeks younger than our Erika —and the Forman twins' age lying part way between Monica's and Erika's—promised good playmate insurance if we could live in Prague.

To live in Prague takes considerable doing. A foreigner is entirely dependent upon some ministry's or organization's sponsoring him or at least certifying that there is a national advantage to his presence. As a freelance person, this posed a problem for me. The Suchý and Šlitr collaboration was still being negotiated, so Dilia, the state literary and theatrical agency, could not yet intervene on my behalf. By suggesting that he wanted me to collaborate on a screenplay with him, Miloš Forman had lined up Filmexport—the Government corporation that negotiates foreign distribution for Czechoslovak films—to make phone calls and appointments for me. But Filmexport was reluctant to commit anything to writing. Forman and Filmexport had agreed that, under the circumstances, my best bet for a sponsor would be the Ministry of Foreign Affairs press department. My credentials as a journalist were more imposing than as a playwright or screenwriter.

"Filmexport says that, even if they or Dilia were to sponsor you, they could never pry loose a decent flat for you and your family," Miloš informed me. "But once the Foreign Ministry accredits you, then you're eligible to have the Diplomatic Service find you a flat just the way they would if you were a new attaché at an embassy here. You might have to pay in American dollars, but you could be worse off. And once you have press accreditation, the Ministry of Interior semi-automatically grants you permission to reside here."

Thus, in mid-1967, I paid my first visit to the Ministry of Foreign Affairs in Prague's largest palace, the Černín. In a rear courtyard, still off limits, of this sprawling building, the body of Foreign Minister Jan Masaryk was found on the morning of March 10, 1948. The Černín Palace was built between 1669 and 1720 for Humprecht Černín, a wealthy landowner and onetime Ambassador to Venice, who, like many

Prague aristocrats, needed to be situated influentially close to the Castle, then as now the seat of the State. Unlike his more complicated, scheming rivals, Count Černín, owner of more than a dozen estates in Middle Europe, allowed his empire to be administered by a staff of exactly five clerks, who were responsible for his chateaus, lakes, farms, books, paintings, and sculptures. "I know," Černín is quoted as admitting, "that these clerks pinch from me, but they value their jobs and are diligent in them. If I had one hundred clerks, I would have one hundred thieves pinching from me, and that might be my ruin."

My contact in the Černín Palace was an equally philosophical youngish man named Milan Glozar, whose brown suit, tinted hornrims, and droning voice would mark him as a loner in any suave gray diplomatic corps, East or West.

From the outset, Mr. Glozar assured me that "there would seem to be no problem about your coming to work and live here." He also informed me, in a manner indicating considerable awareness of Western economics, that I had stumbled into an income-tax paradise:

The only Czechoslovak taxes I would have to pay would be the ten per cent that is automatically withheld from all income earned from Czech sources. Aside from the occasional reprinting of my writing in Czech translations, I had no expectation of earning crowns but, in case I did, my 10 per cent tax deduction would very likely make me eligible for the virtually free National Health.

As for income earned anywhere abroad from American (or other Western) firms, I would be exempt from U.S. taxes on the first $20,000 of 1968 income, if I arrived in Prague no later than New Year's Eve and maintained "bona fide residence" abroad for the full tax year. If my 1968 earnings abroad happened to be, for example, $28,000, I would merely have to pay the tax bill that comes to the head of a family of four struggling to get by on $8,000 a year. After three years of residence abroad, my annual exemption would rise to $25,000.*

Mr. Glozar said I must give his ministry an autobiographical letter telling why and how I wanted to live in Czechoslovakia as well as the

---

* "Bona fide residence" abroad is not to be confused with the better-known exemption ($20,000) for "physical presence" abroad, which involves your being on foreign soil for at least 510 full days during any period of 18 consecutive months. "Bona fide residence" does not restrict the number of days you can spend visiting the U.S. so long as you set up permanent quarters abroad for yourself and your family and settle down in the community. For details, see the latest edition of Internal Revenue Service publication 54.

vital data about my family . . . a letter from some professional organization (the Society of Magazine Writers would do) vouching for me . . . tearsheets of five or six articles of mine . . . and a half-dozen passport photos of each of us. (There were no forms to fill out, which should have made me wary.) Mr. Glozar estimated that we would have all our papers in order by the end of September 1967, a month before we planned to leave Greenwich Village. He anticipated "no trouble at all."

I could already spot the first cloud on the horizon, however, when the amiable Mr. Glozar mentioned that he would not be around to steer us through diplomatic channels. In the fall he would be going to England as press attaché at the Embassy in London. But even before then he was taking all his accumulated vacation time for the summer mushroom-picking season. In Central Europe, mushrooms are not only a foodstuff, but a pursuit and a passion. When they mature, all other activity stops.

"I've been told," I remarked, "that if I ever have any doubts about a mushroom, I should ask a Czech because he's never wrong."

Mr. Glozar leaned back skeptically and said: "An average of sixteen of our people guess wrong every summer. They get mushroom poisoning, which is—if you eat the right, or rather, *wrong* mushroom—a tenday agony with no cure except certain death. The mushrooms you'll buy in stores here are safe, but I am now going to give you the soundest advice anyone can give you for living in Czechoslovakia: Never, never buy mushrooms from a little old lady who comes around selling them."

He pointed to an item in *Rudé Právo* and said: "She's killed three people in one village already this week, and the police are still looking for her."

On this happy note, my session with Mr. Glozar ended. I was so exhilarated by the apparent absence of bureaucratic hurdles that I walked the whole mile-and-a-half back to my hotel sizing up the sights of "my city" as I went.

No sooner had I opened the door of my room at the Alcron Hotel than I realized that my luggage had been searched.

A trail of sugar led from the door to my suitcase. Inside was a box of Cypriot candy I had bought in my previous stopover, Nicosia, for my mother back in Manhattan. The box had been opened, though none of the candy had been taken. Similarly, other parcels had been opened and then re-sealed badly, though nothing was missing. My papers, too, had been worked over; some picture postals from my "Scientology Assignment" folder had been removed and then carefully replaced in my "Thalidomide Assignment" folder.

When you're searched or burgled, your first fear is that the culprit may still be on the premises. And, behind the Iron Curtain, even when you establish that he's not, you still can't be sure you're alone; particularly at the Alcron, your room may be watched or monitored.

I needed privacy to sort out my reactions. Was my visitor a customs agent, the secret police, or just a prying maid? To whom should I protest? Or should I protest at all, thereby establishing myself as a troublemaker even before coming to live in Prague?

To think my way through to a simple conclusion (*viz.:* Having proved to whom it may concern that I had nothing to hide, I might as well ignore the incident), I adjourned to my adjoining john, which seemed like the safest place for solitary meditation. Fully clothed, I sat down on the green plastic toilet seat without opening the inner lid. When I stood up a few minutes later, I saw that my weight had forced the lid through the seat. The lid was now dangling downward into the water.

I couldn't leave it or use it like this. But if I sent for a repairman, "they"—whoever "they" were—might link this strange event to "their" search. So I decided to repair the damage myself.

It took me half an hour to squeeze the toilet lid back through the toilet seat. In doing so, I not only dispelled all the nervous energy released by my discovery, but I also caught my right arm between lid and seat, thereby inflicting two long gashes on myself. For the rest of 1967's long hot summer, I had to wear long-sleeved shirts to avoid looking like a bungled suicide. My Alcron toilet-seat scars healed and faded, though my family doctor said they will never go away entirely. "But," he consoled me, "man is not made of Formica alone."

EVEN BEFORE MY ROOM WAS SEARCHED, I HAD NEVER relished staying at the Alcron in whose cavernous lobby, otherwise known as the "yellow submarine," the transient and fluctuating Prague press corps of Western newsmen sit interviewing each other. An air of transparent corruption pervades the place through good times and bad, renovations and modernization. On that same visit, each of my first four mornings would start off on the wrong foot with the porter handing me a message to "please check with reception."

The reception clerk was a bald, epicene young man. Rubbing his hands with glee, he would greet me in English with the same venal spiel: "Ah, Mr. Levy. I'm terribly sorry and I know you have a confirmed reservation. But we absolutely need your room. You'll have to vacate it by noon today *unless something happens.*"

I was so naive that, when my shocked protests were of no avail, I said: "Well, Filmexport made my reservation so I'll go over there and see if I can make something happen at that end."

"It would be just as easy to make something happen right here," the clerk purred unctuously, but I was too outraged to take the hint. I marched over to Filmexport, which must have used bribery or pressure to make something happen. My room was reprieved but every morning the same ritual recurred.

After four days of this, I went to bed so braced for my morning confrontation that I popped awake at 6 A.M. I dressed and shaved hastily to get out of the Alcron before my nemesis came to work. He wouldn't dare evict me without serving notice first! I sneaked past the porter and onto the street. Heading past Wenceslas Square, I cut through a maze of arcades in the Lucerna, Alfa, and Black Rose passages and was hopelessly out of sight when a familiar purr accosted me:

"Ah, Mr. Levy. So glad I met you on my way to work. I am terribly sorry and I know you have a confirmed. . . ."

"But how do you know you need my room when you haven't even come to work?"

"They called me at home last night," he said, without blinking an eye, "and told me they absolutely needed your room today. But I decided not to make you nervous and ruin your sleep by calling you then."

For a moment, I was tempted to thank him. One does develop a very special relationship with one's oppressor. Instead, after breakfast, I visited Filmexport to "make something happen."

Finally, on the eighth and last morning of my stay, I was able to march to the reception desk and announce: "I'll be checking out of your hotel at eleven-thirty this morning, so you can have your room then."

At eleven-thirty, after turning in my key and paying my bill, I started out the Alcron's revolving door. I was almost safe on the street when I heard the familiar purr of "Oh, Mr. Levy, Mr. Levy."

I thought about completing my exit. But maybe he had a cable for me. So I took the revolving door full circle.

"I just want to tell you," he said, extending a pudgy hand, "that it's been a pleasure serving you and we hope you'll stay with us again should you ever return to Prague."

The hand extended farther, palm upward. In all innocence, I shook it and then bade him a fast goodbye. I was only 45 degrees into the revolving door when I realized the true meaning of our farewell. To confirm this, I took another 360-degree circle tour and caught a good view of the clerk studying his barren palm.

I never stayed at the Alcron again. But the next time I came to Prague, I dreaded walking past it for fear I would see the same clerk still contemplating his empty palm.

On the next to last of my exploratory visits to Prague, I arrived in late afternoon without a hotel reservation. Miloš Forman whisked me off from the airport to the Golden Jug in Old Town Square for a banquet of cold cuts and too much wine. Only after dinner did we start searching for a room for me, but we soon learned that every hotel from Class B-minus to Class A-Plus De Luxe Special was booked solid.

We wandered from one to the other. After being rebuffed at the Hotel Paris, we almost overlooked another hotel in the shadow of the Powder Tower, the gunpowder storehouse that is the gateway to the old town of Prague. But I glanced through the front window and spotted reception desk, porter's desk, mailboxes, and keys—all the trademarks of a traditional hotel lobby. Aside from one night clerk on duty, the lobby was deserted—which augured well for vacancies.

"What about this one?" I asked Miloš.

He seemed startled for a moment, but then the wine stirred his blood and he said: "Why not try?" In we went and Miloš informed the clerk in Czech that I needed only a tiny room for one night.

To my surprise, the clerk replied: "This is not a hotel. And you both must leave."

"That's no way to treat a distinguished guest from America," Miloš responded with amiable belligerence, "just because he isn't a Communist Party official."

The clerk's body tensed and he looked both ways while Miloš blandly recited my *curriculum vitae,* exaggerating copiously. But the clerk kept interrupting to insist that this wasn't a hotel and we must "leave immediately before someone comes." We were only a few blocks from Franz Kafka's birthplace, but I felt as if we had discovered his permanent home.

I offered the clerk a small gift and Miloš began to recite his own biography, but the man was incorruptible, and very scared. When we heard someone coming down toward the lobby, the clerk turned to me with desperation and said to me in English:

"So now I know who you are. And I have seen Mr. Forman's photograph many times. I have also seen all his films, so I must beg you out of admiration to leave or you will both get into trouble. I must protect our guests at all cost. You are a foreigner, so it will be just a little trouble for you. But Mr. Forman is a Czech."

Then, raising his voice so the approaching guest could overhear, the clerk said in Czech, firmly and finally: "I'm sorry, gentlemen, this is *not* a hotel!"

I couldn't fathom what was happening, but the clerk's taut urgency did reach me. I certainly didn't want to risk any incident *before* residing in Prague. Therefore, I propelled Miloš back onto the street but not before we had caught a glimpse of a tall guest with an aquiline profile. In harsh voice but mild language, he was complaining that his telephone seemed to be out of order.

When our heads had cleared and we'd found me a room elsewhere, Miloš told me that we had visited the "Hotel Without a Name." Once known as the Hotel Praha, it cannot now be located in any guidebooks, travel brochures, or even in the local telephone directory. It is kept in spic-and-span though austere order for visiting Communist dignitaries.

It took us until 1968, however, to realize the identity of the Hotel Without a Name's gently complaining guest. Alexander Dubček was, in 1967, First Secretary of the Communist Party in the Slovak portion of Czechoslovakia. On his periodic trips to Prague from his home in Bratislava, he used to stay at the Hotel Without a Name where, to narrow Dubček's maneuvering, President (and nationwide First Secretary) Novotný used to have his telephone service put "out of order."

Chapter 2]

Wednesday 8 July—
Tuesday 31 October 1967

TO MUCH OF THE OUTSIDE WORLD, PRAGUE IS KAFKA TER-
ritory. To a surprisingly large number of Czechs, however, Kafka (who
was born in Prague in 1883 and did most of his writing here) is not
considered "one of us" because he wrote in German. They lump Kafka
with such other German-speaking "outsiders" as Rainer Maria Rilke
and Franz Werfel (*Song of Bernadette*), both born in Prague; Gustav
Mahler, born in Bohemia; Sigmund Freud, born in Příbor, north Moravia; and Albert Einstein, who taught in Prague from 1910 to 1912 and
conceived and published the fundamentals of his theory of relativity
while here. Nevertheless, Kafka is Prague and Prague is Kafka and
does anyone who's been in Prague for long think Kafka wrote fiction?

Consider, for example, the Registration of Foreigners section of the
police department, the place where any alien must go to inform the
authorities of his local address (if you stay at a hotel, the hotel does
this for you) or to seek an extension of his visa, permission to reside, or
even (once resident here) an exit visa. It adjoins the main police headquarters in the Old Town, a few blocks from Kafka's birthplace. My
friends assure me that the Registration of Foreigners building was
never used by the Gestapo.

On my first visit there to extend a tourist visa in 1967 I entered a
waiting room that served four doors numbered 2 through 5. All four
doors and parts of the walls were padded with thick yellow mattresses;
the rest of the room was painted a coarse bilious green. Thanks to the
padding, if you knocked on any of the four doors, you wouldn't be
heard; presumably, neither would any words or screams from inside.
But just to make doubly certain, the waiting room was also filled by
soft music played loudly.

At each of the four doors was a doormat. And on each of the four
doormats stood a foreigner waiting his turn and wiping his shoes me-

thodically. When somebody emerged through one of the padded doors, the person on the doormat would go inside and the first foreigner on a long bench would take his place. The other people on the bench would slide up one seat. The first standee would take the last place on the bench. Britons and Americans, Hungarians and Belgians, businessmen from India and students from Senegal all added color and universality, but very few words, to this intimidating scene.

My first test of will power came when I reached the doormat. Having wiped my feet in the lobby, I was damned if I would submit to this inhuman system by wiping them again.

So far, it was almost as much Menotti (*The Consul*) as Kafka. But when my turn came to leave the doormat and enter the room, I was confronted by an outrageous touch of Kafka: Behind all that padding were the friendliest, most solicitous, and most gracious officials I have yet to meet in Prague.

My first and favorite "interrogator" was a young English-speaking working mother named Mrs. Babecká, who greeted me with a smile, an offer of a cigarette, a word of admiration for my passport photo, and then a squeal of delight: "Your name is Alan? My son is named Alan, too!" She flourished a snapshot of a toddler, explained "Of course we call him *Alánek,* meaning 'Little Alan'," and cooed over some passport photos of my daughters. After a delightful chat, my visa was stamped with a routine extension. Of course, when an answer had to be "no" or "not yet," Mrs. Babecká couldn't change it to "yes," but she sent you away feeling that she was doing her best for you.

The four men and a woman with whom she worked proved equally genial and understanding, even the hulking, glowering plainclothesman I've dubbed "The Brute." Every time I go there, I think about not only Kafka, but the dilemma of the average American in a police state: When you cross the threshold, you are thoroughly conditioned to confess—and even a little disappointed that you have nothing to confess.

My political awareness of Kafka began that summer when I had lunch around the corner from the police station with a friend of Miloš Forman's. Igor Hájek was a young man with pale, pink-rimmed glasses, a crew cut, and a soft round face. Best known as an editor of the Writers Union's weekly, *Literární Noviny (Literary News)*, he was widely respected as the Czech translator of J. D. Salinger and John Updike; he won an important prize for his rendition of the latter's *Centaur.*

Translation is a particularly respected art in Prague because the groundwork for the whole Czech nation was laid by a crusading band of nineteenth-century linguists. They enriched what was outlawed (by the Habsburgs) as a subversive peasant dialect by codifying its mythology and translating the world's classics, hitherto published in German, into the Czech tongue.

"Kafka wasn't mentioned much here after the country went Communist in 1948," Igor told me, "but he really started coming into his own again four or five years ago. There was an International Kafka Congress here that was really a political argument shrouded in talk about literature. The key issue was *alienation*. The East German faction insisted that Kafka wasn't relevant because alienation disappears with socialism. A number of Czechs maintained, however, that a man could be just as alienated working in the Škoda car works as he could at General Motors. He needed to feel that he had a say, that he mattered. And the Czechs hinted that socialist bureaucrats could be as alienated as any others. The issue was really whether or not socialists wanted to see things as they are, which is the only way you can begin to improve them."

The Kafka argument spilled into the pages of Igor's weekly *Literární Noviny* where it continued long after the Kafka conference had left town. And the man in the street picked it up and started reading *Literární Noviny,* not because he cared that much about Kafka, but because he recognized that, unlike so much of what he was made to read, this *did* concern his own situation.

From this point onward, *Literární Noviny* was destined to be a chronic and crucial battleground in a war of words between idealists and ideologists that was just erupting openly when I first met Igor. With its own brand of down-to-earth literary talk about reality, *Literární Noviny* had amassed a circulation of 140,000 and a collection of stern warnings from the Communist Party's Central Committee. At least once, an editor-in-chief had been kicked upstairs to a less sensitive post (managing director of a book publishing house) and replaced by the party's hand-picked choice. "But even then," said Igor, "it didn't take long for the new man to surrender to the insistence of his editorial staff."

That June, the Writers Union held a Congress at which the most outspoken speeches against Novotný's censors, against his definition of "true socialism," and against his pro-Arab posture toward the Middle East were made by three editors of *Literární Noviny.*

President Novotný, whose responses could have been ghost-written by Kafka, insisted publicly that "the Writers Congress was part of a campaign organized and financed from abroad against the celebrations of the fiftieth anniversary of the Great October Revolution" in Mother Russia's womb.

When we were having lunch later that summer, Igor Hájek was surprised nothing worse had happened than a party-ordered reshuffle of *Literární Noviny's* editorial board and removal of some of the louder dissidents at the Congress, including playwrights Pavel Kohout and Václav Havel, from a list of candidates in a Writers Union election.

Almost three months after our lunch, however, the three outspoken editors were suddenly expelled from the Communist Party for "conduct incompatible with membership." Kohout was given a stern official "reprimand with a warning." Worst of all, *Literární Noviny* itself was taken away from the Writers Union. It was put under Minister of Culture Karel Hoffmann, who immediately fired fourteen of the nineteen staffers (the other five, including Igor, resigned in protest) and recruited replacements qualified to apply "party-minded ideological and political criteria to criticism and journalism." The insipid result of their labors was known as "Tales of Hoffmann."

What this whole incident proved, however, had little or nothing to do with culture: The sluggish response of the Central Committee, three months between provocation and reprisal, was the first strong hint that Antonín Novotný was having trouble keeping his house in order.

I was back in New York by then winding up our affairs there. Valerie had already started taking Czech lessons and I joined her whenever I could. During those last weeks in our native New York City, however, we found ourselves having a more severe language problem with anxious relatives and genuine well-wishers who could not comprehend our decision to put not only America, but capital-*W* Western civilization, behind us. They peppered us with disturbing news items and clippings about:

 . . . the "show" trial of a young writer named Jan Beneš for his contacts with Czech exiles abroad. He was sentenced to five years.

. . . the expulsion, after twenty-nine hours of interrogation, of a Swiss journalist known for his friendships within the Prague intellectual milieu, into whose hot center Forman and S + Š were plunging me.

. . . the spectacular defection to Israel of the Slovak novelist Ladislav Mňačko in protest against Novotný's Middle Eastern stand and the Czechoslovak authorities' refusal to publish Mňačko's novel, *A Taste of Power.*

. . . the official kidnapping (and subsequent release) of a Czechoslovak-born naturalized American when a Russian plane made an unscheduled stop in Prague.

. . . the murder of Charles H. Jordan, executive vice-chairman of an American Jewish organization, whose corpse was found floating in the Vltava that August.*

All the omens seemed to read: "Americans, stay home!" For 1967 was a time in America just a little before the full burden of our nation's Vietnam adventure came home to roost. It was not yet a time when you heard what we hear now from home: "All the good people are getting out" . . . "Joannie and I found out last summer that even traveling through Europe and staying in *pensions* is cheaper than just living in New York" . . . and all the other symptoms of deflated hopes and inflated costs. We could not have guessed then that we were going to fulfill the fantasy of half the people of our own generation that we knew in New York. Neither did they; most of them advised us either not to go or to go somewhere else.

My first line of verbal defense in these arguments was to cite President Johnson's own economic efforts to "build bridges" to Eastern Europe. But even liberals deigned to mail me Henry J. Taylor's syndicated column, in which that grand old Cold Warrior (Eisenhower's Ambassador to Switzerland, which he pronounced a left-wing "international center of Communist espionage") assailed this pretense:

. . . Come with me to the other end of the "bridge" and ponder some places tourists seldom see.

Czech President Antonín Novotný . . . lives in medieval Hradčany

---

* Many theses attribute Jordan's death to culprits ranging from the CIA to the NKVD. My own sources in Prague put the blame on an Arab visitor who was still smarting from Israel's victory in that June's "Six-Day War." Jordan's presence in Prague apparently unleashed a passion similar to that which, less than a year later, would kill Senator Robert F. Kennedy.

Castle, kinglike and remote. A glance from him can mean a bullet and a coffin, with a funeral to order. . . .

Throughout the country, every apartment house and group of homes has a communist house warden. His reports even include seeing if you have a good record for going to church. A house warden often stands at a church door checking those who attend.

Taylor concluded by describing the Iron Curtain as an electrified fence "with twists and turns and varying controls [which] runs all the way from Bratislava to Hong Kong":

This is the line of barbed wire, charged with a death-dose of electricity, and of police dogs, Communist sentries, watch towers, Tommy guns and mine fields that holds the Czechs inside their country.

The tall wooden posts, duplicated three tiers deep, have a thick mattress of wire interwoven like a basket between each row. But first you encounter a false frontier. It is a duplicate, except that once you break through (if you can) and believe you are free you are still in Red Czechoslovakia. It is set a mile inland to fool you.

Give or take some exaggeration and hyperbole, these last two paragraphs sketched the Western perimeter of the picture we were about to enter. From the other side, as a onetime visitor to the American Second Armored Cavalry when it was patroling West Germany's border with Czechoslovakia, I had gazed through a telescope at the former Czech village of Eichelberk, which had been razed and leveled for surveillance's sake. Plowed ground makes escapes more difficult. At night, all you could see was a 6-foot-high neon-lit red star. And you could hear an eerie, scraping noise. "What's that?" I had inquired. The American sentry on duty, a sergeant, had intoned dramatically: "That noise you hear is coming to you across the Iron Curtain." Then he had added, more warmly: "But the first time I heard one of those dogs yipping, I felt the same way you do. I thought it was a lion roaring."

So why should I take my family to live amidst such indignities as an Iron Curtain and a Berlin Wall? I could joke that these were no worse than a customs examination at Kennedy Airport. Or I could answer quite candidly that I was willing to expose us to the perils of Prague because I liked the people there and felt at home among them. Or that, with an American passport, I was safer in Prague than in New York City. But all of these responses sounded trivial and insincere even to me as I heard myself speak them.

We were going to Prague, I think, largely on an assumption of mine that in all systems the people are far more decent than the governments that purport to represent them. Rather than try to convince my older relatives of this, I found it simpler to tell them as glumly as I could manage that I had to go to Prague for my work.

In late September, my accreditation still hadn't come and I fired off a cable to Filmexport. I received this optimistic reply by air mail:

> I was talking to Mr. Fárek, who is now the man at the Foreign Ministry in charge of your problem and he assures me that there are no difficulties to get approval for your stay here, and that he hopes to be able to give you the final approval in writing within next three weeks.
>
> As concerns apartment, they told me that in the moment you will get written approval, they will immediately take care of same. Anyhow, they do know that you would like to be here from approximately 15 Dec., 1967, and therefore they will make all the arrangements in time. . . .

We gave notice at our Perry Street brownstone. The Endicott Overseas Movers were coming on the 31st of October to ship our household goods (weighing 2,900 pounds and costing about $1,250 to transport) to Prague, first on the *S.S. Container Forwarder* to Antwerp and then overland to Levy c/o Filmexport, Praha. When three weeks had elapsed without further word, I cabled my Prague address: "ANXIETY MOUNTING STOP PLEASE PROD FAREK TO RUSH CREDENTIALS". Back came a cable reading: "PLEASE CONTAC OUR PRESS ATTACHE WASHINGTON AS SOON AS POSSIBLE FOR INTRODUCTION AND BRIEF TALK STOP EVERYTHING SEEMS OK BUT AMBASSY MUST CONFIRM APPROVAL TO PRAGUE REGARDS".

I had already dealt with the Press Attaché in Washington. I called him again and he said: "It's always a pleasure and I've been meaning to call you, but I forgot your telephone number." I hung on his every word as he continued: "What I wanted to know from you is: I have been reading dispatches about your World Series and I would like to ask how you Americans pronounce the name *Yastrzemski?*"

He had no news about my plans to go to Prague.

Fifteen minutes later, I cabled Prague: "WASHINGTON PRESS ATTACHE SAYS HE RECEIVED NO INSTRUCTIONS FROM

PRAGUE STOP AT MY BEHEST HE IS QUERYING PRAGUE BY MAIL STOP HELP".

A week later, Filmexport cabled: "REGRET CANNOT INTERFERE ANYMORE STOP YOU MUST WORK OUT WHOLE MATTER WITH OUR AMBASSY WASHINGTON REGARDS".

"The hell with this!" I said. Without even breaking the bad news to my family, I went to the ČEDOK * travel bureau near Grand Central, picked up four applications for tourist visas, filled them out, and sent them (along with our passports and $4.00 each) to the visa section of the Czechoslovak Embassy in Washington. Forty-eight hours later, via Registered Mail, we had tourist visas valid upon arrival in Czechoslovakia for up to 90 days.

Tourist visas are Iron Curtain annoyances which exist more for fiscal reasons than for keeping out undesirables. A Western visitor is obliged to exchange—either for prepayment vouchers valid in hotels or else for cash upon arrival—a certain minimum sum per day of stay. In Czechoslovakia 1967, this daily minimum was $3.00 per person over fourteen.**

A brief lesson in Communist economics is in order here:

The Russian ruble is officially valued at $1.11. On the open world money market, however, its actual buying power is 23 cents. The fallout from this artificial effort to maintain the prestige of the ruble is felt as far away as Cuba, where the peso still pretends to be worth a dollar. In general, throughout the Communist world, the ratio between the official price and "what it's worth in real money" is 5-to-1.

This particular unreality has spawned a thriving black market among natives who need hard Western currency if they can ever hope to travel abroad. An army of hotel doorman and sidewalk solicitors will buy dollars from tourists for five times the official rate and re-sell them to natives at *double that price,* but without the State Bank's limit on the number of dollars a native can buy (in Czechoslovakia, $5.00 to $10.00 per person per trip to the West).

When a tourist takes out a visa, then, the State gets at his hard currency dollars before the black marketeers do. The State, which

* ČEDOK, the State travel and hotel agency, is a word contrived from *Č*eskoslovenská *D*opravní *K*ancelář Czechoslovak Travel Bureau.
** In mid-1970, it was raised to $5.00 a day.

needs to buy machinery and other supplies from the West, pays the tourist a "225 per cent bonus rate of exchange" which is considered a good buy by travelers who don't know that 500 per cent is available downtown.

End of economics lesson.

And now we were about to head away from home! On Monday the 30th of October, 1967, friends carted away our washing machine and other trophies we'd sold or donated. On Tuesday, the morn of Halloween, the Endicott movers came and dismantled our last seven years in New York in less than four hours. Watching the whole world she'd known being crated and then trucked away, Erika reverted to thumb-sucking.

All we had left were two cots (borrowed from our landlord) and a sofa bed that would be called for in the morning. We had our tourist visas, though no accreditation, and so, on our last night in Greenwich Village, I think I was still waiting for a Sign.

At 11 P.M., Val and I were just opening the sofa bed when we heard a jolting clunk from our landlord's garden apartment below. I opened our door to find the landlord standing at the foot of the stairs with blood streaming down his head.

He and his wife had been watching television in their living room, which opens onto the garden in the rear. They were clearly illuminated by the picture tube. Any burglar would have known that he wasn't breaking into an apartment whose occupants were out for the night. Hearing a noise, our landlord and landlady had glanced up to see two men breaking in. One had picked up a garden shovel and was smashing the glass door. The other man had been pointing a pistol at them.

The wife had run screaming onto Perry Street, from where she could summon help and yet be near their two children sleeping in the front bedroom. Her husband had picked up the chair in which he was sitting and raised it as a shield. It wouldn't have done much good against the man with the gun, but fortunately he didn't fire. Instead, the man with the shovel had bashed our landlord on the head. Then, hearing the landlady's screams, both men had retreated, climbing the garden wall and disappearing into the New York night.

"Must've been addicts," said the policeman who took the report.

"They'll do anything for a fix and seeing the TV on just meant that they could hock it for heroin."

Thus, on our last midnight in hitherto safe Greenwich Village, I wound up baby-sitting with the landlord's daughters while he and his wife went to St. Vincent's Hospital for repairs. And on that haunted Halloween, I reflected that if the Village—whose bright lights, late hours, and populated streets had made it one of the few New York locales where you could walk at night—held such perils, what did we have to fear in Prague, a city where you could still stroll in the parks at midnight?

Interlude] Let there be light

THAT SAME HALLOWEEN IN PRAGUE, HOWEVER, THERE was a rare and therefore shocking outburst of violence.

For two years, the technical students in the modern dormitories behind the tenth-century Strahov monastery had been without adequate electricity. That night, 1,500 of them embarked upon a candlelight procession toward the center of Prague. "We want light! We want to study!" they chanted—and these words, as well as their march, were construed as a political challenge to the system. Emerging from the park behind Strahov and heading through the rococo Firehouse Square, they were met by a police roadblock and then tear gas and truncheons as they tried to make their way onto Neruda Street leading downtown.

The students threw stones as the police chased them back into the park. Later, police roamed the streets beating up students who hadn't even been in the demonstration. Thirteen students and three policemen were injured, two of the students seriously.

Not one word about the Strahov riot appeared in the Czechoslovak mass media during the remaining two months of 1967. But, like the riot itself, the news spilled out of the park and the wave of revulsion it uncorked spread quickly to the Communist Party Central Committee.

Along with the Writers Congress scandal, the Strahov riot marked the beginning of the end for Novotný's dictatorship. As Ladislav Mňačko observed from his sanctuary in Israel: "It was a revolt of the young. It was the revolt of the generation that grew up under socialism and therefore expected far more of socialism than those who brought the system into being."

And all they had wanted was a little light.

Chapter 3

Tuesday 7 November 1967—
Monday 1 January 1968

TO CUT DOWN ON "CULTURE SHOCK" AND TO DRAMATIZE
the dimensions of our move, I had decided against flying my family
and myself from New York to Prague. Sitting down in a flying restaurant at Kennedy Airport and disembarking at Ruzyně nine hours later
lacked the momentousness I sought. Instead, our rowboat to Prague
would be an oceanliner which made a leisurely two-week sail to
Piraeus, the seaport for Athens. After another fortnight soaking up the
good Greek sunshine, we would fly a Czechoslovak Airlines* nonstop
Tupolev jet for two-and-a-half hours and land in Prague several days
before Christmas.

All across the Atlantic and along the Mediterranean, I regaled my
family with memories of Athens. I harped on the guards in embroi-
dered skirts who would be guarding the Tomb of the Unknown Soldier
across Constitution Square from our hotel. In the square itself we
would have outdoor luncheons beneath the orange trees.

"Oranges in winter?" asked Monica.

"Soldiers in skirts!" Erika marveled.

"Daddy's teasing," Monica concluded.

"Wait and see," said Daddy.

Instead, we docked to a prophetic welcome of tanks and sandbags.
In Constitution Square, each sentry in skirts had given way to a platoon of Greek marines in helmets and battle garb with rifles at the
ready. The oranges were in bloom, but you could scarcely see them for
the anti-aircraft guns. Greece was in the throes of *not* having a coup.
King Constantine had broadcast an appeal to his nation to rise up
against the dictatorship of rightist colonels who had seized power eight

---

* Czechoslovak Airlines (ČSA) is also known by its ticketing code name, OK, which
just about sums up its operations. It and Russia's Aeroflot, however, rank as the
best of the Eastern European (or "salami service") airlines.

months earlier. Then the King and the Royal Family had flown to exile in Italy.

In times of civil emergency it really pays to have a confirmed reservation. Our taxi was halted by soldiers one block from the hotel. When I showed our confirmation slip, a tank swiveled aside and we were allowed to walk through a labyrinth of sandbags to the Kings Palace Hotel. Three soldiers carried our luggage.

"Is it safe?" we asked the concierge.

"There is no trouble unless the King comes back," he said, shaking his head sadly, "and the King isn't coming back."

Two hours later, he phoned our room with some news. The military commander for downtown Athens had given us a pass to march up the street to see Walt Disney's *Fantasia* in English with Greek subtitles. And so we passed our first afternoon together in ancient Greece watching Bacchus and Diana and all their cherubic playmates romp to the tune of Beethoven's *Pastoral Symphony*. The children could tell we were someplace else in the world because periodically the film halted for vendors to tramp the aisles and hawk ice cream, lemonade, and sandwiches. And afterwards in the coffee lounge, one of the girls dropped her water glass. It broke and we were charged eight drachmas (24 cents) by a man who kept murmuring "think nothing of it." We were no longer in the land of the scot-free.

When we left the cinema, all of the tanks and most of the sandbags were gone. By morning, the sentries were back in their skirts and guided tourism as usual had resumed. Europe and the Middle East have lived through too many catastrophes to let them interfere with business one hour more than is necessary.

We scaled the Acropolis on a night of the full moon and retreated down the Plaka to a *taverna* which used to be a mansion of King Otto. There the waiter lit a fireplace for us and the pianist taught the children to play *Frère Jacques*. We rode a funicular up Mount Lycabettus and dropped in on a morning mass at St. George's. We took a bus to Corinth and stood in the agora where St. Paul addressed the Corinthians. The children played hide-and-seek in Agamemnon's beehive tombs and took bows in the ancient theatre of Epidaurus. Best of all, on our last afternoon in Athens, it snowed! We wandered through the Royal Gardens and fed bagels to the ducks, peacocks, pheasants, and stork who accompanied us on our stroll. Miraculously (for Greece), the snow stuck to the orange trees.

"We're in fairyland!" Monica announced.

"Sno-Crop," said Erika, to whom it had all the aesthetics of a frozen orange juice can.

We were between two worlds but limbo can be beautiful. And right now this limbo was King Constantine's in name, but ours to walk through. We were seeing a sight few Athenians have ever seen. The snow stopped at 4 P.M. and quickly blew away from the oranges.

We thought of that scene often in the next few months because we didn't see another orange all that winter. (Our flight, originating in Bagdad and terminating in Prague, left Athens early—at dawn.) In Prague, there were so many shortages that the dying Novotný regime had a standard form answer to queries about the scarcity of any commodity. Whether the item was full-length mirrors or paper clips, the explanation invariably was:

> There have been inquiries about a current insufficiency of FULL-LENGTH MIRRORS OR PAPER CLIPS. We wish to inform you that no major miscalculation on our part in supplying estimated needs is involved. The factory responsible produced its quota of FULL-LENGTH MIRRORS OR PAPER CLIPS and then re-tooled for producing another necessary item which cannot be identified here. However, public consumption of FULL-LENGTH MIRRORS OR PAPER CLIPS exceeded previous norms, which gave rise to the current scarcity. As soon as the present quota of producing other goods is fulfilled, the factory in question will re-tool back to FULL-LENGTH MIRRORS OR PAPER CLIPS, but this will not be for an indefinite period of time.

One always suspected, though it couldn't be proved, that these defensive answers came off a pre-printed pad with only four or five blank spaces to be filled in by some bureaucrat. But the revelation we were all waiting for came that winter, when all the consumer bulletins chorused happily that oranges were now in plentiful supply at the fruit stores. Nevertheless, there wasn't an orange to be had in all of Prague.

The press made its usual polite inquiry (just once) and back came the answer every cynic in Prague had dreamed of:

> There have been inquiries about a current insufficiency of ORANGES. We wish to inform you that no major miscalculation on our part in supplying estimated needs is involved. The factory responsible produced its quota of ORANGES and then re-tooled for producing another necessary item which cannot be identified here. However, public consumption of ORANGES exceeded previous norms, which gave rise to. . . .

A few days later, there was a "further clarification": A trainload of oranges from Greece, routed to Prague via Graz, Austria, had indeed crossed the Czechoslovak frontier, but the train had subsequently been misplaced. The public thirst for information was more than gratified while the oranges rotted on some forgotten railroad siding.

Like the oranges, the Czechoslovak economy was stagnating. The Russians had liberated but looted the country in 1945; after it went Communist three years later, its Soviet masters systematically bled the land of its natural resources, particularly uranium. They achieved such a stranglehold on the Czechoslovak economy that today nine out of ten cars here are driven on Soviet gasoline and two out of three rolls are baked from Soviet flour.

Worse still, unfavorable trade treaties negotiated at Russian behest transformed a small nation famed for its light-industry craftsmanship (china, glassware, radios, and consumer goods) into a heavy-industry hunchback manufacturing the heavy machinery and whole factories needed to make the Soviet Union into the light-industry nation that Czechoslovakia once was. This vision was never realized by Russia, but the effort to achieve it was ruinous to Czechoslovakia. Her heavy-industry output never measured up to world export standards. And within the first decade of grinding out junk to meet artificial quotas, Czechoslovakia's light-industry consumer goods deteriorated in quality or vanished in quantity. By 1964, only a third of 4,000 products surveyed met the rest of the world's quality standards.

The *a priori* logic and illogical priorities of the Kafka bureaucracy within Czechoslovakia have compounded the felony. Two examples from personal experience come to mind:

. . . Two winters before we came, Czechoslovakia had a warm winter. On the basis of that winter's figures, the coal quota was halved for the next applicable winter, three winters thence. This applicable winter was a very cold one that the government officially described as a "coal calamity."

. . . A glass factory in Slovakia is making light bulbs (just the bulbs, not the wiring) for Tesla Electronics. Going through the plant, I am shown the first new automated equipment and assembly line (from America and Japan), which hasn't quite been tuned properly; more than half the bulbs are coming out visibly faulty or shattered. Much of the assembly-line's work is still being done by grandmothers in smocks, who carry the unfinished bulbs in handfuls from one station to the next; the ladies' breakage rate seems lower, except when the manager and I stop to chat with them. I ask what happens to the bulbs when they leave the plant. "They are sent by truck to Tesla in Prague, where they are wired." And suppose you want to buy one in Slovakia? "Oh, after they're finished in Prague, a certain number of them come back here." The vision of these fragile bulbs jouncing along cobblestoned highways on the 500-mile round trip is not comforting. Nor are the manager's words: "Slovakia is underdeveloped and, after all, the raw material for the glass comes from here, so we ought to have a part in the process. And you must understand about what you have just seen that, even in the best glass factories anywhere in the world, a 35 per cent breakage rate is normal; it's the best system of quality control there is. So we're not that far from par as we may seem to you." Later, in the nearest city, I try to buy a light bulb. There are none to be had that day.

Thanks to State ownership, mismanagement, and the removal of all incentives, a nation of small shopkeepers became a maze of indifferent clerks staffing empty counters. Not long ago, a friend of mine went to the stationery store with a shopping list of eight items, starting with air-mail envelopes and ending with toilet paper which, being a paper product, is sold in stores that sell paper. As he read the list, the woman who was waiting on him ticked off her eight answers without looking up:

"There *are* no air-mail envelopes. . . . We had those two years ago, but not now. . . . We were supposed to receive a shipment of them yesterday. . . . All out of these. . . . Only available in a much larger size. . . . We're expecting napkins next week, but don't count on it. . . . They've stopped making those. . . . We sold all our toilet paper yesterday."

My friend turned to leave empty-handed, but first he asked in exasperation: "Well, what *do* you have anyway?"

"We open for business at 8 A.M. and we close at 5 P.M.," the woman replied, still without looking up. And that is often the extent of shopkeeping today.

Services are comparably inadequate. Normal dry cleaning takes twelve to fourteen days; "express" service means one week and a 33 per cent surcharge. (This is in a residential district; downtown, it's twice as fast and the surcharge is 50 per cent.) A good dry cleaner is one who makes you remove the buttons before you give in your coat; otherwise, the machinery will demolish them. Good or bad, all dry cleaning here doesn't remove the spots; it simply laminates them. Worst of all, the cloth dry-cleaning tickets are *sewed* onto the clothes by an invisible army of the world's best seamstresses and can be removed, without damaging the fabric, only by surgical scissors. How one longs for the Spotless Cleaners and their vicious staplers!

By 1956, the Czechoslovak economy was suffering paroxysms which the regime sought to explain rather than cure. "Deteriorating trends were skillfully said to be due to floods in the spring, drought in the summer, rains in the autumn, and frosts in the winter," the brilliant economist Ota Šik remarked sardonically. "At the same time, the political Old Guard knew the true state of affairs; yet they opposed every necessary change."

Despite the desperate need for scientific and technological change, less than 1 per cent of Czechoslovakia's annual investments were in science. Housing construction here takes three times as long as in the West. A linotypist in Prague rides to work on a quaint but dilapidated tram that was built before World War II and then works a printing press of the same vintage. Much of any worker's time is devoted to ingenious patching of the obsolete equipment with which he deals. In 1961, more than a third of the Czechoslovak engineering industry worked from blueprints more than five years old; a tenth from blueprints fifteen or more years old.

Crisis was reached in 1962, when the annual rate of economic growth, already the slowest in all of Europe and the Communist world, ground to a halt. Wages actually dropped, thereby worsening the standard of living and prompting cutbacks in housing construction. A year later, Czechoslovakia was the only nation in Europe to produce less than it had the year before.

Russia and the other Communist nations gave stopgap transfusions of money, but always with the heavy-industry strings that had unleashed the disaster. Finally, Novotný was forced to turn to Ota Šik, the part-Jewish economics professor who had been his fellow concentration-camp inmate during the war.* On several occasions after

---

* I don't know if this was the case with Šik, but a number of Czech Jews we know avoided Nazi extermination by confessing that they were Communists when they were caught in underground activities, thereby distracting their captors from matters of ancestry. Most of these Jews were also, incidentally, dedicated Communists.

Novotný came to power in 1953 (as acting First Secretary of the Communist Party), Šik had pressed their past connection to urge the formation of an economics brain trust. "But," Šik recalled ruefully, "Mr. Novotný doesn't like being instructed by others."

Even after Šik had been called in to save the economy, he was at first refused permission to explain his objectives at the next Party Congress. Thanks to the intervention of several other party officials, he was put on the program but as the last of a long list of speakers. Later Novotný declared that Šik never should have been allowed to speak at all.

Šik's offense was his proposing a New Economic Plan whereby wholesale prices would be determined by market forces instead of by party hacks . . . incentives would be introduced for both workers and management . . . factories would be allowed to dismiss unnecessary workers, reinvest profits, and even distribute them as bonuses to workers. Šik hinted that loans and other technical assistance from the West were required if Czechoslovakia could ever hope to modernize. And he challenged the myth that "socialist ownership could only have the form of State ownership." Šik contended that "personal enterprise based on one's own work and family help is not contrary to socialism because it doesn't constitute exploitation of man by man. It exists in other socialist countries." In all of them, in fact, and particularly in East Germany, the most economically advanced of the satellite nations. Šik added that "Czechoslovakia is the only one to have liquidated, for dogmatic reasons, even the last shoemaker."

Over Novotný's objections, Šik's economic reforms went into effect at the beginning of 1967. Its first small achievement was almost immediate. The Prague Taxi Service was reorganized and a limited number of private car owners were licensed to work as independent cabbies. The reorganization revealed such waste of funds and human energy that a few basic measures were able to transform a municipal enterprise running at a loss into one that showed a profit by the end of the year, even after a raise in wages and a lowering of the fare.

Elsewhere, however, Šik's economic reforms were encountering sabotage at the hands of bureaucrats who recognized that the superfluous jobs to be abolished might well be theirs. To make matters worse, President Novotný himself dropped in at factories, beer halls, and even workers' weddings to crusade against Šik's reforms which were, the

President insisted, "solving shortcomings and difficulties at the expense of workers, pensioners, and other socially-weak strata." Novotný hinted ominously that this was a state of affairs he "would not permit."

Šik's heated rejoinders ("absolute fabrications resulting from a complete lack of understanding") went largely unpublished in the controlled press. But Šik had the ear of a few influential politicians who shared his concern, and the economic situation was coming to a boil when our jet from Athens touched down in Prague the week before Christmas, 1967.

Miloš Forman and Jiří Šlitr were waiting each with a car to help transport our nine suitcases. Suchý had been unable to come, so he sent a cousin to pay his compliments.

Our friends delivered us to the Palace Hotel on the Street of Lords (*Panská ulice*), which parallels part of Wenceslas Square. The Street of Lords is so named because, while only a block long, it houses half a dozen former palaces of the aristocracy, including the American Family Levy's first address in Prague. The Palace Hotel proved old and faded, but pleasantly elegant—with a minimum of the bowing and scraping, tipping and spying that would make the Alcron a hellhole for children. The assistant manager, Milan Horák, showed us to our room and said we could stay as long as we wanted but he hoped, for our sake, that hotel living wouldn't last too long. Pan* Horák pointed to our two double windows and said: "That should be your refrigerator in the winter." Then he told us where we could buy milk and other perishables to be stored on our window sill.

We had one large double bedroom with high ceiling and chandelier, an extra sofa bed and cot, and a round cocktail table for dining-in. Our adjoining bathroom had two sinks, a toilet, a bidet, and a tub with hand-shower and a mysterious cord. When we pulled it, the chambermaid came running. We had given the emergency signal for heart trouble or else a fall in the bathtub.

At the tourist rate of exchange, this nest of ours cost $12.50 a night, including two breakfasts (which fed four amply). For paying directly in dollars or travelers checks, we were given a 10 per cent discount, however. Considering that our five rooms in the Village had rented for $275 a month, the cost of hotel living in Prague was not too much

* Pan = Mr.; Paní = Mrs.; Slečna = Miss.

different for us from apartment living in Manhattan. But we hadn't all been in one room back home.

It was nightfall by the time we had settled in, unpacked, and napped. The downtown stores were staying open for Christmas shopping, although the choice of goods struck us as limited. Monica and Erika were delighted to discover, at the foot of the Street of Lords, the biggest and best department store in Prague: the House of Children (*Dětský Dům*). Four stories high, it is devoted entirely to the needs of children from cradles to skis, teething rings to teen beauty aids, toys to books. In the House of Children are also a special pediatrics pharmacy, one of the best pastry shops in town (with a coffee counter for grown-ups), and the Little Sun puppet theatre and children's cinema in the sub-basements. (Here, children five and over can be left and entertained in a matron's custody while their mothers shop; at night, it is a discothèque, where teen-agers dance in the aisles.)

We bought a toy boat and a toy train for the Forman twins and another train for Kubik Suchý. The rest of our Christmas shopping (Metaxas brandy and ouzo) had been accomplished in Athens.

On our first morning in Prague—for almost our first year, in fact—Wenceslas Square was a shambles. A pedestrian "subway" (meaning *underpass*) was under construction and so was a passenger "metro" (meaning *subway*). The trams were clattering up and down a make-shift wooden trestle. On foot, you couldn't get from one end of the square to the other without several major detours. Wenceslas Square, incidentally, is not a square at all, but a sloping five-block-long boulevard.

Slowed by an icy rain, we made our way to Old Town Square, just missing the apostles registering 10 o'clock. The rain became a downpour as we pushed on toward the Charles Bridge, a brooding Gothic miracle in stone built across the Vltava between 1357 and 1380. Three centuries later, thirty baroque saints in stone cloaks and gilded haloes were added to guard its sanctity. The Charles Bridge is the one sight in Prague that silences the traveler and ends his shrill game of comparisons with other wonders of the world. That is: if he gets to see it. Because it is for pedestrians only, the Charles Bridge is not on the čedok tours; the sightseeing buses cannot traverse it. But once you stand on the Charles Bridge, you know that you are nowhere else but in Prague. "The Bridge is an emotion," the American novelist Marcia Davenport has written, "not only the emotion of response to unique beauty; but it is visibly and tangibly the spirit of Prague."

To my utter dismay that dismal morning, I couldn't find the Charles Bridge.

It was still there, a stranger reassured me. Its right-bank approach was hidden by scaffolding that extended almost a quarter of the way across. Tourism in the summer; restoration in the winter. We mounted a rickety wooden stairway, maneuvered a couple of treacherous catwalks, and at last descended onto the Charles Bridge.

Keeping to the right, I led my family to the crucifixion tableau with the *I.N.R.I.* inscription to the glory of Jesus in gold Hebrew letters. "It was paid for," I explained, "by a fine imposed on a Jew for blashpheming." "Oh," said my wife disinterestedly, pushing onward into the wind. On a clear day, you could see, framing the Romanesque towers at the other end of the bridge, the great green dome of the magnificent baroque St. Nicholas Church, the Prague Castle rising majestically above it, and the Strahov Monastery and Prague's Eiffel Tower, called Petřín. But today you couldn't even see the bridge towers from the bridge.

I hurried my family across. I didn't need to scrape the ice off my glasses to see that only their blue lips prevented them from asking if *this* was what they had come all this way for.

Fortunately, at the other end lay sanctuary—the gay ultra-modern apartment of Gene Deitch, an American film animator, and his Czech wife Zdenka. Gene Deitch, who directed the 1961 Oscar-winning cartoon *Munro,* is one of Prague's better-kept secrets. So are the origins of his cartoons. *Munro** and a number of others, including thirteen "Tom and Jerries," were made in Czechoslovakia on–the–cheap by American film companies through a subcontractor who paid Gene a retainer that would be handsome as a salary even in New York.

Gene, a Californian who had never been to Europe before, flew from New York to Prague in 1959, and has been here ever since. Tiny, blonde Zdenka—who looks like an animated puppet created by Trnka —took our dripping raincoats and told Valerie right off the bat: "Gene wants Alan to live here. We met him last summer and we got on so

---

* *Munro* was based on Jules Feiffer's comic strip about a four-year-old boy drafted by mistake into the U.S. Army. MUNRO: "But I'm only four!" PSYCHIATRIST: "How long have you been feeling this way, son?"

well. And now we can see that we're going to like his three ladies, too. . . . The other Americans living here are either older or political refugees or Embassy people, although some are quite nice."

The Deitches had voluntarily begun our apartment hunt—right after spending four years waiting and trading and wangling and pressuring and maneuvering and finally winning this apartment for themselves. They had won it in the summer of 1967. Once the previous tenant had defected to the West and the Communist Mayor of Prague had intervened on their behalf. "After all," Gene told us, "what good would our experiences and mistakes be if we couldn't put them to some use helping you guys?"

As we shed our boots and shoes, Zdenka brought us airline slippers which she kept for American visitors. (Czechs, when they go visiting, carry their own slippers to protect their hosts' floors.) Then Zdenka handed us hot tea while Gene invited the four of us to Christmas dinner and the two adults to New Year's Eve.

"We'll come to both," I said.

"Christmas definitely," Val corrected. "New Year's Eve if we can get a baby-sitter."

"How do we go about hiring one?" I asked.

"Damned if I know," said Gene. "Everybody here has a grandmother. But ask at your hotel."

"Maybe," said Zdenka, "they have a list of students who'll mind your children free just to practice English on them."

"On New Year's Eve?" I said.

"You must get here that night," Zdenka told us. "We've invited a lot of people, including some who'll be going out of the country or who may know of a flat that's available."

"We'll be there," said Val, "even if we have to take turns."

We took the tram back to Wenceslas Square for a Red Chinese lunch with Miloš Forman, Jiří Šlitr, and his girlfriend Sylva. Anybody who came to Prague as a friend of Miloš was taken to a Chinese meal. Miloš could not believe that anybody else would want to eat such everyday Czech fare as duck and dumplings.

The Chinsky Restaurant is a tale in itself. During the Marxist solidarity of the early 1950's, Mao's mandarins donated it to Communist Czechoslovakia as a "national restaurant." Delicate but modern, with a subdued glow of daylight to it at any hour, the Chinsky was an early victim of the chill between Red China and the Soviet satellites. First, the Chinese chef was summoned home and no replacement was posted to Prague. Then Peking ceased supplying ingredients.

The resourceful Czech chef who took over the kitchen first tried to duplicate his predecessor's specialties with whatever was available on the local market. Later, he threw away the Mao Cookbook, but kept the menu and simply improvised, shaping whatever was available on the local market into highly-spiced dishes worthy of such listings as *Suei-ču-žou* or 'Buddha's Hand' or 'Happiness.' ("Try a little 'Happiness,'" Miloš would croon, plying us with an irresistible deep-fried-diced-veal-and-almonds creation.) In coping so creatively, the Czech chef not only made his Chinese restaurant one of the best in the Occident and perhaps the most unique in all this world—a place where Pilsener beer comes with the meal and it takes a special request to pry loose a pot of tea—but he also endeared the Chinsky to the Czech jet set.

With such regular customers as Forman and Šlitr and various other cultural and political personalities, the Chinsky began to specialize in an added item that wasn't listed on the menu: Hot Grapevine, Prague Style. In the absence of a free press, virtually the only reliable news source (while the facts were still timely) was the kind of sober and soft-spoken table-hopping which went on in the Chinsky that December afternoon (and which goes on during any time of crisis). By the time our last anise-flavored black egg was washed down by the far-from-last glass of beer, the ricocheting question, "Is something going on up at the Castle?" had been answered in fragments that could be pieced together into this mosaic:

The Writers Union rebellion in June and its delayed-action purge in September had shown some politicians that Novotný was staggering. For reasons having more to do with Slovak nationalism and the crying need for Ota Šik's economic reforms, various members of the Central Committee's ten-man Presidium had risen at their October meeting to denounce Novotný's "personal monopoly" of power. No one man should be both President of Czechoslovakia and First Secretary of the Communist Party, they warned, trying to make it sound impersonal.

One speaker however, had been outspokenly blunt. In a long, emotional speech, the hitherto recessive First Secretary of the Slovak Communist Party, Alexander Dubček, had accused Novotný of breaking promises to and discriminating economically against Slovakia.

This had so infuriated Novotný that he had then and there denounced this unknown Slovak as a "bourgeois nationalist," a charge hitherto equated with prison or death.

The October meeting had ended with the issue still unresolved and the intrigues were just beginning. At first it looked as though Dubček would be eclipsed, if not eradicated. He was dropped from Novotný's official party going to Moscow for the fiftieth anniversary of the October Revolution (which is celebrated in November).

Even before Novotný and his favored friends left for Moscow, there was the Strahov student riot. Novotný paid it little heed, but the grapevine recognized its importance. So did Dubček. By the time Novotný returned from Moscow, he found that Dubček had used his absence to bind together the Slovaks, the economists, the surviving intellectuals and university officials on the 110-man Central Committee, and various other "liberals" * in an opposition that was now calling for Novotný's outright resignation from at least one of his two posts. Meanwhile, the students were staging more protests, usually within Charles University, where the faculty was now telling the police they had no legal right to enter the grounds.

In a belated effort to yank the rug out from Dubček, Novotný had sought to undermine him in Slovakia. When that failed, he had sent an urgent S.O.S. to S. V. Chervonenko, the Russian Ambassador to Czechoslovakia. Chervonenko had contacted Moscow. None other than Leonid Brezhnev, the Soviet party chief, had responded to the call. On a flying visit to Prague, Brezhnev had studied the situation and apparently seen it for the first and last time as what it really was—an internal dispute between loyal Communists and not a threat to the international movement. His parting words had been: "Comrades, this is not my affair. It is the affair of the Czechoslovak workers. It is for you yourselves to decide."

Now, said the Prague grapevine, the Presidium and then the whole Central Committee had met. Novotný was definitely out as First Secretary. His resignation would be announced as soon as a successor was chosen, either a relatively conservative economist (when compared with Ota Šik) named Oldřich Černík or the current Prime Minister (head

---

* In today's Communist parlance, a "conservative" is one who leans toward the more Stalinist certainties of governing; a "liberal" leans away or recoils from them. To confuse matters to Westerners, the word "leftist" is still applied to a "conservative" and "rightist" to a liberal. And, since the invasion of Czechoslovakia, the American-made labels of "hawk" and "dove" also have been applied.

of the Cabinet), a popular Slovak named Jozef Lenárt. But the out-spoken Mr. Dubček could not yet be counted out of the running.

One last buzz of gossip electrified the grapevine in the Chinsky that Saturday before Christmas, 1967: "President Novotný has been given his final walking papers, too. The people who've made him resign as First Secretary think he should resign the Presidency, too, after a de-cent interval, say by the end of March."

I jotted down these deadlines. Never having heeded grapevines be-fore, I wanted to test the accuracy of the one Prague lived by.

A conflict in Christmas Eve invitations had been compromised thusly: In the afternoon, we would go to the Formans for cocktails, cookies, and childplay; in the evening, to Jirka Šlitr's for a more for-mal family celebration with Jirka's parents and Sylva and her mother.

The Forman twins, Matěj and Petr, ten months younger than Mon-ica and three months older than Erika, immediately ushered their new playmates into their bedroom, from which our daughters emerged two hours later speaking a smattering of Czech: *"Podívej se!"* ("Look here!") *"Počkej!"* ("Wait!") *"Dej mi!"* ("Give me!") *"To je moje!"* ("That's mine!")

Matěj announced: "I love Monica. I am going to marry her."

Petr said: "And I will marry Erika when we grow up."

Erika stuck out her chin and said: "I won't grow up."

Monica told her: "But you have to grow up! Mommy says so."

Before anything irrevocable could be said, I interposed diplomati-cally: "Well, if Erika does grow up, I suppose she'll want to marry Petr."

"If I grow up," Erika said firmly, "I'm marrying Mommy."

The Formans, a family of four, rented a three-room apartment (kitchens, bathrooms, W.C.s aren't counted in room totals) while Jiří Šlitr, a bachelor, owned a two-story, ten-room villa high on Malva-zinky, one of the seven hills of Prague. Below was the Villa Bertramka (Mozart's Prague address, where he composed much of *Don Giovanni* for its premiere here) and then "our" city divided by the curving Vltava River. Just down the block from Šlitr was the villa of Antonín Novotný, Jr. The President's son was, at the time, head of ARTIA, the "Foreign Trade Corporation for Import and Export of Cultural Com-modities" such as books, periodicals, and phonograph records. This was an altogether fitting and proper neighborhood for the composer Šlitr, whose own stage presence—often composed of sinister ineptitude, tight-lipped deadpan, and nasal whine—bore a startling resemblance to the senior Novotný that was not purely coincidental.

Could the discrepancy between Šlitr's way of life and Forman's, or, for that matter, the rest of Prague's possibly be socialism? Yes—and all you could say about it was that, as in every other system, the distribution of wealth was strictly economic.

As a film director, Forman was paid a straight salary of $100 a month plus, for each film, a flat fee of $1,200 and an $800 bonus upon completion. He was also paid a comparable flat fee for collaborating on the script, which is why a Czech movie director always takes co-author's credit on the screenplay. He did not share in the worldwide box-office receipts from his film; these went to Czechoslovak Filmexport.

Jiří Šlitr, on the other hand, owned a villa because Czechoslovakia is a dutiful member of the International Copyright Convention. In addition to being a "crown millionaire" from domestic song royalties, Šlitr also had a substantial foreign-currency income from songs that did well in Western Europe.

A Prague villa, incidentally, is seldom the manor house of a sprawling Riviera-like estate. The Czechs use the word in the British sense of "a detached or semidetached dwelling house, usually suburban." Šlitr's had been built during his two sojourns in North America. The décor was semi-Scandinavian elegant; leather sofas and swivel chairs in the downstairs living room, which blended into a dining room with an open brick kitchen flanked by a snack bar that doubled as a serving counter. Airy modernity prevails in the houses-beautiful of Prague's jet set and crown millionaires; it keeps the city's baleful stone exteriors from following one home and perhaps oppressing one.

The paintings on the walls looked like Picassos, Mondrians, and Klees.

"Are they originals?" I asked.

"Why, yes," Šlitr replied, deadpan. "All originals—by Šlitr."

They were neither copies nor forgeries, however, but affectionate tributes to other styles he admired and played at emulating in the studio directly above his living room.

Having settled into his villa, Jirka Šlitr had brought his aging parents from their village in the mountains "to live out their lives in the style they deserve near the medical care they'll need." His mother, a sprightly red-faced white-haired gnome of a woman who looked like

Santa's busiest and happiest helper, would keep house for him. That Christmas Eve, she spoke French to the children*, Czech to Valerie, and a little English to me. While the grown-ups sipped aperitifs (which she served), she also fed our children. By the end of my first Cinzano, our hostess was *Teta Pavla* (Aunt Paula) to Monica and Erika and us.

Teta Pavla refilled our drinks and took all four of us upstairs to a piano where she played "Silent Night," "Jingle Bells," and various Czech Christmas carols, though not "Good King Wenceslas," which is virtually unknown here. After a while, we were interrupted by sleigh bells outside the door. Teta Pavla led us down the stairs on tiptoes.

"It is just as I suspected!" she exclaimed. "St. Nicholas came and went while we were upstairs. But look what he brought!"

Now there was a fire in the fireplace. A Christmas tree, which hadn't been there in the living room when we'd arrived, was now alive with sparklers. Beneath it were gifts: a French tie with matching handkerchief and some Guerlain men's cologne for me; a recording of Smetana's *My Country,* and soft woolen scarf, and two picture books of Prague for Valerie; and a doll and chocolates for each daughter. The children ran to the picture window to call their thanks after St. Nick and somewhere between the stars gleaming above and the lights of Prague blinking below, we all think we caught a glimpse of a miniature sleigh and eight tiny reindeer.

The Šlitrs also trotted out their pet dachshund named Uli, after the hero of the show I was to adapt, and he romped with Monica and Erika until it was time for the two happiest little girls in the world to be put to bed in a guest room. That Christmas Eve was the night Erika decided to grow up. "And when I do," she said, taking her thumb out of her mouth, "I'm going to marry Uli."

Every Jewish father has his own worries, I guess.

In the dining room at 10 P.M., the adults sat down to the traditional Christmas Eve dinner: stuffed snails; fish soup (made, we learned after our second helping, from carp entrails); fried carp (the Christmas fish) and potatoes; and a prune compote all washed down by Moravian red wine and the good beer from Pilsen (*Plzeň*). Then we shifted for des-

* Our daughters had been reared bilingually from the cradle. Valerie, a French-teaching native New Yorker, had talked to them in French, I in English. After a few weeks of living among the Czechs and playing with their children our daughters were trilingual.

sert to the living room, where we were joined by Sylva and her mother who had just come from an almost identical dinner with relatives.

The conversation was lively until midnight, when the feature attraction on Czechoslovak Television was a Šlitr and Suchý Christmas program, featuring them and eight new songs written for the occasion. Having filmed it a week earlier at the Semafor, our host could now sit and enjoy it with us. And the program was relaxed too, genial and amusing and as Christmasy as a Yule log. It was the kind of show Bing Crosby might have done on Christmas TV if our networks could ever afford to be as low-key and loose as radio used to be.

At the end, Šlitr watched the final credits, said "OK," and switched off the set. The conversation resumed. That's all there was to it for my collaborator—no "wasn't I great?" or "how'm I doing, Mom?" or "I really should fire that arranger!" or "d'ya think I enhanced my image, Manny?" Just the normally gratified ego of a man looking over a couple of weeks' work well done and looking forward to his next task.

The next meal we ate fourteen hours later was Zdenka Deitchová's* version of a traditional American Christmas dinner. She had opened up her Christmas gift, a rotisserie, at dawn and welcomed us that afternoon with roast turkey and roast chicken, mashed potatoes, wild cranberries, plus all the trimmings. The Deitches' guests were the Levys plus Mr. and Mrs. Herbert Lass and their teen-age sons Andy and Joe.

Herb Lass is "an old socialist from the Bronx." He is a puckish little fellow whom you tend to call "Herbie" until you hear his very smooth and serious voice. It is a voice capable of giving profound analysis to any question including "How are you?"; it is a real Herbert of a voice. At this point, you compromise and call him "Herb." But the voice is, in fact, one that will haunt you in Prague, for at the Castle or Strahov Monastery or Mozart's Villa Bertramka or a dozen other sights where there are coin-operated orientation lectures in English, you may hear a recording of Herb.

Herb came to Prague after the war as an official of the relief organi-

---

* In Czech, female names generally end in *ová*. Pan Deitch's wife is Paní Deitchová. Pan Levy's wife and daughters are named Levyová here. But surnames that have adjectival meanings do not take the *ová* suffix for females; they take the feminine adjectival form. Because Jiří Suchý's last name is the masculine word for "dry," his wife Běla is Paní Suchá.

zation CARE. He loved the city so much that after CARE shut up shop here he stayed on, importing his Vassar-educated wife Hilda, who used to work for Time-Life. Both their sons were educated in the Czech schools. Joe was home for Christmas from Cambridge University in England; Andy would be entering the Prague Film Faculty (alma mater of Miloš Forman and Jiří Menzel, among others) the next fall.

Now Herb was working for Radio Prague broadcasting the daily hour in English. His program was free of discernible propaganda and Herb told me the restrictions had been dwindling steadily. Hilda, who was now an editor of the monthly *Czechoslovak Life*'s English language edition, had similar observations.

Herb and Hilda wouldn't talk much about the 1950's, but I gathered those were rough years for them and for the other half-dozen American families resident in Prague (aside from the U.S. Embassy transients and occasional academic exchangees). Prague's "permanent" American colony included another broadcaster who came here with a French wife and divorced her to take a Czech bride; an economist and his family, whose children have all married Czechs (the economist was now working with Ota Šik); a U.S. Army colonel who defected here from Berlin during the Cold War and found a new career as a teacher in Prague; and a chemistry professor whose postwar research work in America all turned out to be for military or atomic work, which not only offended him but required security clearances.

Some were Communists; some were idealists; one or two were perhaps both. Some were here when communism happened in 1948; others came because it happened here. When mccarthyism afflicted their native land, they couldn't go home again without serious risk. Most of them lived on their Czechoslovak residential permits and didn't apply for renewal of their U.S. passports for fear they'd be rejected and then have to go to court. One told me about a trip he'd made to Castro's Cuba in the early 1960's: "Of course, we had to go first from Prague to Moscow and then from Moscow to Havana nonstop on Aeroflot."

"But why?" I asked. Soon after Castro came to power, both ČSA and Cubana were flying the Havana-Prague direct route.

"They refueled in Gander, Newfoundland you see," he explained, "and the Canadians took a dim view of Americans who traveled without passports."

Even without passports, though, these people clung quietly to their U.S. citizenship. Long after Joseph McCarthy died and Supreme Court decisions began running in favor of passport holders, these Americans in Prague started dropping in at the U.S. Embassy and saying casually: "I have this passport that seems to have lapsed. Would you mind bringing it up to date?" After some delays and cables to Washington, the Embassy would issue them new passports.

The McCarthy years back home were the Stalinist years here, and most of these expatriates were pariahs in Prague. Foreign languages, foreign accents, and foreigners were all deemed dangerous. It was sometimes punishable for a Czech to associate with anything or anyone Western. One of these American couples didn't even dare to speak English to their son until he was eleven years old.

Thus, these long-term Americans in Prague struck me as rather cynical about all ideologies, which is probably why an optimist like Gene Deitch wanted me here to keep him company. Aside from the Lasses, none of them became close friends of ours; they kept their enthusiasms to themselves and their friendships were those that had already been tested by time. These people all look and act a little tired, but not altogether defeated. Their political ideals never worked out. But their other values such as committing your whole life to a love for family or maybe a city seem to have carried them through. They are, without exception, among the nicest people you will ever meet.

It took us most of our first year in Prague to meet all the people I've just described. Meanwhile, at Christmas dinner 1967, we were concentrating on finding a flat for ourselves, and the Lasses tossed out a few leads, which the Deitches said they'd follow up with invitations for New Year's Eve.

Gene said matter-of-factly: "Someone's bad news here is someone else's good news. Somebody dies. Somebody goes to prison. Somebody escapes. And someone else gets the apartment."

Zdenka asked if we had a baby-sitter for New Year's Eve yet. I said I'd get to work on it as soon as we were back at the hotel.

The man to whom I wanted to entrust this problem, Pan Horák, the English-speaking assistant manager, was working the Christmas night shift.

"Do you think," I said, taking a deep breath, "you could find us a baby-sitter for next Sunday night?"

"Certainly, Mr. Levy," he replied, making a note.

I wanted there to be no misunderstanding about this vital quest: "You realize, Pan Horák, that next Sunday night is New Year's Eve.

And we'll be out past midnight, so we'll need the baby-sitter until three or four in the morning."

"Guaranteed hunky-dory," said Pan Horák, showing off his slang. "Tomorrow is a holiday [St. Stephen's Day], but I'll have the baby-sitter to you first thing Wednesday."

"Oh, it doesn't have to be that fast!" I said. "Eight o'clock Sunday night should be fine. That'll give the baby-sitter and the children a couple of hours to get used to each other."

"Then why not Wednesday?" said Pan Horák. "After all, better safe than sorry."

I assented. I had to admire this kind of Czech thoroughness. Even if I had to pay for the time, this preliminary interview between baby-sitter and clients struck me as an excellent practice. They would not be sprung upon each other as New Year's Eve bolts from the blue.

Pan Horák told me to put the matter out of my mind, which I did until we came in from some sightseeing toward 5 P.M. Wednesday. Pan Horák greeted me excitedly: "Mr. Levy, Mr. Levy! The baby-sitter is here!"

I looked around the lobby, but saw nobody who fit the picture.

"Where is the baby-sitter?" I asked.

"In the room," Pan Horák replied.

"For how long?"

"Since before noon."

"That's five hours!" I said. "I'd better go right up there and have a talk with her."

It seemed strange to me that the Palace Hotel would let somebody into our room at all—let alone for that length of time. It also seemed to me, as I took our key and caught the elevator, that Pan Horák was gazing after me strangely.

When we reached the room there was nobody there. I explored the premises hastily. Nothing was missing. But then the children discovered that something new had been added: *A brand-new wooden high chair.*

"The true baby-sitter," we called it for the rest of our stay at the Palace Hotel. I had been taken at my word and that can be an abject experience for any writer.

During our first few days in Prague, I had learned the first reason why our accreditation hadn't come and Filmexport had suddenly clammed up. Our various friends in Prague had prodded the authorities regularly until, one day, they were called by an official who asked the same basic question: "How do you know for sure that this chap Levy isn't a spy?"

Try though they did, there was no way for them to answer such a question convincingly. Talking it out over Christmas, we had all agreed that my best tack was to act as if the suspicion had never been raised and to proceed in the most open, direct, and honest manner toward my own objective. I would take the family with me to my official runarounds. This would very likely exonerate me. But even if it didn't and Monica and Erika happened to crawl on a bureaucrat's desk, overturning his inkwell (as they did once), it would certainly mark me as the clumsiest espionage agent that SMERSH or SPECTRE ever put down on this earth, the kind of agent every country likes to have spying on it because he's so easy to watch.

To which Gene Deitch added this advice: "This is Kafka country, so you keep working on all possibilities official and unofficial until you have the accreditation in your hand and you're actually *in* your apartment. We were told that this apartment was ours and everything was in order, but it took eight months more before we could actually gain access to the place. Everyone I went to see said: 'Why are you worrying, Mr. Deitch? You have the flat. It is now legally yours.' The fact that we weren't there yet didn't bother anyone but us."

To put ourselves into the proper spiritual frame for our first family confrontation with the Ministry of Foreign Affairs, we arrived shortly after 9 A.M. at the Loreta sanctuary, which lies across a slanted, cobblestoned esplanade from the Černín Palace. It is an unlikely combination that works—the stern grandeur of Černín and the tender passion of Loreta.

Built by the Capuchins as a holy shrine during the Thirty Years War (1618–48), the Loreta is the most invitingly feminine church building you will ever enter. Her curves and swirls and slightly buxom bell tower, her cupids and her cloister, all inspire great tranquility and a kind of peaceful exaltation. Here, brooding turns to meditation. The sight of Monica and Erika romping in the inner courtyard's fresh snow brought us a serene joy that is unique to the Loreta, even while the disembodied voice of Herb Lass directed our attention to a remarkable crucifixion scene: The naked figure on the cross had breasts!

"This is the chapel of Saint Starosta," said the recorded Herb, "a devout young virgin who wanted to enter a convent, but whose father arranged a marriage with a wealthy man instead. The virgin prayed for deliverance and, when she awoke the next morning, her prayer was answered: Overnight, she had grown a beard. This so displeased her future husband that he broke the engagement. Her father asked her who was responsible for this outrage. When she replied that Jesus had answered her prayer, her unholy father had his bearded virgin daughter crucified."

To go upstairs to the West Wing of the Loreta, you pay a tiny admission fee. An elderly watchman will then show you to a room housing a priceless collection of jewels, chalices, and monstrances. A monstrance looks like an elaborate hand mirror; its center is where the Host (the holy bread) is displayed for adoration by the worshippers. This room is called "The Loreta Treasury" because it possesses the dazzling "Ray Monstrance"—27 pounds of gold inset with no less than 6,222 diamonds!

These jewels were taken in 1695 from the wedding gown of the Countess Eva Ludmila, who wore all 6,222 of them to her third wedding ceremony when she was fifty. Then, eternally grateful to the Catholic Church for finding her a young husband and sanctioning her marriage to him, the Countess Eva Ludmila had the diamonds made into a monstrance that she donated to Christ.

The latter-day Communists have been scrupulous about preserving and displaying the relics of the aristocracy with no more ranting than the recorded spiel's passing reference to "the pious wives of the noblemen who had to go to immense pains to wring out of the peasants the means for the accumulation of such riches."

Upon leaving the Loreta Treasury, if you turn left, the third portrait on the wall shows a chubby voluptuous lady who might resemble a corseted Mae West if she weren't weighed down by her clothes. She is smiling demurely and just a little smugly. She is the Countess Eva Ludmila in her wedding dress.

The music of the Loreta comes from its carillon. Built by a clockmaker named Petr Naumann in 1694, the twenty-seven bells of Loreta range over two octaves. They chime on the quarter-hour and half-hour and they play St. Mary's Hymn on the hour.

Loreta's music is piped across the square to the Černín Palace, where it inspires the blasé diplomats to glance at their watches and murmur "Eleven o'clock. Time for lunch," or "Three o'clock. Time to go home." Three days after Christmas, however, as soon as the carillon had played and while the great bell was still tolling ten o'clock, we hurried over to the Černín for our appointment with Pan Fárek. Like his predecessor, Pan Glozar, Pan Fárek wore a brown suit and was just as amiable, but much less reassuring. He was a man who, in any of several languages, chose his words carefully.

He did not know when or if my accreditation would be granted. Or how on earth we could find a flat.

"I have 1,300 kilos (2,860 pounds) of household goods on the high seas bound for here," I pointed out.

"Very good!" Pan Fárek exclaimed. "Not everything is available here and in any event, it will save you a great deal of shopping."

"And we have only eighty-four days before our visas expire."

"That should be ample time for us to accredit you once you have a place to live. You see, that's the only hitch. We are delighted with your qualifications and can issue your credentials a few hours after you've settled into a flat. But, if you and your family should be cooped up in a hotel, then we suspect you may write unhappy stories about us."

"My living conditions," I assured him, "have nothing to do with what I am writing—unless I am writing about my living conditions."

"Oh, I admire the way you choose your words, Mr. Levy. And I hope you can find a flat because you truly deserve to be happy here."

"But how do I find this flat that will make us all so happy and lead to instant accreditation," I asked, "if I don't have a permit to reside here?"

"Oh, but to find a flat, you must be a resident."

"And how do I get to be a resident?"

"You take your accreditation into the police station."

"So all I need is accreditation," I said.

"Which you will have as soon as you find a flat."

"But Pan Fárek!" I exploded. "This is pure Kafka!"

"Of course! There is a situation in *The Castle* almost analogous to yours. As you know, this is Kafka's city. You will be shown many houses with plaques saying 'Kafka Slept Here', but, unlike your George Washington, he really did sleep everywhere it says he did. He was very restless. He must have changed addresses every two weeks. Are you familiar with his comic novel *Amerika?*"

"Yes," I said distractedly, "the Statue of Liberty waves a sword."

"So it does!" said Pan Fárek. "But I don't think Kafka meant it to be political."

Monica broke in with: "Daddy, I should like to live here in Pan Fárek's palace."

"I only work here, my dear," said Pan Fárek and, after a few minutes of small talk, he stood up to say goodbye. I would hear from him only in the unlikely event that he had any positive news to report.

To consolidate our negligible gains at this session I said: "Let me sum up my understanding of this conversation: If, on our part, we should somehow manage to find a flat, then we can go ahead and negotiate for it on the assumption that, once I have the flat, I'll be accredited to work and live here."

"I would say so," Pan Fárek concurred. "Unofficially, of course."

"What do you think it all means?" Val asked me. "Anything?"

"I think it means Gene's," I said, "if we're ever going to stand a chance of breaking out of this vicious circle."

Pan Horák at the hotel had laughed with us over the "baby-sitter" misunderstanding. Then he had detailed the Sunday-night chambermaid to make bed checks every quarter-hour while we were away. Thus, when Valerie and I arrived at the Deitches' New Year's Eve party, we had barely unloaded our coats before Gene said: "Tell our friends the story about 'the baby-sitter is in the room, Mr. Levy.'" I did—with Zdenka translating me into Czech at a machine-gun pace—and, as the laughter subsided, a cherubic lady who looked fifty and sounded twenty addressed me in a peculiar brand of Oxonian English:

"If you're dead serious about a live baby-sitter, I've just retired as a secretary and I'd like to supplement my pension. I have no children of my own, but I'd be right proud to take care of yours one or two nights a week. I am quadrilingual: English, French, German, and, of course, Czech."

Her name was Ludvika, but everybody called her Lulka. Even in retirement, she was still a busy lady. Twice a week, she worked for the screening committee which chose foreign films for distribution in Czechoslovakia. She did simultaneous translations of American, British, and French films, a demanding job that had already cost Laurence Olivier and Jean Gabin an admirer. "Clearly though they enunciate," Lulka told me, "they don't move their mouths very much. And half of simultaneous translation is lip-reading."

Her tweedy British, acquired in Czechoslovak boarding schools before the war and cultivated on two trips of a fortnight each to England, bore a certain American flavor, although she had never been to our shores. Years of being around Gene and translating cowboy films had Westernized her vocabulary without adulterating her accent. "If you will be so kind as to excuse me," she said once during the party, "I will mosey around a bit." On subsequent occasions, she was to appear at our door fresh from translating three movies with some outrageous question left over from her day's work: "What on earth is a red herring?" or "a G.O.P?" or "a one-eyed jack?" I would barely have time to answer, for the children would shoo us out impatiently so they could have their Teta Lulka all to themselves.

The baby-sitter problem was resolved by 10:15 P.M. on New Year's Eve. The housing problem lasted until nearly midnight.

First time unlucky. A man who'd been invited abroad for a year had failed to get permission to take his family with him, so he was going for only six months and his family would of course remain in his flat.

Second time uncertain. It certainly was a darling idea of dear Gene to cheer him up by inviting him to this gay little party, said the limp-wristed costume designer. His mother had died of cancer last summer and, as happens more often than we read about, his father had died soon thereafter of grief. Yes, it would be nice if someone could share his "great big empty apartment!" That was why, he added with a tiny shudder, this divorcée with three children was literally running after him. She was still living with her ex-husband because of the housing problem. She had proposed marriage to the designer and he was beginning to find her proposal not only legitimate and businesslike, but advantageous for his own public relations. . . .

Third time lucky! Over the pre-midnight supper (Russian crabmeat; broiled Czech chicken from Xaverov; and Heidsieck Dry Monopole champagne from Reims, $4.00 a bottle for hard currency in Prague), Gene introduced us to a tall and serious middle-aged lady who was intent on joining her husband in England at the end of January. He was a Charles University professor who had gone to a British university in September for a short teaching stint. He had liked it there so much (and been so well-liked) that he had obtained permission at both ends to stay abroad for two more years and to have his wife and two daughters join him.

"We have a long list of Czechs clamoring to sublet our flat," the woman informed us, "but when Hilda Lass told me about your situation, I decided to offer it to you first because it's just about your only possibility. The Czechs who want our flat all have roofs over their heads, maybe three generations under one roof, but a roof nonetheless."

"This is very nice of you. . . ." I began.

"It has advantages to us, too," she said. "The problem with letting a Czech into your flat is that once he's in he's very hard to get out. There are very strong squatter's rights here."

"Even if you're awarded a flat," Zdenka remarked, "the decree says that it's yours only when the previous tenant and his family vacate the premises."

Gene said: "That's why I was so anxious even when we had our decree. They wouldn't let us into the flat right away because it was legally sealed after the previous tenant defected. There was always the chance that the last tenant had left behind a nephew who would get in there and keep us out."

Our landlady-to-be went on: "It might take us months or years in court to move a Czech out of our apartment if we came back and he didn't want to go. But you're Americans, so you have no legal rights at all in Czechoslovakia, just the privileges that your passports afford you. You'd be no problem to us when we come back."

"When can we look at your apartment?" said Valerie, who never did believe in blind dates.

"We'll take it, of course," I said, "but we'd like to look at it too, if we may . . ." My desperation stemmed from growing awareness of the Prague housing situation as well as numerous New York cocktail party agreements that evaporated the morning after.

Valerie flashed me a warning look, but Gene Deitch mediated: "Why don't we compromise it this way? They'll take it and then they'll look at it and then they'll take it again."

"Agreed," said our new landlady, laughing for the first time. "Would you like to come over tomorrow afternoon with the children?"

"We would," I said. "We promised the children lunch at the Castle, so as soon as we can find a taxi or a tram. . ."

"Oh, I'm two tram stops past the Castle," she said, "but it's just as easy to walk from there." And then, as I began to hold my breath, she gave me directions: "You go out through the Castle's first courtyard

into Hradčany Square. Stay on the left side of the street, past the
Schwarzenberg Palace. Do you know the Loreta? . . . You walk past it
and past the Černín Palace. Then, just beyond the Černín, you bear
right into a square with a statue and a great big firehouse. . ."

She went on giving directions. I had been struck speechless, but
from a few thousand years away, I heard a very faint voice—Valerie's—
saying: "We'll take it!"

"DEITCHOVI HAPPENING!" proclaims the elaborate psyche-
delic poster that hung on the Deitches' door that New Year's Eve and
now hangs framed over our bed. Gene had designed it himself and it
ended in red-black-yellow-and-green with the words: "THIS WILL BE
A COMPLETELY NEW YEAR."

No sounder prophecy was ever made for a cataclysmic year in which
both Lyndon Johnson and Antonín Novotný would abdicate peace-
ably, while Martin Luther King and Robert Kennedy, both men of
peace, would die violently. Jacqueline Kennedy, thirty-nine, would
marry Aristotle Onassis, sixty-two +. The French Republic would
nearly crumble in a revolution against Gaullism and Charles de Gaulle
would reap the only reward: a temporary vote of confidence. One could
predict that thousands of soldiers and civilians would die in both Viet-
nams, but not that thousands of children would starve to death in a
land called Biafra. And probably not that Richard Nixon, of all
people, would be elected President of the United States. And certainly
not a war in Czechoslovakia. . .

"Bude úplně nový rok!" "This will be a completely New Year!" was
the toast at midnight in Czech and English. The bells of St. Nicholas,
across the square, tolled in 1968 while we unfurled green and yellow
paper yo-yo's. Zdenka opened the canary's cage and turned Bohouš
loose on his annual flight around the flat, which lasted at the frightened bird's behest until 12:02. Fifteen minutes later, we all sat down to
our first dinner of 1968: shish-kebab and lentils served by a tall and
statuesque Czech girl in a Parisian chambermaid's mini-uniform with
bright yellow panties gleaming beneath black fishnet tights. Her
watchful husband, who had taken over the kitchen from Zdenka, hovered behind her in his high-hatted white chef's costume. When we left
a lentil or two on each of our plates, we were admonished.

"Every lentil uneaten is a missed opportunity," said our new baby-
sitter Lulka.

"Or an unmade crown," said our new landlady.

"Or, in your case, an unmade dollar," said Zdenka. Knowing the economy, I scooped up all our lentils.

Toward 1 A.M., there was the first fight of the New Year. A husband and wife, who had been quarreling for months, had come to the party together. She called this a "reconciliation"; he called it a "celebration." He kept glancing at his watch and on the dot of one, he stood up and said he had to leave. His wife accused him of promising his girlfriend equal time. He denied it. She repeated it. This time he admitted it. In the argument that ensued, he mentioned the dreaded word "divorce" for the first time and stormed out into Malá Strana Square, where a woman in a car was waiting for him.

It was, I suppose, an average New Year's Eve: for us, better than any; for another, worse than any; for all the rest, hopeful and promising and maybe a little frightening. But even if we hadn't landed a babysitter and an apartment that night, it would have been an extraordinary New Year's for us because this was Prague.

At 3:15 A.M., there were no taxis at the stand behind St. Nicholas Church, but there was a fat young man in a party hat with a pink clown's collar. He flirted drunkenly with Valerie, so we moved away and waited for the tram which runs all night at forty minute intervals on the major lines. As we waited in the baroque shadow of St. Nicholas, two young students with dueling swords came clattering out of a side street, fighting all the way.

Everyone stood back a little, but stayed to admire their sword-play which was fast and furious and might have been frightening if they weren't having so much fun. The tram came and we all climbed aboard, including the two young fencers, who put up their swords and paid their fares like ordinary citizens. At Wenceslas Square they, like us, disembarked. Unlike us, they resumed their duel.

"This will be a completely new year," Valerie and I reminded each other.

PART TWO

Apogee:
January Spring

. . . Then you will have clarity, truth,
avowal, as much of them as you desire. The
roof of this wretched life, of which you say
so many hard things, will burst open, and
all of us, shoulder to shoulder, will ascend
into the lofty realm of freedom. And if we
should not achieve that final consummation, if things should become worse than
before, if the whole truth should be more
insupportable than the half; if it should
be proved that the silent are in the right as
the guardians of existence, if the faint hope
that we still possess should give way to
complete hopelessness, the attempt is still
worth the trial, since you do not desire to
live as you are compelled to live.

Franz Kafka, *Investigations of a Dog*

Chapter 4]

Monday 22 January— Thursday 1 February 1968

WHEN WE MOVED IN LESS THAN A MONTH LATER, THE slanted roofs of the street where we live were striped with snow and the barren trees white-laced with frost. Winter is the only time of year when you think of Prague as a fragile, delicate tapestry rather than a massive, overpowering city. The air on our street was clear and the snow stayed clean, a rarity in Prague though not in Hradčany (Castle Quarter) on our high hill far above and beyond the industrial basins.

Our street is only three blocks long, but almost as wide as Park Avenue. Down the middle runs a grassy strip, like Park Avenue's, but with a four-pump Golem gas station and a news stand at one end. Both conveniences are visible without offending the landscape and one wonders why American gas stations must be such uniformly glaring eyesores.

From all angles that day, children were sledding in the street with only an older boy or two keeping ears tuned for the cars that seldom turn onto the block. Our landlady stood on the bedroom balcony watching with pleasure our progress past the nursery school and park that flank the approach from the Castle side. She had told us she lived on a good street in a good neighborhood with plenty of children and now, as on each of our previous visits, the neighborhood was showing itself off to us.

Our flat is on the "first floor," which means one flight up. It is classified as "three rooms." The Czechs count only the large living room with its parquet floors, four double windows, chandelier, dining table seating six (or sixteen, when expanded), marble fireplace housing an ugly radiator whose winter warmth is nevertheless appreciated, high raftered ceiling (when the painters came, we found out that the rafters were plastic), and secret panel leading to a storage closet called the "priest's hole" . . . the children's room with six windows and three beds . . . and the dark stained-oak master bedroom, with its double windows, paneled doors, and unobtrusive balcony. A wooden jalousie, rolled up and down by an inside strap, makes the best Venetian blinds on either side of Venice. One can shutter out night's noises and day's early lights while sleeping and then, upon arising, unveil the wondrous view of Strahov Monastery's green onion domes.

Among the several rooms that aren't counted, my pride and joy lies just beyond the living room's rear door—a sun terrace which our land-lady's husband had enclosed with glass. He used it as his summer study, but I would use it as my year-round office—doing the rest of that winter's writing while bundled up in sweaters; an electric radiator the Tuzex department store ordered from Austria wouldn't arrive until a balmy day in May. But nothing mattered except the privacy and the view. My office could be locked off from the rest of the apartment with shades to conceal myself from children's living-room romps and flirts (no names, please).

Visibility in the other three directions was unimpaired. Here I would spend all seasons of the year at my desk facing over gardens and up toward Ořechovka Hill, where the Suchýs and Formans dwell. Behind me loom the spires of St. Vitus and the Prague Castle; I have chosen to put my back to them, for otherwise I would be so inspired that I would never work.

In winter, I look out upon a hunter's hares dangling from a terrace clothesline. In spring, I watch flowers in bloom yield in splendor to new blossoms, and each morning when my coffee mug and I commute from the breakfast table, all my senses inhale the new fragrances and colors of the day in Prague. In summer there are always children playing in the garden below. One July day in our first summer there, a radio on a window-sill would blare out the latest news of impending crisis while some youngsters jumped rope. The two teen-age girls twirling the rope would be the only ones to heed the radio by exchanging anxious glances. And I would catch myself murmuring aloud at the typewriter in a mixture of bad Czech and English: *"Děti! Děti!* (Children! Children!) I wish you a future!"

In the autumn, I see what the decadent English poet, Arthur Symons, saw when he wrote in 1902:

> Seen from Hradčany, the kremlin of Prague, the city is dominated
> by towering spires, copper-green domes and the jagged, unkempt pat-
> tern of red-tiled roofs. Prague is all red and green. . . . And that

lovely verdure is in evidence everywhere forming vivid patches on the fortifications high above the town where children play on the grass, it is piled obliquely at Nebozízek,* it grows out of the river-bed and immortalizes the river through its shadows and green islands.

All seasons of the year, I see the men of each house beating their carpets on the metal racks planted in backyards for that purpose. The sound of carpetbeating can resemble gunfire. And still I am here, for our rowboat to Prague has brought us through the dusty thump of carpetbeating and the acrid roar of an invasion. I still sit right out in the winter hailstorms and summer thundershowers that pelt my glass study like thwarted lovers. Exposed to public view in three directions, I am still writing away as yet virtually unmolested in the storm center of Soviet-occupied Czechoslovakia.

My phone is monitored, but it is better not to think of myself as being watched. I am more of a watcher, with no greater ambition than to hold onto my post in my glass booth as a hard-working literary concierge. For my domain as concierge is a neighborhood that could not have been dreamt of in heaven, earth, or philosophy.

In addition to my study, our other "uncountables" included (in order of appearance if you enter our apartment and turn left) a small tiled anteroom (with a sink) leading into the toilet . . . a spacious kitchen with a rear balcony, another six-to-sixteen seat dining table, and a small gas refrigerator (which we promptly augmented with the largest Czech electric refrigerator) . . . a good-sized pantry whose window, left a little ajar, provides adequate refrigeration for eight months of the year . . . and bathroom with tub, sink, three medicine chests, storage cabinets, towel and laundry racks, ancient washing machine built like a Con Edison smokestack (soon to be replaced, for $280, by a Siemens washer-wringer that makes its own hot water), a bathside chair, and (alas!) hot water on Wednesdays and Saturdays only. The same hot-water rationing prevailed throughout the building, but over our kitchen sink was a small gas-operated water-heater that provided a trickle ample for dishwashing.

For all of the above, countables and uncountables, our rent came (at the tourist rate of exchange which we were getting then) to $31.48 a month. Rent was just one item on a total bill, payable at the Post Office

* Nebozízek was the former vineyard that ran in a jagged streak from the Eiffelike tower atop Petřín Hill past Strahov to the Malá Strana (Lesser Quarter) where the Deitches live.

every month, that also included utilities (electricity, gas, telephone, and licenses to have radio and TV). This grand total was $41.59.

"Of course, the gas and electric and telephone fees are just deposits based on average previous use," our landlady had explained. "If you make long distance calls, you get a separate bill for them four times a year. Every six months or a year, they read the gas and electric meters and you get either a rebate or a special bill plus an adjustment in your deposit to the new average." *

"And what," I had asked, "would you like us to pay to you?"

Gene had warned me that the lady was a good businesswoman and that I should expect to air-mail a check (drawn upon the hard currency in my New York bank account) to England every month. Bracing myself for hard bargaining, I had been floored by her response:

"You won't pay us anything. You'll just pay the 673 crowns every month at the Post Office so that we can retain legal possession of the flat when and if we return."

Far worse than bargaining was my unsuccessful effort to get her to take something for the greatest gift that anyone in Prague can give you: a place to live. But all she would ask of us was to "wear it and tear it in the best of health—and repair it whenever you have to."

"You can go walking in the park at any time of day or night," our landlady had told us. "And you don't have to be afraid of our Africans."

Before I could say "what Africans?", she had pointed from the window to two black men waiting at the tram stand. They were out of earshot, but they had waved at her anyway.

"On the next block," she had explained, "is Comenius College, a hostel for foreign students. It's all very cosmopolitan here!"

Later, I came to know several of our neighborhood students including a bearded Hindu named Krishna Vishwanath, who was studying at the Prague Film Faculty. There, where the graduate thesis you turn in can be a film, "Vishu" made a remarkable short documentary, *Black and White,* about the social problems of Czechoslovakia's hundred-odd persons of color. It was later shown professionally as an entry at the Oberhausen (West Germany) festival of short films. The screening,

* These reckonings of excess gas and electricity plus annual bills for heat and water, have never cost us as much as $50 per year. Rates have gone up inexorably, however, and our monthly payment at the Post Office for rent and utilities now comes to a staggering $46.67.

however, was interrupted by firecrackers set off by German students who, whatever their politics toward Czechoslovakia, did not want to hear about its race problem.

One of Prague's Africans told me: "Given a couple of hundred more of us, the Czechs would be master racists just like in the West. Any girl who goes with one of us becomes a whore in the eyes of her mother and her neighbors." And the legend of black sexual prowess had been perpetuated here for purposes of convenience: To obtain an abortion, the mother-to-be must go before a committee and the surest way to win a yes is to say that "the father was black."

Or, as one of Prague's Afro-Cubans put it to me: "Statistically, I and every one of my black brothers have each impregnated 48.3 Czechoslovak girls in the past year. So how come we're not getting any?"

Early in our stay, though, we didn't know our student neighbors well enough to have such conversations. One soon learned that a Korean student came from North Korea and a Chinese student from Red China; some were aloof and some weren't, but these traits had little to do with nationalities or politics. The Vietnamese boys and girls came from North Vietnam and were therefore more polite but less responsive than the others. Once at the vegetable store I did hear a fortyish Vietnamese student complain in Czech to the counter man that he had "given the American a better cabbage than you gave me," but I couldn't evaluate the merits of his claim; all cabbages look alike to me.

I did the morning's neighborhood shopping, which is a good way to start learning any European language; the clerks can be very patient and yet very precise about correcting your grammar. I was using the genitive and accusative cases in Czech long before I learned what they were.

The most intriguing of my fellow shoppers were a group of white Slavs who stood on line for yogurt at the dairy store and then ate it right there at a small table reserved for loading. (Very few purchases are put into a paper sack here. You bring your own shopping bag and dump them in.) As these strangers downed two or three yogurts apiece, they would denounce the Czech yogurt in eloquent English!

One morning, consumed by curiosity, I bought an extra yogurt and joined them at their makeshift dairy bar. When I did, all conversation stopped.

"What are you?" I asked them point-blank.

They exchanged wary glances. Then the tallest and blondest of them, a statuesque girl, spoke: "We are Bulgarians."

I told them what I was and that I liked the yogurt fine.

A small, dark young man pouted and then said: "We are medical students here. We practice our English this way because many of our textbooks are in English."

The blonde girl batted her eyes down toward me and purred: "You sound just like John Fitzgerald Kennedy. If I closed my eyes, I would think you were he. Will you keep our secret?"

"What secret?" I asked, all the more intrigued.

"About the yogurt," she replied. "We don't want to offend the dairy lady, so we denounce her yogurt in English, which she doesn't understand." The dairy lady, indeed, stood beaming at the international sophistication with which her little State-owned shop had been blessed. And I learned from my new acquaintances that in Bulgaria the quality of fermented milk is considered a matter of life or early death.

As I finished my yogurt, the girl elbowed me into a corner and whispered about the small, dark medical student: "Be careful what you say to him. He's a member of the Bulgarian Communist Party."

Later, when I left, the small dark chap followed me out and murmured: "Don't trust her. She's a member of the Bulgarian Communist Party."

"Aren't you, too?" I asked him.

"Everybody is," he replied. "You can't go abroad if you aren't. But I joined because I wanted to go abroad. She joined because she wanted to join."

The next time I saw her in the dairy, she cut me dead, without even a "Good morning, Mr. Kennedy!"

Valerie did the heavy shopping that winter and the children tagged along. I still remember the day when both children were feeling under the weather and so they bought a New Wonder Instant Thermometer made in Czechoslovakia. While I stood by with pad and paper to convert the readings from centigrade to fahrenheit, Valerie translated the very explicit instructions:

> Insert in your rectum, your mouth, or under your arm for exactly as long as it takes to read this sentence. Then remove it and you will have your reading.

The thermometer worked, we think. But just as fast as the readings faded in, they faded out. By the time we began to decipher them, the thin red line was retreating. We laughed so hard that the children perked up and went without fever until our ton-and-a-half of household goods (including two thermometers) would arrive from America.

That winter we stocked up at *Tuzex*. This is a legal black market wherein the State converts your Western currency or traveler's checks into a kind of scrip resembling play money, called Tuzex crowns. It may be bought by tourists (once they've exchanged their obligatory daily minimum for normal Czechoslovak crowns) and it must be bought by Czechs who receive hard currency from royalties or relatives in the West or any other source. The Tuzex crown sells at the same "official" rate as the Czechoslovak crown. But the Tuzex crown, in general, buys five times as much.

Tuzex crowns entitle you to shop at a chain of Tuzex grocery, apparel, appliance, automobile, and department stores where you are sometimes stopped at the door and asked to show your *bony,* which is what Czechs call this funny money. Items like vodka or tinned smoked salmon, which are generally available on the domestic market, sell in Tuzex shops for one-fifth the price in normal crowns. Although clothing and West German appliances are in the most urgent demand at Tuzex, I'm using liquor prices because they can most easily be compared with store prices in America: Beefeater gin costs $2.38 a quart at Tuzex; in 1967 and 1968 it was not for sale anywhere else in Prague. Black-and-White Scotch costs $4.20 at Tuzex; it is also available in a few Prague stores for the equivalent in crowns of $46.16 at the official rate of exchange. Ordinarily, the price of imported goods at Tuzex is the "shelf price in country of origin," but sometimes (as with Beefeater), in the absence of domestic taxes, it is even less.

Tuzex is an utterly degrading system whereby a Czech needs help from abroad even to partake of his native land's natural assets. Certain domestic items, such as fine footwear, apparel, clothing materials, and dietetic jam, called *džem,* are available only at Tuzex. Tuzex is so institutionalized that prostitutes who sell their bodies for hard-Western-currency-only are known as "Tuzex girls." *

While I would have been foolish not to take advantage of Tuzex "because it is here," no Czech I knew resented this. Quite the contrary:

---

* The greatest insult a man can speak of a woman in Prague is: "She's a whore who'll do it for Czechoslovak crowns."

Whenever I pointed out that "even though my own cost of living will double or triple when it happens, it'll be a happy day for me as well as you whenever Tuzex is finally abolished," I was immediately put in my place. For if a Czech has a single Tuzex crown (14 cents) to his name, he will defend Tuzex to the death.

One afternoon in late January, for the first time since Christmas, a Tuzex in the Old Town had Kellogg's cereals. A box of corn flakes cost 28 cents and a Variety-Pak 42 cents, with no limit on the quantity you could purchase. All bore the seal of the Kellogg Company of Great Britain, Ltd., in Manchester: "By Appointment to Her Majesty the Queen—Purveyor of Cereals." (Royal culinary historians will have to analyze the significance of the fact that American Variety-Paks feature "40-per-cent Bran Flakes" while the English feature "30-per-cent Bran.")

Clutching their cartons, familiar friends from a former world, the children toddled through the snowy streets of the Old Town. In the Central European winter, it was dark at 4:30 P.M. Passers-by stared at these two little girls chattering in a strange tongue with their faces hidden behind unfamiliar-looking cartons.

"Do you think they resent our having these?" I asked Val.

"Certainly not," she said. "If you try to feed Kellogg's to a Central European for breakfast, he's likely to gag. There's even a sort of puffed rice on the domestic market, but it's not popular." The few Czechs she knew who'd sampled breakfast cereals had rejected them in favor of bread, rolls, pastry, sausage meats, and eggs.

Laden with Special K and Sugar Smacks, we came into view of the cake-tiered Tyl Theatre, where Mozart conducted the world premiere of his own *Don Giovanni* in 1787.* ("My Pragers understand me," said Mozart, who composed his greatest work for them and completed it here as the guest of his mistress Madame Josefina Dušková and her husband at their Villa Bertramka.) One of *Don Giovanni*'s first-nighters was Casanova, who came to town for the event from rural Bohemia. He was finishing out his life by working as Count Wallenstein's librarian and writing his memoirs.

On a winter afternoon more than one hundred eighty years later the day's cars had already fled the downtown streets, the Old Town's gaslights flickered with warmth, and the Tyl's chandeliers blazed with

---

* At that time, the Tyl was named the Estates Theatre. The composer Carl Maria Friedrich Ernst von Weber was its conductor of opera from 1813 to 1816.

grandeur. One could easily imagine oneself a stroller in 1787 passing the theatre and wishing Herr Mozart—always in his lifetime better appreciated in Prague than in Vienna—good luck with his new opera.

We turned right near the House of Children department store. In an arcade still within the shadow of the Tyl, an old man was walking a shaggy tan-and-white collie. The children asked if they could pet his dog and while they did a young couple stopped to pat the children petting the dog. The scene ended when the dog, having sniffed the corn flakes, stalked away.

Once we had a home address to give, I could open a dollar account at the *Živnostenská Banka* (Trade Bank). There are no checking accounts in Czechoslovakia. You pay or send all bills (even for private transactions, if you wish) at the Post Office, which makes a service charge of a few cents for collection and payment and then remits. Banks are for savings and even loans. But I needed dollars on hand to convert into Czechoslovak and Tuzex crowns for domestic expenses or into Travelers Checks (at the regular Stateside rates) or dollars, pounds, francs, or marks (limit of $50 in *cash* per withdrawal; 2 per cent service charge) for trips abroad. Thus, I could keep my financial pump primed by writing a check for $500 or $1,000 on my New York City bank account and allowing six weeks for it to clear and be credited to my Živnostenská account.

I learned to confine my visits to the Živnostenská Banka to one or two trips a month. Banking here is a ritual wherein you stand on line, turn in your passport and visa and other documents, state your requests, and sign several blank forms, which are then typed up on your behalf. After thirty to sixty minutes, when the paperwork of deposit or withdrawal is completed, you are summoned to the cashier's for the final transaction. If it is a complicated matter on a busy day, this can consume a whole morning of your life.

Your only consolation is the Živnostenská Banka itself: an Art Nouveau palace with an overhead museum of Bohemian statuary (farm boys and milkmaids, gargoyles and cherubs, lions and kings) gazing down from the swirling stained-glass ceiling and tapered balconies. At eye level, however, the vista is a hundred bank clerks, men in shirt sleeves, women in smocks, who are no more imbued with their environment than the Černín Palace's diplomats who set their clocks by the Loreta carillon. And perhaps the most remarkable aspect of the Živnostenská Banka is what doesn't meet the eye: There is not a single bank guard in sight.

My most complicated transaction at this time was the purchase of a typewriter. A new Czech-made Consul standard—sleek, gray, largely plastic, and highly recommended by satisfied users we knew—was available at an Office Machines Store for 2,375 crowns ($146.61 at the tourist rate) with a year's guarantee. There was a choice of Czech, German, Russian, or American keyboards. I said I would buy American.

"Very good," said the saleslady. "What organization are you with?"

"None," I replied proudly. "I work for myself."

"Then you can't have one. Only organizations can buy typewriters here. People, no."

"Well, I'll be doing some of my work on it for *Life* Magazine," I pleaded.

"Then you must get a letter from *Life* that they want to buy the machine. But it won't do you much good. *Life* is not an organization* here."

How could it ever be an organization here without a typewriter? "This is impossible!" I moaned.

"You will find," said the woman, not unkindly, "that many things you are used to are impossible here."

I had no sooner left the store in despair than a salesman who had been watching the non-transaction followed me out and fell into step with me.

"You will also find," he picked up smoothly, "that for you everything is possible here. May I invite you for a cup of coffee?"

In his navy-blue turtleneck and tinted glasses, the typewriter salesman looked like a black marketeer. And I suppose he was, in the sense that it was arranged for me to buy the typewriter for 500 Tuzex crowns ($69.94). The typewriter would be ordered by a friend in another *podnik* and then turned over to me.

The typewriter salesman spoke seven languages and had worked in export-import until the mid-1960's, when he had lost his job for presenting a re-organization plan that would streamline the *podnik*. He had begun all over as a laborer in the typewriter factory and had

---

* The appropriate word in Czech is *podnik*, meaning enterprise. In any dealings with the bureaucracy here, *podnik* and *podpis* (signature) are crucial to your vocabulary.

worked his way up to a sales post. He was even allowed out of the country on occasional visits to "safe" territories like Bulgaria and East Germany.

He and his friend delivered my typewriter to my flat a few mornings later. And to grace our disheveled and somewhat barren new home, they also brought an exquisitely delicate stone statue of two lovers entwined about each other.

"It's called 'The Birth of a Song'," the salesman explained.

"It's lovely!" said my wife. "Who is it by?"

"My father," said the salesman. "He was a famous sculptor. My wife and son and I still live in two rooms of his atelier and we have many of his works. But this is one of his best and my father would certainly want you to have it."

"Is he still alive?" I asked.

"No. He died in Theresienstadt the day before it was liberated."

The salesman and his friend left with one apology: Under the circumstances of the typewriter purchase, the friend's *podnik* could not have ordered an American keyboard. So I would have to learn to use a Czech keyboard.

Which I did, though there were problems at first. The keyboard followed the standard QWERTYUIOP pattern for letters, with one seemingly small exception: The Y was where the Z should be and vice versa. For a few weeks, old friends in New Zork Citz were receiving letters from a vaguely familiar Levz in Cyechoslovakia.

Aside from this difficulty, easily mastered, my shiny plastic Consul proved to be an unmitigated joy.* With it, I could do the *háček,* the *čárka,* and the *kroužek,* which are not new dance steps, but essentials of the Czech alphabet. The *háček* (pronounced "hah-check") is the inverted carat over the *c* that causes it to be pronounced "tch." Or, over the name Miloš, it makes him "Milosh"; over Jiří, "Yirdzhi." The *čárka* (pronounced "chahrka") is the stress mark over the *á* and other vowel sounds; it lengthens them. The *kroužek* (pronounced "crow-zhek") is a tiny circle over *ů,* as in the word for house, *dům.* It changes it from *u* as in "put" to *u* as in "rude."

Another useful key, which is an object of great humor in Prague, is

---

* At this writing, almost two years after its one-year guarantee expired, it has not needed a single repair. Back in New York, my only solution to the typewriter problem used to be to trade in old Underwoods for older ones.

the paragraph key §. The § has come to mean bureaucracy here, with its constant references to bygone §s. Suchý and Šlitr once built a whole revue sketch around it. Šlitr was entitled to be addressed as "Dr." because he had a law degree.* Thus, he found the § sign doubly significant: "Here, it is the official symbol of the legal profession, such as it is. Elsewhere, I think, § is the medical symbol. So here, anyone who practices law must be something of a medicine man."

While I puttered with my new toy the typewriter, our new home was starting to lose its vacant look. First to fill up was the pantry. The only grocery that delivers, The House of Food (*Dům Potravin*), a four-story department store at the top of Wenceslas Square, sent a station-wagon bearing almost 1,000 crowns' (more than $60.00) worth of goods. They were mostly Czech products, but there were also:

California asparagus and fruit cocktail (Every can was somewhat dented or otherwise imperfect. We learned later, upon buying some canned Georgia peaches containing skins and pit fragments, that since Communist nations don't buy, but barter, in their dealings with the West, they are natural dumping grounds for factory rejects.) . . . Algerian olives . . . "mandarin oranges" from Communist China and Sparta orange juice (canned) from rightist Greece . . . Turkish-type coffee from Arabia . . . English tea . . . Russian and Polish vodka (about 70-proof; the kind you can drink straight) . . . Bulgarian Cabernet, Rumanian Pinot Noir, and Hungary's dark velvety *Egri Bikavér,* the allegedly erogenous Bull's Blood of Eger.** (The best red wines in this part of the world compare very closely with the better California wines, which is not surprising. The founder of the California wine industry was Count Agoston Haraszthy, a failed Forty-niner from Hungary who transplanted some 200,000 vines from Europe to the fertile soil of Northern California.) . . . Yugoslavian tuna . . . herring from Mother Russia . . . crab from Cuba . . . and Heinz Ketchup and Worcestershire Sauce made in England by Heinz, Ltd., of Hayes, Middlesex. (These two Heinz condiments are status symbols

---

* Šlitr had never practiced law. By the time he'd finished law school, he'd abandoned his original intention of entering the foreign service.

** Once a consistently great wine and still good but erratic, *Egri Bikavér* is another casualty of mismanagement (on the East European market, anyway). The Hungarian wine co-operatives were allowed to mix bad vintages in with good vintages and a *Bikavér* label no longer mentions its year. Of course, the best *Bikavér* is still put aside for export.

here. Even the best restaurants will serve them in the original bottles alongside all orders, even blintzes or caviar. The largest advertising sign on Wenceslas Square when we arrived in Prague was a two-story-high Heinz ketchup bottle.)

Then, at last, our shipment from New York arrived. In this part of the world, Customs inspection of household goods is a civilized ceremony conducted in the home. Our ton-and-a-half of belongings plus a Customs Inspector of indeterminate weight were due to show up together at 1 P.M. At 12:50, however, the State freight agency (*Čechofracht*) called with the news that the handlers down at the Těšnov station had loaded our crate onto the largest truck available that day only to have the truck collapse on the spot. I would have to come down to the station (about three miles distant) to witness the opening of the crate and the loading of its contents onto two smaller trucks.

I phoned for a taxi. But in the ten minutes before it came, our doorbell rang thrice:

. . . First, there appeared a splendid-looking official personage in a military greatcoat and the only gray uniform I have ever seen that actually gleamed! He took off his hat and scarf to reveal equally shiny red cheeks and bald dome. He was clearly the Customs Inspector straight out of Gogol. When we confessed very sheepishly that there was nothing for him to inspect yet, the personage beamed all over and said: "Good! I live in the neighborhood! I will go home and wait until you phone me that it has arrived here." We prevailed upon him to stay for a cup of coffee, which (we had been told) was customary.

. . . Next, the Tuzex department store's delivery truck arrived with our Calex refrigerator and Tesla "Oliver" TV. Made and bought in Czechoslovakia, neither appliance fell under our guest's jurisdiction. But the TV fascinated the personage far more than any of our imports subsequently did. It was a new Czech model that he'd never seen before. We let him unpack it and tinker with it, although the installers weren't coming until the next day.

. . . Finally, a gnome with gray cap, red nose, and black toolkit appeared. He looked like a professional burglar and was in fact the official wire-cutter. (Our crate had been sealed in bond for its journey through Belgium and Germany en route to Prague. His job was to unseal it.) Furious at not finding his work cut out for him, he even declined the traditional cup of coffee. "Now I'll have to go back to Těšnov, another forty-five minutes on the tram," he grumbled. I mollified him slightly by assuring him he could be my guest in the cab that was coming.

On a remote freight platform at Těšnov stood six workmen, their foreman, and another distinguished-looking Customs Inspector. This one bore an astonishing resemblance to Ambassador Arthur Goldberg, but he was nearly blind. With a maximum of ceremony, the gnome cracked open our crate and shook my hand; by now, I knew to tip him. Then the six men unloaded all our belongings into two trucks, pausing only to ask questions about the American goods they had never seen before, particularly the rollaway toy chests (stuffed with goods, because you paid by volume rather than weight) and our double bed. The latter is rarely mass-produced in Czechoslovakia. With the housing shortage, living rooms must serve as bedrooms and so the demand is for convertible sofa beds.

Nothing was missing. When I had signed the pertinent documents and tipped all six men*, I could see that everybody was still waiting around for something. Mr. Justice Ambassador Customs Inspector Goldberg, who spoke the most English in the group, was clearly the spokesman. He peered at me and asked: "Begging your pardon, Mr. Levy, but do you plan to keep this empty crate in your apartment?"

"No," I said. "What do you suggest I do with it?"

The men began to nudge each other with glee and I heard the name Toník cackled several times.

Chief Negotiator Goldberg went on: "If you leave it here, you would have to pay a monthly storage charge."

"I never want to see that crate again," I said. "Can't I just pay a one-time fee to have it destroyed?"

"I think we can do a little better than that," said Mediator Goldberg. He zeroed in his trifocals on the cluster of men two yards away and called: "Is Toník there?"

The youngest of the freight-handlers stepped forth. Labor Secretary Goldberg explained that Toník was the only man there who didn't have a country house, but he had helped the others build theirs and now in 1968 they would work during their vacations to help Toník build his dream house. From his wallet, Toník produced front-and-

---

* The expression here for neglecting this practice, on which communism has made no inroads, is 'tipping à la Chinese." Foreigners in particular are advised to give small tips to all, even the nurse who takes your urine sample or the inter-city bus driver who unloads your luggage.

side view photos of a barren tract near the Vltava, about thirty miles downriver from Prague. He had acquired the rights to it and was ready to build.

"Does he want my crate to be his summer house?" I asked, thinking I was joking.

"I have seen country cabins smaller than this," said Go-Between Goldberg. "But Toník has bigger plans. He would like to use your box as a storage shed at the back of his property. He can keep his tools and supplies there until the house is built. And he will pay you 500 crowns ($30.87, tourist rate) for your box that has come all the way from New York City because it is the biggest and strongest box any of us has ever seen. It has already collapsed our heaviest truck."

He talked of it the way Spaniards discuss bulls. But in the freight-yards of Těšnov as in the *corridas* of Iberia, gestures are more eloquent than words and I silenced everybody by donating my crate to Toník absolutely free with no strings attached.

"I should pay him for taking it off my hands," I said.

If I had shown up in an Uncle Sam suit and given each man a 500-crown tip, I could not have made more friends for my country than I did that icy afternoon at Těšnov. The foreman trotted out a bottle of *slivovice* and toasted "the wealthy Americans and their magnificent boxes."

"Scratch the skin of a Czech and you'll find a capitalist under-neath," someone had said to me. Riding home in the cab of a moving van, I reflected on the paradox of a Communist country where every-man, even a freighthandler, dreams of owning property, even if it's only the size of a crate. One Prague economist has even blamed the material failure of Czechoslovak communism on this mania for country homes: "They worked less than hard in the factory to save their energies for the farm to which the whole family, indeed the whole community, turned their physical and social capacities."

The professor's observation is quite accurate, but perhaps insensi-tive. The Czechs have an admirable capacity not only to endure the worst, but to make the best of it. Perhaps I am inclined to sympathize because I can see it from an American viewpoint:

Try to imagine yourself living and working in Lexington, Ken-tucky, two hours' drive or less from the Indiana and Ohio borders. Then starting one February, you can no longer go to Indiana or Ohio.

For a few years, you bide your time and expect that, when the political heat cools down, you'll be able to go to Cincinnati or Indianapolis or Bloomington or the spa at Sheraton-French Lick Springs. But the situation gets worse, not better, and even in so fair a city as Lexington, you're beginning to feel mightily cooped.

After eight or ten years of waiting, you not only lose hope of traveling, but you lose interest too. Under tight control, the Lexington *Herald-Leader* no longer publishes enticing trivia about the quaint folk customs and picturesque frivolities of Hoosiers and Buckeyes. In fact, what little is printed strongly suggests that the Governor of Ohio is a warmonger and the Governor of Indiana has a skeleton or two in his closet. You don't necessarily believe it, but it's some comfort if you can't go there anyway.

Particularly in an economy where no matter how much or how little you make, there isn't too much you can spend your money on, your interests by then have turned inward. You invest your savings and hopes in a sanctuary where you can legally escape the traffic jams and summer heat of Lexington: a summer house within the state line, maybe on Lake Cumberland or near Kentucky Dam.

Robert Ardrey calls it "the territorial imperative." Norman Mailer pontificates that "politics is property." John Locke enunciated the sanctity of "life, liberty, and property" and although Thomas Jefferson rewrote Locke by substituting "the pursuit of happiness," America has never gone to war to make the world safe for happiness.

Whatever the disease is, the citizens of the Czechoslovak Socialist Republic have it too.

Goldberg rode to our home in the other moving van. It was 3 P.M. when we returned and, to my surprise, the first Customs man had never left. Our television set was "all but installed," he assured us. He had consumed a pot of coffee and now, his shirtsleeves rolled up for action, he was working on his second plate of cold cuts. Goldberg joined the feast while Toník and his cohorts unloaded our furniture under Valerie's supervision. The children were dressing up in the personage's greatcoat, tunic, and visored cap.

"What do you think of your President Johnson?" the personage asked me.

I told him; and, as with every Czech to whom I expressed my views, his response was conciliatory: "But he's the President of the United States, so he must know what he's doing."

To which Goldberg added: "I would not presume to pass judgment on a man until I had sat in his shoes myself."

We talked about Vietnam and then we talked about the Sudeten Germans, three million of whom had been expelled from Czechoslovakia overnight under the terms of the Potsdam Agreement. Each German, no matter how he'd behaved in the war, was sent packing with no more than 110 pounds of luggage. Rather than fall prey to their fellow men, many of these families buried their jewels and other treasures in backyards and forests. Now, after more than twenty years, many former Sudeten Germans—already more prosperous than the Czechs who took over their property—were coming back as daytime tourists and nocturnal diggers for buried treasure.

One could of course rue the critical loss of manpower and technical talent that Czechoslovakia suffered from this postwar, pre-Communist, arbitrary riddance of its German-speaking citizens. But, to our two Customs Inspectors, a Sudeten German is a thorn is a thorn is a thorn.

We had just mopped up the cold cuts and the Sudeten Germans when the moving men announced that all was ready for inspection. The personage stood up, wiping his mouth, and said: "Ah, Mr. Levy, time moves so fast that we can't even begin to take up china."

"China?" I said. "Oh, no, we didn't bring any. We're going to buy our dishes here."

The personage laughed and said: "I meant the Chinese situation."

The inspection itself was perfunctory; it lasted just half an hour and one more pot of coffee. The personage and Goldberg asked us to open a half-dozen cartons and after a few questions we all returned to the kitchen. There the personage explained that a good Customs inspection should always be conducted over coffee because then one gets to know the nature of the person who is being confronted. His verdict on me was that from a Customs standpoint I had "just one visible weakness. The only document entitling you to be here is a ninety-day tourist visa that is almost halfway used up. Clearly, you intend to stay longer. But one of my superiors, going over my reports, might wonder what could legally prevent you from selling these precious goods to Czechs and then leaving the country—legally, of course—before your ninety days are up."

"That's ridiculous!" Goldberg argued on my behalf. "Why, he wouldn't even take any money for Toník's crate!"

As the winter sun began to set and the two Customs Inspectors wrangled, I telephoned the Foreign Ministry and asked for Pan Fárek. Then I put the personage onto the extension phone. The personage immediately stated his name, rank, and title and demanded the same from the startled diplomat. During the wary three-way dialogue that ensued, the Customs Inspector said he would vouch to Fárek that we were indeed moved into the flat if Fárek would vouch for our intention to remain beyond ninety days. After some hedging Fárek said that whatever we were we certainly weren't furniture smugglers. Once Fárek had gone on record, the personage hung up his extension and I thanked Fárek profusely. "As soon as we have our folding chairs un-packed," I added, "we would like to have you up for cocktails."

"Very good," said Pan Fárek. "Which day?"

"The day after tomorrow at four o'clock," I said.

"Good," said Fárek. "I will try to bring your accreditation with me at that time."

Fárek brought along not only the blue six-page booklet of creden-tials, embossed with a Bohemian lion, but also his superior, Dr. Julius Kramarič, who signed the booklet in my presence while we sat at a bridge table laden with champagne and caviar Malossol ($2.80 a jar at Tuzex). Fárek lifted high his goblet and proposed a toast to "the first American journalist accredited to live and work here since Sydney Gruson."

"Of the New York *Times?*" I said. "But wasn't that very long ago?"

"In the mid-1950's," Fárek recalled. "But then the *Times* moved its bureau to Warsaw and there's been nobody else here since."

"The *Times* is still trying, though," Kramarič added. "And maybe your case will help set a precedent that will make it possible again. In any event you are now the Dean of the American press corps here. Congratulations!" *

If I had known what odds I'd be bucking when Forman and Film-export had advised me that journalistic accreditation would be my likeliest foot in the doorway to Prague, I don't think I would have

---

* Some clarification is in order here. I was in fact the first non-Communist U.S. journalist here since Gruson. The *Daily Worker* and *National Guardian* among others were represented by one of the American expatriates here, who works as a part-time stringer.

attempted the impossible. Similarly, eight years earlier when I gave up a newspaper job for freelancing, I'd had no idea of the jungle I was entering. The lesson I've learned from both adventures can be phrased negatively but it is incurably optimistic: If you ever stop rowing long enough to analyze how impossible the journey is, then you'll drown.

Interlude] "I have always loved Russia"

O N   T H E   F I F T H   D A Y   O F   1 9 6 8 ,   T H E R E   H A D   B E E N   A   B R I E F
formal announcement from the Communist Party Presidium: "In the
interests of the division of work . . . and emphasizing the importance
of the function of the President as a symbol . . . the Central Committee decided to separate the function of the President from the function
of the First Secretary of the Central Committee of the Communist
Party of Czechoslovakia. For these reasons," President Novotný had
"requested" to be relieved of his post of First Secretary. The "request"
had been granted and the unknown Slovak, Alexander Dubček, had
been "elected unanimously" to the post.

All votes east of the Elbe are unanimous, but some are more unanimous than others, and the Prague grapevine (which I was beginning to
trust) had it that this vote was perhaps the least unanimous ever.

The new man had been in power less than three weeks when we
moved into our flat so there was no further word on him. It would be
almost three months before I would meet him personally. In January
of 1968, it was too early to tell whether or not, having acquired power,
he would now dump his liberal and intellectual allies overboard.
But, of all the limited possibilities within the Presidium, he was the
most promising, if only because whatever he stood for was the least
known and therefore the least discredited.

"This is my own personal tragedy," he would say, seven months
later, in a moment that may yet re-shape twentieth-century history. "I
have always loved Russia. I have devoted my entire life to co-operating
with the Soviet Union, and this is what they have done to me!" And
then the eyes that had envisioned "socialism with a human face" would
weep bitter tears.

Perhaps his outburst at a moment of national calamity might seem egotistical. But the facts of Alexander Dubček's life would bear out his assertion. And yet there is a good chance that he was conceived in Chicago, not Czechoslovakia.

His restless father, Štefan, was a young carpenter who, early in the twentieth century, saw no opportunity for himself in his native Slovakia, an underdeveloped and oppressed part of Hungary. He left for America and, in 1911, settled in Chicago as a cabinet-maker and then as a mechanic in the factory that made Yellow Cabs. He became an American citizen in 1916, but was quickly disillusioned when barely a year later he was drafted into the U.S. Army and told that he would be sent back to Europe to fight.

Štefan Dubček deserted, but he was caught trying to cross into Mexico and interned for the rest of the war in a camp on the Rio Grande.

It was there, in late 1917, that he heard of the Russian Revolution and Lenin's plea for workers of the world to unite behind the Soviet Union. Facing deportation (the whole world was conspiring to return him to Europe!) after the Armistice, Štefan Dubček decided he would meet Lenin halfway if he had to go back: by giving Slovakia another try, but this time as a Communist.

Back in Chicago while the proceedings were pending against him, Štefan Dubček found work in a piano factory and married another Slovak emigrant. He and she agreed to return to their native land soon after the birth of their first son Julius in 1920. Pavlina was pregnant again when they sailed in the spring of 1921 and Alexander was born on November 27, in the Slovakian village of Uhrovec.

The Slovakia to which they returned was no longer Hungarian. In exile in America during the war, the Czech Professor Thomas G. Masaryk had befriended another political scholar, President Woodrow Wilson, and won Allied recognition of the right of those two ancient Slavic peoples, the Czechs and the Slovaks, to be reunited in one nation after nearly ten centuries of separation. In Philadelphia in June of 1918, Masaryk had drafted the Constitution of the Czechoslovak Republic, a blueprint drawing upon the United States Constitution as his model. On the 28th of October, 1918, the new Republic had been born —and, soon after the Armistice, T. G. Masaryk, nearing seventy, had been chosen President by acclamation.

Slovakia, however, was still undernourished and unfavored, and Štefan Dubček fared no better the second time around, particularly now that he was a Communist. Under the auspices of a movement called Interhelp, the elder Dubček and some Slovak comrades started collecting funds to buy tractors and other machines that would help build an agricultural co-operative in the world's first socialist state. In 1925, the Dubček family set out with an Interhelp group of three hundred Slovaks on a month-long journey that brought them to the Central Asian city of Pishpek (now Frunze). Later, they lived in the city of Gorky and it was there that Alexander Dubček received his elementary and secondary schooling.

During Stalin's pre-war purges, the Dubčeks found themselves unwelcome aliens and so, in 1938, they returned to the Western Slovakian town of Trenčín, disillusioned but still dedicated Communists. As a 16-year-old new boy in town, however, Alexander's most important project was to catch up with the local swimmers. By repeated leaps off a bridge into the River Váh, he could soon dive (according to his mother) "like any other boy from Trenčin." And, once he was one of the boys, his friends then (as now) called him "Sasha."

Communists were outlaws when the Nazis entered Slovakia after the Munich Pact betrayal of September, 1938. (In his quest for "peace in our time," Neville Chamberlain sanctioned the dismemberment of "a far away country of which we know little.") Štefan Dubček continued to work for the party, however, and invested in a railway season ticket. This enabled him to travel on short notice without putting in unnecessary appearances at closely-watched ticket windows. In 1939, when Alexander went to work as an apprentice pipefitter in Trenčín, the lad also joined the Czechoslovak Communist Party. As the Gestapo tightened its grip, Alexander's father became a fugitive. The Gestapo interrogated both of Štefan's sons to no avail, but finally the father was hunted down in 1943 and shipped to the Mauthausen concentration camp.

Alexander Dubček worked as a machine locksmith in a Škoda munitions work from 1942 to 1944. But soon after his brother Julius disappeared into a Partisan brigade, Alexander followed. Now, at Mauthausen, Štefan Dubček was tortured for information about his sons' whereabouts, but he survived. Julius and Alexander fought on in the mountains with the partisans. Julius died in battle on the first day of 1945. Alexander had been shot twice in the thigh a few weeks earlier. He was taken by a priest to a Slovakian seamstress named Anna Ondrisová, who gave him shelter and nursed him back to health. (Anna and

Alexander had met once before in 1932, as youngsters in Russia, where her parents too had gone to aid the Soviet Union.) They were married in a Catholic church in November, 1945, by the priest who had brought him to her.*

When the war ended, Alexander Dubček went to work in Trenčín's yeast factory. But his real career was just beginning, unpaid at that time, as secretary of his factory's Communist party cell.

Anna Dubčeková went on working in a garment factory until 1948, when the first of their three sons was born: Pavel, by 1968 a medical student in Bratislava. The other two children, Petr, 18, and Milan, 15, were also students.

By the time the Dubčeks became parents, Czechoslovakia had gone Communist and working motherhood was a virtual necessity. But Anna Dubčeková was determined to be a homebody and so she declined to return to the factory after her six months' paid maternity leave had expired. Herself the oldest daughter of a laborer and a working mother, Anna had spent much of her childhood looking after her baby brother and sister. "So once I had children of my own, all my real training was to look after them and I knew it should be a full-time job," she said once. And then, hinting at her own unrelaxed childhood, she confided that she had always hoped her children would be only boys so that she would not be persuaded to inflict her own early start as a matriarch upon any daughter of hers.

It was not until 1949 that Alexander Dubček became a full-time paid Communist party *aparatchik:* first as organizing secretary and then as party head in Trenčín. Two years later, he transferred to Slovak Communist Party headquarters in Bratislava. After another two years, he was named head of a Slovak regional committee. Feeling a certain need for polish, he took correspondence courses in law and then, in 1955, enrolled in the Moscow political college of the Soviet Communist Party. He studied there for three years and was graduated *summa cum laude* in 1958. (Any attempt to call him "Dr." Dubček, however, is quelled with a remark that "such titles are only used to hold one's own in negotiating with Germans.")

Dubček had been in Moscow at a time of upheaval in the Commu-

---

* There is a parallel in the life of Alexander Dubček's father Štefan, who escaped briefly from Mauthausen in 1945 and was recaptured by the Nazis. During his spell of freedom, he was sheltered for a while by a Slovakian peasant woman. After the war, he divorced Pavlina, Alexander's mother, and married the peasant woman. Štefan Dubček died on May 31, 1969.

nist world. The impact of Nikita Khrushchev's "Cult of Personality" speech, the subsequent degradation of Josef Stalin, and the 1956 uprisings in Poland and Hungary had all been felt at the party college during Dubček's enrollment there. There had been purges and reevaluations: new theologies for old, though not quite overnight. If Stalin's world had been flat black and white, Khrushchev's was round with shades of gray, and both had careened around Alexander Dubček's eyes and ears while he was living near the vortex of the cataclysm.

His views of these developments are not fully known, but one observation is certain: He was shocked to return home and find that, in Communist Czechoslovakia, nothing had been changed by recent history and Stalinism was more entrenched than ever. But he bided his time.

"Moscow-trained Communist" is an accolade in Eastern Europe, where it carries the same cachet as a Harvard Business School degree does in capitalist circles. Dubček had no sooner unpacked his bags in Bratislava when he was named the local and regional party chief. That same year he was elected to the Central Committees of both the Slovak party in Bratislava and the main Czechoslovak party in Prague. In 1962, he landed on the ten-man party Presidium in Prague and in 1963 he was named First Secretary of the Slovak party.

His rise was orthodox, his manner never flashy. People who knew him a little described him as "colorless," but even his enemies grudgingly used the word "decent" when speaking of him. Though firm with former factory owners, he was never vicious, just realistic. In his party capacity, in fact, he advised and enabled one of these pariahs to return to college; this ex-capitalist is now an eminent chemist. Nobody in Czechoslovakia could say "I was Dubček's victim in the 1950's", and this is indeed a rare tribute to pay to any Communist politician who tasted power in the Stalinist years.

In Slovakia first and later on in Prague, Dubček quietly befriended the literary intellectuals as well as the economic reformers. Thus, when he was ready to make his move, he had, if not their confidence, at least a murmur of goodwill from them. One of the few prophets to foresee that Dubček's accession represented much more than a compromise with Novotnýism was the exiled Slovak novelist, Ladislav Mňačko, who said in Israel: "I didn't think he could rise this high, a man like this, as good as this."

Chapter 5]

Friday 2 February—Friday 22 March 1968

OUR TELEVISION WAS HOOKED UP TOWARD THE END OF our second week in the flat. The installer pushed the button and then jumped backward as though electrified—for he and we had tuned in on the dawn of the Czechoslovak Revolution.

On screen was a handsome face that looked like Henry Fonda's in need of a shave. It was none other than Dr. Eduard Goldstücker, vice-rector of Charles University, former Ambassador to Israel, and veteran of a Stalinist jail. In 1968 he was officially still under a life sentence as a spy and a Zionist; he had been branded a member of the "Rudolf Slánský gang" in the early 1950's and had barely escaped hanging with the others. Quietly released from prison almost a decade later, Goldstücker had made his way back into academic circles and created his first ripple in the "alienation" controversy, from which he became known as "the man who rehabilitated Kafka."

Now, in Alexander Dubček's first major move, Goldstücker had been named head of the embattled Writers Union with the tacit blessing of the Central Committee. He immediately went on radio and TV to announce that *Literární Noviny* (*Literary News*) "taken out of our control by higher authorities last year" had been restored to the Writers Union and would henceforth be published as *Literární Listy* (*Literary Leaves*).

The TV interviewer asked why the name was changed. Goldstücker drawled candidly: "You know, when I bawl out my kids and later on we find out that I was mistaken, my kids and I have an automatic understanding that a way has to be found to keep Daddy from looking like a fool."

That was really all he said. But such a statement was so new to the mass media here that Goldstücker immediately imprinted himself as Czechoslovak TV's most forceful personality ever. Our TV installer left soon after, shaking his head at what he had seen. Other people, I'm told, hung around their TV sets for an hour or two after Czechoslovakia's one channel went off the air. They were waiting to see if anything more would explode in that magic box.

It took another three or four days. But when it became clear that Goldstücker wasn't going back to jail for what he'd said, he had triggered a nationwide binge of free expression. Starting on "Channel One" (as TV is called here no matter where you get it on your dial) and on Radio Prague, freedom of speech spread to the press and the provinces, the factories and the farms, and ultimately to the highest councils of the Communist Party of Czechoslovakia.

For a while, the press had to probe in the dark. "After Dubček's election," said radio commentator Milan Weiner, "the Central Committee and the party apparatus were in complete confusion. All of a sudden, we sensed that the old barriers were gone. The censors still read our articles and commentaries, but they no longer knew what was and wasn't permitted. Before, we used to get phone calls from them complaining about this or that dogmatic mistake in what we'd written or said. Now the phone calls stopped coming. So we went ahead testing whether there were any limits to our new freedom."

I started watching the 7 o'clock Television News every night with either Sylva or our baby-sitter Lulka on hand for simultaneous translations. A few evenings after Goldstücker, the nightly interviewee was a young economist. He fielded some rather technical questions about supply and demand, import and export. He said that these statistics would improve only if controversies were settled and if the workers took an interest in solving them. Even by the standards of American educational TV, the interview seemed dull and stodgy to me. But not to one Czech who had been watching Channel One all his adult life. He called me after the broadcast with at least four reasons to cheer:

"First of all, the economist was young. Up to now, the guest has always been the chief of whatever ministry is involved: a man who is treated with utmost respect befitting his stature and who is far too busy with policy to have any answers at his fingertips.

"Secondly, the questions for once weren't easy. They didn't sound as if they'd been submitted a month in advance. And besides, the interview was live, not filmed.

"Third, the young man conceded that there was controversy, not just unanimous enthusiasm. Until now on TV, everything has been perfect and could only be made a little more perfect still.

"Fourth, he had the audacity to suggest that perhaps these matters hadn't even caught the interest of the people. That's what was interesting!"

Thus, in the early days of the Czechoslovak Revolution, watching TV required a sense of recent history. For example, the televised press conference of a deputy minister of technology struck me as highly unexciting until I learned that it was the first time in twelve years that anybody from that ministry had deigned to meet the press.

In the wake of my accreditation came a mushrooming number of invitations to press conferences, which I found even less edifying than their stateside counterparts and much more fattening. After one or two I stopped going. A typical 10 A.M. press conference in Prague consists of aperitifs, a speech of welcome, open-faced sandwiches with beer or wine, a sermon or two about the subject of the press conference, and then—over dessert, coffee, and cognac—a question period. A press kit and a small souvenir are handed to you on the way out. There were, I learned, a handful of local pensioners who no longer published, but whose press cards served as free tickets to any number of elegant "second breakfasts."

As one of Prague's forty-seven accredited foreign journalists, I was invited to join the annual Ministry of Foreign Affairs press junket to an enormous agricultural co-operative at Bezno, about thirty miles from Prague. "We always see the same co-operative," one of the less doctrinaire Polish journalists grumbled to me, "because it's the only one that works." Nevertheless, most of the invitees showed up—some for the feast and a few to confirm with their own eyes and ears the remarkable news that an American had at long last been accredited.

The State Collective Farm of Bezno perches on a high plateau above the town of Mladá Boleslav where our friend Sylva was born. Arriving shortly before 10 A.M. at the dilapidated castle that is now the collective's administrative headquarters, we were immediately fed a "breakfast" of pork liver, pork tongue, roast pork, an apple-flavored horse radish, black bread, beer, apples, and *slivovice*. Then, donning freshly-laundered white smocks and looking for all the world like three-dozen jolly veterinarians, we were herded from barn to barn to inspect 200 cows and pigs.

For a city boy, the animal farm's first highlight was a semi-automated cow-dung disposer, which did its job almost before the cows did theirs. But, after looking at enough cows and pigs to give us indigestion, we were intercepted by an intense, prematurely balding young schoolmaster who took us through "the part of the farm where young minds grow." His brand-new schoolhouse was as ultra-modern and sterile as any other anywhere in the world. But its blue and yellow pastels blended nicely with the backdrop of sky and nature. Inside was no mere showcase. It was a beehive where the students and a couple of teachers we met radiated the same bustling nervous energy as their headmaster. The classes we walked in on were alive with ideas and even arguments that scarcely slowed down for the guided tour.

I asked the headmaster if agricultural subjects were stressed.

He said: "No. They get enough of that at home. Here we teach them about the rest of the world, and believe me it helps their farming. I myself teach geography and this is my classroom."

His best pupil was giving the lesson—on the American West. Each student had been issued a copy of the December, 1962, issue of *Arizona Highways* magazine.

I asked the headmaster where he had obtained a dozen copies of the magazine as well as maps, travel posters, and picture postals on his walls.

"I write away for anything I want," he said, "and half the time I get back everything I request, sometimes much more!"

A young bureaucrat from the Foreign Ministry who was shepherding us asked: "What department do you write to in Arizona, for instance?

"To the man at the top, of course," said the headmaster. "It's the way people do it in the West. I wrote to the Governor of Arizona and the man I heard back from was an official in his publicity department."

"How many other Governors have you written to?" I asked.

"Usually, I try to deal only with heads of state," he replied. "I am in correspondence with President Johnson, General de Gaulle, the King of Norway. . . ."

Egged on by our interest, he produced a sheaf of letters. He was no megalomaniac, although a number of the replies were form letters accompanying routine enclosures. Some were signed by underlings, though Madame Indira Gandhi had replied with a warm personal handsigned note.

To cap all his triumphs, the schoolmaster flung open a closet to show the world press his treasure: a life-sized autographed poster of Generalissimo Francisco Franco of Spain, with whom Czechoslovakia had long enjoyed no diplomatic relations.

"I am in correspondence with Generalissimo Franco, too," the schoolmaster informed us.

The young man from the Ministry of Foreign Affairs whose job was to keep our trip smooth, punctual, and uneventful began to sweat little beads. Therefore I made a point of remarking to him that it was charming for a man in a little hamlet atop a mountain in Bohemia to be corresponding with the world's statesmen. The young man relaxed a little and said: "I suppose that if Czechoslovakia ever wants to resume diplomatic relations with Spain, it is good that this channel has been kept open."

After our tour, we returned to the chateau for lunch (soup, ham, cold smoked meats, cold raw bacon, and all the trimmings) while a small brass band serenaded us. Then there were speeches of welcome and reports of annual achievement. "After the next meal," we were told, "there will be an opportunity for you to ask questions." With that, we were served a "high tea" of pork chops and cutlets.

An official from Prague stood up and announced, in a very stern tone, that he would "moderate" the question period. This particular individual was the purest specimen of Stalin Gothic I have ever seen in a native-born Czech. Rigid, unsmiling, and unbending, he looked like a hammer-and-sickle hewn from the same stone as Prague's Hotel International.

After several routine questions, a very dapper young man with hornrims stood up. He was Helmut Jungwirth of *Der Stern* and he had been accredited only a few weeks before—not long after Czechoslovakia had resumed trade, but not diplomatic, relations with West Germany.

"You are only 50 kilometers from Prague," Jungwirth began. "Undoubtedly, you are hearing about the political rumblings emanating from the Central Committee meetings. How are the workers on your farm reacting to what is going on there? Has it yet begun to affect their lives?"

Jungwirth asked his question in German. The Stalin Gothic "moderator" eyed Jungwirth darkly and said in German: "Our comrades here have no means and no desire to know what their people are *thinking*. It is not their job to read minds. Next question, please."

One of the press corps toadies popped to his feet with the kind of inquiry that will divert or anaesthetize all controversy: "You say your milk output increased from 1.9 million liters to 3 million liters in a year's time. All this is very good, but can you explain why your other crops didn't increase proportionately in output?"

One of the officials of the collective stood up. Although he sported a bristling mustache, he was a smug looking man who hardly seemed to have any surprises in him until he spoke in German:

"Yes, I can explain. But first I would like to answer the previous question. Our regular meeting with the farm workers usually lasts no longer than one hour. The other night it lasted three-and-a-half hours and all of that extra time was devoted to questions about what is happening in the Central Committee. The people here expressed great satisfaction with what has happened thus far in Prague. They are interested and they will be watching developments carefully and hopefully. Now, to answer the second question. . . ."

For the speaker, it was a polite but quickly calculated act of a provincial official defying centralized authority. For me, it was a moment of truth, the rare kind of truth that would become for barely half a year the rule rather than the exception in a land whose oft-abused motto is *"Pravda Vítězí"*—"Truth Prevails."

A couple of nights after my return from the collective farm at Bezno, my home screen began to explode with a series of televised events that had all the relentless inevitability of a Shakespearean historical drama. In black-and-white Iron Curtain mufti (color TV isn't due here until the mid-70's), a pageant unfolded about the making and breaking of kings. But this was a modern one that weighed heavily on the life of every person watching it.

First, Goldstücker reappeared on TV to tell a panel of university students point-blank: "The world is watching whether we shall be able to do what history has not yet known—to unite socialism with freedom."

He also held up a series of before-and-after official photos of past Czechoslovak Communist leaderships. In the "afters," various historical figures (who had been purged and, in some cases, executed after standing trial with Goldstücker) had been airbrushed out of the pictures.

Meanwhile, under Goldstücker's auspices, the Writers Union's new

Literární Listy emerged as a full-fledged social and political as well as cultural organ. In its first issue Goldstücker picked up the thread of his TV remark by writing:

> I would wish that my words might arouse in the minds of my readers the notion of the unique nature of this moment, the chance which history is giving us—that we might make the attempt of combining that which is inseparable: socialism and freedom. I believe that no revolution in history has ever had such a real chance—and our lot is placing us before the most difficult trial.

His deputy, Jan Procházka, took a more skeptical tone that was to typify the sardonic, show-me crusading liberalism of *Literární Listy.* "The same set of guides and leaders for hell, purgatory, and now paradise!" Procházka exclaimed in print. "This is too luxurious an economy even for such a small nation as ours. And to where will they take us?"

In the pages of *Literární Listy,* noted writers criticized the public performance of the new party leadership as well as the old. Hitherto anonymous sources told harrowing first-hand tales of eavesdropping, suppression, and torture. Several of these exposés concluded with the same disclaimer: "Just in case I am found dead: I want to state that I am quite healthy and in sound mind and good spirits, so I have no intention of committing suicide."

The intellectuals were still suspicious of Dubček, but Igor Hájek, happily back at work at *Literární Listy* after a four-month layoff "which I welcomed as a chance to do some writing of my own and then didn't write a word," was hopeful:

"Dubček knows that winning one of Novotný's two hats was not the end of his struggle, but the beginning, and all the entrenched old-timers will be rallying around Novotný and gunning for Dubček. So he needs our support because we have the loudest and cleverest voices, and now that he's unleashed us, it's our turn to howl. We're using him and he's using us."

As the trumpet of the egghead rang throughout the land, the people's television was discovering an invisible man: the proletarian. Roaming mobile units zoomed in on the man in the street, stuck microphones before his face, and asked him all about socialism and democracy. Sometimes, he answered with questions of his own: "Are you kidding? Do you think I want to go to prison for talking to you?" But often he was eloquent. We saw a minor civil servant awakening: "Yesterday I didn't think I could say what I think. Today I think maybe I can." . . . an old man grumbling at a young newsman: "It's fine for you, but a little too late for me." . . . or a factory hand in his late twenties reflecting on the future: "I hope our children won't be afraid to tell the truth like we were."

One night on TV—live!—a panel of experts analyzed videotapes of these responses. They agreed that what they had just witnessed reflected the need for a secret ballot; clear-cut choices, rather than rubber-stamp ratifications, at the polls; and not only freedom of information, but also a greater flow of information.

Fascinated, the public watched itself perform. But it also eyed these experts who were evaluating its performance for they, too, were new faces on Czech TV. The public began to sense that if all went well, it was watching a preview of the future leadership of Czechoslovakia. Perhaps the most interesting of them was Ota Šik, the dark and peppery economic reformer. Šik never minced words or pulled punches as he jolted a sluggish nation into an awareness of how paltry its purse was:

"Shortages of other consumer goods and services make people buy more food, even though food is relatively expensive. Between 1963 and 1965, workers' families in West Germany and Austria spent 38 per cent of their incomes on food; in Czechoslovakia, 51 per cent. . . .

"Simple facts like these, which I am presenting on television, could not be made public for a long time. The backwardness of production and services must be overcome by fundamental changes in the system . . . if we can ever hope that, in four years perhaps, we will achieve the present level of Austria, which is one of the least economically advanced nations of Western Europe.

"The situation is grave. Ten years ago, the first outlines of [Šik's] New Economic System were conceived. Five years ago, the project was worked out in detail. And yet the country is only at the very beginning of change. If there is another delay, the country's situation and its population's living conditions will grow much worse."

The man in the street was invited to confront experts like Šik directly on TV with such questions as these posed by one worker: "Why is the Czech crown worth so little and foreign currency so much? Why are our prices so high and our wages so low? Why are all the best goods our country produces sold only in Tuzex stores and not for Czech crowns?"

A popular new radio program, "Carousel," was run by a former political prisoner named Čeněk Sovák, who interspersed recorded music and cultural news with tales of people he knew in prison and how they were faring now. Once Sovák took a tape recorder and a carload of ex-prisoners back to a prison where they had all served. They confronted their jailers with their bitter recollections. The jailers denied everything. No matter whom the listener believed, he knew he was hearing broadcasting he would never forget.

Listening and watching, the man-in-the-street still played it close to the vest. Too many times in the past twenty years, he had been robbed of his smallest hopes. So when TV asked him what he thought now, he kept his enthusiasm decidedly low-key: "makes sense" or "not bad." Sometimes he played it flip: "I saw an American movie here last night. Now that's something new!" At other times, he was cynical: "Nothing's going to change. . . . I don't believe any of it."

Channel One, however, didn't stop at mere interviews, analyses, and confrontations. It is one thing to point out that one-fifth of Prague's population lives under unspeakably substandard housing conditions, but it is another to follow the man-in-the-street to his home and go inside to show the nitty-gritty of how people live. We saw three generations, the middle one including brothers and sisters and their spouses, dwelling in one small flat that would be a slum with any people less fastidious than the Czechs. "We have to go out into the hall for water," the head of the family said matter-of-factly. "We've been living like this for ten years, y'know." The camera panned around the premises and you saw that everything he said was true and something had to be done.

Seeing and hearing was scarcely believing, however, when the director of the State Bank of Bratislava, Eugen Löbl, who was also imprisoned in the Slánský trials, went on TV to proclaim that what the Czechoslovak economy needed was 200,000 to 300,000 private enterprises. Taking up Ota Šik's cudgels, Löbl said that "the danger of a restoration to capitalism may have existed in 1949 or 1951, but today capitalism is unthinkable here. To whom should we return what?"

The man-in-the-street didn't believe that 1968 was indeed going to be "a completely new year" until he watched the Czechoslovak team beat the Russians in the World Ice Hockey Championships televised live from Grenoble over the Eurovision (West) and Intervision (East) networks. This was taken as a talisman by several Czechs I knew, one of whom remarked that only then did he "really begin to believe" everything else he had been hearing and seeing: "After twenty years, you can't help thinking that even the sports events are managed by the Russians and between the periods Moscow will telephone our coach and tell him to take it easy. But when the Russians let themselves lose to us in hockey, then anything can happen."

A few days later, for the first time in the history of any Communist Party anywhere, the Central Committee's Presidium decided it would divulge *who* voted *how* at its top-secret meetings.

Even before the good guys and bad guys could be sorted out, however, TV had a new comeuppance ritual that became known as "the nightly *mea culpas.*" Invariably, the 7 o'clock news and sometimes the 10 o'clock news would be followed by familiar faces: the same smug faces who used to boast that there was plenty of coal in the bins and fruit in the stores when the viewers knew damn well that both were bare. But now they filed past sweating as they chanted a new litany: mistakes-have-been-made-in-the-past-and-nobody-is-without-blame-but we-are-now-reappraising-our-thinking-in-accordance-with-the-new-wave-of-progressive-socialist-thinking-in-Czechoslovakia, etc.

Instead of swallowing this, however, their interviewers now thrust the microphones closer and asked bluntly: "But who made these mistakes?"

"Well," said one Trade Unions official as the camera zeroed in on his hands, which he was wringing, "the trouble was that we were operating under the 1965 rules and now they have to be brought up to date."

"But how?" the interviewer persisted. "How can we do it if the same people who made the mistakes are being entrusted with correcting them?"

Camera and mike closed in. Now I could see and almost hear the perspiration dripping from the official's natty mustache.

"I am also being asked that question," he began lamely.

Two nights later, the Television News carried his resignation.

The leader of the Communist Party in Prague, Martin Vaculík, complained that he was being muzzled by the mass media. He was promptly invited to face the nation on TV. After some prodding, he showed up but meekly apologized for the "impreciseness" of his accusation. Later, he remarked that "the criticism made me sweat sometimes, but inside I was satisfied."

Even the Minister of Agriculture and Food, a Dubček adherent, ate crow on the radio. Having remarked that the media were "adopting the manners of bourgeois democracy" and "it's a wonder that they aren't demanding the revival of the . . . fascist party," he was grilled by a panel of editors to whom he admitted that his assertions were unfounded. The editors in turn pronounced him a hypocrite. At the end of the broadcast, one of them "reminded" him that only a few months back, he had said that "if the writers don't leave things alone, they will be dealt with by the Government." The Minister, who was replaced soon after this memorable broadcast, said he didn't remember making such a remark.

These performances were described by one of Goldstücker's deputies as "dancing on eggs." And to compete for public attention, the daily newspapers underwent emergency face-lifts. When we had first come to Prague, items about export sales of hockey pucks were front-page news. After just a few weeks however, the Czech press was clamoring like a chorus of *Village Voices*:

COMMUNIST MEETING AT PRAGUE
MUNICIPAL TRANSPORT ENTERPRISE

. . . Mr. Ludvík Černý, the Mayor of Prague, failed to win the attention of the audience. While endorsing the January decisions and deploring Mr. Novotný's mistakes, he failed to make specific critical or self-critical suggestions. He was often vague, for example, when cautioning the mass media. He said that our relations to the Soviet Union and the international working class movement must not be doubted and that the foundations of socialism must not be attacked. Fortunately, his "criticism" did not carry much weight. In fact, the whole meeting, with rare exceptions, did not distinguish itself with any bright ideas. What was said here amounted to a mere undemanding repetition of problems, which are sufficiently well-known from the press, radio, and television. An observer may have acquired the impression that the municipal transport workers had nothing to change and improve in their own work.

With such coverage, daily sales totals for newspapers rose by 118,000 between January and March in Prague alone to a new high of 557,192. Queues formed at news stands every morning and the skinny eight-to-twelve-page dailies (thinned by a perpetual newsprint famine) no longer wrapped the same day's fish, but were read on the trams and then taken home at night for further study. Jirka Šlitr, who had been collecting my discarded *International Herald Tribunes**, stopped com-

* Published in Paris Mondays through Saturdays in conjunction with *The New York Times* and Washington *Post*.

ing for them. "Our own press is more interesting nowadays," he explained.

The public liked it that way, too. A survey conducted by Czechoslovak Radio indicated that "73 per cent of listeners reject the view that the press, radio, and TV 'should not worry about what does not concern them' and want them to express their own views on events. The number of set-owners who watch the evening Television News rose from 23 to 52 per cent last month. The number of readers of the daily press rose from 54 to 69 per cent and listeners to radio news from 43 to a full 80 per cent. The majority of listeners, 78.5 per cent, do not mind that the amount of time devoted to entertainment has dropped as a result of increased information on internal political questions. A full 96 per cent of those questioned were of the opinion that the public should be informed immediately about all important events regardless of whether they are pleasant or not."

The full glare of these spotlights focused on a man who wasn't there, a powerful but hitherto unknown forty-one-year-old general named Jan Šejna. The nation learned that Šejna was a farmhand who had left school at the age of fourteen and been drafted into the Army as a private in 1951. He made undistinguished progress through the ranks until 1967, when he was suddenly elevated to major general at the "special request of the highest political and military authorities." According to *Literární Listy,* his public voice had first been heard pressing for further and harder sanctions against the writers. Only now, however, was the turbulent flow of uncensored news making it obvious to the people that in late 1967 and early 1968, their country had stood on the brink of military seizure or civil war. General Šejna had been plotting nothing less than a *coup d'état* to keep Novotný in power as First Secretary as well as President.

In December, he had mobilized at least one tank division and made other preparations involving troops to seize the Central Committee. A general named Václav Prchlík, however, had learned of Šejna's plans and, by rallying liberal support, had managed to balk him. Prchlík had then been asked to resign his commission because he had "lost the political confidence of Comrade Novotný." Prchlík's superiors had backed him against Šejna and Novotný, however, and the power grab was dead.

With Dubček's accession, most of the officials who had brought pressure upon General Prchlík were dismissed or allowed to resign. On the 25th of February, however, Šejna fled the country and turned up in Rome with his eighteen-year-old son and twenty-two-year-old mistress, who was first described as the son's fiancée. The embittered wife Šejna left behind promptly set the record straight on that score: She gave out an interview recalling a visit from the mistress, who had introduced herself as "your lawful successor."

By then, Šejna (still accompanied by son and mistress) was en route to asylum in the United States as a guest of the Central Intelligence Agency. Prague's official Communist Party daily, *Rudé Právo* editorialized:

> To what kind of person is the U.S.A. about to grant asylum? In the terms of the lingo, to a diehard Stalinist who has lost his case at home. But *The New York Times* has suggested that the American authorities are likely to ignore the fact that Šejna opposed liberalization at home to the very end. He will be treated as a precious source of information. . . .

Which he actually was! It was Šejna who, during his debriefing by the CIA, told his interrogators about a 1967 episode in Kremlin politics. Soon after the death of the Soviet Minister of Defense, Marshal Rodion Malinovsky, the Politburo had sought to replace him with a civilian Minister of Defense: Dmitri Ustinov, a "Soviet McNamara" who was well-liked by the Russian military. Nevertheless, the military had balked at civilian control and won its case. Marshal Andrei Grechko was named to the post instead. The hawks were in the ascendancy and the fate of Czechoslovakia, or any other slightly divergent Warsaw Pact nation, was perhaps already sealed.

Back in Prague, a panel of three fellow generals convened on TV to dissect Šejna as a philanderer, a profiteer and a disgrace to the uniform. He had also, they said, made off with $20,000 worth of clover, alfalfa, and lucerne grass seeds belonging to the State and smuggled foreign cars into the country. True or false, this repellent quarter-hour of character assassination in a kangaroo court-martial made fascinating television. As the revelations about Šejna mounted, with accounts of rendezvous in the Golem restaurant near the old Jewish cemetery, the nation learned more about corruption in high places than even the worst cynics had imagined.

Though Šejna was clearly "Novotný's man," he was also identified as "a long-time friend" of Antonín Novotný, Jr. The President's son was feeling so much heat about Šejna that he gave an interview in which he admitted that "we have known each other well," but denied that, on orders from Šejna, soldiers had been put to work on construction of the Novotnýs' summer chalet near Slapy Dam and their villa in Prague down the street from Jiří Šlitr's.*

One newspaper actually went so far as to label Novotný, Jr., "an upstart son of functionary hierarchy for whom his close friend, traitor and spy Jan Šejna, was procuring cheap labor" and to implicate young Novotný in Šejna's escape.

A few nights after Šejna's defection was revealed, the Minister of Defense, General Bohumír Lomský, took the video hot seat. Nervously reading from a prepared statement, Lomský disowned Šejna (admittedly a close friend and neighbor) and said he was "shocked not only by his speculations, but also by his cowardice when he, a Communist, left his country and betrayed it for fear of punishment." Lomský added that "the Army belongs to all the people." Certain military maneuvers called at the time of the crucial Central Committee meetings had been, he said, purely coincidental, although they "could have given rise to speculation."

The next day's papers reviewed General Lomský as "unconvincing" and "unfortunate."

When another general, the Deputy Minister of Defense, put a bullet through his head and died while being chauffeured to a board of inquiry, a sick joke heard in Prague cafés suggested that he had feared being sentenced to fifteen minutes on TV.

The joke was told with a minimum of gloating. For the taste of freedom was diluting the taste for blood in the Czechoslovak palate. And once again it was Goldstücker who set the tone.

A panel of students met with him to discuss the last Halloween's Strahov riot. One of them told Goldstücker: "I wasn't even *in* the demonstration. I came out of a movie and there was a policeman who said to me: 'I'm going to tear you to pieces.' "

Goldstücker looked at the lad with fatherly compassion and said:

"My biggest fear is that this Strahov affair will remain in your mind. But life goes on and brings new problems, new risks. . . . The

---

* Later investigations, however, confirmed that soldiers did work on the Prague villa after being informed by Šejna that it was a top-secret "State Security conspiratorial villa" used for high-level meetings and interrogations. The summer chalet was, it turned out, paid for out of funds from the President's chancery between 1963 and 1967. After the investigation started in 1968, the chancery was reimbursed by President Novotný himself.

important thing about Strahov is that not only were the students shocked by what happened there, but so were all the people of Prague. After all, the students are the children of this twenty-year-old socialist society of ours, and now *they* were being treated like enemies of the State."

References to the "children of communism" were what one kept hearing—and not only on radio and TV. A boy named Václav, just turning nineteen, happened to be visiting us with his parents the night Goldstücker was on TV with the students. Václav said: "The Stalinists of the 1950's, they wrote off our parents, but they counted on us. They shouldn't have. I've lived all my life under one system, so I have every right to criticize it."

Václav's father said: "They called them 'children of communism,' but they were our children, too; and they were the ones who started saying what we were still afraid to say."

On the screen, a young cynic was grumbling to Goldstücker: "I think everything that's happening now will all end in fiasco."

"But there is a realistic basis for hope," Goldstücker told him. "You must realize that whatever has happened already will be built upon."

As if to prove Goldstücker's point, the very next night's *mea culpas* starred none other than Prague's Chief of Police.

"I am sorry to say that the events in Strahov are being presented from just one point of view, the students'," he began predictably. But then he made a 180-degree turn of the other cheek as he went on to say: "Yes, we admit the conditions in which the students were living were bad enough. And I must admit that, in the final moments, we lost our prudence as safety officers. True, most of the students behaved themselves. But you must remember that the police were nervous. They were not used to this kind of situation." Then he gulped and, looking right at the camera, blurted out: "I just want to present my apologies to all those persons who were injured."

This was probably a first in the long annals of world police repression. (A few hours later the Chief's chief, the Minister of the Interior, issued a formal apology to the students of Strahov and, a few days later, the Minister was dismissed.) But the television interviewer didn't let the Chief off the hook. He reminded him that since not all the streets of Prague were safe at night for women and pensioners, the police should be worrying about this instead of clubbing students.

The most dramatic and biggest-name *mea culpa* was still waiting in the wings. Dubček's new policy of total disclosure was being applied not only to the present, but to the past. The voting at the crucial party Presidium meeting where Dubček had ousted Novotný as First Secretary was officially divulged. It had been a 5-to-5 tie that had then been resolved in Dubček's favor.

There was a tremor in the land that could be felt that night. Czechs and Slovaks were realizing how close the impossible dream they were living had come to eclipse before they ever would have glimpsed it.

Our guests that night were Jiří Šlitr, his parents, and Sylva. By then, dinner invitations in Prague had come to mean aperitifs at 6:30, watching the 7 o'clock Television News, discussing it over dinner, with farewell brandies during the 10 o'clock Television News. But that night my wife's spaghetti went unnoticed and unappreciated by those who ate it.

"If one man had voted differently," Jirka kept murmuring.

"If Šejna hadn't antagonized . . ." said his mother to herself.

"If Brezhnev had helped Novotný. . ." said his father to himself.

"By a hair," said Sylva over and over, "by a hair."

Other hostesses who were "entertaining" that night reported similar soliloquies.

There were at least two major surprises when the 5-to-5 vote was further detailed:

. . . One of the five who had voted *against* Novotný was his heir apparent, Jiří Hendrych, a party ideologist who had engineered the suppression of the writers in 1967. Hendrych was known as "the only man in Czechoslovakia who could enter President Novotný's study without knocking." His support was taken for granted by the President, but he had felt at the last moment [he said now] that "for two years, Mr. Novotný has been acting alone and isolating himself, speaking to everyone separately." And so he had voted to separate the posts of First Secretary and President. Hendrych also had repented of his acts toward the writers: "I do not hesitate to say that I made a mistake." Whatever his motives, Hendrych's vote was deeply appreciated—though not enough to save his political future. A month later, he asked to be relieved of all his party posts "to facilitate the most favorable conditions for future work in the ideological sphere."

. . . The other surprise involved the "number three" man (behind the President-First Secretary and Hendrych) in the Novotný regime:

Prime Minister Jozef Lenárt, a Slovak. In 1968 Lenárt had been paying vociferous lip service to Dubček and the "rebirth" of the democratic process. But now the records showed that, at the 1967 Presidium meeting when all the chips had been down, Lenárt had been one of the five (Novotný himself plus four others) who had voted for keeping the President in both posts.

We turned to our TV screen for clarification. And, the next night, there was Prime Minister Lenárt looking grim as death. He explained that he was sick with the flu and shouldn't be out of bed, but nothing could keep him off the TV screen at this time. "I have not spoken publicly before," he apologized, "because as a disciplined party member, I had considered it my duty to speak on party soil only."

He said that, at the crucial time, "the name of the candidate for First Secretary was not yet known." Eyes watering, Lenárt pleaded that this was why he had voted the way he did. "When it was decided that the functions would be divided, I myself proposed Alexander Dubček, whom I knew as a sincere and brave Communist who is devoted to the party. This was unanimously approved."

On television, Lenárt now reiterated his unqualified support of the "progressives" (meaning First Secretary Dubček) and dissociated himself from the "conservatives" (which had already come to mean President Novotný). The Prague press reviewed Lenárt's performance thusly: "The Prime Minister made a good impression . . . but he has left open several questions that cannot be overlooked."

One of these was that, in the jockeying for power after the tie vote had been resolved by the whole Central Committee, Lenárt had been the Novotný faction's candidate for First Secretary. The opposition's candidate had been Oldřich Černík. Another deadlock had developed in the Presidium. A cautious Czech pragmatist who sensed that the initial victory might go down the drain, Černík had suddenly withdrawn in favor of Dubček, a Slovak. This had swung enough Slovak votes to win the day for Dubček. Then and only then had Lenárt moved to make the close vote unanimous.

Novotný had been surprisingly acquiescent to the Dubček selection. "Why not him?" he had said, pointing to Dubček, who had been sitting silently throughout the hours of tense negotiations. "Comrade Dubček has no enemies. He has a good party record and I think he would make for the best compromise solution."

Even while Prime Minister Lenárt was pleading his case on TV, his Deputy Prime Minister (another of the five who had voted for Novotný's continuation) was giving a similar performance on the radio. The Deputy Prime Minister even ventured to predict that "Comrade Novotný, who is an experienced and veteran political worker, will certainly not allow his name to be linked with holding up the revival of party and public life. I do not doubt that he will resign from the function of President and thus render a good service to the Republic in the present situation."

But no word came from the Presidential apartments in the Prague Castle, where Antonín Novotný was in seclusion. The sixty-four-year-old former steelworker had ruled the Czechoslovak Socialist Republic with an iron hand since 1957, when he added the Presidency to the First Secretaryship he had acquired after the death of Klement Gottwald in 1953.

In the early days of Dubček, Novotný could still be seen on TV performing innocuous ceremonial functions. The man whose official photo, displayed in every store and office, radiated a cold and wary glint would harangue the nation with ghosted words punctuated by his own jolts of disbelief at what he was saying. He reminded me of a silver-haired elevator operator arguing against automation.

After a while, if we saw Novotný greeting a delegation of women on International Women's Day, the women would then adjourn to a Castle anteroom and pass a resolution expressing their support for Dubček's reforms.

One day, Novotný visited a factory and we saw the workers cheering him. A few days later, we saw a representative of those workers on TV: "We cheered because the President of the Republic had come to see us. But he showed us when he visited our plant that he no longer has the intelligence to lead our country."

There were a few such episodes and then Novotný became the grayest of eminences on the black-and-white home screen. We heard long lists of groups and individuals demanding his resignation, but we no longer saw him.

Oldřich Starý, a distinguished neurologist and rector of Charles University, proclaimed bluntly: "Concentrated power is an awful thing, especially when it is combined with an even more horrible drug —if the leading representative personifies himself as the working class;

if he believes that his person expresses our attitude toward the Soviet Union; if he appears and acts as if he alone were the Communist party. Worse still if he is proceeding from distorted information steadily supplied by people whom he has raised to high posts."

Ota Šik, the economist, was kinder, but just as firm: "An effort should be made to win over the greatest possible number of people for new work. At the same time, dignified conditions for retirement should be established for those leaving their jobs. They should not be treated in the undemocratic way which they themselves have applied to others. . . .

"This is a time for the greatest possible political tolerance and a genuine beginning of a new, humanitarian socialist democracy. I believe that the strong democratic tradition here and the Czechoslovak people's dislike for political oppression makes this country suited for an unprecedented form of socialist democracy. The new socialist society could become a truly attractive community for the working people of the capitalist countries and influence the left-wing movement in the West."

Two newspapers in Bratislava printed open letters urging the President to resign. "If we did not invigorate the economic system with new trends which you opposed, our economy would have collapsed," said the Slovak *Pravda*.* The other, the youth daily *Smena* (*Shift*) wrote:

> We know that it is very difficult to go. It is complicated, it is an art, but sometimes it is extremely necessary. You are lucky enough that you will not go the way many others went before you—people who were more honest and more just—to dark corners, one-room flats, practically without any money and without any hopes. We hope that those years will never come back when people were only being classified as black or white. We are convinced that you have also done many a good thing and just for that reason you will live as a human being, in a dignified way, and without material problems.

The Czech trade unions newspaper, *Work,* entitled its plea "The Art of Leaving." It concluded: "It is not a shame to go when someone else can do the work better. . . . We must learn not only the art of ruling, but also the art of leaving, which is equally important and sometimes even more important. That moment has come."

Agricultural News lashed out with hammer *and* sickle:

* The word *pravda* means "truth" in Czech and Slovak as well as in Russian.

In Antonín Novotný the people, long before January, saw the personification of the stifling, distorting, and falsifying phenomena of an
undesirable political atmosphere. His bad attitude towards the people,
his cool relationship to history, his lack of interest in the minds and
hearts of this nation have brought this President to the very limit of
complete estrangement.

Novotný's nemesis, Dubček, was an entirely different sort of man
who was already beginning to delight the sophisticated Czechs of
Prague as well as his fellow Slovaks. The new First Secretary, age forty-
six, had made an inauspicious TV debut in January. Reading from a
prepared speech, he kept losing his place and looking as insecure as the
spectacles that slipped down his Pinocchio nose from time to time.
Warm and homely, he scarcely seemed to be an inspiring personality,
just a cordial, catalytic one with an angular profile that was a carica-
turist's dream and an endearing political asset. Translating TV for me
one night, Sylva had giggled and remarked: "First enters the nose, then
enters Mr. Dubček." I had laughed too, and quoted the line in a *Life*
article that (I would learn in our first face-to-face conversation) Dubček read and remembered.*

As the first Slovak ruler of Czechoslovakia, Dubček for a while
acted, in the words of one diplomat, "as cautiously as the first Negro
President of the United States might be expected to behave during his
first year in the White House." The format of an early Dubček appearance was fairly cut and dried:

First, a lesser official would deliver a fire-eating oration: e.g., "All
Communist party workers have a right to participate in the party and
to criticize. When that isn't the case, when we see flattery, bureaucracy,
and leading people unable to accept criticism, *then* we are in danger."

Dubček would shake the speaker's hand and give a mild-mannered
but telling response: e.g., "There are fears as to whether the process of
democratization is going too far. . . . Well, that is what we wanted
and what we want. . . . The press, radio, and television have done a
great bit of work by spreading interest in the current events to the
widest masses of the population. Such an interest in our internal political affairs hasn't been evident for ages. This, too, corresponds to the
Leninist requirement for the greatest number of people to understand
political life, to participate in it and . . . in the administration of the
State."

* "A Binge of Free Expression: Czechoslovakia de-Stalinizes in Front of the TV
Cameras," *Life,* April 5, 1968, pp. 62–64.

To which Prague's only afternoon paper *Večerní (Evening) Praha* soon added:

> Today, it can already be stated that the discussions which, until recently, have taken place primarily in the press, radio, and television . . . has come to be the affair of the entire nation. . . . A serious demand is for the assessment of the work especially of Comrade Antonín Novotný. . . .

Now the nightly newscasts were running half-an-hour overtime with announcements of lesser resignations, dismissals, no-confidence votes, sick leaves, and petitions for recall. Miroslav Mamula, head of the nefarious Eighth Department (a special task force of secret police) within the Communist Party Central Committee and one of General Šejna's principal civilian allies, resigned to become an obscure factory hand. Mamula was replaced by, of all people, the steadfast General Prchlík who had thwarted Šejna's coup.

Still Novotný didn't take the hint. And his scheming presence, sealed into the seclusion of the Prague Castle, worried us all. When Dubček stayed home with the flu, Czechs I knew were worried sick. When he flew to Moscow on a State visit, they stopped in at church to pray on their ways to and from work. *"Now* Novotný will make his move,"* they said fearfully.

They had good cause to worry. Upon Dubček's accession in January, he had been invited to Moscow for an official blessing. Now the Prague grapevine (whose timetable for the removal of Novotný from the Presidency by the end of March, if all went well, was proving deadly accurate) had a new tale to tell:

When Dubček arrived inside the Kremlin, he had to wait until his Soviet counterpart, Leonid Brezhnev, finished with a previous caller. Eventually, Brezhnev's door opened and the caller inside proved to be Antonín Novotný, looking mighty hangdog. The fact that Novotný was made to exit via the anteroom where Dubček waited was also a good sign that his last-ditch plea for Russian intervention had failed. Nevertheless, it must have been a terrifying shock for Dubček, who could not have been unaware of the perils of Iron Curtain statesmanship. As recently as 1956, Hungarian Premier Imre Nagy and his Cabinet members were abducted by Soviet police and executed.

In early 1968 as in late 1967, Russia did not intervene, but hewed instead to the original Brezhnev doctrine of "Comrades, this is your own affair." With American prestige sinking in the Vietnam morass, Russia remained unwilling to lose its propaganda advantage by making an ugly move in the goldfish bowl of world public opinion.

Still, there were twenty Russian divisions across the border in East Germany and other Soviet troops stationed in Poland and Hungary (to protect the regimes there) and, of course, in Russia—all of which border on Czechoslovakia. Coupling these realities with memories of past repressions in the neighborhood lands, the most optimistic Czech glanced over his shoulder from time to time.

For even while Novotný still clung to power, the Czechoslovak Revolution was an international affair watched with mixed and volatile reactions abroad. When students surged through the streets of Warsaw and Cracow that winter, they chanted "We Want a Dubček!" They could only have known what was happening next door from listening (illegally) to foreign broadcasts, for the Polish press had kept the Czechoslovak Revolution a dark secret. Now, however, there were official Polish references to "the poison from Prague" and East German rumblings that Czechoslovakia seemed to be "defecting" from the East bloc. Russian intellectuals, though screened from the truth, were informing visitors that "we, too, are waiting for a Dubček of our own."

The Czechoslovak Revolution was having its impact in the West, too. Student demonstrators in the Latin Quarter of Paris chalked and chanted the slogan "Long live Czechoslovak students! Long live Czechoslovak workers!"

All these reactions, positive and negative, were duly reported in Prague as was a newspaper editorial from neighboring capitalist Austria that made the most sense of all:

"If Czechoslovakia's daring experiment succeeds, the West will be faced with a challenge more dangerous than all the threats of communism so far because it would have to be matched with weapons of the spirit, and not with political methods."

Fortunately for nobody, the fearful old men who personify Communism in Moscow, Pankow, Warsaw, Sofia, and Budapest could never quite perceive this. Thus, as early as March, a backlash against the Dubček reforms could be felt inside Czechoslovakia. There were occasional warnings from both conservatives and liberals for the mass media to cool it. A Dubček ally in Prague praised the work of TV and radio, but added that "a dialogue would be better than a series of monologues." In the provinces, a number of Communist party district conferences passed resolutions objecting to "the ways used by various authors writing for the press, radio, and television . . . which do not contribute to a positive trend." Journalists covering some of these meetings were heckled and ejected.

The Party daily *Rudé Právo,* under the ironclad editorship of a diehard conservative Central Committee Presidium member, still sounded like Novotný's trumpet when the chips were down. It printed a lengthy transcript of doubts expressed by workers at the Tesla electronics plant. Wasn't free expression getting a little out of hand? Shouldn't *certain* freedoms be restricted here or curtailed there?

Milan Weiner, radio commentator, took to the air to rebut them:

"I implore you, comrades from Tesla and *Rudé Právo* . . . can you name a single moment in this country's life in which we have had to be ashamed of *too much* freedom and criticism? Or has all the shame and distortion . . . not been associated with unfreedom, oppression, and restriction of criticism? I keep wondering how come some people permit themselves to be again and again misused for aims detrimental to them."

A listener phoned in and Weiner, on his next broadcast, played a tape recording of the conversation:

"I want to ask you, Mr. Weiner, whether there has been anything good in this country over the past twenty years?"

"Of course there has!"

"My name is Josef Záruba and I want to tell you that you have just now talked like an agent of imperialism."

"Well, do come to see us here at Radio and tell us about your views."

"I shall . . . but you're all scoundrels. You're spitting on the republic. You're spitting on the party. You're spitting on everything. Since when have *you* been in the party?"

"Since 1942," Weiner replied. "I joined the party in a concentration camp."

"Well, I am a party member since 1939 . . . but I shall probably not be able to stay in any party of which you're a member. Probably there will have to be *two* parties to fight each other. . . ."

"I'm all for it," said Weiner. "It could be interesting, y'know."

"Interesting, you say?!!" the caller spluttered. "When you're not permitting anybody to speak out!"

Now Weiner concluded his broadcast:

"There you are, Mr. Záruba, we have already let you speak out. And I am not cross with you for having called me an imperialist agent. . . . I do not wish to end on the gallows. But I cannot forget that the road to the gallows begins where fingers are raised in warning. It is my experience that what ended in the darkest period of socialist Czechoslovakia began with suppression of free speech and free criticism."

Everyone was being heard from except President Novotný. The Communist Youth Union called a rally at Slavonic Hall in downtown Prague. Two thousand students and workers filled the ballroom to accuse Novotný of "a reign of terror" and demand his resignation. Television ran two hours of it.

A week later a similar event was held at the Julius Fučík Park of Culture.* This time, 16,000 people showed up. The rally, which was the nearest thing to an old-fashioned American town meeting I have ever seen, lasted from 7 P.M. to 2 A.M. and radio aired it live and unexpurgated. TV filmed it and showed most of it in installments on subsequent nights.

The star of both rallies was Josef Smrkovský, Minister of Forestry and Water Conservation. The name Smrkovský means "of the pine trees" and he was known to Czechs as "the man of the woods and waters." These were my first glimpses of him.

Born in 1911, Smrkovský was appointed to his first Communist Party post in 1932 and served as a trade union and party leader from then on. His personal popularity always worried tyrants, and in 1940 the Gestapo issued a warrant for his arrest and offered a reward of one million crowns. Uncaught, he served as an underground militia commander throughout the war and a leader of Prague's uprising against the Nazis in 1945.

When the Communists came to power in 1948, Smrkovský served as general manager of State farms and Deputy Minister of Agriculture. Again, his popularity put him in jeopardy, this time with his insecure "superiors." In March of 1951, he was arrested as an "anti-State con-

---

* Julius Fučík (1903–43) was *the* martyr of Czech Communist resistance to the Nazis. A journalist, he was imprisoned and then executed by the Gestapo, but not before he had written a book called *Report from the Gallows* that was published in 1945. His dying words were a warning against more war: "People, I loved you, be on your guard!"

spirator" and held in Ruzyně prison (near the Prague airport of the same name) without trial for three and a half years of torture, interrogation, and solitary confinement. In 1954, he was sentenced to fifteen years in prison, but a year later he was released and the verdict was declared null and void.

Such experiences might have shaken one's faith in Communism, but not Smrkovský's. Seeing his persecutors as deformers of the ideal, he determined to cleanse the system from within. And people listened to him because, as with Goldstücker, imprisonment at the hands of those villains were the most impeccable credentials—if you survived. (This status reached such a pinnacle in 1968 that once, at a party, I asked a Czech jokingly, "Why weren't you in jail in the 1950's?" In all seriousness and with the same defensive manner of a 4-F at a V.F.W. bash, he apologized for his clean slate.)

Smrkovský started up the ladder again as a mechanic at a State farm, an agricultural technician in the State forests, and then, for six years, chairman of an agricultural co-operative. Finally, in 1963, he was granted full political and judicial rehabilitation and quickly made his way back into the National Assembly, the Central Committee, and the Cabinet. More of a hero than ever, he was rumored to be the next Prime Minister or even President whenever Lenárt and Novotný would fall.

Round-shouldered and crew-cut, "the man of the woods and waters" still bore definite traces of prison pallor on his wrinkled, grandfatherly leprechaun's face. Viewed on TV, his most distinctive mannerism was shoving his hornrims above his eyes like pilot's goggles, which he did at the first rally while proclaiming that his only regret about the conduct of the press was that it hadn't been unleashed sooner: "If it weren't for journalists and all their media, the party as a whole and our public would not be correctly informed to this day."

At the second rally, Smrkovský spoke of "the tremendous duty of creating in this country a socialism which will be capable of giving a new human content to life, which will lead to a flowering of culture and a new moral code. Many of us realize that it is our very country that is capable of creating a new type of socialist state which will have something to say also to the people of developed Western European countries."

Smrkovský's co-star at this second rally was Goldstücker. And, de-

spite the vast throng egging them on, both men seemed to be addressing themselves to one man—the brooding enigma in Hradčany—assuring him that he could bow out with dignity and not be removed from
power in the brutal way that they once were. The relatively civilized
treatment accorded Nikita Khrushchev in 1964 was cited numerous
times at this last rally.

The next night, President Novotný broke his silence. He telephoned the afternoon paper and explained to a startled editor that he
was bedded down by "gall bladder trouble which had turned into flu."
Now he was recovering, but he still had fever. As soon as he recovered,
he would "come before the public with opinions on current happen-
ings."

Fever aside, that brief telephone chat was the warmest interview
Novotný had ever given to the press.

The next morning, he phoned the afternoon paper again to add:
"I'll be glad to make a public appearance and I hope that I'll have the
chance to do so. I'm ready now and can appear at any time. I repeat: I
am ready. Certain considerations guided me not to appear and I didn't
want to complicate the situation. I had promised this to the comrades
and I kept this promise. But now is the time for me to appear." Meanwhile, his son resigned as head of ARTIA, the import-export corporation for "cultural commodities."

A nation glued itself to its TV for the final act. But, like the elusive
Godot, Novotný never appeared. Instead, on Friday the 22d of March,
1968, at 11:30 A.M., as the National Assembly deputies moved to take
a vote of no-confidence in him (a preliminary to impeachment), Novotný sent them a letter of "comradely greetings." In it, he abdicated
the Presidency "because of the internal situation which at this moment
has prevailed."

His words arrived in time for the noon Television News. There was
a collective sigh of relief, but no dancing in the streets. The most appropriate comment was Eduard Goldstücker's:

"The peaceful and dignified handling of the situation was im-
mensely important. All people, no matter what they think of Mr. Novotný's work, will now gladly and humanely acknowledge that the tradition of heaping mud upon departing statesmen should be forever
forgotten."

It became known that Novotný's last official act preceding his resignation was to write a letter to Goldstücker (in the latter's capacity as

head of the Writers Union) pardoning the imprisoned writer Jan Beneš. And another writer observed in print:

"That was a wise way to go. Not only a writer, but a statesman, too, sometimes needs forgiveness, and much forgiving at that. This departing man will need it, too. For the people could have presented him with a long bill to pay."

Interlude ⌉ The Lonely Sniper

IT WAS A KIND OF JERSEY CITY-MODEL STALINISM THAT the Czechoslovak people lived under. Novotnýism had no ideals, no real program, just a blind instinct to consolidate power and cling to it at any cost. By the time these self-serving reflexes had aged into torpor, the structure of the government ministries (according to *Rudé Právo* itself) had been re-organized more than 100 times—for the betterment not of the masses, but of the bosses.

Novotnýism was the ideological heir of its parent regime, Gottwaldism. But, where the nation's first Communist Prime Minister (later President) Klement Gottwald (1896–1953) was an ambitious, belligerent drunkard who had dedicated much of his life to making Czechoslovakia go Communist for reasons that must have started with belief, Antonín Novotný (born 1904) was a careerist dedicated to keeping Czechoslovakia Communist for the sake of his own personal security.

An analysis of the combined result was delivered at Charles University two days before President Novotný abdicated:

"The character of the totalitarian dictatorship under which we have lived for the last twenty years has certain national peculiarities. One big advantage for the regime was that it was headed by full-blooded Czechs imbued with the Austrian tradition of joviality plus our own disorderly capability as caretakers. Totalitarian dictatorship in the Czechoslovak manner often seemed more chaotic, paradoxical, and comical than tyrannical.

"Apart from a few murders, the government knew as little about what to do with absolute power as an infant does with numbers. A spontaneously spouting geyser of improvised stupidity bubbled forth tirelessly for twenty years in the official press, the tolerated culture, and the speeches of statesmen. But it proved unable, even by extreme effort, to undermine the basis of the socialist set-up here. The natural intelligence of the good-natured people in Slovakia, Moravia, and the Czech Lands always corrected the worst excesses to a bearable degree.

"Another characteristic feature of this totalitarian dictatorship was that, for twenty years, internal political crises were avoided so long as there was something that could be reduced in price. And it must be said that this suited our people fine; it was enough for them.

"The regime survived at the expense of economic effectiveness. It made it possible for one to work less and worse for more money. It insured the legal and economic equality of a laborer with a university professor.* Thanks to this, no noticeable opposition appeared in Czechoslovakia, even during the last decade, when our economic diffi-culties were growing. The State was led to bankruptcy, helped by the taciturn discipline of the controlled but thrifty citizens. . . ."

The speaker of these unflattering truths was a balding, bespectacled historian and philosophy lecturer named Ivan Sviták, forty-two. He was a teacher whose ideas have touched the life of every student of his I've ever met, including our good friend Sylva. To her, Sviták had been not merely a professor, but "the person who opened doors for me, doors to the modern world of art, painting, and poetry. I went to the univer-sity in the Fifties, when all contacts with the West had stopped. But this was the man who said to me: 'There are new things and new ideas. Some are from the West and some are from the East. And there are also old ideas you should know about.' Then he not only told me about Kafka and Camus, but he lent me their books, books which were for-bidden or out-of-print, 'decadent' but delicious. . . ."

For his pains, Sviták had been expelled in the 1960's first from the party and then from the Academy of Sciences as a "deviationist." He had only recently been reinstated and now he could state from aca-demic and even official podiums what he had been saying all along.

"I am what you might call a lonely sniper," he remarked after his lecture on Novotnýism. "I don't think I will go to prison for this. They will not persecute me, at least not now."

With Novotný's downfall, Sviták served notice that he would not be silenced by a mere turn for the better. From his perch in academia, the lonely sniper would continue to strafe the new men with his opin-ions, starting with a prediction that "the harmony between critical in-

* On the same page of the same issue of the same Czech periodical, there appeared the following two HELP WANTED ads: WANTED: bus driver, wage within the limits of 2,800 to 3,400 crowns. . . . VACANT: post of specialist in internal diseases at district hospital—salary: 2,100 crowns.

tellectuals and high representatives of the party and State will vanish. This will happen when the new set of leaders will consider the democratization process completed, which will be at the stage achieved when they come to power."

And this, said Sviták, would never do: "We want democracy, not democratization. At present, we are not very clear on what democratization is. On the other hand, we know quite precisely what democracy is. And apart from the temporary, unofficial and, at any time, revocable abolition of censorship, our country lacks all the attributes of this form of government."

Chapter 6 ⌐

Sunday 24 March—Sunday 31 March 1968

OUR ROWBOAT TOOK US INTO A TIME WHEN WE NO LONGER felt like Americans living abroad. Instead, we were Americans who might have been living in the Hudson Valley around 1784, when the enemy had been vanquished but the revolution was still fraught with peril. Now, at a time when our own nation was wracked by riot and decay, we seemed to be partaking of the American dream's beginnings.

The Government Committee for Tourism had offered my family and me a free eight-day guided tour of Southern and Western Bohemia. Forty-five hours after the President abdicated, we embarked upon our journey through the Czech Lands that Good Prince (not King) Wenceslas had ruled from 928 to 935 A.D. Our rowboat from Prague was a Chaika limousine—and the paradox of glancing, slightly apprehensively, into a chauffeured Russian chariot and perceiving a family of friendly Americans was the kind of small miracle that nourishes the imperishable descendants of Wenceslas.

That week was the false dawn of spring, when the first buds poked through the winter's snow and the warm sun of freedom started cracking the Ice Age of Novotnýism. Like Rip van Winkle, the Czech provincials we met seemed to be emerging from a twenty-year slumber.

After that first warm week of spring, the weather would turn cold again and the buds would wither and die. We might have taken this as an omen if we hadn't known that eventually spring must blossom forth triumphantly. Which it finally did.

Czech or American, once you have lived through such a glorious spring and part of the summer that followed, you have something to live for and die for, even when a cruel, relentless winter descends in August. In the dark time that ensues, you compare and the contrast makes you shiver. But you cannot be sorry that you had those good months.

Or ever forget them.
Or settle for less.

Our guide was named Henrietta, and it was clear from the moment we met her that ours was not going to be a glibly packaged tour. Pinch-faced and repressed-looking, Henrietta was thrice-divorced and sassy in four or five languages. She was in her late forties, part of "the generation that had thirty years amputated from our lives: ten by the Nazis and twenty by the Communists. The Germans closed the schools just when I was to go to college, so I worked in a library and learned whatever I could there."

What promise did the dawn of the Dubček era hold out to Henrietta?

"For me, nothing," she said, as we cruised through the outskirts of Prague. "And for my two married daughters, very little. For my thirteen-year-old son, well, I can hope. But there's always going to be someone who hasn't got the word. People who work in dark corners can't afford to see the light. I brought along two books in English to read at night while we're traveling. One is by George Orwell. . . ."

"*1984?*" I guessed.

"No," said Henrietta. "Do you know *Animal Farm?*"

"Oh, yes. All creatures are equal, but some are more equal than others."

"The pigs, of course. And the other was by Robert Donovan about the six days it took for Israel to put our Arab brothers in their place."

Her Donovan and Orwell, sent by a couple of Californians she once guided, had just necessitated a trip to the "special" Post Office in Maxim Gorki Square.

"You can't have these, of course" the lady behind the counter told her grimly.

"What do you mean?" snapped Henrietta. "Haven't you heard? There's no more censorship."

"I'm not censoring these books. I just can't let you have anything that isn't good for you. But they're insured, so you must sign that they arrived safely."

"Why aren't these two books good for me?"

"Because they're enemy propaganda. If you could read them, you wouldn't want to live in the same flat with them."

"Suppose," said Henrietta, "you give them to me and I'll look at them in the park and decide for myself whether I should take them home." The woman shook her head, so Henrietta asked: "Have *you* read them?"

"Of course not. I can't and neither can you."

After half-an-hour's howling by Henrietta (the very thought of which can make the blood run cold), the turning point came when she asked for the "Book of Complaints and Requests" (*Kniha přání a stížností*). This is a book of numbered forms that every office, store, or eating place must maintain in Czechoslovakia. If you register a complaint in it, you will eventually receive a reply of some sort from whatever higher authority inspects that book. In the 1950's, the answer sometimes was a visit from the secret police, but in 1968, Henrietta was willing to take the chance that this diehard conservative was more scared than she was.

"All right," the lady relented. "You may have these books if you'll pledge never to lend them to anybody."

"Oh, I can promise you that," said Henrietta. "If there are two treasures I want for my old age, it's my books and my friends. And books like these are so precious here that if I lent one of them and never got it back, I'd have lost a book and a friend."

Half an hour out of Prague, we stopped at what was once the village of Lidice. The world now knows the fate of this massacred town where more than 400 people were living when the 10th of June, 1942, began. Lidice is now a giant flower bed and rose garden with a mass grave lined by wreaths and candles. Where the schoolhouse used to stand, there is now a huge statue of a weeping mother, cradling a small child in the folds of her dress.

Back in the car, Henrietta remarked: "Whenever we have Germans coming this way on a tour, East German, West German, it doesn't matter, we make an unscheduled stop here."

"Do they complain?" Valerie asked.

"Only to me," she replied. "The old ones say, 'Henrietta, we didn't do it! Why should we come here and suffer?' I don't give them any answer. But the young ones look and listen."

A mile or two out of Lidice, Henrietta told us of the only time in more than a decade of guiding she had received an official reprimand: for taking her tourists on a detour to the town of Lány, where the

Masaryk family is buried. She was suspended from guiding for three months. Lány hadn't been on a Czechoslovak tourist itinerary for at least fifteen years.

I asked the question Henrietta was hoping for: "How far is Lány from here?"

Immediately, our driver Jaro slowed down and searched for a turnoff while Henrietta replied: "It's sort of between Lidice and our destination for today, Carlsbad. Just a little off the main road. In fact, it used to be on the main road, but after the Masaryks became non-persons, Novotný had the highway re-routed away from Lány."

"Talk about Orwell!" I exclaimed.

"Kafka," Henrietta corrected.

"Whichever it is, we want to go to Lány. You can tell your superior that I insisted upon Jaro's using an old road map."

Jaro was signaling for the turnoff to Lány by then.

For more than a generation, President Thomas Garrigue Masaryk (1850–1937), founder of the Czechoslovak Republic, and his son, Foreign Minister Jan Masaryk (1886–1948) had gone unmentioned in the official press and dismissed briefly (if mentioned at all) by textbooks as "bourgeois nationalists." In 1968, however, the Prague press had begun to praise them cautiously for their devotion to the nation. Then *Literární Listy* had managed to sketch a limbo of ignorance in one profound cartoon: A small boy and his father stand before a statue of President T.G. Masaryk on horseback. And the boy exclaims: "Look, Daddy, a statue of a horse!"

Two Sundays before our visit to Lány had been the tenth of March, twenty years to the day when Jan Masaryk's body was found mysteriously dead in a Černín Palace inner courtyard. It was also the week when T.G. Masaryk was born, 118 years earlier, in semi-serfdom to a Slovak coachman and a Moravian housemaid. And on that Sunday the Czechs had shown that their long memory could not be obliterated by Big Brother and two decades of his Ministries of Truth and Fear spouting Orwellian Newspeak.

Starting that Sunday morning, when thousands of cars and buses had flocked to Lány, the old had wept pent-up tears for those they had admired and lost while the very young had been held aloft so they could see the grave and wonder what the name Masaryk meant. The tenth of March had been a Sunday of windswept snow, but more and more Czechs and Slovaks kept coming. Toward 4:30 P.M., a special train from Prague disgorged several thousand students, who paraded the goodly distance from station to cemetery with banners proclaiming "TRUTH WILL PREVAIL—EVEN HERE?" and "JAN, WE SHALL NEVER FORGET YOU." And one of their number, from the Philosophical Faculty, had made this short speech:

"We stand at the grave of a man who died an unusual death twenty years ago, a great son of a great father. He was a cosmopolitan in the best sense of the word. He said in February, 1948: 'I have always gone with the people and I shall always go with the people.' Let us remember this man at this crucial time in which we hope that people of the quality of Jan Masaryk will lead our nation."

Here where every graveside visitor used to be photographed by secret police, the students had sung two songs that were favorites of the Masaryks and then quietly departed. But ordinary citizens had continued to come. The next Sunday, St. Patrick's Day, a wreath had appeared on Thomas Masaryk's grave with two ribbons saying, in English and Czech, "FROM THE AMERICAN PEOPLE."

Now, on the third Sunday, not a single policeman or plainclothes type was visible. We stood on line to pay homage to the three graves in the corner of the little country cemetery: Thomas Garrigue Masaryk; his Brooklyn-born wife Charlotte Garrigue (whose maiden name her husband had taken as a gesture of devotion); and their son Jan. Our driver Jaro stood on line with us too, and, while we waited, pointed out the grave of the Masaryk butler Procházka*, who had asked to be buried near his masters. That morning, one never would have foreseen the Pandora's Box that rehabilitating the Masaryks and reviving the mystery of the son's death would open upon Czech decency.

A Czech cemetery is such a restful place. In Lány, as elsewhere in the land, were well-kept marble headstones with little glass display compartments featuring tintypes of the deceased, family trophies, newspaper clippings, urns with ashes, and even, on view over one grave, a small plastic Christmas tree. A Czech cemetery is less of a place where the dead decay than one where memories are preserved and the living converge to remember.

Five centuries before the Masaryk dynasty was conceived, the Holy Roman Emperor Charles IV, "supreme ruler of the world," decided he preferred Prague's location and landscape to Rome's or Vienna's and

* Procházka, a common Czech name, is the equivalent of our Walker.

so he built Prague into a city whose wonders still bear his name: Charles University and the Charles Bridge, though he named the mighty Cathedral, begun in his reign, after St. Vitus, the patron saint of all epileptics, humble or regal.

Outside Prague, along the route my family and I were now traveling, Charles IV's scientists stocked the fishponds and cultivated fruit, vineyards, and hops for beer.

Charles IV (1316–1378) was a small, fidgety man who married four times for political expediency. He dressed simply, admitted all petitioners to his presence in Hradčany, and listened to advice from all. But he ruled alone, despite his addiction to the royal "we" as in his "We the Emperor have built, redressed, triumphed."

One day, We the Emperor was hunting near the town of Vary when a fleeing stag led him to the hot spring of the river Teplá. While the stag leapt to freedom, the emperor sipped the water and found that it improved his digestion. The grateful monarch designated the insignificant village of Vary as a "royal city" with appertaining privileges and rights. He even allowed the spa that sprung up around the spring in his lifetime to be named after him: Karlovy Vary—now, literally, Charles' Hot Springs, or, as legions of German health-seekers came to call it, Charles' Bath, alias Carlsbad!

Many Americans don't know that both Carlsbad and its rival Marienbad are both in Czechoslovakia. But once you have crossed, as we did, over the Bohemian Mountains and suddenly caught your first glimpse of Carlsbad gleaming on the hillsides beneath you, you will never again need to be reminded where it is. Alexander von Humboldt compared this scene to "a diamond set in an emerald" and Goethe once wrote that Carlsbad was one of the only three cities where he would like to live; the other two were Rome and his own Weimar.

The valley below was already turning green that first Sunday in spring. As we caught our breath, Henrietta began her spiel:

"Those two large sanatoriums you see there are the Imperial and the Richmond, where your President Roosevelt came trying to cure his polio. Even today, one of them is reserved only for visiting Russian dignitaries. Farther down, near the hot spring, you can see a blue and white building, the Grand Hotel Pupp. Since some time after 1948, it has been re-named the Grand Hotel Moscow-Pupp. I will really start believing in Dubček when he annuls that mismatch. The Pupp, as you will see, is built like a wedding cake with cherubs and swirls and chandeliers and period furniture. Now, for the film festival, they are building a new wing over there which the architects say blends with the Pupp style, but the Czechs call it 'Crematorium Modern' or 'Pupp in an Ice Box.' It will ready for this June's film festival.

"The Carlsbad Film Festival used to be an annual event. But, when the Russians decided they needed a Moscow Film Festival and there weren't any good dates open on the festival calendars, they simply took away every odd-numbered year from Carlsbad and gave it to Moscow. Two years ago, your American entry at Carlsbad was disqualified simply on the basis of its title: *The Russians are Coming!*"

Carlsbad is a spa for the gastrically disturbed. Its management can furnish you with an 88-page anthology (in English) of *Karlovy Vary Medical Reports,* featuring scholarly dissertations on "The Karlovy Vary Mineral Springs as Stimulants of the External Secretion of the Pancreas" and "The Treatment of Diabetes in Carlsbad" and "Balneologic Treatment of Functional Dyspepsia and Constipation."

Balneology, the science of water and bath therapy, is taken as seriously by Czechs and other Middle Europeans as the French take their livers and vichy water. (Our days in Carlsbad and Marienbad were, in fact, sponsored not by the Government Committee for Tourism, but by BALNEA, the national spa administration.) As we came down the mountain and entered the spa city, we saw hundreds of grown men and women (mostly middle-aged) wrapped in winter woolens. They were strolling sedately while sucking placidly from an assortment of small china pitchers. The pitchers, I noticed, ranged in quality from Rosenthal delicacy to souvenir ticky-tacky.

"They take the water from the spring," Henrietta explained, "and then, for the digestion, they must walk around sipping it slowly for an hour or two before each meal."

"They look just like opium smokers!" Val exclaimed.

"You suck the water through the spout," said Henrietta, "so it doesn't cross your teeth. Otherwise, the water will rot your teeth away." Later, as a souvenir, she gave us a "rusty rose of Carlsbad"—a real flower that had been soaked and petrified in the healing waters.

Henrietta had come equipped with some souvenir pitchers, so we sampled the opiate of the people for the first and last time. If you like hot saké, however, then the Carlsbad waters are probably for you. I have no first-hand experience of their mineral values, but certainly the mountain air, vacation atmosphere, and the discipline of a leisurely stroll before meals are all therapeutic.

We were shown through the venerable Number One Bath, starting in a lavish anteroom adorned by a giant mural that brought together several centuries of satisfied customers in one drawing-room scene: Peter the Great, Maria Theresa, Archdukes Ferdinand and Franz Josef, Marie Louise, Chopin and Beethoven (at opposite ends of the mural, so surely the former would have to shout to be heard), Paganini, Mozart, Bismarck, Metternich, Goethe, and Dr. David Becher, the founder of balneologic treatment at Carlsbad.* It is always interesting to wonder what the conversation might have been like if this particular gathering had ever assembled together.

We could not linger long in the anteroom before parting company, however. A very Germanic lady official sent Valerie, Henrietta, and the girls to the left and Jaro and me to the right. The two of us were invited to invade the privacy of an "underwater massage," where a blimp of a man floated in a sunken tub of the healing water while a toothless, grinning old cleaning lady (in a nurse's uniform) vacuumed him with a hose, starting with each toe and going all the way up. The ladies were taken to a similar cubicle to see a huge naked lady sloshing wildly, almost dizzyingly, in her sunken tub. When I wondered later if this was a fitting exposure of our girls to the female body, Valerie said: "Don't worry. She was turning over and over so fast that it was like watching a love scene in an Alain Resnais movie. You see everything, but you see nothing. The only fixed point of reference was a crucifix in her cleavage." Re-united, we paid a visit *en famille* to the ulcer-therapy center of the Number One Bath, where we watched a couple of portly men get mud packs on their chests. The children serenaded them with the Flanders and Swann *Hippopotamus Song*: "Mud, mud, glorious mud!/Nothing quite like it for cooling the blood!"

After our balneologic rounds, we took a funicular railway up Mount Diana and contemplated the glorious view again. Walking down, I couldn't help remarking to Henrietta: "What a beautiful place this would be if there weren't all those sick people around."

"*Ach!*" she said. "The German atmosphere has you talking like Hitler." Then she started filling me in on who comes to Carlsbad now:

* Bottled filtered mineral water from Carlsbad is sold all over Czechoslovakia for everyday consumption (the tap water is drinkable, though frowned upon by the natives). Our own preference is for the sweet golden "original Carlsbad liqueur" called Becher Water.

"All year round, Czechs and Slovaks on the National Health. Carlsbad has enough hotels, pensions, and eighty sanatoriums to accommodate seven thousand patients."

The Seligmans and Schiffs and other American German-Jewish millionaires like the Guggenheims no longer come this way on private trains that used to meet their boats. "But sometimes," said Henrietta, "Carlsbad gets a couple of blue-haired old ladies and their handsome young 'interpreter'—a different chap each time—who fly here in a chartered jet. Fairly recently, we have had the Maharani of Hyderabad and Haile Selassie and the Shah of Iran. And of course we still have the 'banana tourists' from East Germany for the time being."

The East and West German frontiers are only a few miles from Carlsbad. Tourists from diplomatically unrecognized West Germany used to have problems getting Czechoslovak visas, but already the restrictions had been eased to the point that virtually anyone from anywhere could simply buy a forty-eight-hour visa upon arrival at any frontier crossing or airport (and later apply to the police for an extension of up to sixty days).* East Germany being a "comradely" nation with formidable barriers against escape to or infiltration from the West, there were no visa requirements between this so-called "German Democratic Republic" and Communist Czechoslovakia. There were also no bananas in East Germany.

Czechoslovakia's fruit scarcity was oranges, but the Chiquita Banana empire had made numerous trade inroads here and so bananas were no problem. Therefore, a typical Sunday outing for an East German family had become a drive across the frontier to Carlsbad to take the waters, have a leisurely lunch, and load up the Wartburg with bananas for the trip home.

"I think banana tourism is on its last legs," Henrietta informed me. "Herr Ulbricht is already making it harder for his citizens to come here and be contaminated with our ideas. In Prague, ČEDOK gets cancellations of hotel reservations from the East German travel bureau. Then the East German travel bureau calls up its clients at home and tells them: 'Those stupid Czechs! They confirmed your reservation and everything, but now they say there's no room. So you cannot go on your trip to Prague.' "

"Do the East German tourists believe it?" I asked.

* This convenient access for tourists from Western nations ended soon after August 1968.

"Maybe no, maybe yes. But you don't say what you think there. It isn't polite and it's dangerous, the way it was here."

One more visitor from Germany was encountered the next morning, Monday, when I took a digestive (though unwatered) stroll before breakfast. Near the hot spring, I discovered a bust of Karl Marx, a Carlsbad regular until he was exiled from the Continent. (The mural of notables in Bath Number One, having been painted by a Habsburg favorite in 1914, did not include Marx.)

In front of our hotel, the Central, stood a full-length statue of Lenin thrusting his arms out toward the workers. When Henrietta and Jaro asked where I'd been, I replied: "I walked from Lenin to Marx and then back to Lenin. I wanted to know what they thought of the upheaval in Czechoslovakia."

Nudging Jaro, Henrietta asked me: "And what did they tell you?"

"Well, first Lenin said: 'Ask Marx. This must be Marxism.' And so I went and asked Marx and he said: *'Himmel!* This is out-and-out Leninism.'"

Henrietta and Jaro both agreed that, after barely three months there, I joked like an authentic Czech.

Like Karl Marx, Franz Kafka's visits to Carlsbad went unmuralized. But that morning, we stopped at a post office to mail some picture postals and, from the conversation around us plus a few pointed questions, learned just how the Kafka was crumbling.

For a number of years, this Carlsbad post office had doubled as the interception station for all surface mail from neighboring West Germany. This mail was stuck through a wall, behind which was a special room that could be entered only from a special street entrance. The room was off-limits to the postmaster and his staff. For several years, the most they ever saw of that special room was an occasional hairy hand reaching out for letters they were putting through the hole in the wall. Later in the day, most letters would emerge through the same hole after having been, presumably, steamed open and read and re-sealed.

For almost a week, however, no mail had been coming out of the hole. The postmaster had consulted his superiors in Prague and then knocked on the street door for a day or two. Nobody had answered. There had been further consultations with Prague before the postmaster had been authorized to break open the door.

In the room, he had found several days' mail lying unopened, unread, and uncensored. Censorship doesn't end in a fiery blaze; it simply slinks away with neither a bang nor a whimper.

Valerie's mother's wedding china had been made in Czechoslovakia. We had admired its dainty flowered elegance so much that we'd left our own wedding Russel Wright behind and lived off our blue plastic unbreakable MelMac while shopping for new china in Prague. Disillusion had set in fast: A few souvenirish patterns were sold at Tuzex. Nothing good was available for Czech crowns except imperfect or incomplete factory leftovers. "There isn't much good Czech china," one saleswoman told us, "and whatever is good is made for export. Why don't you look for some when you go to Vienna? The best Czech china is for sale in Austria."

We had traced my mother-in-law's china, whose quality we still hoped to approximate, to a porcelain factory near Carlsbad. That Monday, Henrietta was happy to call up and arrange a visit there.

The director himself, a burly, heavy-set man of fifty in a green sweater, showed us around. "Only the making is done here," he told us. "The decisions on production and marketing and sometimes design, too, are made by officials in Prague. Always the best 50 to 70 per cent of our product goes abroad."

I expressed my usual sincere distress that only "hard-currency foreigners" and not the Czechs could partake of the wonders that were made in Czechoslovakia.

"What wonders?" he said with disgust. "Here we make junk. We've been grinding out junk ever since 1950. It used to be that everything beautiful and nice was made right here, and it continued that way from 1948 to 1950. But then Prague decreed that what we were doing here was bourgeoisie-oriented. So the State gave us quotas to meet or else we'd go to jail.

"For most of the 1950's, I had my hands full just to keep them from closing down this factory. We were small and even the quotas we met didn't 'justify' our existence. Whenever I pleaded for our life's blood on aesthetic grounds, I was given official warnings about my own personal safety.

"Finally, I won the factory a reprieve by offering guided tours. I've managed to keep it open as a working museum and salesroom for tourists.

"This was reasonably successful, so they offered to build us a new plant where we could mass-produce souvenir china for the tourists. I told them, as discreetly as I could, to save their money. You can cook the best meals in an old kitchen. A new stove was no answer to the immediate problem."

I asked him: "What is the immediate problem?"

His reply was succinct: "There are two generations of workers here who've been indoctrinated with nothing but bad habits. They can't be retrieved. We must write off these people."

Over coffee, we talked some more about how "Made in Czechoslovakia" used to be an unassailable guarantee of the finest craftsmanship before World War II. Then, after presenting Valerie and me with the special (only two-of-a-kind) coffee cups we had just used, the director gazed up at the Novotný portrait that still watched over his shoulder* and said:

"I think it's safe now to show you my secret. Five or six years ago it dawned on me that a Dubček or someone like him was destined to happen in this particular country sooner or later. It's almost as though we willed him to be, although I never dreamed he would be a Slovak. But whenever he happened I wanted to be ready, because it was even then maybe too late. The old craftsmen were all retired and dying off. So, three years ago, I organized a secret cell. . . ."

He led us down the road to a workshop on the factory grounds. The sign on the door said "Hobby & Recreation Club." Inside, however, nobody was relaxing. We were introduced to the last of the Carlsbad china factory's pre-war craftsmen—four men in their eighties. They were training a handful of apprentices, ages eleven to fifteen.

"We were not allowed to have apprentices," our host explained. "But I chose these boys anyway. Then I called these master craftsmen out of retirement. In the summer, an art professor in Prague sends his students here too, to help these lads with new ideas for designs. "If the old men can train these boys for another three years, then maybe the tradition isn't dead and the oldest boys can carry it on. Maybe—if the boys are good. But the old men tire very easily."

The Moser Glassworks showroom, our next stop, was a museum of shimmering color whose most enticing Bohemian glass goblets, vases,

---

* Post Offices that week reported a run by philatelists on postage stamps bearing Novotný's portrait. The Minister of Posts and Telecommunications also issued a statement that such stamps were still valid, though no new editions were contemplated.

and sculptures (including hand-cut frogs and fish) were primarily for export. We had a late Monday lunch in a mountaintop ski lodge near the East German border: venison stew sopped up with the thick Czech black bread and washed down with the strong, heady, and slightly bitter Pilsener beer.

Jaro cruised us down the mountain for tea at the Radium Palace in Jáchymov (German name: Joachimstal), a sanatorium that stands where Marie and Pierre Curie first isolated radium. When I remarked that the name "Radium Palace" was almost as unappetizing as the Festival of Gas restaurant at the New York World's Fair, the miniskirted young Public Relations officer showing us around said: "I have good news for you. We are in the process of re-naming it." By now, the Radium Palace should officially be known as the Sanatorium Marie Curie-Sklodowska, the last part being Madame Curie's maiden name.

The Radium Palace treats rheumatism with water from its radio-active springs. The cure takes twenty-one to twenty-eight days and the average age of patients is forty-five. "Between forty and fifty, we can start them moving again," said our pretty guide. "After that, we can only treat or help, not cure." Exposure of patients to radiation is care-fully controlled and the staff is given shorter hours than elsewhere plus extra vacation time at a special spa for decontamination.

The Radium Palace impressed me as more run-down and patched-up than any spa in Carlsbad. I asked why.

"There was the war, of course," our hostess replied, "and then we weren't allowed to start up again until 1958. Because of the uranium here, the Russians who liberated us didn't leave the Jáchymov area until thirteen years after the war. The Radium Palace was a barracks. Nobody else was allowed to enter the area except the Russians and the Czechoslovak prisoners who worked in the mines and loaded the trains.

"When the Russians had all the uranium they wanted and the area was no longer productive, they went home. Between the Germans and them, Jáchymov had been bled almost to death. We may never catch up. We have enough of a radioactive water supply to treat 2,100 pa-tients, but our sanatorium's capacity is only 700."

In the village of Jáchymov, our Russian limousine had drawn dirty looks. I had guessed why, but I had also noticed that the people of Jáchymov continued to glower when they perceived we were Ameri-cans.

Henrietta explained: "There was a bad mistake made near here in

1945. Ten days after the Germans left, either the Americans or British flew a bombing mission over here. Maybe it was because of the uranium, but I think it was just stupidity. The people ran out to wave greetings and the planes dropped bombs on them."

Jáchymov also bears a more tangible relation with the United States. It is the cradle of the dollar. In the 16th century, the town's founder, Count Šlik, built a currency system around a coin called the "thaler" from which our dollar derived its name.

We drove through the Hills of Teplá (which means "hot") and the Imperial Forest to arrive by night at Marienbad. Alain Resnais' celebrated film, *Last Year at Marienbad,* was not made here and Resnais, in fact, never saw Marienbad until years later. Nor was his movie ever shown here. "We only vaguely heard about it," a spa official told me, "and we were told it was decadent and not for us. We persisted until we learned from someone who saw it that it had nothing to do with Marienbad. Even if we could have shown it, it would have been a disappointment for us." The film was not even set in Marienbad; its title came from a cryptic conversation about a past encounter there.

Nevertheless, in one of those sublime unions between Art and Nature, much of Marienbad resembles Resnais' imagining of somewhere else.

Even the fussy, but very nervous service in the Esplanade Hotel was late nineteenth-century rococo. In the lobby were bas-reliefs of dancing Victorians and the one that moved was the reception clerk. In my family's two-room suite, all the furniture was delicately brocaded with flowered patterns and framed with gilt. Over every door on the beige walls were white cameo circles—the head of Maria Theresa with her face left out. Each room had tear-drop crystal chandeliers. And on each table were pussywillows in cut-glass Moser vases.

All the rooms on our side opened onto one long balcony where weatherbeaten white statues of lovers gazed down across formal gardens onto the city below. The gardens were floodlit and, after a late supper, we took a stroll through them. The mood was such total Resnais that Valerie and I found ourselves drifting rather than walking. I was not too surprised to hear myself say to my wife, with art-film *savoir-faire*: "Didn't I see you here last year? Or was it next year?"

Before Valerie could put me in my place, three-year-old Erika, who had wandered behind a giant stone flower-pot, piped up with one of her editorial pronouncements: "We don't like the spider who frightened Miss Muffet away."

If the long night's journey from Resnais to Mother Goose (if not to Disney) still hadn't brought me back to earth, a conversation I had over cognac would have. While Valerie was putting the girls to bed, I repaired to the downstairs lounge for a nightcap. An East German of about forty was already drinking there, killing time, he told me, until his mother and father from West Germany would arrive in Marienbad the next afternoon.

I was beginning to discern another function of Carlsbad and Marienbad and, to a lesser extent, Prague: as meeting places for German families that have been split by the Berlin Wall and the sealed-off frontiers of their divided land. Several such poignant family reunions were going on about us during this and every subsequent stay in Carlsbad and Marienbad. It is no secret that what alarmed Walter Ulbricht the most about the Czechoslovak Revolution was its early and sustained emphasis on freedom to travel. If the Czechs relaxed or abolished their border patroling, which they never did, then Ulbricht could envision these sojourns in Carlsbad and Marienbad as escape routes to the West.

The man I met in Marienbad wasn't thinking of escaping. He was a prosperous Party member. He made no secret of the fact that material comforts were indeed improving in the "German Democratic Republic," which has achieved the highest economic level of any Iron Curtain country, largely due to Ulbricht's unsung emphasis on trade with the West and private ownership of small enterprises.* This man simply wanted to see his mother and father.

We talked about what I had been seeing on Czechoslovak Television and he remarked: "We used to be able to get Radio Prague at home. Lately, though, it's being jammed the way Voice of America and Radio Free Europe are."

---

* In 1964, East Germany imported $15.8 million worth of wheat and barley from France; $10.8 million worth of wheat from Canada; and $7.8 million worth of wheat from the U.S.A. Still, East Germany's most important capitalist trade partner is West Germany, which accounts for 35.9 per cent of its trade turnover with the West. . . . Private enterprise in East Germany was publicly acknowledged by Ulbricht in 1968, when he told of a sentimental journey to the shop of a self-employed sausage butcher. Ulbricht concluded with the assertion that he would rather taste that man's dregs than "the coffee that is brewed for the intellectuals in Prague."

In East Germany, a good TV receiver can also pick up West German TV. It is *verboten* to watch Western TV, but people take the risk for slicker entertainment and more reliable newscasts.

At the school my new acquaintance's eight-year-old daughter attended, the children were asked a few months earlier to list their favorite TV programs. Some children listed West German shows. Soon thereafter, their parents were summoned to the police station and lectured ominously.

My acquaintance was among them. But he had enough standing in the Party to complain privately to the headmaster, who said he would warn the teacher. Using children to spy on parents, the educator agreed, did smack of Hitler. And, after all, wasn't there enough of that in *neofascistrevanchist West Germany?* (They speak such shibboleths as one word in this part of the world; other products of overuse are *marxismleninism* and *rightwingopportunism*.)

Three weeks later, however, the same teacher gave a "mathematics lesson" in "telling time." What kind of clock did the student see on TV? One of the Germany's TV's has a circular clock; the other's a linear clock. Parents whose children gave the wrong answer were again reported. This time, second offenders were obliged to "volunteer" to spend their next vacations in a work camp.

"I was lucky," said my new acquaintance. "My little girl knew instinctively, after what the first experience did to her papa, to tell a lie." He put his hand to his head and said: "There were bad times and then better times. But it isn't money or comfort that makes a man lose his patriotism. It's seeing his child grow up as badly as her elders. . . ."

In the morning, we caught our first full glimpse of Marienbad, a city of parks laid out with grandeur and imagination. It is planted with exotic trees that link up, without your ever noticing the transition, with the surrounding woodlands. Even in the heart of downtown, you can enter buildings with yellow and pink and blue facades and, if you exit by the rear doors, step straight into the woods and perfect settings for picnics.

Marienbad (or the Bath of the Virgin Mary; in Czech, *Mariánské Lázně*) used to attract sportsmen as well as kings for its hunting and golf. Carlsbad and Marienbad competed to have the first 18-hole golf course in the Czech Lands and, as with the Concord and Grossinger's, there are conflicting accounts of who won. Finally, though, the bal-

neologists who had defended Carlsbad's superiority as a spa for digestion proclaimed Marienbad's primacy as a treatment center for kidney,
circulatory, and skin diseases.

Today, the strollers sipping the purgative salts from the Spring of
the Cross promenade along a quarter-mile pavilion-like colonnade
lined with shops and statuary and frilled with lacy filigree woodwork.
On weekends, there are band concerts there.

That Tuesday morning, Valerie and the girls chose to go hunting
chocolate *oplatky* (round wafers baked with the local waters*) while a
Jewish balneologist (who, after the war, had changed his name from
the Germanic *Hahn,* meaning "rooster," to the Slavonic *Husák,* meaning "goose-man") took Henrietta and me to inspect "our new gas
chamber, which is not as sinister as it sounds. The vapors improve the
circulation to the organs. This has proved useful in our work with
women who are physically capable of having children, but can't conceive."

After doing a few deep knee-bends with the gas chamber ladies, we
re-joined my family at the Spring of the Cross. The spring lies under
glass at the bottom of a well in the cathedral-like rotunda of the colonnade. At ground level, the spring was surrounded by two circles of
people. On the outer rim, they were lining up with their mugs at a
soda fountain where a lady dispensed the carbonated mineral water
piped up from the spring like beer on draft. On the inner rim, women
were raining coins down the well and trying to hit the glass dome of
the spring.

Thinking we had happened upon the universal Fountain-of-Trevi
superstition, I handed Monica a 5-heller (three-tenths of a cent) coin
with which to insure a return visit. Henrietta stopped our four-year-old
and explained to me:

"These are barren women trying to hit the dome. If Monica's coin
lands there, the legend is that she'll be pregnant in six weeks."

I wasn't ready for grandfatherhood, so I took my money back.

What a difference a day makes—in Czechoslovakia!

Awakening in the ornate elegance of Marienbad, we take a late-
morning drive of a little over an hour and find ourselves in the grimy
industrial city of Plzeň (German: Pilsen), home of the Škoda Works

---

* Plain *oplatky,* served hot at certain hours in certain Prague, Carlsbad, and Marienbad shops, are truly a gourmet snack.

(heavy machinery) and Pilsener Urquell beer. We lunch in the brewery's venerable Dickensian restaurant, the Prazdroj.

Another hour's drive brings us to Blatná, a Gothic castle and church surrounded by a forest game preserve (teeming with deer and hares), a park, and rose gardens. Henrietta willingly scratches two more castles from our day's itinerary, so we can spend the best part of an afternoon there.

Dusk—and Jaro behind the wheel—brings us to the ruin of Vimperk. Henrietta is surprised to find Vimperk in our itinerary with the following descriptive notation: "mountain town, Bohemian crystal glassworks, printing of Korans, artistic costume jewelry made of bone and horn." Henrietta observes: "Whoever put that down hasn't been here since 1947."

For the town itself is now mostly bone and horn. Being Henrietta, our guide doesn't try to avert our eyes. "You may find this educational," she says, and escorts us on a walk around Vimperk. The town is built on a steep hill leading up to what used to be its marketplace. "In 1948," says Henrietta, "they formed a farm co-operative and closed the market, which destroyed the town of Vimperk. Now, if Ota Šik has his way, they're going to re-open the market and let the individual farmers sell their own produce, but nobody else's. It's going to be some mess to clean up, but take a look at the doorways."

On every entranceway, building, on every lamp post, we see beautiful wood carvings. The street lamps switch on and in their dim light (for fewer than half are in working order) we glimpse what might not be apparent in the ugly glare of daylight—that we are in a quaint medieval town which could still be saved if its decay was caught in time.

With a little work, Vimperk could be a tourist mecca like the Plaka *taverna* district in Athens, which is built on a similar slope. Instead, Vimperk is the only slum, rural or urban, we have glimpsed in Czechoslovakia. The town is empty, except for random heaps of garbage and broken glass.

Halfway down the hill is a fourteenth-century Gothic church built by mountain villagers as a shrine for God to protect the area from the winter and summer storms that were their precarious lot. Much of the church is boarded over, but even the boards are broken. Sitting, not playing, in the entranceway are some scrawny inbred-looking children who heckle us in a mountain dialect because Monica and Erika look funny to them.

"There was no work here when the market left," Henrietta says. "So many people went away. Those who stay must take buses to and from jobs that involve long hours far away from here. The bus drops them off at the foot of the slope. Vimperk isn't on any main road. They climb uphill, they eat, they go to sleep. They have no time to take care of their homes, let alone their city."

"How far are we from the main road?" I ask Henrietta.

"Barely a mile," she replies.

"If they just would open a café here and make it a rest stop for the buses," I point out, "they could re-vitalize this town in a year."

"Shhh," says Henrietta, bitterly. "You are speaking pure anti-Communism when you preach the greatest good for the greatest number."

And so, after another two hours' drive, to bed. We sleep in a resort hotel on Lipno Dam near the Austrian border. The itinerary calls for dinner there, but after a day's buffeting by so many contrasts, we are too tired for anything but bed.

In the morning, though, we will be eager to feed the birds and walk in the woods before breakfast. That's the difference a good night's sleep makes—in Czechoslovakia!

Monica and Erika have adopted our driver Jaro, a benign grandpa who dandles them on his sturdy knees several times a day. Each morning, they awaken in a new hotel and clamor for him. Their tinkling cries of "Jaro! Jaro!" are music to Czech ears as well as ours, for the name *Jaro* also means "spring-time."

And early one spring morning, Jaro makes an unscheduled stop near the medieval mining town of Kutná Hora to unpadlock his country home and invite us inside. Apologizing for not lighting a fire, he nevertheless serves us slivovice at 9 A.M. The chauffeur is every inch the master of the house. Particularly in this part of the world, pride goeth with property.

In the days that followed, Jaro and Henrietta shepherded us to a museum of postage stamps . . . "the largest fish pond in Bohemia" . . . and the South Bohemian brewery town of České Budějovice, pronounced *boodyay-oh-vee-tseh*, which is practically *Budweiser* in English. The town's pre-World War I German name was *Budweis*. The original brewers and their recipe came from here. Long before Communism, the brewery family emigrated to America, arriving with little more than their European reputation, which they exploited by giving their new product the name of its old home town: hence, *Budweiser!* The excellent beer that's made in České Budějovice nowadays calls itself *Budvar* but the export label, in English, calls itself, without fear of contradiction or competition, "The Original Budweiser." A provincial fair happened to be in České Budějovice, so we did our sightseeing from a ferris wheel.

We visited a dozen provincial castles which were anything but rustic, including three of the seventeen that once belonged to the Schwarzenberg family: The Hluboká Castle, a 140-room Tudor Gothic chess set of a building containing three Lucas Cranachs, a Breughel, and, in the dining hall, seven magnificent tapestries by Jordaens (commissioned in 1644) illustrating such proverbs as "Hunger is the best cook" and "Like father, like son"; . . . Jindřichův Hradec, a simple, elegant Renaissance fortress of a home with a golden well and a dungeon into which prisoners were lowered by rope and left to starve and die amidst the bones of their predecessors (with the help of the rats, death never took more than four or five days); . . . and the town and castle of Český Krumlov (started in 1279) with its baroque theatre (built in 1748) still in use and its medieval air polluted by the stench from a nearby paper mill.

Český Krumlov and several other castles we saw had two or three bear cubs living in its moat. Our children soon became such sophisticates that their first question about an impending visit to a castle was (and still is), "With or without bears?"

The last of the Schwarzenbergs left Czechoslovakia in the late 1940's, but the family retains ample holdings in Austria, Germany, and Italy. "One of them returns to Czechoslovakia every year or so," Henrietta told us, "to tour their former properties. He says his family could never have afforded to give them the care that the State does." It was one of the few times I heard Henrietta speak a reasonably kind word for communism.

The dedicated $74.08-a-month caretaker of Jindřichův Hradec had a tale to tell. He was a lean, intense young man in his thirties with balding blond hair. His name was Veselý, which means "merry" or "cheerful." That was the way he must have looked when he first came to the castle after passing a civil-service history examination in Prague. Now, after nearly a decade of overwork and aggravation, he was sallow, unshaven, beady-eyed, and sad. He also had the hangdog look of a man who'd done time in prison.

He hadn't, yet. But he did have a prison sentence hanging over him. The "national committee" of the town had discovered tourism and opened a tavern in "his" castle's wine cellar. Veselý had opposed the idea. Two weeks after the wine tavern opened, he had burst into the national committee's regular meeting in an "I-told-you-so" rage. Drunken teen-agers, emerging from the cellar late at night, had broken off delicate fragments of "his" golden well's grillwork to take home as souvenirs. "I have closed down your wine tavern!" Veselý had informed the national committee.

Incensed, the committee had coped with the problem then and there: by ordering the tavern re-opened and by sentencing Veselý to three years in jail for "mismanaging State Property." But his departure for prison had been postponed repeatedly until an adequate replacement could be recruited. Meanwhile, Veselý could be found in the castle courtyard every midnight guarding "his" golden well. Now he could hope that under Dubček his court appeal would be heeded.

On Friday afternoon, we dipped into the Czech province of Moravia for dinner and an overnight stay in the town of Telč. Henrietta bought a newspaper there and when she saw the headline, she kissed it. It read: "CZECHOSLOVAKIA'S FIRST STRIKE IN 20 YEARS!"

In the nearby South Bohemian town of Písek, some 800 workers at the Heavy Current Engineering Works had made Communist history by walking out at the very moment when their plant was to discontinue its production of pushbutton switches and retool to make something else. This semi-annual retooling had long irked the workers. They had only recently learned that whenever they retooled *from* pushbutton switches, another factory retooled *to* pushbutton switches.

Led by the plant's party chief and trade union chairman, the men had demanded continuation of pushbutton switch production as well as independence from the regional headquarters that decreed all this senseless retooling. They also expressed nonconfidence in the two managers they deemed responsible for this absurd practice.

"Can we go there in the morning and see the picket line?" I asked.

For the first and only time, Henrietta said no: "I'm terribly sorry, but unfortunately the strike lasted only seventy-five minutes."

"And then was it suppressed?"

"No. The managers gave in. They agreed to let the plant go on making pushbutton switches. It says that 'the other two demands will be looked into at a more suitable moment.' But the workers were satisfied and went back to work, so let's order dinner and toast the brave strikers of Písek."

All along our route, Henrietta had been buying and hoarding newspapers, and these were the latest political gleanings from Prague:

Last Saturday, the morning after Novotný's abdication, Dubček had been summoned to Dresden in East Germany for "a comradely talk" about his plans. Present were Brezhnev, Ulbricht, Wladyslaw Gomulka of Poland, Janos Kádár of Hungary, and Todor Zhivkov of Bulgaria. There was no precedent for such a summit in the history of the Communist movement.

While little was announced about what transpired in Dresden, it was known that Dubček's interrogators had pressed him for tangible assurance that Czechoslovakia was not scheming to defect from the Warsaw Treaty Organization, their 1955 answer to N.A.T.O.* Dubček had said they would have to take his word for it. Brezhnev had proposed that Dubček invite them to hold Warsaw Pact maneuvers on Czechoslovak soil that June, but Dubček had evaded an answer and flown back to Prague.

There, three candidates for President of the Republic had been put before the Communist Party Central Committee's ruling Presidium:

. . . JOSEF SMRKOVSKÝ, fifty-seven, the Minister of Forestry and Water Conservation (see Chapter Five). "The man of the woods and waters" made it clear, however, that he would prefer a post with more political maneuverability than Presidential statesmanship allowed. Nevertheless, in public opinion, Smrkovský was at the top, and his rating in the Czechoslovak Academy of Sciences polls had soared during the week following the Dresden summit conference. For, shortly after Dubček's return to Prague, one of Walter Ulbricht's ideological mouthpieces, Professor Kurt Hager, had expressed his dismay at the trends in Czechoslovakia. Hager had singled out Smrkovský as a favorite of "Axel Springer's reactionary press" in West Germany and declared: "Smrkovský's actions fill the right-wing forces of Bonn with

* The original membership also included Albania and Rumania, but by 1968 Albania had wandered into the Maoist orbit and Rumania, with its independent foreign policy toward Israel, China, and West Germany, was no longer trusted or invited to such bullying sessions.

hopes that Czechoslovakia will be drawn into their vortex." Smrkovský's record as a long-standing, long-suffering, and unswervingly loyal Communist and anti-fascist was ample reply in itself. Even the Russians, however, felt obliged to dissociate themselves (in Moscow's *Pravda*) from this East German slander. And this in turn surprised Smrkovský, who remarked candidly at one point: "If I were in the Soviet Union's shoes, I would worry about developments here."

. . . ČESTMÍR CÍSAŘ, forty-eight, whose name means "Caesar" or "Emperor." He was the favorite of Prague's students, who marched through the streets that week waving tattered royalist banners and painting and chalking up all of Prague with the shocking *double entendre*: "WE WANT AN EMPEROR!"

Císař, born in northern Bohemia, was graduated from the Philosophical Faculty of Charles University in 1948, the year communism came to power here. The young Ph.D. had been active in the party for two years by then, so he went to work as a career Communist. Serving in the party's agitation-and-propaganda bureau* for almost a decade, Císař rose to deputy editor-in-chief of *Rudé Právo* in 1957; editor-in-chief of a periodical for party intellectuals called *New Mind* in 1961; and, two years later, Minister of Education.

As a Cabinet member, he was progressive and well-liked by students and professors. This liking became loving when, during 1966's May student revels, Císař's own daughter was among those rounded up by the police for chanting impertinent slogans. For his daughter's sins, Císař was banished to Rumania—as Ambassador! By the time Dubček came to power and Císař was recalled to Prague "to assume new duties" that March, he had made of Rumanian President Nicole Ceausescu a good friend for the Czechoslovak Revolution.

. . . GENERAL LUDVÍK SVOBODA, seventy-two, a white-haired old soldier whose last name means "Freedom." A Spencer Tracylike Eisenhower figure, Svoboda symbolized all the old Czech virtues of dedication and craftsmanship that the castle caretaker Veselý was risking jail to preserve and the porcelain factory director in Carlsbad was fighting to instill.

A farm boy born in the Bohemian-Moravian highlands where my family and I were now traveling, Svoboda had evaded conscription

---

* The relatively new English word, *agitprop*, meaning "agitation and propaganda, esp. for the cause of communism," is derived from the Soviet agency called *Agitpropbyuro*.

into the Austro-Hungarian Army of World War I. Instead, he enlisted in the Czechoslovak Legion that fought on the Russian side against the Habsburg monarchy. Afterwards, Svoboda managed his father's farm, but joined the Czechoslovak Army in 1922.

When the Nazis entered Czechoslovakia after the Munich Agreement of 1938, Svoboda went underground as a resistance leader in eastern Moravia. From there he went to Cracow and organized a Czech military unit that fought alongside the Polish Army until Poland fell in late 1939. Svoboda and his men fled to Russia, where the First Czechoslovak Independent Brigade was commissioned under his command. Their exploits became legendary. In the March, 1943, siege of Sokolovo in the Ukraine, Svoboda's brigade and a Soviet battalion repelled an attack by a German tank division for ten days. Eighty-six Czechoslovak soldiers lost their lives at Sokolovo. And Svoboda became one of a handful of foreigners ever to be named Hero of the Soviet Union.

Svoboda's wife and two children stayed behind in Czechoslovakia, working in the Resistance movement. Mrs. Svobodová kept a clandestine transmitter in her home. She helped dispatch fugitives abroad and hide fighters who were parachuted in. When arrest loomed, she and her daughter Zoja went underground. But the Svobodas' son, Mirek, was caught by the Gestapo and tortured to death at the age of seventeen in the Mauthausen concentration camp.

Returning home in muted triumph with the vanguard of the Soviet Army in 1945, Svoboda was still not a Communist. In the coalition regime that governed uneasily from 1945 until it came asunder in 1948, Svoboda served as Minister of Defense, a post he kept for two more years by joining the Communist party in 1948. But his personal popularity among ex-soldiers made him dangerous to the other leaders, both Czechoslovak and Russian. In 1950, it took only a few words from Stalin, to the effect that, all in all, he felt no confidence in any Czechoslovak Army that had Svoboda as head man, to cause the Minister of Defense to disappear from the national scene.

Svoboda was one of the lucky ones, for he surfaced almost immediately as bookkeeper in a Moravian agricultural co-operative. There, he is remembered not only as a gallant outcast, but also as "a proper accountant who rarely made a mistake. And, when he did, he was the one who discovered the error. That is the measure of a big man."

He remained a big man in a small pond for almost a decade until

Nikita Khrushchev paid a visit to a Czechoslovak party congress, looked around, and said: "But I do not see my old comrade General Svoboda!" The general was summoned to Prague, where Khrushchev not only embraced him with a traditional Russian bear-hug, but also insisted that he sit beside him on the rostrum. This was instant rehabilitation for Svoboda. He was named head of the military academy in Prague and elected to the National Assembly (Parliament), where he served until retirement at age seventy.

My final TV view of Antonín Novotný as President had also been, prophetically, my first glimpse of Ludvík Svoboda. The occasion had been a Prague Castle ceremony commemorating the twenty-fifth anniversary of the Battle of Sokolovo. President Novotný extended an official welcome to one hundred veterans of Sokolovo, including General Svoboda, with his usual dispassionate speech about the "neighbor in the west who, after two great world defeats of its aggressive intentions, is again forming militarist and revanchist forces and raising voices calling for a new crusade for the old goals of German imperialist policy."

The next speaker had been General Svoboda, wearing so many medals that he must have been forklifted onto the podium. (In World War II, he received fifty-four Allied medals, including the U.S. Legion of Merit, the French Legion of Honor and Croix de Guerre, and the British Order of the Bath and K.C.B.) His voice was resolute as he told how some of his men had "died prematurely in the years following the liberation as a consequence of war wounds and suffering. Many lived penuriously and some died tragically as victims of the unlawful reprisals of the Fifties. . . . In the spirit of reversal to which the road was opened by the December and January meetings of the Communist Party Central Committee, everything must be rectified that can be rectified. . . ."

Dubček's trip to Dresden must have decided him in favor of Svoboda, for who would be a better choice to placate the nervous Russians than a Hero of the Soviet Union? The tell-tale signal was a spate of front-page interviews with Svoboda, who seemed to be holding open house in his study at Prague's Military History Institute. The editors were sending over their star reporters and you didn't have to read between the lines to tell that a build-up was starting.

Chatting with Svoboda, one interviewer characterized the defection of General Šejna as the country's greatest military scandal since World War I, when Colonel Alfred Redl sold Austro-Hungarian secrets to the Russians and committed suicide when his treason was discovered.

Svoboda retorted: "My dear boy, Redl was a man of character compared with Šejna. . . . Redl's was pure military treason, but this one is only dirt." *

Another reporter spoke of righting past wrongs and Svoboda said: "Let us first of all settle that matter. No, we are not going to engage in witch-hunts. We want only justice. There is, after all, a difference between democracy and demagogy, between democracy and hysteria. We must establish a regime in which quality will always prevail over quantity."

Rudé Právo's visit made his selection all but official. "I am reading the foreign press," Svoboda informed *Rudé Právo*, "and we are in the center of world attention. We have taken upon ourselves a great task: setting an example of true socialist democracy to be followed by others. It's as if all of us have been given a big dose of oxygen."

True, he spoke in homilies. But in a land whose values had been corrupted and inverted over two decades, Svoboda's homily-for-the-day was often yesterday's heresies. There was more warmth in those three interviews than there had been in all the verbiage of Novotný's fifteen years.

As we sat in Telč waiting for supper, the news came over the radio that the Central Committee had unanimously accepted the withdrawal of Smrkovský and Císař as Presidential candidates and then, by the vote of 105 of the 107 members present, adopted the Party Presidium's recommendation (conveyed by Alexander Dubček himself) that Ludvík Svoboda be designated as the most suitable choice for President of the Republic.

The actual election of a President by the National Assembly would take place the next morning in the Vladislav Hall of the Prague Castle. But in Prague that night it was Dubček who called the tune.

A couple of thousand students, favoring Císař, poured through the streets to protest the choice. They were not only disappointed, but vaguely worried by Svoboda's esteem among the Russians. It was after 10 o'clock at night when they reached Central Committee headquarters on the Vltava's far-right bank. But Alexander Dubček was there and he came down to the street to talk with them.

* Redl was also the homosexual hero of John Osborne's recent play, *A Patriot For Me*.

"Why not Císař?" the students asked.

"He is going to have a lot to do right here in the Central Committee," Dubček replied calmly. "I shall need him down here. Up at the Castle, they will be able to get along without him."

A couple of students from Slovakia asked Dubček why he hadn't picked their fellow Slovak and his, Dr. Gustav Husák. A chain-smoking Bratislava lawyer and intellectual, Husák had spent six years of his life (1954-60) in jail as a "bourgeois nationalist" and the last eight years of freedom mapping Novotný's downfall and popular vengeance—whenever the time would be ripe.

"Perhaps I shouldn't say so and be accused of revealing a State secret," said Dubček, flashing the wide grin that almost outdistanced his nose as a trademark, "but we are counting on Dr. Husák to be Deputy Prime Minister."

"What is the guarantee that the old days will not come back?" one student asked Dubček.

"You yourselves are the guarantee. You, the young," Dubček told the gathering. Then, almost to himself, he mused: "Besides, can the old days come back at all? There is only one path and that is forward."

Such optimistic certainties have been spoken and betrayed before in the land we were now touring, the land whose dubious motto is "Truth Prevails." Five-and-one-half centuries separate the tragic parallels and connecting links between Alexander Dubček and Jan Hus, the rector of Prague University (now Charles University) who preached in the Czech language rather than in the official tongue, German. Then, in 1409, Rector Hus declared the university a Czech institution, free at last of its rule by foreigners. The Catholic Church retaliated by barring Hus from his pulpit at Bethlehem Chapel in Prague. In 1412, Hus was excommunicated for denouncing the sale of Papal indulgences, and banished from Prague.

From the South Bohemian town that is now Tábor, he continued to preach and write. To a corrupt church empire divided among three popes, one man's intractable morality was a clear and present danger. In 1414, Jan Hus was summoned from his sanctuary in Tábor to the German city of Konstanz, where a council of bishops had been convened ostensibly to hear his views. Armed with a guarantee of safe conduct, Hus went to Konstanz. There, he was clapped into irons and put on trial for heresy.

Hus would not recant in Konstanz. The council condemned him. Jan Hus of Prague and Tábor was burned at the stake on the 6th of July, 1415, and his ashes were scattered to the winds.

The man died, but not his truth, which shook both the church and its Holy Roman Empire for the rest of the fifteenth century. Back in Tábor, the country poor gathered together to build a new society embodying Hus' vision of the Kingdom of God. A system of Christian communism was introduced, based on the scriptural creed of "love thy neighbor" (though not thy oppressor, the church). Private ownership was abolished in Tábor. Property, money, and valuables were pooled to equip a communal army under Jan Žižka (1370-1424), an impoverished one-eyed country squire who had come under Hus' oratorical spell.*

In 1968, Alexander Dubček of Prague and Slovakia had gone to Dresden to explain his reforms to the theocracy of European communism. Unlike Hus, Dubček was allowed to return home safely and the course he set thenceforth was to shake all of communism to its foundations.

The Hussites had given their mightiest fortresses Biblical names. Mount Tábor was where Jesus appeared shiningly transfigured before Peter, James, and John. And the fifteenth-century walled Hussite city of Tábor—preserved and restored in modern times with a population of 20,000—was where, on the 30th of March, the American family Levy witnessed the making of a president, 1968, on Czechoslovak Television.

Our itinerary called for "Saturday morning sightseeing in Tábor." But the first sight to be seen on that morning in history was the road from Telč to Tábor lined with Czechoslovak flags—"the white-red-and-blue (Henrietta explained); the French call theirs blue-white-and-red and the Yugoslavs, of course, call theirs the red-white-and-blue."

As the early formalities were broadcast over the car radio, Henri-

* *Dollar* has been mentioned as a Czech contribution to the English language. Add to this list the ugly words "howitzer" (*houfnice*) and "pistol" (*pištál*) as gifts from the Hussite Wars. To fight knights on horseback, General Žižka armed his untrained men of Tábor with scythes, flails, pikes, and the first homemade small arms. (The word *pištál* meant, literally, "hand firearm.") He put his armor on wheels. Mounted with howitzers (siege cannon with high angles of fire), his armored farm carts fired easily as they slashed through enemy lines and cut superior forces to pieces. The carts were used for transport and in defense, too, as semi-impregnable barriers surrounding Žižka's foot soldiers. Žižka's military genius has only been fully appreciated in recent times, but it is now more ironic than ever that "the great-grandfather of modern motorized and tank warfare" was a Czech.

etta and Jaro had an argument over whether Svoboda would be the sixth, seventh, or eighth President of the Czechoslovak Republic. Jaro declined to count Edward Beneš twice; Beneš, like our Grover Cleveland, served two terms several years apart. (In Beneš' case, the critical interruption was exile during World War II.) Jaro absolutely refused to count Emil Hácha, the puppet president during the Nazi occupation. In Czech, the "ch" sound is guttural, so the name Hácha was excellent for expectorating.

"Spit all you want," Henrietta told Jaro, "but we can't obliterate history just because we don't like it. That isn't being done here anymore."

"What kind of a president do you think Svoboda will make?" I asked.

"I think," said Henrietta, "that Svoboda will not be a power figure, but a symbolic, ceremonial one too old to compete with Dubček."

"And is that good?" I wondered.

"Well, soon we will know the truth about Dubček," said Henrietta. "If Dubček is a good man or a bad man; whichever he is, now he will be able to perpetuate his goals. There is no longer any powerful opponent like Novotný. But I am beginning to think that Dubček cannot possibly be a bad man. For a bad man would have known better than to give our people a taste of freedom and then take it away. With a man of evil, truth cannot be allowed to prevail."

I noticed that Henrietta was looking five or ten years younger than when we'd started out. "You weren't talking this way last Sunday," I remarked.

"I have been thinking with my eyes open," she said, "and seeing what you've been seeing. And do you know?" Now her eyes were brimming with tears and I heard her brisk voice quavering as she went on. "For the first time in my life, I am happy to be a Czech!"

Granite-jawed Jaro began to cry, too, and so did Valerie and I. This was at a crossing near the railyards of Tábor, where a four-car freight train was being shunted back and forth endlessly. The children laughed at us and then wondered aloud if we all had fever. Meanwhile, on the car radio, an army band played the opening of *My Country,* Smetana's haunting symphonic poem. The first four notes, plucked on a harp, seldom fail to give the listener goose-flesh.

And then the nominating began.

"What are we doing here?" Henrietta screamed at Jaro. "Watching freight trains when these people should be watching history being made!"

As soon as Jaro could clear the barriers, we raced into Tábor and dashed into Hotel Jordán. If anybody had wanted to check in or out that morning, he would have been out of luck. The hotel's entire staff and its guests, some fifty in all, were in an upstairs clubroom watching the election on TV. We joined them without knocking.

The setting for the television drama was familiar to us: the Vladislav Hall of Prague Castle. Vast, barren, and stark in all its stern Gothic purity, the Vladislav Hall was reserved once upon a time for jousting by knights on horseback and nowadays for electing a President of the Republic.

In the TV room at Tábor, a genteel, white-haired old man helped us find four chairs. "He's the night watchman here," Jaro whispered, "but he had a distinguished past before 1950." The old man addressed us in English: "Now we are like Americans. You had your General Ike and now we have our Svoboda, the general whose name means freedom, too."

"But Eisenhower wasn't seventy-two when he took office," said a young father. He was trying to hold his eight-year-old son on his lap long enough for the lad to witness history. But the boy wanted to play with Monica and Erika, so he wriggled away.

"How long is the President's term?" I asked.

"Seven years," said the younger man. "When there are elections."

"Svoboda will serve all seven years," said the old man, "and he'll be re-elected when his term expires like Eisenhower was. I know old men. I am from their generation."

The young father was too polite to say more than: "Let's hope we don't have a State funeral soon."

On television, Alexander Dubček was speaking in the Vladislav Hall:

"Ludvík Svoboda's share in the struggle against fascist Germany as well as his career after the war have made him a living and permanent personification of the friendship between the peoples of Czechoslovakia and the Soviet Union."

The young father remarked: "I was for Smrkovský, but I suppose he'd rather work than be President."

The balloting commenced and the TV announcer observed solemnly: "We took a very hard task on our heads: to show the rest of the socialist nations the way to democratic socialism. Let's hope they'll follow us—*if* we succeed."

The announcer filled in the lulls with biographical details about Svoboda. When we heard that Svoboda collects stamps for his grandchildren, the little boy playing with our girls in Tábor squealed: "You see, Daddy! When our President collects stamps, he doesn't get spanked for it."

The young father said: "That's because he doesn't tear the stamps off letters before anybody can read them."

Bohuslav Laštovička, a Novotný man who still headed the National Assembly, announced on TV that the counting of ballots would begin. When he did, a lady watching with us was so moved that she burst into tears and ran from the room. The TV cameras switched to the Castle courtyards, where thousands of Czechoslovaks filled almost every inch of space as they waited for the certainty of Svoboda's confirmation.

"Look at that!" Henrietta marveled. "It's truly spontaneous! Those people weren't dragooned there in lorries and ordered to cheer." She was right. The spectators looked as avid as tourists at Buckingham Palace hoping to see the Queen. Many had cameras and some of their children were rocking doll carriages. "How I wish I'd be thirty years younger!" Henrietta exclaimed. "You know, I've been promised a three-week trip to America this fall and now I'm starting to believe it's one promise that'll be kept. But once I go, what else will I have to look forward to?"

I began to realize how much those lost thirty years had cost even the peppery Henrietta in adventurousness as well as youth. Remembering Richard Nixon's advice, I said: "Don't be silly! Go while you can."

The votes were counted. Of the 288 National Assembly deputies present, 282 voted for General Svoboda and six abstained.

"Six abstentions!" Henrietta cackled. "You see, this is true democracy!"

I refrained from comment. Our own Lyndon Johnson's speech of abdication announcing that he would not be a candidate for re-election was just a few hours away, but nobody could have known. And who was I to give the natives lessons in democracy?

General Svoboda, no longer in uniform, but wearing a dark suit that made perfect TV contrast with his white hair, was sworn in as President of the Czechoslovak Socialist Republic. From the plain of

Letná, where Stalin's statue once stood, cannons fired a salute. There was a flyover by Mig jet fighters and then the army band played the Czech national hymn, "Where is My Home?", and the Slovak national hymn, "Thunderstorm over the High Tatras."

The deputies lined up to congratulate President Svoboda by kissing him on both cheeks. Several Dubček progressives kissed him on the lips. Valerie remarked: "With a seventy-two-year-old President, there'd better not be any epidemics around."

When the kissing started, the children stopped playing and watched with open-mouthed fascination. "Kiss me the way they're kissing the President," my wife teased Erika.

Erika shook her head. "You're not the President," she said. "You're the Mommy."

Svoboda inspected the Castle's Honor Guard. He also received, on a balcony in the Third Courtyard, a two-man delegation representing students and working youth, who pledged their full support to him.

The new President thanked them. Then, still addressing them but looking right at the camera, he said: "Let the fulfillment of duties become a matter of course. Every citizen must be proud of his work and his children must be proud of his achievements. For the future belongs to you."

"I think he's talking to us," said four-year-old Monica—and I hoped she was right on that glorious Saturday in Tábor.

DR. OTA ŠIK, FORTY-EIGHT, WAS NAMED A DEPUTY PRIME Minister and this went well with those who felt that his overdue reforms were now a matter of economic life and death for the nation. But their enthusiasm was tempered by the more conservative economics of the man under whom Šik and Husák (and three others of varying prestige) would serve as deputies. The new Prime Minister, replacing Jozef Lenárt, was Oldřich Černík, forty-six, who had thrown his support to Dubček in the crucial Presidium balloting for Party First Secretary.

Černík was a balding, slightly pop-eyed and dumpy-looking individual whose actual manner was dapper and silky. He might have been a Seventh Avenue cloak-and-suiter invented by Jerome Weidman and allowed to mellow into grayness, but he was actually a self-made Communist who had worked his way up in the local, regional, and then national party hierarchy throughout the Gottwald and Novotný years. Most of his high posts were in the economic sphere: Minister of Fuel and Power from 1960 to 1963; Chairman of the State Planning Commission (as well as Deputy Prime Minister) from 1963 to early 1968. Even critics who questioned Černík's imagination, academic qualifications, and willingness to compromise always paid tribute to his organizing ability. Some of them hinted that Černík and the more flamboyant, dynamic Šik might make a good team. And, for a time, they did, while Šik was a winner.

Bohuslav Laštovička resigned as Speaker of the National Assembly "because the Czechoslovak people have questioned my attitude toward the current process." The public cheered when everybody's hero, Josef Smrkovský, was designated to replace him. There was a murmur of dismay, however, when the National Assembly's deputies formally elected him as their chief: 188 voted for Smrkovský and 68 against.

This was a clear sign that the Novotnýites, whose stranglehold on power had been broken by Dubček, were not going to settle for a mere toehold or less.

The next Party Congress was a couple of years away, but now a clamor went up for an emergency congress at which more representative candidates could be proposed for office and the public could then vote on them in unrigged elections. (Previous elections had been rubber-stamp ratifications at which the voter approved a slate right before the eyes of party officials. Any overture toward secret or write-in balloting had ominous echoes as soon as you left the polling place.) In the interests of governmental order and continuity, however, Dubček was at first reluctant to undertake such a purge.

This was a period of "Hurrah, but—." Every brave new appointment seemed to possess or provoke a slightly gray element. Sometimes, this was immediately apparent, as in elevating Šik but putting him under Černík's thumb. Sometimes, it only manifested itself a few days later, as in the vote against Smrkovský. And sometimes, as in the inspired replacement of one Václav David, the catch didn't come until still later.

> "Your Foreign Minister? Incredible!" These words of congratulations were conveyed to Czechoslovak diplomats by their foreign colleagues, journalists, and politicians in the past fourteen years. Mr. Václav David was certainly the longest-serving Foreign Minister in this century. Mr. Dean Rusk told him on one occasion: "You could well become chairman of the Foreign Ministers' Syndicate."

Thus had *Literární Listy* begun its crusade against this obtuse man who, for virtually all of the Novotný years, was the Czechoslovak equivalent of our Secretary of State.

A month later, when Novotný was out of power but Václav David still clung to his chair in the Černín Palace, *Literární Listy* carried this dispatch from Karel Král, the Czechoslovak Wire Service (Četeka*) correspondent at the United Nations:

> U.N. diplomats and journalists used to believe that, as long as Mr. David remained Foreign Minister, there was no need at all to pay attention to Czechoslovak diplomacy. Mr. David's policy was even considered "anti-Czechoslovak." He always asked to speak as soon after the Soviet delegate as possible. It once happened that an old text [of a

* *Četeka* is the Czech pronunciation of the initials ČTK for *Československá Tisková Kancelář*—Czechoslovak Press Agency.

David speech] was distributed by mistake. Don't bother to give us a new one, the journalists said, there are no changes anyway.

In Prague, it was said that "where a good diplomat should speak several languages, Minister David speaks only one: Russian!" Thus, there was a national sigh of relief when Václav David's resignation was finally announced. It turned into a cry of joy when the new Foreign Minister was named: Dr. Jiří Hájek, fifty-four, a former university lecturer, Ambassador to Britain, Ambassador to the U.N., and most recently, Minister of Education.

Hájek was a wispy, owlish-looking man with thinning blond hair, thick brown spectacles, and a receding, pointy chin. An alumnus of Hitler's concentration camps (though not Jewish), he was known here affectionately as "the lonely long-distance runner" because of the range of his ideas and abilities, his eloquent championing of unpopular causes in the highest councils, and his daily jogging of eight miles a day. His politics were well-liked, but to the Czechs, the primary fact about Jiří Hájek was cultural: At last their country had a Foreign Minister who spoke seven languages fluently (English, French, German, Spanish, Norwegian, Czech, and Slovak) and who would make a worthy occupant of the Černín Palace ministerial apartment where the cosmopolitan Jan Masaryk once lived.

I went to Hájek's first press conference in the Černín Palace and heard him speak explicitly of Jan Masaryk whose name, for more than a decade, could only be whispered in the building haunted by the mystery of his death. Noting that a look at the map would show that continued alliance with Russia was unavoidable, Hájek thereupon quoted "Jan Masaryk who said that Czechoslovakia is not located between East and West, but between Germany and the Soviet Union."

As former Minister of Education, Hájek was willing to state candidly that much of Novotný's downfall stemmed from a desire among students and young intellectuals to take a giant step away from Moscow:

"They have, for too long, heard only uncritical eulogies of the Soviet Union. And that is rather boring. Now they rebel against it."

The new Foreign Minister said he hoped free discussion of attitudes toward Russia would repair the damage done to Czechoslovak-Soviet friendship by "twenty years of uncritical exaltation of everything Russian" and "stupid pro-Soviet propaganda."

No names were mentioned, but many minds in that room must

have leaped back a month in time to the dark ages when Václav David was Foreign Minister. The name of Václav David was seldom mentioned until it became known that he was to be the next Ambassador to Bulgaria. This occasioned another howl from *Literární Listy,* where my friend Igor Hájek (no relation) was now foreign-affairs editor:

> We are happy to learn that the truly unusual political and diplomatic abilities, sharp wit, tactfulness, erudition, and many other qualities of Mr. David are not going to be lost. . . . Due to the fact that he also happens to be the man who, until the very last moment, gave staunch support to Mr. Antonín Novotný, he is certainly unmatched by any other candidate for the job—which will require experienced and eloquent advocacy of post-January developments in Czechoslovakia. We believe that similar candidates for posts advocating developments which they impaired for long years are fairly numerous. It would be a pity if our more flexible foreign policy forgot about them.

Václav David did become Ambassador to Bulgaria, a safe neo-Stalinist haven from which he could plot his own comeback.

Our friend from Expo '67, Miroslav Galuška, forty-five, was named Minister of Culture and Information. He replaced the detested Karel Hoffmann; but Hoffmann himself had not yet taken his last bow or spun his last web. He was shunted from Cabinet rank to the less prestigious, but highly sensitive, post of Director of Telecommunications. This, in effect, gave Hoffmann control of the machinery of transmitting phone calls, radio and television broadcasts, telegrams and Telexes, as well as a foot in the door of the Post Office, which handled many of these matters.

Not long after all censorship had officially disappeared, a listener phoned in a tip to one of several new radio programs (with titles like "Whom Do You Want to Hear?" and "Songs by the Telephone") that had started up to protect the man-in-the-street's interests. The caller said that a certain office at a certain address was still steaming open mail and intercepting cables. The "responsible administrator" was a crony of Hoffmann's.

The moderator of this telephone tribunal (here in 1968, a moderator no longer moderated; he was a man with contacts and a sheet of unlisted phone numbers) phoned this man at home—on the air. The administrator's wife said—on the air—that her man was "eating his supper. Could you call back later?" The answer, in those newly outspoken days, was no. Her husband came to the phone and categorically denied that there had ever been such an office doing such work.

The program was still on the air when an irate caller phoned in: "What does my superior mean by saying that my office doesn't exist?" In a voice oozing wounded civil-service pride, he spelled out the size, scope, and staff of his eavesdropping operation which (everybody from Hoffmann on down said) was discontinued immediately thereafter.

In newspaper offices, the censors still came to work but read no copy. Bored by idleness, some of the censors played cards or bought everybody coffee or ran errands for those who used to live in fear of them. One even applied for an editorial job. For a while, magazine copy was dutifully delivered to the Censorship Offices on Benedict Street. But now the parcels came back unopened.

By a majority vote, the 300-man apparatus of professional censors passed a resolution calling for their own abolition. But the word was also passed among the worried minority: "Don't be alarmed. This is only a temporary affair."

The last bastion of internal security was a yellowed white-tile building that looks like an enormous public toilet. It crouches in a strategic location at one end of the plain of Letná, not far from where Stalin's statue used to stand. On the other side of the building is the mouth of a tunnel used by cars and buses going between downtown Prague and Ruzyně airport.

This is the Ministry of the Interior—in this part of the world, The Ministry of Fear: police, secret police, counterespionage, and any other shadowy apparatus protecting the State and those in power. Good, bad, or indifferent, the Minister of the Interior is by definition the most dangerous man in the land.

The most powerful criminal in Communist history, Lavrenti Beria (1899–1953), was Minister of the Interior in Stalinist Russia. Four months after Stalin's death, his jittery successors managed to have Beria arrested and later shot to death.

In Communist Czechoslovakia, the post carries many of the same powers and perils. But Svoboda's and Dubček's choice was pure poetic justice, and a refreshing change in the ministry's plumbing. In a self-emancipating police state, this one-line news item rated four columns across page one of the paper that printed it: "Minister of the Interior Pavel walks to work every morning without a bodyguard!"

General Josef Pavel, fifty-nine, was described in one autobiography as "a lifelong wanderer in the garden of communism." Trained in Moscow, he fought in the Spanish Civil War and then, during World War II, with the Czechoslovak Army in the West. He was captured by the Nazis and survived a concentration camp in France. When he returned home, he was the first Commandant of the People's Militia, a blue-uniformed sort of workers Reserve Police Force that played a decisive role in 1948's Communist takeover.

The People's Militia later became an enforcer of orthodox thinking in factories but, by then, Pavel was gone from their ranks. He had been named Deputy Minister of the Interior in charge of public security, a post he resigned in 1950 to protest his agency's interfering in the lives of honest citizens. Eight months later, he was arrested as "an agent of the West." He was held for a week in the vault of a Prague bank and then sentenced to twenty-five years in prison, the first five years to be spent in solitary confinement.

Pavel at first wanted to hang himself with a khaki tie he had managed to smuggle into prison, but he stayed alive to keep the faith that people would otherwise lose in him; suicide would be taken as a confession. Besides, he couldn't help thinking that his arrest was "all a dreadful mistake or else the work of some Western intelligence agency, which must have faked material that would compromise me. Even so, I couldn't understand why anybody wanted to get rid of me this way."

Not content with having him under lock and key, the Gottwald regime sought to extract a confession from Pavel. He had nothing to confess. He was told to "simply repeat what the interrogator says," but he wouldn't. Presented with a written confession, he refused to sign it. He was tortured and beaten unconscious. "When I awoke in my cell," Pavel recalled, "the interrogators were still with me. I heard them whisper that my confession was needed to provide Gottwald with an argument in his next speech. Then I knew who my enemies were! I also knew that they were enemies of the party."

He was released in October, 1955, after almost five years in solitary. Given an obscure post with the Czechoslovak Union of Physical Training, he retired in 1966, still waiting for vindication and not content with the compensation and partial rehabilitation that were offered to him.

"There is injustice that cannot be paid for with money," Pavel remarked during the last days of Novotný. "One thinks that, after returning from jail, everything will be as it used to be in the party. One thinks that, having been a member of the Central Committee before being arrested, one will be asked to come up there and hear an explanation of how it all happened. And one waits to hear what steps will be taken so that no such thing should ever happen again. And then one is disappointed to see that the case is being processed—like most things in this country—in an opportunist way. . . . Now we have been rehabilitated, but we have not yet been returned our human dignity. And that must be done!"

From the moment when Pavel's appointment as Minister of the Interior was rumored until a few weeks after he took office, there were more than two dozen suicides by secret policemen. A Prague police colonel, who headed the interrogation department, hanged himself in the woods of Marienbad and left a note that he feared "a public scandal." A judge was found hanging from a tree in the Bohemian Forest. As vice-president of the Czechoslovak Supreme Court, he had been entrusted with drafting a law to rehabilitate persecution victims like Pavel, and so there were suspicions of political murder. Investigations, however, did more than rule out foul play. They also showed that this high judge had neither a university nor a secondary school education. He had, in fact, begun his legal career by presiding over one of the trumped-up sabotage trials of the 1950's.

Literární Listy and Prague's afternoon papers all ran articles detailing the torture of political prisoners at the Ruzyně jail in the 1950's by "a certain Dr. Sommer," who signed false death certificates to conceal his own handiwork. Three days later, Dr. Josef Sommer, still the physician at Ruzyně, hanged himself in his Prague flat. His daughter, thinking he had gone to work, went to clean his room and found his body dangling from a pipe.

Sommer's death seemed to prey on Pavel, for this was a man the Interior Minister said he "knew all too well. I was under his 'care' as a prisoner in the 1950's. I do not like to remember those days. He was testing me to see how much a man can endure and still be kept between life and death."

Pavel was not a vengeful man and he was reluctant to take drastic measures:

"I should not like to harm anybody and I don't want further injustice to accumulate. On the other hand, I am aware that we cannot do without changes in the police apparatus. . . . Many of the officials who took part in the illegal methods of the Fifties have left the State Security services some time ago. A very sensitive approach must be taken in investigating the individual cases that remain.

"The suicide of Dr. Sommer is related to this. . . . He need not have committed suicide if the visits paid to him and the investigations into his past had been conducted with more tact. In no case, however, does the security apparatus have anything to do with his death."

Most of the offenses being investigated had been committed more than ten years earlier and various statutes of limitations had expired. Pavel said that, where the evidence warranted, he would dismiss people, but might never indict them.

"I don't believe we should engage in indefinite retribution," General Pavel told a visitor to his office. "I want conditions to be stabilized. This is why I am against prolonging the period of statutory limitations. I myself was also arrested and tortured by these very interrogators and yet I feel no hatred for them. I only want to purge my apparatus and make their unlawful methods impossible in the future. This is by no means simple."

To make his point, Pavel showed his visitor a resolution received from the Slovakian city nearest the Russian border:

> The arrival of Josef Pavel at the Ministry of the Interior marks the beginning of stagnation of the security apparatus. . . . We communists working in the State Security at Košice, acting on the basis of the situation at the Ministry of the Interior in Prague, express non-confidence in the work done by Minister Pavel so far.

Pavel spoke of the difficulty he would have replacing many of the signers. He also noted that not all who signed such conservative resolutions were necessarily bad people. Then he touched the letter to his forehead and asked his guest: "Do you realize how difficult my task is?"

In that enormous john called the Interior Ministry, the visitor was seeing perhaps the noblest profile of "socialism with a human face." People like Pavel were the moral strength of Dubček's Spring. But turning the other cheek in a public toilet can be a risky practice. Even after Pavel had started purging his security apparatus, some whom he dismissed literally retained their side-door keys to power.

Chapter 7

Tuesday 23 April—Monday 29 April 1968

First Secretary of the Central Committee
of the Communist Party of Czechoslovakia
ALEXANDER DUBČEK
& Prime Minister
of the Czechoslovak Socialist Republic
Engineer OLDŘICH ČERNÍK
have the honor of inviting
Mr. LEVY, Alan & spouse
to a reception arranged in honor of the
Party and Ministerial delegation
from the
Bulgarian People's Republic
on the 23d of April at 20 hours in the Černín Palace of Prague

This invitation arrived by special-delivery mail a few hours before
the party. Our baby-sitter Lulka couldn't be reached, so Valerie stayed
home and missed out on my first personal encounter with Dubček
(though she would meet him several times thereafter).

I put on my last Brooks Brothers suit and strolled toward the Foreign Ministry, which lies, in relation to our house, just across Prague's
most exquisite square: *Pohořelec,* the Firehouse Square. It takes its
name from a hulking stone structure whose rescue squads, from sixteenth to early twentieth centuries, were on constant call to mop up a
nearby red-light district called the "New World" whenever (as was
frequently the case with quaint buildings and raffish tenants) the
whole neighborhood burned down. But the Firehouse Square takes its
personality less from its firehouse (now a military barracks) than from
its rococo facade of dwellings (some with very Catholic cameo paintings installed in upstairs niches), its pastel colors, and its rounded late
Renaissance arcades that can lead one dryly toward a rainy day's shopping expedition.

Tonight was a four-alarm night in the Firehouse Square, the first time I had ever seen a traffic jam there. Chaika and Tatra limousines, flying diplomatic flags, were backed up for a quarter-mile along Kepler and Neruda Streets (two main arteries among the seven streets that lead into the square). Police with phosphorescent armbands and flashlights were waving them forward and shooing civilian cars away. The American Embassy had sent its Cadillac and its *Chargé d'Affaires ad interim;* Ambassador Jacob Beam was out-of-town.

Nobody but nobody arrives on foot, I discovered. But rather than hire a black Volga taxicab (the usual custom for invited pedestrians) and contribute to the traffic jam, I simply walked up the formal driveway and pretended I was a limousine.

Secret police were all around, some looking obvious in black or brown leather jackets; others, in Jirka Šlitr-model derby hats, trying to look diplomatic. In the parking lot, two dozen chauffeurs and a dozen civilians were gawking at the arrivals.

Having checked my topcoat on the ground floor, I followed the other guests upstairs toward the noise. In the vestibule of a main ballroom, I gazed up to count eight chandeliers and, when I looked down again, I discovered that the other guests were no longer in front of me. They had veered to the right to stand on a short line which I otherwise would have missed. It was not for food and drink, but to meet the hosts.

Prime Minister Černík had been met once before; his handshake was flaccid and perfunctory.

Alexander Dubček took me by surprise. Having read up on regional history, I must have been conditioned to expect a Slovak Jan Hus. Instead, my visceral reaction to this first meeting was an unspoken inner exclamation of: "My God! A Jewish Adlai Stevenson!"

Dubček isn't Jewish and standing six feet three-or-four inches, he is much taller than Stevenson was. The name *Dubček* means "little oak," but he towered above all the acorn people surrounding him.

Nobody was performing introductions, so I mustered my best Czech and said: "My name is Levy. I have written about your country for the American magazine *Life.*"

By then, Dubček's right hand was pumping mine, but when he heard my name, the left hand went to work. It beckoned to the nose, which was indeed as long as it had looked on TV. His shy smile became a big grin and I knew, beyond a doubt, that he had read my *Life* article in which our friend Sylva's remark had been paraphrased: *"First the nose enters the room and, five minutes later, enters Mr. Dubček."*

Dubček's whole face was twinkling. Again his left hand pointed to his nose, but now his right hand was lending dimension to the pantomime. He gestured to the doorway and then, by pinching his nose with two fingers that began to march like feet, he managed to suggest a nose entering a room.

I replied by showing Dubček my wristwatch, which said 8:10. I pointed to his feet, the ballroom, his feet again, and then to the quarter-after mark on my watch—indicating, I hope, that he should follow his nose by five minutes.

Dubček reared back like a stallion and laughed a deep, throaty growl. A lady interpreter had stepped forward unobtrusively and now she told me in English that while Mr. Dubček had understood my Czech, she would be happy to translate my words into Slovak.

I thanked the First Secretary for reading and remembering me.

Dubček responded that he was "grateful to *Life* and to you for the attention you have devoted to Czechoslovakia and my nose."

"I hope," I said boldly, "that the Czechoslovak people will one day be able to read what American periodicals are saying about you."

"Can't they already?" Dubček asked.

"The store at this end of the Charles Bridge has *Le Monde* and the London *Times* now," I replied, "but nothing American yet."

"Have you tried the new store near the Comedy Theatre on Jungmann Street?" Dubček asked me. When I said no, he suggested I drop in there and that I might also ascertain whether *Life* was willing to be sold for crowns.*

I said I thought they would be and moved on into the ballroom.

---

* The popular Čestmír Císař had been named the Party Central Committee's liaison with the hitherto alien worlds of science, education, and culture. At his first press conference, Císař had announced that Czech news stands were now open to responsible Western periodicals that would be of some interest here. They must, however, be sold for Czechoslovak crowns. Heretofore, they were sold exclusively at hotel news stands for foreign currency only. While Císař's announcement meant that now a Czech could have access to Western periodicals, it also meant that the publishers couldn't take their income from sales out of Czechoslovakia (since the crown is neither importable nor exportable). They could, however, spend their profits within Czechoslovakia, on their correspondents' hotel accommodations and other expenses here, for instance. Two issues of *Life Atlantic* and five of *Time* went on sale that summer—starting two months after my chat with Dubček—in the store near the Comedy Theatre. But this, alas, proved to be just a summer special.

"Two minutes and fifty seconds!" said one of the more dogmatic Polish journalists, wearing his perpetual smile. "And what did Mr. Dubček have to say to his American correspondent for almost three minutes?"

I ignored the unctuous possessive and answered blandly: "If you want to know what we talked about, you'd better ask Mr. Dubček himself."

"I will," he said, and to my amazement he joined the line for his second trip.

I didn't linger to see Dubček's response. But I am told that a few days later, a Polish journal carried the item that Mr. Dubček granted a lengthy interview to the correspondent for the reactionary American journals *Time*(!) and *Life* while refusing a request for equal time with a socialist-brother journalist from the north.

In the ballroom, the diplomatic and press corps of Prague stood in taut little circles, almost defensively, while the most elegantly dressed people at the party, the waiters, fortified them from round trays of white and red Czechoslovak wines, Polish and Russian vodka, canned orange juice from Greece, mineral water and Becher liqueur from Carlsbad, and an occasional lox or herring *hors d'oeuvre*. Various catering officials hovered fussily, synchronizing their watches every minute or two, at one end of the room. On the dot of eight-thirty, they flung open the side doors.

Beyond, you could see a corridor with several buffet rooms opening off it. But nobody wanted to make the first move, least of all the Bulgarian guests of honor who stood nearest the food. It is not their instinct to pioneer anywhere and so their tight little circle narrowed around a rotund man who looked like a dour Khrushchev. He was Todor Zhivkov, their Prime Minister and Communist Party boss, a man who calls his drab puppet nation* "Russia's most confident ally. . . . We have been and we will continue to be with the Soviet Union for life and until death." A confirmed foe of "Western moral patterns," Zhivkov had just purged long hair and short skirts from Bulgarian State Television. "Actors nowadays prefer a hair style which makes them look like girls," Zhivkov had proclaimed. "Sometimes you can only tell who really *is* a girl when the camera moves down to the knees

* Film festival gossip has it that the lifeless city in Ingmar Bergman's *The Silence* was patterned after the Bulgarian capital, Sofia.

and you're confronted with one of those miniskirts which are contrary to Bulgarians' sound taste for beauty." His taste being law, knees and page-boys had done a fast fade.*

The caterers beckoned and implored everybody to come and eat. A few military attachés obliged, but most of the guests simply wouldn't budge. Then Dubček, who had just disbanded the reception line, came sauntering in. He walked with a heavy but bouncy sort of promenade lope. Even more than the famous nose, Dubček's walk would enable me to spot him in crowds.

One of the aggrieved caterers caught Dubček's eye imploringly. Dubček nodded and strolled right toward the food. In the doorway, he leaned back like a right-handed sidearm pitcher on the mound and gave a great big friendly sort of "come-on-down!" motion. Many people in the room laughed. The Bulgarian delegation parted and Zhivkov waddled to Dubček's side. It was an amusing contrast in Communist leadership styles.

In Prague, if you're at an official reception to see or meet people, you get on line in the first buffet room. But if you're there for serious eating, you go to one of the last of a half-dozen buffet rooms farther down the corridor and you will be first on line. (The same foods are available in all rooms, though the layouts may vary with the shape of the room.) I had found a way to savor the best of both possible objectives. By filling up my plate with various combinations of lobster, caviar, eggs, mushrooms, onions, and smoked meats in the fifth buffet room, I was able to take my plate back to the first room just as Dubček and Zhivkov were coming off the line there.

The two Party bosses had been together for three days, visiting auto plants, a chemical works, and an agricultural co-operative, so they didn't have much chit-chat left to make with each other. After a few minutes, Dubček devoted his full attention to eating from a plate that was heavy with Hungarian salami and fish. Now he stood alone with his supper, a glass of white wine, and his thoughts in the center of the crowd at the Černín Palace. Though many were watching him the way I was, few approached him. Those who did were greeted cordially in his harsh, almost croaky voice and listened to attentively.

His dark, slightly checked, suit hung a little limply on him as if he

---

* A British journalist, who complained to Zhivkov at a Copenhagen press conference that Bulgarian authorities wouldn't grant him a visa unless he shaved off his beard, won a special dispensation "because the founder of the Communist party had a beard."

might have lost some weight. His dark hair, receding from his high forehead, had been combed and slicked toward the rear, where it was close-cropped and at the base of his skull, blond.

A lumpy, scowling man stood next to me watching Dubček, too, and a journalist introduced me to him. He was Stefan V. Chervonenko, the Russian Ambassador to Prague. Chervonenko spoke Russian with a thick Southern (Georgian) accent. The journalist asked him if it was true that the Czechoslovaks had asked him to stop conferring with Antonín Novotný now that Novotný had been out of office for a month.

Chervonenko parried the question with another question: "Who's been telling you that?" Then he moved off without shaking hands.

A lesser Soviet diplomat remarked during the evening: "Mr. Dubček is a man who listens politely to what we tell him to do and then does whatever he wants to do. He is a man with either the best future or no future at all."

Dubček was still living at the Hotel Without a Name in Prague. His wife, Anna, was commuting from Bratislava for important occasions. She was there tonight, a stocky schoolteacherish matron whose idea of dressing up for a State reception proved consistently to be decorating a plain blue dress with a beaded necklace. Several times, I caught her shyly holding hands with her husband while they waited their turn at one buffet table or another. She clearly missed him, for she was spending most of her time looking after her sons and her mother-in-law at the Dubček home on Mouse Street (*Myšikova ulice*) in Bratislava.

The Dubčeks left the Černín Palace together toward 11 o'clock and the party broke up shortly thereafter. I lingered, trying with no success to coax a Palace official into showing me the courtyard where Jan Masaryk's broken body was found twenty years earlier. But the court was (and still is) sealed off from the view of public or press.

When I departed, the Firehouse Square was deserted, and I contemplated its black-and-gold baroque statue, around which all traffic parts. The figure is a familiar one in the Czech Lands: Saint Jan of Nepomuk, alias John the Confessor. There is hardly a village in Bohemia without some monument to this martyred priest, who died in 1393 but was not sainted until 1729. It is safe to say that Jan of Nepomuk outnumbers Good Prince Wenceslas two-to-one.

Bohemia also had a Bad King Wenceslas—Wenceslas IV, the murderously jealous and drunken son who succeeded Charles IV. The official legend has it that Jan of Nepomuk, Archbishop of Prague and vicar-general of Bohemia, was ordered by Bad King Wenceslas to divulge the confession of his wife. When Jan refused, Wenceslas had him flung into the Vltava River from the Charles Bridge—off the very spot where yet another statue of Jan of Nepomuk now stands. Divergent legends take it from there: A) The river dried up soon thereafter for several days, and/or B) When his body was recovered, his tongue was missing, or C) the rest of him was waterlogged, but only his tongue was intact.

Certain Protestant and secular historians claim, however, that Jan of Nepomuk never existed . . . or that he died of natural causes . . . or that his drowning was accidental . . . or that he was executed for graft . . . or for defying Bad King Wenceslas when the latter converted an abbey into a cathedral without following ritual. Or that his story was a fund-raising gimmick. The skeptics point to the time lag of more than three centuries between martyrdom and canonization and claim that he was sainted only as a Catholic antidote to the enduring appeal of Jan Hus. Jan of Nepomuk, who may or may not have held his tongue, was chosen because his death antedated (by 22 years) that of Jan Hus, who spoke out.

The most notable monument to Jan of Nepomuk is his great silver tomb in St. Vitus Cathedral. But no statue of him is more convincing than the baroque one—with a fish at his foot and the Strahov Monastery looming overhead—that presides over traffic in the Firehouse Square. And that April night, after meeting Alexander Dubček, I didn't ponder legend or fact. But I did have an uncharacteristic religious experience. For I found myself murmuring to Jan of Nepomuk, the Czech expression of thanksgiving: "Good men still live!" *

At that time, what seemed like the lasting monument to Alexander Dubček had just been put before the public eye: the 90-page Action Program of the Communist Party of Czechoslovakia, a remarkable document that codified many of the noble heresies espoused on radio and TV. Seeing them in print, couched in the drab prose of an authentic party document, somehow made the dream official. Now there was a

* *Good Men Still Live* was the Czech title of Romain Rolland's 1923 novel, *Colas Breugnon,* which achieved immense popularity in Czechoslovakia between the wars.

written promise against which a nation could measure its aspirations and achievements. The Action Program touched all bases (including educational and economic reform), but this was the essence of it:

. . . The Fourteenth Party Congress, still more than a year away, would be advanced to early September, 1968, to hasten the objectives of the Action Program and the democratic election of those pledged to its goals. (Any such election spelled doom for Novotný's remnants still clinging to power.)

. . . "The implementation of constitutional freedoms of assembly and association must be ensured *this* year."

. . . "Legal norms must guarantee more exactly the freedom of speech of minority interests and opinions."

. . . "The constitutional freedom of movement, particularly the traveling of our citizens abroad, must be precisely guaranteed by law."

. . . "It will be necessary to adopt, in the shortest possible time, the long-prepared law on compensation for any damage caused to any individual or organization by the unlawful decision of a State organ. It is a serious fact that, hitherto, the rehabilitation of people—both Communists and non-Communists—who were victimized by legal violations in the past years has not always been carried out to the fullest political and civic extent."

. . . The equality of Slovaks (still regarded as a backward tribe by some cultured Czechs) would be expressed in the Constitution and bolstered by renewing the postwar (1945 to 1948) practice of appointing a Slovak second-in-command at any ministry whose chief is a Czech (and vice versa).

. . . There was a pledge to "strive for friendly relations with our allies—the countries of the world socialist community—to continue, on the basis of mutual respect, to intensify sovereignty and equality and international solidarity." But its language toadied no farther than that. And its statement of German policy was enough to make Walter Ulbricht see stars, in any color but red:

> We shall consistently proceed from the existence of two German states; from the fact that the [East] German Democratic Republic, as the first socialist state on German territory, is an important peace element in Europe; from the necessity of giving support to the realistic forces in the [West] German Federal Republic, while resisting neonazi and revanchist tendencies in that country. The Czechoslovak people want to live in peace with all nations.

East of the Elbe, such fair-minded pronouncements were, as late as 1968, fighting words. The German Democratic Republic had already made it clear at Dresden and shortly thereafter that it viewed the democratization of its southernmost neighbor as a threat to its own security. Now it became known, from high official leaks in East Berlin, that "the Czechoslovak party is like a rotten fish which begins stinking at the head." And the head, of course, was Dubček.

But the sweetest-smelling time of year had come to Prague. It was a time when we awoke each morning to find the city glistening and blossoming all around us, a different and more beautiful city than the one we went to bed in. This was revelation; my family had already taken the city on faith and fallen in love with it. For, even veiled by winter and the downtown smog, Prague had been catching Valerie and Monica and Erika by surprise. They would glance around and catch an unexpected view of Hradčany looming over the Vltava; neither was where they had thought it was. "And no matter how many times you see the Castle or the river," my wife observed, "the colors and shadows make them look entirely different, even from hour to hour."

To fall in love with a city, though, you must fall in love with the people as well as the scenery. This too we had done—in a quiet, unspoken way. Věra Formanová was a frequent visitor with the twins and so was Běla Suchá with little Kubik. With various editions of Saint-Exupéry's *Little Prince* in hand, Suchý's Běla and my Val exchanged Czech and English lessons, reading and translating their favorite fable to each other. And Šlitr's girl Sylva, already an old friend, came over twice or three times a week to chat with Val and teach the children Czech nursery rhymes that enabled them to win friends and dazzle their peers in the neighborhood.

A couple of our best friendships here started when our Erika erupted with what she still calls "chicken pops." Prague is still considered the pediatrics capital of Europe, so we had no qualms about calling in a doctor two of the neighborhood mothers recommended. A tall, glamorous lady in her forties arrived, looking like Simone Signoret, and, after a few minutes of laughter behind closed doors, emerged from the children's bedroom to announce in English: "Erika has the chicken pox and that is very good news. If you're lucky, Monica will have it in ten days. They are at the best age to have it: no pockmarks, no infections, no complications."

She and Val and I adjourned to the living room, where she wrote us a prescription that would soothe Erika's skin.

"And what do we owe you for your visit?" I asked after a while.

You're not going to believe it, but this is what the doctor said: "Nothing. It's too complicated. Any doctor who started practicing after 1948, like I did, doesn't know how to charge. And those who practiced before then have forgotten, except for the dentists. Even on the National Health, you won't ever be let into the chair until you've brought him at least a box of tea." *

We offered her a carton of Kents, but she declined.

"I will tell you what I would like," she told Valerie. "I have a daughter who is eighteen going on nineteen and she must take the languages exam for the university. Can she come over and practice languages with you?"

The next day, a slender, sloe-eyed girl came to talk French and English and Czech with my wife. In all three tongues they often wound up discussing current events. "This spring," the doctor's daughter remarked one day, "we pop awake each day to new freedoms like new flowers."

"We hear them too, like birds singing," Valerie confessed. "But do you know something? I sometimes wonder if Alan and I have the right to rejoice with you because we hardly lived here at all under the old way of life. If we'd been here as long as Gene Deitch has or maybe even two or three years. . ."

"That doesn't make any difference," said the doctor's daughter. "Look! It's been getting better here for at least five years, two or three steps forward for every one step back. This is just the start of the third act. We've had political jokes, satires, impersonations for as long as I can remember. The only thing is: we've also had fear. Now we don't."

For the umpteenth time, Valerie marveled at how the doctor's daughter's generation, the offspring of twenty years of communism, had grown up so astutely that they were, as much as anybody, the ones who had brought down the Novotný state. To which the doctor's daughter responded:

* Czech dentistry proved to be excellent correctively, though nil preventively. If you scheduled a semi-annual visit to the dentist, he would ask: "Where does it hurt?" If you would say "nowhere" and spout the virtues of a periodic check-up, he would oblige, but would be likely to ask: "How long have you had this obsession with your teeth?" A request for a cleaning would elicit this question: "Which particular tooth do you want cleaned?"

"The 1950's were the worst time, when they taught lies in our schools. But our parents saved us. My mother wasn't the only one who, when I'd come home from school, she'd sit down with me and say, 'What did you learn today?' I'd tell her we learned this-and-that-and-this-and-that. And then she'd say: 'Well now, *this* is so, but *that* is not so. And *that* is partly so, but it's all wrong about such-and-so. And *that* isn't so, but *this* is so.

"Well, when you're eleven or twelve, the last person you want to believe is your mother. It was so much easier to believe the school. We used to have terrible arguments at home that would tear us both apart. I wanted to believe the school was right and I think I had myself convinced for a while. Until certain things happened.

"Some other boys and girls went to school and sometimes for spite, sometimes from the pressure at home, sometimes just because of honest confusion they would say in school: 'But my mother says *thus-and-so.*' And every now and then, their parents would get in trouble. With some teachers, the children were praised for informing on their parents. Everything was backwards.

"Still, it didn't take me long to sense that any school system which punishes parents for what their children say they said at home can't be very much good. So I just kept my mouth shut in school and, what's really hard for any teen-ager, I listened to my mother.

"Sometimes, I read now that kids like us who are in revolt—and believe me we are!—are really rebelling against our parents. When I hear such things, I'm ready to set fire to someone, maybe myself. Because here, at least, we're rebelling against the system, not against the mothers and fathers who made us see straight. . . .

"I don't know enough about what the kids of your country or England or France are rebelling against. All my life, I've never been able to travel there and find out for myself."

Three or four times a year, back in New York, I used to be wracked by seizures of Going Nowhereness. These blues are the curse of a free-lance soul trying to grow or even just make ends meet in a parochial milieu which considers you only as good as your last (or next) project. Whenever this would happen, I was certain to moan "I'm not getting anywhere!" and likely just to lie down and cry for a day or else bang my head against the bedroom wallpaper. Or I might go for a boat ride to Staten Island or else a subway ride to the wrong end of the 14th

Street-Canarsie line, where I could contemplate the only grade-crossing on the entire New York City rapid-transit system. I remember one night, though I forget why, walking the entire length of Central Park, from 59th to 110th Streets in the hope that some mugger would put me out of my misery. But in a world where one's good intentions are never enough, who can rely upon the bad intentions of others? Eventually, I would fall back upon myself and return to living and working.

In Kafka's Prague, too, the melancholy blues can strike. But all I have to do is go for a walk and look around me. I can tread on stones in Hradčany that have endured for ten centuries or cross a bridge that has stood for six hundred years. I can muse about the artisans who made them and wonder how much their lives differed from today's stoic, steady, almost routine, endurance of impossible situations. And then I hurry home to my work, for it would be slander to tell myself, "I'm not getting anywhere." If I did, my own voice would snarl back and reverberate against centuries of stone: "But I *am* somewhere!"

We had lived in Prague for four months, three of them in our flat near the Castle, when my wife and I agreed that we wanted to make our home here for the rest of our lives if we possibly could. I don't know who began talking about it, but the "hows" and "whats" became nightly topics of conversation among Valerie and myself and our friends. (The children, having settled in among their playmates, simply assumed we would all live here forever.)

Foreigners cannot acquire property in Czechoslovakia, but Czechs can. And there was nothing to stop us from giving funds to a reliable Czech friend to buy or build a house, which he or she could then share with us or rent to us as tenants. Occasionally, desirable old houses, one or two of them in the shadow of the Castle, were put on the market by national committees in need of hard Western currency. Or else one could have a "Tuzex villa" (so called because the supplies and workmen were made available only for foreign currency) like Jiří Šlitr's (whose home had been built for Czechoslovak crowns) custom-built for between $12,000 and $20,000. Land was available on an inexpensive long-term lease from the State at a fixed rental for the duration of your life and your direct descendants'. There were still some choice sites available overlooking the Vltava from Barrandov Hill, near the film studio.

We talked with the Deitches about Zdenka's buying a duplex.

"Then Gene and we can be your tenants," Valerie explained.

"And I, a Czech, am the only eligible capitalist in the quartet!" Zdenka said, with a gleeful cackle.

"But the fact of the matter," Gene said after a while "is that we fought for four or five years to get this flat we're in now and I won't be ready to leave it for another hundred years."

We had to admit that we ourselves couldn't envision a happier place to live in than our own flat. And some of the letters from our landlady hinted that her husband was being offered substantial inducements to remain in England. Our scheming, therefore, turned toward eventually transferring our flat's "official decree" from the professor's family to ours, a much knottier bureaucratic problem.

Home and friendships were enhanced by the creature comforts that came to us through the courtesy of Pan Rott and Paní Soukupová, who dwelled in the basement of our building.

Not quite a concierge, Pan Rott was a red-nosed gnome who stoked the furnaces and made whatever building repairs he could. He, like virtually all of the Czech proletariat, was more hearty than humble, but still extraordinarily class-conscious. "I am an ex-convict," he told me soon after we met. "But I want to make it clear that, unlike the better kind of people with whom you associate, I was in prison for criminal, not political reasons. Still, I was on their side and I had the privilege to meet some of them there."

He also wanted to know my title. With an M.S. in journalism, I was entitled to be addressed as "Engineer Levy," a notion that I immediately banished. When I wouldn't tell Pan Rott, he took to skulking around my door trying to glean my rank from arriving and departing guests. Our guests, in turn, kept me informed: "You know that the secret police are following you, don't you? I mean, there's a decidedly criminal type hanging around here who's asking suspicious questions about your educational background." When I asked Pan Rott to desist, he resolved his dilemma by always addressing me thenceforth as *"Pan Doktor Inženýr Alan."*

Everyday maintenance and cleaning of the building was the responsibility of Paní Soukupová, a dignified and cheery lady who also did some tenants' wash for a fee. She had lived in the building since pre-war times, when she was the servant of the owner, still one of our upstairs neighbors. After his building was nationalized and he was allo-

cated one small flat, Paní Soukupová moved downstairs from her servant quarters but functioned almost the same as before. Her former
master was now the "apartment steward," who, when he came home at
night, computed joint bills (such as water) and relayed tenant complaints to the national committee. One of the other tenants told me:
"During the 1950's, of course, he couldn't be the steward because he
had a propertied past. Paní Soukupová was the official apartment
steward."

"Was she qualified?" I wondered.

"She was," he said, "but that was neither here nor there in those
times. She's a good person and unlike many former servants, she didn't
take revenge on her master. And she was good to the rest of us, too. If
our organizations wanted to send us on a business trip abroad, it had
to be cleared with the party, the district committee, the national committee, and right down to Paní Soukupová. And Paní Soukupová always said yes. She thought everybody should travel."

The Deitches found us a cleaning lady who worked five nights a
week as a charwoman at the animation studio and was willing to work
two full days a week for us. She jumped at our wage offer of 30 cents an
hour and gave us ten times the value. On Tuesdays and Fridays, our
apartment was rendered spotless. Should one of us spill anything, the
whole floor was waxed. My underwear was not only washed but ironed,
contrary to orders. For Paní B., round-faced and red-faced and a few
years younger than us, was a cleaning woman of the old school. She was
also a country girl from South Bohemia, which meant to Zdenka Deitchová that "she is honest as the day is long and you must ask her whether
she bakes." Once the inquiry was made, Paní B. never showed up
empty-handed: twice a week, we breakfasted on the latest strudels or
danishes which she and her mother-in-law were collaborating on.
Sometimes she brought a pot of soup, too. When we had overnight
guests, we would order an assortment of breakfast pastries and pay for
them at the rate of 30 cents an hour plus cost of ingredients. We hesitated to ask what time Paní B. arose to bake them, but they always
arrived piping fresh.

Paní B. lives in a flat the size of ours, but with her husband Adolf
(a bus driver in ill health who can work only part-time), their two
children, Adolf's brother and his family, one sister-in-law, and Adolf's
parents—eleven people in all. We were invited there once and it was as
immaculate as our flat. The tenants, understandably, like to stay out of

there (and each other's way) as much as they can, but they will proudly show you their extraordinary view of the Prague Castle above them.

During the Prague Spring of 1968, after a decade on the waiting list, the B. family was told that a flat for the four of them in Malá Strana (the quaint "lesser quarter" of Prague) would be available within six months. Now their qualifications would have to be reviewed, "just a formality to ascertain that you're still married, all alive, and really have two children living at home." A month later, they were rejected. The inspector had noted in passing that they had their own car, a second-hand Polish jalopy which Pan B. had bought with Paní B.'s extra earnings. Now they were told: "If you have a car, you can't have public housing in the city, where most people don't have cars and have to live where there's public transportation. You must buy a flat in the suburbs and commute from there in your car." * To apply for housing in the suburbs, where the wait is only four or five years, one must pay the full purchase price and start at the bottom of a new list. The B's didn't have the cash and so they continue to dwell in their one room, workers in a workers' republic, wondering whether all the fine slogans they hear will ever, ever apply to them.

* If you don't let the authorities know about your car or if you buy it after you move in, you can have both car and flat.

*This is one hell of a way to run a hospital! The Medical Director plays
the piano and makes pompous ghost-written speeches. Nurses perch on
his piano and the younger doctors' knees. The Head Nurse is in bed
with the sole surviving patient. The First Staff Physician never finished
medical school; the Second Staff Physician never started. And no patient has ever walked out of the Hospital of Antonín Holoček alive.
The Hospital, currently overfulfilling its mortality quota by 30,000 per
cent, is known in medical circles as "the last resort".* . . .

Šlitr and Suchý had a new musical show on the boards at the Semafor, and I'm synopsizing it here. Šlitr was the Medical Director; Suchý
the patient. Jiří Menzel, better-known here as a stage director, directed the play. *The Last Hospital* was an outright caricature of "Doctor" Antonín Novotný and the welfare state he had wrought. Though
the Semafor had been rehearsing it since January, they hadn't been
able to open it until eleven days after Novotný's abdication. Fortunately, S + Š had blessed it with many comic pratfalls and several good
songs, one of which, Růže Růžová ("Pink Rose") waltzed to the head of
Prague's pre-August hit parade.

*At the end of the first act, abetted by the Head Nurse, the patient
defects. But, early in the second act, the battered patient is recaptured
by the Medical Director, who undertakes Instant Musical Therapy, a
silent-movie melange of flickering light, player-piano medication, and
surrealistic sound effects* that had the Menzel "touch."

*When this medicine neither kills nor cures, the Second Staff Physi-
cian obtains the Medical Director's permission to inoculate the patient
with an experimental wonder vaccine. While the dose is being readied,*
Suchý *the Patient engages the audience in a direct soliloquy.* ("*I must
call your attention to the fact that this is not a satire on the Health
Service. . . . When I get well I'd like to get to know about those who*

doctor to the ills of millions. I'd like to know who THEIR assistants are.") Then, as he is injected, medical history is made! But, as is too often the case at the Hospital of Antonín Holoček, the patient dies.

Ultimately—and this was where some 1968 spectators told Šlitr, Suchý and Menzel that they had gone overboard on corn and pessimism—*the Head Nurse* tries to tell the world of Antonín Holoček's sins and to reform his hospital, but she is murdered, too. She is buried with honors, however. ("She undoubtedly made certain mistakes . . . but this in no way detracts from her meritorious service in the past.") Uncluttered by patients or dissenters, the Hospital of Antonín Holoček is at last permitted to achieve its destiny—as a brothel!*

Dated by events, *The Last Hospital* nevertheless thrived as the smash hit of the Semafor's repertory and as a nostalgic reminder of the dark days that lay not far behind.

---

* Played by the Prague pop-singer, Naďa Urbanková, seen by Western film audiences as Viktoria Freie (who initiates the hero) in Menzel's *Closely-Watched Trains.* Her malevolent assistant in *The Last Hospital* was Miloš Forman's wife Věra, starting her comeback from full-time motherhood.

Chapter 8]

Wednesday Morning 1 May—
Friday Noon 10 May 1968

TWO YEARS EARLIER, TRAVELING WITH THE CINCINNATI millionaires, I had happened to be behind the Iron Curtain on May Day—in Moscow. Sunday the First of May, 1966, had been cold, drizzly, and utterly appropriate for the grimmest hardware show I'd ever hoped to witness. The tanks, jeeps, and rocket launchers were not especially modern or startling in themselves. But as they converged upon Red Square—wheeling, snarling, growling, nearly sideswiping, damn near colliding!—it looked, through a cloud of exhaust smoke, as though the Kremlin were under siege. It was all over in ten minutes. Even after the dirty haze had lifted, though, the precarious choreography left one feeling as if one had witnessed a battle.

The rest of Moscow's May Day ceremony was a four-hour "Youth Parade." A thousand-man band in Red Square played marches while people of all ages filed past Lenin's Mausoleum and raised their flowers toward the unseen men reviewing the parade from above. One float featured a small boy perched on a cratered moon balloon playing an accordion. By then, the tanks had long departed and were as invisible as the oligarchy atop the tomb. But their stench of frying grease still filled the air and I consoled myself with the false comfort that, at least while you're behind the Iron Curtain, anything you see won't be used against you.

> Czechoslovak and Red [hammer+sickle] flags are to be hoisted on all State and public buildings from 1800 on 30 April to 0800 on 2 May to mark May Day. On the subsequent occasion of [World War II] Liberation Day, 9 May, State and public buildings will be decorated with Czechoslovak and Soviet flags from 1800 on 8 May to 0800 on 12 May. The public are also advised to decorate their houses in a similar way.
> —official notice, Prague, April, 1968.

The Central Committee of the National Front, the organizer of this year's May Day celebrations, has issued a proclamation emphasizing the tradition of the occasion: the international solidarity of the working people. The proclamation also points out that this year's May Day is being celebrated in the atmosphere of a political spring, combining the ideas of socialism and democracy. It also mentions that this is the year of the 50th anniversary of Czechoslovakia. *The attendance at May Day celebrations will be voluntary. Citizens may attend these celebrations where it suits them best.*

—newspaper announcement (italics mine), Prague, April, 1968.

The 1968 May Day Parade in Prague was an unprecedented and anarchic love feast which ground to a happy halt at the main reviewing stand near the Powder Tower. Instead of passing smartly in review, the marchers simply stopped to gawk at, converse with, and photograph Dubček and Svoboda.

First came a group of old, old legionnaires in frayed, shiny, splendid uniforms dating back to World War I. All the codgers wore medals and some wore hearing aids. There wasn't a tooth to be seen in the whole platoon. One, with more decorations than he could wear, carried a wooden board on which he displayed his surplus medals. With his other hand, he threw a shaky salute which General Svoboda (wearing civilian clothes) returned smartly. It was hard to remember that one or two of these old soldiers might be even younger than the President, who was seventy-two.

The ancient veterans moved out as smartly as they could—and then all order broke down. From the First of May Bridge across the Vltava and on down the National Boulevard came factory delegations, trade union workers, neighborhood committees, "Citizens of Greek Extraction," the Czechoslovak Union of Gypsies, students, large family groups, small families, young couples hand-in-hand, tram conductors and waitresses in uniform, the long and the short and the tall of Prague. The parade started at 8 A.M. sharp and when it finally disbanded at 3 P.M. (at least three hours behind schedule), 400,000 people, more than a third of Prague, had marched and 150,000 of them were still milling about the reviewing stand to hear Alexander Dubček thank them "for a day of smiles" and ask them to go home.

It was not only a record crowd, but a far cry from the days only a year back when 150,000 people were told to march and another 200,000 were told to watch them march and the rest of Prague stayed indoors and sulked. (By making the First of May a "working holiday," the authorities exerted tight control over individual activities.) This year, spontaneity had prevailed and good will had triumphed. Even a handful of extremists carrying such tokens as an American flag; a Hebrew candelabrum; a banner with the Star of David and the words "LET ISRAEL LIVE!" in Czech and Hebrew; and one "DOWN WITH DUBČEK" sign, stood and gawked and waved, like all the rest, when they confronted Dubček and Svoboda.

KAN, the newly formed Club of Involved Non-Party Members (*Klub Angažovaných Nestraníků*) marched and milled. So did the alumni society of former political prisoners known as K231 (*K* for *Klub* and *231* for the number of the Protection of the Republic Act, an obscure Habsburg law passed in the Austro-Hungarian Empire of 1848 and used by the Communists more than a century later to imprison 62,000 Czechs and Slovaks). So did 2,000 Boy Scouts wearing hand-me-down, but beautifully preserved, uniforms from their parents. (Scouting had been abolished as "exclusive and therefore undesirable" almost two decades earlier, but it had been revived and rehabilitated on 29 March 1968.) And, when a uniformed pre-war Sokol physical fitness unit passed in review, the spring air smelled of mothballs.

Wreathed with flowers and smiles, all the uniforms, the crusades, the love, and the gratitude mingled in a happy ball of humanity before the reviewing stand, while overhead banners billowed with the watchful visages of V.I. Lenin, Klement Gottwald, Karl Marx, and his collaborator Friedrich Engels. From the mass below, a dialogue began:

"Dubček! Dubček! Don't let the freeze set in again!"

To which Dubček called down: "We cannot. You keep pushing us."

Some students chanted in unison: "Don't stop democratizing!"

Laughing, Dubček said: "We have no time to stop!"

A man lifted his small son to his head. The boy handed a camera to Dubček, who shook his hand but asked perplexedly: "Is this a gift?"

"No," said the father. "I want you to take a close-up picture of the President for me!"

And so Dubček photographed Svoboda.

Some American college girls, spending their junior year in Vienna, had come to town and joined the parade for the best view. Two of them in miniskirts managed to reach up and give Dubček and Svoboda hearty mountaineers' handshakes that almost took the statesmen's arms off.

Students from the Pediatrics Faculty marched past, flourishing appalling statistics about the lagging birth rate and rising abortion rate. In Czechoslovakia that year, every third pregnancy was being interrupted.

"You're right," Dubček called to the fledgling pediatricians. "More children should be born in Czechoslovakia."

"You have to help us!" one of the students called.

"I have got three already," Dubček replied proudly.

For the first time ever, foreign journalists, usually closely guarded in a special compound, were allowed to wander onto the main reviewing stand from behind. Dubček even said a few words to CBS Television and Deputy Premier Ota Šik gave an interview there to Dutch TV. On the adjacent press stand, we bumped into Sylva. She was with a friend from Radio Brussels who had come to Prague to cover the parade.

Amidst the swirl and gaiety and confusion, Sylva said something she hadn't even dared to think in the years since her Berlin Wall dispatch had been falsified: "I wish I could write about what I am seeing!" An editor of the Socialist Party daily, *Freedom's Word* (*Svobodné Slovo*) was standing beside Sylva. Right then and there, he offered her a reporting job and she nibbled. She would work, not for *Freedom's Word,* but on a forthcoming independent cultural, political, and scientific weekly for which the socialist publishing house had (after a twenty-year hiatus) just been granted funds and newsprint. It would be called *Zítřek,* which means *Tomorrow.*

On the first of May, 1968, tomorrow and *Zítřek* and Sylva's new career all held infinite promise and I rejoiced for her. A beautiful friend in her thirties, who had lived largely by her looks as well as her languages, was beginning anew in a sphere whose rewards I myself sought. And Sylva could, in fact, have the best of both worlds.

"I don't think you should give up your other work, although you will work full time for us while you are here," the editor told Sylva that day, after quickly negotiating salary and working conditions. "But when you travel abroad with Black Theatre or the Semafor, you can send dispatches to us. We won't be in a financial position to send out our own foreign correspondents for a long time, so we would dearly like to have one whose way has been paid."

Sylva looked out at the May Day Parade, but the Berlin Wall was in the back of her mind as she asked just one more question: "And my copy won't be tampered with ideologically?"

"That goes without saying," the editor replied, "but I'll say it anyway." And he asked the American Family Levy to bear witness.

Seven hours at the May Day Parade gave me time to contemplate and meditate upon some of the marchers whose very presence in a socialist society was already being cited by Czechoslovakia's nervous neighbors as "evidence of counter-revolution."

"THOSE AFRAID OF OPPOSITION REALLY FEAR PUBLIC OPINION" said the banner waved by the Club of Involved Non-Party Members (KAN), which drew a friendly wave from Dubček. The Russians were insisting that KAN had "broad and well-organized links with some foreign anti-Communist organizations and parties, first and foremost in West Germany. . . . The agitation and propaganda activity of the club is entirely designed to discredit the Communist Party of Czechoslovakia and the socialist system, putting in opposition to them 'other versions of political organization,' for instance, a bourgeois republic."

KAN was the brain child of the philosopher Ivan Sviták, the "lonely sniper" who was appealing quite openly "to a force with fantastic potential: six million people of voting age who are politically unorganized in our country. . . . We non-Communists want to see liberalization go beyond the limits imposed by the new party leadership. I am less pessimistic now about the chances to achieve real socialist democracy than I was . . . when Novotný was still president. But the deep changes have yet to come. The crucial questions are: Will liberal forces in the Communist Party be strong enough to change the entire structure of political life? And what will be the rights of non-Communist parties?"

He was asked if KAN might not be the basis "for a new political group, a new party, which, if not today, then possibly tomorrow or the day after, may take its place next to the Communist Party?"

"Yes," said Sviták. "The trend is in that direction."

Out of Sviták's evangelizing came a KAN Manifesto signed by 150 prominent men, including some Communist Party members who were made honorarily involved non-members of KAN. The manifesto took human and civil liberties as both its starting point and ultimate objective. Its language was clearly Sviták's:

> KAN must act the way a mongoose does when fighting a huge snake twice as strong as he. The mongoose is maneuvering all the time. He often retreats, then attacks, and again assumes the defensive. He is waiting for the moment when the snake could be seized by its most vulnerable spot and then he gives it the fatal strike.

Three thousand people turned out for KAN's first meeting and subsequent sessions were almost as well attended. Because of rattles from Russia, however, Dubček's officialdom dragged its feet and KAN was never granted its formal license to exist, thus making it that much easier to kill.

"NEVER LET IT HAPPEN AGAIN" said another banner in the May Day parade. This was the motto of K231, which the Russians kept confusing with KAN. But they really needn't have. KAN was a bold attempt to shape the future while K231 was a quiet quest to salvage the past for its 40,000 members who had been imprisoned in the 1950's.*

They had met—a few of these haunted-eyed men and women who all knew each other from the interrogation station at Ruzyně or the torture cells at Leopoldov or the uranium mines at Jáchymov—in a hall on an island in the Vltava. "We have no other political aim than to support the existing political forces of our nation in their effort to achieve a just and democratic social order," said K231's official spokesman. "We don't want to make any trouble for the party or government. We have started this organization to help the authorities. Our club has nothing in common with a political organization."

That was on a Tuesday night. Stressing that their concrete goals were legal rehabilitation and firm guarantees of individual liberties, they had fired off a telegram to Dubček expressing "our esteem for the way in which you are restoring the dignity of human life to our people." And the new First Secretary, who was known to have wept when he gained access to the records of past injustices and to have asked "How was it possible for Communists to behave this way?",

---

* According to K231 statistics, a total of 35,000 persons were wrongly sentenced in Czechoslovakia between 1948 and 1956 and another 27,000 (though less severely) between then and 1967. Overly severe fines and confiscations of property were dealt to 35,000 farmers (while agriculture was being collectivized) and to 16,000 small tradesmen between 1951 and 1967.

clearly had shared their vision. On Wednesday morning, they had petitioned the authorities to let them form K231 and, while their application was still pending, to hold a meeting that Sunday. On Wednesday afternoon, a deputy secretary of the Communist Party Central Committee had granted them interim permission to exist "without imposing any political conditions" on K231 and a deputy Minister of the Interior had granted them a meeting permit. The authorities were also sanctioning plans to form K231 regional and district organizations throughout the country and to hold a K231 national congress later that year. But, as with KAN, final permission for K231 to exist was held in abeyance. . . .

Starting in March, one had read hundreds of little news items that made one yearn to know more about the extent of persecution and terror:

> Dr. František Tržický, former National Procurator and head of a department in the Prime Minister's office, who—together with other former leaders of the Social Democratic Party—was sentenced in 1954 on charges of alleged high treason to 25 years imprisonment, has been fully rehabilitated. In the last two years, Dr. Tržický was a tram conductor.

> Associate Professor Milan Hübl has become new Rector of the Political School of the Party Central Committee. This prominent historian thus returns to the institute he was forced to leave in 1964.

> Of the 50 to 60 persecuted members of its staff, the Philosophical Faculty of Charles University in Prague has so far rehabilitated 28, four of them posthumously.

Sometimes you stumbled onto sad stories when a dumpling-faced granny, whose child was playing with yours, embraced an old friend in the playground and explained to you: "We haven't seen each other in ten years and before that we were together every day for ten years in prison." Or when, in a family emergency, you asked a cabbie to deliver one of your kids home and he said to you in cultivated English: "Sir, I think you ought to be forewarned that you're entrusting your child to a man with a criminal record—fifteen years in prison for hostile activities against the State and I'm on probation until 1971." Or hearing two old men in a beer hall defend their pasts when taunted by their cronies.

"I'll never regret my eighty-three months in jail," said one, "because it's a school nobody on the outside can appreciate. It's the only place where a man's character is revealed in its true light."

The other one turned on his tormentors: *"You're* the ones who weren't free. In prison, we could talk freely to each other and we *knew* how things really were."

Or, as the outspoken and outstanding Czech journalist Jiří Hochman put it: "Among other things, it is the jails that reflect the cultural standards of a nation."

Jirka Suchý's secretary, Dana Paseková, a benign Moravian lady who moonlighted as a dance critic, informed us joyfully that she was taking a leave of absence from both jobs to study for her doctorate "now that I've been rehabilitated!" I couldn't believe my ears: "Rehabilitated, Dana? What on earth was *your* crime?" And Dana replied sadly: "Three crimes. I came from a family that owned property. And my field was sociology, the *bourgeois* science. And my professor had already been denounced so his colleagues wouldn't let me take my examinations or submit my dissertation. Afterwards, for a year or two, I wasn't allowed to work. . . ."

One Sunday on the tram, a shabbily but carefully dressed woman, whose coarse, chapped skin didn't quite obliterate her delicate features, overheard my children and addressed them in flawless Oxonian English. When I asked her where she had learned our language, she replied: "From my governesses. I'm a Lobkowitz, you see." Prague's two Lobkowitz Palaces—one now the Swiss Embassy, the other the headquarters of the Czechoslovak Diplomatic Service—swam before my eyes, along with the Loreta Treasure monstrance, another Lobkowitz holding. Further questioning elicited that "I was one of the lucky aristocrats or 'citizens with coats of arms,' they call us now. I never spent a day in prison, thank heaven for that! But of course I had to leave Prague after 1948. They let me live in a smaller city if I would work as a charwoman. But it wasn't Prague, you know."

"How are you faring under Mr. Dubček?" I asked.

"Much better, thank you," replied the lady Lobkowitz. "I'm back in Prague, am I not? I even have my own two rooms and a job—separating vegetables."

Around the time of the May celebrations, mutual friends arranged for three leaders of K231 to come to our house for cocktails: the president of the club, his wife, and a physician.

The K231 president, sixty-four, was a former professor. He had been working in the Foreign Trade Corporation's tourist division in February, 1949, when he was accused of treason, specifically that he was part of a Socialist Party faction that was unwilling to have the Socialists go along with the Communists in the National Front. For his treason, he spent fourteen years in jail—eight of them in solitary confinement—before being released at the end of 1963. Back in civilian life, he worked first with a shovel and now as a clerk.

A ruddy, white-haired, playful little kewpie of a man, he reminded me of the thin man straining to get out of every fat man. Sure enough, his wife said that he used to be everybody's jolly round family man before prison. His doctor added that, at his low ebb in Leopoldov, he'd weighed 86 pounds and now he was comfortable at 125, though the doctor would like him to add another 15 or 20.

"When you arrived at Leopoldov," the president recalled, "you were told: 'It doesn't matter what your sentence is because you won't leave here. This is where you'll die.' "

"I was the physician at Leopoldov," said the doctor. "They said they would give me all kinds of opportunity to improve my surgical skills—and they kept their promise. But they gave me no medicine, no facilities."

"While I was there," said the president, "he gave me an appendectomy and a hernia operation. Without anaesthetic."

"Be glad you don't have splinters," said the doctor, "from the wooden operating table."

"And I had to hold the lamp for both my operations."

This is the way they reminisced. It was almost as if nobody else was there. Sometimes they jumped when I cut in with a question.

"What happened to your family while you were away?"

The president's wife answered: "We have three children. First, my husband was taken away. And then, a month later, I was taken away because I was his wife and because he wouldn't confess. Our daughters were fourteen and eleven then, but our little son was just two-and-a-half. The two girls looked after him even better than I did, but the authorities kept coming back to take him away. But the girls lied. They said he'd been sent to live with relatives. Lying! That's how our family held together."

"We have two clever girls," her husband said proudly. "They weren't allowed to notify me that my wife was in prison. But they were allowed to send me a parcel. They sent it to my prison addressed to her first name and my last name. I was able to guess the news from that. So the next time I was interrogated, I said I would confess if they would free my wife."

"When I came out," said his wife, "I couldn't go back to teaching because of my two-month prison record. And my children weren't allowed to go to the schools either. So I found work as a night-shift clerk and, during the day, I ran a one-room schoolhouse at home. One room is right because they made us move out of our three rooms now that my husband had 'disgraced' us."

He said ruefully: "My son was ten years old before I saw him again."

His wife went on: "For a fifteen-minute visit, we traveled all night on a train to Leopoldov, which is an hour past Bratislava. When we got there, we were told that we'd been misinformed in Prague: children under twelve couldn't visit. When I pleaded, finally the head guard said: 'All right. We'll pretend he's twelve, but no kissing.' Another guard took us there and said: 'You can do all the kissing you want, son, and you, too, lady. I'll be looking the other way.' But as soon as we got into the visiting room, our son broke into tears and ran out the door."

She was an educated and elegant-looking dowager type, but with the sly mouth of a barmaid and the sharp eyes of a hooker—both, I would guess, the result of two months as a prisoner and fourteen years as head of a family "in disgrace. Many people were unkind to us," she said. "When I asked for the 20-crowns-a-month raise in pay that went with working the night shift, I was told: 'No. You should be paying us for letting you work here.' " Nowadays she was working as a day-shift bank clerk.

Eduard Goldstücker had just sent a remarkable letter to K231:

> Common to all of us is the memory of the most shattering experience of our lives, which devoured an irreplaceable number of our years and marked us mentally and physically for the rest of our days. I do not wish to be immodest and give you advice. I only wish to try and share with you some thoughts whereby I have tried, for my part, to find an attitude toward those years of absolute injustice.

> The demand that all acts of injustice should be put right and that those who violated the law and the fundamental principles of humanity should be punished is quite right. . . . But people are wrong to think that their own humiliation would be wiped out if somebody else were punished.

Goldstücker had remarked that "it is easy to be unjust. Tolerance, one of the preconditions of dignified relations among people, must start within ourselves, with our conscious determination to bring it into life as a remedy. Just because I have been branded all my life by the humiliation meted out to every minority and most of all to that [Jewish] minority to which I belong, just because of that, I am particularly careful in accusing others."

Having said this, Goldstücker had then leveled an accusation that had taken me, though none of my guests, aback:

> I cannot keep silent about the fact that, after escaping the gallows by a hair's breadth, I found enmity on the part of many of the thousands of fellow prisoners, which sometimes bordered on a threat to my own life. . . .

> I should like on this occasion to thank those who did not in those days succumb to mass psychosis, but stood up to protect me or at least adopted a neutral attitude toward me. In my heart, I have overcome spite toward those who added to the injustice committed on me the blow of their hatred.

The K231 president's wife gave a snort, but conceded: "There *is* a snobbery among former prisoners. The ones who were put in prison because they *weren't* Communists consider themselves the real aristocrats."

Her husband added: "Some of them, though not myself, are reluctant to accept Goldstücker and the other Communists who were jailed after we were. They were, after all, part of the regime that put us in prison."

"That's why Goldstücker was attacked in prison," the doctor said bitterly. "In one of his diplomatic capacities, your 'man who rehabilitated Kafka' told the United Nations that what was happening to us wasn't happening."

The president said gently: "The prosecutor who put many of us away was later put in prison himself. You can imagine what happens when you're living and dying in prison and the man who did this to you turns up among you with no more rights than you have, fewer, perhaps, because he's newer to the prison."

"He was kicked and beaten every day of the three years he was with us," said the doctor. "But you must take it as a sign of our humanity that he came out alive." Turning to me, he cautioned: "Don't waste any pity on our prosecutor. After only three years, he was released and rehabilitated—this man who should have been in jail from birth! The rest of us served more than ten years in jail for no good reason and we still haven't been rehabilitated."

"We're not seeking to punish him further," said the president. "We only want to see our rehabilitation and some compensation coming to us as fast as it came to him. That's what K231 is about."

"The criminals, you see, were all mixed up together," his wife said. "Politicals, thieves, murderers, German prisoners-of-war, and Czechs who'd collaborated with the Germans. That's another of our objectives: to sort out all those who claim to be political prisoners and keep the impostors from infiltrating K231 or discrediting our own quest for rehabilitation."

"By virtue of seniority and their own natural adaptation to prison routine, the Nazis were the leaders when we got there," the doctor recalled. "You can imagine how this rankles a political prisoner who survives five years in the concentration camps and then has to spend fifteen more in a Czechoslovak jail run by Nazis."

"The Czech authorities learned from the Nazis," said the president of K231. "When I wouldn't confess at first, I was taken for a car ride blindfolded. When they took the stocking off my eyes, I was in a cemetery. They handed me a shovel and told me to dig my grave. When I did, they drove me back to jail for further interrogation. But I didn't confess until a month later, when I learned my wife was in prison, too."

"How could you stand it?" my wife asked.

"The only kind of faith you can cling to," he replied. "Faith that they wouldn't execute me until they pretended to have a trial because this was their style. And one other thing. In World War II, I had lived in England after escaping the Nazis. So I had a strong British sense of humor about this sort of happening."

"ANYONE WHO DIFFERENTIATES BETWEEN JEW AND NON-JEW, CHRISTIAN OR NON-CHRISTIAN, COMMUNIST AND NON-COMMUNIST, IS IN MY EYES AN IDIOT," read a vaguely ambiguous banner in the May Day Parade. The words were those of Jan Werich, the comedian, who now had his own Sunday-night TV commentary, "What Do You Say About This, Mr. Werich?" *

* The team of George Voskovec and Jan Werich ($V + W$) was to prewar Prague what Suchý + Šlitr ($S + Š$) were to postwar Prague. George Voskovec, who won an

What Mr. Werich had to say was so sardonic and topical—like a good Fred Allen monologue—that it obsolesced overnight. A politician skewered by Werich was likely to alter his style or even his appearance by Monday morning.

Werich himself is not Jewish, but his words were borne by representatives of the dwindling Jewish community of Prague—50,000-strong before the war and down to 2,500 by May Day of 1968. Two days earlier, Werich had gone to the former ghetto of Prague, in the Old Town, to give the principal speech at a ceremony opening the Jewish Millennium, a two-year celebration of the thousand years since Jews first settled in Bohemia and Moravia.

Werich had sent me an invitation. As soon as the postlady brought it, I burst into the kitchen to proclaim to my family: "The Millennium has come!"

Valerie was dispensing multi-colored vitamin pills to our daughters. She said crossly: "Could you come back in a minute or two?"

Erika said: "Daddy, I guessed my pill would be purple. And it was purple!"

Monica said: "So Erika wins. I guessed orange, but it was pink!"

I left the room. The Levys still await the Messiah, by appointment only.

Though not a devout Jew, I am received with slightly greater veneration than at home whenever I visit the seven synagogues which now comprise the State Jewish Museum, as the Prague ghetto is called. By Jewish tradition, Levites (Lev or Levý in Czech; Löw or Löwy in German—Kafka's mother was born a Löwy) are the temple's lower priesthood and always welcome; our symbol is a pitcher and a salver.

Even for an O'Malley or a Lumumba, though, the Prague ghetto is a haunted place with the oldest Jewish Town Hall (sixteenth century) in Europe (in its belfry, a clock with Hebrew ciphers that runs counter-clockwise); a precious silver collection in the Meisel Synagogue, down the block from Kafka's birthplace on the Mayor Mordecai Meisel Street; the Old-New Synagogue, built in the thirteenth century and now the oldest synagogue in Europe still used for worship (it acquired its name in the seventeenth century, when a newer New Synagogue was built nearby); and the exquisite Spanish Synagogue (whose Moorish

---

Off-Broadway 'Obie' in *Uncle Vanya,* has long been a successful Broadway and Hollywood character actor.

interior resembles the Alhambra) housing the world's largest collection of temple curtains (2,200) and Torah coats (4,000) dating back to 1592. Here the most glorious tapestries are displayed on sliding racks with a dazzling swirl of pageantry by a tiny, delicate Jewish lady who calls them "my children; I lost my real family in the death camps."

Prague itself is known as the "mother city of Israel," and if this reputation endures, it has none other than Adolf Hitler to thank. The contents of the State Jewish Museum were brought together from all over the Bohemian and Moravian "Protectorate" by Hitler, who was persuaded by some crafty Czech friends of the Jews to assemble these treasures for a "postwar Museum of an Extinct Race," a display of Jewish decadence. The owners were indeed liquidated, but their wealth and heritage linger on.

In the ghetto, at one end of the Jewish cemetery, there is another monument: the late Gothic-and-Renaissance Pinkas Synagogue, whose barren interior is furnished with just a few candles. But on its walls are inscribed the names, towns, and birth and death dates of 77,297 Bohemian and Moravian Jewish victims of the Nazis. It is meticulously researched. Armed with a few facts, I have found Miloš Forman's mother and the parents of several of our friends here. And you will never feel more alone with the dead than you are with those 77,297 names in their four-walled tomb, the Pinkas Synagogue.

On the other side of the cemetery is a turreted mortuary papered with an exhibit of "Children's Drawings from Theresienstadt"—part of which is usually touring the U.S. and other western lands. The artists all died in 1943 and 1944. Their themes are largely outdoors—with butterflies and flowers, ships and sunshine. They were very cold that winter in the concentration camp and many of the drawings show houses with smoking chimneys. Innocence was when a chimney still symbolized warmth.

I can never leave that mortuary without first taking a minute or two to regain my composure. For the drawing that lives on in my mind shows sunshine beaming down upon a house with chimney puffing and strawberries growing in the garden. The artist is another Levy: Malvina Löwová, born three days before me in 1932 and dead on 19 October, 1944.

In that mortuary, there is also an inscription from the Czech philosophical writer Karel Poláček, who died in the gas chamber of Auschwitz. He was describing a Biblical illustration:

The antichrist brandishing a spear is about to run it through one of the saints. The saint is sitting comfortably waiting and looking as though it has nothing to do with him. I used to think the medieval painters didn't know how to depict emotions like fear, amazement, pain, and so on, and that was why the saints never looked at all interested in their own sufferings. Now I know better. What else was there to do?

To travel between the mortuary and the Pinkas Synagogue, one must cross the oldest of all Jewish cemeteries in Europe. Here, 20,000 bodies are buried, ten or twelve deep in places; and the 12,000 gravestones, fighting each other for space, seem alive in their struggle. Ravens nest overhead and small pebbles rest on every tombstone; when the Jews were in the desert, there were no flowers and so they used pebbles to decorate the graves and keep away birds and beasts of prey. And the tradition has been followed in Prague's Jewish Cemetery, where the scholar Abigdor Kara (who passed away on 25 April, 1439) was the first to be buried and where the last Jew was buried in 1787. Also buried here are ancestors of Justice Louis D. Brandeis and J. Robert Oppenheimer.

The cemetery, known as "the Jewish pyramids," chronicles not only death, but also life and stonemasonry over three-and-one-half centuries. One can spend a day deciphering the reliefs on the markers: pitcher-and-salver, scissors, and grapes carved on one stone, for instance, would indicate that Mr. and Mrs. Levy are buried here and that he was a tailor and she was a fertile wife. A unicorn means that the deceased's name was Einhorn.

Fact, legend, and symbolism all intertwine in the gray gloom of the Jewish Cemetery. It is the alleged birthplace of the Protocols of the Elders of Zion, a fraudulent document purporting to outline the Jewish plot for world domination. It is also the burial place for yet another of us Levys: Jehuda Leva ben Bezalel (1512–1609), otherwise known as the Maharal or "Der Höhe Rabbi Löw." The High Rabbi Löw definitely existed and dabbled in mysticism, but there is some uncertainty as to whether he actually created a *golem,* a 19-foot-tall automaton made of clay and given life by the mention of the unmentionable (in Judaism) letters of the word G-O-D. According to eighteenth-century legend, Rabbi Löw's *golem,* built to protect the ghetto, ran amok and had to be destroyed. But *The Golem* lives on—immortalized in the twentieth century by Gustav Meyrink's 1916 psychological novel, more

Kafkaesque than Kafka, and H. Leivick's 1920 poetic drama, still a staple in the repertory of Israel's Habimah Theatre.

Although some Czechs don't acknowledge such writers as Kafka, the late Max Brod, and Meyrink (who, incidentally, died a Buddhist) as Prague's own because they wrote in German, they do accept the *golem* as theirs. For nobody is more fascinated with automatons than the Czechs. The word "robot," a back formation from a Czech word *robotnik,* meaning "serf," was first introduced to the English language by the Prague playwright Karel Čapek's drama, *R.U.R.* ["Rossum's Universal Robots"].*

The last religious census of Czechoslovakia, made in 1947, showed that 77 per cent of the Czechoslovak people considered themselves Catholics. This made the church a natural authoritarian rival and target for the Communists who came to power a year later. They formed a "Peace Committee of Catholic Clergy" headed by a "peace priest" named Josef Plojhar, who was immediately suspended by the Vatican. Nevertheless, Father Plojhar headed the only "Catholic church" with which the government dealt regularly for two decades. Later, Father Plojhar also became Novotný's Minister of Health and, still wearing his clerical collar, a familiar figure on East European lecture platforms: a churchman who'd seen the light of the red star.

An open confrontation between church and State became inevitable when the Vatican refused to give the party veto power over the appointment of bishops. In one crystal night of terror in the spring of 1950, police raided all of the country's monasteries and shut them down. Hundreds of monks were imprisoned. Others were conscripted into the army or sent to work in mines and factories. The convents were closed. The nation's 10,000 nuns were put to work on farms or jailed or else held idle in two "detention convents." A petition from 6,174 nuns to Minister of Culture Galuška in early 1968 said that "since 1949 we have been living in complete legal uncertainty." They had spent a total of 32,000 years in restricted detention or prison.

In the spring of 1968, all of this was ended almost overnight. A few days after Novotný fell, the "peace priest" Plojhar resigned all his posts, including chairman of the People's (or Catholic) Party. Hitherto the most obliging puppet in the National Front, the People's Party

---

* Karel Čapek is a very common Czech name that translates as Charles Stork.

refused to accept his resignation and removed him instead; his "peace" organization was disbanded. Vatican-approved Roman Catholic bishops were permitted to resume control of six of the nation's twelve dioceses. (Most of them had been promoted without any official announcement in the 1950's because they might have been imprisoned for it. The same applied to a couple of them already in prison; Vatican honors would not have improved their situation.) Negotiations started with the Vatican for the return from Rome of Josef Cardinal Beran, eighty, the exiled primate of Czechoslovakia. Rehabilitation proceedings began for 1,500 priests. Some of them returned to parish duties (in Prague alone, one hundred fifty churches had remained active) while others stayed on their jobs as worker-priests. Nuns were permitted to resume nursing duties.

The Evangelist Church (including Moravian Brethren, Czech Brethren, Church of Brethren, Silesian and Slovak Lutherans, Calvinists and Methodists) as well as the smaller Protestant denominations had been molested far less than the Catholics. Nevertheless, they assumed new vigor in March when a popular woman sociologist was put in charge of the Government Secretariat for Religious Affairs. She rescinded a 1949 freeze on clergymen's wages. Parents no longer ran the risk of harassment at home and work if they asked school authorities for permission to send their children for religious instruction. Clergymen were authorized to teach religion to children who wanted it between the second and the ninth grade; in Bratislava alone, 7,000 children applied. Baptisms and church marriages became customs again, not heresies.

The religious revival was blessed by Dubček at the 1968 May Day parade. Confronted by a banner reading "BELIEVERS HAVE THE SAME RIGHTS AS OTHER CITIZENS," Dubček responded with fervor: "We must protect our believers!"

"DUBČEK HOLD OUT FOR US," said a giant psychedelically-colored umbrella. Beneath it marched a random harvest of the students of Prague: scrubbed hippies and barbered longhairs, tweedy pipe-smokers and turtlenecked radicals, sandaled Honzas (nickname for Jan) and miniskirted Mařenkas (nickname for Marie); and, most improbably, an apple-cheeked country girl in a dirndl decorated with an "I'M ON LSD" button. On May Day, 1968, gaiety ran rampant among the children of communism.

"STUDENT POWER," said another umbrella—and its adherents were already proving to be the most ardent and uncompromising element in the whole Czechoslovak Revolution.

No student leader is typical, but the case of Lubomír Holeček, twenty-three, is perhaps the most significant. In 1965, he and a fellow student at the Economics Faculty, Jiří Müller, attempted to reform the Youth Union which had been the sole organization representing young people between ages 15 and 26 after the Union of Students was disbanded in 1948. The Youth Union had become an ideological instrument of the Communist party, a stepping stone for party careerists, and a well-paid plum for older administrators. Only 26 per cent of the eligible young people actually belonged. In calling for greater representation of the actual interests of youth, Holeček and Müller noted in passing that there could be no real economic and social gains without dismantling the power structure that Novotný had amassed.

Three days before Christmas, 1966, while the students were dispersed on vacation, Jiří Müller was expelled from the Youth Union. The next day, he was dismissed from the university on a technicality. Between Christmas and New Year's, he was suddenly drafted into the Army for his two years of compulsory service.

His friend Holeček carried on the struggle. Unable to get a word about it into the Prague press, he published and distributed a brochure detailing the Holeček-Müller reform program and its personal consequences. He also started issuing a regular bulletin for Prague students. A committee of students was formed to fight for Müller's reinstatement and their meetings were attended by leather-jacketed strangers with notebooks in hand. As one of the committee noted later: "Each of us had to make his own choice, whether to withdraw to our studies or else risk being next on the list. Each of us made the decision in the light of his conscience. Each of us overcame fear for the sake of another."

Holeček was next. At the 1967 National Youth Congress, his reform proposals and his appeal of "the Müller case" were vetoed. On the 26th of August, again while school was out, he was summoned to active duty in the Army. In September, when his faculty reconvened, he was expelled.

"I was given duty on a lonesome hilltop," Holeček reported later, "so that I couldn't agitate in the barracks." But in March of 1968, Holeček managed to come home on leave to Prague. He told his story to 18,000 people at a "Novotný-Must-Go" teach-in. Still in uniform, he was an electrifying speaker. His eyes blazed behind dark sunglasses as he warned that, if communism didn't solve Czechoslovakia's problems soon, his generation would seek alternatives.

Less than a week later, and twenty-four hours before Novotný abdicated, both Holeček and Müller were discharged from the Army.

A public figure, Holeček hadn't even changed to his civilian clothes when he held a press conference and was asked what he would do next.

"I don't know," he replied. "I wouldn't enjoy becoming a full-time orator. But I may have to if the Communist Party's Action Program doesn't meet our minimum requirements."

On May Day, I thought to ask a student friend what had become of Holeček. I was told: "He liked the Action Program well enough, so he enrolled in school and will watch developments from there." Not back at the Economics Faculty, however, but at the Philosophical Faculty, where he would be exposed to the heresies of Ivan Sviták and the dialectics of Karel Kosik, a teacher and Central Committee member who drew upon Czech history to redefine Marxist theory. The Philosophical Faculty was also a place where Luboš Holeček could preach his own beliefs. One of his most ardent listeners was a quiet boy of 19—also a transfer student from the Economics to the Philosophical Faculty—whose name was Jan Palach.

The students didn't stop marching when the May Day Parade disbanded. They re-traced the route of the last Halloween's Strahov riot and wound up in the park near our home at the statue of Karel Hynek Mácha (1810–1836). A moody, Byronesque romantic poet and civil servant who studied at the Philosophical Faculty and died at 25, Mácha holds the same esteem in modern Czech poetry that Rimbaud does in French. Mácha gave birth to Czech iambic verse in what is still considered the finest poem in the language: the narrative *May* ("Long is my journey, vain is all calling."). Mácha depicts the individual driven to revolt by the antagonism of life and external forces, a revolt doomed to failure by isolation. In Mácha, even the individual's destruction is of no avail, for there is eternal recurrence.* All of which has struck a responsive chord in generation after generation of Czech

---

* For the full text of *May* in English, see the handsome 82-page edition published in 1965 by ARTIA, Prague, with translation by Edith Pargeter. For partial text of the poem in Czech plus detailed analysis in English, see Professor William E. Harkins' *Anthology of Czech Literature* (New York and London: King's Crown Press, 1953, pp. 30–58).

youth—traditionally a sedentary crowd with a penchant for talking-it-over: whether "it" be sex, politics, war, or peace.

On the night of May Day, 1968, even a pessimist like Mácha might have rejoiced at the goings-on beneath his statue. One big happy multitude, the students sang and talked and made love and decided to meet again in the Old Town Square the day after next. And it was somewhere between the Mácha statue on May First and the Jan Hus statue on May Third that a new noun entered the Czech language: "Come on down to Old Town Square. We're having a *hydepark.*"

I wasn't in Prague by then, for right after the May Day parade, I made a pilgrimage to Marienbad for another spring rite of the young: The Second International Student Film Festival. Upon arriving, I was handed a 108-sentence phrase sheet compiled by a Prague Film Faculty student to take one over the conversational ropes in Czech, English, French, and German. In so doing, it tells you almost all you need to know about that curiously stilted jet-age Continental cultural tradition, the filmfest, which is held everywhere from a gambling casino in Knokke-le-Zoute, Belgium, to a shopping center in claustrophobic West Berlin:

> 5. Where could I buy some dirty pictures-art books? 6. I am a Press photographer; may I take your nude photo? 7. This is a special camera that needs no film in it. 8. Aren't you Brigitte Bardot? I hope your husband is out-of-town. 9. May I walk with you? 10. I have a groundsheet in case the grass is wet. . . . 15. I'm not a good dancer, but I like holding women. . . . 18. You're drinking very slowly. . . . 21. I know a little game to pass the time. 22. Darling, kiss me, please. 23. It's quieter upstairs in the bedroom. 24. What lovely smooth hands you have, put them here. 25. Let's play strip canasta. 26. I can't marry you because I am too young. 27. I am leaving tomorrow, I'll write soon.

Virtually all filmfests are heavily subsidized, usually by municipal and national governments, for whom the name of the game is not culture, but tourism. To them, a well-scheduled filmfest serves the same objective as a Rotary convention or beauty pageant. It keeps the hotels humming during otherwise semi-slack periods. It enables the peak commercial season to start early or end late. It attracts the press and publicity. And perhaps its glamour will serve as a tourist magnet.

Some one hundred young film students from twenty-one nations brought more seriousness than glamour to the rugged green splendor of

Marienbad. That was a golden time of freedom for Prague's young film-makers to meet and talk and play with—and learn from—their contemporaries in foreign lands. But even while they passed their days in an idyll of games and conversations and round-the-clock screenings, distant drums were reverberating through the mountains that seal Marienbad off from East Germany, Poland, and Russia. It was still the golden springtime of Czechoslovakia's peaceable revolution, but a series of Polish-Czech cultural maneuvers were dramatizing the fear of contagion that ran rampant through Eastern Europe.

An invited guest from Warsaw sent his regrets, but he would be unable to attend because "while the Polish People's Republic has not stopped giving exit permits to Czechoslovakia, it has prolonged the time necessary for their issue to two months." A Czech journalist I knew told me that, when he went on assignment to Poland, he was given, upon arrival, two police bodyguards ("for your own protection") who prevented him from talking to anyone. After forty-four hours in their company, he was bundled onto a plane to Prague ("We can no longer guarantee your safety in Warsaw"). And the rector of the Polish film school in Lodz, who already had his visa for the Marienbad filmfest, was purged for "deviationist and Zionist tendencies" and not permitted to come. Nobody from Poland came to Marienbad.

I had gone to Marienbad as an invited observer. But when Ivan Sviták was unable to get away from Prague for a filmfest panel on "What's Happening in Czechoslovakia," two men were drafted to replace him. One was a professor from the Moscow Film School. The other was myself.

"I am a guest in this country," I told the audience, "so it would be presumptuous for me to give any evaluation or opinion of what's going on here. But, after half a year here, I do feel qualified to tell you what I've seen. Since I'm a foreigner here and most of you are foreigners, there's a chance that my perspective may be a little more detached than a Czech's." Then I told what I had witnessed thus far.

The Russian was a round-faced youngish man who spoke into the microphone in English. He said: "I do not understand why there is so much commotion about what is happening in Czechoslovakia. Or why the Western press in general is saying that we in Russia are worried about this. Our *Pravda* has printed the Action Program in full. It contains nothing that any Russian can object to. We have, in fact, for some time enjoyed the same guarantees that the Czechoslovaks are getting now. Our only dismay is that it has taken Czechoslovakia this long to achieve our level of freedom."

During the panel's discussion period, I said: "I have only been telling you what I've seen with my own eyes. But now I must ask the professor a question about something *he* has seen: Did the Action Program, as printed in *Pravda,* mention freedom to travel and the abolition of censorship?"

The professor replied vehemently: "There is *nothing* about this in the Action Program."

A roar went up from the Czechs in the crowd. There was a babble of refutation and then a complete Action Program was presented to the professor. He had tears in his eyes when I said to the audience as gently as I could:

"I had read a United Press dispatch mentioning that these two passages were omitted in Moscow, but I wanted to know it first-hand. I think we have just seen the most insidious side of censorship—that its victim doesn't even know when he's being victimized."

During the eight days between May Day and Liberation Day, the pressure on the heartland of Europe mounted to an ominous throb. Two days after the parade, First Secretary Dubček, Speaker Smrkovský, Prime Minister Černík, and Vasil Bil'ak, who had succeeded Dubček as party chief in Slovakia, made a sudden Friday-night flight to Moscow for urgent talks in the Kremlin. Returning on Sunday morning, they issued a nondescript official communique about talks "held in an open, comradely atmosphere [where] both sides also discussed topical questions." In Communist official parlance, the adjectives tell the tale: "Open" without any embellishment means that dirty looks and maybe even insults were exchanged. The addition of "comradely" means that the meeting was civilized, though brusque. Happier occasions can range upward from "cordial" to "friendly" to the ultimate in good will: "an atmosphere of complete frankness, sincerity, and mutual understanding," which means it was all bear-hugs and kisses.

At Ruzyně airport, Černík said smugly that "everyone is sure to be satisfied with the results. There was nothing sensational in the talks." He added that Dubček would give the details on Monday. But the interview that Dubček gave the next day to *Rudé Právo* was uncharacteristically fuzzy. The Catholic newspaper pronounced it "so disappointing that people had to tune in to foreign radio stations once again in quest of more facts" and the socialist press deplored "a certain vagueness."

By then, Gomulka of Poland, Ulbricht of East Germany, Zhivkov of Bulgaria, and Janos Kádár of Hungary had flown suddenly to Moscow for still another summit meeting. Its subject was undisclosed, but there was no doubt that it was Czechoslovakia. Its atmosphere was later characterized officially as "an exchange of views," which implied some disagreement. The positions of Gomulka and Ulbricht were never in doubt. But Kádár, who came to power in 1956 behind Soviet tanks, was known to be anxious not to see history repeat itself against his friend Dubček.

Despite (or perhaps because of) what Zhivkov had seen for himself during his April visit, the Bulgarian was denouncing "revisionism which regrettably can be observed in the socialist camp" and proclaiming "merciless struggle to eradicate this evil." Since puppets seldom speak for themselves, his reactions were viewed by Kremlin-watchers as clues to Moscow's thinking. And, with the military mind taking command, Moscow's thinking was definitely hardening.

It became known that in April the Soviet Central Committee had secretly condemned the Czechoslovak experiment as "revisionist." A copy of this resolution, sent to Dubček over May Day, had prompted his sudden mission to Moscow. *Le Monde* weighed in with an added report that, also in April, a powerful Russian general named Alexei A. Yepishev had said that the Red Army was ready to "comply with its duty" should a group of "loyal Communists" in Czechoslovakia request help in "safeguarding socialism." The report was denied in Moscow and Prague and not given too much credence elsewhere: General Yepishev, as Soviet ambassador to Rumania and Yugoslavia between 1955 and 1962, had amassed a reputation as a "dove." But the truth was that now, as chief political administrator of the Soviet Army and Fleet, he had thrown his weight in with the "hawks."

The East *Berliner Zeitung* weighed in with a very "exclusive" report that U.S. troops and eight tanks had already arrived in Prague; West German troops and tanks were also expected momentarily. Though not quite a half-truth, this rewrite of a publicity release did bear a shred of accuracy: An American war film, *The Bridge at Remagen,* was being shot in Czechoslovakia with eight U.S. tanks of World War II vintage, borrowed from the Government of Austria and ferried to Barrandov Studios by a private trucker. Czechoslovak military museums were supplying captured German tanks. The combat troops included George Segal, Bradford Dillman, Ben Gazzara, and Robert Vaughn.

Acting on such "information," Walter Ulbricht's border guards precipitated a new "Berlin crisis" by barring selected cars from the *autobahn*. These "renewed tensions" prompted Ulbricht to plead for 11,000 Warsaw Pact special troops (preferably Russian) to be stationed along Czechoslovakia's western frontier as "reinforcements" for the "beleaguered" Czechoslovak People's Army.

I was on my way home from the film festival. The noon express from Marienbad to Prague stopped in Pilsen, where a jovial middle-aged Czech entered my compartment. Seeing that I was a foreigner, he addressed me first in German and then in French. I answered him each time in Czech and, on his third try, he placed my accent as "English or could it be American?" When I told him, his face lit up and he continued in English: "Oh, thank God I came to Pilsen! I haven't spoken to an American since 1948 and I haven't spoken English since 1950. When you're out of practice, it's a very hard language for a slave."

"A slave?" I said.

"Yes, the *slayvic* people. Czechoslaves and Yugoslaves. And Poles and Russians, too."

"Slavs," I corrected. "There's a big difference nowadays."

We talked all the way to Prague. My New York accent was music to his ears. Reading between the lines of his life story, I gathered that, whether or not he had slaved, he had certainly suffered. He was a historian who had served as a guide with the American Army in World War II "and naturally this made me suspect after 1948." But all he would say about his career was: "Now I am all right again. I work indoors, compiling accident and safety statistics."

He preferred to talk about his mission to Pilsen, which had been an important sentimental journey for him. He had been part of General Patton's Third Army that liberated Pilsen on 6 May, 1945, and he had seen his best friend, "a boy from the Bronx," killed by a sniper that morning. The people of Pilsen had welcomed the Americans, named a street after them, and later that year unveiled a plaque on their Town Hall. The foundation for a memorial statue was laid in 1947.

The Communists, however, made a systematic attempt to obliterate the U. S. Army's role. First, it was said that the liberators weren't really

Americans but Belgians; one of the first U.S. units into Pilsen was in fact composed of Belgian volunteers. Then, the rest of the Third Army was blamed for halting in Pilsen instead of moving on to Prague; the American commander had, in fact, forbidden a force of 7,000 Pilsener volunteers to march on Prague. In the 1950's, the American Street was re-named and the tablet and pedestal disappeared (as did Pilsen's monument to T. G. Masaryk). Party orators referred repeatedly to the "Soviet liberators of Prague and Pilsen."

In the spring of 1968, however, Czechoslovak historians held a national meeting and issued a statement calling for recognition of the role "the Western allies and some Czechoslovak troops from the West" had played in the 1945 liberation. "It is politically untenable, historically wrong, and morally harmful to try to keep this secret," they concluded.

Their most outspoken supporter was Josef Smrkovský, who had led the Prague Uprising that began on the 5th of May, 1945. Smrkovský now made it clear why American troops hadn't gone on from Pilsen to Prague. They had halted in deference to a Soviet-American agreement made in early April, 1945, that had defined Pilsen as a "line of demarcation." The Russian high command had already mapped "Operation Prague" and asked the Americans to let them liberate the capital, which they did on the 9th of May. It was just one of several Big Power sphere-of-influence agreements that put Czechoslovakia where it was by 1968.

Smrkovský went even farther than the historians. He chided the Czechs for failing to erect a monument to their own parachutists who assassinated the Nazi "Protector," Reinhard Heydrich, because they had come from Britain. And he linked this omission to the Stalinist era, which he termed a "dark spot in history [that] concerns all society and all generations. No nation can afford it. For it not only harms its own moral health, but it also sullies the memory of those who once stood at its head and it treads on its best and most vital people who sacrificed even their lives for its future."

On 6 May 1968, Pilsen had honored its American liberators for the first time since 1947. Two days later, the slave who was sharing my train compartment was able to tell me happily: "Thousands of people were there. A new plaque was put on the Town Hall and flowers laid where the monument was supposed to have been. The American national song was played, the American flag was raised, and most important, the American soldiers were remembered." Then he sang all four stanzas of *The Star-Spangled Banner* on the express train to Prague.

I returned home on Liberation Day's eve, when my wife and I were invited to President Svoboda's holiday reception at the Prague Castle. We climbed a red-carpeted marble staircase and, after leaving our coats, wandered through salon after salon until we came to a room where the President and his wife were standing. We introduced ourselves and Svoboda, whose white hair, red face, and blue suit matched the Czechoslovak flag, greeted us warmly. His wife, Irina, told Valerie that her daughter, Zoja, married to a diplomat at the United Nations, was living in New York. When we parted, President Svoboda shook our hands again and, as soon as we were out of earshot, Valerie murmured: "Spencer Tracy lives!" The resemblance was astonishing.

Everyone was gravitating toward the center of the room Dubček was in. Where he was usually surrounded by no more than half a dozen people, Dubček now had a circle of fifty. The innermost ring was formed by Russians; in fact, the party was swarming with them. The commander-in-chief of the Warsaw Pact forces, Marshall I. I. Yakubovsky, had come with a delegation, ostensibly "to introduce ourselves to the newly-elected leaders of this country: the President of the Republic, the Speaker of the National Assembly, and the Prime Minister . . . as well as to discuss the defense of the Warsaw Pact countries." This meant that he was pushing for Warsaw Pact maneuvers on Czechoslovak soil, but the word around the party was that Dubček wasn't saying yes.

Dubček was in an argument with one of the visiting Russians: a younger man, even taller than himself, in civilian clothes. They were talking in Russian. The Russian man was jabbing like a fighter with his finger, his face, his words, and his body. You could see him spitting with anger as he spoke.

Dubček, who never looked at home in ornate castles and palaces, stayed calm, though annoyed. Once, however, his face flushed and he talked back angrily in his gravel voice. Then, after five minutes more of discussion, he rotated his right hand near his hip as if to say "we are talking in circles." Dubček started to walk away and the circle opened to let him through.

The Russian, however, thrust after him. The argument started up again. After a few more exchanges, Dubček stalked off.

We and various Czechs asked some of the Russians present about the identity of their belligerent young countryman. We received such answers as "What Russian?", "What argument?", and "It was just a brotherly chat."

A long holiday weekend had started that Wednesday night. On Thursday, Sylva joined us for the afternoon and for dinner. We explored Petřín Park and its Eiffel-inspired Tower built in 1891 for Czechs who couldn't travel to Paris. Up its 300 outside spiral wooden steps we went, faster and faster as though in a reverse tailspin, while magnificent views of Prague danced dizzyingly around us. Now you see the Vltava, now you don't CLUMP CLUMP CLUMP There's Strahov and behind it is our house Keep moving CLUMP CLUMP CLUMP *Pardon!* CLUMP CLUMP CLUMP There's the statue of Mácha CLUMP CLUMP CLUMP What's the Castle doing over there? I don't know, but isn't it gorgeous from above! CLUMP CLUMP CLUMP CLUMP Watch your heads! Now we're at the top and *voilà* Prague!

On the walk down, Monica said: "Daddy, I like the Petřín Tower better than the Empire State Building because here they let us *climb* all the way up!"

Next to the tower is a funhouse with a labyrinth, historical diorama, and crazy mirrors. It has no recorded sound effects, but the innocent cackles of Prague children and grown-ups seeing themselves as others never see them have exactly the same maniacal sound as the canned howls that emanate from carnival funhouses in the States.

Sylva stayed for a Tartar Beefsteak dinner that night and, after she had helped Val put the dishes and children away, we sat in the living room and reviewed her first week as a journalist. Although *Zítřek* wasn't due to appear for another three or four months, Sylva had gone to work the day after May Day. "I have so much to learn," she told us. "And there is a censorship problem."

"Oh, no, Sylva!" Valerie exclaimed.

"A *self*-censorship problem," Sylva clarified with a laugh. "Any people who have lived under thirty years of censorship must *learn* democracy. Every time I ask a question, I feel as if I have no right to ask it. Yesterday, I was ready to end an interview and so I stood up and started to apologize to the man I was interviewing, a Cabinet minister, for taking up his time. But then he asked me a question and started drawing me out in conversation for half an hour. That was when I got my best material. Later, I thanked him for keeping me there and teaching me how to do my work."

At nine o'clock that night, our whole neighborhood was rocked by explosions. The three of us jumped. It took us about two seconds to remember that Liberation Day—like our own Independence Day—is celebrated with fireworks in the Petřín Park. We settled back with embarrassed laughs, but the look of consternation was not quite erased from Sylva's face. I suggested that, since she was now a journalist, she jot down her reaction. She took out her notebook and wrote: "My generation has lived through too much, but I certainly hope that we shall live through much more." When she laughed almost like the Sylva we knew, the three of us wandered out onto the bedroom balcony and watched the last sparklers evaporate over Strahov Monastery.

"Can we turn on the television a little?" Sylva asked when we'd stepped back inside. We watched the national opera, Smetana's *Bartered Bride,* which was comfortingly familiar. Sylva left at 10 P.M. The trams were still running often and people were out strolling on a balmy night.

At 10:15 the first transatlantic call was put through from New York. It was my literary agent, who had just heard on the radio that Western tourists and diplomats traveling from Warsaw to Prague or Berlin were being sent back to Warsaw. They were told that the reason for their re-routing was "troop movements near the Czechoslovak frontier."

My agent suggested: "Why don't you turn on your television and get the latest news?"

"It's on," I said. "There's only one channel and it's doing *The Bartered Bride.*" I held the phone toward the TV to pick up a tenor singing that "only those who are in love can know what love really means!"

"Do the actors look nervous?" my agent asked.

"No," I said, "but they're probably on videotape."

On this inconclusive note, my transatlantic call ended. Val made some tea while I tried in vain to get some bulletins on the radio. For the situation is not to be taken lightly whenever a Communist country interferes with tourism and hard Western currency.

My wife and I sat up discussing eventualities. It didn't seem probable that the Russians were coming. Clearly, they didn't like what was happening here but, in that fickle neverland known as the Court of

World Public Opinion, they were winning by default, thanks to America's involvement in Vietnam. And surely, in 1968, Russia could not afford a repetition of Hungary in 1956!

On the other hand, the Poles and East Germans had absolutely no prestige to lose. Acting on their own paranoid provocations, they might conceivably invade, with the Russians, of course, pulling the strings while saying blandly: "We're keeping our hands off this dispute, just as we've kept our hands off the internal developments inside Czechoslovakia."

Thus, the prospect of German troops goose-stepping through Prague had to be considered, and my wife and I made a contingency plan that night: In the event of any kind of invasion, the Prague Castle, near our home, would certainly be a key target. As soon as street-fighting ended, we would retreat up Ořechovka Hill to the Suchýs' house, another third-of-a-mile away from the strategic Castle. Our second line of retreat would be the Formans', still another quarter-mile beyond the Suchýs'—and in the direction of the airport.

This, though, was as far away as we were willing to think. For it seemed to us that our U.S. passports were our best assurance of physical safety—better surely than submergence of our identities in any mad stream of refugees. And, in the event of an occupation, I as a writer would want to remain here to witness events and make sense of them.

A couple of relatives phoned from the States and the Bonn bureau of *Life* called with an offer to help us evacuate plus a request that I file a few hundred words before fleeing. I said I was staying; they could phone me three or four times a day, if they wished, but I would file no copy. There was nothing to write about unless *Life* wanted a mood piece. People were still strolling, the trams were still running, and the third act of *The Bartered Bride* was going strong.

I did go out on a midnight walk, however, for I had devised an easy visual gauge of how international tensions were affecting Czechoslovakia.

One block from home stands a lemon-yellow stone complex of Czechoslovak Army barracks—added on to the ancient Firehouse, which was now a military headquarters building. On the night of 9 May, only a lone sentry was awake and visible.

Through the Firehouse Square, bear left and you are at the Černín Palace, the Ministry of Foreign Affairs. There were no official Tatra limousines in the Palace's cobblestoned parking lot. That was a good sign!

I walked four blocks farther through Hradčany to my final checkpoint: the Castle. The President's flag ("TRUTH PREVAILS") was fluttering blithely, signifying that General Svoboda was in residence. The young blue-hatted, white-shirted Castle Guards, armed with carbines, were lounging at their usual casual attention.

I headed home by a different route through the winding cobblestoned streets of the New World, the oldtime red-light district with its narrow green and yellow houses of ill repute now thoroughly sanitized and among the choicer residential addresses in Prague. The New World (*Nový Svět*) is still gas lit by a lamplighter with a bamboo window-pole that catches onto a high hook.

The old lamplighter had retired until dawn, when he would douse his lights, but the New World's one surviving wine tavern, the Golden Pear, was still open and I phoned my "all's well" to Valerie from there. Then, to unwind, I had a cool glass of a dry white Moravian wine called *Poezie*. The cook had gone home, but the two old waiters offered to whip up the house's specialty, also called "The Golden Pear" (*Zlatá Hruška*), a mixed grill of meats and vegetables (whatever was best and freshest that day) invariably crowned with a pear (fresh or canned). I said I wasn't hungry and asked if it had been a quiet Liberation Night.

"After the fireworks, yes," the older waiter said.

"Just couples holding hands," the younger waiter added.

Both of these courtly, gracious men had the same in-bred, built-in, old New World look that went so well with the Golden Pear's walnut benches, tables, and walls. Both of them, in fact, dated back to its capitalist days as a privately-owned inn. Nothing much had changed for them except perhaps the payer of their wages. Their wine and their serenity relaxed me so that I went home and slept nine hours—by which time the crisis had dissipated like the sparklers over Strahov.

Newspapers had halted publication for the holiday weekend. The only Czechs who knew of the "invasion crisis" were the few who still bothered to tune into Western radio broadcasts. To make communications worse, the phone lines to Moscow, Warsaw, and East Berlin had mysteriously gone dead on Thursday, but they were "repaired" on Friday. New York and Washington had, it seemed, been more nervous about the Czechoslovak border than the people of Prague. The first reports from Poland on Thursday afternoon (Wall Street time) had dropped the stock market six points. U.S. State Department sources were chattering off-the-record about "another Hungary."

Toward noon, Gerda Endler, *Life*'s correspondent in Bonn, phoned to say that this would be the last call from there: "It looks like the war is over, Alan. The Poles are denying that they restricted tourist movement and when the tourists say 'But you did—and here we are to prove it!', the Poles say 'It must have been a mistake because you're perfectly free to travel.' The tourists have left Warsaw without any further interference. Still, there were troop movements last night, but they were headquarters units, a few thousand men, and no infantry. I think it was just meant to be a dramatic reminder to Dubček."

The Czechoslovak Foreign Ministry put its best face on the episode with a statement that it had been notified in advance of the maneuvers in Southern Poland and "Czechoslovak political circles consider rumors circulating abroad a provocation."

Among the Czechs and Slovaks who were "provoked" by the scare and by their people's blithe unawareness of it were various mentors and technicians of the free press, radio, and TV. The gun-rattling of May inspired them to make contingency plans that would insure continued expression. All they had to do, in many cases, was dust off blueprints designed in the 1950's for use in the event of an "inevitable West German invasion."

FIRST TRIP TO THE WEST AFTER FIVE MONTHS BEHIND the Curtain: The Vindobona, luxury express train, leaves East Berlin (Ostbahnhof) every morning, stops in Prague mid-afternoon, arrives Vienna (Franz Josef Bahnhof) 2102 hours. First-class fare is $4.80 in crowns up to the Austrian frontier at Gmund and $5.30 in hard currency from Gmund to Vienna. The Vindobona has a good dining car, if you don't mind being served good German beer and good German bread on a train that passes through the land of great Pilsener beer and great black bread. But one further problem: Being East German, the Vindobona keeps its diner closed until it is in Austria, around 8 P.M., whereupon the steward can rush you through the meal and charge you in hard currency. Tonight the train is running an hour late, so it's almost nine o'clock when we and two cranky, hungry children sit down to supper. To make matters worse: The only hard currency I have is a $100 travelers check, for which the steward doesn't have anywhere near enough Western money to make change. A fellow traveler (American from Paris) has $5.00 to spare, so I write him a personal check on my New York bank. The bill, with 10 per cent added for service, comes to $4.97. "Keep the change!" I tell the steward magnanimously. He musters a bow.*

Just out of Tábor, the customs and immigration officers had boarded and, by the time we'd reached the frontier, all passports, exit visas, return visas, and currency declarations had been checked. The officials had disembarked at the last stop on the Czech side, a sealed station guarded by Czech soldiers in green berets. There, a mechanic flanked by two soldiers with rifles had walked the length of the train. He had poked his flashlight under every car and jumped up periodi-

* Good news for travelers! Since 1969, the Vindobona has been operated by the Czechs, who keep their own beer, bread, and hours.

cally to ascertain that nobody was lying on top of the train. The search had taken half an hour.

"Maybe they're looking for another General Šejna," one of the Czechs in our compartment had remarked. But the fact was that just in case Czechs or (more likely by then) East Germans were stowing away, the Czechoslovak Army still kept a true Marxist-Leninist vigil at the border while Walter Ulbricht and Leonid Brezhnev were railing at the Czechs for not protecting their western flank.

Culture shock! That's what we feel from the moment we arrive in Vienna on Friday night to the moment we leave on Tuesday morning. In the taxi from station to *pension,* we are frightened by the neon flooded Kärntnerstrasse and we huddle a little closer. Saturday morning, we go on our first shopping spree. We have a deadline, for Gene and Zdenka Deitch have been in Vienna all week with their car. They are going back home today at 2 P.M., after the stores close, and we can load up their back seat and trunk with our Saturday purchases. The American Family Levy races down the Kärntnerstrasse grabbing up everything that's unavailable or scarce in Prague: forty dollars worth of American and Italian spices plus a spice rack . . . a shopping cart . . . Ritz-type crackers . . . turtleneck jerseys . . . a toilet-paper dispenser and all the soft toilet paper in sight . . . Kleenex-brand Kleenex . . . oil for my Czech typewriter . . . Hushpuppy shoes . . . Johnson's Baby Cream . . . Scotch tape that sticks . . . Number-one-size paper clips (Prague stores have none smaller than 3-inches long; how's that for a symptom of bureaucracy?) . . . Papermate pen refills . . . bourbon whisky and rosé wine (neither stocked by Tuzex) . . . Lassar's paste for the children (who watch it being mixed with mortar and pestle in an old-fashioned apothecary's) . . . dirndls from Lanz . . . and getting my Omega watch fixed (the guarantee is still in effect, but there are no Omega dealers or parts in Prague).

Like peasants flocking to the bazaar, we simply snatch whatever we want from the shelves and, once we have it, look around for the cashier. This is the way it's done in Prague, but not in Vienna. At Steffl's department store, our behavior commends us to the attention of a couple of haughty salesgirls, then the manager, and finally the store detective.

"You don't look as though you're from Eastern Europe," he begins in English, "but you act as though you are. . . . Here, you ask for what you want or point to it and then the saleslady will fetch it and put it in something for you!"

"In a bag?" Valerie asks in amazement. In Prague, you have to ask for a paper bag and the answer isn't always yes.

We promise the detective that we'll try to do better. But then we catch a glimpse of oregano or water-color paint sets or baby aspirin and forget all our vows. We know we are behaving badly, but after almost half-a-year away from the Big Supermarket, we cannot help helping ourselves!

I am happy to see that we are not the only miscreants in Steffl's. Down one long aisle, I see the manager and the detective chasing after someone else who is doing what we're doing. He comes toward me like a mirror image of myself and I see that it's Gene Deitch! Although he gets to Vienna every month or so, he still behaves like an orphan in a candy shop. I try to pretend I don't know him or else Steffl's will think it's been hit by a shoplifting ring.

As Gene passes me, I am fondling six double rolls of a caressingly soft toilet paper with the unforgettable brand name of FEH.

"Put it back!" Gene snarls out of the side of his mouth. "You can get FEH for 20 per cent less at Herzmansky's on the Maria-Hilfer-strasse."

"I will *not* put it back!" I exclaim. "The FEH is here and I am here and what'll happen if I get to Herzmansky and find they're all out of FEH and then I come back here and find that Steffl's has sold all its FEH, too? Then how'll I feel?"

"Look, kid, it doesn't work that way in this part of the world," Gene says with a laugh. "But I wouldn't want our friendship to founder over a roll of FEH, so forget I ever mentioned it."

"Anyway," I say soothingly, "Herzmansky might close before I get there."

Valerie is bristling, however. "Do you mean to say," she asks the manager and the store detective, who have caught up with Gene, "that the same commodity can cost two different prices in the same city?"

Gene and I cackle at how quickly a housewife can forget Western civilization. But the Steffl's officials are struck dumb. Clearly, the challenges to capitalism lurk everywhere. But what are they to make of this one which has come from the East speaking American?

My family went home on the Vindobona without me. I flew on to the Cannes Film Festival for a reunion with Miloš Forman, who had been in America since January. When I asked him what it was like and how it felt to be living in the U.S. of A. temporarily, Miloš cut me off with: "Tell me all about the Prague Spring first and I'll do you a favor by not telling you about the studios in America. That's where the real Stalinists are, at the budget meetings. For a while, everyone was avoiding me—even my own lawyer—and it took me three weeks to find out why: The film I'm going to make in New York was running under budget and I was making the whole system look bad."

In Cannes, Miloš was also waiting for another arrival from Prague: Jan Němec, the movie director whose 1965 *Report on the Party and the Guests* depicted President Novotný as the dapper host at a paltry feast which nobody was allowed to leave. When Novotný had previewed it at his screening room in the Castle, he had suppressed it. Now, barely two months after Novotný's abdication, Němec's *Report* was playing in Prague and was about to be unveiled to the West at Cannes.

Němec's path and mine had crossed only briefly in Prague, usually at the Chinsky Restaurant, though many of our friends had regaled me with tales of Němec's ex-marriage to his screenwriter, Ester Krumbachová.* They had parted amicably, so amicably in fact, that they went on collaborating and also threw a party to celebrate the granting of their divorce.

I happened to be in front of the Carlton Hotel when Němec, a roly-poly, reddish-haired crew-cut cherub of thirty-three, arrived in Cannes. He parked his orange sport Fiat illegally on the Boulevard Croisette. I hurried over to greet him and tell him where to find Forman. But a policeman reached Němec first and started to write a parking ticket.

Němec exclaimed *"Merde!"* and the policeman placed him under arrest.

I fetched Forman and told him how Němec, who had survived Novotný's wrath, was now in the custody of the French police. By the time we reached the station house to bail out Němec, however, he had the situation well in hand. Everybody was laughing and there were introductions all around. Then the officer in charge asked Miloš: "It is really true, M. Forman, is it not, that in Czech the word 'merde' means 'it's going to rain'?"

---

* Ester Krumbachová also collaborated with director Věra Chytilová on the screenplay for *Daisies* (1966), a surrealist tale of two footloose girls. Jiří Šlitr also composed the music. *Daisies* was long denied public showings in Czechoslovakia because of the "outrageous way in which it tramples the achievements of socialism."

Miloš gave the right answer and Němec was released without so much as a parking fine. But for the rest of the filmfest, Němec was accompanied to the thrice-daily rooftop parties by a uniformed body-guard assigned whenever the weather looked threatening. The guard explained that he was there to "protect M. Němec in the event one of our countrymen mistakes his pleasant conversation about the weather for an impertinence."

Even with police protection, however, Němec was challenged to a duel in Cannes.

One night he was in the market for a high-coiffed Ethiopian "Tuzex girl" whose going price, payable in advance please, was 200 francs ($40.00) for the night. With the aid of hard-currency loans from Forman, myself, a publicist, a critic, and a French distributor, Němec was able to scrape together 180 francs. He promised to pay the rest by 9:30 the next morning, and the glamorous Ethiope extended credit. A few minutes past the deadline, Němec delivered in the breakfast room of the Carlton by plunking down four five-franc coins on the table of—*oops!*—the wrong statuesque Ethiope. This one was the wife of a Festival dignitary, who later came looking for Němec to "demand satisfaction."

Němec and Forman gave greater satisfaction inside the Festival Palace. Though no longer topical, Němec's slashing *Report* on No-votný, with its brooding Kafkaesque air of menace-that-can't-quite-be-placed, inspired Renata Adler (then the movie critic of *The New York Times*) to hail it as "certainly one of the best Czechoslovak films ever made" and Němec as "clearly one of the most powerful and universal young directors now at work."

Miloš' *The Firemen's Ball** was leading the Grand Prize field at the halfway mark (according to one of the judges, Louis Malle, who broke jury secrecy) when the festival collapsed a week ahead of schedule. The French Revolution of 1968 had started in Nanterre, spread to Paris, and was now working its way down the Riviera. In downtown Cannes, at lunchtime, Miloš and I saw Frenchmen smashing bank windows and stepped aside while a mob of young people ("the generation my films speak to," Miloš muttered) chased a fortyish businessman through the streets. They were last seen gaining on him. After a leisurely lunch, we returned to the festival just in time for a riot on the stage of the Palace. To show "solidarity" with the rebels outside and "contest Gaullist

---

* *To the Fire, Firemen!* was its French title; *On Fire, My Love!* was its Czech title.

power in the film industry," Jean-Luc Godard and François Truffaut were physically halting the screening of a Geraldine Chaplin film called *Peppermint Frappé,* though not before the lightweight Godard lost his eyeglasses five times and the bantamweight Truffaut was knocked down four times.

Němec and Forman and I sat in the auditorium quietly witnessing this ultra-chic *révolution à la mode de Cannes.* When the filmfest was officially disbanded a few hours later, my two companions had few regrets that no prizes would be awarded. Němec was eager to get a head start on a documentary he was making that would be a hymn to the Prague Spring, a joyous hymn! And Forman was grateful to be leaving Cannes a week ahead of schedule for Prague, where the real revolution was at. I was ready, too, and when it dawned on me that I was just as homesick for Prague as they were, I began to realize how far my rowboat had brought me!

Chapter 9 ⌉

Monday 20 May—Tuesday 25 June 1968

MILOŠ FORMAN LIVES ON A STREET CALLED MAJOR Schramm. He was moving there when I first met him in 1966. I asked Miloš once or twice who Major Schramm was. And why should a mere major have a street named after him? Miloš replied: "I don't know. But he must have been some kind of Communist war hero, a Partisan maybe."

In the spring of 1968, we began to read that, if Foreign Minister Jan Masaryk had indeed been murdered at the Černín Palace in the early hours of 10 March 1948, then the likeliest suspect was none other than the mysterious Major Augustin Schramm.

The question of "who killed Masaryk? Himself or a person or persons unknown?" was revived for the world and raised publicly for the first time in Czechoslovakia by the abrasive philosopher Ivan Sviták in an open letter to the weekly *Student*. Twenty years after the event, Sviták was suggesting that the official verdict of suicide was incorrect and calling for an investigation that would establish whether Jan Masaryk "was the first victim on the road to totalitarian dictatorship." The founder of KAN went on to note "a well-founded assumption that Masaryk was murdered" and added that, as a matter of prestige, the authorities should present all the facts in the case.

Any idea that Sviták put his mind to was, in 1968, an idea whose time had come. In interviews, he mentioned the name of Major Schramm and asked not only who he was, but also: Why was a street in Prague named after Major Schramm, but none after Jan Masaryk? Why was Schramm himself liquidated soon after Masaryk's death? Why, for that matter, did so many who bore some connection with the Masaryk case die or disappear under mysterious circumstances?

Less than a month after Sviták expressed his doubts, *Rudé Právo—
the official Communist Party organ!*—editorialized:

> There is very serious cause to suspect murder. In any case at least,
> the disappearance of potential witnesses—together with a number of
> other circumstances—makes it categorically necessary not to neglect any
> aspect of the case.
>
> The suspicion has been stated and has still not been disproved
> in any way that Jan Masaryk was not only murdered, but that it was
> a political murder and that Major Schramm, an officer in the State Se-
> curity at that time, was involved and so, too, were Beria's "Gorillas."
>
> This circumstance cannot be made light of because it is also gen-
> erally known what a scandalous role the Beria gang played in the
> pogroms on leading and honorable functionaries of the Communist
> Party of Czechoslovakia from 1949 to 1952. For this reason alone, the
> theory is, in principle, admissible.
>
> It is of supreme interest that it be clarified whether Beria's "Go-
> rillas" had a hand in any way in the case of the murder of Jan
> Masaryk or not . . . and we believe that our Soviet friends will give
> us all legal aid possible in this. Beria's criminal clique, after all, com-
> mitted such terrible wrongs primarily against the Soviet people them-
> selves and it was justly punished in the severest possible way twelve
> years ago.

Prague braced itself for Moscow's response to this challenge. Tass
merely labeled any conjectures about a link between Masaryk's death
and the Russians as "mendacious through-and-through" and designed
to "stir up anti-Soviet moods among politically unstable people." But
the official Moscow Communist periodical, *Sovietskaya Rossiya,* chose
to reply with a diversionary overkill straight out of the "so's-your-old-
man" arsenal of yellow journalism. Jan Masaryk, it said, was the son of
a bourgeois nationalist who financed a plot to kill Lenin in 1918.

The Czech press was outraged. "Gross falsification of history," said
the Catholic press. "I am bitter," wrote a trade-union journalist. The
socialist daily confessed to "awkward feelings" and a faint hope that
the whole Soviet response was a fraternal joke. Radio Prague termed it
"beneath dignity."

The man-in-the-street was interviewed. A chauffeur said: "Everything the Masaryks did was filled with humanity. Everyone in this land
loved them." A woman said: "This is the last straw!" A middle-aged
man said: "If the Russians had dropped a bomb on the Prague Castle,
they couldn't have made the Czech people angrier."

A professor of history named Bohumil Černý said: "How could

they? After three hundred years of Austro-Hungarian repression, Thomas Masaryk was the first and only man to realize what had to be done to make a state here. He was a towering figure, a humanitarian, a philosopher who knew his Plato. . . . Our youth worships him, even though they've had no access to his major writings."

Both Masaryks had been non-persons for two decades, but, starting with the pilgrimages to Lány in March, Czechoslovakia was experiencing a 1968 "Masaryk Revival."

In Prague, tram and train conductors started calling out Central Station by its old name "Masaryk Station," though the old name was never officially restored. T. G. Masaryk's bust was returned to the pantheon of the National Museum. Miroslav Galuška's Ministry of Culture and Information set to work reopening the former Masaryk Library in Prague. Most of the library's inventory was recovered from the off-shelf collections of other libraries. But a few of the more valuable items, which had been taken into "personal custody" by high Communist bureaucrats, turned up in second-hand bookstores (*Antiqvariats*) to which their "custodians" had peddled them for personal profit. The dealers had hoarded these treasures with loving care, and in 1968 they returned them, *gratis,* in excellent condition.

A Marxist philosopher's tribute, *Tomáš G. Masaryk,* by Dr. Milan Machovec, was published with this quote from its subject as a frontispiece: "No matter what stand you take, I shall not leave you in peace." Its first printing of 14,000 copies sold out in one morning.

This was the Masaryk Revival of 1968. For some older Czechs, though, two double-takes in a lifetime were too many. Under the heading of "UNBELIEVABLE!", *Agricultural News* reported this incident from an elementary school at Hodkovice-nad-Mohelkou:

> After visiting a family where he saw a bust of T. G. Masaryk, Mr. Oldřich Hyč, the headmaster, told his teaching staff: "We have rehabilitated Masaryk. Now we may just as well rehabilitate Hitler."

The teachers, the story added, dissociated themselves from the statement and took a vote of no-confidence in the headmaster.

The official seal of rehabilitation came when Ludvík Svoboda, on his first stay at the President's country estate in Lány, placed a wreath on T. G. Masaryk's grave. Then Prague's evening paper ran an article that began "Local people in Lány say that so many people haven't been to their village since T. G. Masaryk's days" and went on to say:

Local people judged the occupants of the chateau mainly by their cordiality and popularity with the neighbors. President Masaryk used to mix, talk to, and help local people. President Beneš used to get there only seldom. President Gottwald would often spend the whole summer there, but the walls of the park were then furnished with barbed wire and other entanglements, some of which President [Antonín] Zápotocký (1953–1957) ordered torn down. President Zápotocký was well-liked. This was by no means true of President Novotný, who acted as if he didn't trust people. He had his own summer house at Orlík and a cottage in the park of Lány. It was in that cottage that Soviet Marshals Malinovsky, Grechko, and others were his guests.

President Svoboda visited Lány for the first time at Easter. The gatekeeper says that the President got out of the car at the gate and shook hands with him. Ice began to break step by step. The park was opened to the public. The barriers at the gate disappeared. The new President even suggested that President Masaryk's bedroom should be given its original furniture.

Reading this, my family and I made a return visit to Lány. We paid our respects at the cemetery and then wandered through the chateau's park, which envelops a crystal-clear lake and green boulevards of trees receding into the mist of a springtime sunset like history that had been erased. Hundreds of people were there, but there was ample room to be alone. For everyone on hand, taking a lovely Sunday stroll had become an act of patriotism.

Thus, when Mother Russia slandered Masaryk's memory in the spring of 1968, she insulted every citizen of the nation he founded. Even the American Family Levy felt offended, but that was all we felt. It didn't occur to us then that the resuscitation of the Masaryk case would drive the pan-Slavism of the Russians and the Czechoslovaks beyond the point of no return.

DE-FEN-ES-TRA'-TION *noun.* The act of throwing out of a window, or the result of or subjection to such an act: used specifically with reference to a mode of executing popular vengeance practiced in Bohemia in the later Middle Ages. [<L. *de,* out of + *fenestra,* window]

—Funk & Wagnalls

de-fen-es-tra-tion (dē fen/ i strā/ shən), *n.* the act of throwing a person or thing out of a window: *the defenestration of the commissioners at Prague.*

—Random House Dictionary

So much has been written in the West about how Foreign Minister Jan Masaryk's broken body was found in the courtyard of the Černín

Palace in the early hours of 10 March 1948, two weeks after Czechoslovakia went Communist, that it is almost presumptuous for one who lives in Czechoslovakia to chime in at this late date. If you read the two most authoritative books on the subject,* you will know more than you'll want to know about:

   . . . The mysterious emissary from one "Major Chlumsky," who may or may not have warned Jan Masaryk not to go to his apartment in the Foreign Ministry that night.

   . . . The night duty officer of the Černín Palace who was locked into his office and whose telephone went dead between 2315 and 0210 hours.

   . . . The unnatural fates of virtually everyone connected with the case. The night duty officer was imprisoned for treason from 1949 to 1960. Vladomír Clementis, Masaryk's Communist deputy and successor, was hanged with Communist Party Secretary-General Rudolf Slánský in 1952; when Clementis' widow asked for her husband's ashes, she was told they'd been tossed down a drain at Pankrác prison. The police driver who'd responded to the first call (and found the Communist Minister of Interior already at the scene of the crime) was imprisoned for two years and given no reason other than that he'd "been punished as a warning." The criminologist who investigated the case became a truck loader soon thereafter; in what appears to have been a case of mistaken identity, his brother was arrested and executed. And the police surgeon who examined Masaryk's body died at Prague police headquarters, where, according to the official statement, he mistakenly gave himself an injection of gasoline. When his wife asked to see his body, her request was denied. She persisted—and committed suicide soon after.

   . . . The official communique issued toward noon on 10 March 1948. It gave the time of death as 0630 (several hours after the body was found) and said that Masaryk "committed suicide" in a fit of "sudden insanity" brought on by "reproachful telegrams from his former

---

* *Too Strong for Fantasy,* the 1967 autobiography of the novelist Marcia Davenport, who thought she was going to marry Jan Masaryk and was waiting for him in London when he died (New York: Chas. Scribner's Sons), and *The Masaryk Case,* by Claire Sterling (New York: Harper & Row, 1970). Mrs. Sterling bases much of her case on excrements that were found on Masaryk's bathroom window sill. *"People who commit suicide do not lose control of their bowels,"* she writes in italics, while, *in the final stages of violent suffocation, people do.* She theorizes that, after failing to defenestrate the struggling Masaryk, his murderers smothered him with a pillow and pushed him out the window.

friends in England and America" condemning his "manly and patriotic attitude" toward staying on for a while under the Communists.

Then, one day in the spring of 1968, a man named Vítězslav Kadlčák walked into a Prague newspaper office and said he was "Major Chlumský," a wartime courier between the Czechoslovak underground and Masaryk when the latter had been living in exile in London. With him, Kadlčák brought a file of documents, and added that he had in his possession still others, including one incriminating Major Schramm, who was, he said, an NKVD agent. Kadlčák, alias Chlumský, also appeared on a three-part Czechoslovak Television "special" on the Masaryk case: "Helping the Prosecution," it was called. He was a chunky, loquacious proletarian sort who, whenever he wanted to make a point, would jab his interviewer with a finger and punctuate his utterance with an emphatic "Right? Right!"

This was not, by a long shot on a winding road, the last that would be heard of Major Chlumský. But, at the time, all I noticed was that the most vehement Soviet outbursts (the second was a formal diplomatic protest against the Czech press) coincided with the introduction of Majors Schramm and Chlumský into Prague print, even though the Soviets scrupulously avoided naming either major. It was like monitoring an American strike: the crucial issues are usually omitted from any official list of grievances.

I am not a labor reporter, but I used to be a police reporter and I have always been a behaviorist. Having seen "evidence" lead many a cop and an occasional jury astray, I always kept an eye cocked for guilty behavior: the overeager witness, the evasive victim, or the tiny detail that might loom large in the light of a later revelation or an unexpected twist. And my journalistic instincts told me to keep an eye out for further mentions of the intriguing Major Chlumský.

Perhaps the psychology of the police station doesn't apply to the sanctimoniousness of great nations toward small neighbors. Or perhaps it does. By 1968, twenty years after the death of Jan Masaryk, there wasn't too much else to go on. As had become the case not long after the death of John F. Kennedy, you simply picked your theory and you ground your ax.

Having returned to Prague from Cannes, I found myself giving a guided tour to Miloš Forman of all people—a grand tour of the Prague Spring that had just been dawning when he'd left for America in late

January. I took him to watch a *hydepark,* where he wound up defending *The Firemen's Ball* against a throng of young cineastes. I took him to the store near the Charles Bridge where he could buy The London *Times* for crowns with no questions asked. "It's the last one I have today," the lady said, taking The *Times* out of the window, "but it's closing time anyway and there'll be a new batch tomorrow."

"Keep my money," Miloš told her, "and also keep The *Times* in your window. It will give many people much pleasure when they walk by here tonight."

And I took Miloš to see Dubček, whom he had glimpsed only once before—through a wine-glass darkly, as it were, in 1967 on our tipsy visit to the Hotel Without a Name.

The Central Committee was meeting at the end of May: to ratify Dubček's proposal for advancing the Fourteenth Party Congress to 9 September 1968, thereby creating the first reasonably free elections in twenty years . . . to implement other specifics of the Action Program . . . to consider several overdue rehabilitations of party members . . . and to discuss the status of various other party members, including Antonín Novotný.

Thus, on the first morning of the Central Committee session, Miloš and I walked over to the Prague Castle to watch the official cars disgorge their passengers. Forty or fifty other spectators were already standing under the archway when we arrived.

Dubček showed up early and everybody applauded him. A dozen photographers, including an American from *Look,* held their cameras aloft and snapped him making his way through the small throng. Miloš shook his hand without introducing himself, but Dubček knew who he was and said: "Where have you been?"

"In France and America," Miloš replied.

"It is good to have you back with us. Will you stay?"

"When my work is done there, I'll be here for good."

"Good," said Dubček, "it is important."

(A few mornings earlier, on the stage of the National Theatre, Dubček had addressed a gathering of Czechoslovak artistic and cultural figures: "We Communists are in favor of committed culture. But we don't want to hand out advice on what should be done and how it should be done. . . . Conditions must be created so that we may live in an atmosphere that will help expand creative thinking, fantasy, artistry, and ingenuity as well as open the door to beauty. . . .

("Today, when we are considering the new ways of our society, I should like to win you over to them. We need you and we want to make politics of such high quality that you, too, will appreciate them and require them, in the same way that *we* appreciate good art.")

When Dubček had disappeared, Miloš was able to say to me on the basis of their brief encounter: "All my instincts tell me this is a very good man, a very modest man."

"I know what you mean," I said. "For a moment, I thought he was going to ask you for your autograph."

Speaker Josef Smrkovský and Prime Minister Oldřich Černík were applauded and photographed when they arrived.

General Lomský, the old friend of Novotný's and General Šejna's, had resigned as Minister of Defense, but still held a Central Committee seat. He received a smattering of boos.

Then Antonín Novotný arrived, looking tanned and silvery. All the Czechs on hand, including Miloš, made no sound. They simply turned their backs on their former dictator.

There is no visual record of this impromptu shunning ceremony, for even the photographers turned their backs. I didn't, because I will never join a mob, even if I should happen to be on the mob's side. And certainly not when I am a guest in the country of both the mob and its target.

Witnessing this scene, though, I wanted to share it with someone, but the American photographer from *Look* had also turned his back. I nudged him and suggested it would make a marvelous photo.

"These Czech photographers are professionals," he snapped, "so they must know what they're doing."

I shrugged, and, all by myself, watched the solitary but sprightly figure of Antonín Novotný bound up the red-carpeted marble staircase and vanish into the vast Presidential apartment which used to be his home. Three-quarters of the way around the building, he would enter the neo-baroque Spanish Hall for the meeting, after pausing in the buffet for refreshments.

There, we learned later, an incident occurred to counterpoint the shunning in the courtyard. Over coffee, Novotný was left standing alone. Not even the diehard Novotnýites cared to risk associating with him. But Josef Smrkovský, who had spent a good part of the Novotný years in prison, was the one man who ventured over to chat with him.

It was Smrkovský who told about the incident later. He added that those who were snubbing their ex-President were the same men who used to pat him on the shoulder and fall over each other fetching him drinks. Smrkovský termed their rudeness "uncultured behavior . . . left over from the morals of the 1950's."

Inside the Spanish Hall, it was Dubček who took off the gloves. "Without the holding of an extraordinary Fourteenth Party Congress," he warned, "there can be no guarantee that the new policy is being firmly implemented. . . . Moreover, it was stated at regional conferences that comrades who lost confidence must leave the Central Committee without delay. Mr. Novotný was explicitly mentioned in this respect."

Novotný balked not only at resigning, but also at another item on the agenda: full posthumous rehabilitation of the executed Rudolf Slánský. He even cast vague doubts on the absolute innocence of Slánský and Vlado Clementis, who died on the gallows with him.

Two Slovak orators then rose to rebut him.

A woman who had been associated with Clementis read the former Foreign Minister's last letter, in which he wrote that his impending fate would be "legalized murder." Clementis also said: "I am a lawyer and a Communist and I harbor no illusions."

A stocky, gray-faced man—whose pursed lips and half-rimmed glasses remind one of a dentist who doesn't believe in novocaine—delivered the *coup de grâce*. He was Deputy Premier Gustáv Husák, a Bratislava lawyer who had spent the first half of the Novotný years (1954–1960) in prison as a "bourgeois nationalist." According to the Slovak novelist Ladislav Mňačko, "Husák left his cell with one ambition: to destroy the man who had put him there."

Husák, who scarcely seems to move his lips, but waves his arms a great deal, can be a frighteningly effective speaker. Relating his own experiences almost in a monotone, he concluded explosively:

"I have absolutely no doubt about the political responsibility of Antonín Novotný for the brutal reprisals of the 1950's, for the jailing of innocent Communists, for the cheating on rehabilitations, and for the torture of thousands. Honest people can now join the party only if people like Novotný get out of it."

Antonín Novotný asked for the floor and offered to resign from the

Central Committee. But the two speeches had swayed the Central Committee so drastically that it refused to accept his resignation and expelled him instead.

Then, along with those of six other officials of the 1950's, Novotný's party membership was suspended pending full clarification of his role in the trials. The former President of the Republic and First Secretary of the Communist Party was thereupon asked to leave the Spanish Hall in which he had reigned, but not without first surrendering his membership card, please.

The ambitious politician bent on revenge is in an enviable position once he plants his foot on the ladder. Unhindered by ideology, he has nowhere to go but up, particularly as old enemies start to topple. In the chain-smoking, popular, and sometimes demagogic personality of Gustáv Husák, fifty-five, the Czechoslovak Revolution had spawned an unfettered "realist" who would ultimately rise to meet any occasion. Much of this would be done in the name of "Slovak nationalism," which is usually described, along with his hatred for Novotný, as Gustáv Husák's other unquenchable passion. As a hero and historian of the Slovak uprising of 1944, Husák's sincerity as a Slovak nationalist was unquestionable.

A "harsh presence, with eyes as barren as potholes," Husák has been described by a close colleague thusly: "He gives the impression that he has no idea what joy and spontaneity are. His usual reaction to levity is to frown and readjust his glasses, as though to cover his inability to participate in social exchanges. He is so careful and skeptical [that] it is difficult to reach any agreement with him, but once this is accomplished, he makes every effort to keep its terms." *

I had not (and still have not) met Gustáv Husák, though I was fated to watch him on TV often and, on a May Day yet to come, see him take Dubček's old place on the reviewing stand. Therefore, my knowledge of him is little more than public knowledge, plus two additional tidbits: one semi-exclusive, the other little-noted.

. . . During 1968, I went on a Foreign Ministry press junket to one of several trade fairs that are held every year in the Moravian city of Brno. At breakfast, Thomas Hamilton, a *New York Times* man based

---

* Quoted from an article "In Czechoslovakia Today," by Peter C. Newman, editor-in-chief of The Toronto *Daily Star*. Newman spent his boyhood in Czechoslovakia. Published in The Boston *Sunday Globe* 19 April 1970.

in Geneva, and I found ourselves sharing a press table with a British economics writer and retired Royal Navy commander named Edgar P. Young. Even then, when Husák was still a popular Czechoslovak liberal and "Dubček man," Commander Young was viewing him with two decades of trepidation:

"I met the chap just after the war [in the Beneš days when Husák was a Communist member of the coalition Slovak Board of Commissioners] and I dare say it was the most anti-Semitic interview I've ever had with anybody. The funny thing was: I don't think Dr. Husák had any innate feeling one way or the other about the Jews. But he said that the Jews who were coming back to Slovakia were creating a serious economic problem. He actually *blamed* them for coming out of the concentration camps *alive* and pinching Slovak jobs and property.

"Of course, this was because the Slovaks, on the assumption that all their Jews were dead, had already pinched the Jews' property."

. . . The other person I met in 1968 who had unkind words for Husák was none other than his ally and mentor, Alexander Dubček. Not that Dubček spoke these words to me; he wrote them, in 1959, for a Slovak party periodical called *Hlas Ludu* (*Voice of the People*).* Paying tribute to Slovak party members who were imprisoned or executed by the Nazis, Dubček wrote:

> These arrests . . . allowed nationalistically minded people like Husák and Novomeský† to take over the leadership of the Slovak Communist Party. These men were concerned, in 1943, to retain their links with the bourgeoisie and even to ask the help of the bourgeoisie. This hindered the development of the Partisan movement.

It was an unjust accusation published at a most unfashionable time, soon after Husák's life sentence had been commuted and a few months before he was due for release from prison. It was also a time when even the most deluded Communists had recognized the imprisoning of Husák as a disgrace to the party. Why Dubček, who had refused to make such an attack in 1953 when it was fashionable, chose to do it then remains a mystery. The best explanation I have heard was that 1959 was a time when Dubček was disoriented by having been in Moscow when Stalinism was discredited and returning to Czechoslovakia to find it still rampant and reigning.

---

* Vol. 6, issue no. 34.
† Laco Novomeský, Slovak poet and Communist; close friend of Husák's; a member of the Slovak Communist Party Presidium from 1969 to 1971.

Nowadays, whenever I read or hear that Husák has "done in" Dubček, I'm inclined to agree—but my own sense of theatre keeps reminding me that Dubček had once (and probably only once) hit a man when he was down.

At the time in 1968, though, when Miloš and I stood outside the May meeting of the Central Committee, one would not have named Husák as the greatest threat to Dubček. Dubček's highest-ranking "conservative" opponent was Vasil Bil'ak (pronounced *Bill-yak*), fifty, who had become the party's First Secretary in Slovakia and a Presidium member only when Dubček had moved up to the pinnacle of party power.

"EVERYBODY CANNOT BE DUBČEK" was the caption of one 1968 cartoon showing the stocky, dark-haired Bil'ak (who looks like a punchy, shifty Herblock version of Nixon) trying to model his rangy predecessor's wardrobe. The contrast became even more severe at the Central Committee session when Bil'ak, a fumbling speaker, rose to blame Masaryk and Beneš for the rise of Hitler; proceeded to absolve Soviet advisers of any role in Czechoslovakia's ordeal of the 1950's by quoting a denial from Stalin himself; and then concluded:

"We should pause to examine what is happening in this country. Why has Czechoslovakia suddenly become the idol of a wide range of persons from the Vatican to Bonn? Our working people are deeply disquieted by the growth of anti-socialist forces. Socialism can be constructed only on the principles of Marxism-Leninism. Only the Communist Party can be its leading force."

As of the first of June, Bil'ak was still paying lip service to the Extraordinary Party Congress scheduled for September. He said it could become "one of the milestones of consolidation." But he warned that "it could cause great harm to the party and the state if it were to be prepared in the atmosphere of today," an atmosphere (and a congress) that Vasil Bil'ak was to play no small part in destroying.

The conservatives were fighting a delaying action. On the day when Presidium member Oldřich Švestka, the dogmatic editor-in-chief of *Rudé Právo*, took his turn presiding over the Central Committee session, the liberals literally did not get a word in edgewise. Only conservative speakers were recognized by the chair. But Švestka's day served to dramatize a power struggle that he was losing within *Rudé Právo*, where a "Vote of Confidence" had gone against him by 67 to 1. Švestka was on the way out—his ouster slowed only by word from Moscow that it would be taken as an international affront.

The Dubček leadership was treading gingerly wherever the Kremlin was concerned—sidestepping any looming confrontation simply by turning to some other overdue reform or else granting Moscow some unimportant concession that would buy Prague time toward realizing its long-range goals.

Ever since the Liberation Eve scare, Russia had been sending delegations of persuaders to Czechoslovakia. Marshal Grechko, the tall, ham-handed, and humorless Soviet Minister of Defense, had landed at Ruzyně airport with seven other high officers. They came "to meet the new leadership of the Czechoslovak Army, to exchange experience, and to discuss questions which interest the two parties."

One member of Grechko's delegation was General Yepishev, the chief ideological officer of the Soviet Army. Having been quoted by *Le Monde* as saying that the Soviet Army stood ready to come to the rescue of loyal Czechoslovak Communists, General Yepishev was a focal point of Prague interest. No sooner had he stepped off the plane than he was intercepted by Duňa Havlíčková, a journalist from Czechoslovak Television who thrust a microphone before his mouth and asked him whether the quote was true.

General Yepishev, a plump little man laden with medals, looked around for the kind of help that would have been forthcoming had such a question been popped at him in Moscow. When nobody would rescue him from the journalist, he tried to brush her away. But everywhere that General Yepishev went at the airport, Miss Havlíčková was there too, with her persistent question. Cameras recorded this remarkable comic *pas de deux* and it was shown on that night's 7 o'clock TV News. Miss Havlíčková succeeded in bullying General Yepishev into replying, reassuringly if not candidly: "It is a stupid thing."

Later in the official visit, Speaker Josef Smrkovský asked Yepishev the same question. Smrkovský reported the conversation while being interviewed on Czechoslovak Radio:

"We were having a talk, a very gay talk. We had a good laugh both of us. General Yepishev categorically denied the authenticity of the statement attributed to him by the French *Le Monde*. He said he wished to know how much the Czech journalist got for spreading the false report here."

The Catholic newspaper *People's Democracy* saw this banter as no laughing matter:

> This . . . may be interpreted in two ways. Did General Yepishev mean how many months (of imprisonment, presumably) or how many dollars had the journalist been given? No matter how it was meant, the question touches upon the honesty of Czechoslovak journalists. Nor was it right for Mr. Smrkovský to treat the matter in the way he did. There is very little to laugh about when it is reported that a Power is to intervene. . . . The Czechoslovak press merely quoted the report, giving the source of it, which was the only right thing to do. Laughter of two men will not rectify a grave matter which causes much public anxiety in this country.

A few hours after Grechko's group had touched down in Prague, Soviet Prime Minister Alexei Kosygin had landed—in the company of his daughter Irina—to take the waters at Carlsbad. There, he undertook a "ten-day stomach cure," which he managed to compress into four days and sandwich between conferences with Dubček and Černík in Prague. Dubček and Černík also paid one flying visit to Kosygin while he was in Carlsbad. Both sides worked at maintaining the official pretense that Kosygin's visit was non-political. When asked why he and Černík were flying to Carlsbad, Dubček replied wryly: "As good hosts, we are coming for a visit."

For every one of his four mornings in Carlsbad, Kosygin could be seen filling his pitcher at the hot spring and then sipping while he strolled along the Teplá canal. Although it was late spring, the weather had turned cool and the affable-looking Soviet Prime Minister, sporting a semi-Smrkovský crew-cut, usually wore a dark overcoat and a pearl-gray homburg with a speckled silk band. A recent widower, Kosygin was accompanied only by his daughter, or so it seemed. But when an American journalist came upon him and said "Good morning, Mr. Kosygin!", another Russian promenader stepped between the two men and said in English: "No questions to the Prime Minister."

The only journalist to put any questions to Kosygin had been General Yepishev's nemesis, Duňa Havlíčková. Kosygin granted her a ten-minute interview on one condition: no politics. Their on-camera talk was mostly amiable chit-chat about the weather in Czechoslovakia and the glories of Carlsbad, but it did achieve a slight edge when Havlíčková complained that he had kept her waiting for three days.

"Well," said Prime Minister Kosygin, "I feared that the interview would disturb my rest."

"But you must understand," Havlíčková explained, "that this was the only way that our people would get to see you while you were here."

Kosygin had been an understanding man, and this was the impression he left not only with Czechoslovakia's TV viewers, but also with their political leaders. The official communique had described his three meetings with them as "held in a cordial and comradely atmosphere." The Prague grapevine, still active, had it that in exchange for the sympathetic Kosygin's pledge to argue, not just plead, their case in the Kremlin, the Czechoslovaks had agreed to:

. . . Allow only Communists to fill key government positions, especially in the security services. (This could be lived with for a while because, thus far, all of the high reformers were Communists.)

. . . Bar opposition parties and political groups. (This was a threat to KAN's long-range plans, but it could still function as a club until the right moment came.)

. . . Consult with Moscow and other Eastern allies before making any major political move toward the West, especially West Germany. (No *political* moves were contemplated; only *economic*.)

. . . Strengthen security on the Western borders; permit regular Warsaw Pact inspections of these arrangements; and sanction a week of "limited Warsaw Pact maneuvers"—involving 10,000 to 12,000 infantry and signal troops who would enter the country unarmed—during the month of June.

To the Czechs' and Slovaks' dismay, the first Russian troops started arriving in late May on the very day when the Central Committee was considering Novotný's ouster. The men of these "advance parties" were unarmed, but this wasn't true of the tanks and fighter planes they unexpectedly brought with them. And, as the ground convoys rumbled through Slovakian and Bohemian villages, observers noted that there also seemed to be more men than the number specified.

The Czechoslovak Ministry of Defense kept a tight official lip. The actual number of men was a "military secret"; so was the starting date of the weeklong maneuvers, which would be announced only twenty-four hours in advance.

"Nothing was said about foreign tanks participating in the maneuvers," a reporter remarked at the Ministry's press briefing.

"There are no motorized infantry units without tanks in any modern army," said the official spokesman, a general. "They serve as direct infantry support. Besides, there are only a few of them in the current exercise."

The same answer applied to the air support. The reporters asked whether the Soviet troops were contemplating a prolonged or permanent stay. The general snapped back: "Of course not."

"Then why did the Soviet officers bring women with them?"

"The women are civilian employees. This is a normal thing in every army, Czechoslovakia's, too. There are only a few of them in the current exercise."

A Russian general named Zhadov visited a barracks of Czechoslovakia troops to brief them on the impending maneuvers. According to one enlisted man who complained to *Literární Listy,* General Zhadov used almost the same words that had been attributed to General Yepishev in assuring his unnerved audience that the whole Red Army stood ready if called upon to come to the aid of good Czechoslovak Communists. During a question period, General Zhadov had remarked that the internal political situation here was not quite clear to him. But he understood "that negative forces are misusing the revival process as a weapon against socialism."

With an unknown number of Russian soldiers on their soil professing all sorts of friendship, the Czechoslovak hosts mustered a hospitable front. In the village of Holice, citizens welcomed each convoy passing through with boxes of chocolate and a book about East Bohemia. In Trutnov, the gateway to the Giant Mountains, the same delegation of townsfolk who greeted their Russian liberators with a bouquet of lilacs in 1945 stood waiting with fresh lilacs in 1968. Nearby, a Soviet Army truck that missed a curve and sank its wheels into a ditch was pulled back onto the road by a farmer's tractor and an entire hamlet's willing hands.

The maneuvers didn't start until the last week in June. Dubček and Černík formally welcomed Soviet Marshal Yakubovsky, the Warsaw Pact commander-in-chief. General Svoboda donned his uniform for the first time since he was elected President and inspected Marshal Yakubovsky's honor guard.

The next morning, President Svoboda took Marshal Yakubovsky with him to a friendship rally in the agora of Vimperk, the ruined Gothic mountain village that had so depressed us on our March tour.

By June, Vimperk was being restored, the market re-opened, and the outlook of its citizens re-vitalized. But Marshal Yakubovsky couldn't have cared less. To him, it was a strategic outpost near the West German border.

After lunch, the President took the Marshal to inspect a Frontier Guard unit on the border. The guards presented each of their guests with an Alsatian puppy. Svoboda thanked them warmly and took his puppy home to the Castle with him: "I will give it to my grandson."

Yakubovsky left his puppy in the custody of the border guards: "I will ask about it in due course." He didn't say when.

Josef Smrkovský and nine National Assembly deputies paid a ten-day goodwill visit to Moscow to "learn what our hosts think and make good use of the good things and avoid the bad ones." Without compromises, however, for Smrkovský insisted: "We shall not stop halfway or disappoint the hopes we have aroused."

In the Kremlin, Smrkovský's group outlined the trend of events back home. According to the grapevine (openly published in Prague) the Russian leaders listened politely and then told Smrkovský they had information of their own about "some negative aspects of the Czechoslovak mass media." The meeting quickly deteriorated into a wrangle. Leonid Brezhnev blubbered tearfully that Russia bore nothing but goodwill toward Czechoslovakia. But Soviet President Nikolai Podgorny warned against elements that "would like to drive a wedge between our countries" and then lectured the Czechs and Slovaks on what ungrateful poor relations they were.

"Your economists should do some calculating," Podgorny told Smrkovský, "and explain on your radio and television that . . . the Soviet Union sends grain to Czechoslovakia even at times of bad harvest when we have to buy from the capitalist countries with our gold." Then, with no humor intended, Podgorny added: "*Our* people *never* complain, not to the Central Committee, not to the Supreme Soviet, not to the Government."

Upon his return home, Smrkovský related these conversations in great detail both privately and publicly. And he warned some friends that "we must not underestimate the fears of the Soviet Union. It has in mind not only Czechoslovakia, but the security of the whole socialist camp. Despite all this, the Soviet comrades declared that they don't want to and will not interfere in our internal affairs." Nevertheless, he added, "activities of non-socialist groups" were being "very closely watched" by various socialist embassies in Prague.

A reporter remarked to Speaker Smrkovský that he was spending more time with high-level Russians like General Yepishev and Prime Minister Kosygin than his Czechoslovak constituents might want him to.

"Look," said Smrkovský. "My attitude toward the Soviet Union was formed long before I became a member of the party Presidium. Even after I returned from five years' imprisonment in the Fifties, I still remained a Communist and a friend of the Soviet Union. Whether I am to survive politically will be decided by people voting for or against me. But I won't court popularity by pounding the Soviet Union. I'll remain the same as I used to be, no matter whether you like it or not."

Freedom's Word, the socialist newspaper, surveyed its 38,000 readers, half of whom turned out to be Communist Party members. Nine out of ten favored a strong opposition party or several opposition parties rather than fusion in the Communist-dominated National Front. But Dubček, knowing that this would be a sore spot with the Russians, had taken the tack that an opposition could not be considered until democracy had been developed *within* the Communist Party. And Smrkovský, just back from Moscow, took Dubček's side:

"The problem of having an opposition party in this country is different from the West, where one kind of political structure favors the existing order while the other advocates a change. In this country, only one social order is possible now and in the future: socialism. If anybody wants to call this undemocratic, he is free to do so. But we openly declare that it cannot be otherwise."

Another reporter wanted to talk economics wih Smrkovský: "Mr. Speaker, iron ore from Krivoi Rog in the Soviet Union is transported here from a distance of 3,600 miles. It contains 23 per cent iron. Deposits, say, in Sweden, are much nearer and contain 80 per cent iron. Isn't our economy ailing precisely because of these details?"

"I know what you're talking about," Smrkovský replied. "And I know that things can be arranged so we don't import dirt but concentrated iron. Still, what's happening in this country mustn't bypass Krivoi Rog. We have our experience and we know that economic relations with the Soviet Union are a safety factor we don't propose to disrupt. But we'd like to make better use of them."

"Then why," the reporter asked, "shouldn't Czechoslovakia accept foreign loans from the West?"

These were being negotiated, but the conversation might prove so touchy to his country's Soviet "benefactors" that Smrkovský shifted the subject: "I'm convinced that our progress can become highly attractive for other nations. Many of their people will come to see it through their own eyes. I expect a tremendous upsurge in foreign tourists this year."

"Let's hope the tourists won't wear helmets," said the interviewer.

"Oh, no! I don't believe this would happen," Smrkovský responded. "Every morning, I am reading what the world says about us. . . . And I highly appreciate it that the [foreign] journalists have stopped looking for sensations in our country and have started to realize that something great is in the making here."

His interviewer said: "A French reporter told me that, if the West—and especially France—doesn't do the utmost to help us without political strings attached, it will be guilty of yet another Munich."

"Exactly!" Smrkovský exclaimed. "I should like to thank your friend for those words. Our nation's profound influence on European history goes back to the Hussite period."

"But Hussitism was harshly suppressed."

"I know. It is a joke we sometimes make among ourselves. We say that we should not like to end up in Konstanz"—where Jan Hus was burned at the stake after winning a safe-conduct from oppressors who denounced his heresy.

As the prolific and candid interviews with Smrkovský continued, *Literární Listy* poked fun at him with a cartoon that showed Smrkovský murmuring into a hundred microphones: "Strictly between you and me. . . ." Smrkovský asked the cartoonist for an autographed copy of the original drawing.

Another candidate for honors in consuming Prague newsprint was the party's popular ideologist, Čestmír Císař. Boyish, crew-cut, and bullet-headed with black horn-rimmed glasses, Císař was emerging as the Arthur Schlesinger, Jr. of the Dubček era. He had a pithy analytic pronouncement for every occasion. Announcing the full exoneration of the *Literární Noviny* crew which had been punished after the 1967 Writers Congress, Císař said their only "offense" had been to advocate "too early" what "we all wish now." * While the Russians railed at official tolerance of the press, Císař rebuked "certain leading officials" for "not speaking out in the press, radio and television often enough. The party Presidium has instructed the Communist members of the Government to maintain maximum contacts with the mass media." But, like Smrkovský, Císař was opposed to the idea of an opposition party:

"A new party with the mission of being in opposition . . . would mean the end of the Czechoslovak experiment in creating a model of democratic socialism. A plurality of political parties fighting for power would be against the needs and interests of the people. It would open the way to a return to capitalism, calling to life the danger of a violent clash and the necessity to defend socialism by force."

Several fears were implicit in Dubček's, Smrkovský's, and Císař's opposition to an opposition. With near unanimity, their people had embraced them and thus greased the path for urgent, drastic reforms. But, if there was any counterforce to offset the impact of these men, it was the public's quiet antipathy toward communism, an aversion which absolute freedom of choice might tempt a victim to express at any cost. If an Ivan Sviták were to harangue the Czechs with his theories and some Slovak demagogue were to play upon his land's inferiority complex, the people just might cut off Dubček's nose to spite socialism's face, not because it was a human face, but because it belonged to socialism.

The leaders knew, though, that it would never come to this. Russia simply would not allow it to happen. And, in a showdown, Czechoslovakia would certainly stand alone. Already, "spheres of influence" were being rattled and there were rumors that Lyndon Johnson—in his consuming quest to leave office honorably with either a settlement in Vietnam or a triumphant summit meeting or both—was "playing spheres" with the Kremlin. The Italian newspaper *Stampa* contended in mid-May that the U.S. and U.S.S.R. had already exchanged several messages concerning Czechoslovakia. According to *Stampa,* Russia had assured America that present Soviet policy ruled out any armed intervention in Czechoslovakia. And *Stampa* said that America had declared

---

* The editors themselves expressed surprise when the officials who handed back their party cards in 1968 were the same ones who had gloatingly confiscated the cards in 1967.

it would neither meddle in Czechoslovak internal affairs nor exhort Czechoslovakia to quit the Warsaw Pact.

Thirty years earlier, the Munich betrayal had taught the Czechs a painful lesson in how little their own sovereignty meant to their Big Power enemies or friends. Even so, in 1968, the most anonymous of all Czechs—the sidewalk or wallside graffiti artist—chose his words carefully. To the occasional chalked or painted signs which used to say "U.S. GO HOME" were now appended "FROM VIETNAM; U.S.S.R. GO HOME FROM CZECHOSLOVAKIA." One day, however, my family encountered the last unamended "AMERICANS GO HOME" sign in Prague on their way back from the New World playground.

"But Mommy," said Monica, who had just begun to read, "we *are* going home!"

Russia, on the other hand, was heading toward the point of no return. On Karl Marx's 150th birthday, Čestmír Císař delivered a routine address in Prague, during which he said: "There are such social conditions in this country today that we cannot continue preserving an outdated political system. The dictatorship of the proletariat, regardless of its correct features or aberrations, has exhausted its historical possibilities and functions. Czechoslovakia must search and find a new alternative political system. And genuinely Marxist thinking will help us in it."

For his tribute, Císař was denounced in Moscow's *Pravda* on 14 June, 1968, as "the last of a long line of revisionists, Trotskyites, right-wing Social Democrats, and Jesuits." Císař a Jesuit! In a land where the Jesuits had been the church of the Habsburg oppressors for three centuries, the Russians couldn't have outraged the Czechs more if they'd called T. G. Masaryk a terrorist—which they had already done. But this attack carried particular weight for a number of reasons. It was given generous and prominent space in *Pravda*. Its author was Academician F. Konstantinov, the long-time official propagator of Stalin's theology; and it was the first time a specific member of the new Czechoslovak leadership had been directly and personally attacked by the Russians.

Císař replied coolly and impersonally that Konstantinov "took one half-sentence and one quarter-sentence from the speech on the Karl Marx anniversary; joined them; and insinuated to the author intentions which he has never advocated, taking advantage of the fact that

Soviet readers had not seen the text of the original speech and could not check what the authentic statements were." To the music of the Prague Spring, the Russian leadership was now turning something worse than a deaf ear—a distorted ear trumpet that amplified only the most guttural sounds.

The political metaphors were often cultural that spring. Discussing the responsibilities that the "leading role" of the Communist Party incurred, Dubček's new Minister of Agriculture, Josef Borůvka (the name means "blueberry"), likened the party "to a conductor. The conductor doesn't know how to play all the instruments used in his orchestra. And yet, when conducting, he must recognize which of the instruments are playing badly. But the thing for the conductor to do is not to go and start playing the instrument himself. He must replace the bad player with a good one."

Similarly, Bratislava's *Pravda* editorialized:

> Czechoslovakia must not assume the role of a "Messiah" in the "orchestra of socialist countries." We do not wish to be either the drummer or first violinist, or to sing in unison. Czechoslovak foreign policy will apparently play in polyphony, according to its own score.

Even "Prague Spring," the name the world gave to the Dubček era, had a double meaning for Czechs. For Prague Spring (*Pražské Jaro*) is a traditional monthlong music festival here, featuring such names as David Oistrakh and Elizabeth Schwarzkopf, the Amsterdam Concertgebouw and the Berlin Philharmonic. Prague Spring always ends with Beethoven's Ninth and begins with Bedřich Smetana's *My Country*.

The Charles University weekly, *Student,* was exchanging invective with the Soviet Minister of Education, who claimed to have read in *Student* that it favored having "nothing to do with the Communist Party." *Student* replied that it had said no such thing and consequently the Minister

> is not speaking the truth. . . . Perhaps we *are* stray sheep. But, if the Russian Minister really wants to comment on us, he would do better to come and visit us to hear and see for himself.

On second thought, *Student* editorialized, the Minister had acted so obtusely that "we are not quite sure an official visit would be of help to him."

Student's cheeky style characterized the daily and nightly *hyde-*

parks in Old Town Square; the occasional offshoots near the Mácha statue and on a downtown boulevard, where a pair of newlyweds pitched a tent and honeymooned together to protest the housing shortage; and the dialogue in the student coffeehouses. At one of them, Jan Němec filmed (for his documentary) an American folk-guitarist teaching some Czech students to sing "We Shall Overcome." As soon as the students had an elemental mastery of the song, they began improvising their own additional lyrics, and when they chanted *"We are Dubček's children!"*, even the camera was almost overcome with emotion.

Signs and slogans took on a distinct anti-Soviet flavor. Old official graffiti, quoting Klement Gottwald's proclamation "WITH THE SO-VIET UNION FOREVER!", were still visible, with this postscript appended: "—BUT NOT A DAY LONGER!" Newer signs read "LONG LIVE THE SOVIET UNION—BUT ON ITS OWN MONEY!" . . . "FOURTEEN MILLION CZECHS + SLOVAKS ARE SUB-SIDIZING THE LARGEST UNDERDEVELOPED COUNTRY IN THE WORLD!"

At 10 o'clock one night in Prague's former Masaryk Station (now Central Station), there was a small explosion and then a burst balloon released a shower of leaflets warning against "a return to the days of the fascist puppets Masaryk and Hácha." Similar materials were dropped by an unmarked low-flying plane onto the boulevard that leads from our house to the Bílá Hora (White Mountain) battlefield; they littered the roadway for half-an-hour, whereupon a special sanitation crew appeared. Mailboxes were stuffed with attacks on "revisionists who have crept into the party and state apparatus."

There were other incidents in the hinterlands of Bohemia, Moravia, and Slovakia, where the democratic tide was not yet abreast of Prague's, though it was rising rapidly. But country reflexes, ingrained with twenty years of bad political habits, could not shift with the lightning swivel of a chair in a Prague café, where intellectuals had been whispering truths and heresies to each other for a generation. Thus, at some district and regional party conferences, journalists covering the meetings were still occasionally denounced, heckled, and—in one instance—banished from the hall.

The journalists, however, were riding an irresistible wave of free expression. New journals were being organized by all the political parties that were hitherto silent partners in the lopsided National Front.

These parties had their own daily newspapers, but now they were founding independent weeklies whose editors talked hopefully of having "the same detachment from the daily operation that The Sunday *Times* has from the London *Times.*" The People's Party was founding a new organ to be called *Restoration.* The trade unions were reviving a popular pre-1948 periodical called *World of Work.* Even the Club of Involved Nonparty Members (KAN), for all its troubles, was negotiating with two more respectable organizations to collaborate on a new weekly.

Sylva's new employer, the Melantrich Publishing House of the Socialist Party, was budgeting a press run of 80,000 copies for the 4 September debut of *Zítřek.* Sylva had vaguely remembered and I had never known that *Zítřek* was actually a "cultural continuation" of a distinguished pre-1948 journal called *Free Tomorrow.*

One day, Igor Hájek, the foreign editor of *Literární Listy,* phoned to inform me joyously that *"Literární Listy* is doomed!" He paused to allow me a moment of shocked silence before he added: "In October, we're reverting to our old name of *Literární Noviny.* And we're becoming the weekly supplement of a *new* afternoon daily called *Lidové Noviny* (People's News)."

Igor went on to explain that *"new* is one of those words in Czech that often means *very old.* A newspaper called *Lidové Noviny* used to be the most respected daily of the 1930's in Prague. Karel Čapek was a regular contributor and so was President Masaryk himself for a little while.

"The new *Lidové Noviny* will be a daily of at least eight pages, with our *Literární Noviny* as a Sunday supplement of twenty-four to thirty-two pages. Once a month, we'll publish a foreign version in either English or French with highlights of our most important articles."

"Is it definite, Igor?" I asked.

"Everything is set editorially," he replied. "Our last remaining obstacle is real estate. You've been to our office on Bethlehem Street. It's just barely big enough for *LL,* so we have to find a headquarters that'll house two *LNs.*"

Meanwhile, *Literární Listy,* having completed its installments of the memoirs of Rudolf Slánský's widow, was now serializing Isaac Deutscher's biography of Trotsky. And, as if this were not infuriating enough, A. J. Liehm, one of *LL's* more outspoken editors (and a victim of the 1967 Writers Congress purge) was telling a Congress of the Journalists Union:

"I am not really interested in the pronouncements of those who cannot stomach the freedom of the press. With them, the dilemma is simple. Either they'll win, in which case more than just the free press will disappear from this country's life. Or else they'll lose.

"I am more interested in what the so-called progressives say. They seem to suggest that the free press is needed to serve the renascent process better, that socialism needs the freedom of the press for its own improvement. Very well, socialism needs the press. But does the press need socialism? If so, what for?

"The press . . . did not come into being for the sake of socialism. Industry, agriculture, justice, none of them came into being for the sake of socialism. It is socialism which is to serve industrial, agricultural, judicial development—not the other way around.

"The progressive wing is unable to extricate itself from the captivity of old concepts. It still tends to regard the press as a utility, an ideological instrument, a tool of the party, the government, the system. In a way, the press is all this—but not primarily."

Declaring that the press needs socialism only "insofar as socialism can supply the press with a greater measure of freedom and independence than any other social order," Liehm concluded:

"The press is not here in the role of an applicant who begs for freedom or tolerance. The press and the journalists can offer this society only one service: the service of trying to make everybody in this country know about everything. Czechoslovak socialism can either accept this service and establish a climate for it or else refuse it, in which case it will have pronounced over itself an irrevocable and final verdict.

"Should this happen, we shall start looking for other jobs. We want to serve, but we shall not be subservient."

On the 25th of June, censorship—already suspended—was outlawed altogether. The National Assembly was presented with a surprise bill abolishing the entire censorship apparatus. Drahomír Kolder, forty-two, a beefy, coplike Presidium member, rose in outrage to ask what would protect "certain people" from being "shot down" in the mass media. He was told that the libel and slander laws already on the books were more than adequate.

Then a vote was taken: 197 in favor, 30 against, 17 abstentions. Censorship was extinct, effective that very day. The Czechoslovaks had again done what no other Communist people had ever dared to do. And with that, in the minds of their orthodox neighbors and their own conservative remnants, they had left the pale of communism.

The censors had, weeks earlier, receded into the woodwork of the society they'd terrorized. Now the Ministry of Interior, which administered the censorship apparatus on Benedict Street, had an empty building on its hands. And the Minister of the Interior, General Pavel, with sublime irony, offered the premises to the editors of *Literární Listy* as headquarters for their new daily. Not only was the symbolism perfect; so were the facilities. The editors of *Literární Listy* sent General Pavel a telegram: "MAY GOD REPAY YOU FOR THIS."

Interlude ⅃ Up against the wall in Carlsbad and Berlin

I HAD EVEN STARTED TO THINK LIKE A CZECH. WHEN A cryptic notice came from the Customs Post Office telling me to report there within a week with all my documents "including marriage certificate," I knew what it was about. Our household's 1847 Rogers Brothers silver—which my mother had shipped to us just before flying to Prague for her first visit—must have arrived at last. Any clever Customs official would immediately deduce that I was a shrewd Czech dodging import duties by pretending to receive an unsolicited wedding gift from the States.

"A thousand apologies! We thought you were a Czech!" the Customs man on duty began when I reported into his headquarters off the Square of the Republic. "Of course you may have it duty-free. . . . No, I don't need to see your marriage certificate; you we trust. But I do have to fill out the form, so I'll simply put down 'Tax-Exempt Wedding Gift for Foreign-Currency Foreigner.' Now don't be angry, but just tell me how many days you've been married and then you can have your cutlery."

"Well, you'll have to do some multiplying and subtracting," I said. "Because it'll be twelve-times-three-hundred-sixty-five in August. Plus three February twenty-ninths."

He blinked and said: "Twelve years! I congratulate you!" I noticed that, on the form, he simply wrote "12" without specifying days, weeks, months, or years.

I rushed home, deposited the silver in the kitchen, and whisked my family and my mother off to Carlsbad. We'd been invited for yet another filmfest, one at which the official U.S. delegation screened *In Cold Blood* the day after Robert Kennedy died.*

* Ethel Skakel Kennedy, Robert's widow, is of Czech ancestry, incidentally. The name Skakel is an Americanization of the original name Skácel (pronounced *Skah-*

Guests of the Carlsbad Film Festival are granted one free single room and full board at the Grand Hotel Moskva Pupp. But, because I had brought along my wife, daughters, and mother, we were billeted instead (for free) at the Sanatorium Volgograd* across the canal. When we arrived there on the first morning, the lady at the desk didn't even look up. She simply asked in a bored voice: "What's your complaint?"

"We haven't been here long enough to complain," I replied.

That made her look up. "Who's your doctor?" she asked next.

I saw what she was getting at and explained that we weren't there for treatment. She said that she wouldn't be able to find our reservation unless she had our diagnosis, for the Sanatorium Volgograd's clientele was not indexed by name. Or, as she put it: "Without a complaint, I can't find you." But we prevailed upon her to make an exhaustive search, letter-by-letter. Forty-five minutes later, she discovered us under *Z* for *zdravý*, meaning "healthy."

Then we went to lunch upstairs, where we were served the only unappetizing ham in Czechoslovakia. I asked the waitress for some mustard to drown it in, but she said: "Not without a note from your doctor."

The Sanatorium Volgograd's finest hour, however, was 2300 that night, when Valerie and I returned from the filmfest's evening double feature. (My mother and children, who all shared a room, had already retired for the night.) The building was completely locked up. Fifteen minutes of ringing, pounding, and yoohooing evoked a white-capped nursing sister who leaned out of an upstairs window and threatened to call the police: "We close up at ten. If you're well enough to be out after ten making all this noise, then you don't belong here!"

"But we *do* belong here!" Valerie wailed. "My children are inside."

"Nonsense!" said the lady in white. "We don't take anybody under eighteen as a patient here."

"Please," I begged, "look us up under *Z* for *Zdravý* and you'll see that we belong here."

"Rules are rules. Come back in the morning and ask to see the registrar," we were told as the window slammed shut for the night.

---

tsel) under which her forebears lived in the Moravian town of Újezd u Přerova. They emigrated during the 19th century.

* Formerly the Sanatorium Stalingrad; and before then, the Rudolfhof. Carlsbad's old Sanatorium Washington is now the Sevastopol. Down the street, the M-Club Cinema is now the Kino Kreml, not the hair tonic, but the Kremlin.

We had to take a room overnight at the Grand Hotel Moskva Pupp.

I made just one more trip out of the country—to West Berlin for my final film festival. Originally I'd been scheduled to go there with the Semafor's "Country Beat" band and with Sylva, who was supposed to be their German-speaking mistress of ceremonies during a short engagement at a West Berlin theatre. But this plan had been made before a West Berlin agitator named "Red Rudi" Dutschke led a student insurrection against the Vietnam war and other irritants. For his pains, "Red Rudi" was shot in the brain by a deranged housepainter who claimed that he was a "good German" (and later hanged himself in his cell). Dutschke lost 30 per cent of his vision; West Berlin was plunged into its worst postwar riots; and the West Berlin theatre sent the Semafor a telegram canceling the engagement of the "Country Beat" from Communist Czechoslovakia "because of anti-American feeling in West Berlin."

At Šlitr-and-Suchý's behest, it fell my lot to try to "explain" this absurdity to their disappointed troupers, who were now unpacking their bags without having taken their long-awaited trip. To a man, my listeners blamed their plight on "Red Rudi" and, when I alluded to his "brain damage," one of the musicians said: "He was brain-damaged before anyone ever shot him in the head." Dutschke had earned their contempt, early in the Czechoslovak Spring, by coming to Prague and advising students not to challenge the system they were living under because it had many good and fruitful qualities. As one press account reported the reaction: "The Prague students, displaying the tolerance of real revolutionaries for a fake one, laughed him out of the hall."

The upshot was that I took my mother to Copenhagen to see her off for the States and then went to Berlin by myself, solely for the filmfest in the Europa shopping center. "Knowledgeable" film sources had been predicting for weeks that the festival would not take place. Warning that "Cannes was just a rehearsal for Berlin," radical students from Munich were converging on the divided city to disrupt its filmfest. West Berlin's own radical students warned that opening a filmfest while Red Rudi still lay wounded was an "affront to solidarity." The Munich students and the Berlin students met to co-ordinate strategy for wrecking the filmfest and, in a disagreement over tactics, wound up flinging eggs at each other.

To further complicate matters, some of the key troublemakers from Munich didn't reach Berlin until it was too late. For on the other side of the Wall, Walter Ulbricht was applying one of his periodic squeezes on travelers—and West German radicals are always vulnerable in transit through East Germany. This particular Berlin crisis was designed to create an urgent need for Communist solidarity and thereby scare the Czechoslovak heretics back into the fold, or else isolate them further.

Thus, the Berlin filmfest ran a relatively untroubled (for 1968) course—marred only by the explosion of a stink-bomb (which many mistook for bad cheese) and the mugging of a film critic's wife in the Europa Center's garage.

The students' archnemesis, press baron Axel Springer, threw a lavish reception for filmfest dignitaries in the penthouse of his $25 million skyscraper, which stands right up against the Berlin Wall. "It is a symbol of our confidence," the host explained, "that a free press will eventually overcome concrete walls." I applauded, but I couldn't help thinking that, illuminated by floodlights which Ulbricht's *Volkspolizei* train on their Wall to keep it escape-proof, the spectacle of expense-account nobility gorging itself at the buffet merely highlighted the excesses of both East and West.

Amidst all the fat cats on hand, a slim young lady flashed me a look of shared discomfort and I introduced myself to her. Her name was Gerda and she was studying linguistics (English and French, in particular) in Frankfurt. Like virtually all West German college students, she was required to spend one semester at the Free University of Berlin: "It's part of the reality into which we graduate."

Gerda was working as a filmfest hostess, but she and several others were wearing red carnations as a polite protest against their line-of-duty presence at Springer's.

I asked Gerda a question which had been perplexing me: "I can see how somebody here might be a leftist, or a romantic leftist, but how can anybody in West Berlin possibly be a Marxist? I mean, he has the Wall right there to remind him of how the system must survive."

"I'm neither a Marxist nor a leftist," she said, "but those who are say that Marxism must be given a fair chance. They say that if there were no Wall, then capitalism would suppress Marxism. Maybe they are right. But I think that what is happening in Czechoslovakia now

may one day lead to a fair competition between the systems. I hope
so."

A couple of mornings later, Gerda took me to see Checkpoint Charlie, a few yards from Springer's skyscraper, by daylight. Checkpoint
Charlie looks like a Merritt Parkway toll station manned by American
military policemen with submachine guns. Beyond it, however, you
cannot gather speed, for there is a zig-zag maze with control stations
and huge metal bars (pointed aloft like cannons) which can be lowered
to crush a car.

That is all you can see from the ground, but nearby is a reviewing
stand. Looking eastward, you see, in order of appearance:

. . . First, the Wall, only 10 or 12 feet high, sometimes lower, but
with barbed wire bringing it up to uniform height. Its top layers are
pipes that look like giant typewriter rollers. They are there to prevent
any climber from gaining a grip that will take him up and over the
Wall.

. . . Then a plain strip of dirt. "Heavily mined," said Gerda.

. . . What looks like triangular stacks of logs. They are actually
flares that are tripped by trespassers.

. . . Little huts with open windows and binoculars surveying us. A
Vopo inside waved to Gerda. She didn't wave back.

. . . More manned booths; some seemingly empty huts; and Vopos
patroling in pairs. "To watch each other," Gerda explained. "The
same with the workers who repair the Wall. They watch each other and
the Vopos watch them. The Vopos they send to guard the Wall are
mostly Saxons, who have a reputation for hating Berliners. Even so, a
few of them defect."

I shuddered in the summer heat, for I found myself thinking of
Sylva, whose last article before 1968 had been adulterated to say the
Wall was beautiful.

"When you go to East Berlin," I asked Gerda, "do you go through
Checkpoint Charlie?"

"No," said Gerda. "I take the elevated train, the S-Bahn, to the
Friedrichstrasse Station crossing point. Then I must spend half an hour
clearing controls." She shivered and said: "It's Kafka."

My turn for crossing the Wall came when the filmfest ended. The
only direct flights (on Č.S.A. or East Germany's Interflug) to Prague
leave from Schönefeld Airport in East Berlin. At the Helios travel
agency in downtown West Berlin, you board a bus that stays in the

West zone for all but the last half-mile of the ten-mile journey. The border crossing has the same layout as Checkpoint Charlie, but no American M.P.s.

Zig-zagging toward the first East German checkpoint, the driver suggested we take down our luggage from the racks. When the bus halted, two very young, clean-shaven Vopos came aboard. They studied the driver's credentials, even though he crosses back-and-forth eight or ten times a day. Then they took away our passports and delivered them to a windowless booth from which a hand reached out to take them. A slightly older Vopo came and collected our plane tickets. Two Customs men boarded but did nothing until our documents returned.

After twenty minutes, the older Vopo came back with a plane ticket and a slip of paper stuck into each passport. When he reached me, he said in English: "Mr. Levy? You are authorized to proceed to Copenhagen."

"But I've already been to Copenhagen," I said. "Now I'm going back to Prague."

"Your ticket says Copenhagen," the Vopo insisted.

"My ticket says Prague-to-Copenhagen-to-Berlin-to-Prague and I've used up the first two legs of it."

He studied the ticket and said: "This was issued in Prague?"

"Yes," I said. "I live there."

Reluctantly, he took back the slip, the ticket, and the passport. "You would rather go to Prague than to Copenhagen?" he asked.

"My family is in Prague waiting for me," I said.

"I see," he said. He was inside the windowless booth with my credentials for another twenty minutes. Then he returned with a civilian in a black suit. The new man compared every detail of my passport photo with my face. He nodded and then the Vopo said: "Your papers are in order, Mr. Levy. You may proceed to Prague."

Only now did the Customs men go to work. They asked every East or West German, every Czech, and every East European to open his bags. They merely questioned non-German Westerners about the contents of theirs without laying a hand on anything. For my suitcase, however, they had special treatment. Each of them kicked it twice, and hard!

"Do you want me to open it?" I said. "It's unlocked."

"Never mind," said the older Vopo. The Customs men kicked my bag once more apiece and then left. The Vopo and the civilian followed.

The barricade before us was raised. We crossed another zig-zag and a control point before turning down a tree-lined boulevard adorned with red hammer-and-sickle flags and Macy's Parade-size banners of Karl Marx and Walter Ulbricht. At the other end of this impressive driveway was the airport, which offered nothing more exasperating than a two-hour delay in the plane's departure and a 5-mark charge for a "transit visa."

"I don't have any East German marks," I told the Vopo at the cashier's counter.

"Oh, you had better not," he said, laughing. "If you did, I would have to arrest you as a currency smuggler. The import and export of our money is prohibited. You must pay in West marks."

Prague had a brand-new air terminal when we finally landed at Ruzyně. It was all glass and as impersonal as any world capital's, but a welcome contrast to the old shed with illuminated red star and hammer-and-sickle which used to be our rowboat's port of entry. Treadle-operated glass doors slid open silently as you approached them. Money-changers sat behind open counters rather than in cages, just the way they do at your newest, friendliest Chase Manhattan. The Customs men waved your bags into the country to the accompaniment of soft music. Virtually the only trace of the old austerity was a scowling man behind a plastic Pragocar (affiliated with Avis) counter defaced by a black, hand-crayoned sign saying, in seven languages: "THIS IS NOT AN INFORMATION DESK."

Almost a month earlier, I had been to the airport's formal dedication: a champagne open-house for government and aviation officials as well as the press. Every country whose airline served Prague had sent a delegation.

Airline people are fairly bland the world over, even behind the Iron Curtain, and they invariably speak English, for it is the official language of aviation. (Even when approaching Prague, pilot and control tower communicate in English.) Thus, the two Aeroflot delegates in ill-fitting gray suits had stuck out like sore thumbs. They didn't speak English and they brusquely side-stepped all conversation, even in Russian. They were inquisitive, though, nosing around every cranny of the new building and often taking notes (one would write while the other would see that nobody was looking over his shoulder). They didn't even down their drinks.

"Must be from air freight," one Western airline official had remarked condescendingly.

"I shouldn't wonder that they're from the NKVD," said another.

"They can't have traveled at all in the West," said the first. "They're still wearing Russian shoes, and that's the first thing a Russian buys when he gets out."

The two Russian "aviation delegates" would reappear at Prague's new airport one night in August. But the next time they would not be wearing sheep's clothing.

PART THREE

Antithesis: Capricious Summer

" 'It's a foreigner,' ran the whisper around him. 'He wants to see the grave.' They pushed one of the tables aside, and under it there was really a gravestone. It was a simple stone, low enough to be covered by a table. There was an inscription on it in very small letters; the explorer had to kneel down to read it. This was what it said: 'Here rests the old Commandant. His adherents, who now must be nameless, have dug this grave and set up this stone. There is a prophecy that after a certain number of years the Commandant will rise again and lead his adherents from this house to recover the colony. Have faith and wait!' "

Franz Kafka, *In the Penal Colony*

Chapter 10]

Wednesday 3 July—
Thursday 1 August 1968

PRAGUE'S NEW AIRPORT WAS OPENED IN THE NICK OF time. For everybody was traveling abroad that summer. Not just *almost* everybody we knew, not even *virtually* everybody we knew, but every Czech we knew—except our cleaning lady, Paní B., who had just acquired a summer house—took a "trip out" that summer. Šlitr went to Berlin and Hamburg when he wasn't needed at the Semafor or Barrandov. The Suchýs would be going to England and Yugoslavia in August. Forman's wife Věra and the twins made their first trip out—to Paris, where Miloš was working for a while, and then to visit friends in Belgium. The Doctor and her husband went to Yugoslavia and then Italy.

Our "jet set" friends in the Prague cultural and journalistic community never purported to be typical, but they've usually been either an exaggeration or a harbinger of what's happening. Statistically, 300,-000 Czechs—or better than one in fifty—visited the West during their glorious Spring and summer. And this in itself was a travel record for any Iron Curtain country.

Around the time when it had abolished censorship, Dubček's democracy had effected another reform promised by the Action Program: freedom to travel. Exit visas, which used to require separate, frequently unsuccessful applications for each trip out, were now made "permanent"—meaning in bureaucratese, valid for an unlimited number of trips during a specified period of 180 days and thence renewable. This was the same privilege granted my family and me as resident foreigners. Dubček's gradual timetable called for the exit-visa period to be expanded to a full year and, eventually, for the whole exit-visa rigmarole to be abolished. The right of every citizen to possess a passport entitling him to travel out to anywhere he pleased was now legally guaranteed.

The greatest restraint on travel, however, had never been visas but the $5.00 to $10.00 limit on hard currency officially available to Czechoslovaks going to the West. This was still in effect. The Doctor's daughter and her fiancé spent two days standing on line at the Živnostenská Banka to draw their combined allowance of $20.00. Then, rather than squander a cent of it on transport, they rode the Czechoslovak Railways (for crowns) to the Austrian frontier and hitchhiked the rest of the way to Vienna. There, jobs were waiting for both of them in a perfume factory: his in the warehouse and hers in the accounting office. For their work, they were paid a joint income of $53.84 a week.

The Doctor's daughter wrote to Valerie:

> The person who arranged our jobs, a postwar emigré friend of my parents, has also lent us his villa and his servant while he's away traveling in America. At the end of our working day, we ride a tram for an hour to the other end of town and there is our villa with the servant cooking *tournedos* for us.

She and her fiancé, a lanky, blond, sideburned art student, worked in Vienna all of July. Then, with their accumulated schillings, they could spend August hitchhiking through the Alps into Italy and on to southern France.

Matching the outflow of Czechs was an influx of tourists coming from all over the world to see "the democratization" as well as the older wonders of Prague. New hotels were rising, though not so fast as the demand for rooms. (They included a couple of boat hotels on the Vltava and a spanking-new Intercontinental in the old Jewish ghetto.) Travel in and out of the new airport was booming. ČSA, whose largest Tupolev jet seated 88 passengers, was able to lease from Aeroflot one of the latest Ilyushin-62 long-distance jets seating 132. (This was the four-rear-engine copy of Britain's VC-10 that Aeroflot introduced on the Moscow-New York run which began that summer.) Publicity stressed its two round trips a week between Prague and Moscow, but its most profitable uses were on the Paris and London runs during the rest of the week.

The overflow of sightseeing buses for Strahov and Loreta parked on the street where we lived. Sunday mornings became a piercing babble of *achtungs* as German sightseers armed with spiky walking sticks nearly eviscerated our children, who weren't on the tour and therefore were invisible to them. But who could complain? Prague was too great a discovery to hoard for oneself. And tourism was pure gamma globulin for the economy. Furthermore, under the economic reforms, it had been pledged that a large chunk of ČEDOK's proceeds from foreign tourists would be used to increase the hard-currency allowance of Czechs and Slovaks traveling out.

With all our friends leaving the country, the most exotic and inexpensive place we could think of spending the summer was in rustic Czechoslovakia. And so the American Family Levy's rowboat to Prague was moored, more often than not, at various locations along the Vltava and Sázava Rivers.

For two weeks, Šlitr gave us the key to his rambling log villa near Ledeč, where the first half of *Loves of a Blonde* was filmed. Šlitr's country home was furnished like a Wild West saloon with a piano looming above a mahogany and velvet sunken living room. Raspberries and currants bloomed in front yard and back; a 15-minute circuit of the house before breakfast would bring in enough to feed a family of raspberry buffs for the day. If you went for a hike in the woods, there were blueberries and mushrooms to be picked and the shell of an abandoned Prague streetcar to romp in. Jirka's parents, *Strýček Pepa* (Uncle Joe) and *Teta* (Aunt) Pavla, were there and so was his dachshund Uli. Sylva came out on weekends. Everybody was undemanding and unsolicitous; nobody expected anything of you. If Teta Pavla or Sylva or Valerie felt like cooking, she cooked. If not, there was a trade-union children's camp across the Sázava. We could take three insulated buckets there and buy a hot meal from the camp's chow line.

Near Karlštejn, a fourteenth-century castle, straight out of Prince Valiant, but built for Charles IV, our well-born baby-sitter Lulka long ago inherited a mansion that reminded me of Tara in *Gone With the Wind*. Communism had allotted her two rooms in Prague and one corner room on the ground floor of her country estate, which made Lulka one of the more fortunate Czech aristocrats. She spends her summers there and the year-round tenants defer to her like serfs to a countess. We visited her on a couple of weekends with Gene and Zdenka Deitch. The first time we went there, Lulka served an elegant garden luncheon of freshly-picked fruits and vegetables with home-grown dill, Czech camembert, and home-baked currant pastries. Every now and then, a horn would honk on the main road and Lulka would excuse herself for a minute or two. Gene and I followed her once and discovered that she had set up a roadside stand to peddle her tomato and plum harvests.

"It's part of the economic reforms. Ota Šik says farmers can market their own produce," Lulka explained cheerfully. After lunch, we put the children out to "play store" and business improved.

Monica and Erika found their first Czech "best friend" on one of our several country sojourns that summer. She was a round-faced blonde three-year-old with an endearing little bullfrog voice. Her name was Marianka and she lived in Prague. But we came upon her along the banks of the Sázava. She was croaking into a toy telephone: "Is anybody there?"

Those are the first words a Czech child learns to say into a telephone: "Is anybody there?" For Czechoslovak telephones work even worse than French phones and Czech telephone manners are worse than anybody's. If you telephone a woman and a man answers, you hang up. If the person you call isn't in, the one who answers will hang up. If a man's secretary has trouble understanding your Czech, you'll be left with a *"Ježišmarja!"* followed by dead air or a dial tone. If the secretary calls you for her boss, she'll tell you to hang on, but she won't tell you who's calling and you may never hear from any of them again. Is anybody there?

The games that Marianka taught our children exuded social comment. Playing store with baskets of marbles, Marianka was Mrs. Manager and Monica and Erika were her customers. This is the dialogue I overheard.

ERIKA: "Have you cream?"

MARIANKA: "Saturday."

MONICA: "Morning or afternoon?"

MARIANKA: "We're closed on Saturday."

MONICA: "Then I would like ten eggs."

MARIANKA: "There *are* no eggs."

ERIKA: "And I would like six tomatoes."

MARIANKA: "You can have these, Mrs. They're not very nice, but they're the last two in town."

MONICA: "Have you any nice cabbage?"

MARIANKA: "Only what you see here."

ERIKA: "And lettuce?"

MARIANKA: "This week we have cabbage."

ERIKA: "A loaf of black bread, please."

MARIANKA: "We had bread at the beginning of this week. Come back at the end of next week, Mrs."

MONICA: "And some beer for my Daddy."

MARIANKA: "We've sold all our beer for the summer. Come back next winter, Mrs."

At this point, I was impelled to interrupt the game with an outraged: "This is Czechoslovakia and there's always beer!" Marianka was too polite to contradict an elder, but at the end of July, in the next hot spell, the stores in Prague all ran out of beer, cider, and soda.

Marianka's parents became good friends of ours, too. Nad'a edited *belles lettres* for a Prague publishing house. Her husband, František, was artistic director of an important Prague theatre. Much of their life revolved around little Marianka because she was an only child and Nad'a had half a dozen miscarriages before having her. Nad'a spoke French and said she hoped Marianka would pick up some from Monica and Erika. "Then I will talk French to her, too," Nad'a explained, "and maybe in a year or two she can attend the French Cultural Institute in Prague. Our own schools used to be much better, but they were ruined after 1948, maybe forever. Everything was overhauled on the Russian model. There was a different curriculum, even different gymnastics." Then Nad'a, who talks in aphorisms, added: "The foreign body just can't be transplanted here." I glanced into her deep, dark crow's-footed eyes and knew she was talking about communism itself.

Her husband František wore plaid shirt, khakis, and a 10-liter sombrero that made him look like a cowboy actor in a Yugoslav western. But he sounded like a Czech at the end of his tether when he poured us some beer and told me:

"I signed a petition a month ago, so if the Russians stay and don't go home from their so-called 'maneuvers' here, then maybe I'll hang or go to prison. But, even if I don't and even if I keep my post, who wants it under the Russians?

"I'm forty-three now and thirty of those years have been lost to two totalitarian systems under which I never chose to live. So, if the Russians are settling in for a long stay under one pretense or another, then we are going to Vienna forever. Because if things should ever go back to improving at the old three-steps-forward-and-two-steps-back rhythm, it's going to take at least another twenty years, and I'd be 63. Our Marianka was three this month. For her sake, we can't afford to lose another generation."

He refilled the beers and then perked up a little as he watched the foam go down:

"On the other hand, if the Russians somehow let us have our way, then maybe there *is* hope—for Marianka's generation."

No matter what any conversation was about that summer, it inevitably turned political. July was often damp and chilly. František made a fire one night when we came over to his summer house for dinner.

"Bad weather for mushrooms," I remarked.

"Yes," said František, "but I'm hoping for a long, cool summer. It's better for tempers with Russian troops still in the Czech Lands."

We talked that night about the theatre and the crypto-political role which the arts had assumed during the Novotný repression. František opined that the new freedom of expression was dooming this kind of cinema (e.g., Němec's *Report on the Party and the Guests*) and theatre (e.g., S+Š's *Last Hospital*), for which his own playhouse among others had an excellent reputation. "The political drama on TV every night is outstripping us all," he explained, "and we will have to take a new turn to get people away from their sets."

František said it was too early to predict what that turn would be, although he was sure "it will require a whole new alphabet" and "it probably won't be frivolous." A movie director I discussed the matter with a few days later hazarded a guess that "it may take an extremely serious turn indeed; a kind of dialectic cinema or theatre that confronts the very *idea* of socialism itself—artistically, I'm sure."

Šlitr and Suchý had written and were co-starring in a film that Menzel was directing at Barrandov: *The Crime in the Night Club*. Šlitr was playing an incompetent defense attorney who makes such an unexpectedly good case for his innocent defendant (Suchý) that, in order for the system to survive, both lawyer and client must be sentenced to death. Beyond that point, though, Šlitr told me "we're having ending trouble. If we get it right politically, it's wrong structurally. And vice versa. Politics are stupid!"

One day, while the Soviet troops were still playing their "war games" on Czechoslovak soil, a man brought a petition around to the studio and Suchý and Šlitr and Menzel signed it. This was the "2,000 Words," written by a self-educated ex-shoemaker named Ludvík Vaculík, who was now an editor of *Literární Listy*. It was a plea for the new leaders to stand firm; for the discredited Old Guard to step down or risk demonstrations, strikes, and boycotts; and for the public to "let our government know that we will support it, even with weapons in our hands, as long as it does what we ask it to do."

The most prophetic of Vaculík's "2,000 Words" were his ending.

> This Spring has just ended and will never come back. In the winter we will know everything.

The "2,000 Words" were published simultaneously in weekend editions of *LL* and three other periodicals. It bore the signatures of nearly one hundred other prestigious figures, including artists, scientists, scholars, and the athletes Emil Zátopek and Věra Čáslavská.

The reaction from the Kremlin was chilling. The "2,000 Words" evoked the cry of "counter-revolution" in Moscow. East of the Elbe, that compound label means "poison"—and this was the first time that Russia officially applied it to the Prague Spring.

Various Czechoslovak political leaders (not all of them Novotnýite holdovers) also termed the "2,000 Words" a "call to counter-revolution." Alexander Dubček, in his own easygoing way, at first took the matter lightly, but a few days later he inserted into the prepared text of a speech an expression of "great anxiety" over the manifesto and an "unequivocal dissociation" of himself and his party leadership from its viewpoint. But official Moscow periodicals kept referring to the "2,000 Words" under such ominous headlines as "PURE DEMOCRATS GRASPING FOR POWER" and branding Dubček "soft" on counter-revolution.

Of Dubček's Presidium, only Josef Smrkovský had any kind words for the "2,000 Words." Smrkovský, an ardent and frequent Semafor Theatregoer, remarked that the prime threat to Czechoslovakia did not come from "political romantics" like Šlitr and Suchý and Menzel, but from "the growing attacks launched by supporters of pre-January conditions." This was why Smrkovský felt that the leadership had acted "in haste" and not very sensitively or realistically, in condemning the "2,000 Words."

Dubček had his hands full in the Presidium. Of the eleven members, three—Kolder, Bil'ak, and editor Švestka—were now outright enemies. Of the four so-called "centrists": František Barbírek, head of the Slovak National Council, had come under Bil'ak's wing and had been meeting with the East German ambassador; two others, Jan Piller and

Emil Rigo, were wavering; and only Prime Minister Černík was standing firmly behind Dubček thus far. Therefore, Dubček could rely upon only four Presidium members: himself; Smrkovský; Josef Špaček, forty, a Moravian party leader who had risked his political neck under Novotný to save a liberal Brno magazine; and Dr. František Kriegel, sixty, a paunchy heart specialist who had been fighting for communism ever since he joined the Spanish Republican Army in 1937. Kriegel was now head of the National Front, but to the Russians he was a marked man for three reasons: First, he was a liberal. Secondly, he was born in Galicia, now part of the Soviet Ukraine. Thirdly, he was Jewish.

There were whispers of an occasional 6-to-5 vote going against Dubček in the Presidium. Worse still, the party's administrative apparatus was in the hands of a suave but faceless Central Committee aparatchik named Alois Indra. A onetime railway clerk in Slovakia, Indra, forty-seven, had been Novotný's Minister of Transport for nearly five years. Upon reading the "2,000 Words," he had fired off an I-told-you-so Telex, warning against "counter-revolutionary incitement," to all district and regional committees in the name of the Central Committee. In other Telexes, Indra was preaching against "TV's exaggerating the role of T. G. Masaryk" and deploring the vanishing of "Comrade" as a form of address—even between party members.*

Outside the Presidium, Václav David—the ex-Foreign Minister who "spoke only one language: Russian"—had actually been confirmed as Ambassador to Bulgaria and was packing his bags. But he still held a National Assembly seat in Prague and, from it, he proclaimed that he could perceive no foreign attempts to interfere in Czechoslovak affairs. He accused the mass media of "creating an artificial atmosphere of tension with respect to the Soviet Union and other socialist countries." The Warsaw Pact troops on Czechoslovak soil, he complained, found themselves in the position of undesirable aliens. The mass media were pressing for their departure, while the people themselves were still giving the troops a cordial welcome. David insisted that any delays in departure would be routine, but "the sullen atmosphere . . . will not win Czechoslovakia a good name among her allies."

The maneuvers had ended on the 30th of June. A staff analysis had been held on schedule on the 2d of July in the East Bohemian garri-

---

* Standard tactful response recommended for foreigners who are often offended by this form of address: "I'll be your friend, so must I be your comrade?"

son town of Milovice with Soviet Marshal Yakubovsky presiding and Dubček, Smrkovský, Černík, and Svoboda as guests of honor. The Russian Army was to leave immediately thereafter.

At the briefing in Milovice, invited journalists from Prague found themselves barred by a Russian officer while Russian journalists were admitted. *Rudé Právo's* military correspondent, a Czechoslovak Army officer himself, came in uniform, but was barred too.

That afternoon, the townsfolk in Milovice presented the Russians with farewell gifts and thanked them for not wearing out their welcome. One Russian lieutenant, who spoke English, told a British journalist that every time he saw an "Ivan Go Home" sign in Milovice, he agreed with it: "I think you have a saying in your language: 'East, West, home's the best.' That's the way all of us feel."

Some Russians did leave. A planeload of sixty Soviet generals departed from Prague for Moscow with great fanfare and press coverage. At a border crossing in Eastern Slovakia, a Soviet convoy was greeted by townsfolk and brass bands on both sides of the frontier. The border guards declared open house. The Ukrainian villagers invited their Slovakian neighbors across for a party celebrating the safe return of their boys. The party lasted three days.

These, however, were only token forces. True, six special trains had been dispatched to Milovice to fetch troops and hardware. But there the trains sat in the yards, empty. No more than 10 per cent of the unknown number of Soviet troops had actually left Czechoslovak soil. The others were either inside or else encamped outside many key military installations.

Czechoslovakia's Minister of Defense could only say lamely: "I expect the remaining troops to be withdrawn fast. We are in contact with the representatives of the Joint Command. This is, after all, their responsibility and we believe that they will show understanding. The last time I talked with Marshal Yakubovsky about this thing was on Thursday of last week."

Marshal Yakubovsky blandly attributed the delay to "heavy weekend traffic" on Czechoslovak roads. But highway congestion here is never thicker than the emperor's new clothes. On two weekend round-trips (totaling 200 miles) from Šlitr's during that siege of "heavy traffic," I encountered an aggregate of under 100 cars going in any direction.

Meanwhile, new and hitherto unannounced Soviet "maneuvers"

started up in Hungary, Poland, and East Germany, usually on terrain near the Czechoslovak border. East Germany, where the ordinary male has a forty-six-year military obligation (from ages fourteen to sixty), underwent a partial mobilization and emergency call-up of reservists. Russian tourists en route to Prague were intercepted by Intourist and sent home "because of the tense situation." Future trips to Czechoslovakia by Russian vacationers were canceled for an indefinite period.*

Speaking at a "friendship" rally in the Kremlin's Palace of Congresses, Leonid Brezhnev made a pointed reference to the Soviet "liberation" of Hungary in 1956.

Alexei Kosygin, on a goodwill tour of Sweden, clearly had Czechoslovakia on his mind. In Stockholm, he held a press conference to sum up his impressions of Sweden, but four times he said "Czechoslovakia" when he meant "Sweden." This is not an easy Freudian slip to make in any tongue. When reporters called it to his attention, Kosygin glossed over it with a jovial inanity: "The standards of life in Sweden are very high. But, for that matter, they are very high in Czechoslovakia, too."

From Stockholm, Kosygin flew to Warsaw to meet with Brezhnev, Gomulka, Ulbricht, Kádár, and Todor Zhivkov over the "Czechoslovak emergency." The session lasted all day on the fourteenth of July, a Sunday. When it was over, all of the delegates emerged looking grim. Hungary's János Kádár looked grimmest of all. It was no secret that he was Czechoslovakia's only defender in that room.†

My sixteen-year-old niece from Marblehead, Massachusetts, landed at Prague's new airport on Monday 15 July after a long weekend in London. Nancy was to stay until the end of August, when I would escort her to Paris and chaperone her there while showing her around. Then I was to put her on a plane to Boston and do a *Good Housekeeping* assignment before coming back to Prague.

The phone was ringing when Nancy walked through our door. It was her mother (my older sister) calling from the States at $2.50 a

---

* Later, when 650,000 Soviet visitors would arrive wearing helmets, they would come equipped with spending money, the Czechoslovak crowns allotted to travelers by Intourist.

† According to Erwin Welt, Gomulka's interpreter who later defected to West Germany, Ulbricht warned Kádár at one of several such "Meetings of the Five" that if Czechoslovakia were lost to the Red bloc, then Hungary would be the next to go. "Either you don't understand that," Ulbricht shouted at Kádár, "or else you don't want to understand it!"

minute. My sister had always had mental reservations about our going to East Europe "and flushing your lives down the drain." She had just read the headlines from Warsaw and now she had return reservations on her mind.

"I want Nancy to come home on the next plane," she began.

"Nonsense!" I said.

"Can we talk? I suppose your phone is monitored."

"Even if it is, we can still talk," I said.

"What's going to happen to you?" she wanted to know.

"Nothing. We have U.S. passports, so even if the Russians do intervene we should be safe. Probably, Dubček and Smrkovský will hang within fifteen minutes after the Russians take over. Maybe a day later, our friends who've signed this '2,000 Words' manifesto will start going to jail. . . ."

The transatlantic connection was worse than ever and so were my sister's nerves. After a second of dead air, I heard my sister screaming to her husband: "Joe! Joe! Alan says they've hung Dubček!"

"No!" I corrected. "Not yet. Maybe never. We hope never."

There was a burst of static and then a bulletin from Marblehead: "I hear machine-gun fire!"

By the time my sister had spent $22.50, we'd worked out a compromise whereby in the event of an invasion Nancy would be repatriated on the "next plane out." We didn't discuss the likelihood of there being a next plane out. . . .

The next day, the Presidium of the Czechoslovak Communist Party was having its regular Tuesday-afternoon meeting when it received the result of the Warsaw summit meeting: a letter of ultimatum signed (in Slavic alphabetical order) by the Communist Parties of the Bulgarian and Hungarian People's Republics, the German Democratic Republic, the Polish People's Republic, and the Union of Soviet Socialist Republics.

The letter blasted KAN, K231, and "the forces of reaction" that "unleashed a campaign against the Communist Party of Czechoslovakia." It condemned the "moral terrorism" of the mass media. It branded the "2,000 Words" a "platform of counter-revolution" that was "not denounced and even found supporters in the party and its leadership." And it warned that all this had created "a situation . . .

which is utterly unacceptable to the socialist countries." They therefore demanded an immediate meeting with the Czechoslovak party leadership.

Dubček's Presidium stayed in session all Tuesday night and well into Wednesday afternoon, 17 July, to ponder the "Letter of the Five" and hammer out a reply that refuted it point-by-point, but was nonetheless conciliatory:

> The Warsaw Pact staff maneuvers are concrete proof of our loyalty to commitments of alliance. We gave a friendly welcome to Soviet . . . troops. The presence of our highest party and government officials demonstrated the importance we attributed to the maneuvers. Misunderstandings and certain doubts have been expressed by the public only after repeated changes in the times of departure of these troops from Czechoslovak territory after the end of the exercise. . . .
>
> We agree that the party must thwart the intentions of right-wing and anti-socialist elements. Our party has worked out its plan to do so . . . and is acting accordingly. We can be successful if conditions exist for us to accomplish these aims gradually within a few months. We think that one of these conditions is to avoid an erroneous step which might call to life a power conflict.

The last section of the reply dealt with a continuing wrangle over the form of the inevitable confrontation that must ensue. The five letter-writers wanted *unilateral* talks—that is, Czechoslovakia defending itself against all five at once. Czechoslovakia favored preliminary *bilateral* talks—that is, face-to-face meetings between Czechoslovakia and each individual power, one at a time.

Now the rollercoaster started. On Wednesday, the day Prague replied, Leonid Brezhnev demanded a meeting between the Czechoslovak Presidium and the Soviet Politburo. That sounded good because, by wanting to meet face-to-face, Politburo-to-Presidium, Russians-to-Czechoslovaks, Brezhnev was acceding to bilateral talks. When did he want the talks to be held? On Friday! That much urgency was always bad. Where? In the Slovak city of Košice. That sounded good, but maybe it was bad. Košice is less than fifty miles from the Soviet border. The surrounding areas in Slovakia were still teeming with Soviet troops who had yet to go home.

Then, driving back to Brno from the Presidium meeting, Dr. Špaček, one of the four reliable liberals, was rammed head-on by an American tourist in a Volkswagen. The American was passing illegally in the other direction. Špaček suffered a brain concussion, face cuts, and chest injuries. He would recover, but not in time for a Friday summit meeting in Košice.

Late Wednesday night, Soviet Ambassador Chervonenko flew from Moscow to Prague with a new note from Leonid Brezhnev. Chervonenko arrived at the Central Committee building on the Vltava's right bank to find most of the Presidium still in session, as it had been almost constantly since Tuesday afternoon, and the Prague and world press corps camped in an anteroom. When the journalists saw the Russian Ambassador, they set up such a clamor that the Presidium could hear that word had come.

Chervonenko was ushered in. After half an hour, Josef Smrkovský stepped out for a minute and told the reporters: "Victory!"

The Russian hurried away after another thirty minutes without talking to the press. A few seconds later, Dubček stepped out of the Presidium hall. He marched to a bar cart, poured himself a cognac, drank it down, poured himself another, took a sip, and then permitted himself to speak. "It is hard to repair the errors of twenty years," he said.

The press soon learned that Leonid Brezhnev, apparently having trouble putting his house in order for a trip to Slovakia, had sent a conciliatory message indefinitely postponing the showdown. In it, he purred that the letter from Warsaw had been a warning, not an ultimatum. It was not, repeat not, to be taken as an endorsement of Novotnýism or a call for the return of the past.

Dubček, whose Presidium meeting resumed as soon as he finished his second cognac, made a bold move in the early hours of Thursday. Knowing that a treacherous summit duel with the Soviets still lay somewhere ahead, he would ask the Central Committee to give his leadership a vote of confidence. When the time came, he wanted to confront Russia with evidence that he spoke for the party. He was also gambling that public unity behind him would harden the line between Novotný conservatives and Dubček liberals—thus bringing waverers into the Dubček camp. The Central Committee meeting was convoked for Friday.

On Thursday night, Dubček addressed his nation on television. He was still not a compelling speaker; but Czechoslovak Television had conspired (and here was a plot Moscow never hinted at!) to dramatize his homespun assets and relieve his own podium nerves.

The cameras showed Dubček arriving at the studio in his own car, a not-very-recent Simca. The announcer noted that Dubček frequently avoided the chauffeured limousine put at his disposal by the party in favor of his own car, which he'd driven from Bratislava to Prague one weekend and for whose petrol he paid out of his own pocket rather than with official coupons. "Thus," said the announcer, "Alexander Dubček manages to go around largely unnoticed."

TV followed him right into the make-up room, where the nation watched him banter with the cosmeticians. Then, taking his place for the formal address, Dubček peered forward and began with a kindly: "Dear friends, dear citizens."

The effect of those four words was overwhelming. In homes across the nation, people burst into tears. In taverns, sports clubs, and hotels, beer-drinkers—who had hoisted high their flagons to toast Dubček— were so startled that they let them drop and smash. For Dubček's salutation was an emotional break with twenty years of Eastern Europe's cold cameraderie, where every Communist leader started off with a brusque "Comrades and citizens."

In retrospect, some of us in Prague think it was those four heretical words—*"Dear friends, dear citizens"*—which arrested the thaw in relations and made up Brezhnev's, Ulbricht's, and Gomulka's minds that Czechoslovakia could no longer live.

"We all feel great responsibility," Dubček told the TV audience. "But we are determined to go on pursuing the policy we began after January and which the Czech and Slovak nations wish us to pursue. We paid dearly for the old methods. . . ."

Dubček was by now relaxed enough to *ad lib* a significant, semi-Brechtian quip: "Our people were dissatisfied with the previous leadership. We can't change the people, so we had to change the leaders."

He continued: "Now, after many years, an atmosphere has come to our country in which everybody can publicly, without fear, openly, and in a dignified manner, express his opinion. By an open and honest policy, the party is gradually regaining the public's badly-shaken confidence. Therefore, we proclaim—openly, calmly, but resolutely aware of all that is at stake—that *there is no other way* in which the democratic yet socialist transformation of our life could be accomplished. . . .

"Our country is wedged between the socialist countries and we intend to protect this strategic outpost. Socialism is the apple of our eye. . . .

"We have not betrayed our friends and allies. We have faithfully complied and we shall comply with our obligations deriving from the Warsaw Pact. . . .

"Democracy is a clash of views. But democracy is also conscientious discipline. Democracy also calls for statesmanlike wisdom on the part of all citizens. Unnecessary dramatizing of misunderstandings and short-sighted unleashing of passions would not be beneficial.

"As citizens of a sovereign socialist country, we must be resolute, wise, and aware of our great responsibility to this country, to this people, and to the international Communist movement. What we need most at this juncture is support from all citizens for the leadership of the party and the Government. May your support, confidence, prudence and determination be a dignified response to the challenge of this important moment. May it correspond to the great democratic traditions of our socialist homeland.

"This is what I wanted to ask you for."

When his talk was over, TV let us watch Dubček watching a football match on a studio TV monitor. We could decompress and so could he. After a while, the camera said goodbye to him and concentrated on the football. And we knew that in the showdown impending, Czechoslovakia's cause was in sane, firm hands.

The activist playwright Pavel Kohout had been chilled from the first moment of the telecast. Kohout wrote later:

"When Dubček got out of that car alone, it was too much for me. I couldn't stand it. I'm not for a country of gun-toting bodyguards, but I wanted to offer myself to him as a protection for the rest of the evening."

Instead, in a few days, the burly Kohout would turn his talents to even finer use.

Prague was in the summer slump that afflicts all Europe, East or West, and makes peak-season tourism unrewarding for those Americans who come to see people instead of monuments and each other. Half the population took its vacation in July; the other half would go in August. Everyday services deteriorated or collapsed from overloading and understaffing. No taxis at the terminals. No beer in the stores. Our corner news stand shut down for four weeks. Air mail to and from the States, which generally averaged eight days, now took fourteen. The man you were trying to reach on the phone had "just stepped out of the office for a minute" and would return your call when he came back in a month. In renaissance or repression, some verities are eternal, and this one was called "the cucumber season."

When we were in the city, we had a dairy crisis. Milk comes to Prague in unrefrigerated trucks and is delivered to unrefrigerated stores. Czech children have learned to live with (and like) sour milk, but mine turned up their noses at it. So I rose at 5:15 every morning, staggered out to the dairy store, and bought a bottle that wasn't standing in the sun. When I came home, Valerie would boil the milk, and—if they were lucky, Monica and Erika would have sweet milk all day.

A man who came to dinner rescued us temporarily. He was Tad Szulc (pronounced Schultz) who late that spring had opened Prague's first *New York Times* bureau in more than a decade. A bearish Polish-American, Tad was anxiously awaiting accreditation (which was granted on 19 August!). Over supper, he mentioned that he had no sooner arrived in Prague than he had been offered commissary privileges at the U.S. Embassy. I called the Embassy the next morning. At first, I was told that "Szulc was granted commissary privileges because he *had* to come here, but you *chose* to come here." When I cited President Johnson's policy of "building bridges" to Eastern Europe and pointed out that my coming here helped open the door for Szulc and other American journalists, I was finally told to write a letter detailing why I was a special case "so that we won't have to extend commissary privileges to any Tom, Dick, or Alan who comes here and wants them, too." A week later, we were granted "guest" privileges ($100 a month maximum, payable by check in dollars; no whisky) at the American Embassy Prague Commissary Association.* Our first purchase was several gallon pure-pak containers of frozen, pasteurized, homogenized milk (trucked in regularly from Nuremberg) labeled "U.S. FORCES EUROPE."

I was prepared to dislike this "Big PX," but I quickly learned to love the commissary. A well-kept secret in Prague, it would make a

---

* In the spring of 1969, our privileges were terminated when, in one of President Nixon's early streamlinings, all persons other than Defense and State Department personnel were barred from using American commissaries in Europe. Whereupon one solicitous Embassy wife said to us: "We hope this won't dissuade you from living in Prague."

beautiful advertisement for an America that even New Yorkers no longer know. Standing inside a secluded archway of the elaborate palace which is our Embassy, it is a small country grocery store like the old neighborhood A & Ps. It is presided over by a Czech granny named "Commissary Mary," a devoted enthusiast of and godmother to all people and products American.

"For you, a hard-currency-foreigner, everything is possible," the typewriter salesman had told me early in our stay in Prague. But I would never have dreamed that this included Boston-style baked beans, corned-beef hash, Chef Boy-ar-dee and Betty Crocker, soft-lavender Scott toilet paper (Farewell, Feh!), Coca-Cola for a dime a can*, cocktail onions, Fritos, English muffins, Wisconsin cheddar cheese, and America's answer to balneology, Alka-Seltzer. I had never consciously missed them, but seeing them in our Prague pantry almost brought tears to my eyes. It was an emotion (of old acquaintance rather than homesickness or even nostalgia) that I'd experienced in Carlsbad when seeing my first American film in six months: *Guess Who's Coming to Dinner.* I had wept throughout; not because of the story, not because Spencer Tracy was now dead, but simply because a big, fat, slick American Katharine Hepburn-Spencer Tracy movie was playing at the *kino* and because *I was there!*

At the commissary, I wasn't there much, but I was there! I was alternating one week in the country with one week in the city while my family was living most of the time in the country, where milk and fruit were fresh and plentiful. Gooseberries and currants grew in every garden; in the woods nearby, there were raspberries everywhere.

That was why, whenever we returned to Prague and people asked "Did you see the Red Army in the countryside?", I would answer: "Not unless they were masquerading as raspberries, in which case you have nothing to worry about because we ate them!"

We didn't see any Russians on our periodic vacations. But, in both city and country, I took special pains to avoid one new pitfall—planted arms caches. German and American weapons, some of World War I vintage, started being "discovered" in rural areas near where Soviet

* As one of its economic bridges to the West, Czechoslovakia was negotiating with the Coca-Cola empire for a license in exchange for Czechoslovak sugar. Such an arrangement would have reduced the present cost of 42 cents a can (for imported Coca-Cola) on the Czechoslovak market by 75 per cent, putting it almost within reach of the workingman.

troops were still bivouacked. These were new Russian tactics to justify remaining on Czech soil as well as (it was learned later) independent East German plots to trigger an invasion. I dreamed one night that, on a raspberry hunt, I stumbled on a hoard of weapons and tripped a camera which photographed me as proof positive of a foreign counter-revolutionary plot. The next morning, I warned my family not to examine any strange objects in the woods.*

In the city, whenever we used up a U.S. FORCES EUROPE milk container, we obliterated and destroyed it, to prevent some conservative dustman from stuffing it with "evidence."

The Czechoslovak police were operating even more cautiously. They didn't dare catch the Russian troops in the act of planting the arms caches, for that might lead to a shooting incident or even war. And yet it would be far better for the Czechs if they, rather than the Russians, did the discovering. In other words, find the body before the culprit does. This venturesome game of *habeas corpus* took some doing, but the Czechs are experts at disarmament and they know their territory. More often than not, they made laughing stocks of the Russians.

On one occasion, the Czech police seized an arms cache and didn't announce it. Meanwhile, the Russian news agency Tass printed all the details of the latest "find" complete with the names of its Red Army "discoverers." Tass even distributed a photo (obviously taken before the planting) of the Russian soldiers displaying their "catch." Armed with clippings, the police, who, having dug up the weapons first, now had them under lock-and-key, visited the Russian tent camp and put the sheepish, empty-handed "heroes" through a politely Kafkaesque interrogation.

After several such cloak and digging episodes, General Pavel, the Minister of Interior, was able to announce without any fear of serious contradiction: "It is generally believed that the hiding of arms was a provocation with the purpose of dramatizing the situation in Czechoslovakia."

---

* There was, in fact, an uncharacteristic and unsolved double murder that July in the Prokopské Valley near Prague. Two fourteen-year-olds went swimming at 1430 and were found, at 2400, shot to death. They had been neither sexually molested nor robbed. Rumor hinted that the crime had greater implications and, later, it was claimed that they had stumbled upon "persons unknown" planting an arms cache.

General Pavel's words were just a footnote. By the last week in July, another general, Václav Prchlík, was sharing headlines with Soviet troops. The latter were, as one newspaper put it, "LEAVING A LITTLE." A couple of battalions pulled out across the Polish border but it was no military secret that they bivouacked five miles or less beyond the frontier. The rest remained in Czechoslovakia.

General Prchlík was the honest Army officer who had blown the whistle thwarting General Šejna's attempted *coup d'état*. In the spring, Dubček had rewarded Prchlík by placing him in charge of the Central Committee's own notorious Eighth Department, the party's purgative link with both the military and the security apparatuses. He replaced the hated Miroslav Mamula, crony of both Novotný and Šejna. Prchlík's efforts thus far had aimed to neutralize rather than improve the workings of the Eighth Department. There were rumors that he would eventually liquidate it.

In Prague, General Prchlík gave a radio interview in which he was asked: "Does the Warsaw Pact include any provisions that would allow allied troops to stay on our territory beyond the originally approved period under peacetime conditions?"

Prchlík replied crisply that "every provision of the Pact emphasizes that the deployment of allied troops on foreign territory is dependent upon agreement *between*—repeat, *between*—the States involved." He added that, in his opinion, "the Czechoslovak public, while demanding the departure of troops, doesn't want to disrupt friendly ties with our allies. Our friends should, however, seek to understand the quality of our internal political development."

Two days later, Prchlík held a televised press conference. In shirt-sleeved khakis, he struck me as a balding, jaunty, no-nonsense sort of "operator"—like a fair-dealing Miami bookmaker who would be active in religious fund-raising. He had summoned the press to announce that he would indeed be liquidating the party's control of the military and security apparatuses as soon as a law could be drafted to that effect. But the questioning soon turned from the future to current events.

"How will this law affect the coalition of armies within the Warsaw Pact?" a reporter asked.

Prchlík replied that it was not intended to have any effect outside Czechoslovakia, even though "certain qualitative changes" in the Warsaw Pact were long overdue. This was an opinion that no East European military officer had ever dared to express publicly.

To compound his heresy, Prchlík went into a lengthy critique of the Warsaw Pact's inner workings. First off, he said, all member countries should be made equal. On paper, they were. But in Orwellian actuality, Russia was more equal than all the others put together. The Warsaw Pact Joint Command, Prchlík revealed, was comprised exclusively of Soviet marshals, generals, and other officers. Members from the satellite countries were merely designated as liaison officers. None of them had ever held any significant function or title. The Ministers of Defense of each member nation were made "deputies" to Marshall Yakubovsky, their commander-in-chief, who seldom granted them interviews.

The question was asked again about extended stays on territory of a member country without its consent. Prchlík reiterated the view he'd expressed on the radio and went on to characterize the emergency meeting in Warsaw as part of "a war of nerves." He said that Czechoslovakia would soon demand that experts from the armed forces of every member country should be named to the Warsaw Pact Joint Command.

"We have only one course open to us," General Prchlík concluded. "We shall insist that our State sovereignty must not be violated, that our internal affairs must not be interfered with, and that treaties must be respected."

Miloš Forman had come home from Paris for a few days and I watched Prchlík's press conference with him. "This man is much too astute to be a general!" Miloš exclaimed.

For different reasons, the Russian Army felt the same way. Its newspaper, *Red Star,* accused Prchlík of "slander," revealing military secrets, and playing into Western imperialistic hands with his "irresponsible remarks." *Red Star* added ominously: "The events in Czechoslovakia long ago went beyond the national borders of that country."

Three days after the Russian Army attacked him in print, General Prchlík was removed from his post.

A nervous Presidium forced Dubček to do it. But, even while flinging Russia a bone—Prchlík's—Dubček also sped up liberalization. In the process of firing Prchlík, he also abolished the whole Eighth Department. Even so, Prchlík's admirers were appalled. The playwright Pavel Kohout wrote the general an open letter:

> I do not like it at all when an honorable man is censured at a time when so many dishonorable people are being ignored. If one decides

never to sacrifice a pawn again, then one should not sacrifice a general either.

Maybe it was necessary. But it was a pity. Public morale definitely suffered.

I write this to you in the hope that this will not happen again to anyone and in the belief that I will be able to salute you soon in another important military function.

Three separate Prague Communist Party organizations immediately proposed Prchlík as their Central Committee candidate.

Alexander Dubček was unruffled. A *Newsweek* photographer stepped in his path outside the Central Committee and said: "I'd like to arrange a photo session with you, sir."

The most controversial man in the world that week smiled benignly and said: "I'm afraid I'm a little too busy right now to pose for American magazines." But he did stand still for a minute, during which a few hundred photos were taken for world consumption.

Dubček was feeling good because his gamble on assembling the Central Committee for a vote of confidence had paid off with a unanimous endorsement. Considering that only forty of the one hundred ten members were liberals and that the rest were forty diehard conservatives on the way out plus thirty centrists, this was a remarkable feat indeed. There had been no abstentions by those present, though twenty-two members hadn't shown up.

"If the Kremlin provoked this meeting," one observer remarked, "it was their biggest miscalculation since they sent rockets to Cuba."

Not that pressure hadn't been applied to achieve this result. In place of the tight security usually attending Central Committee meetings in the Spanish Hall of the Prague Castle, the anteroom of the hall had been opened to the public. A steady stream of Czechs had arrived all day bearing resolutions of support. Liberal politicians had taken turns stepping outside the Spanish Hall to greet visitors. This was as close as any Communist public anywhere has ever come to a Central Committee meeting. In fact, an effort to have a live broadcast had been vetoed at the last moment. It might have affronted the thunderers from the east who wanted censorship restored at once.

The thunder had started up again, but now Dubček felt fully armed with public confidence for whatever bilateral summit impended. Another "first" in Communist history was being arranged: the Soviet eleven-man Politburo's first trip abroad as an entity. It would meet with the Czechoslovak Presidium at a "secret site" on Czechoslovak soil, undoubtedly somewhere between Košice and the Soviet border.

Pavel Kohout wanted to be sure that Dubček wouldn't be knifed at the summit by his own balky Presidium. The playwright composed a manifesto and *Literární Listy* published it as a special two-page edition in petition form, suitable for signing and delivering to the Presidium in time for its impending journey. A far more eloquent document than the "2,000 Words," Kohout's open letter to the Presidium began:

> *Comrades:* We are writing to you on the eve of your meeting with the Presidium of the Central Committee of the Soviet Communist Party, during which you will be debating the fate of all of us. As has happened many times before in the history of mankind, the lives of millions will be decided by a few. This is difficult, and we want to make it easier for you by our support. . . .

After reviewing his country's "history of bondage," Kohout went on:

> The moment has come when, after centuries, our country has again become the cradle of hopes—and not only of our hopes. The moment has come when we can prove to the world that socialism is no mere emergency solution for underdeveloped countries, but the only true alternative for all civilized mankind.
>
> We expected that, in particular, all of the socialist camp would welcome this fact with sympathy. Instead, we are being accused of treason. We are given ultimatums by comrades who keep on showing their ignorance of our evaluation and our situation. We are accused of crimes we did not commit. We are suspected of intentions we never had and don't have.
>
> The threat of an unjust punishment hangs over us. And, in whatever shape it may materialize, it may rebound like a boomerang on our judges, too. [And yet it would] destroy our effort and above all leave a tragic blot on the idea of socialism anywhere in the world for years to come.

Kohout climaxed his warning to the Czechoslovak Presidium:

> Comrades, it is your historic task to avert this danger. It is your mission to convince the leaders of the Soviet Communist Party that the process of revival in this country must proceed to its end in a way that is in keeping with the interests of all our countries and those of progressive forces on every continent.
>
> All we are striving for can be summed up in these four words: SOCIALISM, ALLIANCE, SOVEREIGNTY, FREEDOM!

The four words suffer in translation. In Czech, they are *SOCIALIS-MUS, SPOJENECTVÍ, SUVERENITA, SVOBODA!*—a majestic, ringing euphony that builds to the beloved President's name. Kohout's four stirring words became the battle cry of the Czechoslovak Revolution.

The manifesto was addressed to each Presidium member by name as well as to the three alternates who would accompany them to the summit: Bohumil Šimon, Prague's liberal new party chief, and conservatives Antonín Kapek, manager of a large Prague factory, and Jozef Lenárt, Novotný's old Prime Minister. Kohout exhorted them all to tell the Russians "that we need freedom, peace, and time to be worthier and better allies than ever before. In short, speak on behalf of the people, who are no longer an empty concept, but a new force that makes history." And then he addressed the Presidium almost personally:

> It is possible that not all of you hold the same views on everything. Some of you, although you jointly fought for January, are being sharply criticized for your mistakes of the period before January. Such is the lot of politicians. But the seven months since January have proved that nobody is trying to turn this criticism into a vendetta. It would be tragic if the personal feelings of any one of you should prevail over the responsibility that, at this moment, you bear for 14,361,000 people to whom you yourself belong.
>
> Act, explain, but in unity *defend* the road on which we have embarked and from which we will never depart alive. In the next few days, we shall follow your talks with suspense from hour to hour. We are impatiently awaiting your reports. Think of us! Write on our behalf a fateful page in the history of Czechoslovakia! Write it with deliberation, but above all with courage!
>
> To fail this unique opportunity would be our misfortune and your shame. We trust you.

Dated "Prague, Friday 26 July 1968" and distributed wherever *Literární Listy* went, Kohout's manifesto inspired more than two million Czechs and Slovaks to put their names (often their addresses) on the line—even while the Russian Army was still lingering in their land.

Outside the House of Children Department Store in Prague, citizens and tourists (particularly East Germans) queued up all night and all day to add their signatures. The House of Children put its computer at the disposal of the organizers. It recorded 85,500 signatures (on petitions weighing 40 pounds) over the weekend at that one location.

In an economy with scarcities, some consumers get on line first and ask questions next. An old lady saw the orderly queue outside the House of Children, joined it, and asked after a while: "What are we standing on line for?"

"For freedom," she was told.

She stayed on line.

That Friday night, Gene and Zdenka Deitch were watching the late TV news in bed. Seeing the queue, they got up, got dressed, and got down to the House of Children. There they stood on line in a drizzle until, at breakfast-time, they signed. All through the night, trams would halt while conductors and motormen dashed to the head of the line to sign Kohout's manifesto. By the time they raced back, most of their passengers were gone, queuing up themselves.

A Czech on the line heckled an East German behind him: "Look at you! Starting at the top here! That's the trouble with you Germans: you never do anything from the bottom up the way the Czechs do."

No assertion could have infuriated a German more. This one didn't bristle, though. He merely said: "We have no place like this to begin with. But what we see here we want for ourselves as well."

The Czech said: "We didn't *begin* here." Over the hours of bickering and discussion, though, the two men became fast friends, and after signing went off to an early-morning pub together to indoctrinate each other.

Two liberal members of the Presidium, Dr. Kriegel and Speaker Smrkovský, came down to the House of Children to see for themselves. Smrkovský assured his petitioners that "there will be no quislings among us." And he assured them: "Alexander Dubček has expressed the opinion of the whole nation."

In Bohemia, Moravia, and Slovakia, scenes like these on TV melted the ice of Kafkaesque alienation and provincial remoteness which had sealed the people off from their leaders for two decades. A farmer saw a city man 200 miles away signing a petition and talking to Smrkovský and—*Ježišmarja!*—he wanted to play a part in the government, too. Villagers converged on town squares in quest of petitions to sign. Some who couldn't find any ventured to the nearest city or made overnight trips to Prague, sleeping, when necessary, on the benches and floors of the three railroad stations. Railway employees covered them lovingly with blankets, coats, and canvas. It was a scene right out of a Russian novel.

That Saturday [it became known later in the Western press] Presidents Tito of Yugoslavia and Ceausescu of Rumania, Eastern Europe's ranking heretics, concluded four days of secret meetings. They sent private assurances to Alexander Dubček that they were ready to fly to Prague on short notice and keep a vigil there to show the Soviets that they were facing much more than a Czechoslovak faction. Dubček thanked them. He asked them to remain on call, but not to come just yet. He would go off to the summit knowing he had some trump cards to play.

That Sunday, the whole Czechoslovak nation went to church to pray for its leaders. Late that afternoon, the entire Presidium plus President Svoboda converged (mostly by plane) on Košice. From there a special train would take them to a "destination unknown" reliably guessed to be the border town at Čierna-nad-Tisou (Čierna on the River Tisa). Reporters, who had gone there to cover the occasional departures of Soviet troops, had noticed intensive preparations underway for a meeting. When police began escorting both Czechoslovak and foreign journalists away from the area, Čierna became a certainty.

From Košice to Čierna, the tracks were swept clear of sabotage or provocation by vintage autos with railway wheels (like the track car in which the fur-coated collaborationist travels in *Closely-Watched Trains*). The Czechoslovak State Railways operate on standard West European-gauge tracks. The Russian trains run on wider-gauge tracks that extend into Slovakia all the way from the border at Čierna to the iron-and-steel works at Košice. With the entire Politburo aboard and using it as a hotel, the Russian train would pull out every evening and spend the night on its side of the border. Leonid Brezhnev had said that he anticipated a counter-revolutionary attempt on his life.

A crowd had gathered in the station at Košice to cheer Dubček on his way: "Dubček! Dubček! We want Dubček!" The Presidium's special blue train bore the official seal of Czechoslovakia, the Bohemian lion, augmented by a red star for a crown, and still the motto "TRUTH PREVAILS." Looking spruced up and shiny (rather than tanned from a day's swimming near Bratislava), Dubček leaned out of a window to smile and wave.

"Why didn't you tell us you were coming here to meet the Russians?" he was asked.

"Because," Dubček replied, "if I had to tell everybody where I was going all the time, then I'd never get out of my office. And besides, if I had announced I was coming through Košice today, then your women would have mobbed me."

The crowd howled with glee. As the train lurched forward, they called: "Don't let us down. Don't let the Russians get the better of you."

"Nothing to be afraid of," was the last they heard from Dubček as his train gathered speed toward the summit.

Čierna is a dingy town whose one spot of color is a bed of geraniums forming a red star in front of the one small hotel. The community's nerve center was the tan-roofed green railway workers' hall, the Junction Club, down a potholed street from the station. The Slovak equivalent of a Legion hall, the Junction Club was the place to go for beer, *slivovice,* movies, and dancing to a jukebox. But now the Junction Club was the setting for the unlikeliest—and least lasting—summit meeting in Marxist-Leninist history.*

The train arrived in Čierna toward 2100 Sunday and all of the town's 2,500 people were there. The chairman of Čierna's national committee delivered an official welcome. Dubček, Smrkovský, and the others walked around the platform, answered questions, and signed autographs. Then they went to bed on the train.

At 0930 Monday, a green narrow-gauge train backed in on the next track. President Svoboda and the entire Czechoslovak Presidium were waiting on the platform. Leonid Brezhnev was the first to descend. He kissed Svoboda on the lips warmly and shook Dubček's hand brusquely. Behind Brezhnev came Prime Minister Kosygin; President Podgorny; party theoretician Mikhail Suslov; A. N. Shelepin, an up-and-coming technocrat with secret police connections; and half-a-dozen faceless men who held the balance of power within the Kremlin. They and their Czechoslovak counterparts walked in uneasy groupings of two, three, and four to the Junction Club, where a pool of newsmen were admitted to photograph the opening of talks and then asked to leave town immediately.

The talks (it was learned later) began badly. There was no conversation on Monday, just formal speech after formal speech in a pecking order dictated by Secretary-General Brezhnev. His own speech made

---

* In the age of instant landmarks, the Junction Club in Čierna was designated as a historical museum early that August. A fund-raising campaign to "build a new cultural center to replace it" began and ended that same month.

more demands than ever before. Dubček's and Smrkovský's showed more determination than ever. But first indication of how bad things were came when the mild-mannered and hitherto dovish Kosygin, who hadn't been himself since Sweden, objected to the presence of Dr. Kriegel.

"But why?" Kriegel protested. He started to remind the Russians that he was a bona fide member of the Czechoslovak Presidium. . . .

Pyotr Shelest, the Soviet party leader from the neighboring Ukraine, told Kriegel: "You just *are* objectionable; we don't have to explain why!"

But Kosygin said with a snarl: "Tell this filthy little Galician Jew to shut his trap!"

Dubček was outraged! He pounded the table with his fist and said: "Comrades, you're not going to treat *us* like your underlings!"

To which General Svoboda is supposed to have sighed and murmured to Dubček: "You'll get used to it, Sasha. That's how Marshal Konev treated me throughout the war." *

The meeting lasted until 2230, with time out only for meals—which each delegation took in its own dining car. The official communiqué issued that night simply stated that "views and standpoints were exchanged by both sides." To even an amateur Kremlinologist, a communiqué without adjectives is virtually a declaration of war.

The Russian train chugged across the border for the night. At 0254 Tuesday in Čierna, a dispatcher spotted a solitary stroller patroling the platform. It was Alexander Dubček. The dispatcher invited him into his office, where several other night-shift railwaymen joined them.

"You must get some rest, Mr. Dubček," one of them told their guest.

"I can never fall asleep before three," Dubček said. "My usual sleeping hours nowadays are three to seven in the morning." Then the gathering talked about football until 0330, when Dubček re-boarded the blue train.

President Svoboda's turn to speak led off Tuesday morning's session. The Russians were banking on this longtime Hero of the Soviet

---

* I wasn't in the room and neither was anybody else I know well. Such dialogue, therefore, was necessarily pieced together (at the time or later) from aides and mutual friends of one or two men who *were* there, plus various press accounts, whose reliability I've taken upon myself to evaluate and sometimes question. Throughout this first Slovakian summit meeting, I was either in Prague or the Bohemian countryside, with a transistor radio always at hand.

Union to make a conciliatory speech, which could then be used by Bil'ak, Kolder, and Švestka to make Dubček and Smrkovský approach, if not yet toe, the Russian line.

Instead, the seventy-two-year-old soldier came on like the nerviest student radical. He demanded the immediate withdrawal of Russian troops. "Czechoslovak sovereignty is inviolable!" he insisted. As a point of honor, he said, this matter was not negotiable.

Svoboda then told his stunned listeners that he had long felt a need to give Russia's allies more of a say in the Warsaw Pact Joint Command. By this time, his stunned listeners were wondering whether they were hearing General Svoboda or General Prchlík.

After that bombshell, the Russians might have been expected to stiffen. Instead, they grew relaxed, even resigned. Brezhnev waived his original stipulation that everybody speak in turn. The discussion moved swiftly, if not amicably, from then on. The meeting lasted until 1945 hours, when the joint communiqué was issued noting that it had been held "in an atmosphere of comradely frankness." This indicated some attempt at rapprochement, though it was still too early and too cool to tell whether it would take. "No war today," was Jiří Šlitr's greeting. "The situation in Čierna," said Radio Prague that night, "is like that of a hospital operating theatre during a heart transplant. But this is much more dangerous because not the life of just one individual but of all Europe is at stake."

Meanwhile, all over Poland, Hungary, East Germany, and Russia, travelers were noting troop movements toward the Czechoslovak frontier. And, in Bulgaria, which has no common frontier with Czechoslovakia, border guards were turning back thirty-one Czechoslovak delegates to the ninth World Youth Festival in Sofia. Invited by the Bulgarian Union of Youth, they had hiked almost 700 miles through Hungary and Yugoslavia to the Bulgarian border, only to be told that they were "too untidy" to be admitted. The youths produced written confirmation that clean clothes had been shipped ahead to Sofia and awaited them there. Nevertheless, the authorities said they could not come into Bulgaria. The next explanation was that they were "personae non gratae."

Other Czech youths, however, had already made it to Sofia, through whose silent streets they carried signs reading "LONG LIVE DUBČEK!", "DUBČEK'S POLICY IS OUR OWN BUSINESS," and

"WAKE UP, SOFIA, AND FACE THE FACTS." Their pamphlets and even their blank stationery had already been confiscated by the Bulgarian authorities as "counter-revolutionary propaganda." Nevertheless, the youths held an indignant press conference for which they sent out invitations printed on the durable Bulgarian toilet paper.

Bright and early Wednesday morning, Josef Smrkovský appeared on the platform and remarked to his greeters: "I believe we shall leave Čierna smiling even more than when we came here. Rest assured that everything will come off well."

Win, lose, or draw, Smrkovský expected the talks to end that day. So did everyone else in Čierna, Russian or Czech. Three days of serious discussion were the most that the Russians could be expected to budget for any balky satellite.

By noon, most signs were favorable. Late that morning, Kosygin and Smrkovský had gone for a stroll together through the streets of Čierna. There, they struck up a conversation with a ten-year-old boy and took him along on their walk—each with a jovial hand propping up the dumfounded lad from behind. Presidents Svoboda and Podgorny also took a walk together.

True, Leonid Brezhnev had been taken ill that morning, soon after his own ideologist, Suslov, had reminded him that he was starting to talk like Walter Ulbricht. While Brezhnev adjourned to his railroad car, Shelest and Shelepin stepped up the attack on Dubček, warning him that "imperialist agents" had infiltrated his Presidium. "If you really think that there are imperialist agents among our leaders, then there's no point in continuing these talks," Dubček said coolly. He stood up and stalked away to *his* railroad car. A short while later, five of the Russians came to Dubček's car to invite the whole Czechoslovak delegation to have lunch with them. It was the first time the two groups had eaten together. After lunch, Dubček saw fit to pay a call on Brezhnev and Brezhnev saw fit to receive him. That was good.

On the other hand, a joint evening banquet—obviously meant to be a cordial farewell—was first arranged and then canceled at the last minute. Nothing to worry about yet. Just some delay over the wording of the final official communiqué. In the meantime, the daily interim communiqué announced that the cliffhanger—whose Wednesday mood was described as "open and comradely"—would be held over for an unanticipated fourth day.

Most of the straws in the Wednesday night wind were favorable. The troop movements on the other sides of the border had ground to a halt. Three of the eighty Russian tourist groups whose visits to Czechoslovakia had been canceled arrived in Prague all of a sudden; their cancellations, they told ČEDOK, had been "repealed." Brezhnev made a miraculous recovery and rejoined the talks. During his illness, a packet of three letters had arrived at the Soviet train. All three warned of disastrous consequences to world communism should any kind of socialist fratricide ensue. One was from Marshal Tito. One was from Waldeck Rochet, leader of France's Communist Party. One was from Luigi Longo, leader of Italy's Communist Party. Rochet and Longo were particularly important to academician Suslov, who had been working for years to organize a world conference of Communist parties. It was scheduled for 25 November 1968 in Moscow and he wanted nothing to mar the facade of Communist unity.*

Thus, on the fourth day, Thursday the 1st of August, a bargain was sealed and the talks in Čierna ended. The final communiqué was eight paragraphs long. The first four paragraphs listed who had participated and where and when. The next two paragraphs said little or nothing, but in the most archaic Communist language:

> At the joint talks, there was a broad comradely exchange of views about problems of interest to both parties. Both parties exchanged detailed information on the situation in their countries.
>
> The talks between the Politburo . . . and the Presidium . . . were held in an atmosphere of complete frankness, sincerity, and mutual understanding, aimed at seeking ways toward the further development and strengthening of the traditional friendly relations between the Communist parties and nations . . . based on the principles of Marxism-Leninism and proletarian internationalism.

The final two paragraphs announced that, on Saturday in Bratislava, the two delegations would meet for a further talk with the Communist

---

* Another letter, signed by representatives of eighteen European Communist parties, demanded an end to Soviet interference in the domestic affairs of the Czechoslovak Socialist Republic. According to the French Marxist philosopher Roger Garaudy (later purged by his Communist Party for his heresies), Dubček warned Brezhnev at Čierna that any invasion of Czechoslovakia would be condemned by most European Communist parties and Brezhnev replied: "Whoever dares to do that, we have the means of reducing to grouplets." And, according to a *Le Monde* quote from Vasil Bil'ak (later repudiated by Bil'ak) Dubček remarked to him not long thereafter: "Brezhnev is senile. There's no point in discussing anything with him. The Russians are nervous, but I won't retreat just because they are."

parties of Bulgaria, East Germany, Hungary, and Poland. The meeting would last one day.

The short time set for the Bratislava summit meant that the Soviet Union, having held truly bilateral talks with Czechoslovakia, was now summoning its other satellites to rubber-stamp whatever was agreed upon in Čierna. Beyond this, of course, the communiqué shed absolutely no light on what had been decided in Čierna-nad-Tisou.

Nevertheless, the Prague grapevine said that the bargain seemed to be this:

Russian troops would leave in all due haste. Czechoslovakia's internal liberalization would proceed apace, too. But attacks on Russia and caricatures of the Russian leaders, in particular, would cease in the Prague press. Similar treatment of the other four countries' leaders would be, at the very least, toned down. The Russian press, in turn, would cease its anti-Czechoslovak polemics at once.

Being a monolith, the Soviet Union could comply almost instantly. The term "counter-revolution" vanished from *Pravda* overnight. The remaining troops (and even the most imaginative Czech was surprised by how many of them there proved to be) gassed up and headed for the borders.

Being a burgeoning democracy, the Czechoslovak Socialist Republic had a harder task. Dubček's Presidium, immediately upon its return to Prague, called a Thursday-night meeting with the editors of *Literární Listy* (representing the Writers Union) and the slick newsweekly *Reportér* (representing the Journalists Union). They would be asked to soft-pedal the anti-Sovietism and concentrate on Czechoslovak targets, a compromise that Dubček knew they would be willing to swallow as long as Russia kept her end of the bargain. It had turned out at Čierna that *Literární Listy,* in particular, was being read avidly in the Kremlin. Two *LL* cartoons had even been cited as "horrid examples" of where freedom of the press could carry you. One of them showed Brezhnev done up as St. Florian, the patron saint of firemen. He was dousing a house called ČSSR while a tiny Dubček remonstrated: "But it's not on fire!" The other showed Walter Ulbricht in a bare-breasted heroic Delacroix pose. The bearded dictator was waving aloft a bayonet and a banner of "LIBERTÉ, ÉGALITÉ, FREUNDSCHAFT!" The last was one of those chilling German words for "friendship."

While Dubček and Černík were pleading with the editors to cool it, the Czechoslovak public was doing a fast burn over the now uncharacteristic lack of information. Hearing rumors that *LL* and *Reportér* were being muzzled, ten thousand people gathered in Old Town Square. Some of them cried: "We have been betrayed!"

The first reassurance came from Košice with a broadcast by President Svoboda: "In January, we took an important step in the life of this country and its people. . . . We shall not abandon the path we have taken. We shall consistently continue to pursue it." Further comfort came when Josef Smrkovský appeared on a balcony of Prague's Old Town Hall and told the crowd:

"The Bratislava talks will last only about one day, so on Saturday night you'll be able to hear what we've agreed upon. And next week, Czechoslovakia will have an opportunity to welcome our friends. President Tito of Yugoslavia and a Rumanian delegation headed by Nicolae Ceausescu are coming. All this has already been settled. Only the calendar will say precisely when."

Somebody called up to Smrkovský: "Why aren't Tito and Ceausescu invited to Bratislava, too?"

"Because they weren't among the five who sent the letter from Warsaw," Smrkovský replied, sidestepping neatly. "First of all, we must set things right with those who talked in Warsaw. The representatives of Rumania and Yugoslavia agree with us on this."

"We hear that freedom of the press will be curtailed."

"Nothing like that," said Smrkovský, "so why are you asking such questions?"

"Then tell us what it was like at Čierna! Tell us what really went on!"

Smrkovský tried to beg off with: "You can read about it in tomorrow's paper." But his audience would have none of this. A slow, piercing, jeering whistle started up. Then a heckler's raucous yelp penetrated the din: "Why can't you speak freely?"

"I can speak freely and so can you!" Smrkovský snapped back.

Even after almost seven months, it was remarkable that this kind of give-and-take was occurring in any Communist country. It was not remarkable, however, that having tasted of such a dialogue, the crowd thirsted for more. The bickering with Smrkovský continued until the speaker cut it off with:

"Look! We ourselves invited the signers of the Warsaw letter to

Bratislava so we can explain to them thoroughly the direction of our new road. Naturally, we cannot predict . . . but I am convinced that these talks will lead to understanding among the fraternal parties."

The crowd must have agreed with him because, chanting "We want Dubček!", it marched almost a mile to Central Committee headquarters. There, Dubček appeared at a window and apologized: "I must excuse myself to prepare for the Bratislava talks. . . . But, as you can see, we have come back in a fairly optimistic mood."

The chant then switched to "Long live Dubček!" and it persisted well into the night after he had withdrawn inside.

The next day, in a radio talk to the nation, Dubček said: "You can be completely satisfied with the results as well as the spirit of the meeting. We kept our promise to you and we are returning with the same conviction that we took to the talks." And Smrkovský, briefing some editors, remarked about Čierna: "You can believe us, it was no honeymoon."

The impact and the relief, however, were blissful. Jan Procházka, Goldstücker's deputy chief of the Writers Union, remarked in an article:

> Untruths have given way to the truth in Czechoslovakia. . . . Instead of people who didn't enjoy public confidence and popularity, there are now people at the helm who are trusted and liked, which is not a common thing in politics. They are being liked even though they tell the public how badly off this country is. But they say the truth— and this is what everybody appreciates.

Even Deputy Premier Ota Šik, who was still telling the nation how badly off it was financially, could write exuberantly in *Rudé Právo*:

> The unbelievable has happened! A political party which at the beginning of January had reached the edge of its deepest moral and political crisis has won incredibly high moral credit within half a year through its will and determination for reform.

Still, there were those who weren't certain that truth was prevailing. A girl who had heard Smrkovský in Old Town Square told me wanly: "We haven't learned anything to comfort us. Nor have we heard anything to make us unhappy." A member of KAN said: "The worst tragedy that could befall us is not Russian intervention, but compromise. What if our own leaders bargain away our reforms? True, they are better men than their predecessors. But the question you must always ask about any Communist is 'How much better?'" One of

K231's veterans of the Fifties declared succinctly: "I am sure they will betray us at Bratislava."

The world press, having been ejected from Čierna on Monday, had retreated to its home away from home, the Alcron lobby. One day during the Čierna talks, I had dropped in there and witnessed a tableau of how the English-speaking press was obliged to cover the grimmest official confrontation since Munich. I saw a pyramid of men, all ears, lunging upward toward a table-top, on which stood a fat lady interpreter with a tiny transistor to her ear. The world press held its breath while she broadcast bulletins: "Dubček's coming out onto the platform! He looks grim! Wait! He's smiling! Now he's stopped smiling! He's looking under the train for something! Now what are they saying? They say he's not Dubček at all! He's a railway worker!" Truth prevails.

Now most of the journalists were packing their bags for the 250-mile flight to Bratislava and so was I. I went down to the Alcron to send an urgent telex. At the desk, I overheard the veddy Anglophilic foreign correspondent of an American newspaper inform the clerk: "I've come for my battery."

"Begging your pardon, sir. What battery?" said the clerk.

"The one I gave you yesterday to have repaired."

"I'm sorry, sir. You didn't give it to me. I wasn't working yesterday."

"Then it must have been your colleague. Please, I must have it."

"But, sir, I have no knowledge of it and my colleague is off duty today."

"Use your head, my good man. What would your colleague have done with my battery? I absolutely need it for Bratislava."

"If he had it back, sir, he might have put it in this drawer here. But he seems to have taken the key home with him. In any event, I cannot find it. Please don't be angry, sir."

This "don't be angry" is a standard Czech form of apology, but the foreign correspondent was already frothing at the mouth. I could sympathize and I even considered lending him my transistor radio or flashbulbs or whatever it was he needed his battery for. But I didn't realize the true dimension of his crisis until he turned away from the desk and implored the world: "Good Lord, how am I ever going to brush my teeth in Bratislava?"

Interlude ⅃ How are things in Bratislava?

SLOVAKS ARE GIVEN TO ALL SORTS OF EXCESSES, MOSTLY amiable ones: excessive drinking and eating (when in Slovakia or nearby Hungary, order one portion for two persons); courtly mustaches, bowing, and hand-kissing; passionate emotional gestures and infinite sadness. Played on fiddles and the *cimbalom* (a stereophonic Danubian zither), the sweet gypsy music to which Slovaks are addicted can make you cry without your knowing what it's about or even when you do. I am invariably moved to tears by the rustic banality of a folkloric staple that goes:

> Round about Levoča town,
> There's a rushing waterfall.
> Any girl who feels let down
> Can jump to end it all.

"Our sense of tragedy is more highly developed than yours in Prague," I was told soon after I landed in Bratislava on the second morning of August, 1968. "So is our pessimism. The Czechs were under German domination for barely three centuries, so they can scheme and hope. But we were under the Magyars for a millenium, so we know better."

Slovaks are also excessively patriotic—as I gathered simply by observing my hosts in Bratislava (friends of a friend in Prague who found me lodging with them when no hotel had room for me). They insisted on meeting me at the Bratislava airport and showing me the Slovak capital city when I arrived three hours before the summit figures would begin to pour in.

"Three hours!" my host, a doctor, explained. "Anything less than a whole week to see Bratislava is criminal."

"So we won't even show you our airport," said the hostess. But I'd already seen that it was a shed, as Prague's airport used to be. She must have sensed my reaction, because she added: "It's not as modern as the one we hear you have in Prague now, but it makes the traveler feel more at home."

Then they whisked me off by car on a sightseeing tour of Bratislava's Castle (they claimed it made "Prague's look like an air-raid shelter," which it didn't at all); St. Martin's Cathedral (they claimed it made "St. Vitus look like a vicarage"; not so, but it might have compared more favorably if it hadn't been surrounded by a sea of mud instead of cobblestones); and, among a dozen other similar comparisons, a rickety iron bridge which, they conceded, "is not the Charles Bridge. But then the Vltava isn't the Blue Danube, is it?"

I didn't have the audacity to reply "no, but neither is the Danube," so I simply nodded agreeably and tried not to glance at my watch as they raced me from wonder to wonder. Bratislava (population: 262,000; formerly known as Pressburg and Pozsony) is a quaint old Danube port best entered by hydrofoil on the Vienna-Budapest run, but this was no time for sightseeing, and I didn't breathe easily until my formidable hosts deposited me at the railroad station fifteen minutes before the Russian delegation arrived.

Dubček and Svoboda were there. They were spending most of Friday shuttling between airport and depot to extend formal greetings while red carpets unrolled and rolled back. Friday's mood, however, was brusque and businesslike. The ceremonies and signings would come on Saturday; Friday was reserved for welcoming and then bargaining at a "strictly procedural" evening session.

Though all the signers of the Warsaw ultimatum had been summoned to Bratislava to eat their words, it was Brezhnev who looked sheepish and Gomulka and Ulbricht who looked angry. It soon became known that Gomulka's first remark had been to this effect: I don't know why this meeting has been called, since everything has already been agreed upon. Kádár looked relieved. Todor Zhivkov looked dour, but didn't he always? Besides, this was the right pose for what one Prague commentator called a "State funeral with full rites for the Warsaw letter."

The two-thousand-word "Declaration of the Communist and Workers Parties of the Socialist Countries" that was to be issued the next day began with this whopping sentence:

> Proceeding from the fact that the complicated international situation, the subversive actions of imperialism directed against peace and

international security, against the cause of socialism, call for still closer cohesion of the countries of the socialist system, and also taking into consideration that the development of socialism sets new tasks whose solution necessitates further pooling of efforts of socialist states, the representatives of the communist and workers parties of socialist countries found it necessary to call this conference in Bratislava.

The language was Moscow's throughout, and so, for the most part, was the shrill tenor of its tirades against NATO, neo-Nazi revanchism in West Germany, American militarism in Vietnam, and "the aggressive policy of Israel's ruling circles." The whole hymnal of Kremlin laments was rendered in the orthodox fashion. The declaration had been drafted by a committee including Dubček and Černík, Kosygin and Brezhnev. Its obvious purpose was to save Russia's face by making Čierna read like a Russian victory. It was even agreed that, at Saturday's signing, Brezhnev would bearhug Dubček, kiss his lips fraternally, and raise his hand aloft like a flag of surrender, all for Soviet home consumption. And Dubček, who had what he wanted, was amenable to letting Brezhnev savor the moment.

The troops were going. The polemics had ceased. The January reforms and the September party congress could proceed without further interruption. And, embedded within the Bratislava declaration's verbiage, were two paragraphs that mattered the most to Dubček and Černík. For Dubček, there was an affirmation that the specific conditions of each country must shape the kind of socialism that would prevail there. For Černík, there was a foot in the door to West German financial aid, for the declaration took cognizance of a few "positive" forces at work there for "democratic progress," which any Communist nation could support and encourage.

Much of Friday night's haggling was over these two clauses. Otherwise, as one Czechoslovak press briefer assured us, "there isn't a new word or a new thought in the whole document." But here he was wrong. Much later, on close re-examination, it became apparent that, at some moment during Friday night's session, Ulbricht and Gomulka (with or without Brezhnev's connivance) had quietly managed to make one small alteration in the liturgy: *Instead of the customary reference to "non-interference in each other's affairs," the seemingly innocent phrase "mutual support" was substituted.* The whole flimsy fabric (in fact, the sole basis) for the "Brezhnev Doctrine" of limited sovereignty, whereby one Communist nation can come to the "rescue" of another, was thus custom-designed for the Czechoslovaks right there in Bratislava by the craftiest of Polish and German tailors.

Then, because the document had to be reprinted, the signing was postponed from Saturday afternoon to Saturday night. To while away a warm summer Saturday, Kosygin and Suslov went strolling along the banks of the Danube. They chatted amiably with Slovaks and even Western journalists. So did Dubček and Brezhnev, and, when a photographer snapped Dubček pointing out a Danube sight to Brezhnev, the caption claimed he was showing him the way back to Moscow. Slovaks like my hosts were optimistic and more than a bit proud. Their capital city was the center of world attention for the first time since Talleyrand came there in 1805 to sign the Treaty of Pressburg after Napoleon's victory at Austerlitz (also in Czechoslovakia, near Brno). They basked in the presence of world leaders.

When Walter Ulbricht passed by in a limousine, however, he was booed by a few Slovaks and quite a few East German tourists. Later in the day, when all the leaders placed a wreath at Bratislava's Russian war memorial, a Slovak called out: "How's it going, Dubček?" And Dubček cupped his hand over his mouth, leaned past Ulbricht, and stage-whispered: "Don't worry. We're home free!"

The Bratislava Declaration was signed at 7:40 P.M. Saturday in the Hall of Mirrors of the city's Old Town Hall. Two briefings were held for the press. The multilingual Foreign Minister, Jiří Hájek, analyzed the declaration for the foreign press. Prime Minister Černík answered the questions of Czechoslovak journalists. Both sessions were boisterous.

Hájek said that the Warsaw letter, which had triggered the summit conferences in Čierna and Bratislava, "was not discussed today and is now a matter of history."

"But you are a historian, Dr. Hájek," one journalist pointed out. "How can any document become history in less than a month?"

"Because of its contents," Hájek replied with a grin.

"Do you think that the Bratislava Declaration will restore good relations with the Soviet Union and East Germany?"

Hájek replied: "May I ask not to be asked to be a prophet?"

At his session, Černík said he was sure "relations will develop so that our alliance with the Soviet Union and the socialist countries, which secures our national independence, will never be violated."

There was a reception that night for delegates in the Old Town

Hall. Members of all six groups appeared on the balcony to acknowledge joyous crowds shouting "Dubček-Svoboda!" and even an occasional "Long live the Soviet Union!" But it was Speaker Josef Smrkovský who did the talking: "I can assure you we have done good work. Normal life resumes as of tomorrow. Everything is normal!"

The Russians went home by train around midnight and the others left on Sunday. Dubček made a radio and TV speech in which he reiterated that the reforms would continue because "there is no other way." And the Ministry of Defense made the good news official with a one-sentence bulletin: "The last Soviet Army units which had taken part in the staff exercises from 20 to 30 June left Czechoslovak territory on 3 August."

Ivan went home, and "socialism with a human face" heaved one vast collective sigh of relief. But the Czechoslovak Revolution had only seventeen days to live.

Chapter 11]

Monday 5 August—
Tuesday 20 August 1968

IT HAD NOT BEEN LIKE ANY OTHER "CUCUMBER SEASON" and, now that the whole nation could uncoil and vegetate, it was still not going to be like any other "cucumber season." Workers in the Merina textile mill started working one extra "Dubček shift" a month to help Ota Šik rejuvenate the ailing economy. This spirit of sacrifice ballooned into Dubček Clubs with sixteen branches across the country and a Fund for the Republic, to which Czechs and Slovaks donated overtime pay, crowns, gold and silver they had hoarded for years, and even Tuzex crowns. Twenty unrewarding years had dulled, but not killed, the national instinct for hard work and, combined with a rational program at last, the economy could conceivably be saved.

Josef Smrkovský stayed on the job and worked harder than ever at assuring and exhorting the millions who loved him. He journeyed north to the industrial center of Ústí-nad-Labem (Aussig-on-the-Elbe) for three hours of unprogrammed questions and answers.

"Do you think you succeeded in convincing the other Communist delegations that our road is the right one?" Smrkovský was asked there.

"I don't think we convinced them," he replied, "but we went to Bratislava to explain to them in a comradely way that this is our business and we would appreciate their respecting our right. . . . I often hear the question: Was the result of the talks a victory or a compromise? I answer: We managed to maintain what we wanted to. Now, however, we must make up the lost time and prepare for the Extraordinary Congress of the Party."

Around the 7th of August, Brezhnev, Kosygin, Podgorny, and most of the other Soviet leaders went on vacation to Black Sea resorts and government dachas along the Moscow River. Even though two of the more hawkish profiles among the faceless men of the Politburu, Kiril T. Mazurov and Andrei P. Kirilenko, were left in charge of the Kremlin, their functions and abilities were those of caretakers and nobody in Prague worried much about them. General Svoboda took a brief holiday in the High Tatras with his wife and granddaughter and, when they returned, it was reported that the seventy-two-year-old President had climbed the Gerlachovka, the highest peak in the land. Foreign Minister Jiří Hájek and Deputy Prime Minister Ota Šik took working vacations in Yugoslavia. Alexander Dubček stayed in Prague to prepare for the Party Congress on 9 September, but he managed to take a long hunting and swimming weekend in Slovakia.

(One Czech journal reported shortly after this trip: "On the stairway and in the drawing room of the Dubček home in Bratislava, the walls are decorated with hunting trophies, the stuffed heads of stags and roebucks. Above each trophy is a wooden plaque telling where and when this particular trophy was shot and by whom. It came as a surprise to find many heads bearing the name of Alexander Dubček." The reporter didn't need to stress the symbolism of the next revelation: "On the drawing-room floor lies the skin and stuffed head of a Russian black bear. About two years ago, a town called Javorina was gripped with fear because of that bear. Slovak newspapers wrote about the three-day hunt that eliminated this bear, but in the characteristic Communist way it did not identify the man who killed it and brought it home.")

Back in the big city, Dubček, the Great White Hunter of the Tatras, was not without his troubles. At a Presidium meeting, the Bil'ak-Indra-Kolder-Švestka axis was trying to woo the centrists with grumbles that Dubček was enjoying too much personal popularity and this cult of personality was undermining the authority of the rest of the members. Bil'ak was telling the folks back home in Slovakia that "Dubček has become more Czech than Slovak." Furthermore, the task of drafting various resolutions had somehow been entrusted to Kolder and Indra, of all people, and they were dragging their feet. In fact, instead of preparing the resolutions, Indra and Kolder were collaborating on a position paper contending that the forces supporting progressive development were superficial and unstable. Meanwhile, Švestka had cashiered two liberal editors of his own *Rudé Právo*.

Dubček had the strength and the stature to overcome his high-level hecklers and saboteurs, whose days in power seemed numbered. But he told his family he could not go on vacation with them in the near future. His wife Anna took two of their sons to Yugoslavia while the third went alone on a trip to Egypt. Dubček's mother Pavlina stayed home making raspberry syrup. The ready-made raspberry syrup sold in the markets was all right, she told a visitor, but it was not up to her own personal standard. Pavlina Dubček's 1968 output of raspberry syrup had just reached seventy bottles, but she hoped to hit the one hundred mark before summer was over.

Despite the moratorium on anti-Soviet criticism, faithfully observed, the Czechoslovak press remained informative, vocal, and political. When Czechoslovak Television and the Ministry of Technology made a joint announcement that they were reconsidering their 1966 choice of the SECAM system for color television in the 1970's because the rival PAL system "has better technical qualities," it was barely footnoted in the press that the previous decision had been made "in the interests of uniformity with the other socialist countries, particularly the Soviet Union."

The sports pages serialized the memoirs of Czech tennis star, Jaroslav Drobný (living in England), telling why he chose exile after encountering exit-visa difficulties and hints that he might not be allowed to go abroad the next time. Colonel Emil Zátopek (stationed at the Ministry of Defense in Prague) told how, during the Novotný regime, he was forced to run a one-man marathon race against a team of relay runners; his losing the race was to help de-emphasize the cult of the individual. On the amusement pages, the singer Eva Pilarová (co-starring with Šlitr and Suchý in Menzel's *Crime in the Night Club*) told of the restriction and persecution she'd endured after her husband fled to the West. And she noted that "the people who did this to me are still in office."

Any magazine worth buying had something to offend somebody. The Journalists Union's *Reportér* took Czechoslovakia's diplomatic mission at the United Nations to task, painting it in broad strokes as a sort of Playboy Club East still staffed by Novotný-era holdovers. They were, *Reportér* claimed, handling instructions from Prague simply by relaying them onward to Moscow, Warsaw, and Sofia for further consideration. In passing, *Reportér* alluded to U.N. Secretary General U Thant's "tact and Buddhistic perseverance" with the Czechoslovak mission. A couple of issues later, however, *Reportér* printed its regrets at reports that the article had annoyed U Thant. The editors said they were sorry about this because U Thant was due in Prague for a Charles

University convocation on the 23d of August (in connection with International Human Rights Year) and they did not want the Czechs to be ungracious hosts. But they defended the freedom of opinion of the article's author (an anonymous but knowledgeable "X.Y." apparently within the U.N. mission).

Student, published every Tuesday and sold out by 0800, started a series of "Talks in an English Garden" with officials of Radio Free Europe. (Czechoslovakia had stopped jamming RFE broadcasts on the ground that the rebirth of freedom "has taken their breath away.") The first interview provoked so much criticism and created such consternation about a possible Russian reaction that *Student's* editors agreed to postpone the rest of the series. Instead, *Student* campaigned for a resumption of diplomatic relations with Israel and abolition of the blue-uniformed People's Militia: "We would hate to wake up one morning only to see the streets patroled by People's Militia and hear the radio announce that Dubček, the lackey of imperialism, has been put in prison."

The South Bohemian regional press did a local zoo story on

. . . the famous dead duck of Hluboká, still very much alive. Two weeks ago, he was put inside the wildcat's cage as food for the beast. Now, a fortnight later, he is not only uneaten, but you can see that he has the run of the cage. Look how content the wildcat is! He knows he can end the relationship at any time, but right now he enjoys the company. Meanwhile, the duck gets fatter and juicier. The people around Hluboká have adopted him as some kind of omen.

The women's magazine *Vlasta* got into the act with an unprecedented interview of a high Communist dignitary's wife. Shortly before taking off for Yugoslavia, Anna Dubčeková had allowed *Vlasta* to pay her a homey personal visit in Bratislava. A fascinated public learned that the Dubčeks still did not have a live-in maid at their house on Mouse Street, just a once-or-twice-or-thrice-a-week cleaning lady.

"What kind of food does Alexander Dubček like best?" the lady from *Vlasta* asked Dubček's wife. Anna Dubčeková consulted in the kitchen with her mother-in-law, Pavlina, who said: "He likes everything." To which Anna added: "He dearly likes cakes, small cakes filled with curds, plum jam on top, and maybe a sprinkling of poppyseed."

"How does he take his coffee?" asked *Vlasta.*

"No, he doesn't take coffee," Anna replied. "And he doesn't smoke. He likes milk, cakes, and hot soup all year round. Whenever I come to Prague, I make him soup for breakfast."

"Does he take beer or wine?"

"He likes white wine, Rýnský Riesling and Müller-Thürgau," his wife replied. Trite though the dialogue may strike the reader of *Good Housekeeping* or Sidney Skolsky, it made history in the East. It also generated a run on the two wines. And, best of all, *Vlasta* illustrated it with the most engaging photo of Alexander Dubček that has ever been taken. It showed the First Secretary of the Czechoslovak Communist Party high-diving as freely as a bird, just as if the sky would never fall in on him.

Whenever I was in town that summer, I made the rounds of the newspaper offices to research an article that *The New York Times* Magazine wanted on "The Free Press of Prague." It was so quiet at *Literární Listy,* however, that Igor Hájek decided he could get away for a two-week vacation in England. Before leaving, he gave me precise advice for our own impending vacation (the first two weeks in September, we thought) in the High Tatras of Slovakia. "I almost envy you the mountains. They've been mine all my life," were the last words Igor spoke to me.

The offices of the new weeklies, preparing to make their debuts, were much livelier. Sylva's *Zítřek* was due to appear only five days before the Extraordinary Party Congress in September. Sylva was busier than Brenda Starr when I had lunch with her that August. "Today I've already interviewed a movie director and a writer," she told me. "And then I'm going to the studio of a woman sculptor I want to write about. After lunch, I'm to sit in on a group interview with the Minister of Justice and then, if there is any time, I'm to write an essay on something I was talking about over coffee the other day—about the emotional difficulties of having friends in West Germany and yet being such a stranger when I'm there."

"I'm amazed," I said more gratefully than facetiously, "that you have an hour for your friends."

"Oh, I must try," Sylva said with a laugh. "I even have time for a night out on the town with Jirka Šlitr." Consulting her diary, she added: "It will be on the twentieth of this month."

Three titans of communism landed diplomatically in Czechoslovakia during the first half of that month—one right after the other. On the 9th, President Tito of Yugoslavia arrived in triumph. He was cheered all the way from airport to castle with cries of "Ti-to—Dub-ček! Ti-to—Dub-ček!" Tanned, dapper, sandy-haired, and bespectacled at 76, Tito was everything that Czechoslovakia hoped Dubček would become —a national leader who had defied the Kremlin and whose nation had not only survived, but thrived (in terms of Communist economies, that is; Yugoslavia is by no means a rich nation). Tito's Yugoslavia had backed Dubček's Czechoslovakia to the hilt.

Tito himself had worked in a Czech factory before World War I. During his August 1968 stay in Prague, it became known that, back in April on a visit to Moscow, Tito had sat in Brezhnev's office and listened to a tirade against the new Czechoslovak leaders.

When Brezhnev had finished, Tito had said: "You don't know the Czechoslovak working class, but I do."

Brezhnev had warned him: "But it is not the same Czechoslovak working class any more."

And Tito had remarked in a voice thick with sarcasm: "How do you expect it to be the same after twenty years under your system?"

Tito had left Brezhnev speechless in April. Now he left all of Prague toasting him on the 11th of August.

Walter Ulbricht came to Carlsbad the next morning and the weather there has never been chillier. A thousand people waited at the airport to snub him with cold stares; they cheered only Dubček, who was waiting with them. The two leaders exchanged perfunctory handshakes. There were no bearhugs, no lip-kisses, not even the minimum bussing on both cheeks which is the Communist equivalent of "an exchange of views." A doughty little girl in Pioneer Camp uniform was stationed there to present Ulbricht with the ceremonial bouquet of roses dictated by protocol. She was the only Czechoslovak whom the goateed East German patriarch managed to kiss—with a nervous sideswipe that landed on her neck. A joke made the rounds in Prague that the poor girl would have to wear turtleneck sweaters for the rest of her life.

After Dubček had finished signing autographs at the airport (nobody asked for Ulbricht's), the official caravan of cars went to the Villa Javorina, where Kosygin had stayed, too. For the photo session before their talks began, both men stared stonily at the cameras, not at each other. In the afternoon, they took lunch separately.

Of all the "losers" at Bratislava, the seventy-five-year-old Ulbricht had the most to lose. Soviet troops had kept him in power longer than any other Communist dictator in history, but now Moscow had publicly failed to respond to what he considered a clear and present danger. With his own East Germans booing him in Bratislava and signing petitions in Prague, he could guess who would be the next to feel the fallout from the Czechoslovak Revolution. Between Bratislava and Carlsbád, he had been so panicked that he had even made accommodating noises toward Bonn: he was willing to negotiate. But Ulbricht is at his most dangerous at such moments.

His meeting with Dubček was reported to be waspish, if not hawkish. Ulbricht said *he* had interpreted the Bratislava declaration as the signal for a genuine crackdown on freedom of the press. What's more, Foreign Minister Hájek had informally received a West German political leader, Walter Scheel, and this did not sit well with Walter Ulbricht. But he racked up a zero with Dubček, who viewed events in Prague without alarm and made it known that his people did not appreciate Ulbricht's inviting himself to Carlsbad at a time when they were busy entertaining so many important friends. Still, one of the Czechs at the meeting remarked acidly, "we try to respect our guests no matter how suddenly they drop in."

Ulbricht held a press conference at which he said democracy was at its peak in his own country—and indicated that this was as high as anybody else should try to go. Then he flew home on Tuesday the 13th of August. Only later did it become known that, upon landing in East Berlin, he placed a phone call to Moscow. Ulbricht warned that Dubček was unrepentant and incorrigible. The Kremlin's hawkish summer custodians listened closely. . . .

Back in Prague, Nicolae Ceausescu of Rumania came to town on the 15th, amidst talk that the prewar Little Entente (Czechoslovakia, Rumania, and Yugoslavia) was about to be revived. Ceausescu's visit was essentially a re-run of the Tito festivities, though not so joyous. The Czechs were thanking him for standing by them in their July crisis, but they also knew that, despite his defiance of Moscow on foreign policy, he survived only because, internally, he ran a taut police state that posed no threat of democratic contagion. This may also be why Dubček discounted Ceausescu's warnings that week. It was learned (much later) that the Rumanian had cautioned that, while Dubček's goals were admirable, they should be approached slowly. It sounded like wishful thinking by a "nervous Nicolae."

I had intended to stay home and observe the Tito and Ceausescu visits to Prague on TV. I was much more involved in moving my family back home from the country to spend the last half of August in Prague. I was also in the final throes of fittings on what we called my "Dvořák suit"—my first custom-tailored suit. The tailor Dvořák would not hear of my naming the suit after him. He re-christened it my "U Thant suit," for my deadline was a reception for the U.N. Secretary General on the twenty-third.

My blue suit itself was a milestone for me, a final farewell to the boys at Barney's Seventh Avenue and Seventeenth Street and the inbred WASP salesmen at Brooks Brothers who must make even John Lindsay feel like a Jew at a country club. Mr. Dvořák meets you at the Tuzex apparel shop to pick out the best English wool. For the fittings (four in all), he comes to your house. The suit he was producing was the sturdiest, most distinguished, and most utilitarian I have ever had the privilege of owning: two pairs of trousers, each with leather-lined pockets; six pockets inside the jacket; a vest that buttons onto the trousers, thereby holding the wearer together as if he were clad in a comfortable corset. The price was $44.00 to Tuzex for the wool and $65.00 to the tailor for his work. But, more than that, the craftsmanship and the service were reminders to me that I could never quite bear to go home again.

On Friday afternoon the 16th, while Mr. Dvořák, a wispy and wonderfully affected gentleman of the old school, was dancing final attendance on my threads, a Special Delivery (*Exprés*) letter came. It was an invitation from the Foreign Ministry to a farewell reception for Ceausescu at the Černín Palace that evening. Alexander Dubček would, of course, be there. I decided to go and Mr. Dvořák and I happily re-named his creation once again: my "Dubček suit."

It was too late to engage a baby-sitter. Valerie cheerfully told me to take our niece Nancy—who would be leaving for Paris and then Boston in ten days, but who was desperately trying to join a Dubček club before her unforgettable summer would end.

Nancy trotted out her party dress and a shoebag for her high heels (even a three-block walk over Prague's cobblestones can ruin them) and we set out for the Černín. In the Firehouse Square, the police with phosphorescent white armbands and illuminated red batons were directing traffic. I led Nancy up the Černín's sweeping steps and briefed her on behavior at official Communist receptions. By now, I was such an old pro at Prague partygoing that I could hold an hors d'oeuvre and a drink while neatly shaking a hand and making small talk without swallowing the pit in my mouth from the previous ham-and-cherry tidbit.

There were no official greeters or reception committee. Dubček and Ceausescu were still down the road at the Castle putting finishing touches on a Czechoslovak-Rumanian friendship treaty to be signed later in the year. Nancy and I stood around the ballroom chatting with Minister of Culture Galuška and his wife. Then a man from the Foreign Ministry complimented me on my new suit, but asked whether I was in mourning. I had donned a black necktie, which was the only one I had available to go with the suit. We all agreed that there was nothing to mourn nowadays.

Another friend introduced me to a ruddy, stocky man with unshining eyes. He was Zdeněk Hejzlar, who had just been named the new chief of Czechoslovak Radio. Until the spring of 1952, Hejzlar had been the head of the Czechoslovak Union of Youth, a member of the Communist Party Central Committee, a National Assembly deputy and a member of its Presidium, an official of the National Front, and deputy chairman of the World Federation of Democratic Youth. But then he had been "linked" with the "Slánský gang" and banished from Prague. After a decade of degradation—as a forced laborer in the mines and then an auxiliary roller-mill operator in a foundry—Hejzlar had been working obscurely as headmaster of an Ostrava elementary school when the Czechoslovak Radio sought him out in 1968.

I made an appointment with Hejzlar to visit him in his office on Thursday, the 22nd of August, to discuss my "Free Press of Prague" project with him. It was an appointment we never kept.

Finally, almost an hour late, the hosts and their guest of honor swept in—first Svoboda and then Dubček, with his dance-floor strut, bending over to talk with the dark and debonair little Ceausescu. Dubček flashed Galuška and me a smile (he always seemed to like seeing journalists talking to the Minister of Culture) as he strode past. The dining hall doors opened before them and, as soon as they were in, there was a madly dignified dash for the seven buffet rooms. Since Nancy and I weren't hungry, we stayed in the first buffet room and watched Dubček and the Rumanians help themselves to the hot roast meats. They bantered and backslapped and drank. Once, they even indulged in a burst of song that went absolutely nowhere. Another circle of military attachés had formed around General Svoboda and they were trading war stories with the President.

Most people were talking and mixing and mingling and eating. But Nancy just wanted to stand near Dubček for a while and I stayed with her. After a while, we noticed that somebody else was doing the same thing. "Is he a bodyguard?" Nancy asked, nodding toward a bulky figure whose fixed smile seemed to have rusted. "No," I said, "it's the Russian Ambassador." Chervonenko was eyeing Dubček and the Rumanians almost as pensively, or clinically, as he might have eyed the lemon peel in his vermouth. Ceausescu noticed Chervonenko too, and waved an admonitory finger at him. Nobody invited him to join them, which was probably just as well with the Russian Ambassador.

The party was showing signs of breaking up when Nancy and I started to leave at 2245. We stopped at the downstairs cloakroom for Nancy to retrieve her shoebag and switch back to walking shoes. As we were ready to go, the official party came by us. My niece and I stood next to the oaken driveway door like lord and lady of the manor watching Dubček say good night to Svoboda and to the Rumanians, who would be leaving the next day, 17 August.

Svoboda's and Ceausescu's flag-laden Tatra 603 limousines turned left off the Loreta Square, bound for the castle. Dubček and his wife, both looking svelte and radiant (Dubček had lost 28 pounds during the summer's crises) boarded an unmarked, chauffeured Tatra 603, which slowly turned right—toward the Firehouse Square. When we reached the Firehouse Square, we could see the Dubčeks at the traffic island, veering right again onto Kepler Street. They were heading along the tree-lined boulevard that leads past the castle and onto a winding road down Hradčany hill, across the Vltava, and past the Philosophical Faculty toward the Hotel Without a Name.

It was the last time I saw Dubček as the leader of free Czechoslovakia.

Most of the events of the next 96 hours were not known until weeks or months thereafter. The next day—Saturday, 17 August—in response to an urgent telephone call from Janos Kádár of Hungary, Dubček journeyed to the Danube harbor town of Komárno in Slovakia, where

Franz Lehár was born. As Dubček's only friend among his five oppressors, Kádár implored Dubček to slow down the reforms. It might already be too late, Kádár said. Dubček replied that, at his end, it was indeed too late. Not even he could halt the momentum of the Czechoslovak Revolution.

The two friends parted late Saturday in Komárno with weary handshakes. Dubček returned to Prague for more work on the Extraordinary Fourteenth Party Congress, three weeks away. Kádár returned to the Budapest in whose terrible events of 1956 he had come to power behind Soviet tanks. He, who had long regretted and perhaps even repented for the "necessities" of power, did not learn from Moscow until Sunday that Hungary was to invade Czechoslovakia on Tuesday.

The storm signals which had alarmed Kádár over the weekend had become visible in Moscow on Friday, when the moratorium on polemics was broken by *Pravda*'s political columnist Yuri Zhukov, who mouths only the official line:

> Some Prague publications, acting counter to the spirit of the Bratislava Conference, are appearing these days with fierce and slanderous attacks on fraternal parties. . . . A consistent and unwavering fulfillment of the Bratislava Agreement is imperative.

Zhukov singled out articles in *Reportér* as "arrogant, vulgar, and vile" and called attention to a "suspicious synchronization" between attacks on Presidium conservative Oldřich Švestka that were published in *The New York Times* and Prague's *Mladá Fronta* (the Youth Front daily). In neither case did Zhukov challenge the accuracy of the articles.

The Prague press had shut down for the weekend by the time it learned that Moscow had broken the no-criticism agreement. But Brezhnev and Kosygin, recognizing that this meant the hawks had seized control of their Kremlin (possibly with the aid of Marshal Grechko) hurried back to Moscow—just in time for a Saturday vote on whether to intervene militarily in Czechoslovakia. According to most Kremlinologists, Kosygin voted no, along with Suslov, Podgorny, and Gennadi Voronov. Brezhnev, whose only ideology by now must have been fear-and-survival, cast his lot with the obvious winners. By a vote of 7 to 4, the die was cast and Czechoslovakia was doomed.

A steady stream of Russian planes began flying to East German landing strips near Czechoslovakia on Saturday. But Ulbricht, Gomulka, Zhivkov and Kádár were not notified until the next day that their nations would be going to war, too. On Sunday, NATO intelligence officers noted an unusually heavy concentration of military flights across Poland, but these were discounted because it was Soviet Air Force Day and the flights may have been part of the ceremonies. When many of the planes returned to Russia, the Western observers relaxed. Actually, the planes, having ferried men and tanks into final position for an invasion, were going home only temporarily.

On Saturday afternoon in Prague, Alois Indra's staff was working late at his Secretariat when Indra suddenly dismissed them hurriedly. One clerical worker forgot her purse and went back to get it. To her surprise and his dismay, she discovered Indra working the Telex himself. In a rage, he ordered her to leave, which she did, but not before she had noted (for future reference) that Indra was talking by Telex to Ambassador Chervonenko.

On Monday, the Czechoslovak press began hitting back at Yuri Zhukov's attacks in *Pravda.* One of his targets, *Mladá Fronta,* pointed out that "in view of the fact that we don't know the intentions of America's New York *Times,* not even being a subscriber to that daily, we must assume that Zhukov got his information from them regarding the 'suspicious synchronization.' We cannot conceive that an important commentator of the most important Soviet party daily could violate the principles of journalistic ethics to the extent of thinking up such accusations." The Catholic newspaper *People's Democracy* remarked that "Yuri Zhukov calls on quotations from imperialist papers to support his arguments on Czechoslovakia. We, on the other hand, prefer to quote Karl Marx, who said that 'a free press is a spiritual mirror in which a nation sees itself—and self-recognition is the first condition of wisdom.' "

The Russian behavior was Topic Number Two at Prague's *hydepark*—which, ever since July's petition-signing outside the House of Children department store—had remained there instead of at the Old Town Square. Crowds had started spilling out of the park next to the store in the heart of downtown and, for safety's and traffic's sake, the city authorities had just ordered the *hydepark* moved to the spacious plain of Letná across the Vltava River. But, at one end of Letná stands the Ministry of Interior and, even with General Pavel at its helm, the people would have none of this. The *hydepark* remained downtown and, for the few hours that remained to free expression, its re-location was Topic Number One.

On Tuesday noon, Victor Louis, a British-based Russian citizen who had peddled the Kremlin's version of Svetlana Alliluyeva's memoirs and could therefore be presumed to have good official contacts, published a story in the London *Evening News* under the headline: "RUSSIA READY TO CRUSH DUBČEK." Louis wrote that "the honeymoon between the Soviet Union and Czechoslovakia is over and the liberal leaders in Czechoslovakia can expect tougher action from Russia in the coming weeks." Louis' "scoop" was perfectly timed, even if his dates were slightly off. Perdition was only hours away.

Toward 1300 Tuesday, an unmarked plane flew over our neighborhood in Prague and dropped leaflets claiming that Antonín Novotný was "illegally deposed" by a "clique" and therefore remained Czechoslovakia's legal President. Not even Novotný (who seems to have been genuinely uninformed of impending events) took this foray seriously.

At 1400 hours on Tuesday, the Czechoslovak Communist Party Presidium—eleven voting members, three alternates, and a half-dozen party secretaries (including Alois Indra)—assembled in Prague for its regular weekly meeting. Alexander Dubček wanted to talk about the Fourteenth Congress. Drahomír Kolder wanted very insistently to talk about a fourteen-page report he and Indra had prepared. Their analysis of events in Czechoslovakia called for laying aside the Bratislava Declaration signed two-and-a-half weeks earlier and returning to the principles outlined in the original Warsaw letter from the five brother nations.

Everybody had read the Kolder-Indra draft and Prime Minister Černík remarked, almost in passing: "Do you know, it reads just like treason." My sources tell me that the scenario apparently called for Vasil Bil'ak to follow it up by sounding a call for intervention. This would instantly evoke the Warsaw Pact response that was already under way. But, perhaps because of Černík's remark, Bil'ak was more sheepish and tongue-tied than usual. The whole sequence was bollixed; Bil'ak didn't get a word in edgewise. To make matters worse for the traitors, Dubček insisted upon sticking to the agenda, and the Fourteenth Congress came first.

Other treachery that was afoot in Prague moved more smoothly. At 1600 hours, Viliam Šalgovič—a crony of Bil'ak's who was Deputy Minister of the Interior and head of the State Security—assembled a group of his "closest selected fellow workers" and told them what their assignments would be once the troops had crossed the border. One of them, a

Lieutenant Colonel Vaněk, was given the task of stationing "reliable" men outside all capitalist embassies plus those of Yugoslavia and Rumania to keep Czechs from seeking asylum there. Another, Lieutenant Colonel Josef Ripl, was to prevent Czechoslovak Radio from broadcasting the Presidium's response to the occupation. Colonel Miroslav Eliáš, commander of the Ministry's Security Air Squadron and formerly Novotný's personal pilot, and Lieutenant Colonel Rudolf Stachovský, chief of airport passport control, were assigned to aid uninvited arrivals at the brand-new Ruzyně International Airport.

At 1800, Miroslav Sulek, the conservative Director General of the Četeka (ČTK) news agency, returned unexpectedly from a vacation in Russia and gave an order (which was disobeyed) that no news about Czechoslovakia was to be sent abroad without his being consulted first.

At 2000, officers of Warsaw Pact units massed across the border in East Germany, Poland, Hungary, and the Soviet Ukraine, read their troops a month-old letter sent to the Soviet Union by a handful of Prague factory workers asking assistance in halting the counter-revolutionary trend. (The letter had long since been published in Prague and disavowed.) Within two hours, the troops were on their way toward eighteen different land crossings of the Czechoslovak frontier.

Toward 2230, a "passenger plane" purporting to be from Aeroflot contacted the control tower at Prague's Ruzyně airport by radio. The pilot said—in Russian!—that he was low on fuel and requested permission to land. Since all commercial pilots are supposed to converse in English with the Prague control tower, the controllers on duty smelled a rat and told the Russian pilot to call a nearby military airport instead. But, minutes later, no less than three heavy Antonov prop-jets landed anyway. They sat on a taxiway for a few minutes while various shadowy figures went out to meet them. In the Foreign Departures lounge, a dozen "tourists" who'd been cleared by Colonel Stachovský stood up and brandished revolvers. Another detachment of Czech and Russian civilians burst into the control tower and chased the controllers out.

The airport manager had already broadcast and telephoned an alarm ("We have been attacked!"). Now all gas, electricity, water, and heat were shut off to hinder the trespassers. But it was much, much too late.

The first plane proved to be a mobile air-traffic control center.

From it, at least fifty civilians jumped out and scurried toward the airport building guided by Czechoslovak collaborationists. From the second plane came 150 paratroops in steel helmets and camouflage fatigues with machine guns hanging around their necks. They were led by an airborne-unit colonel. From the third plane, two tanks rumbled down a ramp. In the turret of one tank rode an armored-division general.

Even to two or three of the stunned airport workers who were now being rounded up at gunpoint, the colonel and the general looked disturbingly familiar. Illuminated by the floodlights their troops had brought with them, the two commanders proved to be none other than the Russian "airport officials" who had looked so clumsily out-of-place at the terminal's opening celebration a few long weeks ago.

It took the Red Army more than an hour to work its way out of the airport. First, some of the paratroops who should have been securing the terminal were instead looting the duty-free shop. Then, one of the first two tanks to land became embroiled in a shooting incident as it lumbered up a ramp inside the terminal. Startled when a treadle-operated glass door slid open automatically to welcome them, the combat-ready tank crew opened fire. The other tank crew, seeing their brothers engaged in battle, opened fire, too. Between them, they shot up every door in sight. Within half a minute, Prague's two-month-old international air terminal was a shambles of broken Bohemian glass, treacherous underfoot.

This slowed down the occupation—but soon the airport was in working order as a command post. Military planes were landing at thirty-second intervals. As soon as they disgorged their cargo and troops, the planes took off again. This massive airlift would deposit a whole airborne division at Ruzyně by dawn.

Long before then, however, columns of tanks set out along the six-lane Lenin Highway, which leads from airport to city. They were guided by Volga autos from the Soviet Embassy and Aeroflot as well as secret police cars and flanked by infantrymen and paratroopers on foot. They followed the Lenin Highway into the Circle of the October Revolution, a half-mile from our home. There, the detachments dispersed toward their targets. . . .

PART FOUR

Apocalypse:
In the Firehouse Square

"I have a cobbler's workshop in the square
that lies before the Emperor's palace.
Scarcely have I taken my shutters down, at
the first glimmer of dawn, when I see armed
soldiers already posted in the mouth of
every street opening on the square. But
these soldiers are not ours, they are obviously nomads from the North. In some way
that is incomprehensible to me, they have
pushed right into the capital, although it is
a long way from the frontier. At any rate,
here they are; it seems that every morning
there are more of them."

Franz Kafka, *An Old Manuscript*

Chapter 12

Tuesday Night 20 August—
Wednesday Morning 21 August 1968

AT ELEVEN O'CLOCK TUESDAY NIGHT, THE VERY HOUR when history was to render my project obsolete, I finished a draft of my article for *The New York Times* Magazine on "The Free Press of Prague." * I'd wanted to have it roughed out so I could tie together any loose ends during my impending interview with Zdeněk Hejzlar of the Czechoslovak Radio. I took a glass of milk to bed with me, but I was so drowsy that I forgot to drink it.

Valerie and I were awakened at 0430 when the phone rang. Fumbling for my bathrobe, I murmured to Val: "Please don't wake up. It's for me."

"Who calls at this hour?" she asked sleepily.

"My agent," I replied. "He said he'd call, remember?" On Monday, I'd received a cable that Leland Hayward, the producer of *Sound of Music,* was interested in my outline and a few sample pages of my Suchý-&-Šlitr adaptation. The cable from my literary agent had concluded: "Do you want me to represent you or get theatrical agent? Will phone you later in week." Now I remarked to my wife: "It's only 11:30 at night in New York."

Valerie was unimpressed. "That's not even a decent hour to call anybody who's in New York," she remarked, and her own bristling words awoke her for the day.

By now I had my robe on inside out, so I said: "He may have begun placing the call a few hours ago. Excuse me, I'd better get the phone."

I listened to a few minutes of telephone operator gibberish à la Upper Bronx (the international routings go via White Plains) and then some British and German before my agent came on, sounding crisp as lettuce.

---

* Heavily rewritten, updated, and Telexed by me, this obituary was published there on 8 September, 1968 under the title "The Short, Happy Life of Prague's Free Press."

"Alan, what are you going to do?" he wanted to know.

"Well, you've done so well so far that I'd like you to go on with it. Now what about Leland Hayward?"

"Never mind about Leland Hayward! Where's your family?"

Erika and Monica were fast asleep, I told him, and Valerie was wide awake. "But," I went on, "whoever's going to represent me with Leland Hayward isn't a decision I consult my family about."

"Good God! Will you get Leland Hayward off your brain!" screamed the voice at the other end. Then comprehension dawned, at his end. "You don't know what I'm talking about," he went on. "Look out your window, for Christ's sake! The Russians are there! They've landed at Prague airport. Russian, Polish, and East German soldiers have crossed the Czech frontier. They've occupied the. . . ."

"Now look," I said. "I can see out the window and there are a number of people on the streets, but they're all Czechs. I know you start reading the *Times* from the book page, but there was a big crisis in July, then big meetings at Čierna and Bratislava, and now we're going to be let alone for a little while. . . ."

"No, no!" he insisted. "Prague is an occupied city. Radio Prague has gone off the air. All telephones are dead. . . ."

"If all telephones have gone dead," I exploded, "HOW IN HELL AM I TALKING TO YOU?"

"I don't know," he said lamely. But then, gathering certainty, he added: "But it's been on WQXR twice now and it's all over WINS!"

Now I began to talk fast: "Look, you and I went through this kind of scare back in May, but I'd better get off the phone and check it out. If it's true, I'm not evacuating my family if I can possibly keep them here. The Czechs will lose the war very fast, so the only danger will be street fighting at the beginning. And the best thing to do about that now is to stay put indoors. I can't think about Leland Hayward with this on my mind. So call me back tomorrow night, but maybe a little earlier, please."

"Will do. Take care. 'Bye now."

"Goodbye," I said. "Thanks for calling."

I hung up and moved Monica's bed away from the window without waking her or Erika. But my wife was fully awake now and so was our teen-age niece, Nancy, who'd been camping out on our living room sofa-bed. Nancy was trembling, but in possession of herself. "While you were on the phone, Uncle Alan," she said, "I counted twenty-two planes flying over the house. All four-engine. The first was a jet and . . ."

I caught my breath. Because we live very close to the Prague Castle, no planes were permitted to fly over our residential district—except in emergencies.

"As soon as I get dressed," I said, "I'm going exploring."

Nancy said: "I'm coming, too."

I must have been more disturbed than I sounded, for I didn't think to argue with her. But I did notice that she had donned bluejeans and her Camp Ramah sweatshirt, imprinted with the motto in Hebrew: "THE FIRE DID NOT CONSUME US." I had sense enough to warn her that, if the Russians had indeed come, the Hebrew letters could be provocation. Nancy slipped a yellow raincoat over herself.

Accompanied by Nancy this time, I set out on the same route I'd taken during the May 9 "Liberation Night" invasion scare.

Toward dawn on the 21st of August, outside the Czechoslovak Army barracks up the street, all the soldiers were lined up in formation —but unarmed.

"You know," I told Nancy, "I've come home as late as 3:30 in the morning and I've gotten up as early as 5, but I've never been up-and-about here at 4:45 in the morning. So, for all we know, this is their normal reveille."

"Do you think the sentry will understand your Czech?" Nancy asked dubiously.

"Probably," I said, "but I'm not going to ask him." If the rumor proved false, then my spreading it would have made me one of those "American provocateurs" the Russians and East Germans had been railing about.

On our side of the barracks, some fifty people were waiting for the Number 8 tram and shivering in the early-morning mist. On the other side of the barracks, twice as many were waiting for the Number 22, which goes downtown to Wenceslas Square. Prague being an early-to-bed, early-to-rise city, it didn't seem particularly disturbing to find people at the tram stands before 0500. In fact, it was reassuring to watch the trolleys coming and going, with the people squeezing aboard.

We crossed the Number 22 tracks and headed through the Fire-house Square, keeping under the vaulted arcades that bear left toward the Foreign Ministry and the Castle. I took a little more comfort from seeing two cabs at the taxi stand. Every trace of normality tasted delicious this morning. In the Firehouse Square, however, people were talking and arguing about Dubček and Svoboda as well as cursing Ulbricht and Gomulka. They'd been doing this for weeks, but it didn't seem right to me that they'd be standing around doing it at such an hour when every extra minute of sleep was precious.

As with the soldiers, though, I didn't want to "provoke" them with my transatlantic rumor of an invasion. Nancy and I pressed forward in silence.

We had almost turned the corner to the Foreign Ministry when we heard behind us a dull growl that wasn't thunder.

We reversed our steps just in time to see the first tank roar out of the park behind Strahov Monastery, down a steep ramp of a street, and into the Firehouse Square.

It was olive drab and remarkably small, but it was the nastiest sight I have ever seen. On its front and side were strips of white paint or tape —to conceal where it was from (and, I was told later, to help the air support find its own legions; the tape was phosphorescent). It was followed by nine other machines. They growled to a halt in a circle around the statue of Jan of Nepomuk, the martyred confessor.

I knew it wouldn't be wise for shadowy figures to be seen moving inside an arcade. Nancy and I stepped out into the street with our empty hands half-raised. We worked our way back toward the tram stand. There, clusters of people were standing and watching. Their faces were agape.

The lid of the first machine opened and from it there rose—slowly, like a genie extracting itself from a bottle—a figure all in black: black hood, black goggles, black fatigue uniform, and black gloves. The apocalypse had come and the people in the Firehouse Square looked on with the helplessness of inhabitants of a small planet watching the first explorer from Mars land on their terrain. At that very moment, they knew that their world was no longer theirs.

From the lids of the other machines, there emerged earthmen in khaki, pointing automatic rifles. Some of them were holding their weapons by the triggers. They were very young earthmen, but the high-collared costumes they wore made them look like World War I doughboys or even earlier. Both the future and the past, perhaps even the czarist nineteenth-century, had come to Prague with a vengeance.

There were other Martians in black, too, but all eyes—*theirs* as well as *ours*—were on that first Martian. He was *their* leader. He was *our* conqueror. Only two shreds of white showed on this dark manlike apparition in black: a small patch of his face and a map in his hand. And yet, every movement of his body seemed to communicate a very human helplessness of his own. He gazed down at his map and then up at the white-on-red street signs. Then back to his map. Then down each street that opened off the square. Then back to his map. Then over to the crowd as if he wanted to say something to us. Then back to his map, which he lifted before his face for intensive study.

It dawned on us in the square, all of us thinking aloud in a collective sound, half-sob and half-giggle, which pinged like an outbreak of hiccups, that these Martians were lost!

With that revelation, reality registered and all of us, they and we, seemed to become aware that day had dawned, that a 22 tram had rattled into the square and was now rattling out with a clang of its bell, and that one of the taxis, without a fare, was leaving the square. Nobody else did anything, but now people began to grope for words and conversation within this science-fiction hallucination which reality couldn't dispel.

"Maybe he can only read Cyrillic," I murmured to Nancy.

"How do we know this isn't the Czech Army on maneuvers?" Nancy wondered.

I told her the Czechoslovak Army never went on maneuvers with such a flourish.

"But if they're Russians, why don't their tanks have red stars?"

I answered her question with one of my own: "What do you think is under those bandages?"

"I don't know, Uncle Alan, but I want to get out of here!"

The question would be asked many times: *Why didn't we resist?* Well, we did resist! Some of us in the Firehouse Square shook our fists at the invaders; others turned their backs on them. Still others, like myself, raised our hands in the air like victims of banditry, but we, too, shook our heads when the first Martian looked at us imploringly. Confronted by the unthinkable, we resisted by not giving directions. In the dawn, with the gas lamps still aglow, it never would have occurred to us to wrench out the cobblestones from this lovely rococo Firehouse Square and fling them at the invaders; enough of our lives and dreams had already been defaced overnight.

The doughboys covered the crowd by swiveling their rifles and submachine guns in all directions. But they were still letting people pass and Nancy and I walked gingerly homeward.

Then seventeen more tanks, bigger than the first ten, rumbled into the square.

Their commander, also in black, carried a full-color tourist map of Prague and knew his way. He called a few words, which we couldn't hear, to the first commander. The first detachment immediately set off at a brisk snarl down Loreta Street toward Hradčany Square and the main gate of the Castle.*

Nancy and I, heading for home, were cutting across Kepler Street when the second tank commander made a pincer gesture, indicating that his armor should surround the army barracks up Parler Street.

Just then, the one remaining taxi at the stand moved out too, with a loud start and a lurch. Worse still, he headed down Parler Street. The Czech soldiers were lined up, unarmed, under orders to surrender, but it must have looked as if the taxi was alerting them.

Nancy and I jumped out of the taxi's way and onto a traffic island where Kepler crosses Parler. And, as we did, a figure in black leaped from the nearest tank. Now I could see that this Martian, at least, had black boots, too, and I could hear that he was cursing in Russian. He was fumbling inside his black raincoat, from which he produced yet another black object—a long, dark pistol. He took aim at the retreating taxi, which was now directly behind us.

Nancy and I had neither the time nor the sense to drop to the ground. We simply stood there helplessly with our empty hands waved aloft.

I could tell from his reflexes that this Martian in black was not a young Martian. He was very nervous. His right hand shook as he waved the pistol at the speeding cab. The gun crossed Nancy and me once, then twice—all in a matter of a second. . . .

After four turns in his gunsight, we were spared. He steadied himself by catching his right elbow with his left hand, but the cab was now out of range. It had raced past the barracks without pausing. The Martian in black simply shrugged and, still clutching his pistol, climbed back into his tank.

Now I had time to notice that there was another person marooned

* Only later did I learn that the Castle had already been captured a couple of hours earlier—by tanks and paratroops, guided by a Soviet Embassy limousine, coming in from the airport to the side entrance of the Castle. The Russian soldiers and armor in the Firehouse Square had come overland from East Germany.

on the traffic island with us, a rotund grandmother (*babička*) who'd been coming from the opposite direction with two empty milk bottles in a net bag. She must have been taking them back for deposit and perhaps other shopping at the Firehouse Square dairy, which opens at 0500.

Seventeen tanks rolled past our traffic island—on both sides of us— without a soul to be seen, just the guns swiveling to cover us as they passed. Seventeen times I took a deep breath and held it as I wondered whether a burst of gunfire would cut us down or tank treads would run us down. Seventeen times the answer was an unspoken "not yet." But I knew that, from here on out, our life in occupied Czechoslovakia would be an endless game of Russian roulette.

Then the tanks were gone and we were alive again! The whole square stank of grease and burnt rubber, but Nancy and I took the deepest breaths we've ever known. Not the grandmother, though, whose journey to the dairy had been interrupted. What she wanted was information why.

"Those men in black?" she asked near-sightedly. "Are they fire-men?"

"No," I said, telling her gently that "they were soldiers."

"Ahhh, soldiers!" she said, as if that explained everything.

Then I told her what kind of soldiers. She started to tremble. She dropped her bag. Both bottles shattered and, for the first time that morning, people in the square jumped.

"Are you all right?" Nancy inquired.

"How can you ask such a question?" the *babička* snapped back, "when I've just lost my two crowns' deposit because you children like to play jokes on old people?"

We propped her up against a stanchion, told her she'd be all right, and left her to her complaints. Much, much more than two milk bottles had been destroyed in this dreamless daybreak.

PART FIVE

Apostasy:
The Dogs of War

"The hunting dogs are playing in the courtyard, but the hare will not escape them, no
matter how fast it may be flying already
through the woods."

Franz Kafka's Notebooks

Chapter 13]

Wednesday 21 August 1968
from 0530 to 1300

NANCY AND I TOOK A CIRCUITOUS ROUTE THROUGH THE
park and arrived home to hear Radio Prague declaring: "This is the
least understandable thing that could have happened." The children
were still sleeping, but my wife was grinding coffee and asking a mother's question: "What are we going to tell the kids?"

"Tell them the Russian soldiers have come to live with us," I said.

"And do we say we like them?"

"No," I said. "We say the Czechs don't like them any more, but all
we can do is see for ourselves."

We remained indoors that morning while an unimpeded flow of
Soviet tanks and open armored trucks (with soldiers—their rifles pointing, and sometimes firing, aloft—crammed in like cattle) and jeeps and
goulash wagons (mobile kitchens, with chimneys smoking) poured
down the three major arteries visible from our windows or balconies:
Myslbek Street, Kepler Street, and the Boulevard of the Pioneers.

The safest and most informative vantage point, for the time being,
was among the radio and TV and telephone receivers, although twice
that morning I ventured outside.

The first time was at 0745 for milk. But I found sixty-five people,
mostly grandmothers, waiting in line at the dairy and clucking at the
tanks rolling by. So I returned home at once. We had a day or two's
supply in the freezer and I might be able to get more at the American
Embassy. Besides, who could plan more than a day ahead at such a
time?

Twenty minutes later, an unmarked truck hurtled upstream—
squeezing past the tide of tanks headed into the city. From the little
truck, a bundle was tossed out onto our corner. Some twenty men were
huddled around a car radio at the corner gas pump and one of them

opened the parcel. He began distributing its contents and, seeing my neighbors dashing out to get samples, I did the same.

The parcel contained one hundred copies of a one-page special edition of *Rudé Právo* addressed in a banner headline "TO ALL THE PEOPLE OF THE CZECHOSLOVAK SOCIALIST REPUBLIC." *Rudé Právo* reported the invasion, urged readers to keep calm and avoid provocations, and said the Central Committee was calling for "conditional withdrawal" of the troops. It did not say what the conditions were. Nor did it give many facts.

These were the facts I pieced together that morning (and confirmed later) with the aid of a few well-placed, if emotional, phone calls:

During Tuesday night's session at the Central Committee Building, František Barbírek of Slovakia, one of the wavering centrists, kept ducking out of the room whenever the Presidium seemed to be nearing a showdown on the Indra-Kolder report. Everybody knew why. If Barbírek voted no, he'd be in trouble back home, where Vasil Bil'ak still ruled. If he voted yes, he, like Bil'ak, would be in trouble at the Fourteenth Congress in September.

Prime Minister Černík also left the room quite frequently. From an anteroom, he was phoning General Martin Dzúr, who'd succeeded General Lomský as Minister of Defense. The Prime Minister had received reports of faltering communications at the borders and unscheduled landings at Ruzyně Airport. Twenty minutes before midnight, when the Presidium had been in continuous session for nearly ten hours, Černík returned from the phone looking particularly grim. Pallor seemed to have dulled his glowing summer tan. Černík whispered a few words to Alexander Dubček, who gave a convulsive quiver and—bracing himself against the conference table—rose to interrupt the debate with these words: "The armies of the five parties have crossed the borders of our republic and have begun occupying our country."

Amidst the commotion that broke out in the room, a man who was there recalled later that "as far as I could see, Bil'ak, Kolder, and Indra did not seem to be surprised. They looked calm and serene. I think I could also say the same of Švestka. In fact, I would say I saw a faint look of satisfaction on his face." Otherwise, all eyes were on Alexander Dubček, who—when he had restored a semblance of order—managed to say in a voice that kept cracking: "It is a tragedy. I did not expect this to happen. I had no suspicion, not even the slightest hint that such a step could be taken against us."

Dubček, who'd been adhering rigidly to the agenda in order to keep Kolder from disrupting the meeting, now produced a surprise of his own: a letter he'd received from Leonid Brezhnev on Monday night. Dubček had planned to read it under "new business." In it, the Soviet Central Committee reproached the Czechoslovak Communist Party for disregarding the Čierna and Bratislava agreements. It claimed that counter-revolutionary tendencies were reasserting themselves. The rest was a reiteration of the July letter from Warsaw, but in much sharper language.*

Dubček went on reading the Brezhnev letter aloud. Harsh though it was, it contained not the slightest hint that military intervention was in the offing. Dubček had interpreted it as the signal for a new round of meetings or perhaps a last-ditch attempt to intimidate the Fourteenth Congress on 9 September. As he droned its unrelenting words, he interjected: "This is what they keep on saying, but they don't take into consideration what the real situation is. After all, we are taking measures." A little later in his reading, he told the Presidium: "I declare on my honor as a Communist that I had no suspicion, no indication, that anybody would want to undertake such measures against us."

It was when he was done that Dubček, with tears in his eyes, uttered his famous lament: "This is my own personal tragedy. I have always loved Russia. I have devoted my entire life to co-operating with the Soviet Union, and this is what they have done to me!"

Having said this, and amidst reports that tanks were now advancing from two directions upon the city, Dubček called the Presidium to order and set to work drafting a proclamation to be read over the radio. He noticed that Alois Indra was absent and, with great emphasis, demanded to know where he was.

Indra, the administrative secretary whose complicity in the invasion was the best-documented, was on his way up to the Prague Castle, triumphantly certain that he was about to be named the next Prime Minister of Czechoslovakia!

* Even if the Presidium had capitulated to Brezhnev's new message at the start of Tuesday's meeting, it would have been too late to halt the invasion. The message was (to use a *Pravda* cliché) "suspiciously synchronized" to coincide with the Kolder-Indra report and Bil'ak's bungled warning cry.

At the Castle, President Svoboda had retired early for the night. He'd been awakened toward midnight, however, with word that the Soviet Ambassador was in the Castle and asking to see him. Svoboda put on his dressing gown and received Chervonenko. The Russian envoy informed him that, in response to a Czechoslovak invitation as well as various threats to Czechoslovak security from within and without, five of the Warsaw Pact nations had come to the rescue.

Svoboda had dismissed Chervonenko coldly and phoned the Central Committee to say he was coming down there. Before he could dress, however, Alois Indra arrived—accompanied, most reports say, by Jozef Lenárt, who'd been Prime Minister under Novotný. Svoboda received them in his office. He sat behind his desk, but he didn't ask them to sit down.

Indra handed Svoboda a list bearing the names of Cabinet members in a new "Revolutionary Workers and Peasants Government." Indra himself would replace Černík as Prime Minister. Lenárt would move into Smrkovský's chair as Speaker of the National Assembly. Kolder would succeed Dubček as First Secretary of the Party. Editor Švestka (whose name means "plum") would have a Cabinet post and so would his fellow Presidium member, Barbírek. A Slovak journalist named Bohuslav Chňoupek, who had served as a Moscow correspondent, would take over the Interior Ministry from General Pavel. Internal Trade Minister Oldřich Pavlovský, who used to be Novotný's Ambassador to Moscow, would be Deputy Premier. And Karel Hoffmann, now the Minister of Telecommunications, would return to the Ministry of Culture and Information to rescue it from the democratic ways of Miroslav Galuška. Svoboda would be welcome to remain as President. It was nobody's intention, Indra insisted, to bring back Novotný.

The seventy-two-year-old soldier listened silently. Then he shouted one word: *"Ven!"* [Out!] His callers cringed. Svoboda repeated the word once more and both his callers left.*

---

* It took Indra until early 1971 to rise from his 1968 status—an alternate member of the Presidium and its chief *aparatchik*—to full membership on the Presidium. Lenárt's comeback has brought him as high as First Secretary of the Communist Party in Slovakia, the post held by Bil'ak at the time of the invasion. Chňoupek worked in the Foreign Ministry for a while after August. In 1969, he was named head of the Czechoslovak Radio and, after he had purged it, he was sent to Moscow in 1970 as Czechoslovak Ambassador there. In fairness to Chňoupek and other Cabinet designates of "the Revolutionary Workers and Peasants Government of Comrade Indra," not all of them knew that they were on his list. The *known* traitors

By the time Svoboda reached Central Committee headquarters, a sprawling low-slung cream-and-coffee-colored office building on the Vltava Riverfront, some toadies in the marble-pillared lobby were already addressing Drahomír Kolder as "Comrade First Secretary." Shortly after 0100 Wednesday, the Presidium had approved this proclamation:

> To All the People of the Czechoslovak Socialist Republic:
>
> Yesterday, 20 August 1968 at about 2300, the armies of the Soviet Union, the Polish People's Republic, the German Democratic Republic, the Hungarian People's Republic, and the Bulgarian People's Republic crossed the State borders of the Czechoslovak Socialist Republic. This took place without the knowledge of the President of the Republic, the Presidium of the National Assembly, the Presidium of the Government, and the First Secretary of the Communist Party Central Committee. The Presidium of the Central Committee was then in session, preoccupied with the preparations for the Extraordinary Fourteenth Party Congress. The Presidium calls upon all citizens of the Republic to keep the peace and not resist the advancing armies, because the defense of our State borders is now impossible.
>
> For this reason, our army, the Security Forces, and the People's Militia were not given orders to defend the country. The Presidium considers [the invasion] to be contrary to the fundamental principles of relations between socialist states and a denial of all the basic norms of international law.
>
> All leading officials of the Party and the National Front remain at their posts, to which they were elected as representatives of the people . . . according to the laws and regulations of the Czechoslovak Socialist Republic. . . .

There were four dissenting votes: Kolder, Bil'ak, Švestka, and Emil Rigo.

At just about the same moment, director Sulek of Četeka was appearing at his office with an unsigned "official communiqué" to be teletyped to the whole world:

---

have fared no better (perhaps a little worse) than other sympathizers who kept relatively or apparently clean before 21 August. Karel Hoffmann was removed and later reinstated as Minister of Telecommunications, but that's as high as he's risen thus far in post-August Czechoslovakia. Drahomír Kolder remained close (but no closer) to the seat of Party power. In the fall of 1968, an overwhelming number of constituents in Kolder's home district petitioned for his recall as a National Assembly deputy. The outraged Kolder prevailed upon official bodies to ignore this "pressure" in the name of "democratic representation." All of which inspired a humor magazine called *Dikobraz* (Porcupine) to print a caricature of Kolder complaining: "What kind of democracy is this where people can vote against me?"

A Revolutionary Workers and Peasants Government has taken over power in Czechoslovakia and asked the fraternal Soviet forces for aid to help the new Government suppress the counter-revolution.

To their eternal credit, Sulek's own Četeka employees refused to transmit his message and threw him out of their building by "brute force."

Czechoslovak Radio stops broadcasting at 0200, so this was the deadline Dubček's Presidium had raced to meet with its official proclamation. But Karel Hoffmann, the Minister of Telecommunications who'd been seen in Indra's company lately, had ordered his engineers at a relay tower outside Prague to knock off at midnight because there'd be no urgent transmissions in the remaining two hours. Hoffmann had also managed to shut down inter-city phone service from Prague to Brno, Ostrava, and Bratislava. To help Hoffmann keep the Presidium's response off the air, detachments of Šalgovič's secret police were stationed in front of the radio and TV buildings.

Nevertheless, a messenger managed to penetrate the radio headquarters. At 0150 Wednesday, Czechoslovak Radio announced: "Yesterday, 20 August 1968 at about 2300—" Less than a sentence later, most radios in Prague went dead. (Not even those first few words were transmitted to the hinterlands thanks to Hoffmann's earlier shutdown of the relay tower.)

Those who happened to be listening to Radio Prague on the 210-meter wave length heard a new voice begin broadcasting. To Czechs who had been persecuted in the Fifties, the new voice's poor pronunciation and grammatical errors were chilling, for it was the same antiquated Czech (an obsolete Moravian dialect) that Soviet advisers and interrogators were trained (in Moscow) to speak. "Personalities of the Czechoslovak Communist Party," it began, "requested military aid from the Soviet Union because our republic was threatened by counter-revolution and anti-socialist elements which, in combination with outside forces . . ." Soon, one bona-fide Czech accent joined the three Russians. The new voice was quickly recognized as that of an old-time Novotnýite. The new station called itself "Radio Vltava." It was later traced to a Dresden transmitter. Hearing the old Novotný man, however, Czechoslovak listeners immediately began referring to it as "collaborationist radio."

Back at the Presidium, most of the members had dispersed once the proclamation had been sent to the radio. Dubček, Smrkovský, Špaček, and Kriegel remained, with several loyal non-voting secretaries plus alternate member Bohumil Šimon, to keep the Presidium officially in session to the very last. Around 0215, somebody at the radio building rang up the Presidium with the news that Karel Hoffmann had shut off transmissions and was forbidding any resumption of broadcasting. Josef Smrkovský grabbed the phone and, with livid contempt, shouted into it: "Do not listen to that Hoffmann! He is a traitor!"

Some of the traitors were waiting anxiously in the lobby for their uniformed reinforcements to arrive. For a while, however, they were joined only by Alois Indra, returning from his abortive visit to Svoboda. Other traitors deemed it safer to go to the Soviet Embassy and wait there.

President Svoboda had not lingered long. He and Dubček and Černík and the other loyalists had agreed that, as the foremost symbol of his nation's sovereignty, this man whose name means Freedom should remain at the seat of legitimacy, the Castle.

Thinking that the Presidium's proclamation was being broadcast (the radio didn't get back on the air until 0500), Prime Minister Černík had left to convene an emergency session of his Cabinet Ministers in his headquarters across the Vltava. At 0300, Soviet armored personnel carriers and scout cars arrived outside Černík's windows. One detachment of violet-bereted paratroops, their submachine guns drawn, surrounded the building while another detachment burst inside and ordered Černík and the handful of ministers and secretaries in his office to face the wall with their hands up. They were searched and all their wristwatches, including Černík's, were taken and donned by the soldiers. After that, there were twenty minutes of terror while the captives faced the wall and waited for the end. The soldiers, it turned out, had no instructions as to what to do next.

Then an order came for Černík to be taken away. As three Russians marched the Prime Minister to the door, a phone rang and a clerk, who was being held at gunpoint, instinctively reached over and picked up the receiver. "Prime Minister Černík's office," he announced, while the Russians looked on.

The caller was Alexander Dubček, who wanted to talk with Černík.

"You can't talk with him, mister," said the clerk. "He's being taken away with his hands in the air and a bayonet at his back."

"Well," said Dubček. "We are not in such a bad situation yet. You must be calm and stay united with the others there."

"Thank you, mister," said the clerk. He hung up and called after the Prime Minister, who was being led to an armored car: "Mr. Černík! Mr. Dubček says it's not so bad yet where he is." When the Russians realized that the Czechoslovak leadership was still communicating under their noses, they ripped out Černík's phone and smashed his building's switchboard. Černík disappeared in the armored car.*

At the Presidium, Dubček waited. Two or three of his allies (it is said Špaček was among them) pleaded that the leaders should go into hiding or else exile abroad. But Dubček insisted that their place was in Prague among their people. (Špaček, accordingly, stayed.) Čestmír Císař, who wasn't a voting member of the Presidium and hadn't attended its meeting, arrived and joined the discussion.

At 0400, three armored cars led by a Volga limousine from the Soviet Embassy arrived at the Central Committee. An advance party of secret policemen rushed inside to prevent the leaders from leaving their office. Some of the troops sealed off the entrances, but they didn't go inside. They were waiting for the tanks, which could now be seen crawling across all the traffic bridges that span the Vltava.†

The first secret policeman to enter the Central Committee building had the dubious distinction of being bearhugged and lip-kissed by Alois Indra. Then, very piously, Indra asked him to arrange refreshments for the leaders who were about to be interned on behalf of Indra's "Revolutionary Workers and Peasants Government."

In the darkness outside the Central Committee, the tanks gathered and soldiers took up positions a few feet apart with all their guns turned toward the building that housed the doomed Presidium. A journalist from *Youth Front* marched up to the barrel of a Soviet gun and said despairingly in Russian to the soldier behind it: "We are your brothers. I am a Czech." The soldier's commander chased the Czech away. The Czech walked up to another soldier and resumed the dialogue: "In 1945, we welcomed Soviet soldiers in Prague." The commander called, "Do not speak with anyone!" The soldier released the

---

* His staff was interned until 1700 that afternoon.

† Contrary to *Newsweek*'s report that "the first Soviet tanks rumbled across the Charles Bridge into the heart of the city," the Charles Bridge, for pedestrians only, was not used that day by the Red Army. One end of it was under scaffolding for repairs and utterly impenetrable by vehicle.

safety catch on his weapon and said "We will shoot." The journalist backed off.

Some of the troops now entered the building. Dubček was on the telephone when two Soviet paratroopers, armed with light machine guns, burst into the Presidium room. They tore the phone from his hands, ripped the wire from the wall, and lined up Dubček, Smrkovský, Kriegel, Špaček, Císař, and Šimon for the ritual of searching. (They were allowed to keep their watches for the time being.) Then, at the behest of a Czech secret policeman who stood outside the door rather than face the leaders he was betraying, Císař was hustled off to the police station on Bartholomew Street. The others were marched to Císař's offices in the Central Committee and locked in a windowless room with no phones. There, they were fed the cold sandwiches and cakes that Alois Indra had so graciously arranged.

Dubček worked on (and managed to smuggle out) a message to all citizens of Prague and particularly to factory workers in the industrial Vysočany district. He implored everybody to stay on the job and remain in the factories, for such a concentration of strength would offer the capital city protection and perhaps even some bargaining power. In these early hours of shock and revelation, the inevitable nature of the Czechoslovak resistance was decreed.

Dubček could not have seen out, but he must have been informed of what happened just in front of his office building in the early light of dawn. Hundreds of Czechs had gathered outside and were clamoring for their legitimate rulers. Two boys made a dash for the building. As they mounted the steps, Russian troops shot them down with a couple of short, staccato bursts of machine-gun fire. The boys died with Dubček's name on their lips.

Minutes later, a third student defied a Russian tank and was crushed beneath its caterpillar treads.

This was as much of the chronology as I could ascertain on the morning of Wednesday 21 August 1968. Television had come on the air shortly after 0700 with pleas to keep calm, but stand firm: "Don't do anything you'll be ashamed of." Sometimes there was video but no audio . . . sometimes audio but no video . . . sometimes both. The telephone number 24–38–65 was flashed on the screen. Somebody had seen Čestmír Císař being taken away in a car. "Mr. Císař, please, would you call this number if you can?"

(Cisař, of course, couldn't. At police headquarters, we learned a few days later, he was being interrogated by Czech secret police collaborators. They were trying to make him confess that he and Smrkovský had conspired to subvert Dubček and were planning to invite the West German Army into Czechoslovakia.)

At 0825, television announced that "we are moving from one studio to another. Please stay by the TV set. We will broadcast as long as we can."

Meanwhile, the scene onscreen shifted to Ostrava. There, a blond young man choked back tears of outrage while reporting that "some of our citizens are actually chatting with the Russian soldiers. The rest of us are shouting in the streets: *'Long live freedom!'* " Then an older colleague in a turtleneck corrected this impression: "The people of Ostrava have been urged by their leaders to explain to the Russian soldiers that we *want* socialism, but *free* socialism."

In Brno, a haggard, paunchy man showed up at the local television studio to announce that he was "no longer the director of Radio Brno. We have just been occupied." His interviewer then explained why the same fate had not befallen Brno's television: "The Russians were asking how to find our studio and the people of Brno were giving them wrong directions."

The news from Brno was that a worker had shaken his fist at an armored truck and been shot dead. Russians were landing at Brno's airport and commandeering vehicles—buses for their soldiers and Tatra cars for their colonels and generals. These buses and cars were first halted at roadblocks and their passengers were evicted at gunpoint. Then the drivers became chauffeurs with pistols at their necks. "Many Czech Army drivers are being made to transport Russian soldiers the same way," Brno TV warned. "Remember that they cannot prevent it and aren't doing it of their own volition."

Television switched back to Prague, where two commentators were talking it over. One of them had just driven back to Prague from a vacation near the Hungarian border: "I talked with the Russian soldiers. They say they are obeying orders. They know nothing else. They think they are doing the right thing and they wonder why our nation weeps!"

"They will lose," said the other. "They will lose in the court of world public opinion. They will be condemned in the eyes of people everywhere. They will not be able to hold on very long."

A few minutes later, Czechoslovak Television received a telegram bearing "strict orders" from the occupation forces to cease televising at once. The TV employees answered it on the air: "We will only honor an order from our legitimate director-general, Mr. Pelikán." And Jiří Pelikán (whose name means just what you think it means) was nowhere to be found—by the Russians, at least.

(In the early hours of the invasion, a Red Army captain named Orlov and a squad of paratroops in an armored truck had located the TV headquarters in Maxim Gorki Square. Captain Orlov had pounded on the door for several minutes until the night watchman had appeared. "Out of the way! We are going to occupy the television station," Orlov had commanded. The ancient watchman had blinked at him and croaked: "Do you work here?" "Of course not," the Russian captain had replied. "Then you can't come in," said the watchman, slamming the door in Orlov's face with amazing dexterity. Orlov had been trying to make contact with his headquarters ever since for further instructions. But the old man's delaying action had already given Czechoslovak Television an unbeatable head start.)

Several times that morning, TV *began* to sign off:

0850: "The soldiers are firing in the air outside our studio. But we will continue as long as we can."

0940: "These may be the last few minutes we can keep in touch with you. But Radio Prague is still operating."

0958: "These scenes you just saw were from the streets of occupied Prague. And this is Studio C, the only place that has not yet been taken over."

Between then and 1030, a starchy-looking young woman, who could have been a Quaker schoolmarm, read resolutions from glassworkers and steelworkers and hospital workers and patients and balneologists denouncing the invasion. My own memories of TV that morning (and my recurrent dreams of the invasion to this day) usually involve that unflappable lady with her prim serenity. I will never forget the understated eloquence with which she said: "Many radio stations have been taken over. They are full of lies. Please don't believe everything you hear." Or a glimpse of her—while a microbiologist went on-camera to read his faculty's resolution—brushing some fuzz off the shoulder of his jacket.

1050: "These are our last minutes on the air. The Post Office telecommunications center is being occupied and our lines will be cut."

1115: "Dear friends, we still have a possibility to telecast."

A few minutes before noon, TV's sound was cut off (you could hear voices arguing in Russian and Czech in the control room) and a sign flashed on: "WE HAVE STOPPED TELEVISING." Then the screen went blank.

Even before Radio Prague overcame Karel Hoffmann's treachery and was back on the air at 0500, the people had rallied to its defense. People who'd heard the radio go dead at 0150 had thrown on their clothes and converged upon the seven-story Radio building just off Vinohradská (Wine Castle), a boulevard which, for a miserable decade, had borne the name of Stalinova. "It's true! It's true!" an official had called from a balcony of the Radio building. "We have been cut off, but you must tell the city that the Russians have invaded." Cab drivers and motorists had leaped into their cars, turned on their bright lights, and, honking their horns, driven through the city to awaken much of Prague.

(The editors of *Student* had met hurriedly in Wednesday's early hours. Their regular weekly edition had appeared on Tuesday. Before trying to go to press again, they decided to play Paul Revere. They drove to every student dormitory in Prague and woke the sleepers with shouts of "The Russians are coming! The Russians are here!")

At 0515, after Radio Prague had announced the invasion and read the Presidium's communique, a commentator read Dubček's later appeal in a voice as husky as Dubček's and cracked with grief: "Mr. Dubček requests that the Czechoslovak people go to their regular places of work, for that, at this moment, is the only thing possible to do. We are incapable of defending the borders now. Carry out *passive* resistance."

At 0530, Radio Prague began repeating:

"This is a legal Czech radio station. Do not listen to any other. Warsaw Pact troops of our allied nations have crossed our border illegally. The National Assembly is now in session and will protest this violation. An illegal occupation has begun. But everything should be peaceful now and we urge you to remain calm. Do not offer physical resistance. If a foreign soldier tells you about conditions here, assure him that everything was going nicely and calmly until now."

The listeners knew that Czechoslovak Radio would soon be their last link to the world from which they were being brutally sealed off.

In the early dawn, they flocked there again. Thousands of them—some still in pajamas and bathrobes—came boiling up through Wenceslas Square and veering left past the Wenceslas Statue and the National Museum to reach the Radio building a few blocks beyond. "Radio hurrah!" and "Long live free speech!" they shouted. They halted trams on Vinohradská boulevard and, with the aid of passengers and crews, derailed them to form barricades. Empty buses, autos, and trucks were drafted to serve the same end. The dawn's first Soviet assault on the radio, however, was electronic. At 0630 Radio Prague announced: "We are being jammed! We are being jammed! Try to hear us wherever you can find us." But the jamming equipment stationed just across the East German frontier didn't do the job and, a few minutes later, a columnist from *Reportér* magazine sounded the words that were to become the motto of the underground radio, TV, and press: *"Jsme s Vámi bud'te s námi!"* "Be with us, we are with you."

A friend who works at Czechoslovak Radio told me his story a few weeks later:

"On the day before *The Great Befriendment*—we're no longer allowed to use the words 'invasion' or 'occupation,' so we refer to the *befriendment* or the *well-known August events*—I pre-recorded my broadcast. At six o'clock Wednesday morning, my son woke me up and said: 'I'm sorry, Daddy, but the Russians have come!' I got dressed and drove to work. My broadcast had been so optimistic that it would not only be outdated, but in pitiful taste. It didn't even occur to me that regular programming might be altered.

"All the way down Vinohradská, I had to be very careful not to get bopped by trucks with girders that were all—spontaneously, I'm sure— heading to the Radio to make barricades. I showed my pass and was let through. As soon as I got in, I was put to work reading bulletins and appeals.

"Around 7:15, the first Russian troops arrived in the building. They had come in their armored trucks—made in Czechoslovakia by Tatra or Praga, I think—and when they saw the barricades, they dismounted and came the rest of the way on foot, firing mostly into the air. We all came out in the hall to look at them and what really stopped all of us in our tracks was that these people in Russian uniforms weren't Russian. *They were central Asians!* I'm no Communist, but like many of the other Czechs there, I'd always held a deep affection for the Russians and I was a great believer in Slavic brotherhood. But I could tell by looking that these weren't our brothers.

"They came running down the halls pulling little cannons on metal chariots with metal wheels, no rubber on them. It turned out that these were anti-aircraft guns that they were putting on the roof. But these Mongols with antiquated uniforms and these incredible weapons all made me feel that the Czech people were being dragged back through history. Not just back into the nineteenth century, but back to the time of the Huns and the Vandals.

"The next squad of Mongols was supposed to occupy the building. How did they do this? They'd throw open the doors and beckon everyone inside to step out into the hall. Some of these 'Russians' didn't even speak Russian. If anybody argued, they'd start to unstrap their rifles. Everybody came out sooner or later. Then an officer went down the halls locking every door for which he could find a key. But he was very neat and he left each key in the door. So those of us who wanted to go back in for something just went back in. Until the soldiers started firing at random into the offices because they hadn't yet found the room from which we were broadcasting.

"During all this, our best female commentator—Věra Štovíčková—came to work. She said she was a charwoman and they let her in. She made her way to the microphone and went right on the air.

"They spent all morning trying to find the broadcast studio. During the time they were shooting into empty offices, one of my colleagues who used to be an army colonel said to one of these Mongol sergeants: 'Come, come, my good man. That's not how you deactivate a radio station.' And the sergeant spat onto his shoes and said: 'Don't *you* tell *me* how to do my job.' "

The radio, like TV, stayed on the air much longer than even its most resolute diehards expected. At 0736, we'd heard the sound of gunfire outside the Radio building, a woman's voice exclaiming "This is the end!", and a man's voice saying serenely: "Remember what we have been telling you. Let our last words be engraved on your memory: *Be with us, we are with you.*" But then, to everybody's surprise, the voices of Radio Prague were still with us until noon, shortly after an announcer, broadcasting from a studio disguised as a ladies' room, declared: "Outside a lot of blood is flowing and we don't know how long we can continue. It is too hot here now, but at least our consciences are clear. *Be with us, we are with you.*"

Then, with scarcely a 120-second station break, Radio Prague yielded to Radio Free Pilsen ("home of the world-famous Pilsener Beer") and Radio Free České Budějovice (Budweis, "home of the original Budweiser Beer"). Hejzlar's radio people had spent the morning organizing a legal (the Russians called it "clandestine") radio network that now carried man-in-the-street interviews (*"This is too dirty! Too dirty to touch!"*); urgent pleas (*"This is Czechoslovakia calling to the world!"*); a poem of protest from a group of librarians; and even the message of an "Extraordinary Congress" of Pilsen elementary-schoolers, meeting in a playground, to the occupation commander. (*"We are children. We want to grow up free. You also have children. Please go home and look after your own children. They are very much like us. Don't leave them alone without their fathers."*)

The transition from Radio Prague to Radio Free Pilsen had not been as smooth as it had sounded on the air. The Battle of Radio Prague had raged through the Vinohrady district all morning. After the foot soldiers, with their anti-aircraft chariots, had invaded the Radio building, Soviet tanks had arrived—firing into the air and punching their way through the obstacles put before them. One of the overturned Prague buses, however, had a full tank of gasoline and it exploded.

The tanks had to halt. When they did, boys as young as twelve and thirteen clambered aboard. They bored nickel-sized holes in the tanks' reserve fuel compartments and shoved flaming wads of rags and paper through the openings. Five of the tanks caught fire and one of them had to be abandoned. All the occupants escaped, but the whole Russian tank battalion had to pull back for a while.

Two Bulgarian tanks, part of a "token" force that had been ferried across the Black Sea over the weekend to join up with the Red Army, blundered onto the scene during this intermission. One of them was chased away by Czechs tossing home-made Molotov cocktails. A Bulgarian soldier from the other tank, however, opened fire with his machine-gun, first into the air and then into the crowd on the sidewalk. He killed a woman and two unarmed Czech soldiers.

The Radio pleaded with its admirers to disperse: "If you stay out front, there may be a massacre." An hour later, the tanks returned—

preceded by armored cars full of Soviet paratroopers. With complete abandon, hundreds of Czechs surged around the armored cars to argue with the Russians. But then the armored cars began careening up and down all the streets near the radio. The paratroopers raked the area and the buildings with machine-gun fire. A twenty-three-year-old student was bayoneted.

Most of the Czechs fled, a few fell, and two nearby apartment houses caught fire. Several tenants were badly burned, but the Russians would not let ambulances get through to them.

On the Vinohradská boulevard near the battle of Radio Prague, twenty-six-year-old Zdeněk Příhoda halted his motor bike and sat quietly waiting for a Russian truck and two armored cars to pass him. He did not live to see that happen, for (according to his obituary in the underground *Agricultural News*) "the last vehicle did not pass him by in peace. Its driver decided to kill. Brutally and recklessly, he shot the young man, a brother to two brothers and a sister; the son of a widowed mother. Deliberately, eyewitnesses say. . . . He carried no flag in his hand. He was not handing out leaflets. He was doing nothing to provoke a submachine gun. . . . [He was] an honest, straightforward young man who had never done anybody any harm in his whole life. He had graduated from the Academy of Industrial Arts. But, because he was critical of the life presided over by Antonín Novotný, he had not been accepted at the university. So he put on workman's overalls and became a member of [a heavy construction] brigade and that is what he was when death found him."

Statistics are not precise, but at least five Czechs died in the Battle of Radio Prague. And, before the broadcasters were finally evicted from their headquarters, sixty-five Czechs were taken to Vinohrady Hospital with "shot wounds, lacerations, lesions, wounds caused by grenade fragments and shots from tank grenades, very grave and deep injuries, shots in the abdomen, in the neck, in the chest, and compound limb fractures" (according to a young doctor on duty, who said he was "getting my baptism in war surgery").

Not all of these casualties, however, were from the Radio battle. Some of them were brought in from Wenceslas Square, a couple of blocks away. An elderly couple who lived on the Square went out to look at the Radio building. Passing the Wenceslas statue, they were suddenly enveloped by a skirmish that spilled out of a side street. The old man sought to protect his wife with his raincoat. When the smoke cleared two minutes later, the front part of his right foot had been torn away, her right hip bone was crushed, and she was blinded by shrapnel in both eyes.

This was the pattern of violence in Wenceslas Square. It ebbed and flowed in sudden dangerous swirls throughout the day. People would protest by sitting down in the street and then, whenever the tanks bore down relentlessly, darting into the side streets and arcades. Often, however, the tanks came out of nowhere and once—but once was enough for two lifetimes—a tank ran over a mother and child who had been crossing the square.

People tossed mattresses, garbage cans, bricks, crates and branches from fallen trees onto the tanks with apparent impunity, but two students threw rocks at a tank and a swath of machine-gun fire answered back forever by cutting their bodies in half.

That morning, too, the antenna of a tank touched a trolley wire. Frightened by the sudden burst of flame, gunners in fifteen tanks opened fire on the National Museum. People standing nearby were wounded not only by shells, but by fallen plaster. And many were physically stunned by this affront to taste.

Because the Czechs are a people whose nation was founded on culture, I knew before I ever saw it that their pockmarked National Museum would become a monument to 1968's barbaric "befriendment." Nowadays, when so much else has been erased, it stands as *the* monument, an uncosmeticized, telltale case of acne crowning the grandeur of Wenceslas Square.

RUSSIAN CIRCUS IN TOWN! DO NOT FEED THE ANIMALS.

IVAN COME HOME! BORIS IS GOING STEADY WITH NATASHA. LOVE, MOTHER.

BREZHNEV! WHEN ARE YOU GOING TO WRITE "MEIN KAMPF"?

IVAN GO HOME! IN MOSCOW THERE IS A COUNTER-REVOLUTION.

BREZHNEV! HUMANITY IS AS FAR FROM YOU AS WE ARE FROM MOSCOW!

THE SOVIET UNION IS OUR MODEL. LET'S INVADE MOSCOW!

WRECKERS OF THE WORLD, DIVIDE!

WORKERS OF THE WORLD, UNITE—OR WE'LL KILL YOU!

IVAN COME HOME! NATASHA'S HAVING SEX PROBLEMS. YOUR FRIEND, NIKOLAI.

THE BIGGER THE TANK THE SMALLER THE BRAIN.

AN ELEPHANT CANNOT SWALLOW A HEDGEHOG.

IVAN! HOW MANY TIMES MORE ARE YOU GOING TO LIBERATE US?

DON'T LIBERATE US. WE SHALL LIBERATE YOU OURSELVES.

WE USED TO HAVE FIVE FRIENDS. NOW THE WHOLE WORLD IS OUR FRIEND.

WE CONDEMN SOVIET FASCISM!

STAY SOBER! VODKA GIVES YOU A THICK HEAD.

DO NOT HARM ONE HAIR ON THEIR HEADS, BUT DO NOT GIVE THEM ONE DROP OF WATER.

CALLING DR. BARNARD! HELP!!! DR. BREZHNEV HAS JUST TRANSPLANTED THE HEART OF EUROPE INTO THE BEHIND OF RUSSIA.

WHO INVITED YOU HERE?

RETURN DUBČEK.

TO REPORT DEAD AND WOUNDED PHONE 38–20–45.

U.S.S.R. = S.S.

U.N.! S.O.S.!!!

WE WANT CÍSAŘ BACK, NOT THE CZAR.

VENI, VIDI, FUGI!

WE DEMAND A SUMMIT MEETING BETWEEN LEONID BREZHNEV AND JOHN F. KENNEDY.

EVEN HITLER CAME BY DAYLIGHT.

THE GERMANS WANTED US FOR ONLY A THOUSAND YEARS; THE RUSSIANS, FOREVER.

WHAT IS THE MOST NEUTRAL NATION IN THE WORLD? CZECHOSLOVAKIA—BECAUSE WE CANNOT EVEN INTERFERE IN OUR OWN AFFAIRS.

WHAT IS THE SAFEST NATION IN THE WORLD? ISRAEL —BECAUSE IT IS SURROUNDED BY ENEMIES.

PROČ? = POCHEMU? = POURQUOI? = WHY?

WITH BROTHERS LIKE YOU, WE BEG MOTHER RUSSIA TO PRACTICE CONTRACEPTION.

A TOAST OF WELCOME—H2S04!

WE HAVE BEEN DEEPENING OUR FRIENDSHIP WITH THE SOVIET UNION FOR 20 YEARS. NOW AT LAST WE HAVE HIT ROCK BOTTOM.

MAKE LOVE, NOT WAR!

WE SHALL OVERCOME!

Sign carried by three East Germans: WE ARE ASHAMED OF BEING EAST GERMANS!

HELP WANTED: ONE PUPPET PRIME MINISTER, ONE NATIONAL ASSEMBLY SPEAKER, ONE FIRST SECRETARY, ONE NATIONAL FRONT CHAIRMAN. ONLY TRAITORS NEED APPLY. CONTACT SOVIET EMBASSY.

SOCIALISM, YES! OCCUPATION, NO!

EXHIBITION OF SOVIET MILITARY MIGHT ON WENCESLAS SQUARE. ENTRANCE FREE; EXIT NOT GUARANTEED.

"HOW MANY TIMES MUST I TURN OVER IN MY MAUSO-LEUM?"—V. I. LENIN.

LENIN! ARISE AND SEE WHAT IS BEING DONE IN YOUR NAME!

BREZHNEV! COMPARED TO YOU GENGHIS KHAN NEVER EXISTED.

IVAN COME HOME! NATASHA IS A NYMPHOMANIAC. (signed) BORIS AND NIKOLAI.

EAT EGGS A LA RUSSE. THE EGGS ARE OUR FRIENDS.

Sign in a dairy window: FREE OFFER TO ALL OCCUPIERS. WE WILL TRADE THREE BOTTLES OF MILK FOR A THIMBLE OF COMMON SENSE.

THIS IS NEITHER VIETNAM NOR BIAFRA.

PROTECT US FROM SMALLPOX AND COLLABORATORS!

THEY ARE HERE! LOCK UP YOUR WATCHES AND YOUR WIVES!

THERE WAS NO COUNTER-REVOLUTION UNTIL YOU CAME.

YOU HAVE MOSCOW. PRAGUE IS OURS.

PRAGUE IS BEAUTIFUL WHEN IT IS CZECH.

HOME, DOGS! OUR NATION WEEPS. 21 AUGUST 1968.

BOOK EXCHANGE: ONE RUINED LENIN FOR ONE BOUND BREZHNEV.

EXCHANGE WANTED: SOVIET-CZECHOSLOVAK FRIEND-SHIP FOR ANY OTHER PORNOGRAPHY.

Small print at very bottom of a large, otherwise blank placard: *Watch this poster carefully. In a few minutes it will be torn down.*

FOR 20 YEARS WE WAITED. FOR 100 YEARS WE WILL RE-MEMBER.

BE WITH US, WE ARE WITH YOU.

Painted on a wall, a poem addressed to the invaders:

> Welcome, friends, you came as brothers,
> And now our blood flows on our land.
> Welcome, friends, thank you for the roses
> On the tombs of our children.
> Welcome, friends, it is with eyes filled with salt
> That we welcome you.

IVAN COME HOME! YOURS, NATASHA.

NO LIBERTY WITHOUT SOCIALISM. NO SOCIALISM WITHOUT LIBERTY.

A poem addressed to Alexander Dubček ends:

If you are menaced, let our arms be your swords and our bodies your
        shield,
If your path is strewn with thorns, walk anyway; we shall go with you,
But never leave the path of liberty, honor, and justice,
On another road, you would be alone.

Chapter 14]

Wednesday 21 August 1968
from 1330 to 2130

AFTER LUNCH, I TOOK MY FIRST WALK THROUGH OCCU-pied Prague. The convoys were still pouring down the Boulevard of the Pioneers (which leads in from the East German frontier near Carls-bad), but people were starting to venture out cautiously. In order to pass unmolested as a helpless voyeur at the rape of Prague, I decided to put a camera around my neck and a guide book in my hand and, *voilà!*, one Instant American Tourist hewing to his itinerary through thick and thin.

In the Firehouse Square, I avoided the traffic island where I'd nearly met my end at dawn. There were no tanks in the square now, just deep ruts and uprooted cobblestones bearing witness to the heavy treads. But a few yards down Loreta Street stood a petite one-gun minitank with a Russian soldier in the turret checking credentials. If he okayed you, the tank would swivel aside and you could proceed as far as the Foreign Ministry. If you wanted to go onward—toward the Castle—you'd have to clear yourself with a larger tank hulking at the next checkpoint. From the direction of the Castle, I could hear the regular thud of cannon fire and sporadic small-arms fire.

Some fifty Czechs had gathered near the minitank. They heckled the soldier, who was ignoring them. When a commandeered Prague bus brought Russian soldiers in, the crowd jeered and stamped and whistled until it had cleared both checkpoints. A couple of students, waving their bus passes, tried to board it.

The route I had chosen down Neruda Street was still open to pedes-trians. From the top of Petřín Hill, the view was clear and glistening all the way across the curving Vltava. But just beyond where Wenceslas Square would be, a pall of black smoke rose from the apartment houses that had burned in the Battle of Radio Prague.

Walking downhill, I knew that my progress was being monitored in a telescopic gunsight a quarter-of-a-mile away on the right-hand side of the slope. The Russians (according to the radio) were inside the Petřín Tower lookout where we'd spent Liberation Day with Sylva. Halfway down, the buildings of Hradčany Square and then the Castle loomed up over my left shoulder. Atop the pristine elegance of one of the palaces, I suddenly thought I saw a statue move. It was a Russian soldier patroling the roof.

People trudging uphill warned me that, at the bottom, Russians were confiscating cameras, radios, maps, watches, pens, and wedding rings. Hearing this, I veered off through a courtyard, a staircase, and two tunnels, which brought me to the American Embassy.

In the Embassy courtyard, tourists were milling around waiting for the Marines (who wear civilian clothes here) to assign them places in a car convoy to Germany. Upstairs, Alan Tillier of *Newsweek* and Tad Szulc were taking turns at the Embassy's Telex, which Ambassador Beam had put at journalists' disposal. Ordinarily, I'm no fan of American Embassies. More often than I care to remember, they shut up shop or put themselves off-limits whenever you need them most. The one in Prague lies on an unpronounceable (for American tongues) street called Tržiště (Marketplace), but it was functioning smoothly and courteously on most cylinders that day. Commissary Mary offered to sell me some milk, inquired after my family, and said she thought it would be safer for them to stay in Prague "for now, at least."

At the reception desk, where I went to dismantle my tourist disguise, I encountered the real thing. An elderly Floridian was shaking his white mane at the receptionist's brunette beehive.

"I paid in advance for a five-day stay here with all meals and sightseeing included, and by God I am going to stay here for five days!"

The girl, a Czech who spoke English, said evenly: "The Ambassador recommends that you leave now, sir, or as soon as we have assurances of safe conduct from the Russians and the Czechoslovaks."

"Safe conduct to where?"

"Probably to Nuremberg."

"But I've *been* to Nuremberg. And I have prepaid vouchers for everything here. This afternoon, I'm supposed to be doing the Hradčany Castle and eating in the *Veekarky* restaurant. Here's my itinerary. . . ."

The girl's eyes had filled with tears, but the old turkey-neck wasn't looking at anything but his damned vouchers while she said, gripping the desk: "The Castle is closed, sir. It's guarded by Russian soldiers who can't read your itinerary, sir. My country has been invaded, sir, and your Embassy recommends for your own safety that you leave as soon as possible."

The man said he reckoned he'd have "the travel agent who booked me this fool tour blacklisted at every American Embassy in the world." I gave the girl my camera for safekeeping and then went on with my walk—using my guidebook as my sole "tourist" prop and wondering whether I hadn't perhaps chosen the most belligerent of all poses.

A Russian convoy was passing through Malá Strana Square and it took me fifteen minutes to get across the street. Another block and I was on the Charles Bridge, as yet unviolated by tanks, but already defaced with chalked and painted graffiti. "LENIN AWAKEN! BREZHNEV HAS GONE OUT OF HIS MIND!" In fresh red and green were striking intertwinings of red stars and swastikas. A heart with a dagger through it was inscribed "1938 + 30 = 1968." Another equation showed 1938-in-a-swastika equaling 1968-in-a-red-star. "UL-BRICHT = DICTATOR = NOVOTNÝ," said another. Plus "IVAN GO HOME" in fourteen different languages that I could count. A Springtime scratching of "CÍSAŘ!" had been amended to read "FREE CÍSAŘ!" And, on the medieval stone bridge, the baroque statues of Saints Vitus and Wenceslas, Cyril and Methodius, Anthony of Padua and Vincent of Ferrara, and particularly Jan the Confessor of Nepomuk gazed over the ancient Vltava with the stoic resignation of religious sculpture.

At the Old Town end of his bridge, the Holy Roman Emperor Charles IV had been handed a Czechoslovak flag.* But the entire right bank of the Vltava in Prague was an endless olive ring of tanks. Russian soldiers, cradling weapons in laps while waiting for orders, lolled on the tank-tops. They eyed passing girls wistfully and the rest of us warily. Cars couldn't pass, but people could.

Twice, though, I saw tourists with cameras being accosted by soldiers who jumped down from the tanks. In one case, the soldier took away the camera and aimed his submachine gun when the owner protested. In the other case, an Italian actually wrestled with two soldiers. The commotion attracted their superior officer. The officer calmed the

---

* Long after the slogans and "Dubček-Svoboda" signs had been erased, whitewashed, and otherwise eradicated to fulfill the "normalization" agreed upon in Moscow, Charles IV's statue clung to his Czechoslovak flag. It wasn't until early 1969 that the Russians realized it had not been ever thus.

Italian by saying, in sign language, that he would work out the dispute. He inspected the camera, opened it, emptied it of its roll of film, exposed the film, handed the ruined film back to its owner, and then walked off with the camera himself!

The Italian simply sat down on the pavement and cried. There was nothing the two enlisted men, who now tried to console him, could do to cheer him up.

From the Charles Bridge left toward Dvořák Hall, the soldiers were all dark, brooding, uncommunicative Georgians; one knew they were Stalin's people even before one found out where they were from. If you asked any of them a question, he might or might not answer you but he would definitely tighten his grip on his weapon. Sometimes, you would walk past their tanks and see one or another of the very young ones eyeing you. Then you would hear the click of a safety.

It was not a very promising cat-and-mouse game, so after a brief detour to the left of the Charles Bridge I doubled back and went right. This route led to the National Theatre and would put me closer to Wenceslas Square. Besides, aboard the sixty tanks planted in that quarter-mile stretch of riverfront were Ukrainians, neighbors to the Slovaks; some of them, in fact, Czechoslovaks until 1945's re-drawing of boundaries. Strapping, blond, and indefatigably cheerful, they could have passed for a touring troupe of whirling dervishes if it had not been for those dumpy brown uniforms which made them look like overgrown schoolboys playing soldier.

It was there and then that I witnessed the miracle of the *hydeparks*. These free-swinging forums had moved right in among the troops who had come to kill freedom of expression. The new *hydepark* was every second or third tank. Wherever the tankers looked willing to answer questions first and shoot later (rather than the other way around), twenty or thirty Czechs would surround a tank and open a debate. Some were sermonizing. Others were audaciously chalking swastikas and slogans on tanks. Every tank I could see was already adorned with a quote or variation of Brezhnev's rebuff to Novotný: "This is your affair." Now the Czechs were reminding the Russians that "THIS IS OUR AFFAIR."

And asking: "Why are you here?"

The answers the Ukrainians gave were incredible, but transparently sincere: "We thought we were on maneuvers. We had no idea we were going to Prague." Some of them, from Odessa and the Black Sea-coast, still weren't sure where they were. Others had never heard of Dubček. A few were convinced they were "in Nazi Germany." "How come all the Germans speak Czech and Russian?" "Oh, our officer says there are two ways to tell a German. They all dress very well. And they speak three or four languages."

Hearing this, I thought about putting away my English-language guidebook and passing for a good German like all the other Czechs. But, just then, my book and I were spotted by a more perceptive Russian corporal, who jumped down from a tank and—to my utter embarrassment—embraced me like an old friend. Hardly anybody has ever been that happy to see me.

"I speak not a little English," he informed me. "In this moment, you are the first Englishman I see for ever. You are English? Australian?" Realizing, when I hesitated, that he had some kind of prize catch, he stepped back and looked me over closely. "Canadian?"

"American," I said shyly. "American tourist."

He clapped me on the back and shook hands: "You are my first American. Up to now, I am disappointed, for they promised me many."

"Many Americans?"

"They tell me, when I don't want to go, that we will be fighting American Special Forces and revanchist German Wehrmacht. If we take prisoners, I can be interrogator. But you're not a soldier?"

"Definitely not," I said. "American tourist. I have been to Moscow and Leningrad once and I hope . . ."

"Come to Kharkov!" he said. "It's a better city than Moscow, Leningrad, Kiev, and Prague put together." Then he showed me a photo not of Kharkov, but of the girl he'd left behind. I showed him a snapshot of "my family back home" and made my exit as soon as I could.

I put away my guidebook and waded forward through dialogue after dialogue. Passing one tank, I would hear someone asking "Why are you here?" and, two tanks later, I would catch a Russian's reply to a different questioner: "If we hadn't come, the Americans would have taken over in two days." I walked faster, but the dialogue was continuous, and you could follow it as though you were walking down a residential street on the night of a hockey broadcast. I noticed in passing that, while tanks were massed on the riverfront outside Igor Hájek's window, the *Literární Listy* office did not seem to be occupied. But I decided against poking my head inside.

At the National Theatre, I turned left onto the National Boulevard and entered still another world. The gregarious Ukrainians and brooding Georgians were left behind. Now I passed between the blank gazes of two solid lines of Asians poised in their tank turrets like toy samurai waiting to be wound up. I didn't have to think hard to remember that the word *robot* was made in Prague. Now the robots had come to Prague—perchance to destroy the city. But these robots had no idea where they were and couldn't have cared less. They were here to enforce, not to look around.

A few steps farther on, I saw a machine-gun nest and four tanks cordoning off the Viola poetry-and-jazz night club. Inside the Viola's entrance courtyard were two minitanks. The whole Viola was swarming with troops. A musician I knew was watching with faint amusement. He didn't appear as aghast as I was and he worked there!

"All this to put down skiffle singing!" I observed.

"It's all right," he murmured. "They think it's the Writers Union. That's what stupid pigs they are!" (The Viola is at National Boulevard number 7; the Writers Union at numbers 9 and 11.)

"Why haven't they done the same thing at *Literární Listy?*" I asked.

"Nobody knows," he said.

(It took four days for the Russians to discover that the Viola was a night club, not Goldstücker's headquarters, and that the café tables could never have housed a battery of typewriters spawning subversions 2,000 words at a time.)

Starting by seeing black-clad Martian tankers adrift at dawn in the Firehouse Square with obsolete maps and continuing by ear-witnessing the Russian inability to silence the radio, I had already come to realize that the invasion was militarily a bit of a botch rather than the "textbook blitzkrieg," "military masterpiece," and "lightning stroke of strategic genius" that it was already being hailed as by the Western press and NATO intelligence.

True, the Russians had put a quarter-of-a-million troops into Czechoslovakia overnight—half of them, plus 2,000 tanks, into Prague—and more were still pouring in.* But they had wasted a precious hour or two fighting their way into and out of Prague's airport, where resist-

---

* By nightfall, the Czechoslovak Ministry of Defense would estimate the total of invading troops (including token forces from Poland, Hungary, Bulgaria, and East Germany) at 500,000; by the following Monday, at 650,000.

ance was minimal and willing traitors were waiting to receive them.

Whenever I could muster the detachment to think tactically, it kept occurring to me that if the Russians had had a real counter-revolution on their hands and if the Writers Union and *Literární Listy,* the radio and the television, the Castle and the Foreign Ministry had been its real strongholds, then the invasion certainly would have lost vital time and ground. And the invaders would have been in real trouble.

With all due respect to Tad Szulc, I differ with what he wrote in the New York *Times* soon thereafter:

> The Soviet-led invasion . . . provided Western observers with the first opportunity since World War II to watch the Soviet Army in a situation of combat readiness on a large scale.
>
> The invasion, especially the lightning occupation of Prague, was a brilliantly and faultlessly executed military operation in the virtually unanimous judgment of Western observers with military experience.

Which is to say: in the judgment of those who were caught napping, and who would therefore be inclined to overestimate the ability of the rascals who outwitted them.

Only the sheer size of the invasion and the passive nature of the Czech resistance saved the Soviets from heavy casualties. But the weight of numbers was enough to snuff out the candle which the Prague Spring had lit for a world that badly needed hope in 1968.

The invasion worked—but it was a fatal blunder of the soul. It seemed to me then that, by over-reacting in the name of world communism, the scared old men in Moscow, Warsaw, Sofia, Budapest, and East Berlin may have sounded its death knell. I would think that they doomed (or certainly postponed) the chances of a chaotic Western nation like France or Italy ever going Communist. These nations (and particularly their Communist parties) were watching the Dubček experiment and were potentially vulnerable to the inroads of "socialism with a human face." After 21 August 1968, however, voting Communist in the West could be equated with treason. It is an irrevocable choice. If your country should go Communist and then deviate the way Czechoslovakia did (let alone try to vote the Communists *out* of office, which Czechoslovakia never even considered doing), then you may have doomed your fellow countrymen to awakening one morning and finding Martian tanks on the Champs Élysées, tanks on the Via Veneto, tanks on every boulevard. . . .

"It is worse than a crime; it is a mistake," Napoleon's minister of police once said of political murder. His words have lived on—and they may yet stand as the ultimate epitaph for the invasion of Czechoslovakia.

Literární Listy was never occupied, and the reason came out only three weeks after the invasion. That was when the Russians agreed to return the Writers Union to its members once the clamps on free expression had been negotiated in Moscow. A portly general of Engineers came around to "release" the Writers Union on National Boulevard floor-by-floor. "You can have everything back," he said, "except the fourth floor."

"Why not the fourth floor?" the Union deputy-in-charge asked.

"Because that's the headquarters of the nefarious *Literární Listy*," the general replied. "And we haven't been able to find their files." (The Russians made off with subscription lists of many of the periodicals they occupied.)

The Union deputy laughed and said: "But *Literární Listy* isn't in this building. The fourth floor is where we store our back numbers. *Literární Listy* is our publication, all right, but it's over on Bethlehem Street, near the Vltava."

The general was not easy to convince, but the writers insisted on receiving "all or nothing" of their building back. Finally, the general was able to see with his own eyes that the fourth floor was not *LL*'s editorial offices. He thereupon sent for a young lieutenant and snapped at him: "Do you know anything about the address, Bethlehem Street number One?"

"Yes, sir, the address is familiar," said the Lieutenant, racking his brain. "Some false informer told us that it was the headquarters of the nefarious *Literární Listy*. I went over there myself, but it was much too small and unpretentious to be the home of an imperialist-financed counter-revolutionary organ."

As I walked up National Boulevard on the 21st of August, people were chanting "Dub-ček! Dub-ček!" and the robots were clenching their triggers tighter and tighter, but otherwise showing no flicker of anger or interest. Just as they all looked the same to me, all of us under their guns must have looked the same to them.

Now a band of young students swept down from Wenceslas Square. They were bearing the white-red-and-blue Czechoslovak flag, but most of the white field was red. "Here's the blood of a thirteen-year-old boy you shot down!" they called up to the impassive robots. It had been dipped in the pool of brains beneath the boy's head in the square where he lay dying.

The robots just stared. Still, if I ever saw them register anything besides coiled tension, it was then. Some of them glanced around for their officers—all white Europeans, incidentally—as though surprised that the command to open fire had not been sounded. Then the flag-bearers turned right at the waterfront and were out of sight. The robots relaxed into their normal rigidity.

Passing the Perla Department Store (which caught fire while being looted the next day), I saw several youths with bandaged heads racing to catch up with the flag-bearers. One of them was still dripping his own blood.

At the next corner, I turned right onto Wenceslas Square, itself a casualty. Good Prince Wenceslas had survived. But the cobblestones below him were all churned up. The overhead power lines for trams were down. The brand-new trolley stop, which had just emerged from scaffolding, had been demolished. Below it, the roof of the new under-pass, nearing completion when I'd seen it last, had collapsed under the excess weight of the tanks. The Russian troops were using the ruins of the underpass for a latrine.

The National Museum's monumental neo-Renaissance facade still spreadwinged the top of the square. The fountain beneath its steps still splashed merrily the way it had yesterday and the day before. But when you raised your eyes, you froze in your steps. The museum's grimy brown facade was pitted and pocked with hundreds of white spots, "as if evil birds had pecked at it" is the way *Rudé Právo* later described the shell holes.

Tanks still swept through the square every five or ten minutes to rake the air with gunfire and splinter the sidewalks with broken glass. At quieter moments, Czechs wandered through the ruins, taking in sights they'd never forget. Some even tried to reason with the Russian foot soldiers lining the square. A grandmother approached one of them and showed him a snapshot: "This was my only son. He died fighting the Germans in the Ukraine." The Russian soldier prodded her with his bayonet and said: "Stand back five metres."

The troops were under strict orders not to fraternize. But one dash-ing young officer accosted the prettiest girl in sight and, apologizing for his poor knowledge of the Roman alphabet, asked her how to pronounce the name of a street on his orders. The girl told him nothing, except: "If you ever come as a tourist, I will show you my city. But when you come in a tank, I will have nothing to do with you."

There on Wenceslas Square, old Czechoslovak soldiers queued up to throw their medals, earned on the Russian front, into garbage pails that would be delivered to the Soviet Embassy a few hours later.

(The Czechoslovak physician assigned to treating the Soviet Embassy's staff resigned his post on 21 August and personally returned a gold medal the Russians had awarded him for long and faithful service. He said he could no longer specialize in taking care of the men who'd butchered his nation.)

That afternoon in Wenceslas Square, students marched between tank forays. They marched behind Czechoslovak flags dipped in the blood of that terrible day's martyrs. And whenever the tanks came, students planted themselves below the equestrian statue of Good Prince Wenceslas, beneath its carved inscription "DO NOT LET US PERISH, NOR OUR HEIRS," to which someone had appended in chalk: "DUBČEK HURRAH!"

A vigil began then and there on the 21st of August beneath the Wenceslas statue. Two by two, the students of Prague took turns standing guard with a white-red-and-blue Czechoslovak flag and a black banner of national grief while hundreds of others sat in silence with heads bowed. Throughout each day and each night for two weeks, they refused to disperse or even flinch when curfews were sounded by tracer bullets and when tanks fired over their heads (and, at least once, into their midst). They spread flowers by day and lit candles by night to honor their dead. And each dawn and each dusk brought new names to mourn, new heroes to remember, and new blood to stain the Czechoslovak tricolor.

I bore left above the statue and there I caught two glimpses of beauty and obscenity that still haunt me. Part of one side of the National Museum was caved in. An exhibit of Italian statues, many of them now maimed or chipped, looked out onto this vista with more visible emotion than I had perceived among all the robots on the whole National Boulevard.

Still circling the museum, I came around the front again and this time I noticed a tank idling just below the building. Its enormous cannon, pointing skyward, was coated with plaster from the museum it had raped.

At the Radio building, the troops were inside and nobody was broadcasting any longer. A group of key officials had put Radio Prague back on the air for a while. Locked into a room by their captors, they'd managed to reactivate the phone and get through to Radio Free Pilsen, which broadcast their words as they spoke them into the phone. The Russians had caught on to this and shoved the officials out onto a balcony from where, at gunpoint, they were now haranguing a cheering street crowd with speeches, resolutions, and newscasts. Their audience below sent up shouts of encouragement and (whenever a bucket was lowered) sandwiches, too. So here were the last voices of freedom on a small ledge with the people before them (and still nourishing them) and the Russians at their back.

The bus which had exploded that morning and a truck which had been crushed in the Battle of Radio Prague were still lying there. The gutted apartment building around the corner was still smoldering. A homeless tenant was prowling about the ruins in search of charred belongings. All he'd found was a teapot, and of all things, an ikon.

"In one day," he said to me, a stranger, without looking up, "the Russians did more damage to Prague than the Germans did in their first six years here."

He spat when he said "Russians," but not when he said "Germans."

I said nothing. But my silence must have registered my dismay because he gazed up at me and said paternally: "Why are you looking like that?"

"I feel sorry for you," I replied, "but I'm Jewish and, when you say such a thing, I can't help thinking of the people who were destroyed in those first six years."

"Then don't feel sorry for me. Feel lucky for me. Feel lucky for yourself," he said, wearily not bitterly, and showed me a concentration camp number tattooed on his forearm. "I'm Jewish, too."

He went back to his rummaging and I went away, feeling neither lucky nor sorry, just small.

Working my way back toward home, I bypassed Wenceslas Square and took a detour that brought me out in front of my bank, the *Art Nouveau* Živnostenská Banka. Like all the State Banks, it was sealed off by a Russian tank. But, on its door, some Czech bard had posted a poem alluding to past economic ravages as well as current events:

> To protect our poor State bank,
> There is no need for Russian tanks.
> To guard the crap we have inside
> Is a job we do ourselves with pride.
> It's only crap with which we're blessed,
> Our Russian "brothers" took the rest.

I crossed the main street they call "The Moat" (*Na Příkopě*) dividing the New Town from the Old Town. On the Old Town side, I saw the Czech manager of Prague's Russian restaurant, the Moskva, climbing up its marquee. I waited and watched. While the tank outside my bank swiveled toward him, the man on the ladder changed two letters in the sign and re-named his restaurant the Morava. Then he came down unscathed. Prague had a new Moravian restaurant!

I entered the Old Town through the Gunpowder Tower. The "notorious *hydeparks* outside the Old Town Hall" had stood high on the Soviet list of targets. With characteristic overkill, the Red Army had sealed off the lovely medieval Old Town Square and redecorated it with six anti-aircraft guns, a machine-gun nest, and fifteen tanks. Even so, somebody had managed to perform an act of mercy by blindfolding the statue of Jan Hus.

Fronting on the square, the two-century-old Kinský Palace, where Franz Kafka attended grammar school, has been a museum since the end of World War II. By coincidence, its August 1968 exhibition was proclaimed by a red streamer running the width of its rococo facade: "20 YEARS OF SOVIET ART." The Russian machine-gun nest was planted, dead-center, beneath it and photographers with zoom lenses were jockeying to shoot this succinct self-criticism of what two decades of communism had done for and to the Czechoslovak Socialist Republic.

A few blocks away, Red Army Square was living up to its name (which is in Russian) only because it houses another Russian target, the "nefarious Philosophical Faculty" and therefore warranted utmost military attention. In Red Army Square, I spotted a 134 bus and asked the driver if he was taking passengers on his regular route today. When he said yes, I boarded and he handed me my first of numerous mimeographed Ten Commandments that were circulating in Prague:

1. Until our leaders are released, practice passive resistance and go on strike if necessary.
2. Do not co-operate with the occupation forces.
3. Talk Russian to the soldiers, explaining our truths, painting slogans, printing leaflets.
4. If threatened, however, claim you do not understand Russian or any other language.
5. If pressed, play the fool.
6. Support only the *free* television and radio.
7. Try to destroy Russian propaganda and jam their broadcasting.
8. Support all our progressive leaders.
9. Denounce collaborators and others weak in character.
10. Prepare yourself for further steps should the occupation continue.

The bus took a roundabout way home via the Plain of Letná, where Stalin's statue once stood and where the *hydepark* had been officially designated to move. But the Plain of Letná was now a helicopter landing field. I saw forty helicopters (some of them landing and taking off) protected by twice as many tanks. Armed paratroops patroled the plain and scanned our bus as it went by. The passenger next to me stared back and then murmured to nobody in particular: *"Hydepark."*

At home, I found the children chafing only a little at being cooped up in the house. They'd been watching the tanks from the window. Erika had decided: "I don't like Russian tanks because they don't stop to let anybody cross the street." Monica, on the other hand, insisted: "Daddy, I should like to meet the Russian soldier." To her, the Russian soldier was a jolly, overbearing character from a Little Golden Record we'd brought over with us: "A Child's Introduction to the Nutcracker Suite" narrated by Captain Kangaroo. ("Sweet Arabian princess, you are so beautiful you cannot be unhappy. I am only a poor Russian soldier, but everyone says I am a prince of a fellow. I will share your dreams with you if you will let me.")

I told Monica that there would, alas, be plenty of time and ample opportunity to meet the Russian soldier, but today was not the day.

My wife and my niece briefed me on what they'd seen on TV and heard on the radio while I'd been out. Valerie also handed me a list of phone calls to return, and when I'd done so, I could piece together this reconstruction of events in and near the Central Committee building:

Shortly after 0900, a dozen Czech secret policemen had met with three members of the Soviet KGB (security police) in the police headquarters on Bartholomew Street. The meeting was in the office of Lieutenant Colonel Bohumil Molnár, chief of State Security for the Prague region.

Císař was already being interrogated next door by other collaborators. Now Molnár told his henchmen they were to take Dubček, Smrkovský, Kriegel, and Špaček into formal custody. Then he assigned the arrest party to five cars—two Volgas, two Tatras, and a Škoda.

"Should we take guns along?" someone asked.

"I think so," Molnár replied.

They went first to the Russian Embassy, on the other side of the Vltava. There, an elderly Russian colonel and another Soviet officer climbed into the Volgas. All five cars then recrossed the river. Outside the Central Committee, they were joined by a Soviet major in battle dress with an automatic rifle. He was the commander of the detachment that had occupied the building. He led them inside. In the lobby, an aide of "Mr. First Secretary" Kolder was screening a Central Committee personnel roster for a couple of KGB men. He was marking who could be sent home or let in and, on the other hand, who was "unreliable." *

The major had led the new arrivals to room 70 on the second floor, where a bureaucratic-looking Czech in rimless glasses was waiting to brief them. Addressing his fellow traitors, he asked: "Who among you is a hero? Who will go up to Dubček and say: 'In the name of the Revolutionary Workers and Peasants Government of Comrade Indra, you are hereby taken into custody.'?"

For a while, they all shirked this job—but, eventually, a Czech secret policeman known as Hoffman, Sr., volunteered for infamy and memorized the formula. He was accompanied by two colleagues named Dubský and Peroutka. In Císař's office, Dubček, Smrkovský, Kriegel, and Špaček were again searched and they still kept their watches! †

---

* As a result of this list, alternate Presidium member Šimon was taken away by the Russians that night and held in custody in Prague for almost a week.

† Oddly enough, while Colonel Molnár's team had been making its plans, another group of State Security men had been meeting with a KGB man named Vinokurov. The Russian had "explained" the invasion to them, using the assertions set forth by Brezhnev and *Pravda* plus the revelation that Dubček was a "weak-willed person" who had surrounded himself with enemies of socialism—namely, Kriegel and Smrkovský. He added that Císař was a confessed "anarchist." Then, toward 0930,

Then they'd waited until afternoon, when Russians with handcuffs arrived. Before being shackled, each leader was led to his office and given a chance to take along with him anything he wanted to carry "on a trip." Josef Smrkovský was led to his desk, where he fondled the National Assembly Speaker's gavel. But, remembering his four-and-a-half years in Stalinist jails (where tea was served without sweetening) all he took were three lumps of sugar from a tea tray.

"I'll need these where I'm going," Smrkovský had remarked. "I've been there before."

Čestmír Císař had fared better down at the police station. He had answered his interrogators blandly and noncommittally. They'd fed him tea and sandwiches and then, in early afternoon, whisked him off to the Hotel Without a Name—"where Dubček," one of them gloated ominously, "used to live." Císař was brought there to meet with "Comrade Indra," whose puppet Government still needed a breath of life from somewhere, anywhere, even if it had to be the bad breath of a defection from Dubček by a Císař. Nobody who knew Císař, however, worried too much about his making such a move, particularly when word leaked out about his entrance into the Hotel Without a Name's dining room.

Escorted by his secret police captors, Císař had been intercepted by a waiter, who failed to recognize him and asked him unctuously: "Are you with a group, sir?"

Císař is supposed to have replied: "No, but the group's with me."

Also on hand in the dining room of the Hotel Without a Name were two-dozen conservative Central Committee members. Only a few were traitors; the rest were honest conservatives who wanted to hear Indra's side of the story before casting their lots. They were kept waiting for Indra all afternoon and well into the evening. "What's happening?" they asked each other over and over. None of them yet dared to breathe aloud the name of what wasn't happening: "The Revolutionary Workers and Peasants Government of Comrade Indra."

Vinokurov and six Czech secret policemen had also set out to arrest Dubček, Smrkovský, Kriegel, and Špaček. They, too, had stopped at the Soviet Embassy to pick up three more KGB men (one of them a high official who'd been an adviser to Prague's Ministry of Interior until 1962) and a military escort of nineteen tanks. But, by the time they arrived at the Central Committee, it was nearly 1100 and their dirty work had already been done.

That evening after supper, my niece and I took our second walk of the day together through the Firehouse Square. Nobody menaced us this time. When we turned onto Loreta Street, we found that the two tanks had been withdrawn ("They're inside the Foreign Ministry now," an old man told us, "so they don't need to guard it from the outside.") and we could walk as far as the other end of Loreta Street, where it funnels into Hradčany Square.

This opening was stoppered by eight Russian soldiers holding twenty mild-mannered Czechs at bay. These soldiers were armed, but they didn't look inclined to use the weapons hanging from their necks. They were smoking their own North Korean cigarettes. They were young boys, tall, dark, and completely somber. Some were quite pimply. All were very hungry.

"We haven't eaten since we left Dresden last night," said one.

Nobody offered him a crumb. Just the usual: "Why are you here?"

"We thought you were having a counter-revolution," he said lamely.

The longer he stayed in Prague, the less convinced he would sound. There he and his comrades-in-arms stood defending the occupied seat of sovereignty from a score of its anxious citizenry while, inside, who knew what was happening to the President? Some of the Czechs on hand were bold enough to listen to transistors and when they told these sentries that three people were reported dead inside the Castle, one of the boys shrugged and said: "They were killed because they wouldn't leave the Castle when they were able to."

"You say 'they were killed,'" said a Czech. "Who killed them?"

"I didn't," said the soldier. The others nodded glumly that neither had they.

Nobody said anything more. This was the only moment of Slavic brotherhood I'd witnessed all day. Brothers in misery, these Russians were too hungry and weary and ashamed to speak just as these Czechs were too dejected and (tonight at least) too spent even to argue much. Nevertheless, it was a potentially inflammatory situation if it went on very much longer. Hungry soldiers, for whom no real provisions had been made, were confronted by a hostile people who no longer had any love to lose. *My brother, my enemy* . . .

In the darkness, with the spires of St. Vitus Cathedral and St. George's Basilica looming behind him like ghostly apparitions, an older soldier entered this scene. For all Nancy and I knew then, he might have been the man-in-black who had waved a pistol at us in the Firehouse Square that morning—but now I think not. He carried a long pole device and he was gently, almost tenderly, turning on the gaslights of Hradčany Square one by one.

"Who is he?" I asked one of the sentries in Czech. A Russian can understand Czech and a Czech can understand Russian if you speak slowly.

"He's our lamplighter," the boy replied in Russian. "We have two in our battalion."

"What for?" I asked.

"For this," he replied, nodding toward the Castle. "We didn't know what for, but we've been drilling in Dresden since April and today we found out why."

Dresden, the china city up the Elbe, must have been the perfect training ground for occupying Hradčany, and I had the impression that not a pane of glass would be broken or a jewel disturbed inside the Prague Castle.* It was also interesting that such elaborate preparations for an occupation had been launched so soon after the weekend of 22 March, when Novotný had abdicated and Dubček had journeyed to Dresden to plead his case.

The lamplighter went about his work with great delicacy. And, when he had provided enough illumination, we could see what had become of the spacious, beautifully wrought Hradčany Square, where no fewer than five splendid palaces form a glittering pendant to the brooding Castle's main gate. The square was now a garage for tanks! They were parked, side-by-side and back-to-back, for the night. More than a hundred of them!

A collective gasp went up from the crowd. A couple of the Czechs started to cry. Others shuddered, although it was a warm August night.

The old soldier who was a lamplighter looked at the reaction his efforts had provoked and then, without pausing to reflect, he simply took the snuffer part of his pole and applied it to the lamps he had just lit. In a few minutes, the square was veiled in merciful darkness.

I knew that the Czechs would never thank him, but I wanted to. "Thank you," I said softly when he passed near me.

He gave me a despairing look in which I could read that "history

* This impression was later confirmed when the Castle was "released" by the Russians.

will punish us," but all he said was: "Four months in Dresden for this!"

When Nancy and I returned home, Radio Prague was miraculously back on the air ("coming to you from a secret location") and so was Czechoslovak Television, which had reappeared on the dot of 1900 (on a different channel than usual) with the "7 O'Clock News"—some terrifying footage of the day's turmoil in and around Wenceslas Square, my wife reported. So we still had the facts, even though they all verged on the unbearable:

Late that afternoon, Dubček, Smrkovský, Špaček, and Kriegel had been taken away from the Central Committee in two armored trucks; Czechs who'd seen them leave said Dubček looked half-unconscious, more as if he'd been drugged or injected than beaten. When the armored trucks arrived at Ruzyně Airport an hour later, the men had been lashed together in pairs by ropes wrapped tightly around their necks, feet, and hands and knotted near the small of their backs. Prime Minister Černík, in handcuffs, was already at the airport. Prodded by rifle butts, all five men were loaded onto a Russian military transport plane—the propellers of which were already whirring—bound for "a place or places unknown."

None of our neighbors or friends wanted to discuss the implications of that. Radio Prague said it would soon be going off the air again because "we are tired and another long, long night is upon us."

Interlude ⌉ Where were you when the invasion happened?

THE SUCHÝS—JIRKA, BÉLA, AND LITTLE KUBÍK—WERE AT a resort hotel in Yugoslavia. When they came down to breakfast late Wednesday morning, their table was piled high with flowers, Swiss chocolates, and American cigarettes.

"Thank you," Jiří Suchý said to the waitress, "but what's the occasion?"

"It's not just from everyone in the kitchen," she said solemnly. "It's from all the guests in the hotel, too."

"But why?" said Suchý. "Today isn't anybody's anniversary."

"Oh, no, it's out of sympathy for your poor country."

That was how the Suchýs learned their homeland had been invaded.

As often happened, Sylva's Tuesday-night date with Jirka Šlitr had to be combined with business. Toward midnight, they were obliged to join Jiří Menzel and a couple of other people connected with *The Crime in the Night Club*. The meeting place was the Vikárka (or Vicar's Retreat) tavern beside St. Vitus Cathedral within the Prague Castle grounds.

The movie had been filmed and was being edited, but its ending was still up in the air. Nobody was satisfied with the one they had:

Both defendant (Suchý) and lawyer (Šlitr) are on the gallows. Called upon for their last words, they ask to "sing a last song instead," an interminably bouncy number about a "Promised Land that lies across the barbed wire there where the meadow ends." The words and music go on and on and on and on. The villainous Minister of Justice, eavesdropping electronically, is lulled into lethargy; the witnesses doze; and the hangmen fall asleep with their hands still resting on their levers. Then the final credits appear onscreen. . . .

"In the light of Čierna and Bratislava," someone said, "maybe the scaffold should break so they are saved."

"Or else," Šlitr suggested, "the executioners are bought off and they bungle the job."

None of these ideas enchanted Menzel, who insisted that his allegory have a sturdy dramatic structure. The discussion dragged on past 0200, when the tavern stopped serving, but the help didn't have the heart to evict such distinguished customers. During one of the lulls, Sylva persuaded Menzel to serve on her newspaper *Zítřek*'s advisory board. But that was about all that was really accomplished. Toward 0400, they paid their bill and agreed that any new ending would have to await Suchý's return from Yugoslavia.

Then they stepped outside and found the Castle surrounded by tanks.

It took them most of the morning to talk their way out of there. "For the next few days," Menzel told me later, "it was not important for us to do our work. First I thought that now we will have to film an execution. But then, when we all met again, we knew that the ending we already had was the right ending for now."

Šlitr and Suchý and Menzel (and another script collaborator, Josef Škvorecký) had indeed stumbled onto the perfect political metaphor for the time that had come to the land they loved: *still singing with a noose around its neck and the end just a little in doubt.*

On their way back to Sylva's home, crossing the First of May Bridge, Šlitr's car was flagged down and searched by soldiers waving red pennants. One of the soldiers noticed a tear of indignation running down Sylva's cheek.

"Don't cry, little girl," he said in his most Big Brotherly way. "We're not here to hurt you."

"But why did you come?" Sylva protested. "Things were fine and good here!"

"You are wrong, little girl. There was a counter-revolution."

Sylva shook her fist at him: "How can you say that? I was here and you weren't! I saw and you didn't see!"

"Your leaders made you see falsely. But don't worry. The counter-revolution will be put down. Then you will be able to go about your affairs, little girl, and I can go home to my family in Leningrad."

That afternoon, while I was out exploring Wenceslas Square, the radio broadcast the first rumor that Russian troops and Czech police collaborators, dressed in white smocks, were carting away signers of the "2,000 Words" in ambulances.

My wife called Jirka Šlitr in case he'd missed the news. Her heart sank when he answered the phone, but he left her laughing with his dry assurance:

"I'm going to the country for a few days and I'll be leaving right away. I couldn't get my car started, but I've been offered a lift in an ambulance."

That night, the Semafor Theatre, scheduled to reopen with *The Last Hospital* on the second of September, was padlocked by its own personnel. Across the glass doors they hung a wooden sign, on which was carved an excerpt from a Suchý poem: "THEATRE STOPS WHEN THE BURST OF LAUGHTER IS MUFFLED BY THE BURST OF GUNFIRE."

Suchý had phoned that he would finish out his vacation in Yugoslavia and then perhaps go to England to watch further developments. Igor Hájek of *Literární Listy,* who was vacationing in England on the twenty-first of August, went to America on a Ford Foundation grant and then returned to England, where he now teaches Czech Literature at the University of Lancaster. Ivan Sviták, the "lonely sniper" from the Philosophical Faculty, was in Vienna attending a philosophers' congress. When he couldn't get back into Czechoslovakia right away, he went to New York to weigh his future plans. To keep his options open and avoid the label of "defector," Sviták traveled very inconspicuously. But soon after he checked into an obscure hotel on lower Madison Avenue, his room was broken into by a remarkable thief who stole only Sviták's Czechoslovak passport. When Sviták reported the theft to the Manhattan police, his presence made news. The Czechoslovak authorities in America didn't dare to issue him a new passport, and, without one, he couldn't go home again. He went to work at Columbia University instead.

Another Hájek, Jiří, the Foreign Minister, flew from Belgrade to Vienna and then to New York to protest the invasion at the United Nations as a "deeply offensive and humiliating . . . use of force which cannot be justified by any means." *Izvestia* retaliated by denouncing Hájek as "a henchman of the dark forces of reaction and counter-revolution" . . . as a collaborator with the Gestapo . . . AND as a Jew who'd changed his name from Karpeles to Hájek. It turned out that the Russians had the dossiers of yet another pair of Hájeks, but that didn't stop the repeated Soviet references to "Karpeles-Hájek," the notorious Jewish SS man who became a Communist Foreign Minister. In his rebuttal, Hájek noted that he wasn't Jewish, but added that "I wouldn't be ashamed if it were true. We must value a man according to what he does. And, besides, our country has said farewell to racism some time ago."

Czechs back home applauded Hájek's words, though they took with a grain of salt his repeated pledge that once the fight at the U.N. was over (and lost, when Mother Russia dropped veto number 105 in the Security Council), he would return home. But he did.

Two actual "Jews in high places," who also stood high on Moscow's purge list, were out of the country and didn't come back. Ota Šik went directly from Yugoslavia to a professorship at the University of Basle, and with him went his nation's brightest hopes for economic salvation. Eduard Goldstücker took the post of visiting lecturer at the University of Sussex.

Some of Czechoslovakia's finest minds kept trickling away, many into the limbo of exile and others perhaps to fight another day. To my surprise, though, František, the theatre director who'd been our neighbor in the country, remained in Prague.

At 0400 on the twenty-first of August, a friend had phoned him with the incredible news. František, who lives downtown, got dressed to see for himself. His wife, Naďa, pleaded with him not to go out. But their little daughter Marianka, she of the bullfrog voice and the shopkeeper's temperament, consoled her mother: "Mommy, the Russians may be bad, but only bees can hurt you."

Later, I asked František why he hadn't fled to Vienna as he'd sworn he'd do if the Russians ever came to stay.

"If I'd been out of the country, I'm sure I wouldn't have come back," he told me. "But now that they had the nerve to start this while I was here, I want to see it through."

Our typewriter salesman—who'd given me, as a free dividend, a sculpture in memory of Theresienstadt—has a young son. The boy had been taught in school that the Russians were "our liberators" from the

Nazis who'd killed his grandfather. On the morning of 21 August, he looked out of his window and asked his father, who already knew: "Who are those soldiers with guns?"

"Occupiers," said the father. "And you must stay away from them. They're no good."

"Then why don't we call the Russians to chase them away?"

Having earned their vacation currency in Vienna, the Doctor's daughter and her fiancé were hitchhiking through Southern France. North of Marseilles, they rented space in a farmer's barn for the night of 20 August. At dawn, the fiancé awoke to a rooster's *cocorico!* and quietly tuned in his transistor radio. All he could pick up was an ugly babble of voices in which the word *Tchécoslovaquie* kept recurring. At first, he thought he was listening to Karel Čapek's play *Mother*, the tragedy of a woman sending her last surviving son off to war. "But I think Čapek is being acted very badly in French," he told himself. A minute later, it dawned on him that he was hearing the actual agony of his motherland and he began to bellow like a barnyard animal. . . .

He and she considered taking asylum in the West. She spoke fluent French and German as well as adequate English; he spoke French. But she was an only child and wanted to consult her parents first. Her mother and father, however, were still vacationing somewhere in Yugoslavia and considering the same choice.

Despite frantic telephoning, neither generation was able to contact the other. Finally, on the first of September, the daughter and her fiancé made their way back to occupied Prague. They were desperate for word about her parents, who arrived home half-an-hour later.

Long thereafter, I asked the daughter whether she'd ever regretted not staying in the West.

"I could never have made such an important decision in a foreign setting," she replied. "Once all four of us were back in Prague, the only question that remained unanswered was 'Whatever made us think of going abroad to live?' We belong here. We're needed here."

She and her fiancé hadn't been student activists before that August. But when they came back from France, they were.

A lady in Prague called a friend at 0400 on Wednesday 21 August to tell her the bad news. She dialed a wrong number, apologized to the man she'd awakened, and told him what had happened. The stranger said: "It's a good thing."

The International Geological Congress, 4,000 scientists from 90 lands, had started a nine-day meeting in Prague on the nineteenth of August. Some of the delegates were billeted in a house near us. They awoke on Wednesday morning to find the house surrounded by eight tanks. It had been requisitioned as a military headquarters. The geologists inside were sent packing. Several of them were Americans, but one was Russian. He was so ashamed that he removed his name tag and pretended not to speak the same language as the soldiers who were evicting him.

Peter Rehak, a Slovak by birth who'd emigrated to Canada as a boy, was the Associated Press' new correspondent in Prague. Working late at the Alcron Hotel, Rehak's ears picked up two ominous sounds: the squawk of Radio Prague going dead and the uncharacteristic hum of planes in the night sky over downtown Prague.

To find out more in a hurry, Rehak played a hunch: The saboteurs might have failed to turn off an auxiliary public-address system whereby announcements of general interest are piped into restaurants and meeting places. This vestige of Novotný's era of Big Brotherism was virtually impossible to silence.

The Alcron's bars and restaurants were closed, but Rehak remembered seeing such an outlet in the hotel's all-night garage. There, he listened to the proclamation being repeated and, by Telex, he flashed the news to the Western world.*

In Washington, Secretary of State Dean Rusk was testifying on Vietnam before the Democratic platform committee (it was a week before the nominating convention in Chicago) when he was handed Rehak's bulletin. Rusk wound up his remarks, handed the bulletin to Congressman Hale Boggs, the committee chairman, and left with a faint smile, saying: "I think I ought to go see what this is all about." Boggs read the news into an open microphone and this was how America found out. One observer remarked then and there: "The Vietnam doves were just shot down over Central Europe."

* Rehak was never granted formal accreditation by the Czechoslovak Foreign Ministry. In September, 1968, when his temporary permit expired, he was told it would not be renewed. He had to leave his native land on a few hours' notice.

President Johnson already knew. Around the time when Ambassador Chervonenko was paying his midnight call on President Svoboda at the Prague Castle, Soviet Ambassadors in Washington, Paris, and London were making urgent appointments at the White House, Élysée Palace, and 10 Downing Street, where they would deliver the same bald message. President Johnson—who'd accepted, on the nineteenth, a formal invitation to a summit meeting in Russia—at first assumed that Ambassador Anatoly F. Dobrynin was coming to discuss re-wording the joint announcement scheduled to be made in Moscow and Washington on the twenty-second. When Dobrynin instead told Johnson of the action against Czechoslovakia, the President of the United States withdrew his acceptance "more in sadness than in anger," according to one who was there.

Harold Wilson flew home from vacation and recalled the House of Commons for an emergency session, the third August meeting of Commons in its 700-year history.

Charles de Gaulle, awakened at his home in Colombey-les-deux-Églises by a frantic phone call from Paris, invited his Premier and Foreign Minister to come down for an "emergency luncheon." Later, de Gaulle blamed Churchill and Roosevelt for "playing spheres" with Stalin in 1945.

Pope Paul VI was getting ready to fly to Bogotá on history's first Papal visit to Latin America. "The news of the world is not good," he said, when word reached the Vatican. "What we believed no longer possible has, instead, happened. The foundations of international order have been shaken." The Pope said he would "willingly" abandon his journey "this instant" if he thought he could be of any service in the crisis. He couldn't; so he went.

U Thant—ticketed, for once, to be in the right place at the right time—canceled his scheduled journey to Prague so as not to "interfere" with the Soviet bloc's "internal" affairs. "He must have his reasons," our underground radio remarked, "but we certainly wanted very much to see him here."

Shirley Temple Black, of all people, was among the 1,500 American tourists in Prague when the invasion happened. The former child movie star and would-be congresswoman, by then a svelte clubwoman of forty, had come to Prague on behalf of the International Federation of Multiple Sclerosis Societies, of which she was vice-president.

The Hotel Alcron had relegated her to a particularly bleak room (looking out on an air shaft) which she later numbered among her blessings when Russian tanks started shooting their way up Štěpánská Street toward Wenceslas Square.

At the end of a day's "eavesdropping on history," during which she shredded her souvenir photo of Dubček and flushed it down an Alcron toilet, she (and 400 others, including Robert Vaughn and the film personnel of *The Bridge at Remagen*) were evacuated to West Germany in a car convoy organized by the U. S. Embassy.

After flying across the North Pole and landing in San Francisco, Mrs. Black announced on television: "The Soviets are machine-gunning all over Czechoslovakia. They're doing it without provocation in many cases." Further questioning by newsmen elicited that "I didn't see anyone hurt or killed and I'm grateful I didn't. But I heard the screams and the yelling."

Learning the brutal truth first from Dean Rusk's hasty exit and then straight from Shirley Temple's mouth was more than at least one sensitive soul back home could bear. A liberal scholar who works in Chicago wrote me a letter that reminded me a little of my own reactions that morning in the Firehouse Square:

> The news from Prague is almost unbelievable. We are getting it from Shirley Temple, which adds a perfectly bizarre, incredible science-fiction haze. Little Miss Marker has been updated through a time machine and set down in an evil place where virtue is being torn to "tell it like it is." She has the innocence of the eight-year-old whose speech she has never abandoned and her doll's face at forty has the eight-year-old's appearance. She uses rhetoric that could come from the mouth of herself thirty-two years ago or. Dean Rusk today. Come to think of it, *he* talks like Shirley Temple's slightly older brother.
>
> Gene McCarthy said sourly that LBJ *over*-reacted; I am ready to bet that you've stopped payment on your check to Americans Abroad for McCarthy.* Gene says that he would have slept on it and reacted in the morning. Nixon sounded the alarums, blew the trumpets, banged the drums—and for a minute I thought I was reading The Chicago *Tribune*'s Sunday editorial. It was stabilizing in a way. The prize reaction came from Congressman Gerald Ford, who used to call for war against communism every day before breakfast. He said "we shouldn't get mixed up in a communist family quarrel," which put it in a metaphor that even right-wing Republicans can understand.
>
> Where I work, the intellectual, internationally-oriented types simply cluck and talk about "traditional Russian expansion south and so

* The check, alas, had already cleared.

what else is new?" And someone else says, enigmatically but cuisinely, "the Russian bear likes Slovak honey and will go home when he gets a paw full." You should live so long—and that is my way of saying to you, "Take care, Alan."

Chapter 15]

Thursday 22 August—
Friday 23 August 1968

1. In order to insure the protection of the working people and to defend the inhabitants of Prague from the dangers connected with actions of extremist and hooligan elements, I appeal to all citizens of this city not to leave their homes between 2200 and 0500. . . .

2. Until further notice, public meetings and other similar activities are prohibited, effective 2400 hours 21 August 1968.

> —public notice from Lt. Gen. I. Velichko, Commander of Warsaw Pact Forces in Prague and Central Bohemia.

At half-past midnight in our first hours of curfew living, we were awakened by a new sound in our lives: *eh-eh-eh-eh-POOM!* Racing to the nearest window, I heard the noise repeated. I saw four red tracer bullets hyphenate the sky and then I heard the explosion of a live shell. *Eh-eh-eh-eh-POOM!* The Soviet Army had commenced night-firing in occupied Prague, a half-hour ritual that was repeated again at 0230 and twice a night thereafter for a week. Each performance originated from the Petřín Tower near our home, with the machine-guns firing out over Strahov Monastery and the Castle and the Vltava. From Klárov, the tram stop at the foot of Hradčany Hill, Soviet artillery would answer back with resounding salvos. But it was the machine-gun fire that we could see passing over and around the street where we lived. We moved our beds farther away from the windows and put down our shutters as well as our shades. *Eh-eh-eh-eh-POOM* became *eine kleine Nachtmusik* through which we learned to live and the children managed to sleep.

"Exercises" was what the Red Army called this nightly terror that chipped the stone off a few more historic buildings. "Exercises" was what wounded some 50 Prague civilians that first night before we all learned to stay indoors from dusk to dawn; even then, a few more were shot inside their flats. "Exercises" was what destroyed the operating room and damaged the main building of a children's hospital that first night. Children recovering from surgery lay shivering in the corridors until it was deemed safe to evacuate them, while the Red Army played its cruel "war games" with every life in Prague.

Violence lurked everywhere in a city where one used to be able to wander streets or parks at any hour of night. During the night, a policeman, sitting in his patrol car and warning unwary pedestrians to get off the streets, was shot to death from a passing armored truck. A tank riddled a truckload of workmen with machine-gun fire—blowing one man's head off and killing three others. "In order to insure the protection of the working people . . ." General Velichko's notice began.

How alarmingly fast the human mind adapts to tolerating the intolerable! Restaurants which used to be open from 1600 to 2400 now served dinner only between 1100 and 1730 to enable the help to get home before curfew. By the second or third night of the occupation, we, like everyone else, were asking each other such matter-of-fact questions as "Shall I set the alarm clock or rely on the Russians to wake us up in the morning?" and "When is curfew tonight?"

The answer to the latter question was, officially, ten o'clock at night. Actually, though, if you ventured out after eight at night, you were often shot at. Hardly anybody reasoned why. Whenever I asked, I was told "First they steal our wristwatches and now they must learn to tell time." Or: "If a Russian says ten, you're lucky when he means eight. That's the story of our foreign trade."

On Friday morning, shortly after 0900, however, a friend called me with an incredible "tip" that I rushed out to verify, pausing only to remove my wristwatch and leave it at home.

A minor Russian official lived four blocks from us. I knew he was minor because there were only four tanks guarding his home. I went there and asked the tankers what time it was. Two them them answered: "Eleven-fifteen."

I double-checked at two other Soviet checkpoints. The Russian replies were always two hours later than mine. My informant was correct. Moscow time is two hours later than Prague time. The invaders from the east had come to set back the clock, all right, but not in the one way that would make any sense in Prague.

The Russian Army, which also came here to kill freedom of expression, had unwittingly triggered a media explosion of Madison Avenue proportions. For five minutes early that weekend, there were no fewer than twelve television channels broadcasting simultaneously across Czechoslovakia, where before the invasion there had been only one. Remote hamlets which had never received TV suddenly erupted with it, and some of the transmissions were so strong that they were picked up in Switzerland and relayed to the rest of the world from there.

Eleven of the twelve channels called themselves "legal television," although their transmitters were being hunted in vain by the Red Army and secret-police collaborators. These stations were seldom on the air simultaneously. Broadcasting twenty to forty minutes at a time, they ordinarily faded out before they could be traced, signing off with instructions for switching channels ("Now please turn to Channel 8"). But the massed show of strength was calculated to impress the twelfth channel, "collaborationist TV," with what it was up against.

Telecasting, appropriately enough, over Channel One, collaborationist TV offered the clearest picture *technically*. But, since almost any action footage it might show would harm its cause, Channel One confined itself to voice-over propaganda behind its emblem: a still photo of a Prague edifice that caught the invaders' eyes. They could not have chosen a more embarrassing symbol, for the building was the Dalibor Tower, a prison with a long history of passive resistance. Here, the medieval cavalier Dalibor had won public favor by playing, on his violin, music sweeter than the promises of the king who'd imprisoned him.

With legal TV clobbering it around the clock, Channel One proclaimed that its very humiliation was proof positive of Western technology conspiring to subvert the Czechs. But the Czechs, who were using military and civil-defense transmitters (many built in the 1950's, at Soviet urging, to ensure communications in the event of a West German invasion), insisted that they were performing this daily miracle by skillful and daring juggling of existing parts only. To them, it was proof of two truths: the resourcefulness of Czech workmanship and the incredible waste of State-run technology.

The collaborationist Radio Vltava had even worse trouble. Its unconvincing messages were losing out in both listenership and technology. Even with better studio facilities (in Dresden) and the on-again off-again silencing of Radio Prague, Radio Vltava couldn't hold a candle or a kilowatt to a national hookup of legal, but clandestine, stations with studios in living rooms, basements, warehouses, garden sheds, not to mention inside cars and trucks. Once, when Radio Prague got back on the air, it was broadcasting from inside Pankrác prison. The athlete Emil Zátopek hid out in the penthouse of a brand-new twelve-story Prague apartment skyscraper from which he broadcast appeals to the world over the "underground" radio. At one point, the Russians actually found the building and, thinking they'd located Zátopek's transmitter, they shot up a refrigerator.

"Go home, soldiers!" the legal radio pleaded. "Your country will soon need you more than ours ever did. Try to put yourself in our position: Do you imagine the Chinese would ever invade your homeland in order to protect you?"

Appeals to world public opinion were repeated in Czech, Slovak, Russian, Polish, German, Hungarian, French, Italian, Spanish, and English. They were addressed to Boy Scouts and Girl Scouts everywhere ("Help us, please!") and to Bertrand Russell, ninety-six: "Please, sir, you are one of the few people in the world who wondered whether the Soviet Union would really invade us."

It was a plea from the legal radio that made Prague a city of anonymity—and the rest of the country followed Prague's example:

"We have no weapons, but our contempt is stronger than tanks. . . . You know where you live. There's no need for the rascals to know, too. Switch around street signs. Take house numbers off doors. Remove name plates from public buildings. . . . The mailman will find you, but evildoers won't."

And it was from the radio that we learned what went on in the Hotel Without a Name on Wednesday night and Thursday morning:

Wednesday evening, the captive Císař and the waiting conservatives were at last joined by Indra as well as Bil'ak, Kolder, Barbírek, a Soviet military escort, and Ambassador Chervonenko! To the dismay of the honest conservatives on hand who wanted very badly to believe that theirs was the true Czechoslovak outlook, the Russians insisted on staying and participating in the deliberations. Furthermore, when the conservatives asked which Czechs or Slovaks had invited the "fraternal intervention" of the five Warsaw Pact armies, nobody had an answer.

The honest conservatives left the room in disgust as early as they could, although the Russian troops wouldn't let them out of the hotel lobby until 0500 Thursday, when curfew ended. Císař, still in police custody, was taken away into the treacherous night.

The traitors and their dupes remained and wrangled through the night. All they could agree upon was a communique supporting the Presidium's appeal for calm and prudence (without mentioning its protest against violations of international law) . . . promising no return to pre-January conditions . . . praising the Action Program . . . and asking that regional and district party committees begin negotiating with the occupation forces.

Only three men present were willing to risk serving on a new Presidium: Bil'ak, Indra, and Kolder, whose names were appearing all over town beneath the word "TRAITORS!" Toward dawn, the meeting broke up with a further announcement that Bil'ak, Indra, and Kolder would temporarily share the title of First Secretary.

News of this troika was greeted with such public scorn that it was never mentioned again as a ruling body. And Chervonenko's report to Moscow could scarcely have been favorable—for it was some time on Thursday that a corner was turned in the Kremlin and the process of saving (or prolonging) the lives of Dubček and Smrkovský and Černík and Špaček and Kriegel began. Leonid Brezhnev is known to have responded to that day's prognosis from Prague: "Well, if we can't find the puppets, then we'll have to put the strings on the leaders."

Back in occupied Prague, the only respectable newspapers were the underground ones. To counteract this, the Russians instituted an aggressive home-delivery program. Mornings at seven, the houses in our neighborhood were buzzed by helicopters or (on two occasions) four-engine bombers dropping their edition of *Rudé Právo* from what appeared to be rooftop level. Minutes thereafter, flames shot up in the aircraft's wake, not from crashes, but from bonfires fueled by *Rudé Právo*. Even so, the trees were littered for weeks with these ersatz *Rudé Právos*.

I rescued one copy, which didn't take long to read. It was two pages long and I could tell (from the printing and typographical errors) that it, like Radio Vltava, originated in East Germany. It featured an Editor's Note ("After a pause . . . caused by well-known occurrences, the readers of *Rudé Právo* are again receiving their daily newspaper, the organ of the Central Committee of the Communist Party of Czechoslovakia") and a photo showing a dozen Russian soldiers being "welcomed" by two uneasy-looking Czech civilians, who'd apparently just been fed cigarettes by the photographer.

"Make the picture a column wider and you'd see the guns at

their backs," one of my neighbors remarked. "Besides, one of those civilians doesn't even look Czech to me."

The caption, however, claimed that what these two men were saying to their Russian "liberators" was:

"Thank you for coming. This long-organized clique has not been able to kill the soul of our people."

"They would have allowed dangerous instability if you hadn't come."

"Our liberators will go away when the danger of capitalism goes away from our society."

Toward noon, thank goodness, the underground, or legal, *Rudé Právo* would be flung from a speeding truck as it had been at least once a day starting on Wednesday. But now small boys on bicycles were waiting and the paper was distributed to the whole neighborhood within five minutes. Featuring the latest atrocity stories and resolutions, it was six pages long and it had a new motto: *"Only that nation is free which does not encroach upon the freedom of other nations"*— *Karl Marx*. It (and the underground editions of other Prague dailies) were also, alas, much more readable than the early-morning air-droppings:

> On the Cyril and Methodius Square in Karlín, a 7-year-old boy was chalking "IVAN GO HOME" on a wall in Russian letters. A Russian tank passed by and its machine-gun swiveled toward the boy. But the boy was concentrating so hard on his Cyrillics that he didn't see the tank. Realizing the situation, a passing mother, out for some air with her baby, wheeled her pram between boy and tank. In her naiveté, she assumed that even the Russians wouldn't shoot past a mother and her baby just to kill a 7-year-old boy. The tank shot all three dead.

There was also an interview with our friend Miroslav Galuška, the Minister of Culture and Information:

> *Q:* The world continues to be interested in knowing whether any Czechoslovak organ really did ask the Soviet Union for help.
> *A:* No help—especially no military help—was requested from the Soviet Union or any other of the states whose armies have occupied this country. I repeat again: The Government has declared that the occupation of Czechoslovakia is illegal.

Every major Prague newspaper published a daily underground edition. Weeklies were now publishing daily, too, and so were several monthlies, including a women's journal. A brand-new four-color humor magazine was conceived the day the Russians invaded and it was snapped up on street corners two days later. A far more serious journal, *Politika,* scheduled to be published weekly by the Central Committee starting with the original 9 September date of the Fourteenth Party Congress, was born prematurely. Three different issues were published during the first week of occupation. In its second issue, *Politika* disowned Bil'ak, Indra, and Kolder.

Literárni Listy published what proved to be the first of three or four "farewell" issues. In this one, it exhorted its readers:

> Do not allow the hopes of the Czechoslovak people to be destroyed. Should we never meet again, we want you all to love each other, protect each other, and hope for truth. . . . Hold fast until liberty can be guaranteed by those to whom you have given your trust.

LL ended this essay with the title of a bittersweet Voskovec-and-Werich song that is eternally popular here: *See You Again in Better Times.*

One night, when I was hurrying home to beat a curfew, I caught a ride with a middle-aged man who had a small camera clamped to his wrist. "I take black-and-white pictures with this one," he explained. "I keep a cheap wristwatch on my other wrist. When the Russians stop cars to confiscate watches, rings, and cameras, I flash my watch and they grab it without bothering to look at my other wrist. I lost four cheap watches in one day alone, but I haven't lost a camera yet." Then he showed me two other cameras in a compartment under the seat: "I take 35-millimeter color film with this one and 8-millimeter color motion-picture film with the other. But only when my wife is along. She sits behind the wheel while I shoot my pictures. We've been shot at twice."

"Are you a professional photographer?" I asked.

"No," he said. "I'm in a totally different line of work altogether, a very ordinary one. But right now I'm not only a triple-threat photographer, but I'm also one of the publishers of *Rudé Právo.*"

"The good one or the bad one?"

The answer was so obvious that he ignored the question and said: "I'll show you how it's done." He leaned over to open up his glove compartment, which contained three small nondescript machine parts. "While the Russians were still seizing our government and before they started occupying the newspapers, these three parts, which are very scarce and only available here, were taken out of every printing plant in the country. When the Russians came, the printers could honestly tell them that they didn't have the parts to print anything for them.

"But whenever the Russians aren't looking or when there's a printing plant they haven't found yet, everything is made ready and one of several men like me goes there. The parts are slammed into the machine, the presses are run, and then the parts are removed and go back into my glove compartment. It takes under an hour and I don't think they've caught any of us yet."

This free press was one which cost the reader absolutely nothing unless, as it happened occasionally, the Russians opened fire on tram riders who were looking at it. Once, riding a crowded and creaky old pre-World-War-II tram up Hradčany hill from Klárov, I stood on the open platform reading *Literární Listy* until the lady conductor planted herself in front of me to conceal my reading matter from outside view. I peered around her imposing bulk and saw that our progress up the hill was being monitored by foot soldiers, tankers, and an officer with binoculars in a tank turret.

When we had passed out of range, I said to the conductor: "Thank you for saving my life."

"For nothing [*Neni zač*]," she said politely, and asked if she could please have my copy when I'd finished with it.

This was the daily routine of the invasion: curfews, night firing, air-dropped ersatz *Rudé Právo*s, clandestinely delivered legal *Rudé Právo*s and other Czechoslovak periodicals, with the radio and TV always tuned in. There was also the daily stench of cordite, diesel fuel, and exhaust fumes from the tanks. Beyond this, however, each day was different from any other in any man's life.

Thursday 22 August was the day the Russians planted a tank on the Charles Bridge, an affront to fine art that is remembered here in the same breath with the shelling of the National Museum. The objective, the Russians insisted, was tactical: Having failed to silence radio and TV, they were instead "confiscating" transistors and cameras. The tank on the Charles Bridge soon became known as "Checkpoint Charlie." It was crowned by two machine-gunners, back-to-back, and flanked by four infantrymen who stripped pedestrians of their jewelry as well as cameras and radios. I myself was so taken aback with outrage at this unexpected eyesore that, although I recovered in time to pocket my wristwatch and wedding ring, I lost two ball-point pens and a map of Prague to the Russian Army. The soldier who "searched" me didn't lay a hand on me. He merely had me extend my hands so he could see what I had on them and in them. Then he looked me up and down, thereby discovering the map and the pens.

"But the map isn't in Cyrillic," I pointed out in Czech.

"*Ne noozhna* (That isn't necessary)," he replied in Russian.

The soldiers on the Charles Bridge had their hands full, not with loot, but with Czech *hydeparkers* who came out to argue with them while others chalked "NEUTRALITY!" all over their tank. Also chalked on the tank was Talleyrand's advice to Napoleon: "YOU CAN DO EVERYTHING WITH BAYONETS EXCEPT SIT ON THEM."

There were roadblocks on all the bridges spanning the Vltava. All cars and some trams and buses were being halted and searched for printed matter (single copies and bulk distribution) as well as cameras, transistors, and souvenirs. One cartoon of the moment showed a sidewalk bazaar of Russian tankmen, dressed up as Arab merchants, selling transistors spread out on carpets. And small boys took to tormenting the conquerors by painting bricks to look like radios and then walking around with them held to their ears.

Thursday was also the day when more than 20,000 people—one-third of the population of Gottwaldov (formerly Zlín, home of the Bat'a shoe industry) petitioned the National Assembly for the recall of their deputy, Alois Indra, in no uncertain terms: "The citizens of Gottwaldov regret that Indra was ever one of them."

Thursday was the day when Radio Prague began broadcasting the license numbers of secret police cars that were supposed to be rounding up liberal politicians, writers, and editors. Listeners painted these numbers on sidewalks and walls. Small boys walked around with the numbers pinned to their backs. One of the cars in question was spotted by a trucker, who rammed it into a brick wall. Two other cars were incorrectly identified, intercepted, overturned, and mangled. One belonged to an architect. The other victim, ironically, was a delegate to the Extraordinary Fourteenth Party Congress. . . .

Yes, unbelievably, Thursday 22 August 1968 was the day when the Extraordinary Fourteenth Party Congress was convened eighteen days early at 1115 in Prague 9, the Vysočany district, whose factory workers had been urged, in Dubček's last smuggled message, to stay on their jobs to preserve national unity. The setting was, in fact, the ČKD-

Praha heavy-machinery factory. ČKD's manager, Antonín Kapek—a Presidium alternate who'd put in a good word for the Indra-Kolder report at Tuesday night's fateful session—never even found out about the Congress on his premises until it was over.

Starting on Wednesday morning, over the embattled Radio Prague, a worker had read a summons calling delegates to come there NOW by any means possible. And now, while "the dogs of war" * befouled their land and while the mighty of the West wrung helpless hands for them, the Czechs were still turning the clock ahead.

The meeting place had been chosen when the organizers learned of one of many Soviet military miscalculations: The troops had orders not to occupy factories because that would antagonize "friendly workers." Over their legal underground radio, the organizers of the Congress made no secret of its site, on the assumption, which proved valid, that the devious Russian mind would assume the Congress must be going on elsewhere. To further divert the searchers, the local organizers rigged up three "dummy" Party Congresses and the Russians announced thrice that they had thwarted this "secret gathering of rightist revisionist forces, only 17 per cent of whom are workers and many of whom were signers of the counter-revolutionary '2,000 Words.' "

Though Russian troops and tanks were stationed outside every entrance to ČKD, the first delegates had started arriving inside the factory late Wednesday afternoon. They wore overalls, carried lunch pails, and bore the identity cards of night-shift workers (who were dispatched to the "dummy" Congresses). Others came in with the day shift on Thursday. Well-known public figures arrived via ambulance as patients, doctors, nurses, and stretcher-bearers. Unexpected arrivals were taken into custody by plant security officials. If they proved to be authentic delegates, they were issued false identity cards and escorted

---

* The quote is from President Johnson, who reacted a few days later to Soviet hints that they might go into Rumania, too, to mop up the "counter-revolution." (There were Soviet troop movements near Ceausescu's frontier and even brief exchanges of rifle fire across the border.) LBJ told a startled audience of southwestern dairymen holding an August convention in San Antonio: "I say to you and to the world that we must not return to a world of unbridled aggression. . . . In a tragic move, the full measure of military power was applied in Czechoslovakia, where tonight hundreds of tanks surround the capital. Surely it is too late in history for small nations to be denied their right to national existence. The Charter of the United Nations makes this a fundamental right of all nations. There should not be any doubt in the minds of anyone as to where the United States of America stands on a question so fundamental to the peace of the entire world. So let no one unleash the dogs of war."

through a maze of corridors and stairways into the Congress which was held in a hall in the oldest part of the plant.

Almost 1,000 of the 1,540 delegates were there when the Congress opened on Thursday morning, but only five were from Slovakia. At least fifty more Slovaks arrived later in the day and the total number of delegates passed the 1,200 mark by the time the Congress ended early Friday. Virtually all of the missing were Slovaks. At various checkpoints along the way from Slovakia, Russian roadblocks were comparing their identity cards with a roster of delegates and detaining those whose names were similar. One Slovak who didn't make it to the Congress was Deputy Premier Gustáv Husák. His party was halted by Soviet troops in Břeclav, Moravia. Politically, this was one of the best strokes that ever happened to Husák. . . .

Presiding over the Extraordinary Congress was an unlikely chairman: Martin Vaculík,* who had resigned as Prague's party boss after unburdening himself in the Spring's televised *mea culpas*. As a discredited conservative, Vaculík had been invited to Indra's meeting in the Hotel Without a Name. But he hadn't liked what he'd seen. As soon as he'd been allowed to leave, he'd made his way out to ČKD, volunteered to serve the forces of freedom in any way he could, and even named the names of those who "showed themselves to be open collaborators."

The Congress sent an open letter addressed to Alexander Dubček, wherever he was. It began:

Dear Comrade Dubček:

The Extraordinary Fourteenth Party Congress . . . sends you warm comradely greetings. We thank you for all the work you have done for the Party and the Republic. The repeated calls of "Dubček! Dubček!" coming from our youth who carry through Prague the bloodied State flag bear ample testimony that your name has become the symbol of freedom, progress, and sovereignty in our country. We protest against your unlawful imprisonment and [that] of the other comrades.

Then the delegates elected a new, 144-man Central Committee, heavy with liberals and trustworthy centrists. They, in turn, elected a new Presidium purged of Bil'ak, Kolder, Barbírek, and Švestka, who, of course, weren't there. Holdovers (also absent) included Dubček, Smrkovský, Černík, Špaček, and Kriegel. Two other absentees, Císař

* Martin Vaculík, who once shared a cover of *Newsweek* with Leonid Brezhnev, is no relation to Ludvik Vaculík, author of the "2000 Words." Both Vaculíks were later expelled from the Communist Party.

and alternate Šimon, were promoted to voting memberships. New faces on this Presidium included Šik, Goldstücker, Husák, and the radio's Hejzlar (not all of whom were present). Dubček was renamed First Secretary. Věnek Šilhán, an economist, was empowered to direct the new Presidium's administrative apparatus in the absence of Dubček and most of its members.

"Our basic demand is, of course, the departure of foreign troops," the Fourteenth Congress resolved. "If . . . negotiations are not begun with our free constitutional and party leaders . . . and if Comrade Dubček has not made a timely statement to the nation on this matter, the Congress requests all working people to stage a one-hour protest strike at noon on Friday 23 August. The Congress has also decided that, if its demands are not accepted, it will undertake further necessary measures."

Doomed though it was, the Congress was far more than a defiant gesture. The Russians, whose troops finally broke their own rules and entered the ČKD Works two hours after the delegates had disbanded, still refer to it with outrage as if it never existed: "The So-Called Vysočany Congress." For, maneuvering in one cramped corner of a factory surrounded by enemy troops, the Czechoslovaks had nonetheless succeeded in electing a legitimate, representative leadership while their Russian oppressors and willing puppets were unable to produce a government that anyone—even they themselves!—could respect.

The invaders' troubles were not confined to Prague. In downtown Bratislava, on the banks of the Danube, there was water everywhere but not a drop to drink—if you were a Russian soldier. The tankmen had brought a three-day food supply in the form of an unappetizing albeit nutritious concentrate to which one need only add water. Every time the troops approached a tap, however, "friendly" Slovaks would warn them that "the water has been poisoned by the counter-revolutionaries." The Red Army command in Bratislava resorted to helicoptering water from nearby Hungary.

Perhaps the tiniest of Czechoslovakia's 650,000 unwelcome guests was a ten-year-old boy who invaded Bratislava in a tank. His father, a widower who drilled on weekends with a Reserve armor unit, had been put on extended duty the previous weekend for "maneuvers in Hungary." Given no chance to put his affairs in order and unable to find someone to mind his boy, he'd asked his tank commander if he could bring his son along for the ride. The officer, who'd known no more about their mission than the father had, said all right. . . .

Small boys from Bratislava set Russian armor on fire in the Prague style. And even soldiers ordered to "abandon tank!" were reluctant to do so for fear they'd be lynched. Those who did venture out were demoralized by signs in Russian: "FOR WHAT YOU HAVE SEEN HERE, YOU WILL BE SENT STRAIGHT TO SIBERIA."

The Russians, to be sure, retaliated brutally. Outside Comenius University in Bratislava, five-year-old Danka Košanová had the misfortune to be standing next to a fourteen-year-old boy who shook his fist at the tanks. Both were shot to death. A block away, the same tank group killed a seventeen-year-old student and a forty-five-year-old Czechoslovak Army captain.

A nineteen-year-old Slovak enlisted man on furlough was ordered to return to his garrison in Bratislava. Arriving at the city's railway station, he was stopped by a Soviet patrol that, at machine-gun point, admired his brand-new-issue military summer shirt. He was ordered to go behind the terminal and change shirts with a Russian private who was about his age and size. The soldier obeyed, but asked: "Now what am I going to wear? I can't report to my unit in my undershirt." The Russian soldier said he could wear his old shirt, but the Slovak declined: "I couldn't wear a Russian blouse. That would be treason." The young Russian thought for a moment and then, for want of a better answer, shot him dead in his undershirt.

"HUNGARIANS GO HOME! HAVEN'T YOU HAD ENOUGH OF THIS?" said a sign chalked on every Hungarian tank in Bratislava. The Warsaw Pact armies dispatched all of their token Hungarian forces to the Slovak capital and the villages along the Slovak-Magyar frontier. The expectation was that the Slovaks—who had been, after all, their fellow countrymen for a thousand years—would welcome their Hungarian brothers with open arms. Instead, the Slovaks spat even upon close relatives.

In the South Slovakian mining town of Rožňava, the people refused to provide the Hungarian invaders with food, water, or shelter. Eventually a compromise was worked out whereby the occupation forces could be lodged and fed in a miners' school, on one condition: *At dusk, every Hungarian soldier was locked inside the school until dawn.*

East German troops rolled through the Sudetenland as though it was 1939 revisited, but they proved surprisingly docile. What shooting they did was with movie cameras. Anyone who shook his fist at the East German Army was filmed—for Walter Ulbricht's archives of known counter-revolutionaries, perhaps.

Polish invaders proved easiest to demoralize. Sometimes it took nothing more than the truth to do the job. Near Šlitr's country retreat, a platoon of Polish soldiers stumbled out of the woods and rolling hills of East Bohemia and asked: "Where are we?"

"Ledeč-nad-Sázavou," they were told.

"But what country is this?"

"Czechoslovakia."

"Czechoslovakia?!!" they exclaimed. "Then we are going home," said the oldest of them. They disappeared into the woods and were not heard from again in Ledeč.

The racetrack community of Pardubice (population: 57,000) was the only Czech city that still wasn't occupied by Thursday. A delegation of townsfolk met the Polish occupation commander on the outskirts and explained to him that there was no counter-revolution.

"Yes, I understand perfectly," he said—and ordered his men to pitch their camp outside the city limits.

(When the Russians learned about this, they occupied Pardubice themselves. And one Russian soldier was detailed to watch each token Pole assigned to Czechoslovakia.)

Demoralization works both ways. In the historic town of Jičín,* two lonely, drunken Polish soldiers opened fire on two local couples necking on a park bench. They killed one of the boys; wounded one of the girls; killed the other boy's mother and wounded his father when they came out to see what was happening; killed a Polish soldier who tried to quell the slaughter; and wounded another Polish soldier, a Czech soldier, and a woman in a passing car. To the town's long annals was added "The Jičín Massacre of 1968."

It was the Red Army's demoralization, however, that most perturbed the Kremlin—and it was in Prague that it was most visible. On Thursday in Charles Square, a young boy showed a Soviet soldier a bullet-riddled newspaper lined with blood and some flesh: "That is a souvenir of my best friend and this is your work. He was killed yesterday." The soldier almost swooned. Nearby, a very young Russian sol-

* Jičín was the seat of the dukedom of Count Albrecht of Wallenstein (1583–1634), the Bohemian-born Habsburg general and hero of Schiller's dramatic trilogy. In its Wallenstein Castle, the Holy Alliance against Napoleon was signed by Austria, Prussia, and Russia.

dier said: "I wish I could just put away this uniform and walk all the way home."

Confronted by Czechs calling him "murderer!", the average Russian soldier's response was to show that his weapon hadn't been fired. "I did not shoot," became the Russian plea of absolution, but many knew better and not all could live with the difference between what their leaders and what their eyes told them.

Thursday (according to the legal *Rudé Právo*) was when a woman named Alena saw someone she knew sitting on a tank near the Central Committee building: "Kolja, what are you doing here?"

The nineteen-year-old boy in uniform had trouble recognizing Alena because, she says, "in that prehistoric time when I visited the Soviet Union, he never saw such horror in my eyes." Finally, he remembered her and she asked again: "Kolja, what are you doing here?"

"We got our orders. We came, like friends."

"Like friends? But you are shooting at us!"

"I did not shoot."

"What will your sister say when you go back home?"

"I did not shoot. They sent us here." Kolja showed Alena that he had a full supply of ammunition.

"If you didn't shoot, others did and others do. Your people shot a twenty-year-old boy. I'm sure he loved you; we all did."

"We got orders. We were told that there is counter-revolution here, that everything is in chaos."

"Kolja, we had peace here until you appeared. Just imagine this many soldiers coming into Kharkov. The same chaos would break out there, wouldn't it?"

Later, Alena tried another tack: "Kolja, what do you think counter-revolution is?"

"That is when you don't agree with Lenin."

"And Kolja, do you love Stalin?"

"No, he was bad."

"Novotný was just as bad. We didn't want him. We wanted to do everything our way and not according to your model. After all, yours is a big country and your ways must naturally be different from ours. . . ."

"I don't understand this kind of talk. I got orders. . . ."

"Kolja, the people who gave you your orders didn't tell you the truth."

"Why would they lie to us?" Kolja asked, but his voice was wavering.

Alena just stood and looked at him. Dozens of people had asked Kolja "why did you come?" and dozens of times he had answered: "I did not shoot." Alena said she asked the question of several of Kolja's mates "and then I saw a terrible thing happen. Kolja turned his gun on himself, pulled the trigger, and shot himself through the heart." Never again would Kolja say "I did not shoot."

Kolja was the first Russian suicide we learned about. Soon, we knew of at least four more in Prague (all officially described, if at all, as "weapon-cleaning accidents") plus dozens of nervous breakdowns. You could see what was happening even on the stolid faces watching you from the tank tops. They had come on their "befriendment" with three military bands. They had come expecting to be welcomed as liberators as in 1945—*to be loved!* Now they were demoralized. And hungry. They had come with supplies for only three days; after that, their welcomers and the "Revolutionary Workers and Peasants Government of Comrade Indra" would look after them. The situation grew even more dangerous. To heat their field kitchens, Russian troops broke into the Charles University library and stole books for use as fuel. The younger soldiers began to swagger through the streets with their guns held by the triggers.

A Russian soldier named Semyonovich died. He was not a suicide. His automatic, which was hanging over his shoulder, went off and shot him through the back. He might have lived, but his comrades-in-arms responded with such terror that they shot him full of holes.

At home, Monica was pressing me for her introduction to the Russian soldier. On Thursday afternoon, I told her that we might go look at the Castle's caretaker-and-lamplighter brigade for a few minutes on the weekend. But Thursday night was when the Red Army for once heeded Lenin ("In the struggle for a city, everything finally turns upon superiority of morale") and ordered a changing of the guard. Tougher replacements were brought into the city and a couple of the more susceptible divisions were withdrawn. Nobody announced this; it simply started to happen, and I had to cancel Monica's outing. Still, one could almost rejoice that the Russians' spirit was being decimated by Czechoslovak decency and sapped by the 14 million "counter-revolutionaries" outnumbering and outwitting their mighty legions all across the land.

Thursday night, though, was also when President Svoboda decided he'd exhausted all avenues of negotiation in Prague for the release of Dubček and the other captive leaders. He notified Černík's surviving Cabinet ministers that he was ready to go to Moscow to negotiate. They designated General Dzúr (the Defense Minister) and Deputy Premier Husák (who'd just been sprung from his detention in Moravia) to go along with him. The National Front added a non-Communist, Minister of Justice Bohuslav Kučera, head of the Socialist party, to the group.

The National Assembly (Parliament) didn't send anybody directly (though most of the people on the trip were also deputies), but instead warned Svoboda that "under no circumstances should he leave the territory of the Republic."

The President, however, was determined to go—and he added his secretary, his aide-de-camp, and his son-in-law [Milan Klusák, former Czechoslovak Ambassador to the U.N.] to the party. Then he notified Chervonenko that he wanted to go to Moscow. The Soviet Ambassador said he'd find out whether the trip would be "safe," meaning "possible."

Late that evening, "a group of comrades from the Central Committee" came to call upon Svoboda at the Castle. Svoboda agreed to see them. But the President has high blood pressure and, when he saw that the "group" was Bil'ak plus Kolder, he insisted that his physician be present.

Bil'ak and Kolder apparently informed Svoboda that Chervonenko would say no unless he balanced the trip with three of their people. After bickering and negotiating that went on into the early hours, Bil'ak, Indra, and conservative Presidium member Jan Piller* were added to the roster. At 0845 Friday, Svoboda talked to the nation by telephone from the Castle (to a clandestine radio transmitter!) urging "calm and restraint" and pledging continuance "on the path of democratic development of our socialist homeland in the spirit of the January plenary meeting of the Central Committee. We expect to return home this evening. . . ."

* Piller became, in 1970, the powerful boss of all the trade unions in Czechoslovakia.

"Svoboda has sold us out!" moaned the neighbor with whom I heard the broadcast. "I've always suspected that fellow's closeness with the Russians."

"Don't give up too soon," I said. "Old men want to die honorably."

At 0930, a special plane with ten passengers took off from Prague to Moscow. Svoboda's wife told his secretary to tell him not to "eat or drink anything there" and "watch out for drugs."

Around that time on Friday morning, my sister in Marblehead—who'd been trying since Tuesday night—finally broke through to us by transatlantic telephone. She wanted to know her daughter's whereabouts: "Nancy hasn't called us yet. Did you evacuate her to Paris or Vienna?"

"She's right here," my wife said. "Would you like to talk to her?"

"Oh my God! I called to find out where you've evacuated Nancy and you tell me you haven't evacuated her!"

Nancy picked up the extension phone: "Hello, Mom. Look, the Czechs are absolutely cool. They have the Russians climbing the wall and I want to stay here and see this thing through."

"You take the next plane out of there, young lady, or you'll be in worse trouble than Dubček."

The planes to the West didn't fly for another three weeks, but the morning train to Nuremberg, Frankfurt, and Paris was resuming daily service on Saturday—and we booked Nancy on it. "If you have to leave Prague three days ahead of schedule," I consoled her, "be glad you'll be spending three extra days in Paris."

"I can't complain," Nancy agreed. But neither could she stop sniffling.

A few minutes before Friday noon—the hour of the work stoppage proclaimed by the Extraordinary Fourteenth Congress, sixty young Czechs linked arms and, spread across the top of Wenceslas Square, they formed a moving rake that swept downhill from the disfigured National Museum. "Clear the streets!" they cried. "Evacuate the square!" Behind them and before them, the square emptied.

The Russian soldiers lining the square grew edgy. They scanned the Art Nouveau rooftops for snipers. Some of them climbed inside their tanks and battened down the hatches. The gun turrets swiveled to and fro—but there were no targets to shoot at.

Then, exactly at noon, the city exploded in noise. Sirens wailed. Horns honked. Factory whistles tooted and church bells tolled. And the Russians panicked. They fired in the air. They fired at the buildings. They fired at each other. They fired at dust, papers, and posters that a desultory breeze churned up. But, from 1200 to 1300, they were all alone with their tanks and their guns and their consciences.

At the stroke of one, the human rake reappeared, this time at the foot of the square—and young and old, men and women, swept up toward the Wenceslas statue chanting the names in which the Good Prince's heirs had put their faith: "Dub-ček! Svo-boda! Svo-boda! Dooobček!" For once, the Russians looked happy to see the mob.

In our residential neighborhood, the hour of protest was a children's crusade. Monica and Erika joined their playmates in the gardens behind our house and from 1200 to 1300 on Friday, they tinkled their tricycle bells.

Interlude] Tass and Schweik tell it the way it was

THE SOVIET NEWS AGENCY TASS WROTE:

"On 21 August, the illegal radio stations and press stepped up the frenzy of attack on those leading members of the Central Committee who had remained faithful to Leninism. . . . Posters showing a gallows were displayed in Prague, threatening . . . Comrade Vasil Bil'ak. Hostile elements, trying at any cost to aggravate the situation, are committing grave crimes. Thus they arrested Oldřich Švestka, the editor-in-chief of *Rudé Právo,* who happens to be a member of the Presidium, and published a special issue of that newspaper in which they attacked the Soviet Union and other socialist countries. Comrade Švestka was released from captivity by Soviet troops. . . .*

"Illegal radio stations and publications are spreading falsifications of the lowest kind. Certain officials are directly aiding them in this. . . . Among them is Čestmír Císař, who has proved his betrayal of Leninism by a series of public statements. There is Ota Šik, whose revisionist views in the field of economy are equally well known. Now he is working hard abroad as one of the directors of the rightist forces. There is Eduard Goldstücker, who in recent months made many anti-socialist statements in Czechoslovakia and abroad. . . . Ota Šik [and] Jiří Hájek, the escaped foreign minister . . . have announced that they will discharge Government functions 'outside Czechoslovak territory,' which, as a matter of fact, no one has authorized them to do."

An underground broadside, distributed in Prague, told it thusly:

" 'Technology, Mrs. Müller, is a great blessing for mankind,' sighed Josef Schweik to his landlady as he massaged his aching legs. 'Take radio for instance. I walked all through Prague, and then I switched on Radio Vltava, and I saw that my walking was all in vain because I'd

* In reality, Švestka was barred from the *Rudé Právo* building by staffers who felt their editor had betrayed them.

missed the most important things happening in Prague. It was only from Radio Vltava that I learned, on the basis of reliable reports from Moscow—and here I quote their very words, Mrs. Müller—that 'one can see all over Prague how soldiers and officers of the allied forces are fraternizing with the population, how they are answering innumerable questions, how they are assisting the people in evaluating the political situation, and how they are clarifying the noble aims the troops have come to fulfill.' That's what they said, Mrs. Müller, and I'll tell you, if I didn't have all that liniment on my hands, I'd wipe off the tears on my cheeks, that's how touched I am. . . .'

" 'And did they also report, sir,' asked Mrs. Müller, 'that a secret cache of arms was found in the Ministry of Mr. Borůvka?'

" 'That's right, Mrs. Müller, and that also proves what I'm trying to tell you. Prophetic information, that's a feather in anybody's hat. The news that a cache of arms had been discovered at the Ministry of Agriculture appeared in Moscow's newspapers on one day and, true enough, the cache was discovered the very next day by the brave occupation troops. They just confirmed, so to say, that Moscow's *Pravda* prints the truth.'

" 'And Dr. Hájek from the Foreign Ministry is on the run, sir,' Mrs. Müller whispered.

" 'That's right, Mrs. Müller,' said Josef Schweik, lifting his sad eyes for a moment to look at his landlady. 'That Dr. Hájek also has a talent for prophecy, which is hard to find. Just imagine, Mrs. Müller, he was on the run at a beach in Yugoslavia for several days before the allied armies suddenly decided to crush the counter-revolution in our country, even if they had to plow it up from the ground first. And to top it all, Dr. Hájek is now running across the sea to the United Nations, which, for a Minister of Foreign Affairs, is something unheard of.' "

Back in World War I, the good soldier Schweik* outwitted his "superiors" by a kind of docile servility that verged on sabotage.

> "Look here, Schweik . . . Now pay close attention to what I'm telling you. Do you understand closely what I'm saying? Don't make the excuse afterward that there was a buzzing noise in the telephone. Now then, immediately, as soon as you hang up the receiver—"

---

* From the four-volume novel *The Good Soldier Schweik* (1920–23) by the Prague satirist and anarchist, Jaroslav Hašek (1883–1923). The quotes that follow are from the traditional American edition, somewhat truncated, published by Doubleday, Doran in 1930 in the translation by Paul Selver.

There was a pause. Then the telephone rang again. Schweik picked up the receiver and was swamped by a flood of abuse:

"You bloody, blithering, thickheaded, misbegotten booby, you infernal jackass, you lout, you skunk, you hooligan, what the hell are you up to? Why have you rung off?"

"Beg to report, sir, you said I was to hang up the receiver."

Nor were his "enemies" immune to the ravages of Schweikism. Transported as prisoners, Schweik and another soldier heckled the corporal guarding them into a state of utter submission:

". . . according to the instructions issued on November 21, 1879, military prisoners must be conveyed in a carriage provided with barred windows. We've got the barred windows all right. But the instructions go on to say that the carriage must also be provided with a receptacle containing drinking water. You've not carried out that part of the regulations. And, by the way, do you happen to know where the rations are going to be served out? You don't know? I thought as much. You simply aren't fit for your job. . . .

"You see, corporal, it's no joke to escort prisoners like us. You've got to look after us properly. We ain't just ordinary soldiers who can shift for themselves. We have to have everything brought to us. That's what the regulations say, and they've got to be kept to, or else where's your law and order?"

The essence of Schweikism is, I think, the ability to endure repeated rape until you eventually debauch the rapist. Hitler recognized Schweikism as the threat it was when he complained: "The more the Czechs curb themselves, the more dangerous they become!" Hitler's "protector" for Bohemia and Moravia, Reinhard Heydrich, described "the Czech race" as "the reed which bends, but will not break." Meanwhile, Schweik just went on making dates for "after the war at six o'clock."

Under communism, Schweik was demobilized but not deactivated. One Schweik joke of the 1950's went:

President Novotný wants to ascertain what the workers really think of him. Disguising himself with overalls, oil can, cap, and smock, he goes to a factory and asks the laborers: "What do you think of our Mr. Novotný?" Some say "no comment, Mr. President"; others shrug or say "Who's he?" Finally, Novotný comes upon the good comrade Schweik and asks him the question. Schweik shushes him, puts a finger to his lips, whispers "come with me," leads him down several stairs and corridors, makes sure they're not being followed, and finally takes him into a boiler room. There, Schweik bolts the door and turns the boiler on full blast to insure that they can't be overheard. Then and only then does Schweik confide: "To tell you the truth, I like him."

The Russians' turn beneath the guillotine that Schweik built was just beginning when a Prague historian, Zdeněk Mahler, wrote:

> The choices with which [the Czech] people has been systematically faced have rarely been simple like the one in the fairy tale: choose between good and evil. Here the choice has been between the greater and the lesser evil—and only then could there be talk about morality. This nation is not inclined to a Messiah complex; to go after a tank with a broom is not our idea of an act of undiluted courage. Not for nothing was Schweik created here and nowhere else as a character who with supreme humor rises above supreme tragedy—not equating the two, but symbolizing the extremes. Sometimes it is easier to die for something than to live for it.

And all the matters of life and death—Dubček's, Smrkovský's, Engineer Černík's, Dr. Kriegel's, even Josef Schweik's, even the Czechoslovak nation's—were now being decided in the Kremlin.

Chapter 16]

Friday 23 August—
Tuesday 27 August 1968

LUDVÍK SVOBODA'S ARRIVAL IN MOSCOW WAS MANAGED with all the finesse of a Cosa Nostra funeral—financed by the murderers and serviced, perhaps, by Kafka as undertaker. The conquered hero was hailed at Vnukovo Airport with a 21-gun salute. He was presented with flowers and then kissed on both cheeks by Brezhnev, Kosygin, and Podgorny. They rode into town with him in an open car along a road lined with Muscovites who'd been given Friday afternoon off from work to celebrate this "happy reunion."*

The old soldier stared stonily ahead. Once inside the Kremlin walls, he made it clear that he wanted no more ceremony and wouldn't talk with his hosts until he had his leaders back.

I am told that Leonid Brezhnev said bluntly: "No, you have no leaders and that's why we must talk today. Dubček and Černík have confessed their crimes and resigned."

"I don't believe you," is what Svoboda is supposed to have replied.

Brezhnev was furious. Without a Government, he said, the only thing to do with Czechoslovakia would be to dismantle it (as the Nazis had done). Slovakia would become the seventeenth "republic" in the Union of Soviet Socialist Republics while the "backward" areas of Bohemia and Moravia would become a protectorate. The Czechoslovak nation stood on the brink of extinction.

Svoboda didn't crack. He was wearing his Soviet medals. Now he took them off and put them on the table. (One of several contradictory reports claims that he also produced a pistol.) "I am an old man," he said in Russian. "I have seen much blood and war. All my life I have

---

* Two days earlier, Muscovites had sniffed that something was in the wind when *Pravda,* which normally goes on sale at 0700, didn't hit the kiosks until 1100. It contained only the briefest announcement that unnamed Prague leaders had "invited" the Warsaw Pact armies into their country.

seen blood being spilled. I am willing to die. If you do not bring in my colleagues, I will kill myself and you will have to explain why a Hero of the Soviet Union perished in your care."

His listeners all had shrugged their way out of other hypocrisies and disavowed other Heroes of the Soviet Union. Still, being mediocre men, they flinched momentarily at the challenge—and now Svoboda lowered his voice.

"There are two solutions," he went on softly, "political or blood spilling. I don't want to take the bloody solution." But he made it clear that, if anything happened to him or if his leaders were not returned, he had left orders—orders that would reach the people and be heeded!—*to dissolve the Czechoslovak Communist Party.*

The Russians had responded half-a-million strong to crush an imaginary counter-revolution. Now the spectre of the unimaginable, the unthinkable, the unspeakable had appeared before them in the imposing figure and measured cadences of the white-haired President of the Czechoslovak Socialist Republic.

Svoboda was fighting, as perilously as on any battlefield, for the very survival of his nation and the continuity of constitutional government. And whom was he up against? In the words of a Czechoslovak who was in that room: "We were shocked to find ourselves talking not with political dogmatists, but with cynical gangsters. The Russians told us that they didn't care who was the leader of Czechoslovakia—that the important considerations were military and strategic."

The Russian leaders knew by now that their invasion had succeeded, but that it hadn't worked. They gave their guests rooms in the Kremlin and both sides slept uneasily that Friday night. The Czechoslovak visitors were isolated from each other and from any news of developments in their homeland. Meanwhile, back in Prague, Svoboda's wife gave an interview to a friend who called up from the daily newspaper *Youth Front,* underground at the time.

"Are you scared?" the journalist asked.

"Yes," said Irena Svobodová. "But I don't believe he will give in to any pressure. . . . I've known him for a good long time. He's a man of extremely good character. I trust him. And I know how profoundly he was affected by this attack on our Republic by the Soviets and their allies."

"Do you think he went to Moscow expecting a favorable outcome or simply not to have left anything untried?"

"He's known them well ever since his experiences in Russia during World War II. Before he was named Hero of the Soviet Union, he was put up before a Troika Court, which usually meant the death sentence. He got out of that because he kept telling them the truth about himself, because he didn't say, no matter how hard they pressed him, that he was an anti-Soviet agent. He didn't let them intimidate him. He stuck it out and in the end he gained their respect. I'm sure that he is no more likely to compromise now. He will not give in to pressure."

Then, to show that her husband was aware of the people's unity, the First Lady said something that became the subject of many armchair and wine-tavern debates in Prague:

"At first, he was anxious because there wasn't much news from Slovakia. But I know he was aware that some units in Slovakia were ready to go into the mountains in case the occupiers refused to leave our country."

Even before Irena Svobodová's words were published, The Argument had started in my kitchen after curfew that Friday night. Two neighbors had dropped up to share their opinions with me over a bottle of Yugoslav maraschino, the colorless and not-too-sweet liqueur distilled from Dalmatian cherries. One was the man who'd exclaimed "Svoboda has sold us out!" when the trip to Moscow was announced that morning. He was a hawk who favored continued, even expanded, resistance that would force the Russians to set up a military occupation government. The presence of a visible enemy, he said, would prolong the Czechoslovak Revolution.

"Then Dubček and Smrkovský will be dead for certain and probably Svoboda, too," said the other neighbor, a dovish advocate of Schweikism. "And maybe a thousand dead Czechoslovaks instead of the hundred who've died already."

"A thousand?" said the hawk. "Be realistic, man! Knowing the Russians, it would probably be in the tens of thousands. But it would still be better and we'll win much sooner."

I contributed: "My country was lucky. America won a war in 1781 and it took almost two centuries before we really lost one. The Czechs have been fighting the same war with different enemies and you've yet to win it."

"Whatever we've won," said the dove, "we haven't won by waging war."

Now the catechism began.

"North Vietnam never stopped fighting," said the hawk, "and now they've done the impossible. They never lost, so they won."

"But at what cost?" said the dove. "And besides, they're up against the Americans."

"The Indians—Gandhi's, not yours, Alan—practiced our kind of passive resistance for years and they won," said the hawk.

"Against the British," said the dove. "And look what happened to Alan's Indians."

"Look at the Algerians. . . ."

"Against the French. The French aren't the Russians."

"Castro started with eighty-two men on a mountain top."

"Against Batista, not against the Russians," the dove insisted.

"Look," the hawk argued. "You and I have just found out that Pan-Slavism was a myth and our Slavic brothers are coolies in uniform. And there's only one thing that Orientals understand—which is: If you kill me, there are a hundred behind me and, if you kill them, there are another hundred behind them. . . ."

"But that's how they win wars," said the dove, "against Americans and Europeans like us. This may work when the numbers are on your side. But it certainly won't work with 14 million Czechoslovaks up against the Russians with their Eastern mind and 250 million people. They could wipe out Czechoslovakia and re-populate it with just a fraction of the people on their waiting list for housing."

I chimed in with a current joke: "Here and now, an optimist is a man who thinks they'll transport all of us to Siberia; a pessimist is one who thinks they'll make us walk there."

Neither of my guests laughed. The dove went on: "Why do you think the Russians are afraid of the Chinese? Because the Chinese are 700 million strong, so they can afford to lose a couple of hundred million if it means wiping out the Russians. But useless sacrifices won't work here. It's Eastern psychology and we Czechs are novices at it. The Russians live by it."

"And yet," said the other, "after three days, we have the Russians so demoralized that they're replacing the troops in Prague."

"But the point is," said the dove, "that the Russians have the replacements."

Friday night's only real news was that Čestmír Císař had escaped from custody at Prague police headquarters. Friendly secret policemen had spirited him away to a hideout in the countryside, but not before he had phoned the clandestine radio to broadcast, in his unmistakably smooth purr: "This is Čestmír Císař. I am free once again and I send the people of Czechoslovakia a fighting salute. I shall join the new Central Committee as soon as possible. *Be with us; we are with you!*"

On Friday night in Prague, 15,000 Czechs kept a vigil along the road from Ruzyně Airport to the Castle. They were awaiting their President's return. They stood for more than four hours until, long after curfew, the Russians started shooting and the Prague police begged the people to go home. No announcement was made that the delegation was prolonging its stay in Moscow.

In the Kremlin, Svoboda was staking everything on the return of Dubček, Smrkovský, Černík, Kriegel, and Špaček. And he didn't even know whether any of the five were still alive.

(Pessimists as well as optimists in Prague somehow took Císař's escape as an omen that Dubček and the other captive leaders were still alive somewhere. But the delegates in Moscow, negotiating for Czechoslovak freedom, didn't even have access to the news that Císař was free.)

On Saturday morning, the hosts in the Kremlin informed their guests that they would "have to wait a few hours for Dubček and the others to get here." The visitors could scarcely believe their ears, or the Russians' words. But, if it were so, then Svoboda's gamble had paid off and maybe the old general could still save his men.

(Around the same time, the Warsaw Pact commandant in Bratislava, a Soviet Colonel Kavaljov, had an unexpected caller, Pavlina Dubčeková. "I am Alexander Dubček's mother. What have you done with him?" she asked point-blank. The colonel blinked and answered: "We are negotiating with him.")

What had happened to Dubček, Černík, Smrkovský, Kriegel, and Špaček after their departure in shackles from Ruzyně could only be pieced together days later, but this is my best chronology:

On Wednesday night, the five leaders sat on the floor of an aging, unpressurized Russian transport plane flying at a low altitude. During their ninety minutes in the air, they were relieved of their remaining wristwatches (Černík's had been taken away that morning) and from then on, according to Josef Smrkovský: "We were kept so isolated that we had no concept of time. We didn't know how much time had elapsed or even what day it was."

The plane landed at a military airport in Central Slovakia. The prisoners were driven, each in a heavily-guarded armored car, to a barn outside the spa of Sliač, where circulatory disorders have been treated since the thirteenth century. There, they were insulted, mistreated, and even beaten with chains. Kriegel, a diabetic, was denied insulin. Smrkovský and Černík have both said of their ordeal, in virtually the same words, that they feared many times that their lives were at an end. There are even rumors that Dubček and Smrkovský were irradiated with cobalt either at Sliač or later in Russia.*

Sometime on Thursday, the prisoners were moved overland to a lonely mountain villa near the Transcarpathian city of Mukachevo in the Ukraine—in an area that was part of Czechoslovakia from 1919 to 1938. (It was ceded to the Soviet Union in 1945.) Here, it seems almost certain, the five prisoners were scheduled to be executed as soon as the "Workers and Peasants Government of Comrade Indra" could be proclaimed in Prague.† When the five captives complained of not being fed or offered any change of clothes, they were told they'd not be needing either much longer.

On Friday morning, however, they were suddenly moved again to the Ukrainian city of Lvov (the former capital of Dr. Kriegel's native Galicia, which was ceded by Poland to Russia in 1945). Here, they were kept alive in a state of uncertainty which their captors seemed to share. Several times they were told they'd be going back to Mukachevo; at least once during Friday night, though, they were awakened and told they would be ending their days in Lvov.

Early Saturday morning, however, they were bundled aboard a plane and told they were en route to Moscow, which they scarcely be-

* When I first heard these rumors (once or twice from doctors who said they knew that Dubček and Smrkovský were checking into Prague's Sanopz Hospital regularly to "have their blood changed"), I jotted in my diary: "If they should die of leukemia in the near future, I for one will start to think the unthinkable." Smrkovský subsequently was diagnosed as having cancers of the hip and spine, but I also remember one of his associates saying, in the spring of 1968, that "he's a very sick man, but he doesn't seem to know it." Therefore, I've continued to suspend my judgment, for what it's worth. In the rigidly controlled and censored post-invasion Czech press, I've seen the possibility alluded to only once—when *Rudé Právo* of 12 February 1970 printed an interview with Emil Rigo, one of the four Presidium members who, on the morning of 21 August 1968, voted against the proclamation condemning the invasion as an illegal act. Rigo noted in passing that "when they [the leadership] returned from the talks in Moscow, there were rumors that they had been tortured by starvation, infected with cancer, and suchlike nonsense."
† Soviet insistence on such formal "legality" is not unprecedented. A comparable, though not identical, timetable was followed in the 1956 abduction of Hungarian Premier Imre Nagy and the proclamation of János Kádár's counter-government.

lieved. In the air, however, their handcuffs were removed and they were even allowed to wash from a basin of water. When the plane landed at a military airport near Moscow, they were amazed that their captors didn't bother to put the handcuffs back on.

Instead, they were met by Army officers who handed them overcoats to conceal their torn clothes. In the hot August sun, the five condemned men were ushered into Chaika limousines with chauffeurs. They were guarded only by plainclothesmen, treatment almost befitting the heads of a Communist party. The Chaikas sped into Moscow and through a side gate toward the fairy-tale spires of the Kremlin. And there, lo and behold, awaiting them were the entire Soviet Politburo; their own President Svoboda; their Ministers of Defense and Justice; Deputy Premier Husák; and the cursed presences of Bil'ak and Indra, who had doomed them and their nation. It was much, much more than could be fathomed by Dubček's, Smrkovský's, or any other rational mind. Only a Dostoyevsky, whose life was reprieved while he stood before a firing squad, could have comprehended this scene.

"I am quite convinced," Oldřich Černík said when he learned what had transpired, "that President Svoboda saved my life."

Gustáv Husák telephoned the word from Moscow to Prague that Dubček and the others were in the Kremlin . . . that they were negotiating . . . and that they were expected to resume their functions of authority shortly.

In actuality, Dubček and Smrkovský were told by Brezhnev that they were "observers" and, every time they opened their mouths, they were commanded to "shut up." Černík apparently was granted some limited say in the talks. Whether Špaček or Kriegel were allowed to speak (or able to, in the case of the diabetic Kriegel) is unknown, but doubtful. Dubček, at least, was too shattered to say much anyway.

(Smrkovský, five days later, told the Czechoslovak people wryly: "Our 'talks' in Moscow were unusual. You know that we didn't get there all at one time and you also know the circumstances under which some of us got there and 'negotiated'. . . . Our connection with home was restricted. At first, we had little information—practically none. . . . We clashed sharply and repeatedly, both with our 'partners' and among ourselves, but we used every argument that was available to us.")

Having silenced the most articulate liberals in the room, Brezhnev warned the entire delegation: "If you persist in your errors, you will lose an entire generation of your people."

Back in Prague, the news from Moscow was met by relief mingled with uncertainty and disbelief. The Russians had told bigger lies before. Still, it generated a little optimism and precipitated a showdown between Gene Deitch and Zdenka, who'd been arguing since Wednesday over whether or not to flee to Vienna.

Zdenka refused to consider leaving: "Look, Gene, we're winning. When the Russians see that our people won't give them the time of day, they must turn around and go home."

"But they've seen that and they're still here," said Gene.

"But now our leaders are negotiating their departure," said Zdenka. Then she turned to me for support: "Ask Alan!"

"I think they're negotiating their stay," I said. Seeing Zdenka wince, I added gently: "If you're a Czech, though, you need hope to live."

Gene told Zdenka: "I think we'd do better to watch the situation from Vienna and see how it shapes up."

"We can watch it better from here," Zdenka insisted.

"The point is," said Gene, "that right now your Czechoslovak passport has a valid exit visa, which they're honoring today, but may not honor tomorrow. If we wait a week or two until the Russians start kicking out Americans, then it may take two years of filling out papers and pleading with officials at both ends before you'd be let out to join me. We can make a living anywhere in the world and I don't want to be apart from you, baby. We can sit it out in Vienna and then come back in if it quiets down. Or you can stay out and maybe I'll come in on my American passport to wind up our affairs, if it comes to that."

Finally, Zdenka yielded and the Deitches said a lingering goodbye to their charming apartment in the Malá Strana. I could tell that they doubted they would ever see it again. There seemed no place in this awful sphere of influence for a mixed marriage of East and West.

As Gene was getting ready to take the last suitcase downstairs, Zdenka said: "I don't want to upset you. But the free radio just said the Russians are turning back all Czechs from the border at Dolní Dvořiště."

"*Ježišmarja!*" said Gene. "That's exactly where we're going to cross."

"So I guess there's no sense in our going," Zdenka said with great relief.

"C'mon," said Gene. "This invasion is so half-assed that they may not even know where all the border crossings are. We'll head for Znojmo/Hatĕ."

"Gene, Gene," said Zdenka. "It's the Western border. That's what they came to 'protect.' Don't be crazy-stubborn."

"We're going," said Gene. And they drove at top speed to the Western frontier, 100 miles away, without seeing one Russian once they had left the outskirts of Prague.

"I think they've forgotten all about us," said the Czech border guard as he waved the Deitches into Austria.

On Saturday, Radio Moscow and Radio Vltava broke the news simultaneously that "U.S. Special Forces have doffed their green berets and are roaming the streets of Prague in civilian clothes. They are firing on our soldiers and shooting down our helicopters." Russia had headed off a plot by "whining NATO politicians to convert Czechoslovakia from its Warsaw Treaty loyalties and create a corridor to the East for West Germany." There were also "3,000 British paratroops disguised as tourists in Prague." But the emphasis was on the "U.S. Seventh Army Special Forces" who were allegedly operating out of espionage centers at Bad-Tölz in West Germany and Salzburg in Austria. In command of the operation was one "Col. Jerry Sage, an expert in subversive warfare who had organized every possible crime of U.S. intelligence in Southeast Asia and North Africa before taking charge in 1964 of U.S. mobile forces carrying out the silent war against the socialist countries of Europe." A detachment of Special Forces, all speaking either Czech or Slovak, had arrived in Salzburg in July. "From Austria, plainclothed Green Berets penetrated into Czechoslovakia garbed as tourists. Czechoslovak émigrés with forged documents were sent from Bad-Tölz into Czechoslovakia."

The U.S. State Department termed this version "an outrageous lie in all its detail and totality." But its truth or falsity didn't matter to me so much as the heightened suspicion and danger that might envelop my family if anybody believed Radio Moscow.

It is an accepted fact of espionage that there probably were a few stray "spooks" wandering around Czechoslovakia. There always are in any Iron Curtain country just as no country, East or West, is without its visiting Russian agents. But I happened to run up against one of "our boys" in the U.S. Embassy courtyard that weekend.

I didn't notice him among the tourists who were being organized into car convoys for evacuation. But he noticed me and sidled over. He was a long, gangling, very nervous Philadelphia type around 30.

"What's the name of that square?" he asked.

"Which one? The one out there?" I said, beckoning toward Malá Strana Square.

"No, the big one across the river downtown."

"The main drag with the statue on horseback at the top of it?" I guessed.

"Yes, that's the one!" he exclaimed.

"Wenceslas Square," I said.

"How do you say it in the local lingo?"

"*Václavské náměstí.*"

He practiced saying it badly a couple of times. Then he said: "Three o'clock, right?"

"No," I said, glancing at my watch. "It's a little before noon."

"I don't mean what time is it now. I mean three o'clock at Whatzisname Square."

By now I knew that I was involved in something other than chitchat. Peering at him quizically, I asked: "What the hell are you talking about?"

He stepped back and took a second look at me. Then he said: "You *are* my baby-sitter, aren't you?"

"Certainly not!" I said. "Don't you think I've got better things to do during an invasion than change your diapers for you?"

I must have raised my voice, for he started to disappear behind the nearest caryatid. And it suddenly dawned on me, from past wallows in Len Deighton's "fictions," that the "baby-sitter" is the local agent who makes contacts for the visiting agent. A minute to two later, one of the Embassy's Marine guards came over to me and said: "Look, Mr. Levy, that gentleman would appreciate it if you'd forget this conversation ever took place."

"It's bad enough," I remarked, "that to these guys all Czechs must look alike. But when all Americans start looking alike to them, too, then *we're* in trouble."

Over the weekend, Supraphon released a long-playing recording of Thursday's Extraordinary Fourteenth Congress.

Over the weekend, ten notorious figures from Ostrava's underworld signed this resolution:

> WE, culprits who committed penal acts in Metropolitan Ostrava, hereby declare and promise that we will not undertake or develop any criminal activities during the critical situation in our country, in order to free the forces of Public Safety from troubles due to us. We, who are alone even in our own country, find it absurd that we should accept the dictates of the Warsaw Treaty armies in such an intolerable situation where our constitutional leaders are in prison and criminals in foreign uniforms patrol our streets. . . . This resolution of ours is being handed over by us to the Chief of Public Safety in Ostrava for him to take due note of it.

Over the weekend, with repeated postponements of the delegation's return from Moscow, the situation in Prague began to deteriorate. Outside the Soviet-occupied waterworks, three teen-agers in a car were shot (two of them fatally; the third required several operations to save his life) by a Red Army sentry whose commander said they were "counter-revolutionary provocateurs." Their provocation? When the sentry had waved his flashlight at them, they'd reacted by speeding up and beaming their bright lights at him. The Russian officer told the Czech police: "It was their own fault." To which the underground *Literární Listy* responded eloquently:

> World, tremble with helpless terror, with desperate anger, with revulsion and shame for murders! In Prague and in Czechoslovakia, they are shooting at children! They are murdering children! Let us remember: All the dead, all the wounded, all of them, all are victims of the occupiers! They would not have died, they would not have been wounded, if we had not been occupied!
>
> The right is on our side! It is our right to do anything and everything, literally everything, to show our resistance. And if we are being reasonable and not doing everything, that is *our* business, *our* prudence. But we cannot and must not admit, by a mere thought, by a single word, that someone is to blame for his own death. . . .
>
> Prudence and common sense are good weapons, but they can also be, and sometimes are, expressions of fear. Let us separate one from the other! Let us realize that we are afraid, let us realize it and admit it. There is nothing wrong in that. Our courage will be that much greater then and our reasoning that much clearer.
>
> They are the occupiers and they are shooting at us. No one has in-

vited them and they are nothing but murderers. Murderers of defense-less children! Shame on them!

Over the weekend, Russian demoralization reached a dangerous low. A reliable Czech, who wouldn't let war interfere with his mush-room-hunting, was in the woods not far from Prague on Sunday. Seeing a Russian detachment approaching, he hid. First came a squad of men with spades. Behind them came fifty manacled men, clearly Russian soldiers, though their uniforms had been taken away from them. They were being marched there by a firing squad and an officer-in-charge.

The gravediggers worked with great care to lift up two feet of sod. The manacled soldiers were executed in small groups, a single volley for each group. Then the sod and underbrush were replaced. The wit-ness didn't dare leave until long after dark.

Less care was given to burying their dead by the Russians who oc-cupied České Budějovice. Soon after the Russians moved from a forest bivouac to a garrison requisitioned from the Czechoslovak Army, local fumigators went in to decontaminate the woods and found twelve Rus-sian victims of a firing squad wrapped up in a tarpaulin.

In Central Moravia, Russian tankmen bivouacked in fields were ordered to sleep on their tanktops which were often boiling hot. Two who chose to nap instead in the tall grass nearby never woke up. A pair of officers discovered them and put guns to their heads. . . .

The Russians were killing their own not only for insubordination, but also for illness. "We have no doctor in our unit and our officer says that, when we move out, the sick will be left behind, which means the firing squad," an ailing Russian private told a Prague physician. Thus, for humane reasons, doctors were virtually the only Czechs who will-ingly gave aid to the invaders.

Still other Russians died from supplementing their tinned field ra-tions with hand-picked poisonous mushrooms. In one manner or an-other, no more than a couple of hundred Russian soldiers died on Czechoslovak soil—though the Soviet public was given estimates up to 25,000. And every time a mother in Kiev or Kharkov was notified that her son "died fighting the counter-revolution in Czechoslovakia," a few hundred of her neighbors must have been convinced that it really was so.

Even so, the Russians had their hands full back home that week-end. The poet Yevgeny Yevtushenko sent a telegram to Brezhnev and Kosygin. In it, he complained:

I DON'T KNOW HOW TO SLEEP. I DON'T KNOW HOW TO CONTINUE LIVING.
ALL I KNOW IS THAT I HAVE A MORAL DUTY TO EXPRESS TO YOU THE FEEL-
INGS WHICH OVERPOWER ME. I AM DEEPLY CONVINCED THAT OUR ACTION
IN CZECHOSLOVAKIA IS A TRAGIC MISTAKE AND A BITTER BLOW TO SOVIET-
CZECHOSLOVAK FRIENDSHIP AND THE WORLD COMMUNIST MOVEMENT.*

Then, on Sunday noon, while the Czechoslovak and Soviet leaders
were meeting inside the Kremlin, five men and two women sat down in
Red Square and unfurled banners reading "HANDS OFF CZECHO-
SLOVAKIA!" "SHAME ON THE OCCUPIERS!" and "FREEDOM
FOR DUBČEK!"

The protesters included the grandson of the late Foreign Minister
Maxim Litvinov, architect of Soviet foreign policy; the wife of the imprisoned writer Yuli Daniel; the poetess Natalya Gorbanevskaya; and
a prominent art critic.

"Almost immediately," Mrs. Gorbanevskaya reported soon thereafter, "whistles were heard from all ends of the Square and plainclothes agents of the KGB came dashing toward us. They were shouting 'These are all Jews!' and 'Beat them!' They tore the banners from
our hands and beat the art critic in the face until the blood flowed and
some of his teeth broke. Pavel Litvinov was beaten on the face with a
heavy stick. They shouted 'Get out of here, you scum!' We remained
seated."

All were arrested and officially denounced as criminals, drunks, and
dissolute, anti-social parasites. Only Mrs. Gorbanevskaya was released
on bond because she had her three-year-old son with her.†

Inside the Kremlin on that last Sunday in August, Dubček and his
leadership were so effectively sealed off from the outside world (and
even from each other) that they wouldn't have known about the dem-

* Yevtushenko received no reply other than the unexplained banning of his play,
Bratsk Hydroelectric Station, from a Moscow theatre for a week.
† After demonstrating again, on Stalin's 90th birthday, Mrs. Gorbanevskaya was
committed to a special KGB psychiatric hospital for those insane enough to dissent.
The others who joined her in Red Square on 25 August 1968 were found guilty of
"slandering the Soviet people" and given sentences ranging from two and three
years in prison to four and five years in Siberian exile. "But my comrades and
I," the poetess wrote in a letter to Moscow's foreign correspondents, "are happy
that we were able, even briefly, to break through the sludge of unbridled lies and
cowardly silence, thereby demonstrating that not all the citizens of our country are
in agreement with the violence carried out in the name of the Soviet people." Another of the demonstrators, Vadim Delone, 23, a student, told the judges who sent
him to prison: "For three minutes on Red Square, I felt free. I am glad to take
your three years for that." Later, however, in a Siberian labor camp, Delone attempted suicide. He was released after two years.

onstration in Red Square just outside the wall. Nor would they have known that, back in Prague, the National Assembly had unanimously approved a letter to President Svoboda in Moscow telling him that the Parliament and the Government were still functioning . . . expressing full support for the "legitimate new Central Committee and Presidium" elected by the Extraordinary Fourteenth Congress . . . and imploring him:

> Dear Comrade President: Aware of the fact that no written report can fully portray the atmosphere in the cities and concluding from the reports of Tass that Soviet organs are being informed quite distortedly and unobjectively, we consider it an essential pre-condition of your further negotiations for you to be more fully and precisely informed about the real state of affairs.
>
> We therefore recommend that information be given to you by a special consultative group composed of representatives of the Central Committee, the National Assembly, and the Government, whose presence in Moscow you could urgently request.
>
> We also submit for your consideration the suggestion that your negotiations be interrupted temporarily . . . and you return to Prague along with comrades Dubček, Smrkovský, and Černík. You could use this short interval to become better acquainted with the situation and to consult with the appropriate organs.*

Prague's National Assembly headquarters, where the Parliament had stayed in constant session since Wednesday, was now the citadel of official resistance. And it had an unlikely defender.

General Lomský, the defrocked Minister of Defense and friend of Šejna's, still retained his National Assembly seat. And it was Lomský, sometimes wearing his uniform with Soviet medals, who went out into Prague's Maxim Gorki Square and defied the Russians to enter the building. Speaking the fluent Russian he'd learned during his war years in Moscow, Lomský hinted darkly that there were reinforcements within.

Another general, Interior Minister Josef Pavel, had tried to get into his own Ministry on Wednesday but was turned away by the Russian soldiers guarding the door. This proved to be a fortunate bungle, for he was earmarked for arrest by the traitors within, one of whom, Colo-

---

* This letter bears three signatures: by representatives of the National Assembly, the Central Committee Presidium, and the Government. The third signature, that of Lubomír Štrougal, then Deputy Premier, proves most interesting when viewed in the light of his own spectacular post-invasion rise as a hard-line opponent of "The So-Called Vysočany Congress" and other "negativistic" acts of August in Prague.

nel Vaněk, was speculating aloud that Pavel "must be hiding in some cellar, that clown!"

Pavel, who became the object of a vast Soviet manhunt, did go into hiding, but he managed to stay in contact with the surviving Cabinet Ministers. After Radio Moscow claimed that Pavel had fled to the West, he gave an interview to the underground Radio Prague on Sunday.

"As you can see, I'm no apparition," Pavel told the interviewer cheerfully. "I'm sitting here with you in Prague. We are looking out of the window onto the street where Prague citizens are walking. Up there in front, you see runners who bring me messages, which are evaluated here. Then the runners leave again to pass on my orders either in writing or by telephone. As you can see, I cannot telephone from here. I want to tell you that this is not the only place where I work. I have a number of work places like this and I keep shifting from one to the other."

Pavel then pointed out that virtually all uniformed policemen in the land, from traffic cop to border guard, were staying loyal to their chief and their people:

"I am very satisfied with them. A somewhat more complicated situation prevails in the State Security, which has been tainted and some of whose members, it seems, have taken part in unlawful activities. People should be careful here."

On Sunday night at 2145, the Czechoslovak Government received and relayed this cryptic message from Moscow to the Czechoslovak people:

> Dear Fellow Citizens:
>
> We send you cordial greetings on behalf of the entire delegation.
>
> The negotiations have been continuing today and will go on into the night. We know that you are thinking of us. And we are thinking of you. We appreciate your coolheadedness, which is of great help to us here. We ask you to keep it up.
>
> Once more, many greetings, and we are thinking of all of you at home.
>
> Yours,
> SVOBODA, DUBČEK, ČERNÍK,
> SMRKOVSKÝ and the others.

We all knew by then that some *dénouement* was near, but we knew not what. Nor did we know, until later, what brutal terms had been laid down or which one the silenced Dubček was most vehemently shaking his head against: nullification of "The So-Called Fourteenth Party Congress."

His friend Gustáv Husák was the man who, in Moscow, persuaded Alexander Dubček that the Congress lacked legal validity because the Russians had succeeded in preventing so many of their fellow Slovaks (including Dubček and Husák themselves) from attending. Husák resigned from the Congress Presidium and then so did Dubček.

Thus was Slovak nationalism first used by Husák to dissolve Dubček's dream of "socialism with a human face." The Kremlin leadership took notice of Husák's dexterity and, in that very room, began slowly driving a wedge between those two very special, but very different, Slovak politicians. At that moment in Moscow, Alexander Dubček and Gustáv Husák must have passed each other in orbit.

In Prague that night, the Soviet Ambassador met with several of Prime Minister Černík's loyal Cabinet members. Chervonenko promised them that in the light of "favorable" developments in the Moscow talks, the Warsaw Pact troops would co-operate more closely with the Czechoslovak Government in easing the consequences of the occupation.

Minutes later, three of the Cabinet ministers, riding in an official car down Hradčany Hill, were fired upon by Soviet troops from the tank outpost at Klárov. The Ministers of Transport, Mining, and Heavy Industry were unhurt. The Red Army officer who halted them explained blandly that his men had been defending themselves against shots fired from the Ministers' car. Challenged to search the auto for any sort of weapon, the officer shrugged and said: "All right, we're letting you go this time."

The Government filed a formal protest, but the people just said as they'd said many times in the past five days: "There's a Russian promise for you."

The firing on the Ministers signaled the beginning of a wild night-and-day-and-night of terror and emotion that threatened to become the American Family Levy's last hours together in Prague. Or, worse yet, the first guns of World War III. . . .

In the early hours of Monday morning, the American Embassy's roof caught fire, not from Soviet machine-gun fire, but from an attic furnace overheated by two days' steady burning of confidential papers.

The blaze raged out of control for ninety minutes. Prague's fire department could not respond because of the Soviet curfew. But the Marine guards, the Embassy's staff (many of whom were sleeping in their offices), and the American journalists on hand managed to quell it. By the time they did, though, the roof and attic were in ruins . . . the telecommunications center just below them was severely damaged . . . the Telex machine therein was doused with water and disabled (for a whole day) . . . and Tad Szulc, who'd been Telexing when disaster struck, had a broken foot.

Some Russian armored trucks had responded to the blaze, but they'd gone away when the Americans told them their help wasn't needed. At dawn, a Soviet helicopter flew over several times to survey the damage.

One of Tad Szulc's translators phoned me with the news, and right after breakfast I walked downhill to see if I could be of any help to Tad. I arrived just in time to witness the siege of the U.S. Embassy.

The last embers had been doused and everybody was just starting to unwind when three very young Russian soldiers entered the premises. Carrying automatic rifles, they wandered through the courtyard, up a marble staircase, and along the Ambassador's formal gardens toward his orangery—a gazebo-like pavilion, surrounded by fruit trees, almost a quarter-mile back into Embassy territory. There, they climbed a fence and began picking apples.

Two Marines in civilian clothes went out to the orangery. The Russians nodded to them and went on picking apples. The Marines scaled the orangery and there, with a flourish worthy of Iwo Jima, they raised the American flag. Then the ranking Marine, Master Sergeant Bob Gattis, proclaimed to the Russian trespassers: "Boys, those are American apples."

One of the Russians said *"Ne panemajo"* ("I don't understand") and all three of them went on picking apples.

The Embassy's political officer came out and asked them, in fluent Russian, to leave.

"We have our orders," one of them replied.

The diplomat was insistent. The soldiers were surly. Finally, however, they gathered up their apples and left.

Fifteen minutes later, two armored scout cars and an armored personnel carrier roared up Tržiště Street with twenty men inside. The personnel carrier wheeled sharply in front of the American Embassy and halted with its little cannon poking right into the mouth of the Embassy entrance.

The Russians blockaded the Embassy in this manner for exactly ten minutes. Their officer in charge said they were there "to maintain order." Then they withdrew, though for several days they had one or two armored trucks posted 25 yards down the block.

Ambassador Beam left in his Cadillac to register a formal protest—but to no avail in Prague.* Meanwhile, to those of us taking our first deep breath in the Embassy, it was not too hard to envision World War III exploding out of an incident as trivial as the temptation of three hungry Russian soldiers in a garden of luscious American apples. Was original sin that much different?

One stop past the American Embassy, the Klárov tram stand was flanked by two tanks. Our cleaning lady, Paní B., waited there placidly for the Number 22 tram to take her to work at our house, four stops away. She had not been waiting long when she saw a 22 approaching.

Aboard the tram was Mrs. Marie Charousková, twenty-five, the slender mother of an eighteen-month-old girl. Marie Charousková was on her way to the Faculty of Mechanical Engineering to deliver the final portion of her graduate thesis.

Like Paní B. and so many of us in Prague (foreigners included), Marie Charousková was wearing a small swatch of the Czechoslovak tricolor with a tiny black ribbon across it. But, as she descended from the tram, one of the tankmen, standing at ground level, caught her eye and said: "Take that off!"

Marie Charousková smiled sweetly and said: "But why?"

From the top of one of the tanks, a machine-gunner shot her dead.

Paní B. told my wife what happened next: "A car that was passing by stopped. The driver opened his door and two men who'd just got off the tram put the poor girl inside. They said to take her to the hospital. But I could see she was already dead."

Paní B. boarded the same tram and arrived at our house fifteen minutes later, a little out of breath, quivering from shock, but still all too coherent.

* The Soviet Embassy referred him to Warsaw Pact occupation headquarters and Warsaw Pact headquarters referred him to the Soviet Embassy. Eventually, the protest was made in Washington and it was there that the Russians formally apologized.

"Do you realize you might have been shot for the same thing?" my wife said, pointing to Paní B.'s tricolor.

"I wouldn't have taken it off," Paní B. replied firmly. "And suppose I had taken it off? I'd only be calling attention to it, wouldn't I?"

"How could you drag yourself up here after seeing something like that?" my wife wanted to know.

"Look," said Paní B., her voice losing its tremor. "The tanks have been there for five days and five nights right outside our house. To get on line for milk or anything else, I have to walk between them, too. So we go back and forth as little as we can. Once I'm outside, I stay away as long as possible. And once I'm inside, I stay inside."

After the siege of the U.S. Embassy and the shooting of Marie Charousková*, my fear for my family's safety mounted. Once we'd all survived the initial shock, I'd imagined that the worst was over and that very little physical danger remained for holders of U.S. passports who exercised some discretion. But nobody had asked for Marie Charousková's credentials or citizenship before killing her. The American passport? What did it mean in a city of random shooting and sudden death? Just don't reach into your vest to produce it because a Russian soldier might think you're Special Forces and shoot you in self-defense.

Monday afternoon, word came from Moscow that some kind of agreement had been reached. One underground radio commentator described it, without knowing the details, as "a compromise for sure, a rotten compromise, but a peaceful one, the peace of the grave."

The leaders would be home within a day. As an immediate token of good faith, an unspecified fraction of the Russian troops would pull out of Prague that very evening. Curfew for drivers on all Prague streets and all main highways leading from Prague would be 1800. Curfew for pedestrians would remain 2200, meaning 2000 Prague time. The announcement added: "In case of violations, Warsaw Pact forces will take harsh measures. Shooting cannot be excluded."

That afternoon, Czechoslovakia began formal withdrawal of its official protest to the United Nations. And the occupation headquarters announced another of many "further conditions":

---

* "Dead on arrival" at Petřín Hospital, Marie Charousková was awarded her degree posthumously by the Engineering Faculty.

> Representatives of the headquarters of foreign troops stationed in
> the capital of the Republic have announced to the Czechoslovak au-
> thorities that, on the condition that the slogans, inscriptions, and
> posters are removed in the capital, the forces will leave the capital.

A similar edict was issued in Bratislava for the Slovak capital, where a
few Russian enlisted men seized the occasion to make small boys lick
the painted DUBČEKs and SVOBODAs off the walls of public buildings.

Despite all the ominous implications, a kind of false joy prevailed
in Prague for a few hours, perhaps because the citizens needed to be
buoyed for the ordeal ahead. People set about whitewashing the slogans, hoping against hope that maybe the only free speech to be eradicated would be the past week's, which nobody would ever forget anyway. On a treacherously steep rooftop in our neighborhood, I saw a
chimneysweep being besieged by joyous children smearing themselves
with his soot for good luck. Downtown, students suddenly swarmed
around the bewildered Soviet tankmen and pressed cigarettes upon
them. In Wenceslas Square, a blonde with painted red toenails handed
a Russian paratrooper a calling card with her name and the words:
"Our freedom will triumph."

"You shouldn't put your name on things like that," the soldier
warned her with a friendly laugh. "You could get in trouble."

"But our freedom *will* triumph," the girl assured him happily.

I was not at all optimistic, but it certainly was good to see some of
the tanks pulling out. Promptly at 1800 Monday, the outbound convoys of tanks and armored trucks rumbled up Myslbek Street, Kepler
Street, and the Boulevard of the Pioneers. We all watched through the
shutters of the lowered jalousie in our master bedroom. For a while, the
children helped me count the tanks.

"Does this mean I won't get to meet the Russian soldier?" Monica
asked me.

"If we ever visit Moscow," I promised her, "I'm sure you'll get to
meet him. He's much nicer to children when he's there than he is when
he's here."

At 1930, we put the children to bed in their room and Valerie and I
went on watching the tanks go by from our own window. On a park
bench, diagonally across from us, a handful of pensioners and grandmothers were doing the same. They sat out there every day and every

night until the eight o'clock curfew, cackling at the Russian soldiers' antics with the same "what-will-the-younger-generation-be-up-to next?" indignation that they vented on the passing parade of Czechs all year round. The men also traded war stories. Each of those old people was merely living through another chapter of the terrible history of Czechoslovakia.

Ten minutes before curfew hour, the 117th tank I had counted came to an abrupt halt at our corner. Watching from our window, Valerie and I caught a shocking glimpse of just how much Czechoslovakia's free expression must have enraged the Russians.

Out of the turret leaped an officer and two soldiers brandishing carbines. The officer barked a command and motioned to the old people on the bench. They came toward the soldiers with hands in the air.

The two enlisted men darted behind them and poked their weapons into the old men's necks. They marched the people across the street to the corner news stand, directly opposite our windows. The stand had been shut up tight since the eve of the invasion. But the underground press delivery boys had made a point of posting one copy of each edition there for stand-up reading by anyone who had missed getting his paper at home. Our rustic-looking wooden news stand, plastered with newspapers and painted with slogans, had become one of the more eloquent bulletin boards in town.

At gunpoint, the old people were made to strip the stand of its papers, tear them up into small pieces, and then stamp on the pile of them. One of the soldiers playfully tried to make a very old man chew up some of the scraps of newspaper. But the codger pointed to his toothless gums and the officer gestured to his men to be serious. A minute or two later, the officer put a match to the little pile of shredded newsprint.

The old people stood watching it burn while the three Russians climbed back into their tank. After firing into the air, they drove away.

Shooting into the air may be intended as a harmless warning. But when you live one flight up on a downhill slope, you take it more seriously. Valerie and I dropped to the floor as the Russian bullets passed over our windows.

Monica came running in from the next bedroom: "Are you all right, Mommy and Daddy?"

"Yes," I said. "We're fine and don't you worry."

"The Russian soldier wasn't shooting at us, was he?" Monica wanted to know as she climbed into her mother's arms.

"No," said Valerie. "He was just shooting into the air for fun."

"I don't think it's funny," Monica said. "But I did think it was a little funny when he tried to make that old man eat up all that paper, didn't you?"

It dawned on us that after having been put to bed, Monica had crept back to the window and seen much more than any four-year-old ought to see. When Monica had gone back to bed, I told Valerie: "I want you to start packing. I'm staying, but the three of you are leaving tomorrow."

"Just when the trouble is ending?" Valerie protested half-heartedly.

"Even if 99 per cent of the Russians were pulling out," I said, "that wouldn't mean the trouble is ending. And I'd rather be wrong about having sent you away than be wrong about having kept you here."

"I won't go unless you go with us," Val said.

"I can't go," I told her. "I'm an eyewitness to history who happens to be an American writer, so I can do something for the Czechs. And besides, somebody's got to hold the fort here, so that maybe you'll have something to come back to."

That infuriated my wife. "And what about some*one* to come back to?" she snapped. "Do you know what you sound like? The relatives in Poland who didn't have enough sense to get out when the Nazis were coming."

"You may be right," I said, "but at least now I know what made them stay to the end." Our rowboat to Prague was foundering, but it was the best home we'd ever had—and I still wanted to salvage my little corner of the Czechoslovak Spring, even after the Deluge struck. Feeling a little like Noah and sounding too much like John Wayne, I heard myself adding: "I only want to be around here until the good guys win."

After twelve years as my wife, Valerie had just begun to realize she'd married a fanatic. (It was news to me, too.) So she said: "This isn't a place for the children and me right now. We'll come back when you say it's all right again."

"It'll never be all right," I said, "but it'll either be better or worse than this fairly soon."

I phoned the U.S. Embassy and asked them to Telex a friend in Bad Godesberg that Val and the girls would be coming on the morning train to Mainz. Bad Godesberg, the quaint and suitably smug Rhine River bedroom town for Bonn, was the nearest Western oasis where we had good friends. Still, it seemed strange for a Levy to be deporting his family to sanctuary in Germany.

But, once the decision was taken, everything seemed strange. When I hung up the phone, our home in Prague seemed foreign for the first time. The familiar keepsakes that had followed us around the world—our stuffed Fidel Castro (a converted "Mama" doll bought in Havana 1960); our Picasso mother-and-child from his Square period; my Art Nouveau "ESCAPE" sign; and Val's IBM "RÉFLÉCHISSEZ!" sign—no longer seemed familiar to me. Nothing did. My family was going away!

Toward midnight, the tanks were still leaving. I said to my wife: "Do you want to wait an extra twenty-four hours and see how much they have left in the city when this exodus is over?"

"No," she replied. "I've been thinking. Even if every Russian left overnight, I'd be more worried than ever. I'd be afraid they were pulling out of the city so they could bomb it."

"You need calm," I affirmed. "You'll go tomorrow."

In the taxi to the Smíchov station Tuesday morning, we were thrilled to see the President's flag flying again over the Castle and his blue-hatted Castle guard performing sentry duty. The Russian legions had been removed from the Castle, but they were not altogether gone. If you peered through the fences and bushes at the Military Academy across the way, you could see Russian sentries crouching to keep an eye on the Czech sentries.

The tanks were gone from Klárov, where the three Ministers had been shot at and Marie Charousková had been murdered. The only massive show of strength we passed was at the Soviet Tank Memorial near the Újezd playground. Here, a shiny red-starred tank, the first one into Prague in the 1945 liberation, still stood on its pedestal. But ringed around it on 27 August 1968 were eight white-bandaged olive-drab tanks with grim, watchful soldiers protecting this ugliest of symbols from the bitterest of peoples.

Platform Three of the Smíchov station is a place I never hope to see again. Half-an-hour before departure, the 1057 express for Pilsen, Marienbad, Cheb, Nuremberg, Frankfurt, Mainz, and Paris was ready for boarding. The expressions in the train's picture windows and on the platform still haunt me. Whenever someone blandly says "I have *mixed emotions,*" I think of those faces torn apart by feelings—faces with creases that weren't there a few minutes before, but would always be there. Those who were going out to freedom and the unknown beyond looked sad and scared. Those who were seeing them off glowed with joy at there still being a choice and a promise of a future for those they loved, but they also wept with the sadness of separation.

I loaded my family's six suitcases (including enough toys for a two-month stay) into a compartment. When I returned to the platform below, a woman was handing my wife a letter to mail in Germany, telling her son in Canada to stay there. Val said she would post it at the Nuremberg station. Then the woman buried her head on Val's shoulders and they both began to cry.

When the woman had hugged and kissed my wife and left, I asked Val: "Do you know her from somewhere?"

"We met while you were putting away the luggage," Val replied.

The intensity of Platform Three had penetrated to Monica (though not to Erika, who was practicing her German). When I came aboard to say one last goodbye, Monica struggled and thrashed and cried in a way that she hadn't since babyhood. Her own grief and fear rendered her inarticulate. Every time I reached for her, she fought me away. I thought she was angry at me either for sending them away or else for not going with them.

Finally, however, she managed to blubber that: "Daddy—wants to —stay—here. Make him get off the train! Please make him get off now!"

There were still ten minutes, but if I wanted to stay in Prague, she wanted me to take no chances. I climbed down from the train. So there was no farewell embrace for Monica, just the shared knowledge that we were both a little less miserable because I was where I wanted to be and she was on her way to where I wanted her to be.

At 1057 sharp, the train started pulling out. Like everyone else on Platform Three, I walked, then trotted, then ran until the green train passed out of sight and even then I saw it for a good long time.

I was alone now in a Prague that was new to me, where you looked over your shoulder whenever you heard any*thing* behind you and quickened your step whenever you heard any*one* behind you. (In another week, you learned how to tell from the sound of a vehicle whether it was Russian or Czechoslovak; civilian or military; tank, personnel carrier, jeep, or goulash wagon.) I wandered the city alone. At the American Embassy, I called for the camera I had left there on the afternoon of the invasion. But I decided to leave it there for a few more days when I saw two armored truckloads of Russians still stationed just down the street from our slightly charbroiled Embassy. "We're being honored by one of the few public shows of Soviet muscle around town today," an attaché remarked to me.

Inside, Telex service had been restored and Tad Szulc, his foot in a cast, was getting ready to file a story. One of the last of the American tourists, a really gray-flannel-mouthed wise guy from Westchester, spotted the white-red-and-blue tricolors with mourning bands that Tad and I were wearing. The tourist exclaimed fliply: "No wonder we don't get any objective coverage!"

Tad wilted him with a stare and these words: "If you can be objective about indecency then you're just not decent yourself."

I strolled across the Charles Bridge (tankless once more) and, on Wenceslas Square, I saw no Russians posted outside the Socialist party's editorial headquarters. *Zitřek* and several other periodicals had their offices there. I thought I would go inside and inquire after Sylva. But, as I approached the entranceway, I discovered that the building was still occupied after all. A Russian tank and a dozen soldiers had somehow been wedged into a small inner courtyard where you might hesitate to park a Volkswagen.

In my wanderings, I had picked up what little news and gossip there was. The Moscow agreement had been signed on Monday night, though not by Kriegel (who had simply refused it) and almost not by Dubček (who had balked at the last moment, but had been taken aside by Svoboda and, some said, Smrkovský, because they were sure that, if the Russians couldn't get Dubček's *podpis* on the dotted line, they would choose to dismember and annihilate the Czechoslovak nation). Then, once the dirty deed was done, the Russians had thrown a lavish, monaurally festive party for their downcast Czechoslovak brethren. Most downcast of all was Alois Indra, who—on being told that he must return home unanointed in the company of the men he had betrayed—suffered a heart attack that kept him in Moscow for another month.

When the group was delivered to Moscow's airport early Tuesday morning, another member was not among them. "Where's Kriegel?"

Svoboda asked. One of the Russians informed the President: "He will be following you at a later date." The entire delegation (including a rather perplexed Vasil Bil'ak) staged a sitdown strike that lasted two hours. "We're not going back without Kriegel," Svoboda told the Russians. "If you don't bring him to us you might as well put us where you have him."

Kriegel was still in the Kremlin, where he had been standing, hands up, facing a wall for at least three hours. Covered by pistols, "this filthy little Galician Jew" of Mr. Kosygin's was awaiting his end for the second time in a week, surely doomed this time for his heresy and courage in not signing the Moscow agreement. Instead, he was hustled away to the airport. Only then did the delegation board a Soviet transport plane for the three-hour flight home to Prague. Back on home soil, Josef Smrkovský's first recorded words were: "Yes, we have all come back, including Kriegel."

Witnesses at the Prague airport said that Dubček had looked gray, limp, and on the verge of nervous exhaustion. He had a deep gash in his forehead and his hair was now closely cropped, prisoner style. Like a sheepish lad who'd been in a neighborhood fight, he'd shown his family* the shredded remains of the shirt he'd worn to work a week earlier as well as the scars on his back. Then he'd gone into seclusion from everybody, but it was promised that he would address the nation later in the day.

Smrkovský had headed for his office in Maxim Gorki Square. Along the way, motorists had recognized him and honked their horns happily. A bus driver deviated from his route to follow Smrkovský's car into town. Outside the National Assembly headquarters, Smrkovský was met by a crowd waving banners. "Speak to us! Speak to us!" they cried, but the Speaker simply lowered his eyes, bowed his head, and bulled his way into the building. Later, he appeared at an upstairs window and waved to the crowd with both hands tightly clasped. Then the Speaker went and broke the news to his parliament, after which it adjourned without further discussion.

"We are situated in the very heart of Europe," the weary Smrkovský is known to have said at one point, "and the heart is the most sensitive spot of every organism. But unlike the human heart, we cannot be transplanted and must beat where history has placed us."

* Anna Dubčeková had made her way back from Yugoslavia with two of the Dubček boys, though the third son, Petr, 19, was told to remain in Egypt for a while.

Later that morning, a chauffeured Tatra 603 drew up to the Klárov tram stop. From the limousine emerged František Kriegel. He knelt and kissed the sidewalk where Marie Charousková had died. A good friend of Kriegel's happened to be passing and greeted him when he arose. But the friend says that Kriegel was "in a state of shock and didn't recognize anyone at all."

Prime Minister Černík held a briefing for senior officials of the news and publicity media in which he outlined the censorship to come. Reports (printed with varying details in *The New York Times,* The London *Times,* and *The Guardian*) have been denied that, at this session, Černík advised "the best minds to get out of the country while the going is good," but the fact is that such targets as Pelikán of TV, Hejzlar of radio, and A.J. Liehm of *Literární Listy* were shipped abroad in great haste.*

As Tuesday morning became early afternoon, the people of Czechoslovakia still didn't know what fate had been negotiated for them in Moscow, and they were beginning to fear the worst. A lady I met in Wenceslas Square said: "One of two things can happen. They will murder us now or they will murder us later."

Mobile loudspeakers were converging on the Square while we talked. The word was that, to enable them to reach most people, Svoboda and then Dubček would broadcast a few hours apart over the legal, or underground, radio. Černík and Smrkovský would speak on the following days.

At 1440 Tuesday, the joint Soviet-Czechoslovak official communique was read. It lasted eight minutes. The first four minutes were a roll call of those present on both sides. The second half introduced an ugly new word into the Czechoslovak vocabulary:

> An agreement has been reached regarding measures aimed at a rapid *normalization* of the situation. . . .

And, a minute later, in connection with the rapists' "temporary entry into the territory of Czechoslovakia":

> An agreement has been reached regarding conditions of departure of these troops . . . depending upon the *normalization* of the situation. . . .

---

* Pelikán was named Czechoslovak cultural attaché in Rome; Hejzlar, cultural attaché in Vienna; Liehm, the representative of Czechoslovak Filmexport in Paris. They took asylum in the West in 1969, when recalled from their posts to face accusations in Prague.

And finally, of course: "The discussions were held in an atmosphere of sincerity, comradeship, and friendship."

When it was over, the man-in-the-street and I knew as little as we had known before. The communique was followed by President Svoboda broadcasting live from Prague Castle. The voice was firm, the tone was warm, but now the information content was virtually nil:

"After four days of negotiations in Moscow, we are back among you in our fatherland. We have returned together with comrades Dubček, Černík, Smrkovský, and the others. Neither you nor we felt at ease. We were with you all the time in thought, thinking how you were living through those difficult days. We are truly glad to be home among you again.

". . . The recent developments in our country have produced the most tragic events from hour to hour. As a soldier, I know what bloodshed can be caused in a conflict between civilians and an army with modern equipment. Consequently, as your President, I considered it my duty to do all I could to insure that this does not happen, that the blood of peoples who have always been friends is not spilled senselessly, and that at the same time the fundamental interests of our fatherland and its people are safeguarded.

"I do not want to hide the fact that painful wounds caused by these events will long remain. Yet we are truly interested in the renewal of confidence and sincere cooperation between countries linked by destiny and a common road. The place of our country in today's world is in the socialist community and cannot be anywhere else."

Then Svoboda began to lapse into a language which sounded like perfect Czech, but rang in the ear like translations from the pre-1956 Moscow *Pravda*:

". . . When I left for Moscow . . . I saw a *way-out* to the solution of this *complex situation* in the *expeditious normalization* of activity of legislative and other legitimate organs of our socialist state and society and their leading representatives."

He went on to say that the return of the leaders was "the first, but for us very important, step toward the *normalization* of the life of our country." He talked of *"gradual implementation* of the complete departure of the armies" and he warned that "together with the whole National Front, we want to carry on building our country as the real homeland of the working people. From these aims we shall never depart. Naturally, we shall not allow them to be misused by those to whom the interests of socialism are alien. To achieve this, we must now firmly organize our work."

When we had heard it all, the man-in-the-street asked: "What did he say?"

"He said nothing," said another.

"But when will the troops go away?"

"He said 'gradually.' "

"In the Russian dictionary, 'gradually' means fifty years."

An hour after Svoboda's speech, Prague was littered with leaflets bearing just one word—"TREASON!"—and I felt very sorry for this gallant soldier whom history might even condemn for the price he paid to save his nation and ransom its leaders.

I took the 134 bus home. The plain of Letná was down to a dozen tanks and four helicopters. This time, I mumbled "hydepark!" and my seatmate remarked that he expected to find Stalin's statue reappearing at the other end of Letná any day now.

In my neighborhood, there were only a few passing Russian vehicles to be seen, unless you knew where to look. Outside various Russian residences and district occupation headquarters, if you peered closely you would see as many as six tanks concealed in a garden.

Restaurants were open only until 1730 or 1800 so that the help could get home before curfew hour. I realized, as I passed the Golden Pear, that I had forgotten all about lunch, so I dropped in to catch an early supper. The two elderly waiters were surprised to see me and asked after my family and me.

"Evil days," I said, "but we are surviving. My family must be in Germany by now. And you?"

"Bad times," said the older of the two waiters. "My wife died."

"Ohhh," I said. "The Russians?"

"Yes and no. Her heart failed, but it was grief and shock."

"When?" I asked.

"This morning," he said. "The funeral is at the Crematorium the day after tomorrow. Will you have an aperitif?"

I was almost too shocked to speak. But then I realized that his life under capitalism, fascism, and communism must have always revolved around the restaurant and its customers. Small wonder, then, that he was at work. He had two homes in Prague—and the one he slept in was so sad and barren now. Today, with my family gone and myself deferring return to my solitary abode until curfew, I could empathize a little.

I ordered "Tartar beefsteak and a glass of Egrí Bíkavér."

The other old waiter told me with great dignity: "We call it *Steak Imperial* now, but yes we have it. We have no Bíkavér. We don't drink Hungarian wines any more. We do have Rumanian Cabernet." As he spoke, I could see bottles of Hungarian Bíkavér and Bulgarian Cabernet (which is better than Rumania's) starting to gather dust on his shelves. Even in an economy riddled with scarcities, the Czechs were fully capable of a boycott. I ordered the Rumanian red and ate quickly to make it home in time to hear Dubček.

When Dubček spoke, I knew the great dream was truly ending. His slightly gravelly voice was hoarse. The words were his, but delivered in a listless monotone which gradually came to be punctuated by deep breaths, long sighs, and choked tears. At one point, he asked his "dear citizens" for "a little interval before I finish my speech; I think you will know why it is." Some say he fainted; others say the doctor who was at his side gave him an injection that enabled him to go on.

As he spoke—saying that "what happened and what we lived through, the terror, we should forget" and "in a situation like this, it is not the time for free speech and free writing"—you never heard a man less convinced of what he was saying. And yet there was a moment when he heaved a wrenching sigh and said: "There was no other possibility."

When Dubček was done, Radio Free Prague played the fifteenth-century Hussite hymn sung by Jan Žižka's legions as they went into battle. We heard just the music, not the words articulating three recurrent themes: "Don't be afraid of your enemies . . . Power is not all . . . Truth will prevail." Although you might conceivably have guessed these themes from the stirring music, you really had to know what you were hearing before you could appreciate the message.

Thus, even in defiance, the free radio was turning discreet, and in the dark dreamless night that had come to Czechoslovakia, the blackest veil of all was brushing the lips of free expression. "We will not lie," Radio Free Prague promised as its return to normal operations neared. "We may not be able to broadcast the truth, but we will not lie."

Immediately thereafter, *Literární Listy* suspended publication with this statement: *"Literární Listy* will publish only when it is possible to work with one's convictions and conscience. We won't get into the politics of filtered truth." And then *LL* said goodbye in a code that we all understood: "We were with you. We are with you. Be with us."

PART SIX

Nemesis:
August Winter

The explorer thought to himself: It's always a ticklish matter to intervene decisively in other people's affairs. He was neither a member of the penal colony nor a citizen of the state to which it belonged. Were he to denounce this execution or actually try to stop it, they could say to him: You are a foreigner, mind your own business. He could make no answer to that, unless he were to add that he was amazed at himself in this connection, for he traveled only as an observer, with no intention at all of altering other people's methods of administering justice. Yet here he found himself strongly tempted. The injustice of the procedure and the inhumanity of the execution were undeniable.

Franz Kafka, *In the Penal Colony*

Interlude ⅂ Children of Wenceslas

ON THE AFTERNOON OF WEDNESDAY, 21 AUGUST 1968, A
young boy addressed a letter "To All Students of the World":

> As I write this, Soviet tanks are stationed in a large park under my
> windows. The barrels of their guns are trained on a Government build-
> ing adorned with a huge sign: *"For Socialism and Peace."* I remember
> hearing this slogan ever since I was able to grasp the meaning of ob-
> jects around me. But only during the last seven months has this slogan
> slowly acquired its original meaning. For seven months, my country
> has been led by men who wanted to prove, probably for the first time
> in the history of mankind, that socialism and democracy can exist side
> by side.
>
> Nobody knows where these men are now. I don't know whether
> I shall ever see or hear them again. There is much that I don't
> know. . . .
>
> I don't know, either, whether I shall be able to finish my studies or
> ever again meet my friends from abroad. I could carry on and on like
> this, but somehow everything seems to be losing its original value. At
> 3 o'clock this morning, I opened by eyes upon a world entirely dif-
> ferent from the one in which, only six hours before, I had gone to
> sleep.
>
> You will think, perhaps, that the Czech people have behaved like
> cowards because they didn't fight. But you cannot stand up to tanks
> with empty hands. . . . We may be broken physically, but not morally.
> This is why I write. The only way you can help is: Don't forget Czecho-
> slovakia. Please help our passive resistance by increasing the pressure
> of public opinion around the world. Think of Czechoslovakia even
> when this country ceases to be sensational news.

Over the weekend, *Student* had published it in a special underground
edition.

After hearing Dubček's sad speech on Tuesday the 27th, I braved
the impending curfew and made my way down to Wenceslas Square,

where thousands of young people were gathering angrily. I was sure I'd meet someone I knew, and there beneath the equestrian statue of Saint Wenceslas, I met the author of that eloquent letter.

His name was Václav. He was the spindly nineteen-year-old son of a man who worked directly under Dubček. I hadn't seen Václav since March, when he and his parents had visited our flat for cocktails and we'd all watched Goldstücker on TV together.

I congratulated him on his letter and wished him a fate less than martyrdom. But, glancing up at the statue above us, I couldn't help remarking that his very name, "Václav," is the Czech form of "Wenceslas."

Václav corrected me proudly: "On the contrary, Wenceslas is your English form of Václav."

He was not Good King Wenceslas as the British Christmas carol introduces him, but Good Prince Wenceslas, a brave pacifistic ruler who was murdered in 935 A.D. Not only did Wenceslas make the teachings of Christianity the law of his land, Bohemia, but he also practiced what was preached to him by Greek missionaries bearing the liturgy in Slavonic.

When a whole duchy rose in rebellion against him, Prince Wenceslas the Good challenged its ruling duke to fight him in man-to-man combat and thus spare the blood of others. And, convinced that war cost more than it won, Wenceslas bought peace for his small nation by pledging to pay the neighboring German warriors an annual ransom of 120 oxen and 500 marks.

Despite the prosperity that peace brought, Wenceslas' philosophy struck his warlike younger brother Boleslav as shameful. And so Boleslav, known in his time as Young Boleslav the Cruel, had Good Prince Wenceslas stabbed to death while he was on his way to High Mass. Young Boleslav thereupon refused to pay the annual pledge to the German Emperor Henry the Fowler. Instead, Boleslav used the money to raise an army which fought so well and so long that, after many years, the Germans were forced to relinquish their claim. But both Germany and Bohemia were ravaged and ruined by the war. Before the tenth century was out, the farsighted Wenceslas had been sainted.

More than a millennium after Wenceslas' death, the Red Army picked a location to garrison 5,000 of the troops it was pulling out of

Prague under the terms of the agreement negotiated in Moscow. This community's main assets were that it already had an army base (from which 5,000 Czech and Slovak soldiers could be evicted) and it was only one hour by tank from Prague. The town (population: 25,600) chosen by Marshals Grechko and Yakubovsky, with their customary flair for symbolism, was Bohemia's only memorial to Wenceslas' treacherous kid brother. Its name is Mladá Boleslav, meaning "Young Boleslav."*

Beneath the best known of many monuments to Saint Wenceslas, his namesake Václav said to me on 27 August 1968:

"All of us here—we were, we are, we always will be the children of Wenceslas. We'll die to defend what we believe in, but when it no longer exists, then we'll live to fight another day."

"Then why this?" I said, pointing to boys and girls who were lighting candles and unfurling a banner that proclaimed: "SOONER DEAD THAN LIVING ON OUR KNEES!"

"Because we never were the children of communism; because we're no longer Dubček's children," Václav began bitterly, "and because only the National Assembly hasn't discredited itself—yet! So we're going to march on the Assembly building to try to keep them in line."

While we waited for them to march, I asked Václav: "What does your father think of what's happened?"

"They just let him back into the Central Committee building yesterday afternoon," Václav replied, "and he was surprised to find nobody else occupying his desk. He says that all the other Dubček men who've come back keep saying 'We must stick together and not permit a return to the 1950's.' But my father tells them not to worry. He says 'we're not going back to the 1950's. We're on an express train back to the 1940's, a military occupation by Soviet fascism, even if all you'll see will be the puppets dancing.' "

"Then is your father going to quit?" I wondered.

"No," said Václav, "he says that, just because you know what the end will be, you can't do anything that'll hasten the end or make it easier for the Russians. He's loyal to Dubček, so he'll stay as long as Dubček stays."

"Do you agree?" I asked Václav.

"I don't know yet. I do know that's the lesson he and his generation

---

* The whole town of Milovice (population: 4500), also within an hour's tank ride of Prague, became a garrison for another 25,000 Soviet troops.

seem to have learned from 1948, when all the non-Communist ministers except Jan Masaryk resigned and made it a cinch for Gottwald to
take power."

"Do you think that's the lesson your generation has learned?"

"I'm really not sure," he said, as the command to march was given.
"Maybe my generation doesn't want to learn any new lessons. Maybe it
wants to teach the world a lesson or two."

I followed Václav in the candlelight procession from the Wenceslas
statue to the Parliament offices in Maxim Gorki Square, a quarter-mile
away. The crowd was well over 3,000 by then.

When nobody in Parliament responded to their shouts, one of Václav's companions shinnied up a lamppost and called into an upstairs
window: "We ask you to reject the Moscow agreement! Our negotia-
tors were not free men! They were prisoners!"

An official came out to warn them: "Don't offer any provocation or
the tanks will kill you."

"To hell with the tanks!" a student cried. "If there are enough of
us, they won't shoot!"

Before anybody could test this dangerous logic, a youthful and popular parliamentary deputy with horn-rimmed glasses, Alois Poledňák,
appeared at the window with a megaphone and said: "Parliament
doesn't accept the agreement worked out in Moscow because it is tantamount to capitulation before aggression. We will never accept what
has been done to our freedom and sovereignty, believe me! We will not
kneel. But now you must go home quietly."

The crowd booed and someone shouted: "Let the Russians go home
quietly!"

Eventually, the crowd did disband and Parliament did keep
Poledňák's word by passing a resolution condemning the occupation as
"illegal" and insisting upon "the establishment and consistent fulfillment of specific time limits for the speediest possible withdrawal of
foreign troops from our country."* It was yet another last gasp. The
Prague Spring was dying but the children of Wenceslas still had ways
in store to remind the world what had been lost.

---

* In 1969, Poledňák was removed as a National Assembly deputy and from his
other post, czar of the Czechoslovak film industry. This was an administrative job
in which he had, many months before the Prague Spring, opened the gates of
Barrandov Studios to freer expression and created a climate of creativity that the
Western world labeled "the Czechoslovak film renaissance." In 1970 Poledňák was
jailed on charges of "misappropriating State funds" in his film post. In 1971 he was
sentenced to two years in prison for "subversion."

Chapter 17]

Wednesday 4 September—
Tuesday 24 September 1968

> Leaflets stuck to walls and otherwise distributed have appeared in
> Prague (and perhaps also in other towns) containing a text said to be
> the content of the Moscow agreements. The Czechoslovak News Agency
> has been authorized to state that the text of these fabricated leaflets
> does not correspond to the content of the Moscow agreements, whose
> real character was made known to the public in the communique on
> the meeting of the Central Committee of the Communist Party of
> Czechoslovakia of 31 August, the earlier speeches of President Svoboda,
> First Secretary . . . Dubček, Prime Minister Černík, and Josef Smrkov-
> ský, Speaker of the National Assembly, as well as in the communique
> on the results of the Moscow talks of 26 August, signed in Moscow. The
> fabricated leaflets contain a false, inciting text aimed at causing unrest
> and anger in the population.
>
> —official announcement: 4 Sept. 68

The Prague grapevine had taken back its old job from the legal
radio, TV, and press. But the grapevine was no longer a slender thread
of table-hopping at the Chinsky Restaurant or the Café Slavia. It was
now a fat and sassy mass medium which erupted all over town with
whatever truths and rumors could be gleaned. And, because the grapevine's followers now numbered almost everybody, both its sources and
its resources were vaster than they had ever been. Its reliability was
high, which was more than could be said of the official communiques.
The announcement quoted above, for instance, did not say who'd authorized the Četeka News Agency to denounce the grapevine. We knew
that, immediately upon his return, Prime Minister Černík had dismissed Četeka director Sulek, who'd tried to proclaim a Revolutionary
Workers and Peasants Government on the teletype. But we didn't
know anything yet about the integrity of his replacement.*

---

* He had at least enough to get fired himself a few months later. His son, a student,
was imprisoned late in 1969 as a "Trotskyist."

The fact was that the only substantial information to be gleaned from the various speeches about what went on in Moscow was the depth of sorrow in their delivery. There were few, if any, details.

The fact was that virtually all the details "fabricated" by the grapevine were borne out by subsequent events.

The grapevine had it that the "Moskow Diktat" (so Germanically renamed in Prague to remind one of Munich thirty years earlier) listed fifteen basic conditions. Some of them were already known: the invalidating of the Extraordinary Fourteenth Congress and withdrawal of the United Nations protest. Others were pledges of fealty: by Czechoslovakia to the world Communist camp and specifically to the Soviet model . . . by Russia to the spirit of the January, March, and May Central Committee sessions in Prague (though it was this spirit that the troops came to subdue) . . . and by both sides to the Čierna and Bratislava agreements! It was also specified that Czechoslovakia would not pursue an independent line in foreign affairs.

Paragraph 4 of the Moscow Diktat stated:

> Priority is to be given to control over the mass media, which must fully serve the cause of socialism. It is agreed that the mass media will discontinue anti-socialist pronouncements and an end will be put to the activity of groups advocating anti-socialist activities. . . .

This ended the existence of KAN an K231.

Other paragraphs banned the use of the words "occupation" and "invasion." (The Diktat itself referred to them as "the timely and effective measures," a phrase which the censored Czech press took up, along with "Befriendment" and "August Assistance.") The Red Army's presence or whereabouts were to be mentioned only in the most favorable and authorized circumstances.* And there was to be no criticism of the Moscow Diktat itself. To "insure Soviet-Czechoslovak friendship," it was agreed that "all contacts between leaders of both nations after 20 August 1968, including the present talks, shall be considered as strictly secret."

Some versions of the Moscow Diktat listed three other provisos:

---

* As late as 1969, the Czech press circumvented this by reporting in uncharacteristic depth, space, and prominence the attempted rape of a railway switchgirl by "a foreign visitor." The accounts stressed that consummation was thwarted by A) the victim's resistance, B) the arrival of fellow workers to rescue her, and C) the difficulties encountered by the would-be rapist because both he and his victim were wearing uniforms.

. . . Any disturbance in Czechoslovakia henceforth will be taken as evidence of inefficiency on the part of the Czechoslovak leadership [and, by implication, grounds for its removal].

. . . A register of counter-revolutionary forces will be kept by security organs as well as a roster of those who aided them.

. . . Any resistance will be put down by brute force.

The Czechoslovak leadership "pledged to examine the activities of those members of the Government who have been abroad and spoken on behalf of the Czechoslovak Government on internal and foreign issues," spelling the departure of Foreign Minister Hájek and Deputy Premier Šik.*

The Moscow Diktat also specified that "there will be a check on the Ministry of the Interior and new measures to strengthen its leadership." At the end of August, General Pavel was summoned to Hradčany to tender his resignation as Interior Minister. On his way out, he stood for a moment in the gathering gloom of the Castle's second courtyard at dusk. I saw this in a newsreel a week later and, on the sound track, the commentator said simply: "Pavel. Again a wanderer in the garden." †

Let it never be said that the Moscow Diktat ignored the fact that 1968 was International Human Rights Year. It specified:

The Czechoslovak leaders will not permit the discharge from their functions or reprisals against those party functionaries who have advocated socialism, friendly relations with the Soviet Union, and constant struggle against anti-Communist elements.

Which meant the rights of Indra and Bil'ak not to be prosecuted for treason.

* It took the Soviets almost a month to dislodge Hájek from the Černin Palace. He went back to university teaching, but continued to express himself well into 1969, when he told an academic gathering in Olomouc: "I am deeply convinced that the 21st of August 1968 will be recognized as a mistake." Then the newest Czech Minister of Interior started making sinister allegations about "much that is unclear about the conduct of former Foreign Minister Professor Hájek" and the "lonely long-distance runner" was purged from Party and university. In 1970, Hájek was reportedly being interrogated by police and certainly under investigation, but I still saw him periodically strolling with his family, lunching at the Film Club or running in the park . . . Šik sent in his resignation from Belgrade in September before going on to Basle. Although he made several abortive returns, he is now an exile who has been stripped of his Czechoslovak citizenship.
† At this writing, Pavel, 62, lives quietly outside Prague growing strawberries in his garden and looking unconcerned about Western rumors that he'll be tried for treason.

There remained the questions of how many troops would stay how long, and the Moscow Diktat did nothing to answer them:

> The command of the allied troops and the Czechoslovak Army will immediately discuss questions concerning the departure and movement of military units from towns and villages where local authorities can ensure public order.

> The number of troops involved, their organization and deployment will be discussed with the Czechoslovak Army leaders.

There was a glancing reference to the troops leaving once and for all only after "consolidation" of the situation here. But much more attention was paid to "supplies and medical services for the troops" being detailed by an agreement to be drawn up "with the Ministries of Defense and Foreign Affairs. Major disputes will be resolved at the Government level."

In the last of its clandestine issues, the Catholic daily *People's Democracy* quoted a high Government official as saying: "We are told that foreign troops will withdraw when the situation is normal again. But it will not become normal until the troops have withdrawn. This is a vicious circle for which neither side can find a way out." The article was headlined "NORMALIZATION? KAFKA LIVES!"

The Moscow Diktat also contained a vague passage about reparations. But while the Czechs and Slovaks were still counting their casualties and estimating their damages, the Warsaw Pact Armies presented Czechoslovakia with an unitemized bill for $50 million occupation costs, and then assured the Czechoslovaks that, if they'd turn in a bill for the same sum, both expense accounts would cancel each other out and then the whole "Befriendment" wouldn't cost anybody a kopeck.*

I can tell you a story about reparations involving someone I know: an old farmer we met during our summer on the Sázava river. After the Moscow Diktat was signed, a Soviet battalion that had been moved out of Prague bivouacked in the surrounding fields. The farmer kept his distance, but one day a couple of Russian enlisted men appeared and told him: "We are hungry. We are taking one of your pigs." The farmer objected until the Russians pointed their carbines at him. He

---

* Material damages to Czechs and Slovaks have been estimated at $25 million, not to mention 77 dead and 1,000 wounded.

let them take a pig, but he asked them to pay for it. Again the guns were pointed.

The farmer said no more about the matter until he went home from the field that night and told his wife that they now had one fewer pig.

"They can't do that to us!" his wife insisted. "Under the Moscow Agreement, we must be paid. You must go to Benešov and see their commander."

The next morning, the farmer put on his best suit and went to town. A Russian officer listened to his tale and then asked: "If you saw those two soldiers again, would you recognize them?"

The farmer said he would. The officer took him to the next formation of the unit near his farm. The farmer walked through the ranks and, when he spotted the two culprits standing stiffly side-by-side, he identified them.

The officer unholstered his pistol and, with two shots through the head, killed both enlisted men.

The farmer fainted. When he regained consciousness, he protested to the officer: "What have you done? All I wanted was for them to pay me for my pig!"

"Never mind," said the Russian officer. "Now they have paid."

That night at home, the farmer suffered a heart attack, and I heard his story the next time I happened to inquire after his health.

Czechoslovak TV resumed "normal broadcasting" on the 4th of September, by which time censorship required that the routine announcement of Eduard Goldstücker's departure to Sussex be coupled with a denunciation of him from Moscow's *Literaturnaya Gazeta* as "a liberal of many faces" and a criminal who systematically paved the ideological ground for "counter-revolution." The Russian tirade was read by an announcer with solemn disgust while the camera belied these words by illustrating them with a retrospective last look at the Goldstücker TV had taught us to love: motion-picture footage of Goldstücker exhorting a crowd, Goldstücker arguing with students, Goldstücker defending Kafka, and Goldstücker displaying before-and-after photos. Then came slow-motion shots of Goldstücker in the throes of free expression and finally stills, close-ups of that unshaven, handsome, suffering face which, alas, was no longer among us.

TV's commentators looked gaunt and grieving while they delivered their lines in monotones. The newscasters seldom looked up from the sheafs of copy they were reading. But TV was still good to watch, for there was as much mobile footage as ever. We saw Dubček coming to work at the Central Committee and there was a famous girl singer waiting anonymously in a throng of women who came to present him with flowers. Dubček shook hands with each lady, but didn't smile. He was a man in mourning now, but many of our hearts leaped at the sight of him walking free. For we had grieved for this good man, knowing in our hearts that he was already dead, and now he was back among us. Good men still lived!

(Václav's father told me later about Dubček's first days back in the office after his return from Moscow: "When you're a few years younger than the man you work for, you can't help comparing your own condition with his. Well, physically, Dubček astonished me by being in better shape after his ordeal than I was from a week spent mostly at home. Emotionally, though, it was different; and each day, you could see the color ebbing from his face and watch him getting older." Just from watching TV, I could tell that his hair had receded since I'd seen him last [on 16 August!] and it now had a shock of white that wasn't there before.)

The time lag between filming and videocasting was as long as 48 hours, indicating that the rusty mechanism of censorship was starting up creakily. (There was, it turned out, great difficulty hiring censors.) And there were moments which you knew were uncensored, such as the "flower broadcast" that blossomed suddenly on the second night of "normal" telecasting. Around 2145, a movie finished and then TV cameras panned around a cluttered studio with music stands, lighting equipment, unused cameras, tools, and piles of letters casually strewn about. A title flashed on the screen: "BE WITH US; WE ARE WITH YOU." Now the camera whirled to one corner of the room and zeroed in on three men perched on stools. They were the three most outspoken commentators of the gloriously clandestine TV period.

There were no introductions. "The people have been asking what became of us," said the first commentator. "We are here before you. But we must have no false illusions. We cannot back up our ideals."

The second, the man who'd coined the slogan "Be with us; we are with you" said: "You may have been hearing about the 'escape' of our various colleagues to the West. Do not believe all you hear. They went abroad legally and they'll be back. The place of a journalist is here, not somewhere else."

And the third man said: "The Spring was the best time. In the Spring, the flowers at last blossomed and then you could smell the petals and see them in the air you breathed. But then came the wind and the petals began to blow away. The seed was withering down. But tonight I tell you that the seed is still left. And from the plant may yet come new flowers."

Then they were gone. It was as quick as that.

Every night, the newscasts sounded more like the winter baseball roundups—except that the deals were never to the home team's advantage. Dubček was insisting on token payments for each sacrifice he made. Thus, when Hejzlar and Pelikán were removed from the radio and TV, editor Švestka was replaced at *Rudé Právo* by the man who'd edited the clandestine *Rudé Právo* a fortnight earlier.* When Dr. Hájek was finally pried loose from the Foreign Ministry, his formal resignation was coupled with the announcement that "at the proposal of the Government, President Svoboda also recalled Mr. Karel Hoffmann from his office as head of the Central Board of Communications." †

Minister of Culture and Information Galuška was stripped of his title's second half which, under the circumstances, was acceptable to him because the word "information" now meant "censorship."

In early September, Čestmír Císař was "fully released" from the Communist Party Secretariat in order to devote full time to another job he held: chairman of the Czech National Council, an organization working—within the framework of one Czecho-Slovak Socialist Republic—toward federalization, or two separate but equal governments in the Czech Lands and Slovakia. This was, on the surface, a removal from power, but federalization was due to be realized at New Year's. *If* federalization were to happen and *if* the elections scheduled to follow were not proclaimed, then Císař's interim role would become one of longer-range influence. The wily Císař (or his advisers) gambled on both "ifs," and thereby prolonged his official life.

The tormented Dr. Kriegel was dropped from the Presidium, but so

---

* Švestka was demoted to the editorship of an inconsequential party magazine called *Tribuna,* which quickly assumed a measure of importance as an indicator of what Bil'ak and Indra and their supporters were up to.
† Hoffmann was restored to this post in 1969.

were Švestka, Kolder, Rigo, and Barbírek (the last was demoted to alternate membership).

Dr. Kriegel also lost his post as head of the National Front, but he kept his seats in the National Assembly and Central Committee. His political future, though, was clearly so limited that he returned to his medical practice on a full-time basis.

Špaček kept his Presidium seat. Another liberal, Prague party leader Šimon, was elevated from alternate to full Presidium member. Bil'ak and the conservative Piller kept their seats but Bil'ak was replaced as boss of the Slovak Communist Party. His successor was Gustáv Husák. At the time, this seemed like a liberal victory.

During a two-day meeting of the Central Committee on the weekend after the leaders' return from Moscow, both the Central Committee and its Presidium had been expanded. The Presidium had gone from eleven members to twenty-one—the newcomers including Husák and President Svoboda plus a number of liberals, centrists, and unknowns. The one-hundred-ten-man Central Committee had "co-opted" eighty-seven new members—*all* of whom had been delegates to the Extraordinary (and now illegal) Party Congress and were therefore, presumably, liberals.

At that same Central Committee session, Dubček had uttered a self-criticism of sorts: "We didn't take into consideration the strategic interests of our allies. We didn't see the *real* facts. We began to question our confidence in the Soviet leaders' ways of solving problems. In this way, the trust of the Soviet Union in our party leadership was diminished, too. The most important task before us now is to dispel this lack of trust in us." But he didn't recant and he wouldn't repudiate the Prague Spring.

The Russians, it now seemed clear, had settled upon the "salami tactic." They would whittle away at the Czechoslovak Revolution until nothing would be left except the empty shell, and perhaps the skins of the leaders who (the Russians hoped) would have long since lost the esteem of the public. And Dubček would play this losing game as long as he could, but as slowly as he could.

I recognized, too, that I might possibly be drafted into this delaying game as a pawn thrown out to slow the repression. I knew the Czechs well enough by now to even anticipate the script in negotiating with the Russians: "Look, instead of arresting some students, why don't we just expel a couple of foreign journalists instead?" It was the kind of very Czech compromise that would placate everybody—except me.

I decided to make it as hard as possible for them to find any excuse to do this to me by confining my magazine articles about Czechoslovakia to cultural affairs. That would be safe, for a while.

Without a family here, I was adrift in a Prague I'd never really known. There were fewer and fewer Russians to be seen each day, but the parks they'd vacated still stank of Czech disinfectants and we had no illusions that an invisible occupation would be any less brutal than the other kind. The new movies in town were all films I'd seen before (Audrey Hepburn in *My Fair Lady;* Claude Berri's *The Two of Us*) that I knew my kids were now old enough to enjoy. Czechs weren't eating out much these days and the restaurants welcomed me as though I were the only tourist in town (and an American one at that!) with five or six waiters tripping over each other to practice their English and serve my solitary soul. At home, our very kind neighbors' cooking left nothing to be desired—except my wife's.

Telephone service to and from the West was worse than ever, and Valerie and I had one audible conversation during our first fortnight apart. She wanted to know whether to rent an apartment she'd found in Bad Godesberg and whether to enroll the girls in school there. "No!" I screamed, and before the connection broke, we agreed in principle that as soon as Lufthansa (not ČSA) deemed it safe to resume service between Frankfurt and Prague, my family would come flying home.

Valerie's question about school gave me a new realm to explore in occupied Prague. My children being trilingual by now, we had a choice of three kinds of schooling here: Czechoslovak, American, and French. I ruled out the Czech public schools right away because the pressures were already starting. General Ivan G. Pavlovsky, the Warsaw Pact Supreme Commander in Czechoslovakia, had denounced the Czechoslovak educational system as a "nest of counter-revolution" and accused the teachers of trying to destroy a love for the Soviet Union which ran deep in the heart of Czechoslovak children. Red Army political officers, seeking to enter classes in Prague and address the students on opening day, were turned away by teachers. Instead, the soldiers were distributing propaganda booklets to pupils on the streets as they left

school. And General Pavlovsky was threatening bluntly to send paratroops into the schools unless the teachers took a more favorable attitude toward the Soviet Union.

The International School at the American Embassy, down the hill
from us, had British, Indian, West German, and Japanese pupils as
well as State Department kids and American teachers. Tuition was
$300 per semester per child; hours 0900 to 1200 for kindergarten, 0900
to 1500 for all other grades. I liked the idea of keeping Monica and
Erika in contact with their roots, but on previous visits there I'd formed
the vague impression that the children were running the school.

The French Cultural Institute, down the block from the Hotel Alcron, was on the other side of the river from us, but it was a known
quantity. With the exception of a course in Czechoslovak geography
and history thrown in as a gesture toward the host nation, the French
school offered a strict but solid standard education on the same clock-
work timetable that enables the Minister of Education in Paris to
glance at his watch and know exactly what is being taught in every
classroom in his domain. Provisionally, I enrolled both my children in
the French School's kindergarten for four-to-six year olds: Monica,
who'd be five in October, and Erika, who'd be four in November,
would thus both be together for their first academic year.* Tuition was
$16 per month: hours, 0830 to 1300.

I made this choice without consulting Valerie because communications were so spotty. I think I chose not only for my children's sake, but
for my own needs: Rebuilding my rowboat into the sturdy Noah's Ark
needed to carry us through the Deluge intact, I wanted to give us all a
pillar as rigid as Charles de Gaulle to cling to.

Sylva dropped up to cook me a duck on the afternoon of 12 September. "Are you still a working journalist?" I'd ask her each time we met.
The answer always was yes, but this time more emphatically than ever.
The debut of *Zítřek* had been deferred for a month, but it was going
to publish at the beginning of October. *Zítřek* had been granted a
license *before* the invasion—and nobody had countermanded it.

* The children were as happy as *escargots* during their year together in the French
kindergarten. Monica has thrived on French education and, at this writing—two years
later—she's been "skipped" into the French equivalent of our third grade. To avoid
sibling rivalry, Erika transferred in early 1970 to the kindergarten at the American
school, which improved drastically when a new headmaster, Donald E. Kessler, took
over in 1969. In September, 1970, my wife went there, too, for three mornings a week
as French teacher at the American School.

Over an early dinner, we tuned in television and caught the last part of a special performance marking the resumption of concert activities after the invasion. The selection was, inevitably, Smetana's *My Country,* played by the Czech Philharmonic.

The two final movements of *My Country,* "Tábor" and "Blaník," are based on one majestic Hussite hymn, "Ye Warriors of God." It is a melody which resounded frequently through the walled fortress of Tábor. But Smetana also applied it to the sacred mountain of Blaník, where the defeated Hussites are supposed to wait, in deep slumber, for the time when they will again be summoned to the aid of their land. Gently, the hymn surges into a march and then the thunderous glory of the resurrection of the Czech nation.

TV's concert camerawork, which usually focuses on conductor and musicians, did not pay much heed to Karel Ančerl and his orchestra. Instead, it wandered about Smetana Hall picking up audience faces just as they dissolved into tears. Sylva and I saw strong men weeping . . . a young boy, uncomfortable in coat and tie, putting his finger into his collar to give himself breathing room and then yielding to choking gasps . . . a spinsterish lady sobbing widow's sobs . . . and others, striving mightily for restraint, clutching their neighbors' arms for support.

It was more than television. It was all music and emotion and, of course, Sylva and I wept, too. When it was over, we could see our own gratitude reflected in the tears on those faces of concertgoers and we found ourselves applauding at home, too, as if to thank Ančerl and Smetana for affording the Czechoslovak people that last vestige of free expression: a good cry.

The *quid pro quo* for General Pavel's ouster as Interior Minister proved to be the dismissal of his treacherous deputy, Šalgovič. The two events were not linked on the newscasts, but the announcement of his removal also specified that he had fled the country he'd betrayed and that the State prosecutor would prefer charges against him if he ever came back. The Prague grapevine had it that Šalgovič was in Dresden preparing the "evidence" for future trials involving three different "anti-state espionage centers: the journalists, the economists, and the Jews."

"I'm not the least bit worried," a Jewish economist, who dabbled in journalism, told me. "Šalgovič wouldn't dare show his face in this country and, in case he did, he's the one who'd be in danger—not I. But, if you ever hear that he's back in Czechoslovakia and crawling back into power, would you mind giving me a phone call?"

I said I would, for Šalgovič was certainly a triple threat who bore watching—and I knew that the economist would be preoccupied with salvaging the wreckage of Ota Šik's economic reforms while the nation started helplessly back down the old road to ruin.

To help sustain the economy, the Brno Trade Fair, scheduled for the first week in September, opened only a week behind schedule. The official invitation would serve as a safe-conduct pass and an excuse for me to glimpse provincial "normalization" in passing. With an American journalist who'd rented a Ford Cortina from Avis-Pragocar, I made the six-hour drive to Brno.

Along the way, we stopped for coffee in the town of Havlíčkův Brod, and two old codgers came over to our table to inquire: "Are you Americans?" When we said yes, they asked: "Are you here to liberate us?"

"I wish we were," I said, "but no. The best I can do is share your sadness and tell about it."

"One day," said one of them, "your black soldiers will come again to liberate us. I was in Pilsen in 1945. . . ."

This longing for armed Negroes in their streets was not something these farmers shared with their white American counterparts.

In a field just outside Havlíčkův Brod, we were treated to an unexpected display of Soviet weaponry. We came upon fifty Russian soldiers standing with automatic rifles pointed toward the road, though aimed aloft. We slowed down to see what they were guarding, which turned out to be fifty more Russian soldiers urinating in the field. When an officer gave a command, the fifty men in the field buttoned up their flies and picked up their rifles while the other fifty men stacked arms and watered the crops themselves.

"No wonder," said my companion, "Tass calls them the 'relieving armies.'"

At the opening ceremony in Brno, the Foreign Trade Minister (or highest-ranking representative) of each participating nation was introduced. There was no applause (but no booing, either) for the Russian, Polish, Hungarian, East German, and Bulgarian officials. There was loud applause for the British and French and, particularly, Rumanian and Yugoslav delegates. Like the Bohemians of Prague, the Moravians of Brno knew how to express themselves discreetly but clearly.

On display at the Trade Fair were the latest Polish Fiats and Bulgarian Renaults (made under licensing agreements) . . . a workman-like Yugoslavian washing machine . . . and a brand-new Hungarian computer, in front of which stood a young hostess wearing on her ample bosom a provocative red button that said, in eight languages, "ASK ME ANYTHING!"

"Tell us," I heard a man from Brno ask her, "how many counter-revolutionaries there were in Czechoslovakia a month ago and how many there are now?"

"We specialize in data retrieval," she replied primly, "not ideology." But, to her credit, she blushed.

The Polish journalist who had protested my "lengthy" chat with Dubček in April was at the Brno Fair in September. He had continued filing "hate" dispatches during the intervening months and, therefore, as soon as he arrived in Brno, he was joined by a uniformed Polish Army lieutenant who escorted and guarded him all the time he was there.

I myself had a Russian escort. When I checked into the press billets at the Hotel Družba* on Lenin Street, I was asked if I would mind sharing my room with another journalist. My roommate proved to be a friendly, apple-cheeked Russian, thirtyish, in a gray flannel suit. He worked for the Novosti news agency, he said, handing me his calling card. He spoke excellent English and the first thing he said in it was that he hoped his presence didn't embarrass me.

"Not at all," I said. "Maybe the Moravians put us together because they want the Big Powers to settle the Czechoslovak question once and for all."

He laughed, but a little later he asked me for a favor. "I just got here from Moscow," he said. "So someone must tell me what is true and what isn't. Was there a counter-revolution here?"

"Not before the 21st of August," I replied.

"This K231? Was it infiltrated by Nazis?"

"I suppose one or two may have crept in. Everyone with a prison

---

* The word *družba* in old Slovak meant "best man at a wedding" while in Russian it means "friendship." Since 1948, the Soviet meaning has predominated and many enterprises had their capitalist names transformed into Družba.

record would like to have been a political prisoner. But most of these people, just about all of them, I'd say, are people who got a bad deal from the State in the 1950's. No matter what the State gave them now, it couldn't give them back what they lost."

"And my two colleagues, Zavarikin and Nepomnyaschit, whose press helicopter was shot down and they burned to death. Who killed them?"

"The Russians say their helicopter was shot down. The Czechs say the helicopter exploded in mid-air and crashed. I'm inclined to believe the Czechs. . . ."

"And I'm inclined to believe the Russians," he said. "I knew both of those men."

"Look!" I said. "Just consider the number of troops who were put into this little country overnight. Over a period of three days, it came to more men than the United States has put into Vietnam in six years. But very few people died. Now that's a credit, in a way, to your army as well as a credit to the Czechs—because, in such a situation, there are bound to be clashes. Can you go along with my line of reasoning thus far?"

"Of course," he murmured.

"Now do you suppose that the death toll could have been so relatively low if the Czechs had been toting weapons or sharpshooting at helicopters? And, besides, it just isn't their style of resistance."

"No, it isn't," he admitted. "I've been here before and I've read all four volumes of *Schweik*. They do things differently."

He asked at least fifty more questions—about KAN, *Literární Listy*, Ivan Sviták, General Prchlík, everything!—and I answered as knowledgeably as I could. Later, we went drinking at Brno's Hotel International, where a good rock band wearing turtlenecks, and an excellent girl singer wearing leopardskin slacks, did a creditable "Yellow Submarine." All sorts of businessmen were dancing lumpily with girls they weren't married to. Across the room, U. S. Ambassador Beam was wining and dining a large party.

"They call Brno the Manchester of Moravia," my Russian friend remarked, soaking up this scene.

"It looks like Dusseldorf East to me," I said.

We talked much more, and, in the early morning hours just before retiring, he thanked me and said: "Most of our people at home don't know any of these facts."

I said: "I hope you believe me."

"I do. And I'll still believe you when I go. But I think that, after two or three days among my associates, I'll begin to believe again that my friends in the helicopter were shot down by Czechs. So forgive me for that. And I won't forget all that you said. I'll try to measure events here by those truths." He started to say good night, but then he interrupted himself: "You know, my friends and I, we who travel, are the ones I start to feel most sorry for. The other people don't know the truth and it's fairly easy to live with lies when they're reasonably consistent. But we have to shuttle between truth and lies."

"It must be a terrible trip," I said, "and that's why I feel so sorry for the Czechs. They're just starting on the return leg."

He gave me a look of sorrow that wasn't a man's, but a trapped animal's. Yet, because he was a man, he held my gaze almost commandingly, and it seemed as if he wanted me to remember that look. . . .

A few months later, a trusted Czech journalist friend of mine went to Moscow on business. I took the liberty of giving him a letter of introduction to take along. My Czech friend happened to be visiting the Novosti office early in his stay. There, he asked for my Russian acquaintance from Brno. The editors had never heard of him.

My Czech friend's first reaction was: "Uh-oh! Siberia for him for listening to Alan!" He stopped asking about the poor chap, but one of his own friends in Novosti asked to see the name and telephone number.

"Don't pursue the matter," the Novosti official warned my Czech friend. "That's an NKVD number. We have no control or knowledge of who gets press cards and calling cards from us. He must have been in Brno to compile dossiers."

I didn't know any of this when I left Brno on the third Sunday in September. It is always thrilling to return to Prague from anywhere, but never more so than when I came home to find a telegram waiting: "LUFTHANSA FLYING AND SO ARE LEVYS. SEE YOU 1030 MONDAY, LOVE VALERIMONICA."

They landed at Ruzyně just in time for the opening of the French School* and for Monica's fifth birthday party. The party was really an

---

* One of our friends in New York, whose schools were shut down by strikes from September to November, wrote that she envied "the undisturbed education your little girls must be getting in Prague."

"open house reunion" and it seemed as if everybody we knew in Prague was there: the Doctor with her husband, daughter, and son-in-law-to-be; they brought a whole miniature puppet theatre complete with heroes, devils, and a wizard who the kids insisted was "the wicked witch with a beard" . . . a neighbor with a charm bracelet that included Dubček and Svoboda . . . our cleaning lady, Paní B., with a beautiful book of Czech nursery rhymes in English (subcontracted in Prague by a London publisher) . . . and, of course, our children's playmates and schoolmates. Sylva appeared with a box of candy and sent a very ornate Art Nouveau telegram (available at every Prague post office). It was Monica's first telegram and she was almost as proud of it as we were of her when she was able to sign for it.

With each gift there was a card or else a few spoken words of gratitude for my staying on throughout and my family's coming back to share the thin as well as the thick with the Czechs. And we could only say that we would stay on in Prague as long as the authorities would let us, which we hoped would be forever-and-a-day.

Interlude ⅂   Song of Comenius

THE GIFT THAT JIRKA ŠLITR GAVE MONICA FOR HER birthday was what he called "a 45-counter-revolutions-per-minute" Supraphon record in Czech of a choking, torchy ballad that went:

> May there be peace in this land;
> May malice, envy, fear, and conflict go away;
> May the direction of your affairs be returned
>   thy hands again, O Czech people!

It was an unlikely lyric, but the song—conceived in the heat of August's invasion—became the reigning pop hit of Czechoslovakia. It was also an unlikely gift, for the song was by neither Šlitr nor Suchý and it was, in fact, about to dethrone their waltzing "Pink Rose" from the top of the charts.

The new champion was titled "Marta's Prayer" in honor of its interpreter, Marta Kubišová, twenty-six. The land's third-ranked female vocalist (behind Eva Pilarová, and Helena Vondráčková) until she sounded her "Prayer," Marta not only zoomed to Number One overnight, but also became a national heroine and a target for the Russian cultural plainclothesmen who were reportedly arriving to "normalize" the intellectuals. There was, however, little that could be done to silence a song that was on everybody's lips.

The lyricist for "Marta's Prayer" was the unlikeliest of all counter-revolutionaries, Jan Amos Komenský (1592–1670), best-known as the pedagogue Comenius, "Teacher of Nations." Born in Moravia and dead nearly 300 years, Comenius wrote the words after 1620, when the Habsburg victory in the Battle of Bílá Hora (White Mountain) just outside Prague doomed the Czech Lands to three centuries of German domination. His line about "the direction of your affairs" is also carved into the base of the Jan Hus monument in Prague's Old Town Square.

His success as a pop-song writer might have pleased Comenius, who championed relating education to everyday life by teaching in the vernacular and emphasizing contact with the environment. Every child who picks up any kind of Illustrated First Reader today is holding a direct descendant of Comenius' *Orbis Pictus* ("The World in Pictures"), the first such text for children. How far ahead of his times Comenius was and how slow the world was to respond to his ideas is evidenced by Goethe's recollection of his own childhood a century later: "There were no books for young people. . . . Except for *Orbis Pictus,* no book of that kind reached my hands."

By the time *Orbis Pictus* and his greatest work, *Didactica Magna,* were published, Comenius was a prophet banished from his native land. He moved on to England, Sweden, and elsewhere, championing educational reform, equal opportunities for women, and a handful of other causes, before dying in Holland* still believing that "if all men were to learn all things in all ways, all men would be wise, and the world would be full of order, light, and peace."

When Jirka Šlitr quoted this to me, he added with a half-laugh: "If you think we can sell this to Pat Boone, Alan, let me know and I'll write the music."

Šlitr's involvement in the success of Comenius and Kubišová, however, was strictly inspirational. The censorship apparatus was starting up so slowly and with such emphasis on the press that it would take some time before theatre and film would be molested.

At first, with the Semafor closed and signers of the "2,000 Words" rumored to be facing imminent persecution, Šlitr had stayed away from his villa and holed up in a loft he'd rented somewhere on Wenceslas Square, painting in such privacy that not even Sylva knew his studio's address.

But then, in September, President Svoboda invited Šlitr and several other prominent artists up to the Prague Castle. On the President's piano, Šlitr played Debussy and Khachaturian and Šlitr (a ballad called "Celestial Love") for the white-haired hero. And Svoboda took

* The 300th anniversary of Comenius' death was commemorated in 1970 by UNESCO and almost every European nation (with ceremonies, postage stamps, etc.) during International Education Year. A world movement of Czechoslovak refugees (170,000 in all) was founded in Naarden, Holland, where Comenius was buried (though it will have its headquarters in London).

the occasion to remind his guests, in a statesmanly manner, that their share in the life of Czechoslovakia was a pillar as well as a solace.

Thus began the finest hours of Jirka Šlitr's career. He came away from the Castle and made his fellow entertainers and fellow intellectuals feel an obligation to remain and an obligation to work. He told Jiří Menzel that "we're all lucky to still have a few months left in which to communicate a little more sense of liberty to the people." And, without waiting for Suchý to make up his mind in England, Šlitr announced that the Semafor would reopen on 25 September 1968 with "some program or other."

One afternoon, Šlitr and I had lunch downtown with the wife of a prominent poet. She hinted that her husband was considering leaving the country.

Šlitr almost choked on his cheeseburger. Then this gentle, fastidious man said, with a harshness I'd never heard from him: "He must not even think of that. He must not even take a long temporary trip. And you must tell him that!"

"How can anyone tell a poet anything?" the wife said. "And, besides, you know him and you know me and you know we're considering divorcing."

Šlitr was undaunted: "He must realize that he is somebody who made people laugh and think and who has respect. These are bad times and it gives thousands of people comfort just to know he is here among them."

He could have been talking about himself, too.

Another who stayed, at great personal risk to himself, was Jan Němec. His cinematic hymn to the Prague Spring had wound up as a savage eyewitness documentary of the August invasion and all it destroyed. Hastily smuggled out in time for September's New York Film Festival, Němec's twenty-five-minute *Oratorio for Prague* stirred a Lincoln Center audience to its feet in silent tribute. Němec's *Oratorio* was never publicly screened in Prague.

Its August moments—a Russian soldier piecing together a torn-up Czech newspaper to find out why he was in Prague; a hand reaching for Němec's concealed camera—were the most sensational. But when I saw it in Paris a few months later, the Springtime moments were what made it too much for a survivor to bear.

Chapter 18]

Wednesday 25 September—
Thursday 21 November 968

SEPTEMBER AND OCTOBER WERE A BITTERSWEET TIME
when a resident of Prague went to bed at night and often awoke to
find life no worse—or perhaps a little better!—than it had ever been
before. True, one grasped at straws, but it still wasn't hard to tell oneself: "Well, we touched bottom in August and have nowhere to go but
up" . . . or else "Things are looking up" . . . or sometimes even
"You know, I think maybe we're going to win!" Survival was, in itself,
a victory.

A five-day work week went into effect. The first Czech rosé wine in
history went on sale, a Grazie from Moravia. The Number 8 tram became two cars long instead of an overcrowded one car. And, on 25
September, the Semafor Theatre reopened with Jiří Menzel directing
The Devil from Vinohrady, starring Jiří Šlitr. This was a revival of a
1966 Menzel-Šlitr hit, a semi-one-man show (the first act was Šlitr solo;
in the second, he was joined by two girl singers) updated with topical
sarcasm. Apologizing for the slightly dim lighting, Šlitr also managed
to sum up the state of the economy in what became an oft-quoted line:
"We have ten reflectors—nine are from the West and one is from the
East. The one from the East doesn't work. Still, we like the one from
the East."

On opening night, the second act of *Devil from Vinohrady* was electrified by an honest-to-goodness "surprise guest appearance" by the
gnomelike Jiří Suchý, who flew home from England that very afternoon. When Suchý pranced onstage, the orchestra struck up S + Š's
lilting, sardonic "Calypso of a Happy Land" ("where the people don't
work and get paid in advance"). There were 45 minutes of curtain calls
and encores including some "old anti-war, anti-Nazi protest songs" by
Voskovec and Werich and concluding with Šlitr's mockery of "Oh My
Darling Clementine" sung in Russian.

After the opening-night party in the subterranean Semafor Club, Valerie and I took a taxi home. At the entrance to the Letná tunnel, our cab was suddenly cut off by a Russian tank and covered by three armed men in the turret. They were merely asserting right-of-way (which they didn't have) and our cabbie yielded with alacrity. But shame and outrage lingered all the way home.

"They're not supposed to be here any more!" Valerie protested to me. True enough, the Russian armor had been moved out of the parks and off the streets of Prague, though the closed jeeps continued their regular nightly patrols. But a small armor contingent and a couple of dozen sentries were always on view in Haštalské, an off-the-tourist-path square in the Old Town of Prague. There, the Class-C Hotel Haštala ("It's Class Z-minus in our book now," a ČEDOK guide assured me) had been converted into Soviet military command headquarters for the Prague 1 district.

"They're probably on a night prowl from Haštalské," our cabbie had said as he gave the tank plenty of elbow room.

Haštalské was never one's destination, just a place you were passing through on your way to somewhere else; and so the sudden sight of Russian armor looming up in the Old Town's medieval gloom came as a double and oft-repeated shock. When Kosygin flew into Prague in early autumn for a ceremony at which Černík signed a humiliating "Agreement on the Temporary Stationing of Soviet Troops in the Czechoslovak Socialist Republic"*, Haštalské was designated as Prague's only physical reminder of the presence of an occupation army. There were never more than half-a-dozen big armored vehicles on view, but even these were enough to bring back total recall of the 21st of August. They were also ample reminder that thousands of men and hundreds of tanks were on call in Milovice and Mladá Boleslav.

The Hotel Haštala was an ugly symbol, but its Old Town neighbors took it in their stride. I once overheard one of them giving a lost

---

* "Some of the contingents [estimated at 75,000 to 100,000 men] which entered the country on 21 August 1968 will remain on Czechoslovak territory for an unspecified period for the purpose of ensuring the security of the countries of the socialist community from the growing revanchist efforts of West German militaristic forces." No further reason was given in the Agreement. Ironically, it was also specified that the Western border would remain fully under the direct protection of Czechoslovak troops, which it does to this day, with the Red Army stationed farther inland. In October, the agreement was ratified by the Czechoslovak National Assembly, where only four deputies dared to vote against it. One of them was Dr. František Kriegel.

passerby directions: "You go through the square, you bear left past the soldiers, you turn left at the next corner, and then you spit."

At the end of September, 1968, the National Assembly of Czechoslovakia commemorated the thirtieth anniversary of the Munich Pact with this proclamation:

> All those who participated in the Munich Agreement in any way were severely afflicted later. Munich entered history also as bitter evidence of the low level of international morals, which allowed the sacrifice of a small allied state and its people to the power of a brutal neighbor.

Rudé Právo noted that the history of small nations is lined with "various crossroads" at which decisions involving their fate and very existence are taken by more powerful nations. And *Youth Front* dared to remark that Czechoslovakia's current plight was "rather reminiscent of thirty years ago, but perhaps the rest of the world would rather concentrate on the 1968 Olympics." After that, denunciations of the "Munich Pact" became euphemisms for sentiment toward the "Moscow Diktat."

Two weeks after the re-opening of the Semafor, Šlitr and Suchý and Menzel had another first night at Prague's Cinema Sevastopol: *The Crime in the Night Club*. The film's last twenty minutes—Šlitr and Suchý singing away with necks in nooses—were, alas, its best. In the hour that went before, the pratfalls didn't land, the gags didn't jell, and the symbols were sometimes too obvious, sometimes too obscure. "It is a picture I prefer to forget," Menzel told me later. "If you ask me what went wrong, I say it is my fault, it is on me. It is a film I made for people instead of for Jiří Menzel." *

I had one little anecdote to cheer him up. On my way out, I had spotted one of the new Soviet culture cops—a correspondent who, at press conferences, didn't ask questions, but gave sermons. I had asked him how he'd liked *The Crime in the Night Club*.

He had shrugged and said: "Well, I'm not one for light entertainment. But the newsreel that's with it, *that* should be banned."

Gradually, Soviet "advisers" were moving back into the passport and visa offices and the key ministries where they hadn't been seen since the late 1950's or early 1960's. "Our nurses" is what the Czechs

---

* *The Crime in the Night Club* has not been distributed in America.

called these unsmiling strangers who looked over their shoulders, listened in on their phone calls, and kept telling them "this is the way *we* do things." One Czech official informed me privately that I stood fourth on the list of foreign writers due to be wiretapped. Later, he told me that all wiretaps were being delayed because the Russians were unwilling to use the equipment that the Czechs had dismantled, but kept in working order, during the Prague Spring.

"The KGB," he told me, "insisted on importing its own equipment from Russia because they don't trust anything of ours. It took more than a month to get here and when it did, it turned out to be a primitive kind of switchboard that can monitor no more than thirty telephones in all of Prague!"

There were so many different lists of wires to be tapped that there was no room in the Top Thirty for the KGB's fourth-ranked imperialist propagandist. The Soviet switchboard was quickly put to work eavesdropping on various high officials, embassies, and domestic talent. But additional equipment was on order from Moscow, so my wife and I kept our phone conversations brief and uncompromising—as it suddenly occurred to us that we always had done, even in the Prague Spring.

When *Zitřek* (*Tomorrow*) dawned in October, we were introduced to Sylva the writer. Our dearest friend read the way she talked. An article by her, "Post-August Diagnosis," began:

> I am feeling all right. At the same time, I think I shouldn't.
>
> I am feeling all right. But I hear the other people saying: "Recently, my fingers keep trembling." . . . "Lately, the children have started wetting their pants and sucking their thumbs again." . . . "I am not sleeping well." . . . "I wake up at two in the morning and, until four o'clock, I have to read." . . . "Many people are dying of heart attacks." . . . "I simply can't eat or work nowadays."
>
> Even in the taxicab, too, I hear: "It takes only a bottle to get drunk." But who can get drunk all the time?
>
> I am feeling all right, so I have obviously been excommunicated from all the troubles that surround me. Perhaps, in such a case, I should find the help of a doctor because I have this peculiar feeling.
>
> To be truthful, I sought the help of six of them. . . .

Sylva's basic question was: "Are we sicker after August of 1968?" The consensus, curiously enough, was that adults weren't sicker—at least, not yet. An internist told Sylva that August's shock elicited healthy reactions and summoned "such a reserve of powers" that people were, if anything, better for it. The doctor in charge of Prague's "HELP!" phone* informed her that "our number of calls received decreased, in late August, from an average of sixteen a day to an average of eight. Now the figure is starting back up, but it's nowhere near sixteen yet." A psychiatrist exclaimed that, for the first time in a decade, his clinic had an empty bed! He said that at times of catastrophe, when people have something "real" to worry about and feel a closer link with that abstraction called the State, mental disorders diminish: "I think the nation is living through a physiological state of sadness, which it mobilizes as a defense. But, attention please, this is not an illness." The worst time for mental health, he added prophetically, was during the Novotný dictatorship "when people used to break down over incredible trifles. August was a shock, but . . . it was a shock related to the model of life. August wasn't normal, God forbid, but man is given the opportunity to get over it. What he breaks down over is boredom, the stereotyped, uncomplicated situation."

A woman pediatrician told Sylva that children under seven were taking it hardest: "They couldn't understand their parents' sudden loss of interest in them. They wondered what they had done wrong. And so we saw children who had been eating without help asking their parents to feed them or tell them fairy tales while they ate."

Thanks to such serious personal reportage by Sylva and other staff members, *Zítřek* became the most significant, readable, and infuriating journal of post-August Prague. And a couple of other new weeklies were allowed to publish. The trade unions came out with their hard-digging investigatory journal, *World of Work*. And, most audaciously, the Writers Union put forth a new organ called *Listy,* a clever but guarded vestige of the old *Literární Listy.*

Where the quarter-page logotype of *LL!* used to appear, there was now just *L   !* The exclamation point was drawn like a dangling medal —and inside its round dot was imprinted a tiny, apologetic *"Pardon II."*

Late that October, when Czechoslovakia's fiftieth birthday was being celebrated in a rueful way, *Listy* dared to print this "Salute" from Edith Pargeter, an English translator of Czech literature:

---

* If you're in Prague and thinking about committing suicide or running amok, dial 29–79–00 and ask for *"Linka důvěry"* ("trust line").

There were times when your language was driven out of the cities and forced to take to the hills, where the villagers sheltered it and the shepherds kept it alive, until the circle of writers and thinkers brought it back in triumph with poetry and song.

There were times when alien regimes enlisted the renegades among you, and turned them as weapons against your finest sons. . . . Of the sorrows of small nations there is nothing you do not know, nothing you have not survived.

Nevertheless, when the tide of tyranny has receded, you remain; still beautiful, still erect, still durable, like Prague herself, "richly blessed and richly cursed". . . . Until in recent years you . . . began to create a new society—the achievement of your maturity, the sum of all you had learned of man's rights and duties in relationship with his fellow-man. No nation has yet made a perfect society. Not every nation has tried. Few have ever come near to succeeding. You at least saw in the distance the image of the thing desired, and in truth and good will advanced towards it. . . . That is glory enough. Few have ever done so much. It was not your fault that the way was barred. It was your splendor that, even when you were forced to a halt, you neither gave back nor turned aside. . . .

What have you given? What have you to show? A people warm of heart, temperate of mind, not given to self-vaunting, not given to violence, generous to the stranger, and immeasurably responsive to any warmth or goodness from others. A thoughtful people, quick to feel but slow to demonstrate feeling, open and vulnerable to love, and blazingly honest; gifted in friendship; once gained, loyal for life. What nation, we ask, has given more? A wealth of music such as few even among much larger countries can match, a poetry worthy to stand with any, a lively, honest and penetrating presence in the arts of theatre and film. And more. . . .

Did you not hear the loudest, most triumphant roar of approval and acclaim that filled the stadium in Mexico when the Olympic Games began? Not for any broken record, not for any gold medalist. For your team. For your flag. A tribute from the whole people of Mexico and the representatives of the whole world. You do not know how far your voice carried, how many have heard and passed on the words of your writers, students, workmen, housewives, acclaiming justice, choosing liberty, arguing for truth.

You do not know how far your light shone, how many steps groping in semi-darkness it illuminated, how many lamps it has lit in minds continents away from you. They will not all be quenched.

The events that began with Czechoslovakia's fiftieth anniversary celebration on Monday 28 October 1968 marked the end of our bittersweet phase of cautious optimism. It had lasted only a few weeks.

That holiday weekend, the Crown Jewels of Bohemia were put on their once-in-a-decade public showing at the Castle. The people of Prague took the occasion to reaffirm their faith in these symbols of Czech sovereignty and so did we—by standing in line for half a day in order to pass solemnly before that simply, but breathtakingly, displayed fourteenth-century crown of Charles IV on a red pillow flanked by a sceptre and gold ball.

On Monday, at a formal ceremony in the Spanish Hall of the Castle, Dubček droned, with an eloquent lack of conviction, through a sermon warning against the perils of German revanchism past, present, and future. Outside, thousands of Czechs were storming the Castle gates with chants of "Russians go home!", "We want freedom," and "Masaryk! Masaryk!" The policemen who pushed the demonstrators back were sympathetic and polite. But the people now knew that their leaders were no longer in touch with the masses.

That afternoon, there were riots outside the Soviet Embassy and the Hotel Haštala. Students shouted "Down with Brezhnev!" and "Long live Dubček!" They burned copies of *Pravda* and taunted the Russian guards. Inevitably, a Russian colonel came out of the hotel. He ordered four of his soldiers to arrest a West German student who was taking pictures of the Soviet armor. But the Prague police physically wrested the German from the arms of the Russian soldiers, took him to safety, checked his papers, and then released him.

That night, 8,000 people booed Ambassador Chervonenko and Soviet Deputy Foreign Minister Vasily Kuznetsov* outside the National Theatre when they showed up for a gala performance of Smetana's *Libuše*. When the police took the two Russians inside, two Czechs refused to give up their box seats to make room for them. Chervonenko and Kuznetsov stalked back to their Chaika and rode home early to the Russian Embassy.

Winter came uncharacteristically early to Prague in 1968 with snow flurries in October and deep snows in November. "What do you expect?" people said. "We're a Russian colony now, so we have a Russian winter." And, in the cold days that followed the 28th of October's "fes-

---

* Kuznetsov, who had been sent to Prague to oversee the normalization, was referred to by Czechs as "Our Protector," an allusion to Gauleiter Heydrich's title during the Nazi occupation.

tivities," we entered a period of continual crisis with small triumphs and large defeats always looming up before us. It was a time when the clock ran backward. You would go to bed at night and wake up months or even years earlier.

Josef Smrkovský addressed a meeting of law students and sounded an urgent warning: "I beg you not to engage in a demonstration. . . . If one took place, would it be surprising if tanks appeared? If you demonstrate, we may all be sorry. . . . The nation is not here to perform heroic deeds and die."

A girl student inquired about provisions in the "Treaty on the Temporary Stationing of Soviet Troops" and Smrkovský replied vaguely that there were definite limits.

"They have already overdrawn!" somebody shouted.

Almost everybody laughed, but not Smrkovský. "I know why you're laughing," he told the students. "You think any agreement can be torn up or may not be observed. Yes, it's true that each year hundreds of agreements are violated. But, even so, we must not give up the humanistic idea that agreements between nations can be signed and should be honored."

Smrkovský's warning was timely because November was a month of anniversaries whose symbolism would not be lost on the populace. The first target date was 7 November, the official fifty-first anniversary of the Bolshevik Revolution.

The Soviet flag was required to be displayed on all public buildings. But, in Bratislava on the eve of the holiday, every red flag that was raised was torn down and set afire by roving bands of young people. The Slovak National Theatre ballet company was dancing Tchaikovsky's *Romeo and Juliet* when 4,000 students appeared in the square outside to demand that a huge Soviet flag be removed from the building.

A platoon of ushers immediately obliged. The official explanation was, believe it or not, that "the show must go on."

In Prague, police and People's Militia and the Czechoslovak Army sealed off a fifteen-block area surrounding the National Theatre to avert a similar incident during *Swan Lake*. Even so, flags were burned elsewhere in town and, on a main downtown shopping street, a crowd surrounded a Soviet patrol jeep, banged on it with their fists, and spat on it until a Soviet officer jumped out of the back seat and shot into the air.

Before the holiday was over, 167 persons had been arrested in Prague alone. For the first time since the Ṣṭrahov riot a year-and-a-week earlier, police used tear gas and night sticks to disperse crowds of their own people. The Czechs who were arrested were all released after a few hours without any charges being placed against them.*

Nine visiting Western journalists, including an American wire-service correspondent, were thrown out of the country for "abusing their tourist visas," "reporting on [Soviet] troop movements," and presenting the disturbances "in an unfavorable light."

The nastiest spectacle of the day, though, occurred in Prague's Olšany Cemetery, where both Franz Kafka and the Unknown Soviet Soldier are buried. To the latter's tomb went Dubček and Černík—flanked by Russian diplomats and generals—for a wreath-laying ceremony. And it was there that Czechoslovakia's Stalinist past first reappeared with a vengeance. Some 500 old-time party hacks—lady apartment stewards, male block wardens, and assorted incompetents who had enjoyed power in the 1950's—had been mustered as an audience. Now they burst into cries of "Long live the Red Army!" and a fervent rendition of the *Internationale*. Stunned, Dubček's lips quivered with outrage. But then, being a born Communist, he managed to mouth the words of the hymn, though no sound emerged.

Later, on Dubček's way out, the old fools shook their fists at him and cursed him as he brushed past them. His teeth were clenched until he forced a smile that mocked them with its sadness.

Around that time, I asked Václav's father how his boss, Dubček, was faring. Václav's father replied:

"It's amazing! He's more himself than ever. He doesn't talk about his experiences in Russia; and, whenever he speaks of the Russian leaders or their intentions or policies, he's much less ironic than any of the rest of us.

"I have only one explanation. He couldn't find any other way to go on, except to do something that isn't too hard for the human animal to do. If you spend the first forty-six years of your life loving the Russians

---

* A student named Zbyněk Tvrdík, however, was beaten on the head in a police station (in the presence of two other students) on 7 November before being released. Later, he complained of headaches and, on 23 December, he died from the aggravation of an aneurism in the left middle cerebral artery. The policeman involved was sentenced to 20 days in prison!

plus one week of utter horror in their hands, you put that week out of your mind and try to live in the light of the other forty-six years."

"Is it that easy for him to do?" I wondered.

Václav's dad said: "It is, when a man has no other choice left."

On 8 November, the Communist Party's Presidium ordered an "indefinite suspension" of the Central Committee's own weekly, *Politika*. No reason was given, but *Politika*'s unswerving devotion to Dubček's ideals were undoubtedly what condemned it.

On Sunday the 10th of November at the inconspicuous hour of 0800, the Czechoslovak-Soviet Friendship Society held a meeting at the Lucerna cavern in downtown Prague. The Friendship Society's membership had been decimated by August's "befriendment," but it still was able to muster an audience of almost 2,500. The same 500 who'd spat on Dubček were there, of course, augmented by various old-time party-liners and a few ambitious younger careerists who were greeted by one Russian officer thusly: "Allow me to call you 'dear comrade collaborators.'"

The keynote speaker was none other than Václav David, the discredited Foreign Minister who'd accredited me. Now Ambassador to Bulgaria, he had come back to Prague to proclaim that the arrival of Warsaw Pact troops had smashed "the hopes for a counter-revolution." He was followed by a Red Army song-and-dance ensemble flown in from Dresden for the occasion.

Russian newsmen were admitted to the meeting, but not Western or even Czechoslovak journalists. TV confined its coverage to the arrival of the invitees. It wasn't allowed to show us the angry mob of patriotic Czechs who'd been waiting outside since dawn. They were there to avenge the unreported (but widely discussed) abuse of Dubček at Olšany Cemetery three days earlier. They spat on a Soviet Army colonel and his medals. They hurled garbage at the Red Army vehicles that drove up. And an umbrella-wielding old lady bopped the head of Emmanuel Famíra, the official portrait painter of Gottwald, Zápotocký, and Novotný. Famíra, then 68, once boasted that he had been "collaborating with the Soviet Union for 35 years." *

On the 12th of November, Dubček informed students that their

* Famíra died in 1970 and was given a State funeral.

demonstrations had "damaged normalization and our innermost interests, both national and international." He warned that any public marches would be halted by force.

On the 13th, Gustav Husák, in his capacity as Deputy Prime Minister, announced a ban on all demonstrations.

Husák's star was visibly rising and reddening, though the Soviet build-up of him was being handled with relative restraint. But, whenever Soviet *Gauleiter* Kuznetsov made his official rounds of the high Czechoslovak leadership, his talks with Dubček were described as "an exchange of views," with Svoboda as "frank and comradely," and with Husák as "warm and friendly." Where the Polish press labeled Dubček "moody . . . emotional . . . naive," Husák was praised for calling the Moscow Agreement "an honest understanding between honest people."

Husák insisted at all times that he had no intention of undermining Dubček: "We do not have identical views on every detail, but we are looking for a joint solution and we hope to find it soon."

This "solution," which boded ill for Dubček and his followers, was to be taken up at a Central Committee meeting over the weekend of 15 November. In the wake of the riots, the hard-line minority and the Russians would be pressing for tighter clamps on freedom. The omens did not strike me as propitious. Trudging over to the Castle's late-night post office one snowy evening, I was halted at the main gate by two men in brown leather jackets.

"You can't to into the Castle," one of them told me.

"Why not?" I asked him. Then, seeing many official limousines and chauffeurs clustered near the Spanish Hall, I said: "Is it because the Central Committee's still in session?" Heretofore, one had always been able to wander through the Castle even when the Central Committee was meeting there.

The secret policeman looked at me with new interest. "You're not a foreign tourist," he said. "And you speak some Czech."

I had spoken as freely as ever (which was now a mistake in some circumstances). And I didn't like where the questioning was leading, so I said: "All I want is to go to the Post Office. It's still open now."

"You're not a journalist, are you?" he persisted.

Before I could answer, his partner said: "Look at the letters in his hand. Let him go to the Post Office."

So I went and mailed my letters and, when I came out, both of the leather boys bade me good night. "Sorry to have delayed you before," said one of them, "but I had to make sure you weren't an American journalist."

"I didn't know there were any still around," I said cheerfully. Since then, I've stayed away from the Castle on Central Committee nights and, just in case I stumble onto one, I always carry a picture postal addressed to my mother, which I've yet to mail.

The Prague grapevine had it that the policies made inside the Castle that weekend were just as severe as the security outside. It took more than a week before they became known—and then our worst fears were borne out.

The Central Committee passed a resolution pledging fealty to the Action Program, the post-January reforms, and particularly to the Soviet Union. It also criticized the undue haste with which the January reforms had been enacted. Most of this "November Resolution" embodied the sentiments expressed by Gustav Husák in his speech before the Central Committee session. "As a ruling party," Husák complained, "we had one leg cut off and the other got a kind of thrombosis." The amputated limb, he explained, was the secret police apparatus; the diseased one was the press. And he blamed both ailments on "party irresponsibility."

From that moment on, all party proclamations confused matters further by paying tribute to "the spirit of the January politics, the May declarations, and the November resolution." This was like building a utopia based on the ideals of Adam, Eve, and the Snake.

The Presidium, which had been expanded to twenty-one men just two-and-a-half months earlier, remained the same size. But now power was concentrated in a so-called "Inner Presidium" of eight men who would formulate policy that the rest of the Presidium would (presumably) ratify.

Dubček would be the nominal head of this Inner Presidium. Smrkovský, too, was one of the chosen eight. But a third dependable liberal, Špaček, was cast adrift among the Outer Thirteen. The salami-slicer was cutting thinner and thinner.

The true strength of the Inner Presidium now lay in the only three members with whom the Russians were dealing: the increasingly "realistic" and accommodating Černík . . . the ambitious Husák . . . and Lubomír Štrougal, forty-four, a slightly flabby Gray Eminence who had once been lean and mean and orthodox enough for Novotný to have made him his Minister of Agriculture at the age of thirty-five and his Minister of Interior at thirty-seven. But he had lost Novotný's confidence at just the right time for his career, in 1967. At one heated meeting, where Novotný chided him for allegedly being a ladykiller, Štrougal won new admirers with this cool response: "It is true that these hands have held many a woman's bottom. But they are not bloody like yours."

Štrougal, an aparatchik par excellence, had started out in the Dubček era as a Deputy Premier. And now he was ticketed to become Communist party boss in the Czech Lands when federalization would start on New Year's Day.

There was one other development from "the spirit of . . . the November resolution." Effective at the end of the month, Czechoslovakia was banning all trips to the West "not conforming to the interests of the State" and voiding all "permanent exit visas."

The 17th of November was the official Day of The Students, commemorating the date in 1939 when a spontaneous display of grief erupted at the funeral of a student, Jan Opletal, slain by the Nazi occupiers. Adolf Hitler had retaliated for the outburst by closing the Czech universities, deporting 1,000 students to concentration camps, and having nine of their leaders publicly executed in Prague.

The 17th of November 1968 was a white Sunday that began with a solemn mass in St. Nicholas Church, where young people, many holding hands, crammed their way into every baroque nook and cranny. A busload of police sat discreetly in the old stone square outside—ready to come running if trouble erupted. Other police buses were parked wherever *hydeparks* had sprouted in the Prague Spring.

Russian tanks in Milovice and Mladá Boleslav were placed on "first-degree alert" there. Task forces of Soviet infantry had been moved by night into the courtyards of Prague police stations. Far more disturbingly though, Czechoslovak Army tanks stood on the outskirts of the city—ready to be used against their own people.

Despite the ban on public demonstrations announced by Deputy Premier Husák, the Bohemian-Moravian Students Union staged a "quickie" march on Wenceslas Square that Sunday night. The Union had been formed in May by, among others, Jiří Müller and Luboš Holeček, the boys Novotný had once silenced by drafting them into his army. Several thousand students marched up the Square, lingering briefly—just long enough to hear their leaders proclaim, from the steps of the bullet-pocked National Museum, that "because processions like this have been forbidden, we will instead stay off the streets and occupy our faculties for three days starting Monday morning. We cannot accept the destruction of January's reforms."

Then they disbanded. That night, their ten demands were posted on walls all over Prague. Their program included abolition of the "temporary press censorship" that had been restored in August; freedom of assembly and travel; cultural, literary, and scientific freedom; guaranteed personal and legal security for individuals; and removal of officials who have "lost the confidence of the people. . . . Those who conduct the nation's policies—both foreign and domestic—must do nothing that conflicts with the United Nations Charter or Declaration of Human Rights."

These were perfectly reasonable demands in a completely unreasonable situation.

On Monday morning, the students of Prague went to class carrying suitcases, lunch pails, and inflatable mattresses . . . and in school they remained. So did their teachers and even some of their headmasters and rectors. Prominent writers and scientists came to lecture them and stayed on. By day, Šlitr and Suchý and other popular entertainers made the rounds of the schools to perform for the students. At night, in every theatre in the land, a student appeared just before the curtain rose and read the ten demands. Thus did each performance start with the echo of thunderous applause.

"Oh what a lovely occupation!" the Doctor's daughter chirped when she phoned us from her college on Tuesday.

"Never mind that!" my wife snapped. "Are you all right?"

"Well, I could probably use a good washing, but nobody seems to mind."

"I mean: are you safe?"

"Is any of us safe? Look, when I first heard of the strike, I was a little bit afraid. And when I went to school today and saw the buses of policemen, I was a little more afraid. But once you're inside and with a lot of other people who feel the way you do, you're not afraid at all. It's just, well, it's very fine fun!"

"Fun?" said my wife.

"Oh, it's not so much the politics—the politics are hopeless, aren't they?—it's getting to know other kids you've met before, but never had time to be friends with. And the professors are just great!"

Unlike August's military occupation, November's student occupation was a kind of inspirational camp meeting in which the participants talked and sang and reaffirmed their faith in what Alexander Dubček had stood for even while the embattled Dubček himself was warning the students of the "gravest possible consequences." The boys and girls also sang a new genre of music for the mild-mannered Czechs: "student hate songs." The most singable, to the tune of "John Brown's Body," buried a catalog of villains from recent Czech history, one to a verse. When everybody's candidates were safely *"mold'ring in their graves,"* the final line was a snarling: *"And we'll have paradise!"*

To keep out provocateurs and avert accusations that outside agitators were responsible, the strike leaders had barred all but invited guests from the schools: "We can admit no journalists, either Czech or foreign, to our faculties during this strike. Please don't be angry. It could be bad for our cause."

At the barricades, though, one of the leaders talked with the Washington *Post*'s Karl E. Meyer, who flew in from London to cover the strike:

"Of course we don't scream, we don't [all] let our hair grow to flamboyant lengths, we don't use four-letter words. People who ask why we're so different from Western student radicals seem, if you'll excuse me, a little bit thick.

"We are an occupied country: do I have to remind you? We know if we make a mistake the whole country pays, not just us. . . ."

"Here—please underline this point—we are not fighting against the Establishment. On the contrary, we are fighting for what the whole country, including the Government, is fighting for—the right to run our own land."

Inside their schools, the students busied themselves researching and painting slogans on placards and walls. All their signs were scrupulously attributed to their sources: "SOME PEOPLE HAVE TO BE TAKEN IN SMALL DOSES—Ralph Waldo Emerson" and "TO BE OR NOT TO BE? THAT IS THE QUESTION—Hamlet." Jan Hus was quoted in some places "THEY HAVE THE POWER BUT WE ARE GOING TO WIN" and paraphrased in others "THEY HAVE THE TANKS BUT WE HAVE THE TRUTH."

The three-day strike was extended for a fourth day. When it ended, the Doctor's daughter was glowing. "I am fine," she said soon after returning home, "but my mother is very angry with me. She spent a whole day preparing nine different cold meals for me to take along. When I came home today, she unpacked the picnic hamper and there were the same nine meals. I hadn't eaten the whole time."

She paused before adding, almost rapturously: "That's how beautiful the experience was: For four whole days, I never even knew I was on a hunger strike!"

"Do you think," I asked Václav, "there'll be another strike soon?"

"Oh, no," he said. "You must remember that we're students. We never do the same thing twice."

Another of the strikers had been twenty-year-old Jan Palach, born in the year when communism came to his native land. He was a disciple of the student leaders Holeček and Müller (and particularly close to Holeček). But Jan Palach himself (his friends called him "Honza") was not cut out to be a leader.

In the shock of August, this shy and skinny youth had heeded his instincts and bolted to West Germany. But he had returned to Prague because he didn't feel at home anywhere else. In November, he sat-in quietly at the Philosophical Faculty. And, as you are meant to do there, he listened and meditated.

THAT FALL, THEY FINALLY OPENED THE BRAND-NEW
pedestrian underpass—with shops, stalls, and the first escalators in
Prague—beneath Wenceslas Square. On the verge of completion in late
August, its ceiling had caved in under the weight of the Soviet tanks
that shot up the Square. Now it was as good as new; shiny, glassy, and,
like the airport, one of the only places in Prague that didn't look like
Prague. But it didn't stay sleek and unblemished for long. A day or two
after it opened, a Russian window-shopper walked right through one
of its plate-glass storefronts.

The Russian (a civilian) was treated, but the store window was
replaced by a wooden fence. News accounts explained that it would
take six months to obtain a new plate-glass window. (With the best
Bohemian glass and even plate glass, priority is given for export rather
than home consumption.) Inspired by the event, a truly underground
hydepark sprouted. The temporary fence was plastered, painted, and
chalked overnight with mocking slogans, such as "HE CAME, HE
SAW, HE WALKED THROUGH GLASS!"

Realizing that they would soon have an insurrection on their
hands, the authorities expedited a new plate-glass window in six days
instead of six months. But the story doesn't end there. A couple of
weeks later and a quarter of a mile away, Jiří Trnka had an exhibition of his fairy-tale paintings and sculptures. The art gallery had a
plate glass wall on which was fixed a sign that said, only in Russian,
"BEWARE! GLASS!"

Chapter 19

Sunday 24 November 1968—
Friday 24 January 1969

JUST BEFORE THANKSGIVING, 1968, THE MINISTRY OF Foreign Affairs ran a three-day press junket to Ostrava for the foreign press. We would see the "normalized" mining city (population: 252,000) known as "the iron heart of Moravia," just a few miles from the Polish border.

The Ministry's luxurious Europabus was only half full so I was able to take a whole double-seat. The journey would take six to eight hours and I wanted to be comfortable.

About ninety minutes out of Prague, a skinny figure in a brown leather jacket rose from a front seat and cried, in a sort of mid-west-inflected English: "Stop the bus! My flat's going to catch fire!"

The driver pulled over as fast as he could. And a Foreign Ministry official said in Russian, with rather strained politeness: "I know your language, Mr. Bolshakov. What seems to be the matter?"

"I left my new electric iron plugged in," said the young Russian. "We have to go back to Prague at once."

"We have telephones here. Suppose we telephone Prague from the next town," said the official. It took forty-five minutes to get the call through to another Russian in Prague, but he promised to hurry over and disconnect Bolshakov's iron.

During the wait, I took a close look at Bolshakov. He was about twenty-five and handsome in a sallow, loutish way. With a cigarette dangling from the left side of his mouth, he struck me as a young punk trying to be the young Belmondo trying to be the young Bogart. Young Bolshakov was, I learned, representing *Komsomolska Pravda,* the Soviet Young Communist League's newspaper, otherwise known as *Youth Truth.*

After another three hours back on the road, we stopped for sandwiches, beer, and coffee in a small town's tavern. Two miles farther on,

Bolshakov popped up again, this time from the back of the bus. "We must go back!" he proclaimed. "I left my Canadian cigarette lighter on the table in that damn restaurant."

Back we went to retrieve his lighter. It was a Ronson.*

When Bolshakov reboarded the bus this time, he plunked himself down in the vacant seat next to me. No introductions were made. He knew exactly who I was and a good bit more than I knew about him.

(At this time, I hadn't yet learned about the NKVD connections of my Russian roommate in Brno. But various remarks of Bolshakov's later indicated that he knew I was friends with "Forman and Menzel and other Jewish movie directors." I didn't even bother to tell him that Menzel isn't Jewish and Forman is only part-Jewish.)

"Well, that's a relief," he said, igniting a Gauloise with the lighter he'd just rescued. Then he turned to me and said disarmingly: "Y'know, I not only have the face of a loser; I *am* a loser."

Any man who can play word games in a foreign tongue has won my admiration for the time being. So I responded with chit-chat: "When I lose things, I seem to lose them in threes. So what do you think you'll lose next?"

"I hope to hell it isn't my new Czechoslovak shoes," he said, lifting his feet to show me his newest acquisition from the House of Footwear on Wenceslas Square. "I must admit that our Soviet shoes aren't the best. Shoes are why I took this assignment. Believe me, I'm not here because I have any liking for the Czechs."

He was starting to lose me, but he went on: "I mean, it's very hard to be a Russian in this country. People won't talk to you. People won't invite you. Some clerks in the stores won't even sell to you."

I responded quietly: "My friends tell me it's also very hard to be a Czech in a Russian colony."

He swiveled to look at me accusingly: "You talk like one of them, for Christ's sake!"

"I've been here since 1967," I said, "so I've lived through the same 1968 that the Czechs have."

"I know, I know," Bolshakov said soothingly. "And I try to be objective no matter what my feelings. I try to talk to at least three counter-revolutionaries every day."

---

* In later conversation with another journalist, Bolshakov claimed that he had never been to the U.S., though he had seen "all I wanted to see of it" from the other side of Niagara Falls.

I was beginning to hope he would tick me off as one and go fulfill his quota somewhere else. I had never met a young Stalinist before. In fact, it had never occurred to me that there were still such animals in the generations under forty. I wanted out—for this conversation was taking a dangerous turn.

But I was not to be spared. "I'll tell you what the Czechs are," Bolshakov went on. "They're flagellators!"

He had a gift for taking me by surprise. "I beg your pardon," I said. "My English isn't as good as yours. Doesn't that word you're using have something to do with whipping?"

Bolshakov wriggled one arm out of its shirtsleeve to give me a graphic definition: "You and I, if we get a scratch on the arm, we bleed and then we let it dry up. Right? But not the Czechs. They're flagellators! They'll whip the cut and whip it and whip it until it bleeds all over again and festers and becomes poisonous." He was so caught up in his performance by now that he was making a whipping gesture over and over with a sharp arm motion that you could actually hear.

"What the hell are you talking about?" I wondered.

"I'm talking about the National Museum!" he snapped back. "I have to go by there and look at at that eyesore every morning on my way to work."

I wanted to say "Who shot it up?", but all I said was "Your experts, our experts, and the Czechs all say it can't be repaired, you know. Something to do with the kind of stone."

Bolshakov lifted his feet again and said: "Any people who are clever enough to make shoes like these can certainly fix up a museum."

There was nothing I could say that would do him or me any good. But he insisted upon rambling on in his faultless western Pennsylvania dialect about the "decadent Czechs" and "your KAN" and "your K231." So I did the only thing you can do when you're trapped on a bus by a bore. I reclined my seat, closed my eyes, and dozed off.

After fifteen minutes, the bus bounced a little high and I came slightly awake. Somebody was talking to me or, rather, at me. I opened one eye long enough to see that it was still Bolshakov ("persecution with an inhuman face," I thought later) and lapsed back into my coma for another forty-five minutes.

I awoke to discover that he was still talking to me.

While my eyes blinked at the unreality of the monologue, my ears picked up Bolshakov's latest words: "I'll tell you how decadent the

Czechs are! Do you know what they do? They—take—fashion—photographs—in the Jewish Cemetery?"

Half-awake, I snapped back: "Well, I'm Jewish and it doesn't
bother me! So why the hell should it bother you?"

There was a click and I thought momentarily that I had been shot
for my words. As a matter of fact, I had been—but only by a camera.

My eyes opened wide to take in the ambush. A Nikon had been
hung on the back of a seat diagonally opposite mine. The other seats
had been adjusted, while I slept, so that the camera could focus on me
without obstruction. A Russian photographer still knelt on the seat
whose back held the camera. When Bolshakov had needled me into
snarling like an imperialist dragon, the cameraman had simply pushed
the button and filmed me. Now the photographer's work was done. He
was grinning cockily and flashing me a high sign which meant in any
language: "This is going to be a beaut!"

I didn't smile back, but I said to Bolshakov, as calmly as I could: "I
suppose my picture'll be in tomorrow's *Youth Truth*."

"Eventually, perhaps," he said, turning his attention elsewhere.

Choked up with fury and anxiety, I didn't say another word to him.
After a while, Bolshakov changed his seat and started to heckle the
lady from *L'Humanité,* who handled him much better than I had.
("You've been to Russia, Madame? Is there really any significant difference between our champagne and yours?" "Yes, ours travels better.")
In Ostrava, Bolshakov kept busy baiting officials and copying down
subversive materials from bulletin boards. He didn't try to speak to me
again. But, rather than risk another six hours on the bus with him, I
bought a plane ticket back to Prague on Tuesday night.

The people of Prague were being subjected to Russian journalism,
too—in the form of *Zprávy* (*News*), a four-page Czech-language weekly
version of *Pravda*. *Zprávy* was printed in East Germany, distributed in
Prague by Soviet armored trucks, and handed out on street corners by
insistent Russian soldiers with burp guns. It was causing a major litter-
bug problem.

One bitter cold afternoon, outside the Main Post Office, I saw an
armored truck deposit a Russian soldier on the corner with 500 copies
of *Zprávy* that he started handing out. It was clear that he had orders
not to leave the corner until he had given away all 500.

The first three dozen copies he gave away were flung down angrily on the sidewalk. Then an elderly and tidy-minded Czech gentleman came along and said in Russian: "Why don't you give them all to me, son?"

"Only one," the Russian soldier replied.

"Look, son," said the old man. "You see what's happening to them. Now you and I have a common interest. I don't want to see the streets messed up with newspapers and you don't want to stand out on this freezing corner for another hour or two until you've given away your quota." Here, I could perceive a flicker of interest in the soldier's stolid mask. The old man went on: "So, if you give me the papers, I have a friend with a car. He and I can take them down to the Vltava River and dispose of them without anybody knowing. Then you can go back to your room or, with the extra time you have, you can go shopping at the shoe store or maybe they'll even let you into a movie house if you'll check your rifle in the cloakroom."

The old man's crooning, seductive vision had evoked a dazed daydreaming look on the soldier's face. But he had carried it too far with his "rifle in cloakroom" detail and this snapped the soldier back to reality.

Pressing a copy of *Zprávy* into the old man's hands, he reiterated: "Only one."

Kuznetsov wound up his three-month stay in Prague at the end of November and turned the reins of his protectorate back to Ambassador Chervonenko. Just before Kuznetsov left, Dubček lodged a strong personal complaint about the slanders in *Zprávy* and Kuznetsov responded: "When *Rudé Právo* reads like *Zprávy,* then there'll be no need to publish *Zprávy.*"

On December's first weekend, Dubček, Černík, Svoboda, Husák, and Štrougal were summoned to Kiev for a secret meeting with Brezhnev. And this time, unlike July, they came flying to answer the call. Brezhnev, who did most of the talking that weekend, was in a good mood. He greeted each of his visitors with a "double Khrushchev"; that is, a bearhug and kisses on both cheeks. The rest of the talks did nothing to dampen his spirits. Dubček and Černík made formal speeches. Then Štrougal took the floor to dispute some points Dubček had made. For once, a meeting between the Czechoslovaks and the Russians was shorter than anticipated. There was even time for a two-hour wild pig hunt.

The meeting in Kiev was announced only after the delegation had returned to Prague. And the people were outraged!

First of all, the Presidential flag—saying that "TRUTH PRE-VAILS" and signifying that the President is in residence—had waved aloft all weekend while Svoboda was in Kiev. It was a petty deception, but it was a long time since any President, even Novotný, had lied to the people about this one symbolic detail.

Then Josef Smrkovský, who hadn't been invited to Kiev, let it be known that this was a sample of "closed-door policies, which I utterly hate." Minutes after he had spoken out about this to a gathering of journalists, Smrkovský learned what the most crucial item on the Kiev agenda had been: Russian insistence on Smrkovský's own removal.

Smrkovský declined to resign. He told the press that he wouldn't bow out pleading ill health or any other excuse. He had undergone his physical check-up just ten days earlier and "I was surprised myself how healthy I was. . . . I think that I have no right to abandon the front I was helping to form earlier this year. Our time—well, this is a struggle that has been joined by millions of people. Should I betray them now?"

The answer was deferred for a month. The Christmas season had come to Prague almost as early as it does in America and there was an unofficial moratorium on crises.

Christmas follows much the same pattern in Prague as in New York, although there are fewer goods in the stores. At first, the shoppers in the trams are jovial and benevolent. But, by mid-December, they are harried and frantic. Men stop giving ladies their seats (a discourtesy otherwise seen here only in heat waves when men are too exhausted to be gracious). Tram conductors shut doors prematurely and motormen carry their jam-packed human cargos one or two stops past their destinations.

Virtually the only special feature of Christmas shopping in 1968 was that you encountered vast numbers of Russian civilian shoppers; particularly in the six-floor House of Footwear on Wenceslas Square, you began to sense the depth of the flood of "advisors" who'd followed the troops into Czechoslovakia.

The first "Christmas Tree of the Republic" to stand in Old Town Square in more than twenty years was lit by Irena Svobodová, the President's wife. And, as Christmas neared, there was a small miracle in

Wenceslas Square: Suchý and Šlitr re-opened *The Last Hospital* at the Semafor. Their allegory was intact, but with an epilogue and a few details added. In the new ending, the Medical Director (Šlitr) of the brothel was advised that his customers were complaining with alarming vehemence. To which he now responded: "Have no fears! I am calling up my brother and all will be O.K."

Another important change was in Suchý's epic death scene, where, after falling victim to incompetent surgery, he struggled to put himself together with desperate sewing and patching. But his effort came to naught when a voluptuously evil nurse (portrayed by Miloš Forman's wife Věra) playfully bit off the thread. And, as Suchý gazed heavenward, he used to spout the Princess Libuše's prophecy of Prague's grandeur: "I see a great city whose glory reaches to the stars!"

In December of 1968, however, the dying words that Suchý actually spoke were: "I see a great city beneath a red star!"

My "permanent accreditation" and our residence permission would both expire at the end of the year. My accreditation was renewable any time *after* 15 December, which was a Sunday; our residence permit, which was based on the renewal of my accreditation, had to be applied for two weeks *before* expiration, meaning a 17 December deadline. Therefore, with barely twenty-four hours to maneuver in should there be any trouble, I had made an appointment with the appropriate official at the Ministry of Foreign Affairs for 1000 on Monday, 16 December.

The Schweikian gatekeeper at the Černín Palace was in one of his Kafkaesque moods when I appeared: "Your official is not in today."

"But he made a ten o'clock appointment with me," I insisted.

"You must have made some mistake with the language."

"Please, would you phone his office and make sure?"

The old man dialed and said: "The line is busy."

"You see?" I said hopefully. "He must be there already."

"No, somebody else must be phoning, too, and getting no answer."

Just then, a Bulgarian journalist showed up. He also had a ten o'clock appointment with the same official for the same purpose.

"You see!" the gatekeeper clucked at me triumphantly. "You don't have a ten o'clock appointment with him after all! This man does!"

The conversation might still be raging today if the official in question hadn't appeared and greeted us rather distractedly: "Good day!

Good day! But where is Mr. Szulc?" It turned out that he had a ten o'clock appointment with Tad, too. "If Mr. Szulc comes, you'll have to excuse me. My secretary will take your accreditation booklets and stamp them with our seal. Then I'll sign them when I'm done with Mr. Szulc. But I must have a private talk with him." He shook his head sadly.

Just then, Tad Szulc arrived, looking anxious. He was ushered into a room where visitors were received; the same paneled, indubitably bugged, room where my family and I had begun our battle to settle in Prague one long Christmastime ago. While the Bulgarian and I chatted in the lobby of the Černín Palace, I noticed a higher official, looking very stern, join the two men in the visitors room.

A few minutes later, both officials emerged with Tad Szulc. Tad looked grimmest of all. He had been expelled, with forty-eight hours to get out of the country.

Tad shook hands with both officials and said: "Thanks for everything. I know this isn't your fault." The officials said nothing. Then Tad handed the lesser official his accreditation booklet and hurried out. When Tad called me later to say goodbye, he told me "they say I committed military espionage."

My own booklet was signed and handed back to me by the lesser official. I saw that my annual renewal was for just six months, through the 30th of June, 1969. I asked why.

He looked heavenward (or was it toward an overhead microphone?) and said with a groan: "Everything must be done in half-measures nowadays. That's our new policy. You can be renewed just as easily every six months as every year. Believe me, Mr. Levy, things could be much worse."

When I took my booklet down to the police station, the same genial people were still working there. They extended my residence permit for six months, the duration of my accreditation. But they also cut my "permanent exit visa" from its previous 180-day validity to 90 days. I asked how come.

"We like to keep closer track of our foreigners," the man on duty said. "But you can't complain. We Czechs have it much worse."

Alan Tillier of *Newsweek*, a British subject, was next to go. He hadn't yet received accreditation, but it was pending. On the Thursday before Christmas, Tillier was in his room at the Alcron when several men in brown leather jackets knocked on his door, took him to the police station, read him (first in Czech and then in English) a Novotný-era law on divulging State secrets, accused him of violating it, stamped his visa papers "CANCELED," and gave him five hours to drive to the Austrian border.

I happened to be at the Foreign Ministry's Christmas party later that afternoon when *Time*'s man-at-the-Alcron brought the news of Tillier's expulsion. The Foreign Ministry officials, including the two who'd handled Szulc's expulsion, were genuinely shocked. They had not been informed by the Ministry of Interior.

Thus, there were now two arms of the Government in the business of expelling journalists. After New Year's, there would be four. Upon federalization, Czechoslovakia would be blessed with three relatively independent Ministries of Interior; one for the federal republic, one for the Czech Lands, and one for Slovakia, plus a not-very-independent Foreign Ministry. Plus, I supposed, the KGB and NKVD.

With Tillier well on his way to the border, the question that ricocheted around the Černín Palace cocktail party was: "Why were he and Szulc thrown out?" The Foreign Ministry's boot had clearly been twisted by the Russians to get the Czechs to expel Szulc, but the officials who did it didn't really know why the dirty deed had been decreed. Tillier's departure made the reason more apparent:

Shortly after the invasion, the Russians had issued, in virtually every language read by man, 4-million copies of a 192-page book called *On Events in Czechoslovakia:* a compendium of *Pravda*'s truths, other slanders, and doctored photographs. Subtitled: "Facts, documents, press reports, and eyewitness accounts" and credited only to a "Press Group of Soviet Journalists," it had quickly become known as "The White Book." *

Then, in the fall, the Czechoslovak Academy of Sciences' Institute of History had quietly published (for research purposes by members and scholars only) a meticulously documented 494-page "Black Book" called *Seven Days in Prague,* telling just how and by whom the country had been betrayed. The "Black Book" was vaguely alluded to in the Prague mass media, but never quoted therein. Editors had been warned that the Russian response to any excerpts from it would be

---

* "The White Book" is a classic example of one of the few consistencies in Russian and East German journalism: their utter reliance upon and frequent quotation (or distortion) of Western sources. Apparently, their editors and readers know that their own press cannot be trusted for political information.

fatal. Gustáv Husák was already making sinister allegations about the financing of research and publication costs. . . .

Two American periodicals had printed substantial excerpts from "The Black Book" under New York datelines: *Newsweek* and *The New York Times.**

Valerie's parents traveled from America to spend our second Christmas in Prague with us. It was a joyous occasion despite the adversity of the times and Monica's coming down with the mumps. On the night before Christmas, the Doctor made the rounds vaccinating the five of our seven other dinner guests (including three eligible bachelors) who had never had the mumps.

Two pheasants, a gift from a hunter, had been hanging outside our pantry aging properly under the watchful eye of Paní B. On the twenty-third of December, she had pronounced them ready for cleaning and thereupon spent four hours on one of the most grueling plucking jobs we have ever had the misfortune to witness. When she was done, the pheasants were clean—and, stripped of their plumes, barely big enough to feed two people each, but hardly thirteen. A turkey was located and pressed into service moments before the stores closed for the holiday.

Some childless neighbors brought home a Christmas tree from the Bohemian forest, decorated it in their flat with silvery Christmas balls and nursery-rhyme ornaments (cats playing fiddles, etc.) plus American peppermint candy-canes that Val's parents had supplied, and then smuggled it into our living room on Christmas Eve. The children were led into a darkened living room that was suddenly illuminated by the lights of a ceiling-high tree towering over a mound of gifts. When Erika had put her jaw back together, she announced that "next to Daddy, Grandpa, Dubček, and Svoboda, I love Santa Claus the most."

At midnight, the muted Channel One televised High Mass from the medieval St. Jacob's Church in the Old Town of Prague. We saw that even a sheepish Antonín Novotný, Jr., had come to worship—and the camera panned to his Mercedes-Benz parked outside.

On the feast of St. Stephen's, the day after Christmas, we went to St. Nicholas Church for the traditional mass composed by J. J. Ryba, a

* The "Black Book" was later published in America under the title of *The Czech Black Book* (New York: Praeger, 1969). It was edited by Robert Littell, the *Newsweek* editor who brought a copy of the original document out of Czechoslovakia that fall.

Czech contemporary and (in the sphere of church music, at least) peer of Mozart's. An organ, an ensemble of baroque instruments, a 200-voice chorus, four soloists from the Colegium of Sacred Music, and 2,000 worshippers were jammed into the baroque splendor of St. Nicholas where you felt that Christmas was really happening. Parents held babies and lovers held hands, for religion had become a bastion of shared faith and a form of rebellion (as it was in the beginning) here in occupied Czechoslovakia. And there burst forth a sound that might have thrilled heaven or toppled the Kremlin. But was anybody listening?

Almost in answer, Bolshakov struck!

On 27 December 1968, Moscow's *Komsomolska Pravda* carried an article called "HOW IT IS BEING DONE," by V. Bolshakov. It was a long attack on Jiří Menzel (who owed his success to "the active participation of Zionist organizations") and Jan Němec (a "defector to the West," although he was and still is in Czechoslovakia) and Miloš Forman, who was home on a holiday visit and who brought me Četeka's translation:

> Miloš Forman is young, like many other directors who are setting the tone in the Czechoslovak movies today. His fame, though great, arose only recently. . . . His pathological hate against common people . . . is purposeful. He does not pillory the middle class—the voracious and wolfish philistines. With his camera, he keeps a sharp eye on the Czechoslovak working class, which he presents as just a gang of blunt and greedy . . . yahoos. One can call Forman's pictures a vivid, illustrated edition of the counter-revolution's program, "The 2,000 Words Manifesto". . . .

Now, in the best Bogart-Belmondo tradition, special investigator Bolshakov unmasked the *real* conspiracy:

> It is not by chance that these young directors have been fawned over with praise and dollars in the USA. And it was no freak of chance that the American weekly *Time*, in its first December issue, cited among the chief merits of Forman's *Firemen's Ball* that those who attended the party were "functionaries of the Communist Party."
>
> In Prague, I met by chance the correspondent of the *Life* magazine Aaron Levi. We began a conversation and it turned out that Levi, whose anti-Soviet convictions go without saying, came to Czechoslovakia solely to cooperate with Forman. At the moment, he is writing a scenario for his next movie. In fact, it was Levi who "discovered" Forman's "masterpieces" for the West and it was due to his activity that

the movies of Forman, Menzel, and Němec received such wide publicity in the United States.

The mere fact that such movies could have been made in a socialist country played an excellent trump card into the hands of these professional anti-Communists and anti-Soviets of all shades.

It made lively reading. The otherwise muzzled Czech press leaped at the opportunity to reprint such Stalinist propaganda in its entirety. "WHAT THEY ARE WRITING ABOUT US," one journal headlined it. We were all asked for comment. Forman took it upon himself to point out that "his name is Alan Levy, not Aaron Levi." The editor who called me for comment asked me what I thought of "the clearly anti-Semitic version of your name."

"Oh, I'm sure it wasn't that at all," I said cheerfully. "Mr. Bolshakov must have learned English from a Japanese tutor and that's why 'Alan Levy' came out 'Aaron Levi.' "

I was putting a cheerful face on it, but I remember that, when Miloš first started reading me the Bolshakov article, I kept wandering over to the window to see if I was being shadowed yet. For the terror had struck. Until then, I had been doing my work inconspicuously and, under the circumstances, serenely. But I had now been singled out, labeled, and branded with the yellow star of Aaron Levi, the anti-Soviet dybbuk who had polluted the mainstream of Czech worker-and-peasant cinema. Now, at best, it would be harder to do my work unnoticed among the people and hills and stones and smells I loved so much that I could scarcely live without them. . . .

The Czechoslovak Film Journalists Union issued a formal protest against Bolshakov's "slanderous, insulting, and unqualified" attack on all of us. And I would suspect that it was the official nature of this protest that saved my skin in Prague. For, in the two weeks between Aaron Levi's debut in *Komsomolska Pravda* and the Union's protest to Moscow, I was a hot potato to the officials with whom I had to deal. I could actually hear the chill at the other end of the telephone line. After that, social engagements with them were, for the most part, at an end.

This was not the case with our non-official friends. "Congratulations, you certainly stood up to the Russians!" was their general theme. Just as some writers yearn to be banned in Boston, foreign correspondents are supposed to dream of denunciations in some kind of *Pravda*.

Perhaps it's a spectacular way to go if you're ready to go and if your boss relocates you somewhere better. But it's no joy when you know nowhere better to go and when you're living on your own in a land that is militarily occupied by tens of thousands of the *Pravda*'s armed readers.

Between Christmas and New Year's, dislodging Josef Smrkovský from power became the personal crusade of Gustáv Husák. And Husák's little hatchet was once again the cause of Slovak nationalism for which he'd once been imprisoned. Federalization was due to start on 1 January. Constitutionally, the new Federal Assembly would be headed by the Speaker of the old National Assembly, Smrkovský, until the next general election, which the Russians weren't going to let happen for a good long time. But Husák said that, inasmuch as the President (Svoboda) was a Czech "whom we all respect and acknowledge" and inasmuch as the Prime Minister (Černík) was a Czech "who is fully supported," the third high state function should be held by a Slovak.

A unifying force was turned into a divisive maneuver. Federalization was discredited before it ever started. The proposal made no sense at all to Czechs or most Slovaks. Wasn't Dubček a Slovak, for God's sake? Yes, but Husák had arbitrarily ruled party posts, even the seat of monolithic power, out of consideration in this matter.

Petitions, protests, and strike threats poured in from all over the land. Husák's small villa near Bratislava was stoned by irate Slovak workingmen. Portraits of Smrkovský appeared bearing the inscription in Slovak: "SLOVAKS ARE WITH YOU!"

On New Year's Eve, with his status still in doubt, it was Josef Smrkovský himself who delivered this poignant toast to the Czech and Slovak nations over the radio a few minutes before midnight:

"Only a few minutes divide us from the end of the year, one of those fateful years for us that end in the number eight;* a year which brought enough joy, hope, and sorrow to last for years. At this moment, we can hardly evaluate what kind of year it actually was. But one thing we know for sure: In these unforgettable 366 days, we learned a great deal. It was a great school."

Then, turning to the coming year of 1969, Smrkovský said:

* The Czechoslovak Republic was born in 1918; dismembered in 1938 at Munich; communized in 1948; and reborn and repressed in 1968.

"A wise man wrote that confidence is presupposed certainty. And, if such confidence has been created among us, it was just because of the unforgettable certainties opened up to us by the unforgettable January of 1968.

"Therefore, I wish you all, Czechs and Slovaks and all the others—and forgive me for the immodesty: myself, too—that the calendar should not change; for next year to begin with January and to begin in its spirit, in the spirit of the best that we have created together. . . . It is of this I am thinking when I raise my glass of our wine."

We were at Gene Deitch's again as we had been on 31 December 1967, when we had found our baby-sitter and our home in Prague. (The Deitches had returned in early fall.) But this time the special toast was: "May 1969 *not* be a completely new year!"

The Doctor was on night duty at her children's hospital. She had been hoping to display the first baby of the New Year on TV. But, after hearing Smrkovský on the radio, she forgot all about glory and called her daughter at home. "Did you hear the radio, too?" they both asked each other. Then they both had a good cry together over the telephone.

New Year's Eve in Mladá Boleslav: home of the Škoda auto works and now also the V.I. Lenin Barracks of the Red Army. Every fifth person who now walks the streets of Mladá Boleslav is a Russian soldier. Armed troops patrol the sidewalks in pairs. In Mladá Boleslav, the occupation of Czechoslovakia is visible and real.

In the stores, the Russians have been spending their freshly issued crowns as though they were scrip. *"I like these shoes. I'll take two hundred pairs."* "What size, tovarich?" *"All sizes. I'll have no trouble selling them when I get home."* . . . *"Three hundred skirts for the girls I left behind me."* Since long before Christmas, the shops of Mladá Boleslav have been bare.

Is it any wonder then that, on New Year's Eve, a couple of dozen revelers at a bash in a local club hang out a sign reading "NO RUSSIANS INVITED"? Aren't they entitled to an evening of escape? They are left alone until they start leaving in the early-morning hours of 1969. As they come down the steps, the first dozen celebrants are arrested and taken to the V.I. Lenin Barracks, where they spend all of New Year's Day and have their heads shaved. The rest remain at their party for another twenty-two hours spent crouching in terror.

All through the night of the third of January, 1969, the Prague Castle was ablaze with light and crawling with secret policemen. Dubček had convened an emergency meeting of the Presidium in response to an ultimatum from Brezhnev: The dumping of Smrkovský, already a month overdue, must be accomplished at once. Replacing him with a Slovak was a good idea, but the Slovak must be ex-Prime Minister Jozef Lenárt. Otherwise, Czechoslovakia must await the consequences. . . .

That weekend, Soviet troops and tanks rumbled around the vicinity of Prague and several other cities. They tied up traffic, set up roadblocks, and fired shots into the air, all in the name of "showing the flag" to Smrkovský's supporters, who were legion.

On Saturday, the 4th of January, 1969, the Presidium issued a stern warning to the people that "society cannot continue to live and work buffeted in clashes and strains on the verge of a political crisis in which tragic conflict could result from trifling causes." It also gave assurances that "conjectures on an attempt to remove Mr. Smrkovský from party and state functions and to remove him from political life are not based on fact."

Then, having denied these wicked intentions, the Presidium set about fulfilling them. Smrkovský, however, was adamant. He stood on his constitutional rights of office. He would have to be dragged screaming from his chair; particularly, he hinted, if he were to be replaced by such a ghost of Novotnýism as Lenárt.

Sometime that weekend, a weary Dubček phoned Brezhnev and told him that Smrkovský might possibly be demoted, but he could never be removed. And Lenárt could not possibly be installed in his place.

Everybody at Dubček's end held his breath. And, after a moment, Brezhnev sighed and yielded. His message was: Get Smrkovský out of that job any way you can.

Husák thereupon proposed his own man—a faceless Slovak bureaucrat—for the post, but Smrkovský resisted the idea and the Presidium failed to rally round Husák's Slovak.

Smrkovský knew he was pushing his luck, so now he sacrificed himself. He would step down one echelon if his own Slovak friend, Petr Colotka, a liberal ex-Deputy Premier, would be designated Chairman of the new Federal Assembly. The Presidium agreed that this was indeed a "way out." Colotka was named Chairman and Smrkovský would stay on as his First Deputy Chairman as well as Speaker of one of the two houses of the new parliament.

The people of Prague had admired Gustáv Husák until the end of August and detested him thereafter, but they had never really seen much of the man. This particular information gap was remedied forever on the Friday night after the Smrkovský compromise, when Czechoslovak Television treated us to more than half an hour of Husák haranguing a meeting of factory chairmen in Slovakia.

Still smarting from his setback at the Presidium, Husák put on an arm-flailing, demagogic performance the likes of which I have never seen before or since in Czechoslovakia:*

"There are people in Prague who put a knife at our throat. They say they are for Dubček and Svoboda, Svo-bo-dahh and Dooob-ček [here, Husák mimicked the Czech people's litany in mincing Slovak], but what are they really for? They ask for strikes! Now what would a strike do? It would hurt the economy. It would hurt the workers. . . .

"Certain people speak today about policy making 'behind closed doors.' Does this apply to collective discussions by elected party and Government bodies? Or does it mean private meetings of little groups of people who—without any mandate from party or public—meet surreptitiously in their flats to think up provocative acts, launch campaigns, and influence the brave people through the mass media?"

Husák found virtually nothing good to say about 1968's January Spring. During this time, "there were other forces which formally adhered to socialism, but were, in fact, opposition forces . . . propagating destructive activities. . . .

"Some in the mass communications are honorable, some have been abusing power, and some have been instituting action against our nation. Some measures will have to be taken. . . .

"Journalists say that officials should be criticized and that it is necessary to control the leaders. But I ask who controls the journalists? They think themselves to be the owners of the mass communications facilities. Something will have to be done to control them."

---

* Husák has since muted his oratorical style, but he remains the only ranking Czechoslovak leader who speaks to audiences without notes. At the summit, he is addicted to dryly recurrent phrases like "Wild West" for America; snickering at his own jokes; and, as with most orthodox Communist leaders, doubling as cheerleader by applauding his own words.

And so it went. When it was finished, a Czech who was watching the telecast with me took a deep breath and said: "That finishes Husák politically. The people here are too cultured for such a man."

Prime Minister Černík submitted to a TV interview the following Wednesday. "We can say without a doubt that the situation in our country has now quieted down."

At 1500 the next afternoon, Thursday 16 January 1969, Jan Palach stood on the steps of the bullet-spattered National Museum, took a lingering look down at the statue of Good Prince Wenceslas, doffed his overcoat and pinned a note to it, placed his briefcase (containing an identical note) on the ledge of the museum fountain, doused himself with the contents of a can of benzine, and struck a match.

A dispatcher at the trolley stand beside the Wenceslas statue saw a figure coming toward him "burning from head to foot." The dispatcher flung off his own overcoat even while the blazing torch that was Jan Palach cried: "Throw your coat over me!" With that, Palach stumbled and fell. The dispatcher was able to stifle the flames with his coat. An ambulance came two minutes later and the dispatcher rode in the back with Palach. "I—did it—myself," Palach gasped along the way. He had "highest-degree burns over 85 per cent of his body," according to the hospital, where his condition was described as "very grave."

The contents of Palach's note were never published officially in Czechoslovakia, but copies were posted all over Prague later that night. Signed "Torch No. 1," it began:

> With regard to the fact that our country is at the edge of hope-lessness, we decided to express our protest and awaken the people . . . in the following way:
>
> Our group is composed of volunteers who are ready to burn them-selves for our cause. I had the honor to draw the first lot and I have gained the right to write the first letter and set the first torch.

The note went on to warn that, unless censorship was abolished imme-diately and *Zprávy* was prohibited, "further torches will go up in flames."

Palach's deed shook the Czech nation as nothing else had since Au-gust. Self-immolation was an Eastern cure which had already spread from Buddhist temples to the gates of the United Nations and the Pen-tagon. But who could have imagined a Central European student setting fire to himself? And particularly a Czech, with his people's instinct to survive and endure.

Jan Palach lay dying for four days—visited only by doctors, nurses, family, and one fellow student who was admitted by Palach's request: the strike leader and onetime Novotný conscript, Lubomír Holeček. And Holeček hinted that he knew who Torch Number 2 would be.

On the next-to-last day of his life, Palach told one of the attending physicians that "it was my duty to do it and there will be others." The doctor said that Palach's mind was "clear and logical. He sees himself as another Jan Hus, as the second Czech in our history to burn for truth. Jan Hus let himself be burned for it and Jan Palach thought it was his duty to do the same. Jan says he has no regrets."

That Sunday, on television, a woman newscaster wept as she read the brief bulletin: "Jan Palach died quietly. His body could not stand the strain of the burns."

On the radio, Holeček read the words that Palach had dictated to him three hours before dying:

"My act has fulfilled its purpose, but let nobody else do it. . . . Let the living make their efforts in the struggle. I say goodbye. We may still see each other."

The next afternoon, 200,000 people—one-fifth of Prague's population—converged on Wenceslas Square to place wreaths where Jan Palach fell. They passed beneath a death mask of Palach—ringed by black crêpe—gazing down upon his legacy. Then, led by students and young Czech soldiers with flags of mourning, they filed in an orderly procession through the streets of the Old Town to the Philosophical Faculty in Red Army Square, which was instantly renamed Jan Palach Square.

At noon on Friday 24 January 1969, sirens sounded and then there were five minutes of silence in Palach's honor. People stopped in their tracks. Soldiers and policemen saluted. Men bared their heads to the wind. Trams and buses and taxis halted. The whole city froze like the tableau in *Sleeping Beauty* once she pricks her finger and the spell is cast. Then, at 1205, the city came back to life.

All that afternoon and night, Jan Palach's coffin lay in state in the courtyard of Charles University's oldest building, the Carolinium. From an upstairs window came requiems by Bach and Dvořák played by prominent organists taking two-hour shifts. The coffin lay beneath a statue of Jan Hus surrounded by huge fields of flowers. An honor guard of professors in satin and velvet medieval robes was almost lost to the eye amidst the forest of wreaths. Outside, the slowly moving line of the bereaved snaked for two miles through the winding cobble-stoned streets of Prague's Old Town. It was cold and damp out, but we shivered for more reasons than one during our four-hour wait on line. "What a country we live in!" exclaimed the man behind me. "Where the only light for the future is the burning body of a young boy!"

WHEN JAN PALACH DIED, THIS IS THE OBITUARY THAT *Reportér,* the Journalist Union's weekly, printed:

> Goodbye, Josef Schweik:
>
> No, I do not say this to you, nor does the generation that remembers you and the last fifty years of the Republic. I do not say it, for without you we could scarcely have endured what we were living through. Indeed . . . the nation that took recourse in the protective wings of Josef Schweik could never be annihilated. So it is, verbally. We all knew how to do it in spite of all the bossing, all the compulsory participation in meetings, all the foolish parades, resolutions, and "fulfillment of plans." We were able to laugh at the pseudo-idealism which was poured into our heads and we accepted it as a welcome sparring partner to our conditions. . . .
>
> This attitude suddenly broke down in our last tragic days. Something happened which is out of character for our centuries-old resistance. Something from ancient antiquity, from Greek tragedy, was breathed on us all. Suddenly the deed of one student cut the Gordian knot of the Czech nation. No, this is no exaggeration! The switch was literally turned off for our generation which, though it remembers something, fails to comprehend its meaning and stands now only with its hat in its hand.

And so the author, M. A. Tesař, reiterated: "Goodbye, Josef Schweik. The coming generation has surely parted with you. What will be its perspectives? What will be its fate? What will be its end?"

Chapter 20

Saturday 25 January—
Thursday 7 April 1969

THE FUNERAL OF JAN PALACH WAS ONE OF THOSE events, like John F. Kennedy's or Rudolph Valentino's, that will never leave you if you were there. I used my press credentials to get into the Carolinium courtyard. Palach's mother was there, a squat but trim woman in black with a thin veil. She was flanked by her older son and his wife. The latter was a pretty girl, also in black, very pale, with her nose glowing red from weeping. The mother ran her hand along the pale oak coffin and said: "My beloved son, my son, what have you done? He was my favorite son." And, in a tone that might have been Dubček's on the night of 20 August, she also said: "I never believed a thing like this would happen."

The eulogy was by Dr. Oldřich Starý, rector of Charles University*: "Jan Palach's heroic and tragic deed is an expression of a pure heart and the highest degree of love for country, freedom, and democracy. This torch will arouse all people of good will to continue . . . along the road of building a human, democratic, undeformed socialism in our country. . . . Jan Palach brought to the altar of his home the highest possible sacrifice. It will remain in the memory of Czechs and Slovaks and millions of people elsewhere." And the dean of the Philosophical Faculty added these words: "Let us promise here that we shall do all we can so that such sacrifices will no longer be necessary."

When the ceremony was over, the bells of 150 churches in Prague tolled, the organ played Dvořák, and the pallbearers slid the coffin into a plain black hearse. A fleet of black Volga taxicabs had been reserved for the family, but the mother said "I can still walk" and then so did

---

* Dr. Starý later took asylum in the U.S. while on a Ford Foundation grant. Walking near Columbia University in September 1969, he was mugged by three men, two of whom were captured. The third, however, escaped with Starý's briefcase containing important papers.

everyone else. The empty black taxis at the front of the procession had an impact of their own, like riderless steeds.

After the taxis came three students bearing a huge Czechoslovak flag and fighting to keep it unfurled in the wind and steady rain as they plodded through cobblestoned streets ankle deep in muddy water. They were followed by the entire faculty of Charles University and other academic figures in their medieval red and black and gold cere-monial robes. Among them were the Minister of Education and the former Foreign Minister Jiří Hájek.

Now came rows and rows of students bearing flowers and then a U-shaped ring of students—boys and girls—holding hands like Israeli hora dancers to keep spectators from breaking through to the coffin. Just behind them came the hearse, crawling in stately solitude. Then a brass band, from the ČKD Works, playing mournful hymns. Then the mother and son and daughter-in-law and relatives. And then thou-sands of students behind a long black banner.

The procession passed through the Old Fruit Market, where there had been no hint of orange or grapefruit for months; turned left at the Powder Tower and down Celetná Street, past an old mint, past the early-day cubist "House of the Dark Mother of God," past the Vul-ture's Tavern with its medallion of Socrates on the facade, and into the Old Town Square.

Half-a-million people waited in the Square, leaving just a path of space that the students (who organized and policed all of Friday's and Saturday's events) had cleared for the procession. From the balcony of the Kinský Palace, where Kafka went to school, trombonists played fu-neral fanfares. The bells of the Týn Cathedral tolled. From the obser-vation tower above the Town Hall clock, a choir sang a Hussite hymn. The one sound I couldn't place was a weeping, sniffling echo that rum-bled like distant cannon. But when I looked around me and saw thou-sands of faces, particularly the old faces, contorted with grief, I recog-nized what I was hearing. Not until later, when I went to wash my face, did I realize that I had been crying, too.

The procession moved down Pařížská Street toward the empty Stalin monument, but swerved left into the ghetto and circled the an-cient Jewish cemetery before halting in the new Jan Palach (formerly Red Army) Square. There, the ČKD band played the national hymn. Then the mother and the family mourners boarded their black taxi-cabs. They and the hearse drove off to Olšany Cemetery, where Jan

Palach was laid to rest not far from the grave of Franz Kafka and the Tomb of the Unknown Soviet Soldier.

And the rest of us stood, with the Czechoslovak flag, in Jan Palach Square outside the Philosophical Faculty and the Dvořák Hall concert auditorium. Across the Vltava and up Hradčany Hill, the Castle was still visible, but entirely gray in the darkening mist. And I know that I will always recall the sister-in-law's red nose and that mournful castle whenever I think of the funeral of Jan Palach.

Sylva wrote her first words about Palach a couple of weeks later in *Zítřek,* which published her thoughts under the headline: "THE VOICE OF MAN IS THE VOICE OF GOD, BUT WHEN?"

All the things we value—truth, man's dignity, the necessity of living a real life—acquired a new sense through this terrible deed.

But Sylva's own mind had never left Jan Palach Square, where the students' official-looking street markers were now being removed. The square was reverting to its old name: Red Army Square.

Sylva made the rounds of the municipal bureaucracy to ask why. The official reply was that the new name would "disorient" tourists with old maps. But weren't tourists and natives already disoriented by Prague's having two Red Army Squares at different ends of town? And weren't tram conductors calling out the stop there as "Jan Palach Square"?

Sylva's crusade was foredoomed, but her interviews were enlightening.

One of the officials asked Sylva: "Don't you remember all the chaos of the 1950's [when street names were Stalinized]? What would Prague look like if everyone wanted a street named after his grandfather?"

"But this is an unusual case and we are living in a very exceptional time!" Sylva exclaimed.

"What's exceptional about this time?" he asked, smiling blandly, but speaking in a tone that implied she had better leave well enough alone. "Look at you," he went on. "You have a nice sweater and new boots that come up to your knees."

Sylva got out of there fast but she printed the dialogue in *Zítřek.*

The Russians watched the national agony caused by Palach's death in semi-silence, though Tass did term his act "anti-socialist provocation." Next to nothing was heard from Dubček during this time, but it became known that he had experienced a nervous collapse over Palach's deed and was confined to his bed for a fortnight. At precisely the moment when Richard Nixon was being inaugurated as the thirty-seventh President of the United States, another President, Ludvík Svoboda, seventy-three, went on Czechoslovak Television to praise the twenty-year-old martyr as "a man of pure character with pure intentions," but warning that "one spark can create a big fire which could claim many victims." Svoboda went on to say:

"As a soldier, I can appreciate the self-denial and personal courage of Jan Palach. As President and a citizen of our Republic, however, I cannot hide the fact that I do not agree with this method of expressing political standpoints.

"I have just received the shocking news that another young man has tried in Pilsen to repeat the act of Jan Palach."

The nation writhed in shock and horror. It didn't matter that the human torch in Pilsen (who died later in the week) was a twenty-five-year-old brewery worker with divorce and drinking problems. He was a man, and the initial impact was the same. Before a week was out, four more Czechoslovaks had set fire to themselves—one, a convicted thief, at a catafalque honoring Palach in Brno—and an eighteen-year-old Prague student, Blanka Nacházelová, had killed herself with gas. She left a note saying she acted "for the same reason as Jan Palach, but without his courage."

On the steps of Budapest's National Museum, an eighteen-year-old Hungarian student set fire to himself and died. There were related attempts in Austria, Yugoslavia, and Argentina. Across Western Europe, thousands of students marched on Soviet Embassies and trade offices to protest for Palach. U Thant sent his official regrets. The Vatican, without quite condoning Palach's suicide, compared it to the sacrifices of early Christian martyrs and said such protests "deserved the gratitude" of the world. Pope Paul VI, who led prayers in St. Peter's Square for Czechoslovakia and its people, said "we cannot approve the tragic form taken on behalf of [their] aims, but we can uphold the values that put self-sacrifice and love of others to the supreme test."

At the National Theatre, Arthur Miller's *The Crucible* (which is called *Trial by Fire* here) was substituted for *The Bartered Bride* as well as comedies and ballets in the week's repertory programming. And Arthur Miller himself came to Prague soon thereafter. He heard someone denigrate Palach's act as a "superindividual gesture." Miller retorted:

"Palach's death was like a work of art. People, and often society, protest against a great work of art because it forces them to make comparisons—making them feel smaller if they don't tend toward greatness, freedom and truth. It provokes them and places such great demands on them that it puts them to shame. . . . A hero is a man sacrificed by others, which is why they deny him. A hero illuminates truth, which is why he is exposed to fire and sacrifice."

Miller's words were printed in *Listy*. His was a metaphor that every Czech and Slovak could understand—though their leaders tried not to.

The time that followed Jan Palach's funeral was, in general, a period of letdown when everybody had the willies. People found it harder to do their work or go about their business. They just stood around waiting for something to happen or for Torch Number 2 to ignite.

It was also a time when the kind of official gangsterism practiced here in the late 1940's and the 1950's (not always under domestic auspices) reasserted itself on the fringe of this tormented society. A liberal official in Ostrava was visited and terrorized in his home one night. A Prague TV commentator was interrogated endlessly about a possible passport violation. A few notable Prague intellectuals began to sense (though they couldn't yet prove) they were being followed or wiretapped. In the provinces, a handful of people disappeared by way of police stations.

In early February of 1969, the press carried this brief announcement:

> Mr. Vitězslav Kadlčák, alias Major Chlumský, who allegedly stirred up a campaign around the death of Mr. Jan Masaryk, professing that he had been murdered, now stands on trial at the Prague 1 Borough Court, being accused of libel and the defamation of the Republic and her representative.

It seemed significant to my police reporter's nose for official cover-ups that, of all the charges and countercharges flung over Jan Masaryk's grave in 1968, Chlumský's was the first one selected for reprisals. He had been placed under arrest as early as 8 September 1968.

By the time I went down to the court, the Chlumský case had been adjourned until 20 February. The judiciary had not yet been fully purged and the magistrate was intrigued enough to give Major Chlumský time to fetch some evidence which he said would document his case. He claimed to have, among other documents, the minutes of a secret meeting held in Klement Gottwald's home immediately after Masaryk's death. Among those claimed by Chlumský to be present were Gottwald's son-in-law Alexej Čepička* and Stalin's emissary Valerian Zorin. According to Chlumský, Gottwald opened the meeting by saying: "At last we've gotten rid of this cripple, and it's suicide. We needn't worry about popular unrest. . . . Now we'll have to see to it that Clementis† keeps his mouth shut. He's saying queer things, he's crying like a baby. He must be prevented from babbling at the funeral. . . ."

On the 18th of February at 0550, Chlumský was returning to Prague from a north Bohemian hideaway. Driving his old Škoda carefully near the Gothic town of Louny, Chlumský braked for a railroad crossing. He noticed that, a fair distance behind him, a new Moskva car braked suddenly and skidded a little.

Just beyond the crossing, Chlumský slowed down and swerved to get by a black Volga that was standing in his lane with its parking lights on. As he passed, he heard a pinging noise and then the tinkle of glass as his right window broke.

"My first thought," he said later, "was that my car had brushed the other car. Then my head began to sting. I put my hand up near my right ear and felt something sticky. I started to brake, but then I saw another car—the Moskva—gaining on me very quickly and I realized what was happening.

"I pressed down on the accelerator, but the other car was stronger and kept gaining on me. I knew there was a porcelain factory a few hundred yards ahead and I hoped there would be people there to help me. But we were still in front of a farm when the Moskva drew even with me. I'm not a Catholic, but I tell you I prayed!"

In desperation, Major Chlumský said he decided to make one last thrust, by ramming his old Škoda into the Moskva. He leaned back to brace himself for the impact and as he did so his driver's seat flipped

---

* Čepička had been under investigation for his role in a 1947 bomb attempt on Masaryk and two other ministers. He became the first Communist Minister of Justice in 1948. Still alive, it was he who preferred charges against Chlumský two decades later.

† The Deputy Foreign Minister, hanged with Rudolf Slánský in 1952.

over backwards and Chlumský was tossed into the back of his own car. His Škoda swerved off the road and overturned in a snowbank. As he lost consciousness, he heard shots fired. . . .

When he awoke at the hospital in Louny, his first question was about a brown briefcase that he said had been beside him in the car. But neither the police nor the trucker who'd called them knew anything about it. Almost immediately, the police in Prague, thirty miles away, issued a statement that Major Chlumský had experienced "an automobile accident." Later, they claimed he had either faked or staged the incident to divert attention from the absence of evidence to support his case.

The head surgeon at Louny told reporters who went there that Chlumský had arrived "in a grave state of shock and unable to move. It was absolutely impossible for him to simulate this condition, above all the uncontrollable trembling. . . . Personally, I think that what saved [him] was the seat's falling back: the first bullet passed through his beret and grazed his scalp, while the others only pierced his coat and scarf. The police surgeon from Ústí-nad-Labem was called in, and he thought that another injury, on the left ear, was caused by a bullet also. I couldn't conceive of anybody knowingly taking the risk of faking such an incident, or being shot at in such a way. . . ."

Police in Louny wouldn't let reporters look at Chlumský's car. Most indicative, however, of the shadowy quasi-official determination to discredit Chlumský was the experience of the Catholic newspaper, *People's Democracy*. Minutes after the shooting, an editor in the Prague office heard about it. He phoned the hospital in Louny, where a doctor began describing Chlumský's injuries. Suddenly, the phone connection broke. The editor placed the call again. This time, he was informed that all phone connections to Louny were out-of-order and it would take twenty-four hours for them to be repaired.

Undaunted, the editor left the newspaper office, whose phones were known to be monitored, and went to a friend's apartment nearby. From there, he placed a call to a private home in Louny, and it was put right through.

Chlumský recovered, but his trial was adjourned indefinitely— until, that is, his pursuers could be guaranteed a more responsive judiciary and a more sympathetic press. Hence, his last published utterance was made while he still lay in his hospital bed in Louny:

"They are now making such a hubbub about my documents. Well, they were never of such importance that Czechoslovakia should become Chicago. And in today's Czechoslovakia, ever since last August, they no longer have any special value."

In this shadowy time of the Chlumský shooting, there were also determined efforts to tarnish Palach's suicide and related events. Thus, a Central Committee member named Vilém Nový came up with the "revelation" that, while Palach was in West Germany in 1968, he had experimented (under imperialist auspices) with a liquid form of "cold fire" used by Indian fakirs and circus fire-eaters to perform their daily miracles. According to Nový, Palach went into Wenceslas Square thinking he would catch fire, but not burn seriously, and this miracle would be interpreted as divine endorsement of his demands. But, at the very last hour, his fellow student conspirators had, unbeknownst to Palach, substituted normal benzine for his "cold fire."

Similarly, the most infiltrated of the three Interior Ministries now produced the first full text of the suicide note from the girl who'd gassed herself "for the same reasons as Jan Palach." This version implied that she was forced to take her life:

> My dears: When you read this letter, I shall no longer know about it. Believe me, what I have done is not out of conviction. I was forced to do it. I did not have the terrible courage of Jan Palach. I am therefore dying in this way. It is much easier for me, but it is cruel; I want so much to live. When a black Mercedes sounds its horn three times at exactly 0830, I shall pull down the blinds and open the gas. I don't want to, but I must. Please forgive me, forgive me. I can't get out of it any longer. This is better than acid in the face. Goodbye and forgive me, BLANKA

Palach's suicide note hadn't been published. This one was. And, though its language was Czech, its heavy-handed style was unmistakably that of only one genre in the world: the East German detective story.

"Cold fire, fakirs, and a black Mercedes! This is all a bit too rich for our taste," remarked the trade union journal *Work*. Then, referring to Hitler's 1933 ploy of political arson, *Work* concluded: "Let us hope that we won't have a Reichstag fire."

One of my friends' interpretations was even more succinct: "It smells as if the Šalgovičes are coming home from Dresden."

He meant it figuratively, but we found out (a month after the fact) that the betrayer of Prague was indeed back, this time in his native Slovakia. He had even been proposed for the steering committee of the Congress of Slovak Anti-Fascist Fighters, the alumni society of World War II partisans, among whom Šalgovič admittedly had a distinguished record. A professor from Bratislava, however, had risen to challenge Šalgovič for omitting from his *curriculum vitae* "the fact that . . . on 20 August 1968 at 1600, that is seven hours before the entry of the troops and at a time when the President of the Republic, the Prime Minister, and the First Secretary . . . knew nothing, he was issuing instructions to his closest selected fellow workers as to what they were to do when the troops crossed the border."

Šalgovič had pleaded in reply that all he did was order his men not to resist the troops of the five countries because he did not have the heart to shoot at those with whom he had fought side-by-side in the fight against fascism.

"This is cheap self-appreciation," the professor had noted in pointing out all the questions that Šalgovič sidestepped. And the congress rejected Šalgovič by a vote of 211 to 206, with 120 abstentions. But it came as a jolt that, already, there were 206 people in Czechoslovakia who were willing to vote in favor of Šalgovič.

I phoned my Jewish economist friend with journalistic leanings as I had promised to do if Šalgovič ever came back. My friend was "out of the country indefinitely."

On 25 February 1969, the twenty-first anniversary of the Communist takeover and exactly a month after Jan Palach's funeral, another human torch came flaming out of a boiler room (where he had doused himself with cleaning fluid) onto Wenceslas Square. A Prague police major tried to put out the blaze. The major was hospitalized and on the danger list for two days; the boy was dead on arrival. A suicide note found nearby identified him as Jan Zajíc, eighteen, an engineering student from the north of Moravia. He signed himself "Torch Number 2."

By then, the police were able to conceal his suicide note "in keeping with valid Czechoslovak norms." The press could only carry a three-paragraph routine obituary. But Jan Zajíc had mailed a separate letter to his family—and this was made public by his fellow students:

Dear Mother, Father, Brother, and Sister:

When you read this letter, I'll be dead or very near dead. I know what pain I cause you by my deed, but please don't be angry. Unfortunately, I know I am not alone in this world—I don't do this because I am unhappy with life, but precisely because I love life too much. Perhaps I'll make it better for you by my act. I know the meaning of life and I know its highest value. But I want too much for you, for everyone, and that's why I have to pay so much.

After my act, don't lose your spirit. Let Jaček [his brother] learn more so that he may avenge me and the same for Martička [his sister]. You can never agree with injustice no matter what it is. My death binds you to that.

I am sorry I couldn't see you again and couldn't see all I loved so much. Forgive me for disagreeing with you so much. I sent Jaček's photograph back to him. I loved and esteemed him very much—not just him, but you all. Don't allow them to make me out a madman. Give my regards to the boys, to the river, and the woods.

He ended with "goodbye and forgive me."

In a postscript, Jan Zajíc asked to be buried in Prague so that his act would be recorded "in the eyes of the world." His request wasn't granted; neither the authorities nor the people of Prague were ready for another funeral like Palach's. But thousands traveled to Jan Zajíc's home town for his funeral. This funeral, though, was watched and policed by the Red Army. During the procession along an icy road, one of the slow-moving cars skidded a little. Fearing that the auto was coming at him, a Russian soldier opened fire on it and shot a woman passenger through the liver and bowels.

I don't know whether the woman lived because *Zitřek,* which sent two of Sylva's male colleagues to Zajíc's funeral and printed an account of the shooting incident, received a stern warning from the censors to drop the subject. But *Zitřek* put on the record the circumstances which drove Jan Zajíc to take his life. On Svoboda Street, directly across from the boy's school and his dormitory, the Red Army had evicted the Czechoslovak Army from a barracks, torn down a sign bearing the motto "WE ARE A SERVICE TO THE PEOPLE," and replaced it with "LONG LIVE SOVIET-CZECH FRIENDSHIP." During a winter "coal calamity," when the town shivered without heat, Jan Zajíc had watched the Russians unload tons of coal freighted in from the Soviet Union for their own use. And he had told a classmate: "I like to live, but I'll never be able to live here together with them."

Thanks almost exclusively to *Zitřek*'s reportage, Jan Zajíc earned a niche in the long pantheon of Czech martyrs named Jan (John): the Bohemian King John of Luxemburg (father of Charles IV) who perished in the Battle of Crécy in 1346, urging his charger into the thick of the fray even after he'd been blinded . . . the confessor Jan of Nepomuk (1393), the heretic Jan Hus (1415) and his one-eyed general, Jan Žižka (1424) . . . the student Jan Opletal (1939) . . . the statesman Jan Masaryk (1948) . . . and now, in 1969, Jan Palach and Jan Zajíc.

Another Jan, Jan Amos Komenský, alias Comenius, who died in exile in 1670, had helped Marta Kubišová win the televised Golden Nightingale (*Zlatý Slavík*) singing competition in early 1969 with his "Marta's Prayer" lyric. We had seen Mr. and Mrs. Alexander Dubček sitting in the front row. Later, we saw photos of Dubček congratulating Kubišová with a backstage kiss and lifting a glass with her and another singer. Then, during this peculiar gray period of 1969 when the NKVD seemed to be regaining and tightening its grip on the police apparatus, somebody took a pot shot at Marta Kubišová's upstairs window.

Hardly anybody was willing to heed the victim's own suspicion that it was the work of "some kind of jealous lover." Clearly it was, at the very least, part of a political assassination plot.

A week later, however, the Prague press carried a one-sentence announcement: "Film director J.N. confessed that he was the man who shot at Marta Kubišová." J.N. had to be Jan Němec, who'd been dating Marta recently and whose *Oratorio for Prague* had infuriated the Russians. Obviously, some diabolical purge conceived in Moscow was working to take both Kubišová and Němec out of circulation.

And yet, there was Němec in the Chinsky Restaurant, washing down his black eggs with Pilsener beer and admitting, with a cheerful wave of the chopsticks, that it was all true:

"It was a lovers' spat. She wasn't answering the phone or letting me come see her, so I got in touch by firing a shot through her window. A policeman turned up right away and said: 'Here, here, you can't do that, y'know.' So I jumped into my car and drove away. The police chased me into the outskirts and, when I saw I'd never lose them, I jumped out of my car and ran across a field. There was a country tavern near there and who did I find drinking there but some friends of mine!

"I spent the rest of the night there and rode back to Prague with them. Next morning, I reported that my car had been stolen. The police had it and were very suspicious, but my friends swore I'd been with them all night; they honestly remembered it that way! Later, when my friends kept being called back to the station house for longer and longer interrogations, I decided it was time for me to face the music.

"By then, Marta and I had patched up our quarrel. So we went hand-in-hand to the police station. I confessed. She said she didn't want to prosecute. They gave me a lecture and took away my gun. I suppose that's all we'll ever hear of it. Fortunately, I was dealing with the criminal police, not the security police."

Before long, Němec was dealing with both. Němec had been collaborating with playwright Václav Havel (*The Memorandum*) on a screenplay. Hearing a rumor that the Russians wanted the Czechs to tighten censorship by installing *pre*-censors in newspaper offices (instead of calling editors on the carpet *after* publication—which is the way it still stood then), Němec and Havel sent President Svoboda a wire imploring him to resist this demand.

They received no reply. They weren't even able to ascertain whether their message had ever reached the President. After a decent interval, they took copies of it to the Prague press, whose editors thanked them for their support and apologized for no longer daring to print such fighting words. Around this time, Havel and Němec began to have a vague impression they were under surveillance.

Havel invited a relative, who was an electrician, over to install an overhead lamp fixture in his study and to poke around. The relative discovered a curious hole in the ceiling. With a long screwdriver, he extracted an extraordinarily sensitive miniature microphone and at least a yard of cable.

Havel immediately phoned the nearest police station where, after several calls, he was told that a policeman would arrive shortly and that he should "safeguard the evidence"—which his relative had already done by tying microphone and cable to his stepladder.

The moment Havel hung up, there was a noise from the hole in the ceiling and it began to rain plaster. With one mighty tug, the cable was yanked loose from the ladder and up through the ceiling. The microphone, however, fell onto Havel's desk, where his wife offered to stand guard while Havel phoned the police and his relative ran out of the flat and up the stairs.

By the time the relative had obtained a key to an attic storeroom overhead, there was nothing inside but a hole in the floor and a putty knife. A neighbor with a camera offered to photograph all the evidence. The Havels summoned a number of editor and writer friends to serve as witnesses and moral support.

When, more than an hour later, a plainclothesman showed up, he told the gathering that he wasn't authorized to take a report, merely to put the microphone into custody. But he wasn't willing to give Havel a receipt for the microphone. Havel refused to hand it over. The plainclothesman phoned headquarters and, after another hour, was joined by two uniformed patrolmen who also declined to take a report or give a receipt. After trying in vain to persuade Havel to "be a good fellow and not make a fuss," they informed him that it was not their province to investigate events of this character. When Havel asked who *was* competent to investigate, they said they didn't know and left.

Havel later published his version of this adventure, with pictures, in *Listy*. But he knew he would not have the last word. . . .

On Friday evening 21 March 1969, there was something to cheer about! At the World Ice Hockey Championships in Stockholm, Czechoslovakia defeated Russia, 2–0, while all of Europe watched. The crowd in the arena could be heard chanting "Dub-ček! Dub-ček!" That midnight, thousands of Czechs left their TV sets and poured through Wenceslas Square. They waved their flag, chanted the score, and painted "2:0" all over the "VISIT LENINGRAD" windows of the Russian airline Aeroflot.

They wanted to storm the Wenceslas statue, too, but they were thwarted by the ingenuity of Deputy Premier Štrougal, whose star was rising in the East almost as fast as Husák's. After various sit-ins and candle-burnings in Palach's honor, Štrougal had the monument landscaped overnight (in the dead of winter) with an impenetrable garden of shrubs, hedges, and lush, prickly flowers. By the 21st of March, this many-splendored, many-pronged counterattack had become known as "Štrougal Park."

The hockey crowd took Štrougal Park good-naturedly and went away, chanting "Wait 'til next week!" So did a couple of Russian civilians who happened into the Square and were jeered sportingly. For each team plays each other twice and the return match between Czechoslovakia and Russia came on Friday the 28th.

Czechoslovakia won again, 4–3. And, this time, the cheering that erupted from every home literally shook the city. In my neighborhood, thousands of students and hundreds of Czechoslovak soldiers roared out of hostels and barracks and headed downtown to celebrate. Hundreds of thousands of Czechs converged upon Wenceslas Square, where Štrougal Park vanished like an enchanted forest. The numbers "4:3" blossomed on the base of the Wenceslas statue and everywhere on the Square. And the Aeroflot office was pulverized to a fine powder by youths who trampled its model planes and fed its furniture, its travel posters, and its pictures of Lenin into a sidewalk bonfire. A few police on hand stood by grinning and let the violence run rampant for more than an hour until one of their own was slightly injured. Then five busloads of helmeted riot police arrived with tear gas and truncheons to disperse the crowd.

The next day, the cabinet ministers for the Czech Lands met and their Government issued a reasonably firm, but understanding, "Standpoint Toward the Friday Night Disturbances." The riot was, after all, no wilder or more destructive than some college weekends in the States, and much briefer. But Josef Grösser, the new, hard-lining Czech Minister of Interior, was not content with his Government's reaction, so he issued a statement of his own on Monday. In it, he announced Friday-night stonings of the V. I. Lenin barracks in Mladá Boleslav, attacks on various other Soviet garrisons, and the burning of a Soviet Army vehicle in Ústí-nad-Labem. He also indicated that he didn't consider these disturbances spontaneous.

Simultaneously, Moscow's *Pravda* railed against "organized nationalistic manifestations, prepared in advance" and focused on Josef Smrkovský, who'd been working late on Friday night and happened to be riding home in an official car that was trapped and caught up in the Wenceslas Square revels.

Then, when Marshal Grechko and Deputy Foreign Minister Vladimír Semyonov descended upon Prague unannounced, it was clear that they had come as hatchet men.

They bore a letter from the Soviet Politburo, which warned that the tanks were back on first-degree alert and would restore order if the leaders would not.

In his first conversation with President Svoboda, Marshal Grechko began bluntly:

"We have all read *Schweik* and that's all that's happened here so far. Now we want some tangible results."

The Presidium was now so stacked that it promptly issued a public rebuke to Smrkovský for participating in the "anti-Soviet hysteria." Dubček went on TV to warn the nation that "because of these events we will again have to pay a high political price. I would like you to know that the period we have for normalization is not unlimited."

This was not enough. Grechko told Svoboda that an additional 20,000 troops had already been brought into the country. The Red Army stood ready to occupy the key cities if, as Grechko put it, "you don't clean that bad flock out of your party, government, and country."

Various hard-liners and old time Novotnýites, particularly a couple of Army generals, called upon Marshal Grechko at his villa near our home. Fearing a military coup backed by Soviet armor, President Svoboda embarked on a strenuous "inspection tour" of Army garrisons in Bohemia, Moravia, and Slovakia. . . .

While Grechko was in town, *Zítřek* had the bad timing to come out with a front-page photo of the Friday-night hockey bonfire above a Schweikian "ODE TO JOY" by Vladimír Škutina:

> Whoever happened to come out that night could have, without exaggeration, understood the fun and exhilaration of the carnivals in Rio and/or Havana.
>
> Nobody organized it. Nobody called it together. Nobody directed the program. Not the counter-revolution, either. The nation simply had its fingers above its head and went to commune. It was a joy not only because of our hockey players, but we felt just a little proud of ourselves, too.
>
> We needed to show ourselves that we hadn't thrown in the towel yet. That as far as feelings, pride, and hopes are concerned we are optimists evermore. That we don't need rifles for moral victory and fair play. On the contrary, when the enemy doesn't have a rifle, he's on the skids. . . .

And that was the end of *Zítřek*. The issue was confiscated. The journal was banned. And Sylva was out of a job.

Svoboda's "tour" brought the troops back into line. But somewhere along the journey, the fight went out of the weary old soldier. Impressed by the "quiet atmosphere" in Gustáv Husák's Slovakia, Svoboda came back to Prague and threw in his lot with the "realists" on the Central Committee.

On Thursday 17 April 1969, the Central Committee met in the Spanish Hall of Prague Castle. Alexander Dubček asked to be relieved of his post as First Secretary and to be replaced by Gustáv Husák. The request was granted.

The twenty-one-man Presidium was cut back to eleven members. Dubček and Černík retained seats on it for the time being. But Smrkovský and Špaček were dropped.

To appease the public, Dubček was named Chairman of the Federal Assembly, the post that Smrkovský's Slovak friend Colotka now relinquished after three months. The game of playing musical chairs on a downhill slope was in full swing.*

Husák's inaugural address was characteristically blunt and outspoken. This was not a man who pretended (or fooled himself into thinking) that everything was perfect and could only be made more perfect still. He was on the public's wave length. He knew what people were thinking and wanting and bothered about. But he would distort any or all of these for his own ends:

"I know that people will say 'Here comes another Novotný era!' But we *must* discipline the party. We *must* call to account Communists who are against party policy. . . . Everything has its limits, including our tolerance. We expect the wide participation of the masses, of every citizen, in creating our policy, in realizing it, and in controlling it. We are not giving up on any fundamental principles of our post-January policy. But we have to know what to do and when. Keep quiet. Preserve peace. Support our course."

And the people, sick unto death of where their resistance had brought them, simply groaned, but took it lying down. Hardly anybody wanted to talk about it any more, but the truth was that freedom had been an ordeal. At the time, it seemed easier to live without it.

---

* On the same date, Nikita Khrushchev celebrated his 75th birthday in the seclusion that such a non-person is granted and one of Marshal Grechko's predecessors, Georgi Zhukov, published memoirs rehabilitating Stalin as a vigorous leader, wise diplomat, and polite person.

Interlude]   On the beach and in the barn

I ALSO TOOK THE NEWS LYING DOWN, ON A DOUBLE-thick bath towel spread across some jagged stones of a rocky beach in Yugoslavia. Sick and tired of politics myself, I'd escaped—a week before Dubček's downfall—with my family for a ten-day spring vacation on the remote Dalmatian isle of Hvar. Climbing and playing and swimming and sunning myself, I scrupulously avoided the one news stand, which sometimes carried papers from the mainland.

But, when people learn you're from Czechoslovakia, you can't stay isolated from politics. The hotel gave us a discount, which we hadn't asked for, because of where we were from. And it seemed as if every native we met showed us the gun he kept in his desk drawer, just in case the Russians tried to come there, too. Virtually everybody, too, said he had provisions and ammunition stashed away in a cave he knew.

Knowing Czech, we could talk with people: they understood our Czech and we fathomed their Serbo-Croatian. A man who worked at the dock told us: "Czechoslovakia is *kaput*. But it will be a different, bloodier story here and the Russians know it."

Probably so. On the 21st of August, Marshal Tito had ordered a mobilization and a detailed inspection of defenses. This revealed that, between the Hungarian border (the logical point of entry) and the capital (Belgrade), Yugoslavia was protected by a total of two customs officers and two militiamen. Even where there were defenses, the Red Army could have been at Zagreb in six hours and on the Adriatic Coast in another six hours. This had led to a vast re-organization of Tito's military command. Numerous generals known to be chummy with the Russians were pensioned off.

I listened respectfully to all this and agreed that it would be a different, bloodier, and undoubtedly longer struggle if it happened in Yugoslavia, but with the same ending.

Then, on Friday morning 18 April 1969, the only other people on the beach had a transistor and it was tuned to the BBC. . . .

We landed in Prague on the 20th, the eve of the Doctor's daughter's wedding. The next morning we rode with a friend to an intimate and mysteriously delightful Romanesque church, dating back to the eleventh century, on the banks of the Sázava river. The wedding was the first performed by the priest since his emergence from prison and (a few years thereafter) the return of his parish.

Afterwards, the guests all posed for wedding pictures on the church's lawn. Some Russian soldiers were bivouacked nearby. Seeing people in city clothes congregating on a weekday, they sent out a patrol jeep to look us over. The patrol said nothing, but seemed to take a particular interest in my family and me. They went away and came back after a few minutes with an officer. He stared at us, too, and then left us alone.

The wedding feast was in the barn of Konopiště, the castle from which Archduke Francis Ferdinand set out for Sarajevo (now in Yugoslavia) on the eve of World War I. Now, peasant ladies in dirndls barbecued chickens and shish-kebabs, which we washed down with Slovakian wines and Pilsener beer served in earthenware crocks.

One of the wedding guests, a newspaper editor who'd joined the Communist Party "for idealistic reasons" in the 1930's, when it was illegal, shouted a toast to "the ideals of January, which justified my idealism after 30 years." He was philosophical, if not optimistic, about Dubček's successor.

"Husák may be even worse than we think he is," he said, "but at least now the Russians will listen to him."

"And *then* say *ñyet*," said another guest.

"I suppose so," said the editor with a shrug. "But they'd have deaf ears or worse for Dubček."

Less than a month later, I hailed a cab and who was behind the wheel but the same "idealistic" editor. Or rather, ex-editor. He'd been dismissed from his high post for "misapplying the words of Marx and Lenin to criticize an allied nation." But he was one of the luckier ones because he was purged early. Soon, the taxi and tram companies were instructed not to hire any more unemployed journalists or teachers as drivers or conductors because such work put them right back in contact with the public.

Chapter 21 ⅃

Monday 21 April—
Wednesday 30 July 1969

VÁCLAV'S FATHER HAD GONE TO WORK FOR DUBČEK ON one condition: that his superiors give him, in advance, a signed but undated letter accepting his resignation. Otherwise, one cannot just quit the Central Committee. One must be given permission to resign.

Minutes after saying goodbye to Dubček, Václav's father started cleaning out his own desk. He also affixed a date to his resignation. The date he put down was a safe interval before Dubček's downfall.

Thus, when Gustáv Husák came around to tour his new headquarters and say hello to the staff, Václav's father tried to say hello-and-goodbye by handing Husák his resignation.

Husák recognized the trick for what it was and said so. The two men wrangled over the document's validity for a few minutes and the scene was growing very edgy until Husák suddenly interrupted himself to say: "Why are we carrying on like this? I was going to fire you anyway."

A realist from start to finish, Husák thereupon accepted the resignation.

Soon thereafter, Husák left for Moscow to claim his ransom. He was known to be making two requests: 1) a hard-currency or gold ruble loan to keep the economy afloat, and 2) the abolition of *Zprávy*. He came back with no loan and only a promise that *Zprávy* would cease publication soon.

This was one promise which Russia kept. A few weeks later, the Editorial Board of the Central Group of Soviet Troops Temporarily Stationed on Czechoslovak Soil announced that the current *Zprávy* was its farewell issue. No reason was given, but everyone remembered Kuznetsov's remark to Dubček that "when *Rudé Právo* reads like *Zprávy,* there will be no need to publish *Zprávy*."

In the editorial purges that now hit every newspaper, *Rudé Právo* came to read like *Zprávy* or maybe even like Bolshakov. There were articles headlined "HOW *ZÍTŘEK* PREFABRICATED PSYCHO-SIS" and "I ACCUSE THE HUMAN FACE" (the latter by Famíra, the Stalinists' portrait painter). And this is the way *Rudé Právo* soon read:

SONS LIKE THEIR FATHERS

Soviet troops are helping us to ensure the inviolability of our western frontiers which are simultaneously the frontiers of the whole socialist world. . . .

When they came, they did not get the welcome of their fathers [in 1945]. The right-wing politicians and anti-socialist forces in the mass communications media succeeded in confusing a considerable part of the population: "They are occupiers who came to enslave us, to deprive us of freedom," they said. But even this lie is short-lived. Soviet troops have been here for eleven months now. Emotions are quieting down despite the fact that various "fighters for freedom and humanity" are trying by all possible means to maintain anti-Soviet hatred in this country. More and more people are coming to realize that they were deceived. Those who come in contact with the Soviet forces learn what they are really like and have no doubt that they came to us not to suffocate socialism or deprive us of our freedom, but for the very opposite reason: to help us defend socialism and freedom.

Listy, Reportér, and other "offensive publications" were shut down the way *Zítřek* was and so was *Studentské Listy,* a short-lived successor to *Student,* which had disappeared after August. The Bohemian-Moravian Student Union of Holeček and Müller was also disbanded. And even the magazine *Mateřídouška (Mother's Soul),* for readers between five and eight years of age, was rebuked for printing a poem called "Robbers." It depicted medieval raiders who came from the steppes wearing primitive footwear. As *Rudé Právo* pointed out: "Under Habsburg domination and Nazi occupation, people in this land have learned . . . to read between the lines."

The rewriting of history gathered up a full head of steam. To Gottwald's most famous quotation, "WITH THE SOVIET UNION FOR-EVER" was added the phrase "AND NEVER OTHERWISE!" The Presidium issued a public apology to Bil'ak, Barbírek, Kolder, Piller, Rigo, Švestka, Lenárt, Indra, and other top leaders "who were accused of collaboration and treachery . . . on the basis of unfounded allegations and fabrications."

Like naughty schoolboys, hundreds of organizations all over the country were now required to write thousands of letters apologizing to the Indras and Kolders they had "slandered" in 1968. They apologized also for their "disorientations in August" and for "rightist and anti-Soviet tendencies." The finest hours of Czechoslovak broadcasting became known as "the well-known August hysteria of the radio."

To avert demonstrations or comparisons, there was no May Day Parade in Prague in 1969. And, perhaps because of Russia's Czechoslovak embarrassment, Moscow's military parade on May Day was not only canceled in 1969, but "permanently" abolished. Moscow's flower parade, however, went on.

That spring in Prague, the party's Control and Auditing Commission—which usually specializes in purges, not rehabilitations—issued an official communique:

> The Commission discussed a report on the results of an investigation into the activity of Viliam Šalgovič . . . who had been accused in connection with the August events.
>
> The accusations were broadly published by mass communication media without any verification of facts which led to the creation of an atmosphere of hysteria against his person, to the slandering of his person and his family.
>
> Proceeding from a report by the Ministry of Interior and its conclusions and from the investigation of the Commission, the . . . Commission rejects all accusations against Viliam Šalgovič, since his conduct in such a complicated period was in harmony with the laws of the republic, and expresses full confidence in him.

Šalgovič was named Czechoslovak military attaché in Budapest and later chief of the party's purgative apparatus for Slovakia. On Šalgovič's fiftieth birthday later that year, President Svoboda awarded (but did not personally present him) the Order of Labor for "exceptional merit in defense of socialism."

Colonel Eliáš, who betrayed the airport, was named chief of Czechoslovak Airlines, and Colonel Vaněk, who betrayed the Ministry of Interior, was put in charge of exit visas. There was a definite Gilbert and Sullivan flavor in the air.

On 22 May 1969, Suchý and Šlitr unveiled a new musical revue called *Jonáš & Dr. Mattress*. The first-act "curtain" came when S+Š were singing a Brechtian ballad about the 1950's in Prague. Two men in the plainclothes uniform of the secret police (gray or black suits and black bowlers for indoor wear) entered and obliterated the two stars by planting before each of them a giant flowerpot bearing a Christmas tree. Intermission! This frightening, yet amusing, finaletto was S+Š's tribute to both censorship and Štrougal Park.

Their second-act finale was a protest song, "Against All," in which S+Š denounced Plans, Parties, laws, virgins, Boy Scouts, smog, mud, fear, wealth, and particularly:

> Against those who, despite our protests,
> Keep talking nonsense.
> We are 100 per cent angry men
> With hearts full of defiance
> And eyes brimming with rage
> So we'd advise nobody to toy with our feelings
> For nobody in the world can resist the two of us
> Because we know how to laugh.
> We know that laughter makes people into giants,
> It makes children stronger than armies.
> Laughter is infinitely good for you
> But not—when it is—behind your back!

Hand-in-hand with the insidious "rehabilitations" that were being exacted by August's "winners," there were purges on all levels of the Communist Party. Thousands of regional and municipal officials either lost their posts or else resigned when required to sign resolutions that were intolerable to them. The vast majority of officials, of course, remained on the job as long as they could.

At the May Central Committee meeting, Gustáv Husák announced the final ousters from the Central Committee of František Kriegel, Ota Šik (still carried on the membership rolls) and others "who can't be convinced, who stick to un-Marxist attitudes. To them we must say farewell."

Šik wasn't there to defend himself, but Kriegel was on hand to speak out. "Today's meeting," the old radical Jewish doctor began quietly, "will consider that several comrades be dropped from the Central Committee and I am among them. This is because I voted against the Treaty for the Temporary Stationing of Soviet Troops on the territory of our republic. Through this, I exceeded party discipline."

Kriegel pointed out that many of the members sitting in judgment of him had direct or primary responsibility for "the fact that dozens of innocent people met an unworthy death at the hands of the hangman; that thousands and tens of thousands were condemned for long years of torture and prison" as well as for "the protracted economic crisis which has led us to the present situation and which cannot be altered by palming off the causes on the last few months."

Already, there was an official campaign afoot to blame the economy's ailments on its absentee doctor, Ota Šik. Kriegel pointed to a former Novotný Minister of Trade and protégé, who had just denounced Šik, and said: "I was confounded by his short memory. Does he believe that he 'ministered' for twenty years . . . without sharing responsibility for the crisis?"

He pointed to others present and identified them by name, including Jozef Lenárt. And, in each case, Kriegel asked: "Has he no responsibility?"

Kriegel went on: "To load all this on the post-January period is much too transparent a maneuver. There are attempts to shift responsibility onto other people, but these can't succeed. There is too little time for me to talk of large problems, but everybody knows what I'm talking about. Of course, tough sanctions are demanded against opponents of the Treaty for Temporary Stationing of Troops. It is also known that I refused to sign the so-called Moscow Agreement. I refused because I saw it as a document which completely bound the hands of our republic. I refused it, therefore, since it all happened in the atmosphere of military occupation without the benefit of consultation with constitutional bodies and in contradiction to the feelings of the people of this country. . . .

"The treaty lacks specifically the basis of a normal agreement: that is, that it be signed voluntarily. The treaty was signed in an atmosphere of political and power coercion. . . . It was signed in the presence of hundreds of thousands of foreign troops and a huge military-technical arsenal. The treaty was not signed with a pen, but with the muzzles of cannons and machine guns."

Sometimes—when you had been bored out of your senses by the repeated drumming of *Rudé Právo* and the monotones on radio and TV and the many official proclamations of the Husák regime—you began to wonder whether the Prague Spring and the August invasion might not have been hallucinations. But one voice like Kriegel's had the impact of a flare in the dark.

Somebody had referred to "the so-called August events." Now Kriegel asked angrily: "Is someone trying to say that August 1968 was no event at all?"

Coming back to his imminent removal, Kriegel concluded:

"I consider it unjustified. The goal is transparent and aimed further than my person. It is well-known that recent developments . . . mean a wide-reaching restoration process and efforts to legalize August. . . .

"The tempo is quickening to the point where the party is isolated from the people and the leaders are isolated from the party members so that the party changes from a moral and political leading force to an institution which is almost exclusively a power organization. . . . The history of the past two decades is rich in its warnings of tragic experiences."

The text of Kriegel's speech was suppressed, but office workers across the land mimeographed it and circulated it despite grave official warnings against "circulating illegal leaflets." And Kriegel, for his "recalcitrance," was immediately expelled from the Communist Party as well as from its Central Committee.

It was only a year since the session at which Antonín Novotný had received a lesser party punishment for his sins.

The entire municipal Presidium of Prague's Communist Party, including its leader, Bohumil Šimon, resigned rather than implement Husák's hard line. Josef Špaček was dropped from Brno's party leadership. Party members who signed the "2,000 Words" were expelled— and often removed from non-party jobs, too. The outspoken General Prchlík, who had been dismissed from his party post even before the invasion, was demoted to private and ordered to report to Pankrác prison for daily interrogations preparatory to a court-martial for treason.*

Colonel Emil Zátopek, the country's most beloved athlete, was stripped of his rank, cashiered from the Army, expelled from the Party, and removed from all his athletic coaching jobs, paid or unpaid. That spring, this world-famous non-person went to a sports event at which Prime Minister Černík's presence was announced. Many of the 40,000 fans booed Černík roundly, but they cheered even more loudly than

---

* In 1971, Prchlík was sentenced to three years imprisonment for "frustrating and jeopardizing the activity of state agencies" in his 1968 press conference.

that when they discovered that Zátopek was also in the audience. After a few months, Zátopek found employment driving a water-sprinkler truck for the Prague Sanitation Department—but he was fired when pedestrians, who recognized and saluted him, created a "threat to public order." *

Eugen Löbl, the Bratislava banker who'd been jailed with Goldstücker in the Slánský trial, left the country for good. Löbl became a lecturer at the University of Southern Illinois and then a teacher at Vassar. He was expelled from the Communist Party for "behavior abroad at variance with present policy of the Central Committee as well as with the basic principles of the party and Marxism-Leninism."

In London, Kamil Winter, former editor of Czechoslovak TV's news and current affairs department, took asylum in the West, declaring:

"I have been convinced, since 2300 on 20th August, that the Czechoslovak people should have been allowed to take up arms against the foreign invaders, regardless of the outcome. . . . I have been convinced since 26th August 1968 that the Czechoslovak leaders should have refused to sign the Moscow Diktat. I have been convinced since 27th August 1968 that, having been forced to sign it, these leaders should have collectively resigned after their return to Prague."

Löbl, Winter, Šik, and Goldstücker were the publicized "defectors," but there were now some 90,000 to 100,000 lesser-known Czechoslovak émigrés in the West. Where the "Class of '48" tended to cluster in the United States and England, the "Class of '68" gravitated toward (in diminishing numerical order) Canada, Switzerland, West Germany, Australia, and the United States. A good many, too, passed through or languished in Austria's overcrowded refugee camps.

These were almost all people whose skills and ingenuity could scarcely be sacrificed by their motherland's infirm economy. Thus, President Svoboda offered an amnesty (no punishment for the sin of going or staying abroad illegally, but strict accountability for any other sins) to any refugee who came home before 15 September. The news, however, that trickled out of Czechoslovakia to the West was scarcely of the "wish-you-were-here" variety:

. . . Near Carlsbad, a Czech soldier refused to obey a drunken So-

---

* In 1971, Zátopek recanted, telling *Rudé Právo* he was now "sorry that I was one of those wild ones who really poured oil onto flames which could have spread into a fire that would have threatened the socialist world."

viet officer. The officer shot him. Another Czech soldier shot the officer and sprayed bullets at various other Russian soldiers. The Russians fired back. A few hours later, some Czech soldiers drove to where some Russians were drilling and ran them over with an armored car. Casualty estimates in the Carlsbad area ranged from twenty to thirty-two dead and nearly one hundred injured.

. . . Arrests began in late July of 1969 with the jailing of "provocateurs . . . aiming to stir up disturbances and other troubles" around the 21 August anniversary of the invasion. The first criminal prosecution involved a twenty-five-year-old theatre employee in Ostrava. Charged with "inciting," he was held in prison without bond "pending criminal prosecution." An Ostrava writer named Ota Filip was given eighteen months in prison for "criminal acts" of "hostility to the Czechoslovak socialist system." The evidence used against him made it clear that, for some time, his outgoing mail had been opened and resealed en route to its destination. It came as no surprise when, a little later, the new party boss for Ostrava and Northern Moravia was introduced. He was Miroslav Mamula, Novotný's and Šejna's discredited crony who'd preceded General Prchlík as head of the party's purgative apparatus.

In Prague, the editor of a cultural magazine got eight months in prison for shouting insults outside the East German Embassy—or, as the muzzled Četeka put it, for "offenses not related to his editing of the periodical."

The arrests were surprisingly sparse, but the rumors about impending ones (plus the regime's shrill warnings about imperialist-led demonstrations on 21 August) created a new depth of jitters—and a few jokes, such as this dialogue in jail:

"How long a sentence did you get?"

"Eight years."

"What did you do?"

"Nothing."

"Then there must be some mistake. For nothing you get twelve years."

I pride myself on possessing a certain radar which tells me, immediately upon entering, whether somebody—male or female—is reacting to me across a crowded room. And one disenchanted Monday morning in

July of 1969, I went into the barbershop of the Palace Hotel and immediately detected a violent tremor caused by my entrance.

One of the six men waiting for haircuts was leaving as fast as he could—which wasn't too fast because he was on crutches from some kind of recent injury. It was Miroslav Galuška, whom I'd first met with Šlitr and Sylva in Montreal, where he was head of the Czechoslovak pavilion. I'd met him again on numerous occasions in Prague during his year-and-a-quarter as Minister of Culture, but I hadn't had a long chat with him since the night of 16 August 1968, when he and I and his wife and my niece had stood around waiting for Dubček and Ceausescu. Muted attacks on Galuška had started up recently, but he'd stalled them a bit by resigning and accepting an assignment abroad for which he was highly qualified—as head of the Czechoslovak pavilion for the 1970 Osaka Fair.

I wanted to congratulate him on his new post and console him about his injury, but he flashed me a look that was either warning or terror. I knew it was a squint I'd never seen in his open, jut-jawed face before. I also knew that, in this tense interim before taking up the job in Japan, it was certainly best for him not to have any domestic contact with Western journalists. So I said nothing, but the barber did:

"Where are you going, Minister Galuška? Your turn is the next but one."

"I-I must make an important telephone call," Galuška stammered, clattering his crutches. "I didn't know it would take this long."

"So where are you going?" the barber persisted.

"To the lobby, to use the hotel phone."

"Be my guest," said the barber. "Use mine."

"No, no, I can't talk here," Galuška said, leaving as fast as his crutches would carry him.

I looked to see if anybody was following him and the barber watched, too. Nobody else was to be seen.

Minister Galuška's turn for a haircut came after five minutes. The barber held the chair vacant, explaining to his quizzical customers that "it's for Minister Galuška, who's going to Osaka soon."

After ten more minutes, though, I saw Minister Galuška's reflection in the barber shop window. He was standing in the shadows of the Palace Hotel leaning on his crutches and chain-smoking.

After another five minutes, a car appeared and he practically fell into it. I was relieved to see that it was his own car with his wife behind the wheel. The barber, also watching, winked at me.

I was still third in line for a haircut, but the barber now beckoned me into his vacant chair. "You can have Minister Galuška's turn," he told me, "because you're what made him leave."

At a July meeting of "readers of *Rudé Právo* and *Tribuna*," it was reported that

> much criticism was addressed against the former leadership of the party. . . . It was the view of many taking part that it would be incorrect for the burden of the rectification of mistakes to be borne by Gustáv Husák, but also that Comrades Dubček, Smrkovský, Císař and others should also speak frankly about the past period. This is important also because, if certain circumstances are not clarified, it will be difficult to overcome views held by the general public that "the Russians are to blame for everything."

Dubček and Smrkovský took this in silence, but Čestmír Císař, still head of the Czech National Council, held a press conference in which he cleared all the ideological hurdles by glibly alluding to "the complex political situation which you all know" . . . "so-far valid legal norms" . . . and "former ruling circles." Without ever criticizing Dubček directly, Císař nevertheless embraced Husák's hard line. True, he spoke with a dry academic detachment and maybe even the suggestion of a wink. But his words were grist for *Izvestia*'s mill. I had to close my eyes so I would only hear, not see, the old Císař purring as smoothly as ever:

"Therefore, although we didn't like to, the representatives of the party had to take administrative measures against the press as a solution to the crisis in the country. We consider these only temporary, as Czechoslovakia is a country with a long tradition of free speech.

"I don't think it is the end of freedom of speech—as some think. But this freedom of speech . . . does have its limits.

"We shall all sleep off our political hangover and get up one morning with a clear head that represents common sense."

A schism had opened even among the fallen heroes of the January Spring. A few weeks before Císař's press conference, I had found myself sitting next to him at the Prague premiere of *Timon of Athens*. František Kriegel was sitting a few rows behind us. At intermission and at the subsequent party, both men had cut each other dead.

On the same day that I listened to Císař's lullaby, though, I was riding in a cab with my wife when we passed below the plain of Letná. On the empty base of the former Stalin statue, somebody had painted—in huge white letters—"DUBČEK!" (It was eradicated the next day.)

"Whose statue do you think will stand there one day?" the driver said. "I think Stalin's."

Valerie said: "I think Svoboda's. When he went to Moscow in August, he did what had to be done."

And I said: "I still think it will be Dubček's. He did what couldn't be done."

Maybe, though, it will be a statue of Karl Marx, whose dictum that *economics is all* may resolve the destiny of Czechoslovakia. Coupled with the general *malaise* that summer, the renunciation of Šik's reforms and the return to obsolete methods generated a widespread lethargy that outlasted the cucumber season:

. . . You can't get a taxi, but if you do, the fare is now 30 to 50 per cent higher than before. The private cab drivers, who owe their existence to Šik, are being driven out of business by reorganizations of their co-operatives and new regulations (aimed at them) such as a requirement that all taxis must have four doors. Meanwhile, the public cab company is once again undermanned, overworked, unreliable, and unprofitable.

. . . The girl who's writing your plane ticket glances at her watch, sees that it's lunchtime, and goes to lunch without a word, leaving your unfinished ticket lying on her desk and you standing agape at the counter.

. . . The long-distance and information operators just don't answer the phone on weekends—and their weekends now seem to extend from Thursday noon to Monday noon all year round. In 1969, Prime Minister Černík was heard to grumble about the whole nation working a three and one half day week.

Nobody, but nobody, cared about his work any more, except those who wanted to hang onto their jobs or get somebody else's in the purges. Officials in industry told you confidentially in 1969 that no branch of the economy was producing at more than 35 per cent of normal and, even in the controlled press, the news items seemed to bear them out:

SHORTAGE OF MEAT AND EGGS

Czechoslovakia is feeling a great shortage of meat and eggs. The situation is the worse as no egg imports have been secured and pigs won't be ready for slaughter until the end of this year. Leading representatives of the management of purchasing organizations advise that the market would be supplied with imported pork especially in the third quarter of 1969.

The egg supply was estimated at 100-million below normal. And Czechoslovakia, the birthplace of Prague ham and any number of unique and wonderful sausages, must rely on Mother Russia's benevolence—at a price—for her pork. The sly little jokes that accompany such shortages were back:

Q: What is 45 yards long and eats only potatoes?

A: The line at the meat shop.

The housing statistics for 1969 were even more appalling. *Rudé Právo* reported in July that "Prague now has 90,000 applicants for flats. . . . Six thousand flats are built in Prague annually. In the first half of this year, only fifty-four flats were completed."

The Czechoslovak crown—unconvertible; dumped on the Vienna black market by refugees; and useless in scarcities—was soon exchanged on Prague's sidewalk black markets at 60 or 80 to the dollar (ten times its official worth) in 1969; a year earlier, it had been worth 35 or 40 to the dollar there. And an old slogan of the 1950's was heard again: "We pretend to work and they pretend to pay us."

Interlude ⅃ "Treat them as a talisman"

I'VE TRIED TO KEEP THIS NARRATIVE AS CHRONOLOGICAL as possible, but now I must double back in time to May of 1969. Two episodes happened then that, for a long while, struck me as symbolic of my own peculiar status as an American living in Soviet-occupied Czechoslovakia.

On Friday 16 May 1969, a rumor, which had been officially denied for almost four months, came true. A Swedish journalist had been expelled in January for printing a hint of it. But, at 1030 that Friday in May, I dashed out on a neighborhood errand without bothering to take my passport along, and on Parler Street, one block from home, I saw it happen! The Russian Army was moving into the firehouse! Their only troops in Prague had been transferred from Haštalské in the Old Town. They were coming in the back way, six personnel carriers full of them, perhaps 150 men, but they were there.

Well, almost. For a green coal truck happened to be blockading the back entranceway. Back in August, the Soviet commander wouldn't have hesitated to ram it. But now he must have had orders to arrive inconspicuously. So what he did instead was post four men with rifles to seal off that block of Parler Street. Then an officer and two enlisted men started interrogating the pedestrians on the street—one by one—as to whether they had anything to do with the coal truck that was "interfering with Warsaw Pact military operations." They also checked identity cards. And there I was without any—but with an American accent.

The Russian team was almost up to me when there was a disturbance at one end of the street. Two coalmen—Schweiks in sootface—had emerged from a beery "second breakfast" in a corner tavern. They were having trouble getting back to their truck because the Russian sentries wouldn't let them through. The officer hurried over to tell them that they had seriously hampered a Warsaw Pact troop movement.

The coalmen listened in amazement and then one of them tapped the officer on his high collar with one grimy finger and said *"Kdepak!"* —which is an all-purpose Czech word meaning roughly "Come off it, man!"

The two sentries started to unshoulder their rifles, but the officer simply said grimly that the two Czechs had thirty seconds to remove their truck.

They took a minute-and-a-half. Then the troops entered and the street was re-opened. By Sunday, on the Dlabačov Street side of the firehouse, there was a red-and-gold sign announcing, in Cyrillic, that this was Prague Military Command Headquarters for the Central Group of Soviet Soldiers Temporarily Stationed on Czechoslovak Soil. There were officers, in their high boots and baggy blue pants, promenading with their dumpy ladies, and enlisted men, in their doughboy togs, looking homesick.

"They are here. I am here. We are here," I jotted in my notes—and went on with my work. One-and-a-half drafts of this book have been written just one block from Russian occupation headquarters.

While the Russians were moving into the firehouse, our four-year-old Erika was lying in a Prague hospital awaiting urethra surgery. It was successful—thanks to the best urologist and the only American instrument for doing the job in the whole land.

After eight days in the surgical hospital, Erika was moved to a children's hospital for another week of recuperation. There, a woman doctor was in charge of the ward and she treated Erika and her parents at least as well as everyone else there. But, one day, a native came to visit Erika, and, on his way out, the doctor took him aside and said: "They seem like very decent Americans."

"They *are* very decent Americans," our friend said he replied.

"Communists?" the doctor asked.

"Certainly not!" our friend said, giving her a brief fill-in on us.

"But there must be something bad about them," the doctor insisted. "Or else why would they still be allowed to stay here?"

Our friend could appreciate the logic of the question, but he had no ready answer for it. Instead, he gave the doctor his own prescription: "Don't ask around about them and just be glad they're here somehow. Treat them as a talisman."

PART SEVEN

Mortuis:
From Then to Now

And when, after finishing his work in the
shed, the coachman went across the courtyard in his slow, rolling walk, closed the
huge gate, and then returned, all very
slowly, while he literally looked at nothing
but his own footprints in the snow—and
finally shut himself into the shed; and now
as all the electric lights went out too—
for whom should they remain on?—and
only up above the slit in the wooden
gallery still remained bright, holding one's
wondering gaze for a little, it seemed to
K. as if . . . now in reality he were freer
than he had ever been, and at liberty to
wait here in this place usually forbidden
to him, as long as he desired, and had won
a freedom such as hardly anybody else
had ever succeeded in winning, and as if
nobody could dare to touch him or drive
him away, or even speak to him; but—
this conviction was at least equally strong
—as if at the same time there was nothing
more senseless; nothing more hopeless,
than this freedom, this waiting, this
inviolability.

Franz Kafka, *The Castle*

Chapter 22]

Wednesday 20 August 1969—
Tuesday 15 December 1970

THE LONG-ANTICIPATED AND MUCH-HERALDED "COUNTER-revolutionary" riots which the Husák regime had been promising in speech after speech began on the 19th, two days before the official anniversary of the "entry of friendly troops." Toward dusk on the 20th, I walked downtown to see who was there.

At the Old Town Hall, I started to meet people covering their noses and dabbing their eyes with handkerchiefs from tear gas. One block from the foot of Wenceslas Square, I stood with a few hundred Czechs who were quietly watching the "fighting" on the square.

It was a very one-sided fight. Thousands of people were just congregating and chanting "Doob-ček! Doob-ček!" or "Husák Rusák" (a derogatory way to say "Husák is a Russian!"). And, every two or three minutes, the police would attack them—with tear-gas bombs and water cannon fired from armored military trucks on which had been painted (in white letters) the words for "POLICE." The crowd would retreat through the beehive arcades off Wenceslas Square and then reappear, chanting "Geš-ta-po!"

The people in my throng took up the cry, too—though I, being a foreigner, kept my mouth shut. Then the police attacked us and we all ran through the winding streets of the Old Town. A couple of people (one of them an old lady) picked up the tear-gas bombs and tossed them back into the armored trucks, where they exploded. Everyone cheered and the police (wearing white helmets) retreated and regrouped for the next charge.

I took shelter under a ledge of the Tyl Theatre, where *Don Giovanni* premiered in 1787. But nothing was sacred that night and, when a tear-gas bomb ricocheted off the ledge and exploded a few feet from me, I started racing with the rest of the mob.

I say "mob" although this was a crowd of decent people: young couples holding hands even as they ran; middle-aged men and women who were weeping even without tear gas; and quite a few upstanding citizens I'd met on more dignified occasions.

Working my way up the square between charges, I met Jiří Suchý. For half an hour or so, I exchanged news of the summer with him—though our conversation was interrupted eight or nine times by gassings and sprayings. Suchý runs very fast—and, with each police charge, I would make a mad dash only to run up against Suchý surveying the scene. Then we'd pick up our chat where we left off.

It was almost a festive evening—as the annual running with the bulls must be in Pamplona. But, in Wenceslas Square, the amateur toreadors were howling "Doob-ček!" and "Geš-ta-po!" And the bulls were now their fellow countrymen, not the Russians. Czech police and Czech troops (and even, some contend, Czech prison guards) were unleashed to chase Czechs through the streets of Prague with tear gas and water cannon. The streets were soaked, though it wasn't raining.

Czech tanks came into town toward 2200 and I started hearing live gunfire. Two people died and 350 were arrested in the fighting that followed. But I'd walked a few blocks away to where the trams had been re-routed. During the ride home, I saw barred buses hauling people off to jail.

The next day, the actual anniversary, had been designated as a day of silent protest: no going to restaurants, cinemas or theatres; no riding the trams, etc. I walked downtown with thousands of people, some of whom lived six or seven miles from their jobs, who were all walking to work. The trams were empty, except for a few old people and an occasional younger person. (I know of one marriage which started to deteriorate that day when *she* walked to work and *he* rode.) Wenceslas Square stank of tear gas still hanging in the air. The streets were patroled by police, soldiers, People's Militia, and men in World War II partisan uniforms—blue-gray knickers, suspenders, and boots; plus rifles and red armbands to show that they were authorities, not outlaws, this time around.

That night was much the same as the night before—only this time I met Václav, alias Wenceslas. He was weeping.

"Tear gas got you?" I asked.

"Yes and no," Václav replied. "The gas gets it going, but do you know what keeps me crying? Some of my friends were drafted. . . ."

"As punishment?" I asked.

"No, in the normal course of conscription. And I just met two of them. The same two who were throwing Molotov cocktails into Russian tanks a year ago were throwing tear-gas bombs at their own people today."

And Václav began to bawl.

The ghastly spectacle of Czechs fighting Czechs provided Husák's regime with an excuse to enact tough "Emergency Laws" that could automatically imprison, remove, or even banish from Prague a student, a teacher, an editor, or anyone else who protested. And this is what finally broke the back of the Czechoslovak resistance.* But Husák's name wasn't on the proclamation that wiped out the last legal vestige of "socialism with a human face." It was a State document, not a party document—and so it bore the signatures of the President, Prime Minister, and Chairman of Parliament: Svoboda, Černík, and Dubček.

Šlitr had sat out the summer in his country home, but it had not been a good time for him, either. Sylva had been there, too, but she was struggling to break the bonds that tied her up, in some minds, as "Jiří Šlitr's property." We learned (from mutual friends, not from Šlitr or her) that, in late summer, she moved all her personal belongings out of the room in Šlitr's country house where she had spent most of ten summers. But they still remained close friends. "I felt he needed me," Sylva told me much later, "but he would never say so. And the truth is that I also needed him."

When Šlitr returned to Prague in September, he found most of his milieu intimidated. A new Czech Minister of Culture was tightening the lid on films (Menzel's most stunning film, *Larks on a String,* was screened only at Barrandov for friends and then suppressed) and theatre (Edward Albee's *A Delicate Balance* and Molière's *Ode to a King* would eventually be withdrawn because of "provocative reactions by audiences").

A number of pithier moments were dropped from the Semafor shows, but Šlitr and Suchý still had worries. If one of them circumvented a controversial lyric by humming the lines, knowledgeable audiences would sometimes sing out the words from their seats. Or, when curtain calls justified encores (the first of which invariably used

* At this writing, the "Emergency Laws"—like the "Temporarily Stationed" Soviet troops—are still with the Czechs.

to be Šlitr's Russian "Clementine"), Šlitr would ask the audience: "What would you like me to do next?"

The audience would hesitate just a split second which Šlitr would seize to interject: "Umhmm, umhmm, umhmm, you're scared!"

Then another minuscule pause and he would add: "I'm scared, too."

With perfect timing, he had succeeded in saying the unspeakable without really speaking. Everyone knew where he and Suchý still stood.

When Václav returned to college that fall, his faculty had a new rector and some new teachers. (Václav recently encountered his one-time music professor, who is now conducting a streetcar.) Some courses in history, philosophy, and particularly sociology had been suspended. So had the obligatory lectures on Marxism-Leninism, not out of any disillusionment, mind you, but because the authorities wanted to be doubly sure "the correct people" were teaching *their* religion.

It was indeed a religion with the new Minister of Education, the third since the invasion. For this one was somebody special: Jaromír Hrbek, a Lysenko geneticist and devout atheist (as a professor, he was known to schedule exams for Sundays) who contended that "scientific socialism, Marxism-Leninism, is a world viewpoint so right, so crystal clear, so noble, non-dogmatic, and capable of growth that its program can truly be formulated like a poem in prose."

Dr. Hrbek started out the 1969–70 school year by proclaiming that the entry of Soviet troops in August of 1968 "was necessary; it was not aggression, it was not perfidy, it was not occupation." Before the academic year was out, "measures" (ranging from reprimands to dismissals) had been taken "for political-professional reasons" against 12 per cent of the "more than 20,000 leading educational workers" in the Czech Lands alone. Eighty-two students in the Czech Lands were expelled for political reasons; 415 received other punishments; and 45 representatives of the student movement were still under investigation.*

---

* Academic education was not the only strong traditional institution that was dismantled virtually overnight. The 1970 edition of the nation's top sports event, the Spartakiad, held every five years in Strahov Stadium, was canceled; the prospect of 104,000 gymnasts and 250,000 spectators assembled nearby would be enough to intimidate the Russian garrison a quarter-mile away. The Boy Scouts were re-abolished

The previous year, Václav had obtained faculty approval to embark upon an ambitious literary project: a detailed study of George Orwell. But now, in the Hrbek days, Václav found that Orwell's books had again vanished almost completely (one volume of essays remained) from the university library shelves. Soon thereafter, Václav was told that "we're cutting your work load in half." Six of his twelve chapters (including those on *Animal Farm, 1984,* and *Homage to Catalonia*) were dropped from his outline because "their subject matter is now taboo."

Václav didn't greet this as good news. All fall and all winter, he plodded ahead preparing all twelve chapters. In the spring of 1970, he confronted his two most sympathetic professors with the budding reality that they had a small cultural revolution on their hands. The professors were understanding, but worried. They invited Václav to one of their homes and tried to argue him out of it. And when that failed, they came up with a "very Czech" solution: Václav wrote his Orwell paper in English, which his faculty's "unsympathetic" professors don't read. He wrote six double-sized chapters instead of twelve singles, but with everything he planned to write intact except the bibliography at the end.

In the nearly three years I've known him, Václav has grown very proper, almost prim-looking. His jazzy turtlenecks have given way to conservative neckties; prescription sunglasses have yielded to rimless *pince-nez.* He told me:

"Now I dress like a nice young man is supposed to look to his stodgiest elders—every mother's choice for son-in-law. That way, maybe they won't see how dangerous I am. The fashions of freedom don't matter to me any more; it's the freedom itself. And that's what a lot of us are engaged in now, a careful but constant testing and probing to see how far we can safely push back toward freedom."

---

as "useless." Christmas Eve's midnight masses at St. Jacob's and St. Nicholas were advanced, on a couple of hours' notice by the authorities, to 4 P.M. In another instance (that of a research institute in a branch of medicine), the founder was fired; his staff quit, too; and the bureaucrats were forced to advertise in a professional journal for a qualified replacement. Only one man felt he had the credentials to apply and that was the man they'd dismissed. They took him back, but with a lesser title, and then his disciples came back, too. And the purge has reached from the highest rungs of power to the very bowels of a diseased society—tapeworms caused by the ousting of so many pro-Dubček meat inspectors that, for the first time in modern Czech history, it is now unsafe to eat Tartar Beefsteak in Prague.

Škutina, the author of *Zitřek*'s "Ode to Joy"; Havel, the wire-tapped playwright; Jiří Lederer of *Literární Listy;* and Ludek Pachman, an outspoken chess champion and journalist, were jailed at various times and accused of "anti-State acts"—but only Škutina has actually stood trial at this writing; he was given two years for "slandering the republic and approving a criminal act" while writing for *Zitřek*. Škutina took his case to a higher court; on appeal, his sentence was more than doubled—to four years and two months! Pachman was in jail for more than a year awaiting a trial that has yet to happen: while waiting, he suffered skull fractures that the authorities say were inflicted by another prisoner.

Jan Němec and Marta Kubišová were married in the fall of 1969, around the time when both were made non-persons. He was blacklisted at Barrandov. Her newest recordings were halted on the Supraphon production line; her concerts were canceled; and so was the Golden Nightingale telecast at which, as incumbent, she would be obliged to defend (and, no doubt, retain) her title.

The newlyweds retired to his country house on Slapy Dam where, he said, "we can live off the land and our royalties." He let his blondish crew-cut grow nearly as long as her witchlike coif. As her dowry, she had brought into marriage three cats and a dog; he supplemented it at Christmas with his present to her, a donkey.

The only cloud over their idyll was a lawyer some friends engaged for Němec after the shooting scrape: to help him put his anarchic affairs in order in case there would be other brushes with the law. Early in 1970, the lawyer—as a matter of routine for him—went to pay Němec's auto tax. This called the attention of the authorities to the indisputable fact that, in a dozen years as a car-owner, Němec had never before paid his auto taxes. With heavy penalty charges and back tax costs looming, Němec would like to fire his lawyer for his costly diligence, "but now he's got me where I can't afford to."

The case of Jan Masaryk's 1948 death, re-opened in 1968, was officially closed toward the end of 1969. The report stated:

> Masaryk was not able to cope with the slanderous and condemning stand of the Western press, which criticized his positive attitude to the February events of 1948 and his readiness to continue co-operation in Klement Gottwald's Government.

Then, after noting "Masaryk's established habit of sitting in the open window with crossed legs," the report concluded with a verdict of suicide-or-accident:

> Masaryk undoubtedly was sitting in the window on that night from 9 to 10 March 1948 and tried in this way to counter insomnia. There, his depressive mood intensified and finally resulted in a sudden decision to jump out of the window. Or—in case of the other possible version—Masaryk could, as a result of physical exhaustion, lose balance or orientation in the window and fall out. Both versions can explain all the known traces and none of the evidence contradicts them.

Major Chlumský was "exposed" in a ninety-five-minute TV documentary and *then* brought to trial. He was found guilty and sentenced to twenty-six months in jail.

Of 1968's "men of January," only two old Soldiers remain on the job: General Svoboda, presiding listlessly over the liquidation of the Prague Spring, and Defense Minister Dzúr, collaborating actively with the Central Group of Soviet Troops (the phrase "Temporarily Stationed" is now largely omitted).

Čestmír Císař's balancing act brought him to almost the same end as the straightforward Dr. Kriegel—but a year later. In 1970, Císař stepped down from the Czech National Council and was expelled from the Communist Party. He now holds a clerical position in our neighborhood with the State Landmark Preservation Commission in the Firehouse Square. I see him around every now and then.

Kriegel, at sixty-two, has been pensioned off and forbidden to practice medicine. He remains, however, an inveterate first-nighter at the Semafor and a few other Prague theatres.

Prime Minister Černík stepped down to Minister of Technical and Investment Development in January, 1970, and Lubomír Štrougal became the Prime Minister. Five months later, Černík resigned from the Government altogether and was suspended from the Communist Party pending an evaluation of his conduct in 1968. In December 1970, Černík was expelled from the Party.

Alexander Dubček's descent was both more gradual and more spectacular. A month after he signed the "Emergency Laws," he was dismissed from the Presidium. Less than a month later, in mid-October 1969, Dubček lost his job as Chairman of the Federal Assembly. That

December, he was named Czechoslovak Ambassador to Turkey, but he was not cleared to go to Ankara for nearly a month—until he had resigned from the Central Committee, too. When he departed from Ruzyně Airport, one of the Czechoslovak Airlines girls handed him a bouquet of flowers; for that, she was fired. Arriving in Istanbul to change planes, he was mobbed by admirers and had to hide in a men's room until the flight to Ankara was ready. In Ankara, he paid his first diplomatic call to the Soviet Ambassador.

In May, he was summoned home on a pretext that his mother was ill. He never went back to Turkey. In June, he was dismissed as ambassador and expelled from the Communist Party. Now, at this writing, he lives quietly in his two-bedroom house on Mouse Street in Bratislava, tending its garden, painting a fence, or doing the family shopping every now and then.* When they meet him, his friends and neighbors keep the encounters brief, for his sake as well as theirs. If an occasional stranger greets or even applauds him, he slips away as soon as he can. His behavior has been discreet, but the one thing he has been firm about is his refusal to recant on the reforms of 1968.

Thus, Dubček's image as a hero persists inside as well as outside Czechoslovakia. After the August riots of 1969, Černík denounced him and said he misled his colleagues in his dealings with the Five Powers in the summer of 1968. In the fall of 1969, President Svoboda publicly branded Dubček "inconsistent and lacking the principles characteristic of Leninism," but privately made it clear that whatever Dubček's mistakes, he was an honest man and "as long as I am President," there would be no political trial for Dubček. Husák said that Dubček "was expelled from the ranks of our party because, in the relatively short time he headed it, he brought our party to a disintegration such as it had never known." And *Rudé Právo* labeled Dubček "unprincipled, compromising, cowardly . . . weak and two-faced. . . . The legend of Alexander Dubček was created deliberately for many months by a big apparatus of reactionary forces."

The legend, however, would not crumble. Unable to demolish it, Dubček's enemies set out to smear it instead. They circulated a "photo" showing a naked Dubček fondling a naked Marta Kubišová in bed. (Apparently it was a mccarthyesque job of "composite" copying; the original photo, with the same bodies but two entirely different

* In 1971, it was reported that Dubček was working as a minor official of the Regional Forestry Administration in Bratislava.

faces, had appeared earlier in a Danish pornographic magazine.) They also said that the reason Němec fired a shot into Kubišová's bedroom was that Dubček was there at the time.

The pop singer and actor Václav Neckář (who played the hero of *Closely-Watched Trains*) paid a courtesy call on the police to find out why Kubišová wasn't being allowed to keep a concert engagement with him. At the police station, he was shown the "picture" and asked: "That lady, doesn't she look like Kubišová to you?"

"Well," said Neckář, "I *have* been in her dressing room, but I've never seen her naked."

"But it *could* be Kubišová, couldn't it?" the official persisted.

"No, sir, it couldn't. Because she's a very puritanical girl and would never do such a thing."

"Still, just looking at the picture, it could pass for her, couldn't it?"

Neckář took a deep breath and answered: "Like I said, I have never seen Miss Kubišová naked. But I *have* seen her underwear hanging. Miss Kubišová wears a [European] Size One bra, while this girl in the picture, if she ever wore a bra, would clearly require at least a Size Three."

In Sussex in September of 1970, visiting professor Eduard Goldstücker gave an interview to Richard Reston of The Los Angeles Times. "You didn't see the first of May, 1968?" Goldstücker asked Reston rhetorically. "Well, there were huge groups of hippies marching past Dubček and Svoboda shouting, smiling, making jokes, throwing flowers, giving them their sandwiches to eat because they were standing there for several hours. It was moving proof of what the first ray of hope for freedom means to people, especially young people. We saw in those short few months so many talents appearing among the young, talents in statesmanship. That is all crushed.

"Now imagine the young generation, of which each member is now required to recant everything he believed with the whole enthusiasm of his young soul two years ago. It is utterly rejectable, utterly nasty, treacherous, criminal!"

The bronze marker has been removed from Jan Palach's grave in Olšany. A miniature Štrougal Park keeps appearing and disappearing over the little curbside monument on the spot where Marie Charousková was shot getting off a tram. Like everyone else in Prague who didn't know these two young people, we nonetheless take their loss personally.

And there is another bereavement which is intensely personal to us —but which we must share with everyone in Prague: On the day after Christmas, 1969, in his art studio on Wenceslas Square, Jiří Šlitr died under the most mysterious of circumstances. He was 45. And it was his and our best friend Sylva who found his body, plus another's. . . .

That fall, theatre people had been put under intense pressure to sign self-criticisms or pledges that they saw the drama as, first and foremost, a faithful arm of socialism, which they would exercise accordingly. Signers of the "2,000 Words" were being hounded to recant. Among those who obliged was our friend František, the theatre artistic director who'd been our neighbor during our summer of 1968 along the Sázava.

"It's too bad about František, isn't it?" Šlitr had remarked at our Thanksgiving Dinner.

"He hasn't said a word about it to me," I'd said, "but we're still good friends and he's already invited us out for any weekend next summer."

"He's still my good friend, too," Šlitr had said. "An actor or an executive, if he doesn't sign, then maybe he has no job, no work, nowhere to go. Suchý and I are the lucky ones. If it starts happening to us, we won't sign: we'll stop performing. We would both hate to—but at least we can live on our royalties and stay home and write . . .

"If we must go," he went on, turning from the other guests to me, "you must give us many American ideas for songs and shows and maybe children's books."

After two years of interrupted, but always felicitous, collaboration with Šlitr, I'd already known that our show wasn't just a one-shot venture. But I was glad to hear this from him. Everything we did together was so challenging and rewarding that I wanted to work with him all my life.

Suchý—like myself, eight years Šlitr's junior—had the same sense that Šlitr would outlive us all. And so, to be sure, did Šlitr. In 1967, a Prague magazine asked him: "Will you ever stop working with Suchý?" To which Šlitr had replied: "When one of us returns home from the Crematorium alone, that will be when I shall be obliged to look for another collaborator."

The last time I saw Šlitr—Monday 22 December, 1969—was Prague's coldest day in modern memory. That morning, it had been 16-below (Fahrenheit!) and I had seen a bride's wedding bouquet turn brown as she'd stepped from car to church. Šlitr had come over that afternoon to do some work and exchange (but not open) Christmas presents. Sylva was coming to our house for cocktails and dinner at 1730, but Šlitr had promised his mother he'd be home for dinner at 1800. Still, when Sylva didn't show up, he decided to wait for her. He accepted a Beefeater martini ("I'm driving, but it's Christmas, it's cold, and it's imported") while declining our invitation to stay for dinner ("My mother's already started the paprikash").

Christmas cooking had already begun and the gas was exceptionally low. So was electricity. While we talked, our part of Prague experienced its third power failure of the day. When Sylva arrived toward 1900, she discovered us worrying about her by candlelight. She had left for our house on time, but failed to find a cab; taken a tram that had been immobilized on Hradčany Hill when the electricity went off; and walked the last mile to our home.

Šlitr and I took turns putting a glass of cognac to Sylva's icy lips. When she had thawed, but not yet removed her coat, Šlitr donned his and said to her: "I wanted to know: Are you still going to the mountains for the holidays?"

"No. My father has the flu," Sylva replied, "so I will be here all the time from Christmas to New Year's."

Jirka, who was planning to be home for the holidays, too, said: "Then I will be seeing much of you."

To which I heard Sylva say, in soft but anguished Czech: "No, you won't! Please, Jirka."

You have to know the Czechs to realize that such an exchange is their equivalent of a raging domestic quarrel. Inhibited by a lack of housing and privacy as well as by memories of the 1950's thought-control, they rarely raise their voices or speak with audible passion. Instead, they send each other subtle signals. Sylva was fighting to assert her own identity independently of Šlitr.

Sylva ate Christmas dinner with her parents; Šlitr with his. But the day after Christmas is also a holiday here, St. Stephen's Day (as in *"Good King Wenceslas looked out/ On the Feast of Stephen"*). Sylva went to the Šlitrs' on 26 December to have dinner with Jirka, his parents, and his sister's family, who had come in from northern Bohemia for the day. Dinner was scheduled for 1730 to enable the visitors to start their drive home at a decent hour.

Šlitr had driven off at 1400, saying that he had a "short meeting" at the art studio and then a 1600 appointment with his arranger, but promising to be home at 1700. When the arranger called the house at 1730 to say that Jirka had not yet appeared, Sylva phoned a few friends to ask if they'd seen him. Then she and Šlitr's brother-in-law went looking for him in the latter's car.

The brother-in-law, a machine technician, was one of the three or four men who had ever been to Šlitr's art studio. He had gone to fix the gas heater a year earlier. He remembered the studio's location and, nearby, in the shadow of the Wenceslas statue, he and Sylva discovered Šlitr's red West German BMW sports car parked along the uncrowded (on the holiday) Square. But Šlitr responded to neither the downstairs buzzer nor their frantic knocking on the third-floor studio door. A tenant of the building said he'd seen Šlitr go in, but not out.

Sylva and the brother-in-law went to a police station on Cracow Street. An officer told them: "Every year, there are hundreds of people who disappear from Christmas to New Year's. If we went looking for every one of them, we wouldn't have the manpower to do the rest of our work. . . . And when it involves someone like Mr. Šlitr, well, don't be angry, but you know people are going to say it's political if we go breaking down his door."

They argued with him to no avail. Finally, though, another policeman took them aside and said: "Look! Last year, I said the same thing to some people, and a girl died because we didn't go. I'm off duty now, so I'll help you. But, if Mr. Šlitr makes trouble about this, you're on your own."

Toward 2200, they broke in with the aid of an instrument that looked like a tire iron. The off-duty policeman looked inside first.

"It's gas," he said, "and there are two of them in there. The other one's a girl."

This much was certain: Šlitr and the girl were killed by gas leaking from a two burner mini-stove—on which nothing had been cooked. If they had wanted heat, a gas radiator, in perfect working order, stood unused a few feet away. Gas pressure in the building had not been low at any time that day—for it was not primarily a residential building and hardly anybody would be cooking. (Gas pressure all over the city had been OK, too, because people were eating mostly leftovers.)

The two people on the studio couch had not been wearing many clothes. Šlitr had tried to pull himself up by clawing at an adjacent coffee table, but the tablecloth had wrapped itself around his right hand. The girl looked as though she'd been sleeping serenely.

The girl was a red-headed eighteen-year-old student. She had a hyphenated name, for her parents were divorced, her mother had remarried, and so the girl had tacked on her mother's new name.

This next information was more circumstantial: Entries in Šlitr's diary indicated that their liaison had been going on for two or three months. The girl had recently told two high-school friends that she was fighting with Šlitr because he wouldn't be seen with her in public. She had indicated that she would have one more talk with him about it before Christmas. If he still said no, she'd hinted, then the whole world would know by New Year's that she was Jiří Šlitr's girl.

(Ironically, even the one obituary that mentioned the presence of a "girlfriend," in *Rudé Právo,* didn't mention her name.)

Near the bodies were two empty bottles of an inexpensive Czech cognac. Much was made of this detail—and it is perhaps the most perplexing of all. Šlitr's tastes ran to the imported; Pilsener beer was the only Czech beverage he drank. And he rarely took even one glass of anything hard when he was driving. The police would not tell Šlitr's parents whether or not the liquor or sedative contents of the bodies were unusual. But the family did learn that there was more than one autopsy. They are convinced that the girl drugged his drink and then gassed them both. Sylva and I think so, too.

Sylva required remarkably little comforting. "I'm all right," she told me a few days later. "Once the policeman said Jirka wasn't alone, well, I felt a little better just because he wasn't all by himself when something bad happened. Otherwise, I felt nothing. It had nothing to do with whatever I might have said to him—or didn't say. It was his affair."

The police called Šlitr's death a "gas accident." United Press International, identifying Šlitr primarily as a "signer of the 2,000-Words Manifesto," called him a probable suicide. In West Germany, where some of his songs were popular, the press said he'd been "hounded to death" for refusing to recant.

The most tragic certainty was that Jiří Šlitr was gone and the Czechoslovak public took it as personally as we did. "At the worst possible times, he was the one man who could make us laugh—and think!" was the refrain of many strangers who sent condolence notes to his family or Suchý or the Semafor.

When the author of the "2,000 Words," Ludvík Vaculík* heard the news, he pecked out another proclamation on his typewriter:

> Jiří Šlitr died? At first, one doesn't want to believe such information. But then one realizes that, nowadays, the worse the information, the truer it probably is. So it is true: Šlitr is dead. I have the feeling that something extraordinarily evil has happened. Why him, when there are so many harmful people in the world? . . . A part of Prague has fallen through the floor.

Vaculík was inevitably bitter, mocking, and suggestive:

> . . . no incompetent can give us anything to replace Jiří Šlitr, even if he killed himself, and I feel somehow pleased about this. No measure, no resolution, no decision can ever train the stupid noise of engines to make a single tone of such music as Mr. Jiří Šlitr used to compose. Therefore, on the occasion of his death, I also repeat defiance to myself.

On 27 December 1969, the morning after Šlitr's death, Ludvík Vaculík's proclamation was posted on the Semafor Theatre's door. A day or two later, a couple of secret policemen came to the Semafor's office and asked an employee to remove the tribute because it was "causing crowds to collect." The theatre complied.†

(Not long thereafter, Suchý was forced to resign as the Semafor's artistic chief because unrecalcitrant signers of Vaculík's "2,000 Words" were no longer permitted to hold key executive posts. Suchý was, however, allowed to retain the "lesser" functions of author and star.)

Šlitr, a lawyer by training, left no will. By New Year's Day, 1970, his bereaved parents knew why. Someone phoned and said "there's a souvenir of your son" they ought to see. Then they were visited by an elderly lawyer; his wife, a notary public; their thirty-five-year-old daughter (a successful, but not well-known, screen writer whose movies include *The Star* and *We are Looking for Daddy*); and her illegitimate child, a chubby four-year-old girl with the wide, thin-lipped Šlitr fam-

---

* Now awaiting trial on anti-State charges.
† Šlitr's wine-drinking companion, the puppeteer Trnka, outlived him by only five days. Trnka was already on his deathbed when the tragedy happened, but his doctors would not let his family tell him about Šlitr.

ily mouth. According to a child-support document signed by Jiří Šlitr at the time of birth, he was the little girl's father.

In the absence of any other document, the child (with her guardians) became the sole heir to Šlitr's fortune and homes. Šlitr's own lawyer confirmed that, at the time when Jirka had indeed signed the paper, he'd urged him to make out a will. But any will would have had to take cognizance of the child—and Šlitr wanted, in his parents' lifetimes, as few records of the affair as possible. He fully expected to be alive himself when his child would be twenty-one and on her own.

Šlitr's aged, ailing parents had no fight left in them. ("Never out-live your children, Alan," his mother, Pavla, told me.) Acknowledging their grandchild's claim, they made plans to vacate the villa in which their son had wanted them to live out their years.

Prague that winter was like a city in wartime, with more gas crises and power failures (a January, 1970, blackout akin to New York's one-night disaster of 1965 lasted three nights here); a flu epidemic that closed the schools for two weeks; and a bumper crop of the unheralded minor shortages that make everyday life a battle here. My Christmas present from Šlitr—a comic drawing of a woman from his fall exhibit of erotic art, Šlitr '69—could be framed, but without glass. No Bohemian glass (or any other kind) was in stock.

While the Communist Party and the Government wrestled with a faltering economy by changing Prime Ministers (Štrougal for Černík), Šlitr's survivors were finding the Czech Way of Death as difficult as the Czech Way of Life. Due to flu deaths, a coffin scarcity, and a shortage of fuel to burn, bookings at Prague's Strašnice Crematorium required a month's notice. Thanks to Šlitr's prominence, however, he was granted a funeral there on 6 January 1970, eleven days after dying.

Prague's place of last farewells was thronged that afternoon. More than 1,200 mourners squeezed into the modern, antiseptic, and eternally cold main hall while thousands more stood and shivered outside. Even an ordinary funeral there is a very theatrical event. A curtain parts and, on stage, there sits the coffin, very tiny atop a huge catafalque. Flowers separate the mourners from the ritual; in Šlitr's case, there were enough wreaths to festoon the whole Berlin Wall. After an oration from the pulpit (Suchý: "If a man lives fully and happily in the time that has been allotted to him . . . there should be no reason for grief"), an organ on the balcony plays a final hymn.

At Šlitr's ceremony, the organ was augmented by trumpet and drum—which played two compositions. The first, from *Jonáš*, was an S + Š anti-war song that had become an anthem of nostalgia for the Prague Spring and now for Šlitr: "Sure, I Was Once Alive." The second melody, symbolizing Šlitr's thirst to be a big fish in a bigger pond, was Leonard Bernstein's "Tonight."

Just as the music reached the part where Stephen Sondheim's lyrics say *"Today the world was just an address/ A place for me to live in,"* coffin and bier, on a treadmill, began moving upstage. At the rear of the Crematorium stage, two emblazoned doors slid open to admit them. Then, to the final bars of Bernstein (*"Good night, good night. . . ."*), the gates closed on Jirka Šlitr for the last time.

One who came to pay his respects was the stoop-shouldered, crew-cut Josef Smrkovský. Deposed, denounced, and forced by politics to retire at fifty-eight, he now carried a cane. (Later in 1970, we learned that he had bone cancer.) Some youths in the crowd started to chant "Smr-kovský! Smr-kovský!" The police moved in, quietly but firmly, to forestall a demonstration and prevent the death of Jirka Šlitr from being further politicized.

For the death of Jirka Šlitr was not political. Even a man who takes a heroic stand and sticks to it can also find time to make a mess of his personal life. He may not necessarily be a hero to those, particularly the women, who love him and think they know him.

Amidst any kind of politics, including the kind where facade is now all, life goes on, death goes on. The end of Jirka Šlitr was either a crime of passion or else an accident of passion, for passion, too, goes on —even here, where so much love and so much emotion has been spent, wasted, and fatally betrayed.

When Jiří Šlitr died, our Czech friends and neighbors asked us anxiously if we planned to stay now that one of my original reasons for coming here was gone. And I said: "We have all the more reason to stay now that we have some of our own ghosts in the walls of the city."

They were glad, for they take a whiff of faint hope (and some risk) from every day my family and I are here among them. Of course, away from my typewriter, I'm as helpless as they are—but, in the meantime, here we stay and here we want desperately to remain.

It's the week before Christmas once again and I don't really know where I'll be living on Christmas Day. Four days ago, while I was at Ruzyně Airport seeing my mother off to New York, a well-laid trap netted the secret police sixty-five pages of this manuscript—including a chapter about the last days of August 1968.

There are unedited duplicates safely in the West, though that's not where I particularly want to be myself. Anyway, the matter is out of my hands for now. After the usual inquiries by the American Embassy and Czechoslovak Ministry of Foreign Affairs have proved ineffectual, there is nothing to do but wait and, in my case, work. I want very badly to finish my book right here in Prague, where it happened. Besides, you don't get in touch with the secret police; they get in touch with you.

It looks bad, but our leaky rowboat has brought us this far; and so I, for one, offer myself as a hostage to your hopes, Czechoslovak people.

Prague, 15 December 1970 at 1215.*

---

* On 12 January 1971, after a three-hour interrogation by the chief of the Prague secret police, the author was expelled from the Czechoslovak Socialist Republic. He and his entire family were given forty-eight hours to leave the country; their apartment was sealed by the police. The train on which the American family Levy was deported crossed the Austrian frontier at 0630 on 15 January 1971.

This book was set on the linotype in
Baskerville. The display face is Bell.
It was composed by H. Wolff Book
Manufacturing Company and printed and
bound by Halliday Lithograph Corp.
The design was by Jacqueline Schuman.